Traditions of the Fathers

Traditions of the Fathers

The Book of Mormon as History

Brant A. Gardner

GREG KOFFORD BOOKS
SALT LAKE CITY, 2015

Copyright © 2015 Brant Gardner
Cover design copyright © 2015 Greg Kofford Books, Inc.
Cover art, "Mormon, Prophet Warrior," by Joseph Brickey, used with permission.
Published in the USA.
All rights reserved. No part of this volume may be reproduced in any form without written permission from the publisher, Greg Kofford Books. The views expressed herein are the responsibility of the author and do not necessarily represent the position of Greg Kofford Books.

ISBN 978-1-58958-665-9

Also Available in ebook.

Greg Kofford Books
P.O. Box 1362
Draper, UT 84020
www.gregkofford.com

2019 18 17 16 15   5 4 3 2 1

Library of Congress Control Number: 2015945209

For John L. Sorenson,
who opened the door.

Table of Contents

Preface xi
Introduction xv

1. Finding a Lost People 1
    In the Beginning: The Bible as Paradigm 3
    The Pre-Critical Use of External Evidence 10
    Scholarship Joins Faith 17
2. Reading a Lost Book 25
    Reading the Book of Mormon 26
    Reading through the Text's Analytical Layers 29
    Reading through an Ancient Document's Translation Layer 32
    Reading through an Ancient Document's Composition Layer 35
    Reading Archaeology against the Book of Mormon 37
    Reading from a Solid Foundation 40
    This Reading 52
3. A Prophet without Honour 55
    Judah in Its World 56
    Judah and Its People 59
    Lehi of Jerusalem 65
    Israel's Sin According to Lehi (and Nephi) 68
    Israel's Sin and Lehi's Family Dynamics 74
    Lehi as a Fleeing Prophet 75
    The First Camp 77
4. The Lehite Exodus 83
    Returning for the Brass Plates 85
    The Importance of the Brass Plates 88
    Lehi's Prophecy: How Long is a Year? 92
    A Tree in a Dream 95
    A Tree in Stone 98
    Shazer and the Failed Bows 101
    The Place Which Was Called Nahom 105
    Eastward to Bountiful 108
    Bountiful after Privation 110
    Sailing to the New World 112
    Nephi Ends a Book: Nephi Starts a Book 114
5. Book of Mormon Geography in the New World 119
    Where in the World? 121
    Which Sidon River? 125
    Directions in the Book of Mormon 129
6. Nephites in a New World 151

  The New Neighbors 151
  Becoming Nephites and Lamanites 154
  The Lamanite Skin of Blackness 159
  Establishing the People and the City of Nephi 164
  New World Peoples in Nephi's Community 168
  DNA and the Book of Mormon 170
  Nephi: Prophet and Author 175
  Defending the Community 180
  King by Popular Demand 184
  The Nephite Egalitarian Ideal 188
7. The Nephites in a Dark Tunnel: From Jacob to Omni 191
  Pre-Christian Christianity 191
  Early Economic and Social Tension 197
  Early Religious Tension 204
  Nephites in Armed Conflict 208
  Emerging from the Dark Tunnel 211
8. Nephites Arrive in Zarahemla 213
  A New World Fleeing Prophet 214
  Zarahemla before the Nephites 216
  The Ancestor, Mulek 217
  Merging Peoples in Zarahemla 220
  Translating a Stone 224
9. A New Covenant Made, then Unmade 229
  A New Covenant of Unity 230
  Clues to Culture in Benjamin's Speech 235
  Unmaking Unity: Churches 238
  Unmaking Unity: The Reign of Judges 242
  The Voice of the People 245
  A Mesoamerican Model for Nephite Judges 251
  The Nephite Confederacy 253
10. The Cultural Context of Nephite Apostasy 257
  Elements of Nephite Apostasy 258
  Cultural Manifestations of Apostasy 259
  Syncretization of Nephite Beliefs 261
  Bridging the Nature of God 263
  Bridging Heavenly Expectations 265
  The Divine King Replaces the Heavenly King 267
  The King, Ritual, and the Replacement of the Messianic Expectation 268
  Explaining Nephite Apostasy 271
11. Kinship: Tribes and Households 275
12. Glimpses of Lamanite Culture 281
  Zeniff Returns to the Land of Nephi 281
  Culture as Explanation: Ammon and King Lamoni 285

Horses, Chariots, and Other Anachronistic Nouns	289
The Overking and Subordinate Kings	300
The Treatment of Important Captives	302
Culture as Explanation: Anti-Nephi Lehies	303
13. "The Tribulations of our Warfare"	311
Why Did Lamanites War Against Nephites?	312
Seasonality of Warfare	316
Tactics and Order of Battle	317
Big Numbers and Missing Bodies	320
14. The Gadianton Robbers in Typology and History	325
The Narrative Role of Secret Combinations	325
A Plausible Identification of the Gadiantons	327
Two Millennia of Disappearing and Reappearing Secret Combinations	337
From Threads to Tapestry	341
15. The Dreadful Groanings	343
The Geology behind the Descriptions	345
A Recent Reconstruction	350
16. A Bridge Too Far: Quetzalcoatl and Jesus Christ	353
From Native to Spaniard: Through the Mirror, Darkly	354
Topiltzin Quetzalcoatl: King in Tula	357
Ehecatl Quetzalcoatl: The Deity in Heaven	358
Ce Acatl Quetzalcoatl: The Deity on Earth	360
Old Things Are New Again	364
17. Mormon and the Nephite Demise	367
The Mesoamerican Cumorah	373
The New York Cumorah	375
18. Jaredites in the Text	381
The Translation of the Jaredite Record and the Tower	382
Finding Large and Mighty Men	387
Approximating a Jaredite Chronology	388
19. Jaredites in the New World	393
Jaredites, Olmecs, and Warfare	397
Jaredites, Olmecs, and Texts	398
Jaredites, Olmecs, and Geography	399
20. Historicity and Futurity	401
Geo-spatial Convergences	403
Geopolitical Convergences	406
Chronological Convergences	406
Cultural Convergences	407
Productive Convergences	408
From Traditions of the Fathers to Future Stories	408
Bibliography	411
Index	445

Table of Figures

Figure 1: Lehi's trail..84
Figure 2: Izapa Stela 5 99
Figure 3: Mesoamerica and the Book of Mormon...............................123
Figure 4: Limhi's expedition and two rivers..126
Figure 5: Mesoamerican directions..132
Figure 6: Compass 132
Figure 7: Tenochtitlan from Codex Mendoza......................................133
Figure 8: Nephite conceptual world 144
Figure 9: Directions from Bountiful or Nephi.....................................145
Figure 10: Battle litter graffiti from Tikal..296
Figure 11: Trade Routes 314

Preface

Latter-day Saints have a paradoxical relationship with the Book of Mormon. Joseph said that it was the keystone of our religion, but his contemporaries preferred to preach from the Bible.[1] We sing Primary songs about it but rarely sacrament meeting hymns. We affirm that it arrived through an angel but want to see evidence of its divinity in the dirt of history. Much of it is as old as the Old Testament but we claim that it was written for our day.[2]

Like the Old Testament, the Book of Mormon revolves around stories.[3] Both scriptures represent the work of editors telling stories from history to teach current readers how to live in the present.[4] When we read those stories, we create a personal story as our own lives reflect and intertwine with the actors in the text. We end up with stories about stories.

Even though the stories are set in history, we can tell our Book of Mormon stories without any concern for history. There are moral stories, inspiring stories, and stories that springboard us into a discussion of our doctrine. Parley P. Pratt told perhaps the model inspirational story of his first experience with the Book of Mormon:

---

[1] Joseph Smith, et al., *History of the Church of Jesus Christ of Latter-day Saints*, 4:461. "I told the brethren that the Book of Mormon was the most correct of any book on earth, and the keystone of our religion, and a man would get nearer to God by abiding by its precepts, than by any other book." For early missionary avoidance of the Book of Mormon, see Grant Underwood, "Book of Mormon Usage in Early LDS Theology," 49–50.

[2] Ezra Taft Benson, *The Teachings of Ezra Taft Benson*, 58: "We must make the Book of Mormon a center focus of study because it was written for our day. The Nephites never had the book, neither did the Lamanites of ancient times. It was meant for us."

[3] Grant Hardy, "Introduction," *The Book of Mormon, The Earliest Text*, vii: "Most recent holy books consist of doctrinal expositions, ritual instructions, moral codes, scriptural commentary, or devotional poetry. The Book of Mormon, by contrast, is narrative—a much rarer genre of religious writing."

Norman F. Cantor, *In the Wake of the Plague: The Black Death and the World It Made*, 17. "The scientific method had not yet been invented. When faced with a problem, people in the Middle Ages found the solution through diachronic (as opposed to synchronic) analysis. The diachronic is the historical narrative, horizontally developing through time: 'Tell me a story.'"

[4] There is a voluminous literature discussing the development of the present form of the various books in the Old Testament. One of the important assumptions about the editorial process is referred to as the Documentary Hypothesis, or the idea that there are four different editorial strands discernible in the Pentateuch. For an overview of LDS reactions to this theory, see Kevin L. Barney, "Reflections on the Documentary Hypothesis," 57–99. David Bokovoy, *Authoring the Old Testament: Genesis–Deuteronomy*, provides an introduction to the Documentary Hypothesis for an LDS audience.

Although most of the Book of Mormon is the result of the way that Mormon told the stories, Moroni is responsible for telling the story of the Jaredites. Nephi, Jacob, and Enos tell stories from their own histories that have meaning greater than recounting history.

I opened it with eagerness, and read its title page. I then read the testimony of several witnesses in relation to the manner of its being found and translated. After this I commenced its contents by course. I read all day; eating was a burden, I had no desire for food; sleep was a burden when the night came, for I preferred reading to sleep.

As I read, the spirit of the Lord was upon me, and I knew and comprehended that the book was true, as plainly and manifestly as a man comprehends and knows that he exists. My joy was now full, as it were, and I rejoiced sufficiently to more than pay me for all the sorrows, sacrifices and toils of my life.[5]

For Pratt, reading the book was sufficient. He read it and it was *true*. It wasn't true because he researched the origins of the Native Americans. It wasn't true because he understood the complexities of Hebrew religion prior to the exile. It was simply true because it spoke that trueness to his heart and soul. Some modern Saints have that same kind of testimony, but many hope for a different foundation for their faith.

The physical book that the early Latter-day Saints held in their hands described an ancient people who were in some way the ancestors of the Native Americans. Those same peoples were frequently on the mind of the young nation as it less than gently pushed them out of its way. The early saints' Book of Mormon stories incorporated the Native Americans not just as descendants of the book, but also as proof of the book. For many then, and many now, a spiritual witness yearned to have a more temporal witness to lean on.

This book is a historical story. Much of this Book of Mormon story I have told before. I attempted to cover both history and religion in *Second Witness: Analytical and Contextual Commentary on the Book of Mormon*.[6] That comprehensive approach makes it more difficult to see the flow of history apart from the larger number of themes addressed. Only the persistent reader will piece together the history that is interwoven with other topics. Hence this book—and hence the reason this book borrows, and sometimes directly copies, material from *Second Witness*. However, even for those who might have read some of this material before, this story is told more directly, more concisely, and with what insights have become available since the commentary was published. This book contains my stories about the Book of Mormon—the stories as best I understand them and as best I can explain them.

I would like to thank Neal Rappleye and my son-in-law, Ezery Beauchamp, who read earlier versions of this book and provided useful suggestions. Grant and Heather Hardy read a version of this manuscript. Grant provided a thoughtful critique that required rethinking or strengthening many of my ideas. Stephen Smoot performed some much appreciated footwork in chasing down a particular reference. Mark Alan Wright and Lawrence Poulsen have both served as able sounding boards for various ideas. Where they triggered ideas that have found their way into the text, I have so noted. Mark Wright is also the co-author of Chapter 10. Mark's wife Traci provided the graphics included with the text. Curtis L. Sorenson graciously revised the maps he created for *Mormon's Codex*, changing the base map to grayscale and adding

---

[5] Parley P. Pratt, *Autobiography of Parley P. Pratt*, 20.
[6] Brant A. Gardner, *Second Witness: Analytical and Contextual Commentary on the Book of Mormon*.

indicators for the directions in chapter 5. Lavina Fielding Anderson has become much more than an editor of text. Her voice sits in my head often enough that she may have co-written some of this book without knowing it.

In the interests of internal stylistic consistency and clarity for the reader, I have standardized abbreviations of books of scriptures in parenthetical citations, including in quotations. I have made lowercased words of those that are in all capitals in the King James Version (e.g., LORD becomes Lord), and removed the italics that appear in the King James Version passages. Italics or bolding in scriptures indicate my emphasis.

The organization that was known as FAIR (Foundation for Apologetic Information and Research has changed its name to FairMormon. I have not changed references to FAIR when that was the legal name. Readers should be aware that FAIR and FairMormon are the same organization. Links to FAIR currently redirect to FairMormon.

I have differentiated Book of Mormon men with the same name by a subscript when there is the possibility of confusing them. Thus Alma$_1$ is Alma$_2$'s father and Mosiah$_1$ is grandfather to Mosiah$_2$. I have elected not to use the subscript to mark the first Nephi, though I have added it for clarity for his much later descendants with the same name. Similarly, the time and context are typically sufficient to distinguish Chief Captain Moroni from his later namesake, Mormon's son.

I have also intentionally used the divine name Yahweh to describe the Nephites' God. In so doing I am attempting to represent Nephite understanding without the added baggage of terms that modern readers might interpret differently without even knowing they had done so. Yahweh was God to the Nephites. Yahweh was their Messiah. Understanding that the name and title to refer to the same being is essential to understanding the Nephite descriptions of their God.[7]

---

[7] I first laid out this argument in Brant A. Gardner, "Monotheism, Messiah, and Mormon's Book," presented at the 2003 FAIR Conference. That presentation was updated in Gardner, *Second Witness*, 1:214–22.

Introduction

> And it came to pass that the Lord commanded me, wherefore *I did make plates* of ore that *I might engraven* upon them the record of my people. And upon the *plates which I made I did engraven* the record of my father, and also our journeyings in the wilderness, and the prophecies of my father; and also many of mine own prophecies *have I engraven* upon them. (1 Ne. 19:1)

Nephi's description of the plates is dramatically and repetitively physical. The words on the plates are important, but those words required intense human labor to produce them. Nephi *made* the plates. Upon those metal plates, Nephi *engraved* the words. He did not paint, but employed a more laborious physical means of preserving those words. Plates that Nephi made and engraved, along with those Mormon engraved, were delivered to Joseph Smith in September of 1827.[1]

Joseph did not begin translating until Martin Harris returned from New York in February 1828. For five months the physical plates represented sacred hope, but for Emma they were often just part of her day. In her 1879 account she recounted: "The plates often lay on the table without any attempt at concealment, wrapped in a small linen tablecloth, which I had given him to fold them in. . . . I moved them from place to place on the table, as it was necessary in doing my work."[2]

From Nephi to Joseph and Emma, the Book of Mormon was intensely physical, intensely tangible.[3] The tie to the physicality of the plates was broken when the Angel

---

[1] 1 Ne. 19:1 refers to the creation of what we know as the large plates of Nephi. This chapter introduces Nephi's record of the creation of the second set of plates, which we call the small plates of Nephi. Although the specific reference to making and engraving are for a different set of plates, the small plates were made and engraved in the same way. They too demonstrate the physical presence and labor associated with the record. There is no indication that Mormon made the plates upon which he made his account, but he too engraved his account on metal.

King Benjamin similarly speaks of the physicality of Nephi's plates: "And behold, also the plates of Nephi, which contain the records and the sayings of our fathers from the time they left Jerusalem until now, and they are true; and we can know of their surety because we have them before our eyes" (Mosiah 1:6).

[2] Emma Smith, "As Interviewed by Joseph Smith III, 1879," in *Opening the Heavens: Accounts of Divine Manifestations*, 130–31. Michael Hubbard MacKay and Gerrit J. Dirkmaat, *From Darkness unto Light: Joseph Smith's Translation and Publication of the Book of Mormon*, 15 records that Katherine Smith, Joseph's sister, had a similar experience interacting with the covered plates on a table while she was cleaning and dusting.

[3] Dan Vogel, *Joseph Smith, the Making of a Prophet*, 98, provides an interesting highlight to the physicality of the plates. Not accepting them as ancient, Vogel nonetheless accepts them as physical:

> The construction of such a book would have been relatively easy, There were scraps of tin available on the Smith property and elsewhere in the vicinity, and during the several hours Joseph was separated from Emma the night they went to the hill and on other

Moroni removed the plates in June of 1828 after the loss of the first 116 pages of the translation. According to David Whitmer's 1885 testimony they were never returned,[4] although Lucy Mack Smith's recollection suggests that they were. In her first manuscript she recounts Joseph's experience with a divine being:

> An Angel stood before me and answered me saying that I had sinned in that he [sic] had delivered the manuscript into the hands of a wicked man and as he had ventured to become responsible for this man's faithfulness he would of necessity suffer the consequence's [sic] of his indiscretion that he must now give back the plates into the hands of the angel from he had received them [sic]
>
> But said he[,] it may be if you are sufficiently humble and penitent that you will receive them again on the 22 september.[5]

Whether the plates were present during translation or not, they definitely became a physical presence a year later. In June of 1829, three witnesses saw them. A few days later, eight more men testified that they had seen and handled the plates.[6] John Whitmer testified in 1839: "I handled those plates; there were fine engravings on both sides. I handled them."[7]

After the testimony of these men, there were no more experiences with the physical plates. For all who have come after, there is only the text of the Book of Mormon, not the tangible physical presence of the plates from which that text was translated. For those few for whom the Book of Mormon was as tangible as it was for Nephi and Mormon, none denied that physical experience even if they might have questioned later religious experiences.[8]

For those contemporaries who did not experience the physicality of the plates, the Book of Mormon was often seen as the product of imagination.[9] Matthew Roper notes:

> occasions, he could have easily set up shop in the cave on the other side of the hill or in some corner of the forest. Using a pair of metal shears, it would have been easy to cut a number of 6 x 8-inch sheets. A hole punch, nail, or some similar instrument could have been used to make three holes along one edge of each plate. Then it would have been a matter of passing three wires or rods through the holes and bending them into rings.

[4] David Whitmer, "As Interviewed by the *Chicago Tribune* (1885)," 154.
[5] Lucy Mack Smith, *Lucy's Book: A Critical Edition of Lucy Mack Smith's Family Memoir*, 424–25.
[6] John W. Welch, "The Miraculous Translation of the Book of Mormon," 97.
[7] Whitmer, "As Interviewed by the *Chicago Tribune*," 159.
[8] Richard Lloyd Anderson, *Investigating the Book of Mormon Witnesses*, 181–82: "[The several witnesses] occasionally witnessed to other spiritual experiences supplementing [their testimonies of the Book of Mormon], but at no known time did any Book of Mormon witness retract his printed testimony. The first Mormons knew the witnesses and kept track of them through reliable reports—and always insisted that none modified his testimony."

An excellent compilation of materials providing background on the witnesses' testimonies of the plates and later relationship with the church may be found in the FairMormon wiki, "Book of Mormon witnesses."

[9] An interesting recounting of early newspaper accounts of the Book of Mormon is Donald Q. Cannon, "In the Press: Early Newspaper Reports on the Initial Publication of the Book of Mormon," 4–15.

On 26 March 1830, the *Wayne Sentinel* reported that the Book of Mormon had been published and was available for sale. Early reactions in the press to its publication varied from charges of blasphemy or contempt to amusement. On 2 April 1830, the *Rochester Daily Advertiser* wrote, "The 'Book of Mormon' has been placed in our hands. A viler imposition was never practised. It is an evidence of fraud, blasphemy and credulity, shocking to the Christian and moralist". . . [The editor of the *Cleveland Herald*] considered it "one of the veriest impositions of the day."[10]

It was impossible to immediately reconcile the conflict between the faithful declaration that the Book of Mormon was *real* and that of the rest of the world that it was a "vile imposition." At the time when the Book of Mormon was first published, there was no assembly of evidence to support faith in its historicity, although the early Saints quickly adapted popular speculations. The idea that Native Americans descended from the lost ten tribes had been circulating in books and community lore by that time.[11] Those ideas worked themselves into the stories the Saints told as evidence to support faith.

The Book of Mormon declares itself to be "an abridgment of the record of the people of Nephi, and also of the Lamanites" (Title Page). Whatever else it may contain, if there were no physical "record of the people of Nephi" there is little compelling reason to see the Book of Mormon as more than a novel or theological treatise—more interesting for its own history than the history it proclaims.[12] The historicity of the Book of Mormon makes tangible the revealed restoration. Even now, when the tangible is long distant from the physical plates upon which it was originally written, the keystone of our religion depends upon that original physicality.

The Book of Mormon can be read apart from history—discussions of the principles it teaches are most often written from the perspective of the relationship to the

---

[10] Matthew Roper, "Early Publications on the Book of Mormon," 44.

[11] Richard E. Bennett, "'A Nation Now Extinct,' American Indian Origin theories as of 1820," 31: "Professor Mitchill, on meeting with Martin Harris in February 1828 and after studying carefully his so-called Anthon transcript set it down as a genuine linguistic record of an ancient American people which was 'now extinct' and 'which he named.' A delicate people he called 'Australasians' were ultimately destroyed by a hardier, more warlike Asiatic people in a protracted series of ferocious wars culminating in one final battle of extermination, which both Mitchill and Governor Clinton traced to the Boughton Hill region near Palmyra, New York." See also Dan Vogel, *Indian Origins and the Book of Mormon*, chap. 3.

[12] Terryl L. Givens, "Foreword," xiv makes a similar point:

> As "inspired fiction," the argument runs, there is still much spiritual profit to be found in the volume, even if its origins are mired in fraud or delusion rather than grounded in pre-Columbian prophets inspired of God. For a variety of reasons, such efforts at a kind of religious détente may be well intentioned, but they are untenable. The book's unambiguous account of its own construction, as well as the historically defined reciprocity between Joseph Smith's own moral authority as a religious leader and the sacred status of the book inseparably wedded to his claims and career, admits of no simple divorce.

modern reader. This is a perfectly appropriate way to use a religious text.[13] Grant Hardy's *Understanding the Book of Mormon* and Joseph M. Spencer's *An Other Testament* provide excellent discussions of the text that do not require history as a background to the analysis.[14] In spite of the ability of readers to interact with the text as though it never existed in history, believers nevertheless accept that it did, even when they understand little of that history.

Conflicts over the Book of Mormon have not been of history, but of historicity. History studies the past and historicity studies the authenticity of the events recorded in a text from that past.[15] The question of the Book of Mormon's historicity is both simple and paramount: If it has historicity, it is a translation of an ancient document, just as it claims. If it has no historicity, then it is a modern document making deceptive claims about history (even if it could be seen as inspirational).[16]

This dilemma places the Book of Mormon in a tenuous position among texts declared to be scripture. It has no historical provenance. Unlike the Old Testament, it isn't *old*. Although the manuscript tradition of the Old Testament is solid only as early as about 200 B.C. (based on some of the Dead Sea Scrolls), it is still certain that the majority of the Hebrew Bible was established before 200 B.C. In contrast, there is no manuscript and indeed no information about the Book of Mormon prior to 1823.[17]

For the Bible, one may argue whether a particular event had historicity, but one cannot argue that the text itself has no historicity. The Bible can have a history and not be a history.[18] The Book of Mormon, on the other hand, cannot. The English text of the Book of Mormon has a known production date that begins in 1827. The Book of Mormon therefore presents a very simple either/or case. Because the English text is obviously modern, the text itself is either modern or, as it claims, ancient. If it is ancient, then its

---

[13] Nephi indicates that "I did liken all scriptures unto us, that it might be for our profit and learning" (1 Ne. 19:24). This description provides the model for using scripture from a previous time as an exemplar for current living.

[14] Grant Hardy, *Understanding the Book of Mormon: A Reader's Guide*. Joseph M. Spencer, *An Other Testament: On Typology*.

[15] Paul Y. Hoskisson, "Introduction," in *Historicity and the Latter-Day Saint Scriptures*, vii.

[16] Anthony A. Hutchinson, "The Word of God is Enough: The Book of Mormon as Nineteenth-Century Scripture," 1, suggests that "members of the Church of Jesus Christ of Latter-day Saints should confess in faith that the Book of Mormon is the word of God but also abandon claims that it is a historical record of the ancient peoples of the Americas."

This position attempts to separate spiritual value from historicity. It is certainly true that many can extract value from a text whether it has any historicity. The spiritual value of the Book of Mormon lies in its theology, not its history.

[17] Joseph Smith dates his first vision of Moroni to September 21, 1823 (Joseph Smith-History 1:27). This was the first indication of the existence of the Book of Mormon. It became much more widely known when the translation began in 1827. Of course the physical plates are the connection to antiquity, but they are no longer available and are not referenced in any ancient text yet discovered.

[18] This is the argument of a number of modern writers on the Bible. See, for instance, Thomas L. Thompson, *Mythic Past: Biblical Archaeology and the Myth of Israel*.

presence has no reasonable explanation and one must carefully examine the "unreasonable" explanation of its divine revelation and inspired translation.[19]

The early Saints implicitly understood the Book of Mormon in this context. Terryl L. Givens describes the relationship those early Saints had to their special book: "Looking at the Book of Mormon in terms of its early uses and reception, it becomes clear that this American scripture has exerted influence within the church and reaction outside the church not primarily by virtue of its substance, but rather its manner of appearing, not on the merits of what it says, but what it enacts."[20] The Book of Mormon stood and stands as a sign of a modern prophet. Its presence declares an open heaven with an interested and active God. It can do those things best as a translation of an ancient text. Only as a "record of the people of Nephi" does it have the power to declare its own extra-worldly connections and establish our extra-worldly hopes. As history it is a miracle. As not-history it might be called a "pious fraud."[21]

Both the first affirmations and the first reactions to the Book of Mormon implicitly acknowledge the fundamentality of the text's claim to historicity. For the early believers the miracle of translation was a fact that declared a prophet. Early disbelievers avowed its modern origin and claimed Joseph Smith as the sole (and unimpressive) author.[22] The battle lines of disagreement in early discussions of the historicity of the text had little to do with an examination of history. They were apologetics grounded in the faith-based assumptions of both sides of the issue. The two clear positions were either that one might accept new scripture or that the Bible

---

[19] Noel B. Reynolds, "Introduction," in *Book of Mormon Authorship: New Light on Ancient Origins*, 3: "One striking thing about the Book of Mormon is that if . . . tests confirm its antiquity, we have no plausible alternative to Joseph Smith's explanation of its existence. And that explanation asserts the existence of God directly." Daniel C. Peterson, "Introduction," *Review of Books on the Book of Mormon*, vi, note 4: "It would be rather difficult to believe the Book to be ancient and authentic and *not* regard it as scripture."

[20] Terryl L. Givens, *By the Hand of Mormon: The American Scripture that Launched a New World Religion*, 63–64.

[21] Vogel, *Joseph Smith, the Making of a Prophet*, xvii. The issue of "pious forgery" has also been applied to the Bible, although those who have done so have not used that term. See William G. Dever, *What Did the Biblical Writers Know and When Did They Know It: What Archaeology Can Tell Us about the Reality of Ancient Israel*, 273 note 49.

[22] Daniel C. Peterson, "'In the Hope That Something Will Stick': Changing Explanations for the Book of Mormon," xii–xiv.

Francis W. Kirkham, *A New Witness for Christ in America*, 267 quotes an article from the *Palmyra Reflector*, 21 January 1831 (date calculated from the information on page 262):

> The age of this modern prophet is supposed to be about twenty-four years. In his person he is tall and slender—thin favored—having but little expression of countenance, other than that of dullness; his mental powers appear to be extremely limited, and from the small opportunity he has had at school, he made little or no proficiency, and it is asserted by one of his principle [sic] followers, (who also pretends to divine illuminations,) that Joe, even at this day is profoundly ignorant of the meaning of many of the words contained in the Book of Mormon.

was sufficient. The text was historical if you believed in Joseph Smith as a prophet and modern if you believed Joseph Smith was a fraud.

Now approaching two hundred years later, we may point to a body of discoveries that can allow for a deeper understanding of the historical context that the faithful declare produced the Book of Mormon.[23] Hugh Nibley was a pioneer of the modern scholarly approach to the Book of Mormon. Over half a century ago, he declared that "no one can know too much about the Book of Mormon."[24] Both he and others he inspired have demonstrated that, not only can we not know too much, but that there is still much to know.

The Book of Mormon is no longer the intensely physical presence that it was for its writers or for Joseph and a select few. It becomes not physically but intellectually tangible through increased knowledge. For believers, understanding the historicity of the Book of Mormon provides an enriching background that can deepen our understanding of and experience with the text. For those who do not have that same faith, a sufficient goal is to create an argument that allows for an understanding of why we believe.[25]

---

[23] Hugh Nibley's writings on the Book of Mormon have opened this new era of scholarly convergences. Building on the foundation he established are various scholars who have written under the auspices of the Neal A. Maxwell Institute for Religious Scholarship (including its previous incarnation as the Foundation for Ancient Research and Mormon Studies). A single-volume discussion of some of their more important findings is *Echoes and Evidences of the Book of Mormon*, edited by Donald W. Parry, Daniel C. Peterson, and John W. Welch. *The Interpreter Foundation* is a more recent location for the publication of similar work. See www.mormoninterpreter.com.

[24] Hugh Nibley, *An Approach to the Book of Mormon*, 1.

[25] Givens, *By the Hand of Mormon*, Author's Note, unnumbered page: "My focus . . . has not been on whether the Book of Mormon or the account of it given by Joseph Smith is true. Rather, I have tried to examine why the Book of Mormon has been taken seriously—for very different reasons—by generations of devoted believers and confirmed skeptics."

1

Finding a Lost People

The Book of Mormon was a polarizing text even before it was officially available in March of 1830. The Book of Mormon was seen as either a new revelation or a new imposture. The editor of the *Cleveland Herald* was quick to reject: "Many will be shocked to learn there are those sacriligious [sic] enough to contend that a new bible has been given to the children of men. But it is even so."[1] Enthusiast or critic, the response to the text was conditioned by each reader's religious expectations.

When Thomas S. Kuhn began his study of the structure of scientific revolutions, he posed a scenario that is relevant to our study of the historicity of the Book of Mormon:

> Instructed to examine electrical or chemical phenomena, the man who is ignorant of these fields but who knows what it is to be scientific may legitimately reach any one of a number of incompatible conclusions. Among those legitimate possibilities, the particular conclusions he does arrive at are probably determined by his prior experience in other fields, by the accidents of his investigation, and by his own individual makeup. What beliefs about the stars, for example, does he bring to the study of chemistry or electricity? Which of the many conceivable experiments relevant to the new field does he elect to perform first: and what aspects of the complex that then results strike him as particularly relevant to an elucidation of the nature of chemical change or of electrical affinity?[2]

Since the publication of the Book of Mormon, every reader has approached the text with some kind of previous understanding which has informed the way she or he has perceived the text. Those experiences have yielded just what Kuhn suggests; "a number of incompatible conclusions." With respect to the Book of Mormon, each

---

[1] Matthew Roper, "Early Publications on the Book of Mormon," 44.
[2] Thomas S. Kuhn, *The Structure of Scientific Revolutions*, 3–4.
V. S. Ramachandran and Sandra Blakeslee, *Phantoms in the Brain: Probing the Mysteries of the Human Mind*, 134:

> At any given moment in our waking lives, our brains are flooded with a bewildering array of sensory inputs, all of which must be incorporated into a coherent perspective that's based on what stored memories already tell us is true about ourselves and the world. In order to generate coherent actions, the brain must have some way of sifting through this superabundance of detail and of ordering it into a stable and internally consistent "belief system"—a story that makes sense of the available evidence. Each time a new item of information comes in we fold it seamlessly into our preexisting worldview.

reader comes to the text in some way ignorant of the field. We attempt to understand it according to our "prior experience in other fields." That might be prior experience as a member of the Church of Jesus Christ of Latter-day Saints or of another Christian religion, or as scientists, historians, or more likely some combination of experiences.

Since it was first published, both believers and unbelievers have subjected the Book of Mormon to continual examination. As the fields of experience have changed over time for both the faithful and the non-believers, the explanations of the Book of Mormon have also changed. These explanations exhibit a dynamic reciprocal relationship between those who accept the Book of Mormon as scripture and those who do not.

When it was first published, both believers and critics had similar backgrounds in the Bible, although each used that background to argue their opposing views of the Book of Mormon. As new information or new approaches to history became available, they were applied to answering the enigma of the Book of Mormon.[3] When the "accepted model or pattern"[4] (or "paradigm" in Kuhn's terminology) used to examine the Book of Mormon changed, both believers and critics offered arguments to support their position within the new paradigm. New experiences and improved fields of expertise led to new explanations. As believers increased in sophistication in the fields of history, archaeology, and anthropology, their new explanations stimulated a critical response related to those perspectives. Similarly, criticism based on increased sophistication in the fields of history, archaeology, and anthropology required appropriate faithful responses within the parameters of those disciplines.

Nevertheless, the availability and application of a new paradigm to the question of Book of Mormon historicity has never created a clean break from previous paradigms. New paradigms simply do not immediately supplant the old.[5] The disagreements within the same paradigm dialectically lead to better and more refined responses to the opposing view. Unfortunately, participation of the older paradigms in the conversation simply leads to frustration and confusion, particularly in the complex problem that results when a critic raises issues from the old paradigm with an apologist rooted in the new (or vice versa). The slow and messy movement from one paradigm to another within the believing tradition has also seen the difficult process of having faithful Saints arguing among themselves, not about whether the Book of Mormon is true and historical, but how one accommodates that historicity as they separately understand both the evidence and the Book of Mormon.[6]

---

[3] Terryl L. Givens, *By the Hand of Mormon: The American Scripture that Launched a New World Religion*, 91–116, provides his view of the development of LDS apologetics concerning Book of Mormon historicity. Perhaps the clearest example of this dynamically interactive relationship starts with Hugh Nibley, *An Approach to the Book of Mormon*. As a manual of study for Melchizedek Priesthood quorums, Nibley introduced the body of the Church to a new way of thinking about the historical context of the Book of Mormon.

[4] Kuhn, *The Structure of Scientific Revolutions*, 23.

[5] Ibid., 19, notes this phenomenon in the development of scientific paradigms.

[6] For example: Edwin G. Goble, *Resurrecting Cumorah*, 10, 13:

In the Beginning: The Bible as Paradigm

If you lose something as important as ten tribes of Israel, it makes sense to look for them. In the late eighteenth and early nineteenth centuries, many found them among (or as) the Native Americans.[7] It was a predictable identification. Joseph Smith's contemporaries tended to use the Bible as a principal source of all information, both religious and scientific. According to the typical reading of Genesis, all populations were descendants of Noah's post-flood family (Gen. 10).[8] Adam Clarke's Bible commentary, written between 1798 and 1825, underscores this belief: "Eusebius and others state (from what authority we know not) that Noah was commanded of God to make a will and bequeath the whole of the earth to his three sons and their descendants in the following manner:—To Shem, all the East; to Ham, all Africa; to Japheth, the Continent of Europe with its isles, and the northern parts of Asia."[9]

Unfortunately, with the entire ancient world assigned to Shem, Ham, and Japheth, there was no son of Noah left to explain the native populations of the New World. Nevertheless, the European settlers in the New World could hardly ignore the people they were displacing. Into that theological and epistemological void came the remarkable idea that the Native Americans could be encompassed in the biblical definition of the world's races and resolve the issue of the lost tribes of Israel at the same time.

> Some people want to convert others to their point of view in the guise of "defense of the Church," when the Church itself takes no stance on the Geography. Some have a testimony of the New York Cumorah, and they are searching for the rest of the pieces that go along with it. They know that other settings do not feel right to them. . . .
>
> Overconfident Book of Mormon Theorists have merely *chosen* to reject the brand of rationality supplied by the theorists that disagree with their setting.
>
> Also Bruce H. Porter, and Rod L. Meldrum, *Prophecies and Promises: The Book of Mormon and the United States of America*, Preface:
>
> Much of the information presented here has hitherto been the subject of relatively unsympathetic review by an array of scholars who maintain that geographically speaking the only correct setting for the Book of Mormon lies in Mesoamerica. The authors of this work acknowledge that the information set forth within these pages does not necessarily harmonize with that view.

[7] Dan Vogel, *Indian Origins and the Book of Mormon*, chap. 3 provides background on the development of the theoretical and theological discussions of the identity of the natives of the Western hemisphere. By Joseph Smith's time the most popular idea was that the Native Americans represented remnants of the lost ten tribes of Israel, though other opinions were still present.

[8] Carl S. Ehrlich, "Noah," 558, "In many respects Noah was a second Adam. The genealogy of Genesis 5 makes his birth the first after the death of the progenitor of humanity. Like Adam, all people are his descendants. God's first command to the primordial pair to 'be fruitful and multiply, and fill the earth' (Gen. 1:28) is echoed in God's first command to Noah and his sons after the flood (Gen. 9:1)."

[9] Adam Clarke, *The Holy Bible Containing the Old and New Testaments*, 1:84. Italics in original silently removed.

The seeds of this idea were sown almost as soon as Europeans began to attempt explanations of these new people. Seemingly Christian traits among the Central American natives rapidly led to the hypothesis that St. Thomas—the wandering apostle—had preached to them.[10] Tradition taught that Thomas had preached in India, and these were, after all, Indians. For some early Spaniards, the Native Americans were St. Thomas's lapsed converts.

The Natives-as-remnants-of-the-ten-tribes explanation popular in the English-speaking world borrowed the nature of the Spanish arguments without similarly borrowing their conclusions.[11] Unfortunately, both Spanish and English based their conclusions on evidence that resulted from their limited understanding of native practices.[12]

Proponents of the lost ten tribes theory were quick to note similarities between Hebrew and any Native American language. Elias Boudinot's *Star in the West; Or a Humble Attempt to Discover the Long Lost Ten Tribes of Israel Preparatory to Their Return*

---

[10] Jacques Lafaye, *Quetzalcoatl and Guadalupe: The Formation of Mexican National Consciousness, 1531–1815*, 177–206, provides an excellent overview of the St. Thomas literature.

[11] Justin Winsor, *Narrative and Critical History of America*, 115–16, provides an extensive overview of this literature:

> The identification of the native Americans with the stock of the lost tribes of Israel very soon became a favorite theory with the early Spanish priests settled in America. Las Casas and Duran adopted it, while Torquemada and Acosta rejected it. André Thevet, of mendacious memory, did not help the theory by espousing it. It was approved in J. F. Lumnius's *De extreme Dei Judicio et Indorum vocatione, libri iii.* (Venice and Antwerp, 1569), and a century later the belief attracted new attention in the *Origen de los Americanos de Manasseh Ben Israel*, published at Amsterdam in 1650. It was in the same year (1650) that the question received the first public discussion in English in Thomas Thorowgood's *Jewes in America, or, Probabilities That the Americans Are of That Race. With the Removal of Some Contrary Reasoning, and Earnest Desires for Effectual Endeavors to Make the Christian* (London, 1650). Thornwood was answered by Sir Harmon L'Estrange in *Americans Not Iewes, or Improbabilities That the Americans Are of That Race* (London, 1652). The views of Thorowgood found sympathy with the Apostle Eliot of Massachusetts; and when Thorowgood replied to L'Estrange he joined with it an essay by Eliot, and the joint work was entitled *Iewes in America, or Probabilities That Those Indians Are Judaical, Made More Probable by Some Additions to the Former Conjectures: An Accurate Discourse Is Premised of Mr. John Eliot (Who Preached the Gospel to the Natives in Their Own Language) Touching Their Origination, and His Vindication of the Planters* (London, 1660). What seems to have been a sort of supplement, covering, however, in part the same ground, appeared as *Vindicia Judacorum, or a True Account of the Jews, Being More Accurately Illustrated than Heretofore*, which includes what is called "The learned conjectures of Rev. Mr. John Eliot." Some of the leading New England divines, like Mayhew and Mather, espoused the cause with similar faith. Roger Williams also was of the same opinion. William Penn is said to have held like views. The belief may be said to have been general, and had not died out in New England when Samuel Sewall, in 1697, published his *Phaenomena quaedam Apolcalyptica ad Aspectum Novi Orbis Configurata*.

[12] Brant A. Gardner, "Crucible of Distortion: The Impact of the Spanish on Native American Oral Tradition," examines the ways in which information about the Aztec deity Quetzalcoatl was distorted and reshaped from the native traditions into new forms as the Spanish fathers attempted to understand this new world and its people.

to Their Beloved City, Jerusalem (1816) began with a comment that, to a modern linguist, clearly indicates his unfamiliarity with the principles of historical linguistics:

> The Indian languages in general, are very copious and expressive, considering the narrow sphere in which they move; their ideas being few in comparison with civilized nations. They have neither cases nor declensions. They have a few or no prepositions—they remedy this, by affixes and suffixes, and their words are invariably the same in both numbers.
> All this, if the writer's information be correct, is very similar to the Hebrew language.[13]

To this tenuous connection, he added even more dubious linguistic proof. Boudinot's clinching argument was the undeniable remnant of Jehovah worship. He described a Native American ceremony:

> He begins the dance, after once going round the holy fire, in solemn and religious silence. He then in the next circle, invokes *yah*, after their usual manner, on a bass key and with a short accent. In another circle, he sings *ho, ho*, which is repeated by all the religious precession, till they finish that circle. Then in another round, they repeat *he, he*, in like manner, in regular notes, and keeping time in the dance. Another circle is continued in like manner, with repeating the word *wah, wah* (making in the whole, the divine and holy name of *yah, ho, he, wah*.) A little after this is finished, which takes considerable time, they begin again, going fresh rounds, singing *hal-hal-le-le-lu-lu-yah-yah*, in like manner; and frequently the whole train strike up *hallely, hallelu, halleluyah*, with great earnestness, fervour and joy, while each strikes the ground with right and left feet alternately, very quick, but well timed.[14]

The description of the ceremony appears to be reasonably accurate, but the description of the language surely is not. The listener/recorder discerned sounds, but made sense of them by familiarizing them into a full Anglicized Hebrew hallelujah chant and the specific invocation of Jehovah (again Anglicized rather than reflecting the more likely Hebrew pronunciation, transliterated as *Yahweh*).

Boudinot did not stop with just language similarities, however. He also suggested that the Indian ceremonies "are more after the Mosaic institution, than of pagan imitation."[15] He recorded one tribe's legend about crossing a mighty river on dry land as the great father opened the waters.[16] This same tribe believed that they had a book like the white man's long before the white man, but it had become lost.[17] These are

---

[13] Elias Boudinot, *Star in the West; Or a Humble Attempt to Discover the Long Lost Ten Tribes of Israel Preparatory to Their Return to Their Beloved City, Jerusalem*, 91–92.
[14] Ibid., 207–8.
[15] Ibid., 190.
[16] Ibid., 187.
[17] Ibid., 110–11.
The declaration that the Native Americans already had a book like the Bible upon the arrival of the Europeans shows up in other sources. A second source for North America is Charles Beatty, *A Journal of a Two Months Tour*, 90:

> A sober intelligent Indian, inquired of an English trader, when in one of the Indian towns, whether the English had not a book (meaning the bible) among them; and, being informed that they had, the Indian told the Englishman, that, that book was once, or long

very suggestive themes—though perhaps even more suggestive of the nature of cultural contact than specific content. They appear only in Western lore about the natives, or as clear Native American borrowing from stories the Christian missionaries told.

Very similar arguments are made in Ethan Smith's book, *View of the Hebrews* (originally published in 1823 with a second edition in 1825), which assumes them to be so compelling that "the question continually recurs, whence came things like these among the natives of our continent, or the American savages, unless these savages are the very tribes of Israel? No evidence is furnished that such a variety of Hebrew rites is found among any other people on earth, except the Jews."[18] In such a climate, it would

---

ago, theirs; and that, so long as they kept it, and acted according to it, their God was kind to them, and they prospered.

Also see a similar account in Gerónimo Mendieta, *Historia Eclesiástica Indiana*, 538. The theme of a native book that paralleled the Bible became a common theme widely separated in time and space, but doubtless owing to similar impulses rather than an actual text.

[18] Ethan Smith, *View of the Hebrews*, 108. Ethan Smith found this argument so compelling that when some objected to his first publication by indicating that the Afghans might, for similar reasons, be the remnants of the twelve tribes, he responded: "But should the Afghans prove to be of Israel, they may be from a tribe, or scattering people of ancient Israel, who tarried behind when most of that people set off for this continent." (Ibid., 212).

The scriptural basis for his conjecture comes from the Apocrypha:

In 2 Esdras xiii. 40, and on we read; "Those are the ten tribes which were carried away prisoners out of their own land, in the time of Osea, the king, whom Salmanezer, the king of Assyria, led away captive, and he carried them over the waters, and so came they into another land." Here is the planting of them over the Euphrates, in Media. The writer adds: "But they took this counsel among themselves, that they would leave the multitude of the heathen, and go forth into a further country, where never man dwelt; that they might there keep their statutes which they never kept (i.e. uniformly as they ought,) in their own land. There was a great way to go, namely of a year and a half." (Ibid., 47).

The New English Bible quotes these passages differently:

They are the ten tribes that were taken into exile in the days of King Hoshea, whom King Shalmaneser of Assyria made captive. Carrying them off beyond the river Euphrates, he deported them to a foreign country. But then they resolved to leave behind the gentile population and go to a more distant region never yet inhabited, and there at least to be obedient to their laws, which in their own country they had failed to keep. As they passed through the narrow passages of the Euphrates, the Most High performed miracles for them, halting the flow of the river until they had crossed over. Their long journey through that region called Arzareth took a year and a half. They have live there ever since, until this final age. (2 Esdras 13:40–46).

not be surprising for Joseph Smith to produce a book that declared that Native Americans were descended from the lost ten tribes.[19] What is surprising is that he didn't.[20]

The northern kingdom of Israel "lost" its tribes in 722 B.C. when the Assyrian king Shalmaneser V forcibly put down an Israelite rebellion and captured the capital city of Samaria, deporting many from the land.[21] That is over one hundred years before the Book of Mormon begins in the southern kingdom. Lehi's family came from a different time and different kingdom than the lost ten tribes (though he was descended from a northern lost tribe).[22] Rather than ten tribes, the Book of Mormon (for the most part) tells the story of a single family.[23] Nephi certainly drew parallels between his family's fate and the lost tribes of Israel, but they linked his people to the promises of Israel rather than the lost tribes.

In a religious environment expecting a book demonstrating why the Native Americans were the lost tribes of Israel, Joseph produced a book that managed to avoid

---

[19] Dale Morgan, *Dale Morgan on Early Mormonism: Correspondence and a New History*. Dale Morgan suggests that Joseph Smith's "cultural environ was, however, so rich in suggestion that the idea [to write a text explaining the American Indians] may have occurred to him independently." See also Vogel, *Indian Origins and the Book of Mormon*, chap. 3.

[20] John Gee, "The Wrong Kind of Book," 307–29, discusses his perception of what was expected of a book on this topic and how the Book of Mormon differs. I agree with his analysis but offer different contrasts between the Book of Mormon and what might have been expected.

[21] Siegfried H. Horn, "The Divided Monarchy: The Kingdoms of Judah and Israel," 130–31.

[22] Dan Vogel, *Joseph Smith: The Making of a Prophet*, 121–22. understands this difference, but ascribes it to Joseph's astute story making.:

> Early writers experimented with several possible Jewish migrations: a flight from Sennacherib about 700 B.C., navigation during the time of Solomon, and a flight from the Romans when Jerusalem was destroyed around A.D. 70. The theory which received the greatest support and captured the popular imagination of many in Smith's day identified Indians with the lost ten tribes of Israel. The situation was such that Josiah Priest could write in his book, *American Antiquities*, published in Albany, New York, in 1833: "The opinion that the American Indians are descendants of the lost ten tribes, is now a popular one, and generally believed.". . .
>
> To settle the controversy, Smith switched the location of Israelitish departure from the northern kingdom of Israel to the southern kingdom of Judah, specifically to the capital city of Jerusalem, and changed the time from 734 to 600 B.C. in order to have the migration party leave prior to the Babylonian captivity, which the author believed occurred about 600 B.C. This innovation made the task easier because a southern migration placed the story within familiar ground and allowed the narrative to draw from Old Testament prophets, especially Isaiah, whom the northern kingdom would not have known. To write about a northern migration would have required more inventiveness.

[23] In spite of the clear differences, the Book of Mormon story is easily subsumed into the lost ten tribes mythos. For example, Armand L. Mauss, *All Abraham's Children: Changing Mormon Conceptions of Race and Lineage*, 48–49, comments: "The story in the Book of Mormon made no attempt to account for all the lost tribes (though their continuing existence was clearly acknowledged). Rather, the book was linked to the popular genre by its account of certain Israelite 'stragglers' (as they might be called) who found their way to the Western Hemisphere before the Babylonian captivity of 589 B.C.E. brought a final end to the Davidic dynasty in Israel."

virtually every popular idea that was used to support that connection. The popular evidences of remnants of Hebrew language are entirely absent from the Book of Mormon. The popular discussion of remarkable Jewish rituals is also absent.[24] The religious intellectual society was primed for a book about the link between Native Americans and Israel, but it was not prepared for a book that used the seed of Israel in the New World to create a new scripture to accompany the Bible.

Nevertheless, these differences do not appear to have been noted or even been important to believers. The Bible furnished the paradigmatic expectation that Native Americans should be explained by the lost ten tribes. That biblical expectation and its secular expression were co-opted by the new Saints as proof the Book of Mormon in spite of its inapplicability to the Book of Mormon. Parley P. Pratt declared: "[The Book of Mormon] reveals the origin of the American Indian, which was before a mystery."[25]

Boudinot and Ethan Smith had discovered the origins of the Native Americans in the lost tribes, and Pratt saw the Book of Mormon as solving the very same question. LDS authors even readily adopted the very "proofs" that Native Americans were lost Israel and used them as support for Book of Mormon historicity.[26] Both critic and believer shared an explanatory paradigm but applied it differently—one supporting the Bible's lost tribes and the other the Book of Mormon's remnant of Israel.[27]

Quite apart from the biblically based desire to explain the Native Americans, the Bible was the quintessential measuring stick for the authenticity of the Book of Mormon. The earliest arguments against the Book of Mormon were not about its historicity, but its biblical verisimilitude. One of the earliest theological reviews of the Book of Mormon came from the pen of Richard McNemar, a prominent Shaker and former Presbyterian minister, who received a copy of the Book of Mormon as part of the early missionary journey to the "Lamanites" (D&C 28:8). In January 1831 he wrote:

> Whatever benefit the Indians may derive from this book of Mormon certain it is we can derive none. Its endless genealogies & Chronologies, afford no light to a Believer. In

---

[24] The Jewish rituals are absent from explicit discussion, but there are textual traces that allow for the recreation of some that appear to inform the action of the text. See Terrence L. Szink and John W. Welch. "King Benjamin's Speech in the Context of Ancient Israelite Festivals," 147–223 and Stephen D. Ricks, "Kingship, Coronation, and Covenant in Mosiah 1–6," 233–75.

[25] Parley P. Pratt, *A Voice of Warning, and Instruction to All People*, 112.

[26] These claims persisted into the early years of the more scholarly approach to the Book of Mormon. See, for example, B.H. Roberts, *New Witnesses for God*, vol. 3 chap. 32, "External Evidences – The Hebrew Origin of the Native American Races—Hebrew Relics"; John A. Widtsoe, *Seven Claims of the Book of Mormon* ("Claim Four: The American Aborigines Are in Part of Hebrew Descent"); Josiah E. Hickman, *The Romance of the Book of Mormon*, chap. 8, "Traditions and Beliefs Indicate That the Indian Aborigines Are of Hebrew Origin"). On page 99, Hickman quotes Boudinot citing Adair. Similar ideas even found expression in General Conference. See Antony W. Ivins, *Conference Report, April 1909*. Unfortunately, those ideas and authors have not withstood the scrutiny of modern scholarship.

[27] Book of Mormon peoples as a remnant of Israel: Title page, 1 Ne. 15:14; 19:24; 2 Ne. 28:2; 30:4; Alma 46:23–24, 27; 3 Ne. 5:23–24; 10:17; 15:12; 20:10, 16; 21:2, 12, 22–23; 4 Ne. 1:49; Morm. 5:12; 7:1, 10; Ether 13:6–8, 10 (Moroni's interjection about the Lehites).

the New heavens & earth these old things are not to be remembered neither come into mind. We can have no idea of a new & better generation starting up from those brass plates. Or that the seed of Joseph is any better to begin with than the other tribes whatever Ghost they may have to minister. It will prove to be the same old unclean spirit or the spirit of an unclean devil. In all the history of those American churches there is a not [sic] a lick about any cross against the flesh. Or any association on the principle of the self denial, Water baptism was their all.

To give heed to those cunningly devised fables [which?] minister strife rather than godly edifying may suit an apostate but not a settled believer the law of Christ is not written on plates of brass or kept in boxes of stone but on fleshly tables of the heart & kept in the chh. To which we do well to take heed.[28]

McNemar made no analysis of historicity. It was sufficient that the Book of Mormon is not the Bible. Only a month later, Alexander Campbell, one of the leaders of the restoration movement, offered a longer critique. That critique still focused on the comparison between the Bible and the Book of Mormon rather than any historical issue:

1. Smith, its real author, as ignorant and impudent a knave as ever wrote a book, betrays the cloven foot in basing his whole book upon a false fact, or a pretended fact, which makes God a liar. It is this: With the Jews, God made a covenant at Mount Sinai, and instituted a priesthood. . . .

2. This ignorant and impudent liar, in the next place, makes the God of Abraham, Isaac and Jacob, violate his covenants with Israel and Judah, concerning the land of Canaan, by promising a new land to the pious Jew. . . .

3. He has more of the Jews, living in the new world, than could have been numbered any where else, even in the days of John the Baptist; and has placed them under a new dynasty. . . .

4. He represents the temple worship as continued in his new land of promise contrary to every precept of the law, and so happy are the people of Nephi as never to shed a tear on account of the excision, nor turn an eye toward Jerusalem or God's temple. The pious Jews in their captivity turned their faces to Jerusalem and the holy place, and remembered God's promises concerning the place where he recorded his name. . . .

5. Malachi, the last of the Jewish prophets, commanded Israel to regard the law of Moses till the Messiah came. And Moses commanded them to regard him till the Great Prophet came. But Nephi and Smith's prophets institute ordinances and observances for the Jews, subversive of Moses, 500 years before the Great Prophet came.

6. Passing over a hundred similar errors, we shall next notice his ignorance of the New Testament matters and things. . . .[29]

Although critics such as McNemar and Campbell viewed the Book of Mormon unfavorably against the Bible, believers used the biblical paradigm to support the Book of Mormon. A recently baptized William E. McLellan wrote of one of his missionary efforts in 1831:

---

[28] Christian Goodwillie, "Shaker Richard McNemar: The Earliest Book of Mormon Reviewer," 144–45. Bracketed text Goodwillie's.
[29] Alexander Campbell, "Delusions (February 10, 1831)," 91–93.

> We attended our appointment. A numerous concourse of people attended, —I think about 500—If ever I felt small, and felt my dependence on God, now was the time. To have to ascend the judges [sic] bench and face Judges, Lawyers Doctors Priests and people. But I arose with confidence in Elijah's God and gave them a brief history of the book of Mormon, of its coming forth &c, Then reasoned upon and expounded prophecy after prophecy and scripture after scripture, which had reference to the book and to these days. . . .[30]

Paul Gutjahr gives other examples of the perceived harmony between the Bible and the Book of Mormon:

> Mormon converts frequently speak of how they came to a faith in Smith's teachings by reading the Book of Mormon and the Bible side-by-side. One such convert, Eli Gilbert, wrote that upon receiving a copy of the book of Mormon, he "examined the proof; the witnesses, and all other testimony, and compared it with that of the bible (which book I verily thought I believed.) and found the two books mutually and reciprocally corroborate each other; and if I let go the book of Mormon, the bible might also go down by the same rule." Luman Shurtliff, another early convert to Mormonism, agreed: "When through reading, my mother asked me what I thought of the Mormon book. I told her that I was satisfied that the Book of Mormon was not made by man and I did not believe any man living by his knowledge of the Bible could do it and have it harmonize and agree with prophets, revelations and teachings of Christ and the apostles as that book did."[31]

This biblical perspective remained, but was augmented by the groundwork already established for using antiquities to demonstrate the connection between Native Americans and a sacred book. That evidentiary thread developed into the next wave of support for the Book of Mormon's relationship to antiquity. These two early approaches to the text may have been slightly sequential, but co-existed for decades if not nearly a century.

The Pre-Critical Use of External Evidence

It didn't take long to realize that if the Book of Mormon told a history of Native Americans, one might see evidence for the Book of Mormon in the artifacts left by bygone Native Americans. There is some indication that this possibility was understood very early and that it was the object of some trepidation. In a second-hand account of a second-hand account, Apostle LeGrand Richards related: "I have never seen this in print, but I heard President Callis make this statement: that after the Book of Mormon came forth the Prophet Joseph was terribly worried . . . and he said, 'O Lord, what will the world say?' And the answer came back, 'Fear not, I will cause

---

[30] William E. McLellin, *The Journals of William E. McLellin: 1831–1836*, 39. McLellin was baptized August 20, 1831, and preached this sermon September 10, 1831.
[31] Paul Gutjahr, "The Golden Bible in the Bible's Golden Age: The Book of Mormon and Antebellum Print Culture," 36.

the earth to testify of the truth of these things.'"[32] The attribution to Joseph cannot be directly confirmed but may perhaps be indirectly confirmed by David Whitmer's 1883 recollection: "When we [the Witnesses] were first told to publish our statement, we felt sure the people would not believe it, for the Book told of a people who were refined and dwelt in large cities; but the Lord told us that He would make it known to the people, and people should discover the ruins of lost cities and abundant evidence of the truth of what is written in the Book."[33] If the promise was that lost cities and evidence of civilization would be discovered, we can understand why those two elements of archaeology were the focus of early Saints' antiquarian interests.

One of the more short-lived scholarly explanations of Native American origins may have had its most lasting influence among Latter-day Saints. Professor Samuel Mitchill of Columbia College had worked with the Five Nations (Mohawk, Oneida, Onondaga, Cayuga, and Seneca). He began to develop his own ideas about their origin. Richard E. Bennett summarized Mitchill's threefold interpretation of Native America history:

> that three races of Malays, Tartars, and Scandinavians contributed to make up the American population;
>
> that the Tartars eventually overwhelmed and destroyed the other two races over a fairly long period of time; and finally
>
> that the final battles of extermination were fought in upstate western New York not too far south of Lake Ontario.[34]

Bennett also notes that: "De Witt Clinton—a student and admirer of Mitchill, a keen observer of the Iroquois and the other Five Nations Indian tribes, New York City mayor, later governor of New York, and one-time candidate for president of the United States—ardently subscribed to this theory."[35]

The inclusion of the obviously light-skinned Scandinavians as a destroyed people, combined with a final destruction in western New York, must have welcome corroboration for the early Saints. The Book of Mormon phrase "white and delightsome" as well as the final battle around the New York Hill Cumorah appeared

---

[32] LeGrand Richards, *Conference Report, April 1955*. Charles A. Callis was born in 1865 and immigrated to the United States in 1875, so his statement was at least second hand prior to Elder Richards's second hand reference.
Mark Alan Wright, "Joseph Smith and Native American Artifacts," 1–2 quoted both Richards and Whitmer. I express appreciation for a copy of Wright's paper and permission to quote from it. I acknowledge his research as the source of these two statements.

[33] David Whitmer, "James H. Hart Interview, Richmond, Missouri, 21 August 1883," 96.

[34] Richard E. Bennett, "'A Nation Now Extinct,' American Indian Origin theories as of 1820," 42.

[35] Ibid., 43. A more recent discussion of Harris's visit to Mitchill and Anthon is found in Michael Hubbard MacKay and Gerrit J. Dirkmaat, *From Darkness unto Light: Joseph Smith's Translation and Publication of the Book of Mormon*, 39–59.

to have scientific corroboration.[36] That Dr. Mitchill was one of the wise men Martin Harris consulted during his trip to New York when he famously met Dr. Charles Anthon may have abetted the acceptance of Mitchill's theories.[37]

I have found no direct corroboration from any early Latter-day Saint of familiarity with Mitchill's theory, but those ideas need not have come directly from Mitchill. Mitchill's ideas influenced a work that became an important source of evidence for the Book of Mormon. In 1833 Josiah Priest published his *American Antiquities: Discoveries in the West*, which used the remains of earlier Native American populations as evidence for the remnants of the lost tribes in the New World. His use of archaeology doesn't come close to modern standards, but it reflected the opinions and general scholarship of the day. He began:

> We shall now attend more particularly, to the evidence of an ancient population in this country, anterior to that of the present race of Indians, afforded in the discovery of forts, mounds, tumuli, and their contents, as related by eastern travelers, and the researches of the Antiquarian Society, at Cincinnati. But before we proceed to an account of the traits of this kind of population, more than already given, we will remark, that wherever plats of ground, struck out into circles, squares and ovals, are found we are at once referred to an era when a people and nation existed in this country, more civilized, refined, and given to architectural and agricultural pursuits, than the Indians.[38]

Priest used the mound-building cultures along the Mississippi as the model for his ten tribes theory. Early Saints were quick to accept his evidence in support of the Book of Mormon. Terryl L. Givens notes:

> [Priest's book] prevailed among Joseph Smith's followers in particular. Priest's book was referenced or excerpted five times in the church's *Times and Seasons*, and eight years later it contributed to the first sustained attempt to connect the Book of Mormon to North American antiquities, Charles Thompson's 1841 *Evidences in Proof of the Book of Mormon*. That work borrowed extensively from Priest's accounts of ruins in Ohio and Tennessee and juxtaposed them with descriptions of Nephite fortifications and defenses. The parallels were, to Thompson's mind, "sufficient to show to the public that the people whose history is contained in the Book of Mormon, are the authors of these works."[39]

The association between the mound builders and the Book of Mormon still has its proponents. The modern argument follows the same basic logic, often using the same sources.[40] Nevertheless, the emphasis on the Mississippian cultures was gradually

---

[36] See Chapter 6, "The Lamanite Skin of Blackness," for the use of "white" as a metaphor rather than an indication of pigmentation.

[37] Stanley B. Kimball, "The Anthon Transcript: People, Primary Sources, and Problems," 6–7, discusses how he identified "Dr. Mitchell" as Samuel L. Mitchill of Columbia College.

[38] Josiah Priest, *American Antiquities and Discoveries in the West*, 83–84. Italics silently removed.

[39] Givens, *By the Hand of Mormon*, 97.

[40] Edwin G. Goble and Wayne N. May. *This Land: Zarahemla and the Nephite Nation*; Phyllis Carol Olive, *The Lost Tribes of the Book of Mormon*; Porter and Meldrum, *Prophecies and Promises: The Book of Mormon and the United States of America*.

overshadowed as reports of new and more spectacular discoveries in Mesoamerica surfaced. In February of 1833, the following appeared in *The Evening and Morning Star:*

> A late number of the London Literary Gazette, contains a letter from Lieut. Col. Galindo, at Peten, in Central America, giving some idea of those antiquities which rescue ancient America from the charge of barbarism. These ruins extend for more than twenty miles, and must anciently have embraced a city and its suburbs. The principal edifice is supposed to have been a palace, formed of two rows of galleries, eight feet wide, separated by walls a yard thick; the height of the walls to the eaves is nine feet, and thence three yards more to the top. The stones of which all the edifices are built, are about eighteen inches long, nine broad and two thick, cemented by morter [sic]. . . .
>
> REMARKS. We are glad to see the proof begin to come, of the original or ancient inhabitants of this continent. It is good testimony in favor of the book of Mormon, and the book of Mormon is good testimony that such things as cities and civilization, "prior to the fourteenth century," existed in America.[41]

Colonel Galindo's notice was the beginning of the information that began to flow from Mesoamerica. Readers excitedly learned of the evidence of impressive cultures that dwarfed that of the mound builders. In the eclectic and uncritical methods of the day, the new cultures were proof of the Book of Mormon just as the mound builders had been. The 1842 publication of Stephens and Catherwood's *Incidents of Travel in Central America, Chiapas, and Yucatan*, made such an impression that several of those cities were touted as Book of Mormon sites. An unattributed editorial passage in the *Times and Seasons* reports:[42]

> Since our "Extract" was published from Mr. Stephens' "Incidents of Travel," &c., we have found another important fact relating to the truth of the Book of Mormon. Central America, or Guatimala [sic], is situated north of the Isthmus of Darien and once embraced

---

[41] "Discovery of Ancient Ruins in Central America," 71.

[42] Because this editorial is not signed, there is some question about its authorship. Joseph Smith was editor at the time and therefore might have been the author. If that is the case, then we have Joseph Smith endorsing a Mesoamerican location for the Book of Mormon (although it is also likely that he had a rather inclusive view of Book of Mormon lands that still incorporated North American lands).

Historian Ron Barney, personal communication, does not believe that Joseph would have been the author of this passage. He suggested, based on his experience with Joseph Smith's papers, that Joseph simply wouldn't have written that. On the other hand, John L. Lund, *Joseph Smith and the Geography of the Book of Mormon*, 57–65, 87–104, discusses evidence that he finds supportive of Joseph as the author of these strong statements about Mesoamerica and the Book of Mormon.

Matthew Roper, Paul Fields, and Atul Nepal, "Wordprint Analysis and Joseph Smith's Role as Editor of the *Times and Season*," 1–2 provides a different type of analysis from Lund's but which comes to the same conclusion. Matthew Roper, Paul J. Fields, and Atul Nepal, "Joseph Smith, the *Times and Seasons*, and Central American Ruins," 85–97 use both historical and stylometric evidence to support Joseph as the author. Importantly, they note: "Regardless of who wrote the *Times and Seasons* editorials linking the Book of Mormon to Central America, it is difficult to argue that Joseph Smith was unaware of or would have disapproved of the content of the editorials."

several hundred miles of territory from north to south.—The city of Zarahemla, burnt at the crucifixion of the Savior, and rebuilt afterwards, stood upon this land as will be seen from the following words in the book of Alma:— "And now it was only the distance of a day and a half's journey for a Nephite, on the line Bountiful, and the land Desolation, from the east to the west sea; and thus the land of Nephi, and the land of Zarahemla was nearly surrounded by water: there being a small neck of land between the land northward and the land southward." [Alma 22:32]

It is certainly a good thing for the excellency and veracity, of the divine authenticity of the Book of Mormon, that the ruins of Zarahemla have been found where the Nephites left them: and that a large stone with engravings upon it, as Mosiah said [Omni 1:20]; and a *"large round* stone, with the sides sculptured in hieroglyphics," as Mr. Stephens has published, is also among the left remembrances of the, (to him,) *lost and unknown.* We are not agoing to declare positively that the ruins of Quiriguá are those of Zarahemla, but when the land and the stones, and the books tell the story so plain, we are of opinion, that it would require more proof than the Jews could bring to prove the disciples stole the body of Jesus from the tomb, to prove that the ruins of the city in question, are not one of those referred to in the Book of Mormon.[43]

The Central American ruins were significantly more impressive than those of the mound builders, and the connection to the Book of Mormon was made on no better evidence than their impressiveness. The Book of Mormon suggested cities and civilized Indians. The Lord had promised evidence of cities and civilized Indians. The mound builder ruins suggested cities and civilized Indians. The Central American ruins suggested even greater cities and more civilized peoples, and therefore they were even more "appropriate" remnants of the civilized Nephites.[44]

---

[43] "Zarahemla," *Times and Seasons,* 927.

[44] Grant Underwood, "Book of Mormon Usage in Early LDS Theology," 49–50.

> The first half of the nineteenth century probably saw the relationship between science and religion reach its apex. In America, where the twin ideals of Scottish Common Sense philosophy and the Baconian inductive method reigned supreme, the association was especially congenial. During this Indian summer before Darwin seemingly dealt the death blow to biblical literalism, a plethora of publications confidently set forth the "evidences of Christianity." The undergirding faith of this literature was simple. "The God of science was after all the God of Scripture," explains religious historian George Marsden. "It should not be difficult to demonstrate, therefore, that what he revealed in one realm perfectly harmonized with what he revealed in the other. The perspicuity of nature should confirm the perspicuity of Scripture."
>
> Such, too, was the faith of the Saints when it came to establishing the authenticity of the Book of Mormon. No one doubted for a moment that what explorer John L. Stephens was discovering in Central America and the Yucatan in the early 1840s was tangible testimony to the book's truthfulness. The tower at Palenque was surely the temple mentioned in 2 Nephi 5; the ruins of Quiriguá almost certainly the city of Zarahemla; and the Isthmus of Darien (Panama) the "narrow neck of land." Extracts from Stephens's book, *Incidents of Travel in Central America, Chiapas, & Yucatan,* were published in church periodicals with considerable jubilation. "It affords us great joy," wrote the editor of the *Times and Seasons,* "to have the world assist us to so much proof."

At this point in time, neither secular nor LDS thinkers spent much time working on the dating of the sites. No one worried about whether any of the discovered civilizations had existed during Book of Mormon times. Nor did the excitement over Mesoamerican cities replace the interest in the mound builders. It was a time when virtually anything was accepted as a proof, and the early Saints were happy to chase the latest finds and integrate them into previously accepted models.[45] It was a time for eclecticism, not rigorous scholarship.[46] Dan Vogel reminds us: "Archaeology, anthropology, linguistics, and other disciplines were still in their infancy at the time, and scientific answers were yet on the horizon. Although a majority of the early writers came close to modern thinking on several points regarding Indian origins, they did not arrive at their ideas through scientific investigation but rather through philosophical speculation."[47]

---

[45] Matthew Roper, "Limited Geography and the Book of Mormon: Historical Antecedents And Early Interpretations," 254–55.

All nineteenth-century writers on Book of Mormon geography apparently assumed that the place where Joseph Smith found the plates and the hill where the Nephites met their destruction were identical. Aside from this one point, however, the diversity of nineteenth-century opinion is striking. Yet this fact has not been fully appreciated by students of the Book of Mormon or their critics. Did Lehi land in Chile? Cobiga, Bolivia? Lima, Peru? A little south of the Isthmus of Darien? Or "on the Pacific side of the southern part of Central America"? Where was the land of Nephi? Was it in South America? In Ecuador? Bolivia? Venezuela? Or was it in Central America? Guatemala? Was the land of Zarahemla in Colombia in South America? Further north in Honduras? Or in Mexico? Was the river Sidon the Magdalena in Colombia? Or was it the Usumacinta in Mexico? Was the narrow neck of land in Panama, at the Isthmus of Darien? By the Bay of Honduras? Or was it at the Isthmus of Tehuantepec in Mexico? Was the land of Desolation near the Isthmus of Darien? Honduras? Yucatán? Or in the United States between the Mississippi River and the Rocky Mountains? Were the Jaredites destroyed at the hill in New York or in Honduras in Central America? It is worth emphasizing that these points of disagreement are not over peripheral or insignificant matters but over key elements that are central to any discussion of Book of Mormon geography. The fact that there was such wide disagreement during the first fifty years after the publication of the Book of Mormon strongly suggests that no one view prevailed. It also indicates the absence of an authoritative stance on the subject.

I agree with Roper that there was no authoritative stance. However, I disagree that these ideas necessarily represented different models. I doubt that there was even the idea of creating a model. Rather, these ideas floated independently of each other, and were accepted and acceptable even where modern readers see conflicts among them.

[46] Tyler Livingston, "Book of Mormon Geography in Joseph's Day," provides a review of opinions of geography from various early Saints recorded during Joseph Smith's lifetime. Livingston provides an interesting chart that shows the number of references to different geographic correlations, and it is clear that all had some acceptance, and many were seen as equally possible.

More information is available in the FairMormon Wiki: "Nineteenth Century: Statements during Joseph Smith's lifetime: Part I – 1829–1840."

[47] Vogel. *Indian Origins and the Book of Mormon*, 7.

16 *Traditions of the Fathers*

Orson Pratt is an excellent example of the non-critical assembling of data from all sources into "proofs" of the Book of Mormon. In August of 1843, Wilford Woodruff wrote: "[Orson Pratt] spoke in an edifying manner concerning the Book of Mormon its history what it was &c. That it was a History of nearly one half of the globe & the people that inhabited it, that it gave a history of all those cities that have been of late discovered by Stephens and Catherwood, that it named those cities."[48] Pratt certainly never attempted to reconcile a Mesoamerican setting for some cities with the idea that the entire hemisphere (in his understanding, literally "one half of the globe") was populated by Book of Mormon peoples.

By 1866, Orson Pratt had created a correlation that used Panama as the narrow neck of land and distributed locations over the entire hemisphere. He accepted the New York drumlin as the Hill Cumorah and correlated the Sidon River with the Magdalena River in Columbia. He was not particularly careful in the distribution of his cities. For instance, he locates most of the Book of Mormon cities in Central America but Bountiful south of Panama, even though the Book of Mormon requires that Bountiful be north of the majority of Nephite cities.[49] Pratt's ideas were incorporated into the footnotes of the 1879 edition of the Book of Mormon, when he also formatted it into our current chapters.[50] No doubt their presence in the footnotes lent authority to Pratt's opinions, even though the information was removed from the footnotes for the next edition in 1920.

Removing Pratt's notes did not, however, reduce their general acceptance. Janne M. Sjodahl published his *An Introduction to the Study of the Book of Mormon: A Suggested Key to Book of Mormon Geography* in 1927. It continued the tradition of the eclectic acceptance of evidence from the entire hemisphere and across time periods uncorrelated with the Book of Mormon.[51] This model gained the luster of tradition, remaining the primary explanatory paradigm for the Book of Mormon for over 100 years.

Of this period in LDS history, Mark Alan Wright concludes:

> The Saints were surrounded by Native American material culture virtually everywhere they settled. There are only a handful of events that indicate that Joseph was directly interacting with or commenting on them. He does not seek them out, but rather only comments on them when they happen to come to his attention. . . . Almost without exception Joseph seeks to sacralize Native American artifacts by placing them within the context of scriptural peoples or places, the very scriptures he helped bring to light. The

---

[48] Wilford Woodruff, *Wilford Woodruff's Journal*, 2:282, August 27, 1843; *History of the Church*, 552.

[49] John L. Sorenson, *The Geography of Book of Mormon Events: A Source Book*, 159.

[50] Roper, "Limited Geography and the Book of Mormon," 232.

[51] Janne M. Sjodahl, *An Introduction to the Study of the Book of Mormon: A Suggested Key to Book of Mormon Geography*. Sjodahl accepts the New York Hill as Cumorah (5–8), highly speculative linguistic connections (156–97), as well as archaeological data ranging from South America to the New York region.

artifacts and the scriptures had a symbiotic relationship in his mind; the scriptures provided the history of the objects, the objects proved the history of the scriptures.[52]

Scholarship Joins Faith

For much of the last half of the nineteenth century, the Saints were more concerned with the scholarship of soil, water, and community creation than they were about the relatively esoteric question of where the Book of Mormon took place.[53] As the Saints were able to move beyond taming a wild land, they began to tame intellectual frontiers.[54] Between 1907 and 1909 four professors trained at eastern Universities were hired for Brigham Young University: "Henry Peters, an M.A. from Harvard; Joseph Peters, a Ph.D. from Chicago; Ralph Chamberlin, a Ph.D. from Cornell; and William Chamberlin, trained at Berkeley and Chicago."[55]

Along with this expansion of interests from physical necessity to intellectual electives came a renewal of interest in the Book of Mormon. By 1890, Book of Mormon geography appears to have become a prominent Sunday School hobby but had not yet attracted the attention of the trained scholars. President George Q. Cannon noted in an editorial that year in the *Juvenile Instructor*:

> There is a tendency, strongly manifested at the present time among some of the brethren, to study the geography of the Book of Mormon. We have heard of numerous lectures, illustrated by suggestive maps, being delivered on this subject during the present winter, generally under the auspices of the Improvement Societies and Sunday Schools. We are

---

[52] Wright, "Joseph Smith and Native American Artifacts," 16–17. Slight change in punctuation to improve clarity.

[53] Sorenson, *The Geography of Book of Mormon Events*, 17, "In the early pioneering period in Utah no attention seems to have been given to this subject [Book of Mormon geography], as shown by a complete absence of significant printed statements for more than fifteen years."

Brigham H. Madsen, "Reflections on LDS Disbelief in the Book of Mormon as History," 87: "The hardships encountered in crossing the plains and establishing Zion in the desert Great Basin, plus the long fight with the United States government over polygamy, left little time for scientific investigations of the historicity of the Book of Mormon."

[54] Leonard J. Arrington and Davis Bitton, *The Mormon Experience: A History of the Latter-day Saints*, 253–55. The push for education naturally led to a desire for better trained teachers. See James B. Allen and Glen M. Leonard, *The Story of the Latter-day Saints*, 527–29.

Perhaps indicative of the more probing nature of Book of Mormon discussions at this point is the work of B.H. Roberts. See Davis Bitton, "B. H. Roberts and Book of Mormon Scholarship: Early Twentieth Century: Age of Transition," 60–69.

[55] Thomas G. Alexander, *Mormonism in Transition: A History of the Latter-day Saints, 1890–1930*, 171. James B. Allen and Glen M. Leonard, *The Story of the Latter-day Saints*, 529: "The challenge of secularism in religious education was indeed a real one. The scientific method discounted experiences that could not be tested and demonstrated; therefore, the element of inspiration and revelation in the writing and interpretation of the scriptures was increasingly challenged. On the other hand, the new methodology was producing important information that Church teachers could not ignore if they were to respond intelligently to students' questions. Perhaps this movement to greater secular learning was too rapid for some. Some of these pioneers were fired a few short years later."

greatly pleased to notice the increasing interest taken by the Saints in this holy book.... But as valuable as is the Book of Mormon both in doctrine and history, yet it is possible to put this sacred volume to uses for which it was never intended, uses which are detrimental rather than advantageous to the cause of truth, and consequently to the work of the Lord.

We have been led to these thoughts from the fact that the brethren who lecture on the lands of the Nephites or the geography of the Book of Mormon are not united in their conclusions. No two of them, so far as we have learned, are agreed on all points, and in many cases the variations amount to tens of thousands of miles. These differences of views lead to discussion, contention and perplexity; and we believe more confusion is caused by these divergences than good is done by the truths elicited.[56]

Although ultimately concerned because of the contentions that arose, President Cannon did not believe that the investigation should necessarily end:

The First Presidency have often been asked to prepare some suggestive map illustrative of Nephite geography, but have never consented to do so. Nor are we acquainted with any of the Twelve Apostles who would undertake such a task. The reason is, that without further information they are not prepared even to suggest. The word of the Lord or the translation of other ancient records is required to clear up many points now so obscure that, as we have said, no two original investigators agree with regard to them....

Of course, there can be no harm result from the study of the geography of this continent at the time it was settled by the Nephites, drawing all the information possibly [sic] from the record which has been translated for our benefit.[57]

In 1903 the Church held a convention at what would become Brigham Young University. The conference was devoted to discussions of Book of Mormon geography. Participants included Benjamin Cluff Jr., Robert Holmes (who had written "Geographical Sketches of the Book of Mormon," B. H. Roberts, and James E. Talmage.[58] Two decades later, Talmage, who was by then an apostle, took part in the preparations for a new edition of the Book of Mormon. He noted in his journal on January 14, 1921: "In addition to other committee work I attended an afternoon session of the Book of Mormon committee, at which preliminary arrangements were made for hearing some of the proponents of different views on Book of Mormon geography. Many varied and conflicting views concerning the location of Book of Mormon lands have been advocated amongst our people; and not a few maps have been put out. With all precautions taken to make plain the fact that these maps have been intended as suggestive presentations only, we find some people accepting one map and others another as authoritative."[59]

None of these geographies appears to have had any more rigor than earlier ones. While not examining the question of geography, B. H. Roberts nevertheless began to look at

---

[56] George Q. Cannon, "Editorial Thoughts—Book of Mormon Geography," 18.
[57] Ibid., 18–19.
[58] "Book of Mormon Students Meet. Interesting Convention Held in Provo Saturday and Sunday," 108–10. The article consists of excerpts from a *Deseret Evening News* article May 25, 1903.
[59] Trevor Antley, "The Talmage Journals: The Book of Mormon Geography Hearings, 1921."

archaeological evidence that might support the Book of Mormon. Brigham D. Madsen notes: "In his 1909 publication Roberts concluded that after looking at studies of the latest scientific examinations of ruins in Central and South America, he was convinced that there was no conflict between them and the claims of the Book of Mormon and that much of the archaeological science supported the Joseph Smith account."[60]

By at least 1917 a more limited geography centered on Mesoamerica had been proposed. Michael D. Coe notes:

> Probably the most careful scholar to work in this tradition [intellectual study of "Book of Mormon geography"] was Louis E. Hills of the Reorganized Church in Independence, a

---

[60] Brigham D. Madsen, "Reflections on LDS Disbelief in the Book of Mormon as History," 88.

After his 1909 work, B. H. Roberts prepared some documents between 1922 and 1927 which were never intended for publication. These documents frankly discuss difficulties and issues with the Book of Mormon, many of which are directly related to Roberts's acceptance of both a hemispheric geography and the Book of Mormon peoples as the sole source of populating the Americas. B. H. Roberts, *Studies of the Book of Mormon*, ix–xi, gives his intention not to publish this material and the dates he wrote it.

The idea that Roberts may have lost his testimony of the Book of Mormon is certainly incorrect at least after the preparation of his first investigation. In a letter to President Heber J. Grant, dated March 15, 1923 (editor Brigham D. Madsen argues that it should be 1922), recorded in Roberts, *Studies of the Book of Mormon*, 57–58, Roberts states:

> In writing out this my report to you of those studies, I have written it from the viewpoint of an open mind, investigating the facts of the Book of Mormon origin and authorship. Let me say once and for all, so as to avoid what might otherwise call for repeated explanation, that what is herein set forth does not represent any conclusions of mine. This report herewith submitted is what it purports to be, namely a "study of Book of Mormon origins," for those who ought to know everything about it *pro et con*, as well as that which has been produced against it, and that which may be produced against it. I am taking the position that our faith is not only unshaken but unshakable in the Book of Mormon, and therefore we can look without fear upon all that can be said against it.

Sterling McMurrin, "Brigham H. Roberts: A Biographical Essay," xvii–xviii, highlights the difference between Roberts's manuscripts and his faith:

> Roberts's "A Book of Mormon Study" must speak for itself. But those interested in the author's conclusions set forth in the manuscript should not neglect the statements affirming his belief in the authenticity of the Book of Mormon that appear in the letters that are a part of the record of the controversy that resulted from a reading of the manuscript by Church officials. The contrast of his manuscript, composed as an attempt to come to grips with a basic problem that he apparently believed would yield to scholarly analysis, with his affirmation, in the heat of controversy, of his faith that the objective foundation of Mormonism is not to be doubted raises the interesting question of what Roberts did in fact believe about the Book of Mormon in his latest years. That he continued to profess his faith in the authenticity of the book seems to be without question, despite the strong arguments and statements in his study that would appear to explicitly express a conviction that it is not authentic.

The most charitable reading of Roberts's faith is to take him at his word. His scholarly study was to present challenges that he expected would be resolved, and his continued affirmations reflected his heartfelt belief.

man whose contributions to the subject have been systematically ignored by Salt Lake City circles. Prior to his work, it was generally assumed that the locale of most of the cities in the Book of Mormon was to the south of the Isthmus of Panama, in contradiction to the stated belief of Joseph Smith (among those subscribing to this view were James Talmage and the Reorganite "American Archeology Committee"). In 1917, Hills published his *Geography of Mexico and Central America from 2234 B.C. to 421 A.D.* He went over many of the Mexican historical sources (admittedly at secondhand, since he based himself largely upon Bancroft) to arrive at his main conclusion: the narrow neck of land described in the Book of Mormon was the Isthmus of Tehuantepec, so that Zarahemla comprised the lands immediately to the east of it (Guatemala and British Honduras), and Bountiful the lands to the west.[61]

For the Utah Latter-day Saints, a plausible date for the beginning of serious scholarly study of Book of Mormon geography comes two decades later, in 1938.[62] John L. Sorenson describes the event: "The years 1938 and 1939 proved important. For the first time in eleven years the *Improvement Era* (July 1938) published a piece on the geography of Book of Mormon events. Lynn C. Layton had written about a wholly new phenomenon—an internal model. Finally, after 108 years, a Latter-day Saint had showed that it was possible and even desirable to develop such a map. While it is difficult to imagine that coming up with this concept took so long, it is nevertheless true, as far as I can find[:] this sort of map had never been published before."[63] J. Alvin Washburn and J. Nile Washburn later published their own internal map, which added the very important aspect of scale to the problem. When they discussed the scale in miles, the Book of Mormon was shown to cover a much smaller area than the entire continent. They did not tie their internal map to an external geography.[64]

Although those early internal maps were an important step forward in establishing the criteria for locating the Book of Mormon in the real world, the Saints still awaited someone with academic training in appropriate fields to move the discussion to a new level. That era is easily traced to M. Wells Jakeman, who obtained a Ph.D. in ancient history with an emphasis on Mesoamerica. In 1939 he joined with Thomas Stuart

---

[61] Michael D. Coe, "Mormons & Archaeology: An Outside View," 42–43.

Givens, *By the Hand of Mormon,* 277 note 31, points out that Hills's model was the first centered on Mesoamerica, adding that "it was widely introduced to Latter-day Saints by Jesse A. and Jesse N. Washburn beginning in the 1930s."

[62] It is perhaps unsurprising that the intensification of scholarly emphasis on the Book of Mormon should come during this time period. It was generally a period in which scholarship was being applied to the gospel. Alexander, *Mormonism in Transition,* 272–306 describes the important impact of B. H. Roberts, James E. Talmage, and John A. Widtsoe on the development of LDS doctrine. Their writings created or at least supported the atmosphere promoting more serious investigation of the Book of Mormon, using the same academic tools that those three had acquired through their university educations.

[63] Sorenson, *The Geography of Book of Mormon Events,* 31, punctuation as in original. He also notes, on the same page: "We shall see, however, that while Layton published first, he may not have been the first to work seriously at making an internal model—probably the Washburns were."

[64] Ibid., 35–36.

Ferguson (a lawyer) and Franklin S. Harris Jr. (a physicist) to create "The Itzan Society," which was dedicated to examining Book of Mormon geography and connections to archaeology and the remaining historical literature from Mesoamerica. By 1940, Jakeman had developed a model of Book of Mormon geography that was limited to a small region of Mesoamerica, stretching from the southern Guatemalan border to Mexico City.[65] Mesoamerica has become the increasing focus for research into Book of Mormon historicity. Today, LDS scholars with training in history, archaeology, or anthropology most often accept a limited geography theory with the events localized in Mesoamerica.[66]

The study of the Book of Mormon moved well beyond geography with the arrival of Hugh Nibley at BYU.[67] In 1948 he published an article in the *Improvement Era* entitled "The Book of Mormon: A Mirror of the East."[68] That article ushered in an era of intense scholarship on Old World connections to the Book of Mormon. Nibley's brand of scholarship not only inspired readers but also inspired students to follow his path and become conversant with the ancient Near East.

---

[65] Ibid., 37.

[66] The following is a list of publications by authors whose educational background I know. It is not inclusive of all Mesoamerican theorists, for some have accumulated their information outside of the formal academic training. I am aware of others who have not currently published anything I can cite. In cases of multiple possible citations, I list the most representative, or failing that, simply representative. Although they advocate a Mesoamerican setting, they often disagree about where and how the Book of Mormon took place in that Mesoamerican setting.

Joseph L. Allen, *Exploring the Lands of the Book of Mormon*. This book is now in a second edition, prepared with his son: Joseph L. Allen and Blake Joseph Allen, *Exploring the Lands of the Book of Mormon*. John E. Clark, "Archaeological Trends and Book of Mormon Origins," 83–104. William J. Hamblin and A. Brent Merrill, "Swords in the Book of Mormon," 329–51. Richard F. Hauck, *Deciphering the Geography of the Book of Mormon: Settlements and Routes in Ancient America*. V. Garth Norman, *Book of Mormon Geography—Mesoamerican Historic Geography*. For his map, see V. Garth Norman, "The Definitive Mesoamerican Book of Mormon Lands Map." John L. Sorenson, *An Ancient American Setting for the Book of Mormon*. Mark Alan Wright, "Deification: Divine Inheritance and the Glorious Afterlife in the Book of Mormon and Ancient Mesoamerica."

The exception is represented by Bruce H. Porter, whose biographical statement indicates undergraduate training in Semitic languages, a master's degree in Middle Eastern studies, and Ph.D. in the history of religions with a minor in anthropology. See Porter and Meldrum, *Prophecies & Promises: The Book of Mormon & the United States of America*.

[67] Paul C. Gutjahr, *The Book of Mormon: A Biography*, 104, "Various attacks on the *Book of Mormon* via the German Higher Criticism, a lack of archaeological evidence, and a reluctance among many Saints to use the book as the fundamental element in Church evangelism met their most formidable foe in the towering intellectual figure of Hugh Nibley (1910–2005). Incredibly erudite and able to conduct research in more than a dozen languages, . . . perhaps his greatest contribution to Mormon scripture research was his basic scholarly approach."

[68] Boyd Jay Petersen, *Hugh Nibley: A Consecrated Life*, 248. John Gee, "A Tragedy of Errors," 97 note 10, provides more bibliographic information: Hugh Nibley, "The Book of Mormon as a Mirror of the East"; essentially reprinted as "Men of the East," 25–42.

With Jakeman and Nibley, Book of Mormon studies had champions of the scholarship of both the Old and the New World. It is perhaps a testament only to the greater availability of firm data that the Old World context of the Book of Mormon has received so much more attention from LDS scholars than that of the New World.[69]

Hugh Nibley's vigorous defense of the Old World cultural and historical background of the Book of Mormon led to President David O. McKay's suggestion that Nibley provide a series of lessons for the 1957 Melchizedek Priesthood manual. It was an effort perhaps above the grasp of many who would use it, and Nibley's biography documents that, without President McKay's enthusiastic support, it would probably never have become a priesthood class manual.[70] Both the presence of that manual and the implicit endorsement behind it set a tone of acceptance for a scholarly approach to the Book of Mormon.

The transition from pre-critical acceptance of all evidence to the more careful examination of qualified evidence has been gradual. Along with the increasing contribution of trained scholars has come a gradual shift in the perception of what might qualify as a Book of Mormon geography. While it is clear that most Church leaders accepted the hemispheric geography theory at least through the first half of the twentieth century (and some even longer), there are indications of a growing acceptance of the limited geography theory (though without official endorsement).

Important in highlighting this shift was the publication of two articles John L. Sorenson wrote for the *Ensign* (September and October 1984) which laid out some of the reasons for seeing Mesoamerica as the location for the majority of Book of Mormon events.[71] While far from an ecclesiastical endorsement, Sorenson notes that "what was signaled by this request and publication of the pieces was that it was now permissible, and perhaps even desirable, to discuss the topic openly. Such a position was easier to adopt because of the progressive passing from the scene of older church authorities who had been strongly committed to the prevailing hemispheric model with which they had grown up."[72]

The Church has not and does not endorse any particular Book of Mormon geography a position that I consider theologically and pragmatically sound. As Sorenson pointed out, however, it appears that it is "now permissible, and perhaps even desirable" to use the tools of scholarship to approach the topic. Perhaps the most important of the subtle messages that the limited geography theory is acceptable (if not accepted) is the prominence of that theory in important publications. Articles dealing with Book of Mormon history in the heavily edited and vetted *Encyclopedia of Mormonism* demonstrate a strong bias for the limited geography theory while still

---

[69] A brief synopsis is found in Gutjahr, *The Book of Mormon: A Biography*, chap. 6.

[70] Petersen, *Hugh Nibley: A Consecrated Life*, 249–51.

[71] John L. Sorenson, "Digging into the Book of Mormon: Our Changing Understanding of Ancient America and Its Scripture, [Part 1]." John L. Sorenson, "Digging into the Book of Mormon: Our Changing Understanding of Ancient America and Its Scripture, Part 2."

[72] Sorenson, *The Geography of Book of Mormon Events*, 45.

maintaining official neutrality.[73] A similar Mesoamerican bias is seen in the more recent *Book of Mormon Reference Companion*, and Sorenson's *Mormon's Codex*, both published by Deseret Book.[74]

The attempts to establish Book of Mormon historicity constitute a story of changing opinions and developing understanding. The Church has never declared a prophetic mandate that could direct researchers. Rather, General Authorities understand that some questions require more evidence or revelation not yet received. For this reason, Anthony W. Ivins noted during the April 1929 general conference: "There is a great deal of talk about the geography of the Book of Mormon. Where was the land of Zarahemla? Where was the City of Zarahemla? and other geographic matters. It does not make any difference to us. There has never been anything yet set forth that definitely settles that question. So the Church says we are just waiting until we discover the truth."[75]

In the years since 1929 we are still "just waiting until we discover the truth." However, we are now possessed of more information than was ever available before. Much of the advance in research in the last forty years places us in a position where we may hope that we are now closer to understanding the Book of Mormon in its historical context.

---

[73] John E. Clark, "Book of Mormon Geography," 178: "Although Church leadership officially and consistently distances itself from issues regarding Book of Mormon geography in order to focus attention on the spiritual message of the book, private speculation and scholarship in this area have been abundant" (176). "The official position of the church is that the events narrated in the Book of Mormon occurred somewhere in the Americas, but that the specific location has not been revealed." Clark is necessarily broad in his descriptions, though he is known to personally accept the limited geography theory.

William J. Hamblin, "Book of Mormon, History of Warfare," 162–66. David J. Johnson, "Archaeology," 62–63. Daniel C. Peterson, "Book of Mormon Economy and Technology," 172–75. Martin Raish, "Tree of Life," 1486–88.

[74] [No author indicated] "Geography," 288: "The specific locations of the ancient Book of Mormon civilizations are unknown. And the Church of Jesus Christ of Latter-day Saints does not sponsor research with the intention of ultimately designating an exact geography. Instead Church leaders emphasize the spiritual messages of the record and its cardinal purpose. . . ." Nevertheless, the article also notes (289): "The most widely accepted models today locate all of the Book of Mormon cities and geographical features in Mesoamerica (i.e., Middle or Central America)." John E. Clark, "Archaeology," 70–72, mentions only Mesoamerican information for the New World.

David Rolph Seely, "Chronology, Book of Mormon," 196–204, mentions a possible Mesoamerican connection. William J. Hamblin, "Jaredite Civilization," 435, "A combination of archaeological and chronological information makes it plausible that the core lands of the Jaredites in the New World could well be equated with Mesoamerica."

Joseph L. Allen, "Quetzalcoatl," 668–70. V. Garth Norman, "Stela 5," 740–44.

[75] Anthony W. Ivins, *Conference Report*, April 5, 1929, 15–16.

2

Reading a Lost Book

The Book of Mormon can be a polarizing text. It claims to be a translation of an ancient text that had multiple authors, editors, and even translators.[1] Many who have examined it suggest that it was created in the fertile imagination of a relatively uneducated frontier farmer.[2] Many approach the text as a spiritual guide that does not necessarily have any relationship to ancient history. A discussion of how the Book of Mormon as history may only be of interest to those holding it to be a translation of an ancient text.

Nevertheless, a discussion of the Book of Mormon as history should not simply proceed from that faith-based assumption. Terryl L. Givens explains: "How do the particulars of Joseph's past worlds hold up? If his collapse of the sacred into the temporal is to succeed, if we are to see his project as truly historical rather than as simply mythic, then ultimately, the worlds of the Nephites and Jaredites and of Enoch, like the words of Adam and Abraham and Moses and John that he recovered, cannot resist examination as the historical records they purport to be."[3] Understanding the Book of Mormon as history will come only examining it as a historical record finds the same kinds of evidence for historicity that might be expected of other historical records.

The fact that the Book of Mormon has no known textual history prior to Joseph Smith increases the difficulty in discovering whether the Book of Mormon represents history, but it does not necessarily disqualify it as a historical record. Scholars are not

---

[1] Joseph Smith is the declared tlranslator of the text into English, but there is the slight possibility that Oliver Cowdery contributed something during his otherwise failed attempt (see D&C 9:1). It is more sure, however, that Mosiah translated the twenty-four plates of Ether and probable that Moroni edited the book of Ether from Mosiah's translation. See Brant A. Gardner, *Second Witness: Analytical and Contextual Commentary on the Book of Mormon*, 6:159–60.

[2] For examinations of the range of explanations that opponents propose for the Book of Mormon's production, see Richard L. Bushman, *Joseph Smith and the Beginnings of Mormonism*, 120–28. Daniel C. Peterson, "'In the Hope that Something Will Stick': Changing Explanations for the Book of Mormon," xi–xxxii. This 2004 article is a revision of his 2002 "The Protean Joseph Smith." See also Richard H. Cracroft, "'Had for Good and Evil': 19th-Century Literary Treatments of the Book of Mormon," 4–19.

[3] Terryl L. Givens, "Joseph Smith: Prophecy, Process, and Plenitude," 67.

unwilling to accept a text as historical if it exists only in a late copy and/or in a different language.[4] The ultimate tests are in the text itself and how well it fits into its declared time period and cultural context. The Book of Mormon helps us fix its events in time, but understanding the cultural and historical context is part of the difficulty in understanding the Book of Mormon as history.

Reading the Book of Mormon

Steven Pinker wrote: "A thematic core of an argument structure is a specification of a conflation class defining a kind of possible verb meaning in a language, including a specification of which arguments are 'open arguments' or variables."[5] Surely there are professionals who breeze through that sentence, mentally agreeing or nuancing its conclusion. I am not one of them. I understand each and every word, but I am missing the requisite background that turns that particular combination of words into something meaningful.

It is a problem we face in the Book of Mormon without even knowing it. The Book of Mormon seems to declare by theological imperative that it has a plain meaning.[6] That assumed plainness sets the expectation that it should be simple to read, interpret, and understand. For example, in the context of a discussion of Book of Mormon geography, Phyllis Olive declared: "Because the Lord delights in plainness, and because the Book of Mormon was translated by divine means, this author feels we can trust that the scriptures, including any directional designation, were translated into language even the simplest of us could understand."[7] The perception that the text has an obvious meaning also informs Earl M. Wunderli's geographical understanding: "We can examine. . . what the Book of Mormon itself says. One advantage of this approach is that this internal evidence is fixed, readily available, and easily verifiable."[8]

---

[4] One example from Mesoamerica is the *Histoyre du Mechique*, which exists only as a French document from the sixteenth century. Although the document is in the wrong language with no extant Spanish source, it is yet considered an important document representing Aztec culture and history. See Henry B. Nicholson, *Topiltzin Quetzalcoatl: The Once and Future Lord of the Toltecs*, 18–19.

Nevertheless, questionable provenance can still create an atmosphere of distrust. Michael D. Coe, *Breaking the Maya Code*, 229, discusses the Grolier Codex, which for years was considered a forgery:

> The dénouement of the Grolier Codex affair was that it is now considered authentic by almost all those Mayanists who are either epigraphers or iconographers, or both. . . .
> The irony of the whole business is that if Brasseur de Bourbourg had come across the Grolier while rummaging around in archives during the mid-nineteenth century, it would be accepted by even the most rock-ribbed scholar as the genuine article.

[5] Steven Pinker, *Learnability and Cognition: The Acquisition of Argument Structure*, 74.
[6] 2 Ne. 31:3 "My soul delighteth in plainness."
[7] Phyllis Olive, "The Book of Mormon Lands of Western New York."
[8] Earl M. Wunderli, "Critique of a Limited Geography for Book of Mormon Events," 162.

In spite of such "plainness" however, proponents of different geographies read the very same texts differently. Of them, Wunderli suggests that "what the book says seems to have been largely disregarded or misconstrued by the limited geography theorists."[9] Unfortunately, the only thing that is plain is that if someone else's interpretation differs from yours, they have "disregarded or misconstrued" the text. Plainly, the Book of Mormon is read in the way the reader elects to reads it.

Perhaps the most fascinating demonstration of the problems inherent in reading the text comes from opposing interpretations of the very same word. John A. Tvedtnes criticized Brent Lee Metcalfe's reading: "One must also note that Metcalfe seems to be reading the term *land* as if it referred to the entire New World. But people like the Nephites, coming from a Hebrew-speaking environment, would have understood it quite differently [—as a limited region]"[10] The word in the text is the same, but each scholar is applying a different meaning to the text. Each makes a very opposite case based on the very same word. At one point, Tvedtnes exclaims: "Can the same passages really be used as evidence for and against the Book of Mormon or the limited geography theory?"[11] In short, yes.

The claim of "plain meaning" has also been asserted for the Bible, to which William G. Dever responds: "Believers who read only modern English translations of the Biblical text, often unaware of the long transmission process, speak of the 'plain meaning' of Scripture. If there were any such thing, we would have none of the violent controversies that have always surrounded the interpretation of the Bible—beginning already in antiquity and continuing through every popular and scholarly school, both Jewish and Christian, to this very moment."[12]

As with Pinker's discussion of verb arguments above, meaning derives from a context that informs the words just as much as it does from the words themselves. Tvedtnes and Metcalfe can see very different meanings for the word *land* depending upon the context they associate with it. Adam S. Miller states it this way:

---

[9] Ibid., 197.
[10] John A. Tvedtnes, "Reinventing the Book of Mormon: Review of Brent Lee Metcalfe, 'Reinventing Lamanite Identity,'" 97;. Brent Lee Metcalfe, "Reinventing Lamanite Identity," 20–25.
[11] Tvedtnes, "Reinventing the Book of Mormon," 95.
[12] William G. Dever, *Recent Archaeological Discoveries and Biblical Research*, 8. As an example, Thomas L. Thompson, *Mythic Past: Biblical Archaeology and the Myth of Israel*, 36, notes:

> Debate and disagreement about how the Bible was to be used for history hardened the process of such selective affirmation and increased conviction that the theological meaning of a biblical tradition hung on an understanding of the stories as reports. Questions about the accuracy of what had become the imaginary equivalents of war correspondents, created burning issues for historical scholarship over two generations. The historical scenarios involved in the debate took on a life of their own. The nature and validity of the Bible was being defended in these debates, but the texts themselves were hardly seriously consulted. "Plain readings" were preferred. The presence or absence of collapsed fortifications and the nature of nomadism and its relationship to the villages of the South Levant were matched to harmonized readings of the Bible.

> Texts are not static recordings but dynamic, meaning-making machines. The strings of letters, words and sentences on a page create meaning when we turn the machine on by reading it. As a machine with precisely positioned, interlocking parts, a text clearly cannot produce just any meaning whatsoever, but it is nonetheless true that it can produce a variety of meanings depending on the questions brought to bear by its reader. Texts, as meaning-making machines, are responsive to our engagement with them.
>
> For example, if we read a text historically, then that text will produce information about the time and place that it describes or the context and setting in which it was produced. . . If we read a text doctrinally, then the history and specificity of the text will recede as the machine produces general information about what beliefs and principles may be normative and binding for members of the Church.[13]

Reading the Book of Mormon historically is a separate enterprise from reading the text doctrinally. Even in doctrinal readings, approaching the text for the doctrine important to the read is different from reading the text to understand doctrine according to the declared writer. Both is secular and sacred history, reading the Book of Mormon as an ancient text will assume different contexts that determine meanings. As John L. Sorenson cautioned: "In general the 'religious' realm in the lives of ancient peoples cannot be equated with our current use of that term. Our civilization and language are so different form theirs that it is unthinkable that we could automatically translate concepts from their record to our minds without qualification."[14]

A text from history is an artifact. The most famous Mesoamerican text is the *Popol Vuh*, a sacred document from the Quiché Maya.[15] It combines mythology and history without obvious separation, other than the mythology speaks of much older history. It represents the culture that created it. It doesn't define and often doesn't explain that culture. It rather represents unconscious acceptance of the cultural assumptions and pressures relevant at the time of its creation.[16] Discovering the conditions and

---

[13] Adam S. Miller, "An Experiment on the Word: Introduction," 3.

[14] John L. Sorenson, "Religious Groups and Movements among the Nephites, 200–1 B.C.," 164.

[15] *Popol Vuh: The Sacred Book of the Maya*, translated by Allen J. Christenson. *Popol Vuh, Volume II: Literal Poetic Version, Translation and Transcription*, translated by Allen J. Christenson.

[16] Bruce J. Malina, *The New Testament World: Insights from Cultural Anthropology*, 2:

> What do . . . Bible translations offer you? At most they let you, a foreigner, get to know what those first-century Greek-speaking folks are saying. But what someone says and what he means to say are often quite distinct. Should you tell your girlfriend that you love the gold of her hair, do you mean that her hair will make an excellent hedge against inflation? And why would you want a hedge against inflation rather than a fence, a wall, or a stand of trees? The words we use to say and speak do in fact embody meaning, but the meaning does not come from the words. Meaning derives from the general social system of the speakers of a language. This is why what one says and what one means to say can often be quite different, especially for persons not sharing the same social system. By translating the Gospel of Matthew into English, what we do is transplant our first-century Syrian Hellenists into our modes of saying, and all too often we presuppose that what they say embodies our modes of meaning as well.

culture that were relevant at the time of a text's creation should explicate the text in ways that the wrong production culture would not.[17]

The Book of Mormon isn't a text from history. It declares that it is the translation of a text from history. Thus the expectation that it should reflect an ancient culture that produced it will be mixed with the virtually inevitable presence of the world of the translator that presents the text in terms that make sense to the culture and time of the translator.

The complexities of understanding a text in translation require that we pay attention to these unconscious cultural assumptions. We may expect that regardless of the relationship of the translator to the text, the mindset of the original authors of a document should bleed through the translation. The ancient mind behind the text should show in the pressures to which Book of Mormon peoples responded, the history which influenced their actions, and the culture which governed the nature of their responses.

Reading through the Text's Analytical Layers

The Book of Mormon declares a dual creation. Only the plate text is ancient. The translation is inextricably associated with Joseph Smith. This means that our task is not only to discover the culture that produced the text, but to carefully unravel the threads that tie the ancient text to its more modern translation.[18] This dual production complicates the issue, but the path to understanding can be illustrated by the long history of dealing with the text of the Bible and its relationship to history. The Bible, in English, is also a translation. The King James Version is an extremely popular English translation, but that translation clearly creates potential issues for historicity, such as the presence of dragons and unicorns.[19] As does the Book of Mormon, the Bible faces possible differences between a known history and a textually asserted history. The Bible confronts similar issues about whether the textually asserted history might reflect actual events or only myth and literature.[20]

---

[17] From his perspective as a science fiction author, Orson Scott Card, "The Book of Mormon, Artifact or Artifice?" suggests that the problem of cultural assumptions would make it obvious if Joseph Smith had written the Book of Mormon according to his own time's unwritten rules: "[Joseph Smith's] work should proclaim itself to be a phony on every page today. This is because every storyteller, no matter how careful he is, will inadvertently confess his own character and the society he lives in. He can make every conscious effort, he can be the best educated scholar you could possibly find, but if he tries to write something that is not of his own culture he will give himself away with every unconscious choice he makes. Yet he'll never know he's doing it because it won't occur to him that it could be any other way."

[18] Although this book simply accepts a particular definition of how the Book of Mormon was translated, I have elsewhere presented my evidence supporting that definition. See Gardner, *The Gift and Power*.

[19] For dragons, see Deut. 32:33; Job 30:29; Psalms 44:19. For unicorns, Num. 24:8; Job 39:9-10.

[20] Certainly there are many who accept the Bible as authentic history, without acknowledging any issues when compared to external ancient histories. There are others, however, who suggest that there is much that the Bible asserts to be history that may not actually reflect events as they occurred. For example, Israel Finkelstein and Neil Asher

Baruch Halpern provides an interesting analogy that he created to describe approaches to the Bible. It is appropriate to our discussion of the historicity of the Book of Mormon:

> The image of the map clarifies [the various approaches to the Bible as history]. The map, say of Europe, includes cities and highways of the tenth century, of the eleventh century and so on, continuing into our own time. In effect the confessionalist maintains that all those cities were on the map from the start, that God created Europe, and the map, in the tenth century. Critical study divulges that this is not so, that some of the cities and highways appeared later, and it is the job of the historian to determine when each town, highway, and so on, was added. Negative fundamentalists, however, date the whole map by its latest elements. Because the map reflects a view from the twentieth century, they argue, it cannot be used to get at earlier times.[21]

Just like the Bible, the Book of Mormon has its confessionalists who accept the text uncritically. They are likely to assert that all aspects of the text, including the English translation, faithfully represent its ancient origin. The Book of Mormon is also susceptible to what Halpern calls "negative fundamentalists" precisely because it has a publishing history that is demonstrably related to the nineteenth-century American Northeast.[22] As with the Bible, the negative fundamentalists will date the entire text from these most modern elements. As with the Bible, the historian's task

---

Silberman, *The Bible Unearthed: Archaeology's New Vision of Ancient Israel and the Origin of its Sacred Texts*, 76, discuss the contrast between the Bible's story of the Israelite conquest of Canaan and the archaeological record: "Archaeology has uncovered a dramatic discrepancy between the Bible and the situation within Canaan at the suggested date of the conquest, between 1230 and 1220 bce. Although we know that a group named Israel was already present somewhere in Canaan by 1207 BCE, the evidence on the general political and military landscape of Canaan suggests that a lightning invasion by this group would have been impractical and unlikely in the extreme."

John Dominic Crossan and Jonathan L. Reed, *Excavating Jesus: Beneath the Stones, Behind the Texts*, 25–26, provide an example of how the potential conflicts between text and archaeology might be resolved. Luke 4:16 says that when Jesus came to Nazareth, he went into the synagogue. No first century synagogue has (yet) been discovered anywhere in Galilee, let alone Nazareth. Nevertheless, Crossan and Reed note: "In the Jewish homeland at the time of Jesus, the term *synagogue* referred primarily to a *gathering*, and less to a *building* with an accompanying, well-defined liturgy" (p. 26, italics theirs).

[21] Baruch Halpern, *The First Historians: The Hebrew Bible and History*, 4.

[22] John E. Clark, "Archaeological Trends and Book of Mormon Origins," 85–86: "The rival hypotheses about the [Book of Mormon's] origins implicate four knowledge worlds of diverse content and undetermined relationship: the ancient world, the nineteenth-century world, the twenty-first-century world, and the Book of Mormon world. Environmental or naturalistic explanations see the book as a hoax tethered to its nineteenth-century background. Thus, all details mentioned in the book should conform to knowledge and speculations available to Joseph Smith before the book was written in 1829. Mormon explanations see the book as history and situate it in the ancient world."

is to sort out the middle way, to analyze the various roads in the Book of Mormon "map," and to discern the time period in which they were created.[23]

John Dominic Crossan and Jonathan L. Reed approach Halpern's map analogy by suggesting that working with the Bible and archaeology is a pursuit of "parallel layering, an interaction between the layers of an archaeological mound and the layers of a gospel text."[24] Understanding the Book of Mormon similarly requires a parallel layering or interaction between the text and historical information. However, because we have the text only in translation, it also requires that we carefully attempt to separate at least the two obvious layers of information, the original plate text and the English translation. The declared production culture is different for each layer, and each of those two layers will and should display evidence of the cultural and temporal assumptions prevalent at the time of production. Our task would be infinitely easier if we had (and could read) the original plates of Mormon, but we do not. Lacking the plates makes our task more difficult, but not impossible.

There are ways that we can use the modern text to examine its possible relationship to a different and ancient culture. In archaeology, contextual clues can help date when the various roads of Halpern's map analogy were laid down. Textual archaeology requires contextual clues to determine the time and culture that created the text. We are looking for the production culture of each "road" in the text; that is, the conditions and assumptions prevalent when each layer of the text was produced. In this book, I will be most interested in the correlation of the plate text to the culture and time that produced it. The final complication of the stated production of the Book of Mormon is that it really consists of three layers of text, not two:

> **English translation:** Occurs in the nineteenth century.
> **Composed text:** Occurs in the late fourth century.

---

[23] C. Wilfred Griggs, "The Book of Mormon as an Ancient Book," 260:

> The major weakness of such criticisms is the one-dimensional approach taken to problems which the Book of Mormon presents. The assumption that any parallels between the world of Joseph Smith and the world of the Book of Mormon, real or imagined . . . , are sufficient to discredit the Book of Mormon is naïve. The challenge of the Book of Mormon lies elsewhere. It claims to be an ancient book, and it must be examined and criticized in terms of this claim.
>
> If, as Joseph Smith states, it is a translation, any modern language source material which the translator found useful or helpful in his translating efforts cannot be used *ipso facto* as evidence against the authenticity of his work.

Griggs is responding to suggestions that the appearance of certain phrases in a modern text necessarily suggest that the Book of Mormon is modern. If the Book of Mormon is ancient as claimed, then modern phrases may easily be ascribed to the translator rather than the original text. As Griggs also notes, one cannot take a one-dimensional approach to the text. Multiple approaches and types of data must be brought to bear to properly understand the text in an ancient context.

[24] Crossan and Reed, *Excavating Jesus*, xvii.

32 *Traditions of the Fathers*

Source materials for the composition: A collection of documents spanning a thousand years of Nephite history, combined with a record of the Jaredites produced perhaps around 200 B.C.[25]

The success of any attempt to separate these layers will only be seen in the ability of the reconstruction to productively explain the features of the text.

Reading through an Ancient Document's Translation Layer

In the case of a translated text, the translation itself is an interpretive layer—adding yet another cultural interaction with the artifact. Avoiding the inherent interpretations behind the translation is the reason that serious study of any text originally written in a different language should be based on reading it in that original language.

The Italian adage "traduttore, traditore" (the translator is a traitor) recognizes that something is always lost in translation. Depending upon the expertise of the translator, sometimes we have less information than the original provided, or sometimes meanings have been added that were not in the original. Words in different languages may overlap in meaning, but typically not with precision. When the words are combined into idioms, comprehension becomes even more complicated.

The problem of inter-cultural translation is highlighted by Mary Miller and Karl Taube. They discuss the problems associated with using the word "god" or "gods" to describe Mesoamerican concepts of the supernatural:

> There has been considerable debate concerning the concept of gods and divinity in ancient Mesoamerica. The 16th century Spanish chronicles make frequent and direct references to *dioses*, or "gods." However, it has been justly noted that European terminology may have grossly simplified complex concepts of sacredness and divinity. Among the 16th century Zapotecs, the term *pee*, signifying "breath, spirit, or wind," expressed the concept of divinity. This animistic force caused movement—all phenomena or maternal [sic] things that expressed motion were attributed a certain degree of sacredness. Among the Aztecs, the term for sacredness was *teotl* which, like the Zapotec *pee*, referred to an immaterial energy or force similar to the Polynesian concept of mana.[26]

Because the Book of Mormon expressly states that it is a translation, normal procedure dictates that we read it and analyze it in its original language. In this case, it is impossible. We only have the text in translation. There is no option but to study it in—and therefore as—translation.[27] Analysis of the nature of the Book of Mormon

---

[25] I am reserving the analysis of how the plate text was created and what it might contain that differs from what is seen in the translation layer for a future work. A discussion of the source materials is well beyond what I intend to deal with in this book. I have outlined some of those sources in Brant A. Gardner, *Second Witness*, 1:16–20. See also John L. Sorenson, "Mormon's Sources," 2–15.

[26] Mary Miller and Karl Taube, *An Illustrated Dictionary of the Gods and Symbols of Ancient Mexico and the Maya*, 89. Abbreviations for "century" silently expanded.

[27] That we have a text only in translation does not automatically disqualify the text as ancient. For example, *The Apocalypse of Abraham* exists only in Slavonic. Its translator and editor, G. H.

suggests that there are places where an argument can be made that it is not a perfect representation of the underlying plate text, just as all translations are related to—but not perfect representations of—an original. It is not only possible that some translation errors would exist in the Book of Mormon, but virtually certain that they do.[28] Of course, this understanding is easily acceptable for secular translations, or even scholarly translations of sacred texts. It is harder for some faithful to believe that the Book of Mormon should be understood in the same way because its translation is tied to divine influence.

A simple example will suffice to demonstrate the problem of over-reliance on the English translation layer to determine historicity. The Reverend M. T. Lamb published an influential critique of the Book of Mormon in 1887. One of his arguments highlighted what he felt was anomalous vocabulary: "If, therefore, upon a careful examination we find the Book of Mormon filled up with words and phrases and forms of expression that are known to be entirely *modern* . . . then 'counterfeit' must be written across its pages, and its author be held responsible for the sad results of a wicked imposture."[29] He declared: "There are many words used in the book that have a *Greek* or a *Latin* origin *later* than six hundred years before Christ, and many others wholly *modern*. The following are only a few: 'Faculties,' 'Popular,' 'Priestcraft,' 'State of dilemma,' 'Synagogue,' 'Bible,' 'Jews,' 'Gentiles,' 'Church,' 'Baptize,' 'Barges,' 'Immortal,' and others."[30]

Box, *The Apocalypse of Abraham: Edited with a Translation from the Slavonic Text and Notes*, describes the book as "thoroughly Jewish" in character, a point from which he asserts with fairly strong assurance that it was "probably" composed in "Hebrew or Aramaic . . . at the end of the first or the beginning of the second century A.D." The apocalypse's next step was a translation into "Greek," and from which the Slavonic version was created. The earliest Slavonic text is from the first half of the fourteenth century. (PDF, p. 7).

[28] Gardner, *The Gift and Power*, 185–93.
[29] Martin Thomas Lamb, *The Golden Bible; or The Book of Mormon. Is It From God?* 218.
[30] Ibid., 219.

A modern version of this argument is found in Earl M. Wunderli, *An Imperfect Book: What the Book of Mormon Tells Us About Itself*, 105–9. In this section Wunderli describes sets of English words that appear in texts associated with different authors. After discussing words associated with Jesus in the King James Version and those associated with Jesus in the Book of Mormon, he concludes: "The Book of Mormon idiom differentiates the New World Jesus from the biblical one. The Book of Mormon Jesus is indistinguishable from the Nephite writers. The Book of Mormon Jesus uses ten of the fifteen idiomatic words, including the harsh term *abomination* and the meaningless *expedient*. The biblical Jesus begins no sentence with *now*, as the Book of Mormon Jesus does" (109).

Wunderli does not comment on the fact that neither the biblical Jesus nor the Book of Mormon Jesus ever used any of those words. Jesus didn't speak English. Even the New Testament Greek is probably a translation of what Jesus said. Even an Aramaic quotation would probably be a remembrance rather than an actual quotation. It would be more interesting to find disparate translators who agreed than to note their differences.

This criticism would be appropriate and devastating if the Book of Mormon declared English to be its original language.[31] Of course, that declaration alone would be sufficient to show it false as English itself postdates early Book of Mormon times. As a translation, however, the presence of modern words is simply a lexical choice on the part of the translator and has no bearing on the antiquity of the document being translated.[32]

There are three concepts that might describe the possible relationship between the English Book of Mormon text and the language on the plates. It might be a literal translation, a functional translation, or a conceptual translation. Each of these describes a differing relationship between the translation text and the underlying source text. The strictest is the literal translation. Such a translation would attempt to retain as much of the original as possible, allowing for the fact that it is not always possible to have a precise correspondence between two languages. A functional translation attempts to adhere to the source text but may use different words or concepts to convey the meaning rather than concentrating on finding the equivalent of a specific word. Finally, a conceptual translation attempts to retain the sense of the original but permits itself to express that sense in a much more flexible way. After examining the data available that might tell us what kind of translation the Book of Mormon is, I have suggested that the majority of the text best represents a functionalist translation.[33] That analysis informs my discussion of some of the historical issues in the text where I see what might be anachronism as one of translation rather than an issue in the original plate text.[34]

When we read the Book of Mormon for evidence of the culture that produced it, we must therefore be very careful any time an argument is presented that depends on

---

[31] Nibley *An Approach to the Book of Mormon*, 5–6, makes this point with his typical wit:

> Today some critics are fond of pointing out that the Book of Mormon is written in the very language of Joseph Smith's own society That is as if a professor of French literature were to prove Champollion a fraud by showing after patient years of study that his translation of the Rosetta Stone was not in Egyptian at all but in the very type of French that Champollion and his friends were wont to use! The discovery is totally without significance, of course, because Champollion never claimed to be writing Egyptian, but to be rendering it into his own language.

[32] L. Ara Norwood, "Ignoratio Elenchi: The Dialogue that Never Was: Review of James R. White, *Letters to a Mormon Elder*," 336–37. Norwood discusses White's argument, which is very similar to M. T. Lamb's—that the Book of Mormon contains anachronistic words, including "adieu." Norwood replies: "Of course 'adieu' is originally French, as are a vast number of English words, but it entered the English vocabulary by the fourteenth century. Indeed, the word was part of Joseph Smith's personal vocabulary, with the basic meaning of 'Fare thee well' – a very poignant and sublime valedictory statement."

[33] Gardner, *The Gift and Power*, 241–47, presents the conclusions to the analysis. While the majority of the translation is functionalist, the other translation types appear on specific occasions. For example, the manuscript evidence shows that Joseph spelled out the first occurrence of unusual names. In addition to exercising specific control over the spelling, several find correspondences in ancient Near Eastern texts. That process suggests that where names were concerned, the translation process was literalist rather than functionalist. See chap. 15.

[34] See Chapter 12 "Horses, Chariots, and Other Anachronistic Nouns," for a more complete discussion of translation anachronisms.

vocabulary to make its case (either English vocabulary or a putative underlying Hebrew). It is precisely at the level of vocabulary that we have the most uncertain connection to the original plate text. None of this means that we can ignore the English text or construe it at will. It means we have to work harder.

Reading through an Ancient Document's Composition Layer

By definition, an ancient document comes from a time period long before our own. The passage of time alone assures a difference between how a modern reader understands the text and the way the writer believed it would be understood. The problem becomes more complex as we cross a cultural as well as a temporal gap. For example, we tend to read the Bible and the Book of Mormon as though people just like us wrote them. E. Randolph Richards and Brandon J. O'Brien elaborate:

> By the Holy Spirit, God continues to speak to his people through the Scriptures. It is important that Christ's church retain this conviction, even as it poses certain challenges for interpretation. We can easily forget that Scripture is a foreign land and that reading the Bible is a crosscultural experience. To open the Word of God is to step into a strange world where things are very unlike our own. Most of us don't speak the languages. We don't know the geography or the customs or what behaviors are considered rude or polite. And yet we hardly notice. For many of us, the Bible is more familiar than any other book. We may have parts of it memorized. And because we believe that the Bible is God's Word to us, no matter where on the planet or when in history we read it, we tend to read Scripture in our own *when* and *where*, in a way that makes sense on our terms.[35]

Reading ourselves into the text is possible because documents do not always encode all of the information we need to properly understand them. Bruce J. Malina and Richard L. Rohrbaugh explain:

> Biblical authors, like most authors writing in the high-context ancient Mediterranean world, presume that readers have a broad and concrete knowledge of their common social context. By contrast, "low-context" societies are those that assume "low" knowledge of the context of any communication. They produce highly specific and detailed documents that leave little for the reader to fill in or supply. Since the United States and northern Europe are typical low-context societies, readers from these societies expect writers to give the necessary background when referring to something not shared by all in the society.
>
> The obvious problem this creates for reading the biblical writings today is that low-context readers in the United States frequently mistake the biblical writings for low-context documents. They erroneously assume that the author has provided all of the contextual information needed to understand it.[36]

---

[35] E. Randolph Richards and Brandon J. O'Brien, *Misreading Scripture with Western Eyes: Removing Cultural Blinders to better Understand the Bible*, 11.

[36] Bruce J. Malina and Richard L. Rohrbaugh, *Social-Science Commentary on the Gospel of John*, 16–17. Elizabeth Wayland Barber and Paul T. Barber, *When They Severed Earth From Sky: How the Human Mind Shapes Myth*, 17, call this phenomenon the "Silence Principle": "What everyone is expected to know already is not explained in so many words."

They continue: "Because the reader must interact with the text and 'complete' it if it is to make sense, every text invites immediate participation on the part of the reader. Texts thus provide what is necessary, but cannot provide everything."[37] When the unstated context is supplied from our modern time and culture rather than the one that produced the text, Malina and Rohrbaugh note that "as a rule, nonunderstanding—or at best misunderstanding—will be the result."[38] The disjunction between the cultural context for the writer and reader led William G. Dever to warn: "The Bible cannot simply be read at face value as history; nor, of course, can any other ancient text be so read."[39]

It is therefore unsurprising that many Book of Mormon proponents and detractors have such a hard time agreeing on any interpretation of the Book of Mormon. At the extreme contrasting positions, they are reading two entirely different books, even though the actual text is the same. The believer's translated ancient document encodes assumptions and interpretations that are both unavailable and inapplicable to Joseph Smith's world. The non-believer's text contains only information that derives from a nineteenth-century context.[40] Richard L. Bushman cautions: "The preconceptions of the modern age led Mormons as well as critics to see things in the Book of Mormon that are not there."[41]

Of course, reading the text against a cultural background necessarily requires that we define what that background might have been. For that reason, the initial assumption that the Book of Mormon might be historical requires that we resolve the question of Book of Mormon geography. Only by locating the Book of Mormon in space (the Book of Mormon declares the applicable timeframe), can it be located in a cultural context. No proper understanding of an ancient Book of Mormon is acceptable without correlating the way the ancient composition layer interacted with its environment. (See Chapter 5).

---

[37] Malina and Rohrbaugh, *Social-Science Commentary on the Gospel of John*, 9.

[38] Ibid., 14. See also Richards and O'Brien, *Misreading Scripture with Western Eyes*, 13–15.

[39] William G. Dever, *Recent Archaeological Discoveries and Biblical Research*, 5. William G. Dever, *What Did the Biblical Writers Know and When Did They Know It?* 19:

> An apt metaphor for understanding literature may be to regard it as a form of "symbolically encoded thought and behavior," words being the specific symbols chosen and language the code. To the extent that we can "break the code"—difficult at best with ancient texts—we may be able to read the symbols and thus penetrate behind them to the reality that the author sought to express. To be sure, symbols (including verbal ones) are only "signs" pointing beyond themselves, and therefore will always remain somewhat enigmatic. Yet "reading" symbols is possible; and it is not mere guesswork unless it is ignorant of the language, vocabulary, grammar, or syntax of the symbols, in this case the texts. Texts, however encoded, are not "mute" but historians are sometimes deaf.

[40] Grant Hardy, *Understanding the Book of Mormon: A Reader's Guide*, xvii: "[The Book of Mormon] can certainly be read as a product of the nineteenth century, but this requires treating it as an indirect or coded source; one must start with the assumption that it is something very different from what it professes to be."

[41] Richard L. Bushman, *Believing History: Latter-day Saint Essays*, 122.

Reading Archaeology against the Book of Mormon

Dan Vogel and Brent Lee Metcalfe encapsulate a common critical opinion of the New World setting for Book of Mormon: "Had the Book of Mormon been what Joseph Smith said—not an allegory with spiritual import but a literal history of Hebrew immigrants to America—this should have been verified by now. Instead, the varied inhabitants and exotic locales in the Book of Mormon remain elusive; what some would term 'Book of Mormon archaeology' is non-existent."[42]

In spite of their firm declaration that archaeology does not support the Book of Mormon, John E. Clark clearly sees the situation differently: "Archaeology and geography support the Book of Mormon to the same degree, and for the same reasons, that they support the Bible. Both books present the same challenges for empirical confirmation, and both are in good shape. Many things have been verified for each, but many have not."[43] Of those "many things" that he suggests have found empirical confirmation, he notes: "The overall trend in the data over the past 175 years fits the expectations for the Book of Mormon as history rather than hoax."[44] How do we have such different opinions on what archaeology has and has not done relative to the Book of Mormon?

On the one hand, it can be stated with great certainty that there is no artifact or location in the New World that can unambiguously be called Nephite. On the other hand is Clark's declaration: "Book of Mormon cities have been found, they are well known and their artifacts grace the finest museums."[45] Clark intentionally made this stark contrast to expectations because he needed to emphasize an important point. Understanding how the Book of Mormon fits into archaeological evidence differs significantly from archaeology of the biblical region. Both the continuation of cultural memory and the abundance of ancient texts point us to locations and peoples and help in declaring the ethnic and cultural identities of the peoples living in the excavated sites. Neither the historical memory or extant texts assist us in understanding most New World sites from Book of Mormon times.

It is this problem of identification that led Clark to clarify his intentionally startling statement that we have indeed found Nephite remains: "They are merely masked by archaeological labels such as Maya, Olmec and so on. The problem then is not that Book of Mormon artifacts have not been found, only that they have not been recognized for what they are."[46]

The simplest example is the Olmec that Clark mentioned. We have their remains, but no positive identification of the language they spoke. We do not know what they called themselves and the name we use, Olmec, is the result of an early

---

[42] Dan Vogel and Brent Lee Metcalfe, "Editor's Introduction," vii.
[43] John E. Clark, "Archaeology, Relics, and Book of Mormon Belief," 42.
[44] John E. Clark, "Archaeological Trends and Book of Mormon Origins," 95.
[45] Clark, "Archaeology, Relics and Book of Mormon Belief," 42.
[46] Ibid.

misidentification. They certainly called themselves something else. Suppose that they has actually called themselves *Hayaw.[47] We could accurately restate Clark's declaration about Nephite artifacts as "*Hayaw cities have been found, they are well known and their artifacts grace the finest museums." That would be a true statement even though there is no city and no artifact that is identified as *Hayaw. They are all called Olmec.

Even in the infinitely better understood Old World, archaeology continues to have questions and potential issues when compared to the very different types of evidence found in texts. Even in the Old World, problems of identification still arise. William H. Stiebing describes the problem for the Bible:

> Correlating archaeological sites with places known from ancient texts is also not always a sure thing. Cities like Jerusalem, Athens, and Rome have remained occupied since antiquity, so their locations are not in question. But the sites of many other places must be determined from clues found in ancient written material, and sometimes there are two or three possible archaeological sites for a given town or city. Archaeological excavation occasionally solves such disputes by uncovering on a site written evidence of its ancient identity. But the locations of many ancient cities known from texts remain debatable.[48]

A related issue is that a location with modern meaning may have no ancient significance. Nazareth is a well-known biblical location because it is associated with Jesus Christ. The site may even be located archaeologically, but it appears nowhere in nonbiblical history, as John Dominic Crossan and Jonathan L. Reed observe:

> Outside [of] the gospels and the early Christian texts that rely on them, there are no pre-Constantinian citations referring to Nazareth. It is never mentioned by any of the Jewish rabbis whose pronouncements are in the Mishnah or whose discussions are in the Talmud, even though they cite sixty-three other Galilean towns. Josephus, the Jewish historian and general over Galilee during the first Jewish revolt in 66–67 C.E., refers to forty-five named sites there, but never to Nazareth. It is unknown in the Christian Old Testament. Even though Zebulun's tribal allotment in the Bible catalogues some fifteen Lower Galilean sites in Nazareth's vicinity, it is not counted among them (Josh. 19:10–15). It was absolutely insignificant.[49]

Complicating even Old World history are the times where there is an uneasy fit between texts and archaeology.[50] Ephraim Stern points out the limitations of the

---

[47] Søren Wichmann, *The Relationship Among the Mixe-Zoquean Languages of Mexico*, 566, lists *haya(w) as the proto-Mixe-Zoquean word for "man." Proto-Mixe-Zoquean is the leading candidate for the language of the Olmec.

It isn't unusual for peoples to use some form of human/man as their name. There is no evidence that this name was used, but there is some logic behind the choice.

[48] William H. Stiebing, Jr., *Out of the Desert: Archaeology and the Exodus/Conquest Narratives*, 34.

[49] Crossan and Reed, *Excavating Jesus*, 18.

[50] Dana M. Pike, "Israelite Inscriptions from the Time of Jeremiah and Lehi," 194–95:

> Archaeological excavation produces two broad types of evidence: nontextual artifacts—ranging in size from beads and seeds to monumental architecture—and inscriptions or

archaeological record with respect to a text: "Herodotus mentions that in the third decade of [Psamtik's] rule, the Scythians arrived in the area. Even if this event really occurred, it left no distinguishable mark in the archaeological record."[51]

With such issues found in Old World archaeology, it is unsurprising that they are also present in New World archaeology. Kent V. Flannery found little archaeological evidence supporting the textual descriptions of Postclassic warfare in Oaxaca.[52] Travis W. Stanton and M. Kathryn Brown note: "Ethnohistoric and ethnographic data, however, should not be taken at face value. Pre-Columbian cultures were transformed shortly after the first Spanish expedition set foot in Mesoamerica. Problems can arise when comparing textual and archaeological data from different periods. Furthermore, we must remain acutely aware that each ethnohistoric and ethnographic document we use was written from only one point of view and that for each view of reality there are many others. These same problems apply to iconography and hieroglyphic texts."[53]

As a final complication, archaeological evidence may also flatly contradict a text, as in this example Crossan and Reed provide:

> Luke also presumes that a tiny hamlet like Nazareth had both a synagogue building and scrolls of scripture. The first presumption is most unlikely and . . . no evidence for a first-century synagogue building was discovered at Nazareth. The second presupposition is questionable—scrolls were mostly an urban privilege and, most likely, lectionary readings came later.[54]

---

texts. Both types must be coordinated with each other in any serious effort to understand the life and times of ancient Israelites or any other people. While inscriptions may seem more readily accessible and understandable than many artifacts are, they, like artifacts, require careful interpretation in order to be employed productively. Authentic Israelite inscriptions (distinguished from forgeries, for which there is, sadly, a flourishing market) are available to us as they existed over twenty-five hundred years ago. They are valuable primary documents not susceptible to tampering or editing, having no transmission history (in contrast to the Bible). As such, ancient inscriptions are of great importance to any study of Israel's past.

However, all archaeological evidence must be coordinated with biblical data to effectively understand ancient Israel. On the one hand, because of its vast size and the great span of time it covers, the Bible preserves historical, cultural, and religious data that would otherwise be unknown if we had only the relatively small corpus of ancient Israelite inscriptions. On the other hand, the Bible has inherent limitations for students of ancient Israelite history and culture because of its focus on religious themes. For example, little if anything is recorded in the Bible about King Ahab's political or military activity during his twenty-year reign or about the plight of the agrarian class of Judahites who remained in the land after many from the upper and middle classes were deported to Babylonia in the 590s and 580s B.C. Thus biblical data must be carefully employed and coordinated with what is learned from inscriptions and artifacts.

[51] Ephraim Stern, *Archaeology of the Land of the Bible*, 2:107.
[52] Cited in Travis W. Stanton and M. Kathryn Brown, "Studying Warfare in Ancient Mesoamerica," 13–14.
[53] Ibid., 14.
[54] Crossan and Reed, *Excavating Jesus*, 30.

That Luke misses certain historical details does not disqualify his general witness of the Savior. It simply says that he was not an eyewitness to a particular episode and that he misunderstood or was misled by the sources he consulted or by the individuals whom he interviewed. Writers who create their works long after the events may make similar mistakes, yet still present a "true" history. This point is particularly important for the Book of Mormon because Mormon, writing over four hundred years after most of the events he describes, strongly edited and reshaped his material.

Part of the resolution of the conflicting statements from Vogel, Metcalfe, and Clark lies in the nature of the expectations of what evidence should support the Book of Mormon. Like Vogel and Metcalfe, Simon G. Southerton declared that there has been little archaeological support for the Book of Mormon. What he used to demonstrate that absence of support tells us more about his expectations than about archaeology:

> Anthropologists and archaeologists, including some Mormons and former Mormons, have discovered little to support the existence of these [Book of Mormon] civilizations. Over a period of 150 years, as scholars have seriously studied Native American cultures and prehistory, evidence of a Christian civilization in the Americas has eluded the specialists. In Mesoamerica, which is regarded by Mormon scholars to be the setting of the Book of Mormon narrative, research has uncovered cultures where the worship of multiple deities and human sacrifice were not uncommon. These cultures lack any trace of Hebrew or Egyptian writing, metallurgy, or the Old World domesticated animals and plants described in the Book of Mormon....[55]

Southerton's expectations, and therefore what he declares has not been found (that should have been) is a variation on the problem of Nephite artifacts. Although the absence of time-appropriate metallurgy continues to be an issue for Book of Mormon historicity (see Chapter 6), the rest of his list depends upon the assumptions brought to both the text and to archaeology. As with Nephite artifacts, the answers may easily be that we have found appropriate remains but not recognized them. Many of these will be discussed later in this book.[56] The approach to Book of Mormon historicity depends heavily upon the way we approach the data in the text and its plausible relationship to what is known from history and archaeology.

Reading from a Solid Foundation

Michael D. Coe is one of the better known Mesoamerican archaeologists of the passing generation. Unlike most non-LDS archaeologists who dismiss the Book of Mormon, he at least read it before passing judgment.[57] He notes:

---

[55] Simon G. Southerton, *Losing a Lost Tribe: Native Americans, DNA, and the Mormon Church*, xv.

[56] The absence of ancient Christianity is discussed in Chapter 7. Questions about Old World domesticates may be as much a question of translation as archaeology. See Chapter 12.

[57] Michael D. Coe, "Mormons & Archaeology: An Outside View," 40, "Members of the faith have often accused outside critics of ignorance, and often rightly so, on the grounds that almost none of them has ever read the Book of Mormon, and are unacquainted with Mormon history,

In hundreds of motels scattered across the western United States the Gentile archaeologist can find a paperback Book of Mormon lavishly illustrated with the paintings of Arnold Friberg depicting such scenes as Samuel the Lamanite prophesying on top of what looks like the Temple of the Tigers in Chichen Itza, Yucatan.

Any curious archaeologist can hear guides in L.D.S. visitor centers from Sharon, Vermont, to Los Angeles confidently lecturing that the Nephites built the Maya "cities" and expounding on other subjects that are usually the preserve of experts in these matters. Small wonder that the outside archaeologist often feels bewilderment if not downright hostility when confronted with things he is sure cannot be true.[58]

Unfortunately for LDS Book of Mormon enthusiasts, Coe's description of the archaeologist's "bewilderment if not downright hostility" is not hyperbole or simple ignorance of the Book of Mormon. In most cases, it is a legitimate conclusion based on much of what the enthusiastic faithful claim for the Book of Mormon. It is not an indictment of the Book of Mormon as much as it is a sad reflection of the state of our Book of Mormon apologetics. In many ways, the greatest obstacle to understanding Book of Mormon historicity has been our own amateur theories and theorists.[59]

Parallels as a Problematic Methodology

Thirty years ago, Martin Raish lamented: "I am discouraged by the poor research, misleading conclusions, and general lack of rigor far too often permeating the majority of the commentaries [on the Book of Mormon]. An indiscriminate mingling of fact with fiction often results from such methodological laziness and thus tends to discredit the whole endeavor."[60]

He described one occasion where this methodological laziness nevertheless impressed the untrained audience to which it was presented:

---

values, and scholarship. While not myself a believer in the Mormon faith, I should warn readers that I have tried not to commit these sins of omission."

Michael D. Coe, "The Mormons: Interview [with] Michael Coe." Coe provided a response to the question "How would you describe the attitude of most professional historians to orthodox Mormon archaeology?" In part, he replied: "I think that for the Book of Mormon, even though they don't know much about the Book of Mormon or Mormonism, they take the whole thing as a complete fantasy, that this is a big waste of time."

[58] Coe, "Mormons & Archaeology," 40.

[59] Chris Heimerdinger, "A Lost Generation of Scholarship." "This phenomenon of non-LDS scholars lashing out against 'Mormon Mesoamericanists' is still very much ongoing. Really, it's merely a subset of the same struggle that Latter-day Saints have faced since the *Book of Mormon*'s initial publication. And if we are to be honest, some of the ridicule and/or criticism has been justified. Latter-day Saints, because we often have well-established testimonies of the *Book of Mormon* beforehand, are at times all-too eager to promote certain archeological findings before all of the 'research ducks' are lined up."

[60] Martin H. Raish, "All that Glitters: Uncovering Fool's Gold in Book of Mormon Archaeology," 10. More recently, Daniel Peterson remarked of John L. Sorenson: "While he is a committed proponent of the historicity of the Book of Mormon, Sorenson has also criticized the shoddy scholarship that some have used to defend it. This, too, has been a valuable contribution." Daniel C. Peterson, "Advancing Book of Mormon Scholarship."

Several years ago I attended a presentation that consisted of pairs of slides juxtaposing objects from the Old World with similar ones from the New. The point was to show so many Old/New World correspondences that those in attendance could see for themselves that people had sailed across the oceans in ancient times and had influenced the cultures of the Americas.

One pair of images that I especially remember matched the mask of Agamemnon from the royal tomb in Mycenae with an example of Mixtec jewelry from Oaxaca, Mexico. But while many in the audience were ohhing and ahhing at the apparent *resemblances*—both were, after all, gold faces—I was pondering their equally notable *differences*. For example, the first was nearly life-size, portrayed a real person, and was fashioned from a single lump of gold, while the latter was only three inches tall, was an image of the god Xipe Totec, and was made by the lost-wax casting process.

This sort of slipshod "scholarship"—that shines light on only those bits of information that support the argument at hand while ignoring everything else—has always annoyed me.[61]

Well-intentioned armchair scholars have infused their discussions of the Book of Mormon with just this kind of looks-better-than-it-is argumentation.[62] Often the similarities between an Old World and a New World culture are assumed to indicate a New World borrowing of the Old World trait.[63] R. John Williams provides a wonderful example of the problems inherent in such assumptions:

> Part of this paper deals with a unique and complex book whose authenticity and historicity we are asked to accept on "faith." The book claims to arrive as the secondary translation of some magnificent testimonies containing the story of a family whose intercontinental travel takes them beyond the lands known in the Bible. It speaks of "great wonders." It recounts the story of Adam and Eve (slightly revised, of course). There are bloodthirsty, brutal people who threaten the faith of believers with certain death, thwarted at the last minute by divine intervention. At one point the day actually turns dark. At

---

[61] Martin H. Raish, "Review of Paul R. Cheesman and Millie F. Cheesman, Ancient American Indians: Their Origins, Civilizations and Old World Connections," 21.

[62] John L. Sorenson, "Instant Expertise on Book of Mormon Archaeology," 431:

> What is the harm from such publications? First, they train the reader that serious, critical thought is unnecessary and maybe even undesirable, that any source of information will serve no matter how unreliable, and that logical absurdity is as good as sound analysis. Second, the reader gets the false impression that all is well in Zion, that the outside world is being forced to the LDS point of view, and that the only role LDS scholars need play in Book of Mormon-related studies is to use scissors and paste effectively. Third, the underlying complexity and subtlety of the Book of Mormon are masked by a pseudo-scholarship to which everything is simple.

[63] Perhaps the most dramatic list of parallels is found in Thomas Stuart Ferguson, *One Fold, One Shepherd*, 57–72, which provides a thinly documented list of 311 items that are found in Mesoamerica (at various places and various time periods) and which also occur in the ancient Near East (at various places and various time periods, not necessarily correlated even in time with those listed for the New World).

A much more sophisticated use of the methodology is found in Diane E. Wirth, *Parallels: Mesoamerican and Ancient Middle Eastern Traditions*. Wirth does not argue an exclusive importation by Book of Mormon peoples but clearly implies some kind of causality implicit in the parallels. She does not, for instance, allow the possibility of independent invention, even when there is ample reason to look to a common model rather than an imported idea.

another, the land becomes "infested by robbers," and the more evil people even participate in cannibalism. It tells of great kings who offer to convert to Christianity. It demonstrates an uncanny knowledge of guerrilla warfare tactics. It has inspired stories of magical salamanders that turn white when placed in fire, and of course it speaks of wonders and magnificence "beyond description." It has even had an indirect influence on the manner in which we refer to Native Americans. But the original text, unfortunately, no longer exists on this earth, and we are left only with the assurances of a "translator" that the testimony contained in the record is "true," although we do not, in fact, have even the complete text as it left the hand of the translator/scribe.

I am speaking, of course, of *The Travels of Marco Polo*, written by one Rustichello of Pisa, a romance-writer who spent time in jail with Marco Polo in 1298 and claims to have recorded Polo's narrative as Polo told it to him. . . .

But, more to the point, why have I introduced this complex medieval narrative in such a way that my readers are compelled to find parallels between Polo's Travels and the Book of Mormon? Of course, since I ask why "my readers" are "compelled" to find parallels between the Book of Mormon and the *Travels of Marco Polo*, I am speaking already of a certain horizon of expectations. To present that particular series of details, invoking key words like "faith," "miraculous," "scribe," and "guerilla warfare," while omitting other elements like "Marco Polo," "1298," "China," and "Emperor," I am playing a "trick" on "my readers" that works only because I am already intimately familiar with the discursive parameters of *Dialogue* [the journal] readership. I am forcing a particular interpretation, based on my objectives within a particular interpretive community.[64]

It is simply too easy to manufacture impressive parallels by the descriptions that present the parallels. The problem of finding appropriate methodologies for making a case for Book of Mormon history leads us to Dever's suggestion that "in history-writing of any kind, the choice of method is fundamental, because to a large degree it determines the outcome of the inquiry. Where you arrive depends not only upon where you think you are going, but also upon how you decide to get there."[65]

In critical literature, the abuse of comparisons is called parallelomania, a term Samuel Sandmel coined for a similar methodological issue in biblical studies: "We might for our purposes define parallelomania as that extravagance among scholars which first overdoes the supposed similarity in passages and then proceeds to describe source and derivation as if implying literary connection flowing in an inevitable or predetermined direction."[66]

Douglas F. Salmon discussed the problems of the method:

> For the purposes of this discussion, a "parallel" is the occurrence in a separate text of a key phrase, idea, or term that closely matches the same one found in the text under consideration. That parallels exist in a wide variety of texts—separated temporally, geographically, and culturally—is an undeniable fact. The challenge is to adequately explain what the existence of the parallel means. Does it mean that there is some type of

---

[64] R. John Williams, "A Marvelous Work and a Possession: Book of Mormon Historicity as Postcolonialism," 38–39.
[65] William G. Dever, *Did God Have a Wife? Archaeology and Folk Religion in Ancient Israel*, 8.
[66] Samuel Sandmel, "Parallelomania," 1–13.

relationship between the two texts? Did one of the authors know the work of the other, either directly or through some intermediary text? If no relationship between the texts can be established, how do we explain the similarities in thought? Is it simply coincidence, or is there some other theory that can adequately explain the similarities?[67]

Too often, the questions that must be asked of the parallels remain unasked. Without controls, comparisons are frequently simple parallelomania. John F. Hobbins discusses the overly exuberant use of the methodology:

> Parallelomania is the practice of overdoing supposed similarities between texts. Very loose and even non-existent parallels are dressed up as stringent parallels with the result that the sense of a particular text is mis-specified or over-specified on the basis of another. It really doesn't matter if texts A and B derive from the same milieu (however defined) or from discrete milieu. The obsession with "parallels" overlooks the fact that wherever there are similarities, *there are also differences*. If a scholar notes *similarities only* between text A and text B, rite A and rite B, religion A and religion B, chances are, she is on a binge of parallelomania. Said scholar has a disease, but it is not incurable. It is treatable if the patient is willing to go through detox and remain within an accountability structure thereafter.[68]

It is a caution that James R. Davila underscores: "In general, a parallel only has meaning when placed in an overall context of differences."[69]

A wonderful, tongue-in-cheek examination of parallels as proof of Book of Mormon plagiarism is Jeff Lindsay's essay "demonstrating" that the Book of Mormon was cribbed from Walt Whitman's "Leaves of Grass." Lindsay writes with irony:

> While I will discuss examples in more detail below, please note that the parallels between Whitman and the Book of Mormon are not only strong in terms of themes and common elements, but strong and convincing right down to specific expressions from Whitman copied verbatim in the Book of Mormon. Normally a plagiarist will change a few words or modify their order to cover the crime to some degree, and Joseph often did this. But apparently sometimes he got so sloppy that entire phrases have been lifted verbatim from Whitman, and not just two- or three-word phrases, but sometimes entire FIVE-WORD PHRASES! Here are a few examples, some of which we shall treat more fully later:

---

[67] Douglas F. Salmon, "Parallelomania and the Study of Latter-day Scripture: Confirmation, Coincidence, or the Collective Unconscious?" 130.

[68] John F. Hobbins, "A Contrastive Approach to the Study of Ancient Texts."

[69] James R. Davila "The Perils of Parallels (lecture)." Benjamin L. McGuire, "Finding Parallels: Some Cautions and Criticisms, Part Two," 79–80 provides an extensive quotation from Alexander Lindey's book *Plagiarism and Originality* which expands on the problem of the importance of the differences. Lindey provides nine specific criticisms of the method ranging from the problem of ignoring differences to the distortion created by the selection of only certain elements.

Gordon C. Thomasson underlines this issue. "Daddy, What's a 'Frontier'?" 4–5: "Upon finding a possible parallel between the Book of Mormon and some bit of early American history, it is all too often assumed that the source for the idea has been found and further study is neglected or even ridiculed. Such an at best naïve, reductionist approach ignores the fact that where parallels occur they almost invariably related to what are perennial questions—themes which recur in countless religious histories—and which are by no means unique to the Burned-over District in space or time, and/or may correlate even more significantly with ancient evidence than it does with the more recent."

Five-word Phrases Common to Whitman and the Book of Mormon
- **The meaning of all things.** Whitman: "My knowledge my live parts, it keeping tally with **the meaning of all things**, . . ." 1 Nephi 11:17: ". . . nevertheless, I do not know **the meaning of all things**." (Tellingly, this passage is in a scene of prophecy, and the lifted passage from Whitman is associated with "prophetical screams.")
- **Of the souls of men.** Whitman: "Of the progress **of the souls of men** and women. . . ." Alma 40:7: "I would inquire what becometh **of the souls of men**. . . ." The same phrase is also in Alma 40:9 (a double blunder!).
- **By day and by night.** Whitman frequently uses the phrase "**by day and by night**," a five-word phrase found also in 3 Nephi 4:21: "safely **by day or by night**."
- **The beginning and the end.** Whitman uses this phrase more than once. One example: "But I do not talk of the beginning or the end." Given Whitman's emphasis of this term, it should be no surprise to find it also in the Book of Mormon, specifically in 3 Nephi 9:18, where we read that Christ is "the beginning and the end."
- **The righteous and the wicked.** Whitman speaks of "all **the righteous and the wicked**," which is parroted in 3 Nephi 24:18: "Then shall ye return and discern between **the righteous and the wicked**, . . ."
- **The face of the earth.** This tell-tale phrase is one of the most common phrases in the Book of Mormon, repeated an astonishing THIRTY-EIGHT (38) TIMES! Examples include 1 Nephi 1:11, 1 Nephi 10:12, 13; 1 Nephi 12:5, 1 Nephi 14:12; Alma 13:22; etc. It's source is a classic Whitman passage about the prophecies of seers and other spiritual topics, which we'll discuss in more detail below. (Thanks to Dr. Walter Reade for pointing this one out to me.) In fact, this actually should count as a SIX-WORD PHRASE, for Whitman speaks of things that are "**on** the face of the earth," and many of the 38 plagiarized Book of Mormon passages have "**upon** the face of the earth." The minor change of "on" to "upon" hardly conceals the crime of plagiarism. Thus, in all fairness, we have a SIX-WORD parallel—absolutely fatal to the cause of defenders of the Book of Mormon!
- **The Son of God shall come.** Actually, this should also be counted as a **six-word parallel**, for Joseph Smith directly plagiarizes six words from Whitman's phrase, "**The** true **son of God shall come** singing his songs," vainly trying to disguise his crime by dropping the word "true." But with almost insane abandon, Joseph then repeats Whitman's phrase THREE TIMES in the Book of Mormon (Alma 9:26, Alma 11:35, and Alma 21:7). (Thanks also to Dr. Walter Reade for this one!)[70]

Of course, the problem is that the Book of Mormon would be copying from a work published about twenty-five years later. Parallels between the Book of Mormon language and words or very short phrases found in contemporary texts are no stronger than those Lindsay describes for *Leaves of Grass*.[71] Even when the lists of such

---

[70] Jeff Lindsay, "Was the Book of Mormon Plagiarized from Walt Whitman's *Leaves of Grass?*"
[71] The most recent phrase comparison suggests that the 1819 *The Late War Between the United States and Great Britain From June, 1812, to February 1815*, is a significant source for the Book of Mormon. Chris Johnson and Duane Johnson, "How the Book of Mormon Destroyed Mormonism."

similarities are extensive, they do not rise above coincidence or the common vocabulary for common religious themes.[72] Parallels are a problematic methodology no matter who uses them or whether one agrees with the thesis they are used to support.[73] Although much historical work, particularly in the New World's dearth of pre-Conquest documents, requires comparisons to fill in gaps, the potential for false parallels is sufficiently strong that parallels should be used only with the greatest caution and control.

For responses, see Benjamin L. McGuire, "The Late War against the Book of Mormon," 323–55, and G. Bruce Schaalje, "A Bayesian Cease-Fire in the Late War on the Book of Mormon." Schaalje, a statistician, examines the statistical model necessary to make such a distinction.

[72] A fascinating example is Timothy W. Henline, *Absolute Proof that the Book of Mormon Is Fake*. The entire book is a compilation of similarities in vocabulary. An example selected at random (88):

> BOM Mosiah 28:4. And thus did the Spirit of the lord work upon them, for they were the very *vilest of sinners*, And the Lord saw fit *in his infinite mercy* to spare them; nevertheless they suffered much *anguish of soul* because of their iniquities, suffering much and fearing that they should be **cast off forever.**
> COM[mentary] Gill: Heb 12:3 "some of them are the **vilest of sinners**, (Henry, Clarke)
> COM Clarke: Jam 5:20 "him back to God, who, **in his infinite mercy**" (Henry)
> COM Gill: Job 7:121 "but great **anguish of soul**;" (Henry, Clarke)
> KJV Lamentations 3:31 For the Lord will not **cast off forever**;

Bold and italics in original. I have silently removed some internal notations and underlining of the scripture references. I believe that Henline does conclusively demonstrate that Joseph Smith used the religious language common to his day. I disagree that the nature of that vocabulary in a translation indicates that the Book of Mormon is a pastiche of phrases excerpted from commentaries.

[73] Even the best of us have, at times, succumbed to the method of evidence by lists. John L. Sorenson, "Ancient America and the Book of Mormon Revisited," 85–92 presents classified correspondence lists of cultural items that are in the New World and the Old World. They are presented only in a list and provide no information on the nature of the similarities, the comparative dating, and whether the information might be seen as independent invention.

John L. Sorenson, "Reading Mormon's Codex," is a paper he gave at the 2012 FAIR Conference. In that paper he discusses "420 correspondences that tie the Book of Mormon to the picture of ancient Mesoamerican civilization constructed by archaeologists and other researchers." His list of correspondences in the paper is not qualitatively different from his 1969 list. A major difference is that, instead of listing parallels to the Old World, these are "correspondences" to the New World.

John L. Sorenson, *Mormon's Codex* is the book that fleshes out the correspondences he summarized in the 2012 FAIR Conference paper. The simple correspondence list does not appear in the book, though the type of comparisons he makes often leans more to parallels than to a more rigorous comparison of convincing trait complexes.

An important addition to the literature on the problems of parallels is McGuire, "Finding Parallels: Some Cautions and Criticisms" (in two parts). In this essay McGuire analyzes a work claiming a modern origin for all of the major themes in Mormonism by comparisons/parallels to the information environment surrounding Joseph Smith. McGuire's essay is an important caution for anyone attempting to use parallels as a methodology.

Convergences as a Methodological Foundation

Some form of comparison between text and history is always required to discern historicity. Texts are always compared to archaeology and/or other texts. Sometimes even artifacts require explanation by comparison or analogy to similar artifacts from another culture. Comparisons must be made. The problem cannot, therefore, reside in an absolute deficit in any methodology that makes comparisons, but rather in the way the comparisons are made and made to be significant. One important type of controlled parallel is ethnographic analogy. Dever explains his version of this method:

> One aspect shared by both biblical scholarship and archaeology is a dependence on analogy as a fundamental method of argument. . . .
> The challenge is to find appropriate analogues, those offering the most promise yet capable of being tested in some way. Ethnoarchaeology is useful in this regard, particularly in places where unsophisticated modern cultures are still found superimposed, as it were, upon the remains of the ancient world, as in parts of the Middle East. Analogies drawn from life of modern Arab villages or Bedouin society can, with proper controls, be used to illuminate both artifacts and texts, as many studies have shown.[74]

Sorenson's *Mormon's Codex* and this book were both in preparation for a few years prior to publications. During that time, Sorenson and I had some limited communication. When I saw an early table of contents for what would become *Mormon's Codex* I was struck at how much the two books appeared to be developing along similar lines even though we had not communicated. Now that *Mormon's Codex* has been published and my own book's focus and argument have clarified, the two have fewer similarities than suggested by that much earlier table of contents.

However, one of the similarities that struck me was that both Sorenson and I had read Dever's *What Did the Biblical Writers Know and When Did They Know It?* Both of us had been impressed with Dever's concept of "convergences" and both of us had leaned heavily on both that term and our understanding of the subtle difference in methodology that Dever suggested it represented.

As with the general outlines of the two books, our two different perceptions of a methodology built upon convergences has also diverged. Sorenson explains his evolved concept:

> Dever's term convergences has many synonyms—correspondences, parallels, analogies, similarities, agreements, conformities, counterparts, and congruencies. Each has a slightly different shade of meaning. Convergence may suggest distinct processes that end up with similar results; parallel connotes a general or unfocused degree of similarity; analogy points to likeness in form without any particular historical connection implied between the features compared. The comparisons upon which this book relies will usually be called correspondences, in the dictionary sense of "a particular similarity." Occasionally, synonymous terms will be employed to avoid excessive repetition, but no variation in meaning is intended when that is done. (*Mormon's Codex*, 16)

---

[74] Dever, *What Did the Biblical Writers Know and When Did They Know It?* 77–78.

In my book, the shades of meaning that Sorenson spells out might apply to a term used as simply a lexical choice. However, I am suggesting that a methodology may be attached to some of these terms, and those methodologies are much more distinct than are the dictionary definitions. Therefore, while Sorenson shifted his vocabulary (and implicit methodology) to a more open correspondence, I have elected to use "convergence" as a more rigorous requirement for linking a text to the historical and archaeological record.

The pragmatic result is a dramatic difference in the way we present our arguments. Where I have elected to build a chronological argument, Sorenson uses a thematic approach in much of the book. That leads him to use correlations from multiple time periods and perhaps different locations to establish a parallel, or correspondence between something in the Book of Mormon and something similar in Mesoamerica. As has always been the case, Sorenson has important insights. I believe that the chronological presentation of the material will not only aid the reader in understanding how the Book of Mormon fits into a generalized picture of Mesoamerica, but how it fits into the particular picture of Mesoamerica at particular times and places.

As a result of my orientation, I suggest that we will be best served by an approach applied with great success in the field of historical linguistics. Bruce L. Pearson describes both the problem and the solution:

> Sets of words exhibiting similarities in both form and meaning may be presumed to be cognates, given that the languages involved are assumed to be related. This of course is quite circular. We need a list of cognates to show that languages are related, but we first need to know that the languages are related before we may safely look for cognates. In actual practice, therefore, the hypothesis builds slowly, and there may be a number of false starts along the way. But gradually certain correspondence patterns begin to emerge. These patterns point to unsuspected cognates that reveal additional correspondences until eventually a tightly woven web of interlocking evidence is developed.[75]

Pearson's linguistic methodology describes quite nicely the problem we have in attempting to place the Book of Mormon in history. We cannot adequately compare the text to history unless we know that it is history. We cannot know that it is history unless we compare the text to history. We cannot avoid the necessity of examining parallels between the text and history.

The problem with the fallacy of parallels is that it doesn't protect against false positives. What is required is a methodology that is more recursive than simple parallels. We need a methodology that generates the "tightly woven web of interlocking evidence" that Pearson indicates resolves the similar issue for historical linguists.[76]

---

[75] Bruce L. Pearson, *Introduction to Linguistic Concepts*, 51.
[76] McGuire, "Finding Parallels: . . . Part 2," 62.

> The process of recognizing parallels. . . is first and foremost the assembly of a data set on and from which new analysis will need to be based. On first sight, the similarities must evoke some appropriate theoretical explanation. But upon reflection and with the

History is not a hard science, and there is no way to construct a repeatable experiment with the data. History is a construction based upon data which interact with the way the historian perceives the data. Jacques Barzun and Henry F. Graff remind us that "only a divine being would have a perfect and complete knowledge of the event—'as it really happened.' Outside our imperfect knowledge, the event has no independent existence; it is not hidden in some 'repository of the real' where we can find it."[77] Although biblical historian Thomas L. Thompson draws some controversial conclusions,[78] I nevertheless agree with his basic definition of the nature of writing history: "History is by definition anachronistic. It is not objective—something that exists in the past, waiting to be uncovered—for the past is in ruins and exists no longer. If, when we write our history of ancient Israel, we write a history that is reasonable and makes sense, it is a history that makes sense to *ourselves*."[79]

When we examine data from antiquity, we are recasting information that made sense in another cultural world into something that makes sense in ours. In the case of the Book of Mormon, we are recasting their written experience to make sense against a very different (and very modern) way of seeing the world. Nevertheless, Dever promises us that "it is possible to learn about the past, not simply by amassing more bits and pieces of disjointed 'evidence,' but rather by coordinating the pieces of evidence and situating them within a context relating knowledge to a deliberate quest."[80] This is a process he has called a "convergence"—when the evidence from the ground corresponds in time, place, and meaning with the descriptions of the text.

The idea that one may understand history by making comparisons of similarities is dangerously close to the fallacy of parallels, as Dever recognizes: "Of course one may object at this point that seeking such 'convergences' was just what the now-discredited older 'biblical archaeology' sought to do. The critical difference between that and what I propose here has to do with the independent but parallel investigation of the two sources of data for history-writing, and the subsequent critical dialogue between them that scholars must undertake."[81] Although we may lay parallel arguments, they converge only under more tightly controlled conditions and often require specific argumentation to demonstrate the convergence.

This may be one of the most important methodological processes for the Book of Mormon. Reminiscent of Pearson's discussion of historical linguistics above, the problem is not that parallels are inherently useless, but that they must be used

---

collection of each new data set, one will begin to evaluate and analyze not only the data but also the previous theories themselves. . . . The process of comparison in the light of new data sets must also cause us to reformulate . . . the theories themselves.

[77] Jacques Barzun and Henry F. Graff, *The Modern Researcher*, 179.
[78] Thompson is one of the revisionists who see little or no "history" in the Bible and is therefore one of the scholars against whom Dever pointed his arguments in *What Did the Biblical Writers Know and When Did They Know It?*, 23–52.
[79] Thomas L. Thompson, *Mythic Past: Biblical Archaeology and the Myth of Israel*, 68. Emphasis Thompson's.
[80] Dever, *What Did the Biblical Writers Know and When Did They Know It?* 70.
[81] Ibid., 106.

carefully and critically and must be woven into a web of interrelated evidence. In the case of the Book of Mormon, the inability to positively anchor any New World location to the Book of Mormon means that we do not have the luxury of accepting single convergences as Dever might. The Book of Mormon will require sterner stuff. We will require a larger number of convergences, and even then, we will require more than simple convergences.

What the Book of Mormon will require is a number of complex correspondences that are interrelated between text, time, and place. Martin Raish contrasts the typical parallel lists with the more interconnected requirements that I am suggesting must form the basis for understanding Book of Mormon historicity: "Many LDS writers provide what I call shopping lists to prove their points. They assemble rather impressive-looking lists of words, customs, and architectural features which are found both in the Old World and the New. The longer the list, of course, the greater the 'proof.' Unfortunately such an approach is rarely of any real value. . . . To be meaningful, such a list must cite a *complex* system. . . or a *unique* manner. . . which is found *only* in the two cultures in question."[82]

The concept of convergences provides for the complex system that Raish indicates. It is reminiscent of a dictum from the United States Supreme Court John W. Welch quoted: "Circumstantial evidence is often as convincing to the mind as direct testimony, and often more so. A number of concurrent facts, like rays of light, all converging to the same center, may throw not only a clear light but a burning conviction; a conviction of truth more infallible than the testimony even of two witnesses directly to a fact."[83]

Multiple aspects of the culture must converge in time and space in non-random ways for us to understand that there is a real convergence between the text and the evidence from archaeology. They must be unique to that setting and not items that simply mirror natural independent invention based on similar human experience.[84] However, once there is a basic structure of complex correspondences in place, the reiterative process suggests that we may then find place for some correspondences that are insufficient in themselves to establish the pattern, but are useful to elaborate the pattern, just in the way that creating cognates in historical linguistics can find additional data following the discovered relationship between two languages.

---

[82] Raish, "All that Glitters," 13.

[83] John W. Welch, "The Power of Evidence in the Nurturing of Faith," 36.

[84] Wirth, *Parallels*, provides a number of fascinating connections between the Old World and the New. However, some that appear most arbitrary also have a natural explanation. For example, she describes what appears to be a unique and fascinating correspondence between fish and birth that occurs in both Egypt and Mesoamerica. However, she also notes: "A fish was used to represent a human embryo due to the natural habitat of a fetus in a watery embryonic fluid before birth" (79). That naturalistic context is the same in Egypt and Mesoamerica. It is certainly possible that both cultures had discovered an embryo at a stage where it has gills, thus leading to the comparison to a fish. A connection to a biological datum available to both cultures is as plausible as cultural contact—in fact, is more likely.

The iterative process is perhaps even more important in a Mesoamerican context than for much of the rest of world history. While we do have the advantage of a literate people, we don't have the luxury of many texts. Much of the details that we have about religion must be reconstructed by used late descriptions, even post-Conquest descriptions, and using those to see if similar concepts can be discerned for earlier periods. Fortunately for the methodology, this appears to be the case. Perhaps the best example is the great Maya work called the Popol Vuh. Gabrielle Vail and Christine Hernandez explain:

> The stories told (or retold) in the Popol Vuh are of great antiquity, as indicate by comparing particular episodes to iconography represented in Preclassic contexts, including a series of stelae at Pacific coastal site of Izapa (not necessarily inhabited by Maya speakers) and from depictions on the San Bartolo murals. . . .
>
> The San Bartolo murals and Classic period ceramic vessel scenes provide clear evidence that different regions elaborated on the events that are later described in the Popol Vuh as occurring in primordial time. A number of specific episodes are included in these sources—the most important referring to the resurrection of the maize god and his overcoming of the Underworld lords—that are not part of the Popol Vuh. This supports our interpretation that the story recorded in the Pop Vuh during the sixteenth century is regional variant of a narrative that can be traced back a millennium and a half prior to that.[85]

Nevertheless, there are also identifiable later influences in the Popol Vuh, so comparisons must always be made with caution.[86] Mesoamerica was home to multiple different peoples with distinct languages, but it is known as a cultural area because there are overarching similarities that cross ethnic, political, and linguistic boundaries. Vail and Hernandez indicate "that this is the case can be seen by comparing the principal themes in the Popol Vuh with the mythic traditions from elsewhere in Mesoamerica. Commonalities include a focus on twins/brothers, a journey to the Underworld to create the present race of humans, the formation of the earth from a crocodilian's body, the existence of previous eras (before the creation of humans), the planning and carrying forth of a destructive flood to initiate a new world era, and the importance of foundational rituals. Each of these themes forms a core element of creation narratives related in indigenous texts written during the colonial period by Yucatec Maya speakers, as well as Nahuatl speakers from highland central Mexico."[87]

Telling the Book of Mormon history against known events for the time and place hypothesized for the Book of Mormon should display those underlying convergences. At times, the overall outline of the convergences in both time and space will open the opportunity for convergences of ideas or practices that might be inferred based on information from a different time that appear to retain continuity with earlier practices. The essentially conservative nature of Mesoamerican religion and culture allows us to use this information with care.

---

[85] Gabrielle Vail and Christine Hernandez, *Re-Creating Primordial Time: Foundaton Rituals and Mythology in the Postclassic Maya Codices*, xxi.

[86] Ibid., xxii.

[87] Ibid., xxi.

Ultimately, the convergences cannot prove the Book of Mormon, but should allow us a richer understanding of it. As we find ways in which the Book of Mormon reflects a particular culture at a particular place and time, we may then expect that such a culture may also aid in understanding potentially problematic aspects of the text.

As Donald Harmon Akenson put it: "Heuristic fictions, unlike hypotheses, are evaluated not by whether they are proved or disproved, but by their fecundity."[88] When the underlying convergences produce an improved understanding of the text, we may begin to assert that we have found the location (and time) which produced the plate text. The descriptions in the text must converge with the data for the target place and time. The data for the place and time must then converge with the text's descriptions to enrich those descriptions. It is a recursive process that builds its case from multiple examples rather than depending upon a single definitive connection.

This Reading

Of the myriad possible ways to read the Book of Mormon, I choose to read and tell it both *in* history and *as* history. Methodological considerations for establishing the historicity inform my choices in the particular stories I have chosen to tell—but intentionally do not structure it. I am interested in the story of the Book of Mormon as part of the historical and cultural changes that have occurred in a limited region of Mesoamerica appropriate to the times covered in the Book of Mormon.

The vast majority of Mesoamerican archaeology deals with peoples and cultures that were probably not directly involved with the Book of Mormon. The geography I follow in constructing this story is only tangential to the locations where the better-known Mesoamerican peoples lived. Nevertheless, there are many similarities across Mesoamerican cultures even when there were specific differences. Those cultural similarities allow us to understand certain aspects of Book of Mormon history by ethnographic analogy to the better-known peoples. Ethnographic analogy differs from a parallel in that what is being demonstrated is human similarity, not specific connections. When we see similar peoples acting in similar ways, we are not suggesting causality, but human commonality. The Book of Mormon, as a book produced by people living in the region influenced by larger social, political, and cultural trends, we can see those same aspects of history reflected in the Book of Mormon, many times during the same time periods in the text as they are found in archaeology or linguistic reconstructions.

Nevertheless, what is known from the reconstruction of the history of those peoples provides the cultural and historical setting that we can also see mirrored in the actions and motivations of those who are the subjects of the Book of Mormon.

---

[88] Donald Harmon Akenson, *Surpassing Wonder: The Invention of the Bible and the Talmuds*, 33.
Karl J. Weintraub, *Reference Answers*, "Heuristic," defines "heuristic fiction": "Of or relating to a usually speculative formulation serving as a guide in the investigation or solution of a problem: *The historian discovers the past by the judicious use of such a heuristic device as the 'ideal type.'*"

The most important result of understanding the Book of Mormon in history should be better understanding the Book of Mormon. However, I also value the ability to provide a strong argument for the Book of Mormon's historicity. Establishing a firm foundation for its historicity will improve the position of the Book of Mormon as seen from the position of both believers and non-believers. Elder Neal A. Maxwell admonished: "Let us minimize our personal errors which enemies could exploit. Let us conquer the weaknesses which critics could work upon. . . . Let us be articulate, for while our defense of the kingdom may not stir all hearers, the absence of thoughtful response may cause fledglings among the faithful to falter. What we assert may not be accepted, but unasserted convictions soon become deserted convictions."[89] He also believed that one of the results of such a rigorous defense of the Book of Mormon would create the conditions where "there will be a convergence of discoveries (never enough, mind you, to remove the need for faith) to make plain and plausible what the modern prophets have been saying all along."[90] To be plain and plausible means that we will be able to see how the Book of Mormon fits into the ancient world.[91]

Various LDS artists have attempted to help us "see" the Book of Mormon through their visual depictions. Drawing upon histories with which they were more familiar, artists have depicted Book of Mormon peoples as though they continued the dress and customs of pre-Exilic Israel, or perhaps some interesting combination of visual clues from multiple lands and times.[92] Although such illustrations provide a powerful visual addition to the Book of Mormon text, they do not relate to any actual culture in which the Book of Mormon peoples would have lived.[93]

A similar perceptual mismatch often colors the way many see the Book of Mormon. Perhaps cued by LDS artists, they find it difficult to "see" the Book of Mormon against what is known of Mesoamerican peoples. Metcalfe and Vogel declare: "The more we learn, the more inconceivable the Book of Mormon version of

---

[89] Neal A. Maxwell, "All Hell is Moved," BYU Devotional address, November 8, 1977.

[90] Neal A. Maxwell, *Deposition of a Disciple*, 49. This comment was made in the context of a question about whether to fear secular scholarship. Remarkably, his response presumed that faithful scholarship would be armed with the same critical tools as the secular scholars. He urged: "Latter-day Saint scholars will show the way by being able to read firsthand such ancient texts rather than relying on secondary scholarship, as was the case earlier in this dispensation. We will be able to read such texts through a Latter-day Saint lens rather than relying solely upon able Protestant and Catholic scholars, of whom it is unfair to expect full sensitivity to the fulness of the gospel's doctrines and ordinances."

[91] Sorenson, *An Ancient American Setting for the Book of Mormon*, xx: "This model is *plausible*. That means that the setting described could reasonably have been as I represent it. Like a small replica of an airplane or steam engine, this model works, in the sense that the parts fit together to explain point after point in the Book of Mormon that seem inexplicable otherwise."

[92] One need only view Renaissance artists' representations of the life of Christ to see how common it has been to interpret history in terms of anachronistic clothing and settings.

[93] Anthony Sweat, "By the Gift and Power of Art," 229–35 discusses the issue of art and verisimilitude, noting the typical emphasis on the emotive power of art over historical accuracy.

ancient America becomes."[94] What they find inconceivable, I cannot conceive in any other way. Therefore, in this reading of the Book of Mormon I will tell its story as I have come to see it. It is a story of the complex interactions with peoples, places, and concerns that mark the larger flow of Mesoamerican history. Lacking the artistic talent to depict Book of Mormon life visually, I must use text to illustrate text.[95] Sometimes the story will manifest the multiple interrelated convergences that can tie the text to a time and place. Sometimes, the iterative use of those convergences will support other descriptions that can enrich our understanding of the text based upon the times and cultures more tightly determined.

Perhaps because the Book of Mormon is a religious text, it is most frequently read ahistorically. Reading without any grounding in a real history, we do not think about why events occur. They simply happened—perhaps for some divinely didactic purpose. We may extract the divine lesson when we perceive God's pattern in quotidian chaos, but it was the quotidian that engendered the chaos, not God. Understanding better the way the lives of these ancient people interacted with their natural and social environment, we may perhaps better see patterns of divine interaction in our own chaotic lives. Very much as do we, the people depicted in scripture led lives that more often dealt with daily problems than divine realities. Perhaps if we may learn to see them more clearly, we may more clearly see ourselves in their mirror.

---

[94] Vogel and Metcalfe, "Editor's Introduction," vii.
[95] The best visual interpretation of the Book of Mormon against Mesoamerica is John L. Sorenson, *Images of Ancient America: Visualizing Book of Mormon Life*.

3

A Prophet without Honour

A prophet is not without honour, save in his own country, and in his own house. (Matt. 13:57)

An enemy invasionary force cut its way through Palestinian lands. The prophet had predicted this disaster, but the king had not listened. Now this irresistible force was on Jerusalem's doorstep and destruction appeared sure. It was 701 B.C. and the Assyrians had carried away the people of Israel, the Northern Kingdom. It was 597 B.C. and the Babylonians had already enslaved and deported the social elites of Judah, the Southern Kingdom.[1] Yet Jerusalem stood. Separated by a century, these two events were eerily parallel. Both had been preceded by a king intent upon reforming Hebrew religion by destroying idols and centralizing worship in Jerusalem—first Hezekiah and later his great-grandson Josiah.[2] Kings in both eras

---

[1] Isaiah is the prophet proclaiming warnings before the Assyrian invasion. See Isa. 20, and 30:1–10, 31:1–3 for Isaiah's opposition to the alliance with Egypt that led to the war. Jeremiah is the major prophet of the Babylonian invasion (Jer. 11:9–12, 12:16–17). Zephaniah also prophesies at this time, preaching of a coming catastrophe (Zeph. 1).

[2] For Hezekiah, see Siegfried H. Horn, "The Divided Monarchy: The Kingdoms of Judah and Israel," 131–32. "Hezekiah is described in the Bible as a good ruler who initiated a series of important religious reforms when, as sole ruler, he had had authority to do so. These reforms included abolishing illegitimate sanctuaries and destroying cult objects throughout the county (2 Kgs. 18:3–4), thus centralizing worship in the Jerusalem Temple."

For Josiah, Norman K. Gottwald, *The Hebrew Bible: A Socio-Literary Introduction*, 371:

> [The Deuteronomist History] connects [Josiah's] reforms with the discovery of the lawbook in the temple, undoubtedly some form of the laws in Deuteronomy. Chronicles, on the other hand, pictures the reforms as having begun prior to the finding of the lawbook. It is widely thought that [the Deuteronomist History] has telescoped several stages in the reform efforts which can be reconstructed as a succession of widening moves: (1) purification of the Jerusalem temple, (2) purification of outlying Judean holy places, (3) discovery/public presentation of the lawbook and a decision to centralize all worship at Jerusalem by closing outlying shrines, and (4) extension of purification and centralization to all the newly controlled territories in the coastal plan and northward into Samaria, and perhaps also into Gilead and Galilee.

picked the wrong ally and attempted to stand against a northern invader. Both failed. Yet Jerusalem stood.

The parallels must have been unavoidable. They had to have informed Judah's national understanding. The miraculous delivery of Jerusalem a century before must have fueled Judahite faith that Jerusalem would also continue after the Babylonian domination. After all, Babylon had not destroyed Jerusalem but had installed a puppet king, Zedekiah (2 Kgs. 24:15–17).[3] Judah had survived foreign political domination before and many doubtless believed that it would again.

It is into this world that Yahweh sent prophets to warn that this time could be different.[4] Jeremiah, Nahum, and Zephaniah all have writings collected in our Old Testament, and all were active during this general period.[5] It is in this world that Lehi received a call to witness the coming destruction of Jerusalem. This world into which Lehi was called informed both his message and the nature of his flight from Jerusalem. It explains why Lehi was a prophet without honor in his own country, and even without honor among some of his own family.

Judah in Its World

In 641/640 B.C., eight-year-old Josiah ascended the throne of Judah after the assassination of his predecessor, Amon.[6] Both politically and religiously, Josiah was seen as a restoration of the Davidic line. Josiah's great-grandfather, Hezekiah, had been a religious reformer. Much of what Josiah accomplished paralleled his great-grandfather's reforming efforts which had faded during Amon's reign. Josiah's youthfulness at ascension and the assassination of Amon suggest that much of what is credited to king Josiah may have been due to those who guided him.[7] Perhaps some of those providing guidance had been part of Hezekiah's reforms. Josiah's reforms echoed Hezekiah's.

---

[3] Kenneth A. Kitchen, *On the Reliability of the Old Testament*, 44: "In the seventh year (598/597), Nebuchadrezzar could march west for a time of reckoning. Jehoiakim slipped his net, by dying, leaving his son Jehoichin to face the music. The Babylonian Chronicle notes that Nebuchadrezzar II 'besieged the city of Judah [i.e., its capital, Jerusalem] and on 2nd of Adar [15/16 March 597] he took the city and seized the king. A king of his own choosing he appointed (instead), received its massive tribute and sent them to Babylon.' The siege is that of 2 Kings 24:10–11."

[4] Those known to be contemporary with Lehi included Nahum, Habakkuk, Zephaniah, Jeremiah, Ezekiel, Uriah ben Shemaiah (Jer. 26:20–23), Ben-Yohanan ben Igdaliah (Jer. 35:4 LXX [Septuagint version]), the prophetess Huldah (2 Kgs. 22:14–19), and probably others (2 Chr. 36:15–6; cf. Dan. 1:1, Zech. 1:7, Matt. 21:36). See *Book of Mormon Critical Text*, 1:5.

[5] Norman K. Gottwald, *The Hebrew Bible: A Socio-Literary Introduction*, 390–97.

[6] John Bright, *Jeremiah: A New Translation with Introduction and Commentary*, lxxxviii.

[7] Nevertheless, Josiah is often given the credit. Horn, "The Divided Monarchy," 137: "Josiah apparently was raised by a pious tutor who had continued to live in the religious tradition of Hezekiah, for young Josiah proved to be a deeply religious man." That Josiah's actions parallel those of Hezekiah is clear and certainly points to some connection to that time. It is simply likely that more than a single tutor was involved in the reinstatement of the reform program.

Josiah assumed the throne at a time when the might of the Assyrian empire was waning. The Assyrians had dominated the political and cultural landscape at least from the time when they invaded Jerusalem in Hezekiah's reign. With time, however, their control lessened. For a brief period, Josiah and the city of Judah over which he reigned enjoyed an absence of foreign dominance.[8]

Roland Kenneth Harrison describes how Babylon began to fill the political vacuum during the lifetime of Lehi's contemporary, Jeremiah: "During the four decades in which Jeremiah prophesied, momentous events took place in the ancient Near East, beginning the very year that the prophet received his call. The death of Ashurbanipal [last of the great Assyrian kings] was the signal for Babylon to assert her independence under Nabopolassar (626–605 B.C.), and this, along with the resurgence of vitality in Egypt under Psammetichus (664–610 B.C.), was to have an important bearing upon the course of life in the southern kingdom of Judah."[9]

Psammetichus presided over an increased economic prosperity in Egypt that hinged on expanded trade. Egyptian goods had always flowed to world markets, but until the reign of the Saite kings (Psammetichus was the first to designate Sais, in the Western Nile Delta, as his capital city), they had been carried by Phoenician traders. Now, Judahite trade flourished.[10] Donald B. Redford describes the favorable trade relations that Egypt maintained with the Mediterranean region: "Despite the turmoil of contemporary politics in western Asia, Egypt continued to enjoy relatively free access to the products it craved: wine and alum from Phoenicia, medicinal herbs from Palestine, aromatic substances and bitumen from Transjordan; and from across the Sinai, to be tapped at Gaza, flowed a stream of exotic products from South Arabia."[11] Lehi's lifetime falls within one of the four times of peak Egyptian influence in Syro-Palestine.[12]

The brief respite from foreign domination occasioned by the collapsing Assyrian empire was about to be filled by the rise of Babylon. Before that eventuality became inevitable, the third Middle Eastern superpower attempted to make its own play. Egypt endeavored to shore up the remains of the Assyrian empire in order to use it as a buffer against Babylon. Although the reasons for this action are not entirely clear, the result is: Josiah resisted the forces of the Egyptian pharaoh Necho II (also spelled

---

[8] Horn, "The Divided Monarchy," 41. "During these years the Assyrian empire naturally crumbled; Assyria could no longer effectively control its western possessions. It was in the period before Babylonia took over these possessions that Josiah extended his influence, perhaps even political control, over considerable parts of the territory that had formerly belonged to the kingdom of Israel (and had been administered more recently as Assyrian provinces)."

[9] Roland Kenneth Harrison, Introduction to the Old Testament, 2:803. See also Israel Finkelstein and Neil Asher Silberman, The Bible Unearthed: Archaeology's New Vision of Ancient Israel and the Origin of its Sacred Texts, 281–82.

[10] Donald B. Redford, Egypt, Canaan, and Israel in Ancient Times, 434. John Gee, "Egyptian Society during the Twenty-sixth Dynasty," 280.

[11] Redford, Egypt, Canaan, and Israel in Ancient Times, 435.

[12] John S. Thompson, "Lehi and Egypt," 264. Thompson notes that Gregory D. Mumford listed the four times as 1450–1400 B.C., 1250–1150 B.C., 925–850 B.C., and 750–600 B.C.

Neco) and died in battle in 608 B.C. Josiah's twenty-three-year-old son, Jehoahaz was crowned by popular demand but lasted only three months. Pharaoh Necho's power over Judah was sufficient that Jehoahaz was taken to Egypt as a prisoner. Necho installed Jehoahaz's twenty-five-year-old brother, Jehoiakim (who had pro-Egyptian views), as the king.[13] When Jehoiakim was killed, his son Jehoiachin became king; his reign lasted only three months and ten days. It wasn't a good time to be a king in Jerusalem.

Kings of Judah from the Assyrian to the Babylonian Invasions[14]		
King	Years	Relationship to Previous King
Hezekiah	715–687/686	Son
Manasseh	687/686–642	Son
Amon	642–640	Son
Josiah	640–609	Son
Jehoahaz II	609	Son
Jehoiakim	609–598	Brother (installed by Egypt)
Jehoiachin	598–597	Son
Zedekiah	597–586	Uncle (installed by Babylon)
	586 fall of Jerusalem	

Judah had become the buffer between the expanding Babylonian influence and Egypt. It was a doomed position. In 598/597 B.C. Babylon victoriously entered Jerusalem and ended Jehoiachin's brief reign.[15] Then, like Egypt, Babylon installed a new king for Judah, Jehoiachin's uncle, Zedekiah. As a result of this invasion, Babylon deported "all Jerusalem, and all the princes, and all the mighty men of valour, even ten thousand captives, and all the craftsmen and smiths: none remained, save the poorest sort of the people of the land" (2 Kgs. 24:14). Although the text describes a devastating depopulation, not even counting those who died in battle, Kenneth A. Kitchen notes: "The Hebrew figures. . . are entirely consistent in scale with the range of figures for deportations from Israel practiced earlier by the Assyrian kings. Two facts here are worthy of comment: the relative modesty of almost all these figures compared to what the total populations of Israel/Samaria and Judah/Jerusalem would have been; and the status of the people taken away, and those left behind. The idea that the Babylonians carried *everybody* from both Jerusalem and Judah off to Babylon is true neither archaeologically nor to the biblical record itself."[16]

Such was the state of Judah in the first year of the reign of king Zedekiah, the year in which Book of Mormon events begin. Babylon had triumphantly entered Jerusalem and had carried many away. However, large numbers were still left, and it was to them that Yahweh sent "many prophets, prophesying unto the people that they must repent, or the great city Jerusalem must be destroyed" (1 Ne. 1:4). One of them was Lehi.

---

[13] Horn, "The Divided Monarchy," 142–43.
[14] Chart compiled from information in Kenneth A. Kitchen, *On the Reliability of the Old Testament*, 31–32.
[15] Kitchen, *On the Reliability of the Old Testament*, 44.
[16] Ibid., 67. Italics in original.

Given the rather obvious fact that Babylon had already conquered Jerusalem and destroyed much of its elite social structure through deportation, it is little wonder that "the Jews did mock him because of the things which he testified of them" (1 Ne. 1:19). They might have wondered how Lehi thought it could get worse. Babylon was already there. Jerusalem yet stood, and the people probably believed that it could not be destroyed, however precarious their personal existence might be.[17]

Judah and Its People

James H. Charlesworth highlights an important issue in discussing ancient Israel: "I have found surprising two claims emphasized by scholars. First, they rightly point out that in Second Temple Judaism, the historian cannot distinguish between religious and political issues. Then they continue by stressing that Jesus had no interest in politics and that his revolution was strictly religious."[18] Although Charlesworth is addressing issues in understanding Jesus, the problem is similar for discussing anything related to politics or religion for virtually all time periods in the ancient world. Understanding that there was no real division between politics and religion doesn't make it any easier to analyze an ancient culture. Our perceptual categories see divisions where the ancients did not. We may still speak of the political aspects of certain actions, or the nature of the religion, even when both politics and religion were part of the same conceptual system underlying all of society.

---

[17] David Rolph Seely and Fred E. Woods, "How Could Jerusalem, 'That Great City,' Be Destroyed?" 596.

    At least six interrelated factors . . . contributed to the Judahite belief that Jerusalem could not be destroyed: (1) The historical traditions of the spiritual heritage of Jerusalem, "that great city," suggested to many that the Lord would naturally preserve this holy place from destruction and desecration by the enemies of the covenant people. (2) The Jews misunderstood some of the Lord's promises in connection with the covenants that he had made with them. In particular, they misunderstood the promises made to David in the Davidic covenant. (3) The miraculous preservation of Jerusalem and its inhabitants when the Assyrians besieged Jerusalem (2 Kgs. 18–19) in the days of King Hezekiah (701 B.C.) further reinforced the belief that the Lord would preserve his temple and holy city from the enemy. (4) The city of Jerusalem was fortified and prepared for siege. Hezekiah had heavily fortified the city against the Assyrian siege in 701 B.C. with massive walls and towers (2 Chr. 32:2–8) and had even prepared a water source inside the city for the inhabitants of the city to endure a long siege (2 Kgs. 20:20, 2 Chr. 32:4, 30). Thus the inhabitants of Jerusalem believed they could endure a long siege brought about by their seemingly impregnable walls. (5) The recent reforms of Josiah (640–609 B.C.), who had cleansed the temple and led his people in a ceremony of covenant renewal (2 Kgs. 22–23), had given certain people of Judah an undue sense of self and community righteousness that they believed would surely preserve them from any threatened destruction. (6) Assurances were given by false prophets, who promised Jerusalem and its inhabitants peace, safety, and preservation from the enemy instead of the destruction and exile prophesied by Jeremiah and Lehi. These false assurances were readily accepted by many since they were the words that they wanted to hear.

[18] James. H. Charlesworth, *The Historical Jesus: An Essential Guide*, 107.

It is particularly important to understand the interrelationship between politics and religion if we are to understand what we would perceive as the religious climate into which Lehi was called as a prophet. As a prophet, he was clearly part of what we understand as religion. However, much of his message can be fleshed out only against long-term pressures that involved both the political and religious realms.

While the Hebrews have rightly been called a people of the Book, it is also quite certain that, for much of their history, the vast majority of the people had no access to that book, the Bible, nor could they have read it if they did.[19] The Bible is, in the words of William G. Dever, "'a minority report.' Largely written by priests, prophets, and scribes who were intellectuals, above all religious reformers, the Bible is highly idealistic. It presents us not so much with a picture of what Israelite religion really was, but of what it should have been—and would have been, had the biblical writers only been in charge."[20]

Therefore, Dever cautions that the "Pentateuch (or 'Five Books of Moses') and the historical works in the great national epic sweeping from Joshua through Kings are problematic as 'sources.' These texts cannot simply be picked up and read in a straightforward manner as though they constitute objective factual history in the modern sense, based on contemporary eyewitness reports."[21] Their problematic nature does not derive from any suggestion that they do not report historical events, but rather that, as Kitchen notes, "As in the Near Eastern chronicles, the writers of Kings (and Chronicles) had no need to *invent* history; they merely *interpreted* it in terms of the beliefs they sought to express."[22]

What they interpreted was a historical process that witnessed a dramatic shift in the nature of the Hebrew people. Throughout the reign of the judges, Israel was both politically and religiously based on kinship.[23] Beginning with the pressures that led to the establishment of the Israelite monarchy, Israel shifted its political and religious focus away from a kinship base and more toward a centralized government and a centralized religious administration. It wasn't a rapid shift, or one that had been completed by the time of Zedekiah. Baruch A. Levine notes that "it is probably reasonable to assume that the clan continued to serve as the basic economic unit in biblical societies throughout the First Temple period and that clans still owned most of the arable land in common,

---

[19] Christopher A. Rollston, *Writing and Literacy in the World of Ancient Israel*, 134. Van der Toorn, *Scribal Culture*, 11. William G. Dever, *Did God Have a Wife? Archaeology and Folk Religion in Ancient Israel*, 60.

[20] William G. Dever, *What Did the Biblical Writers Know and When Did They Know It?* 173.

[21] Dever, *Did God Have a Wife?* 64.

[22] Kitchen, *On the Reliability of the Old Testament*, 49.

[23] Baruch Halpern, "Sybil, or the Two Nations? Archaism, Kinship, Alienation, and the Elite Redefinition of Traditional Culture in Judah in the 8th–7th Centuries B.C.E.," 291–338 provides an excellent description of this process of religious and political development. For example, he notes (p. 299): "The segregation of Yhwh's cult from that of the ancestors may have been a relatively late development." Thus, the older underpinnings of a clan-based ancestral cult form the base on which the development of an exclusive Yahwistic religion was built.

either within a larger tribal framework or . . . within an administrative, regional districting system. The clan system seems to have broken down to a degree in the postexilic period, when the individual landowner comes into prominence."[24]

This gradual shift away from clans and toward a recognizable state periodically put the two aspects of Israelite society into conflict. What we have in the Bible is the record of the view from the centralized religious elite. John Baines reminds us that this was not the only possible perspective: "While it may prove almost impossible to relate the accessible ideology of the elite to the broader society, it is necessary to bear constantly in mind that ideology may not be representative of a complete society's views and that in some way it will have been created against the background of a much larger social group whose beliefs are nearly inaccessible."[25]

We learn of the religion espoused by this much larger, and perhaps more ancient and traditional group through both what the Bible writers condemned and through the archaeological record that provides a picture of the material culture that underlay the Bible's literary culture. When we do that, we begin to understand that, as Halpern discusses, "Conflict between the state and popular practice was coeval with the state in Israel. The state advanced the interests of its god, Yhwh, and of his divine minions at the expense of traditional mantic arts, ritual specialists, and the ancestral cult."[26] Translated into anachronistic terms, some of the religious reforms being implemented by the centralized authority had more to do with politics than religion.

The need to concentrate political power in the person and place of the king in Jerusalem naturally led to a similar concentration of religious power in the person and place of the king. Through both de facto political influence and more subtle literary recasting of Israel's religious history, the almost inherent messiness of the religion of the masses was increasingly codified into the religion of the Book.

In the earliest forms of Hebrew religion that can be reconstructed, there is a presumed heavy influence from the language and literature of the Canaanite peoples who were already in the land when the Hebrews arrived.[27] Even the idea of kingship and some temple practices may have had Canaanite roots.[28] It is certain that the

---

[24] Baruch A. Levine, "The Clan-Based Economy of Biblical Israel," 451.
[25] John Baines, "Contextualizing Egyptian Representations of Society and Ethnicity," 343.
[26] Halpern, "Sybil, or the Two Nations?" 303.
[27] Amihai Mazar, "Remarks on Biblical Traditions and Archaeological Evidence Concerning Early Israel," 86:

> The great influence of Canaanite language, literature, and mythology on the biblical literature indicates continuous cultural development from the 2nd to the 1st millennium B.C.E., in ancient Israel and the incorporation of Canaanite elements into Israelite culture at a rather early stage of its history. The carriers of these Canaanite literary traditions could have been surviving Canaanites who continued to inhabit the coastal and northern plains of the land of Israel, as indicated by archaeological research. These Canaanites would have been assimilated into Israel from the 10th century on, as indicated both by the archaeological evidence and in biblical passages such as 1 Kgs. 9:20–21.

[28] Frank Moore Cross, *Canaanite Myth and Hebrew Epic*, 144.

frequent conflict between Yahweh and Baal in the people's religious devotion indicates that there may never have been a pure Yahwistic religion among the Hebrews in their promised land, at least until after the Exile.[29]

From the perspective of the Yahwistic religion, there were obvious remnants of non-Yahwistic religion that continued to be practiced among the people who did not live in Jerusalem. Certainly Hezekiah's reforms included purging of some of these foreign religious elements from Israel. However, religion still had political implications. As Halpern notes: "Hezekiah's policies disenfranchised the clans, advantaging court parties. Rural priests lost access to agricultural revenues, and the tradition that Hezekiah registered them suggests that, like the rural population, they came under state control. The elite critique damning the rural cult was now codified in classical prophecy: Amos, Hosea, Isaiah, and Micah."[30] Or, as Halpern more bluntly reported: "Village folk culture was discarded in favor of centralized, canonized authority."[31] In spite of the sweeping reforms, archaeological evidence suggests that much of the rural religion changed very little, if at all.[32]

With the institution of kingship in Israel and the temple cultus, both institutions of Canaanite origin, the old myths became resurgent. In hymns like Psalms 29, 93, and 89B (verses 6–19), the mythos of creation appear, unsullied by historicizing, for example, by reference to the Epic theme of the victory at the Reed Sea. With the close of the monarchy and the end of the classical (pre-Exilic) prophecy, the older theologies of history which interpreted Epicthemes, the Yahwistic, Deuteronomic, and Priestly, give way to a new synthesis of mythic, royal ideological, and literary forms (now freed from their older cultic functions) and the Prophetic tradition that harked back to the league. The Song of the Arm of Yahweh in Isaiah 51 is a superb example of this new synthesis, in which the old Exodus is described in terms of the Creation myth and in turn becomes the archetype of a new Exodus. The old Songs of the Wars of Yahweh were transformed into descriptions of eschatological battle (Isaiah 55:1–3).

[29] Mark S. Smith, *The Early History of God: Yahweh and the Other Deities in Ancient Israel*, 11: "The monarchy generally maintained a special relationship with Yahweh; Yahweh was the national god and patron of the monarchy. Israelite "service" (*'bd) only to Yahweh in the monarchic period eventually developed into a notion of universal service to Yahweh. Though monotheism was ultimately a product of the Exile, some developments leading to it are evident in a variety of religious expressions dating to the monarchy."

[30] Halpern, "Sybil, or the Two Nations?" 321. Also (p. 317): "Kings says Hezekiah 'removed the high places,' the foci of folk religion. . . . In all, we may assume that Hezekiah suppressed rural worship, but not worship at state centers."

[31] Ibid., 336.

[32] One of the ways that this may be deduced is from the evidence of the rural cult of the dead. Smith, *The Early History of God*, 162, notes: "The practices in the Bible concerning the dead belonged to Israel's Canaanite heritage. Feeding the dead, consulting the dead, and mourning the dead were all part of Canaanite religion. Ancient Israel continued most of these practices in juxtaposition with Yahwistic cult" [internal references silently removed]. Following the reforms, Richard S. Hess, *Israelite Religions: An Archaeological and Biblical* Survey, 338, observes: "The archaeological evidence suggests that, despite reforms mentioned during the reigns of Hezekiah and Josiah, there was no change in the popular view of treatment of the dead."

These sweeping religio-political reforms did not last longer than Hezekiah's reign. His son Manasseh restored much of the rural cultic activity. While the Bible certainly sees that as apostasy, a modern historian might equally see the move as appeasing the majority of the population whose access to their traditional religious expression had been cut off.[33] Nevertheless, we see the same combination of reform of the rural cult and centralization of political and religious authority in Jerusalem in the reforms Josiah instituted.

Margaret Barker describes some of the elements of Josiah's reform program, implemented during Lehi's lifetime:

> King Josiah changed the religion of Israel in 623 B.C. According to the Old Testament account in 2 Kings 23 he removed all manner of idolatrous items from the temple and purified his kingdom of Canaanite practices. Temple vessels made for Baal, Asherah and the host of heaven were removed, idolatrous priests were deposed, the Asherah itself was taken from the temple and burned, and much more besides.[34] An old law book had been discovered in the temple, and this had prompted the king to bring the religion of his kingdom into line with the requirements of that book (2 Kgs. 22:8–13, 2 Chr. 34:14–20). There could only be one temple, it stated, and so all other places of sacrificial worship had to be destroyed (Deut. 12:1–5). The law book is easily recognizable as Deuteronomy, and so King Josiah's purge is usually known as the Deuteronomic reform of the temple.[35]

The serendipity of finding a lost book right at the beginning of series of reforms has raised the question of the book's authenticity. The combination of the timing and the nature of the text strongly suggests that it was compiled soon before its discovery.[36] Nevertheless, this does not mean that the book was invented whole cloth at this time. It is much more likely that it redacts older traditions into this new form. Norman Gottwald comments:

---

[33] It is certainly contrary to traditional biblical interpretation, but is quite possible that Manasseh faced a populace with some of the same complaints as we see in the Book of Mormon when the rural population of Antionum complains that the Zoramites have introduced a new mode of religion that has excluded them from their traditional ways of worship. See Alma 31:11–12; 32:2–5.

[34] Raphael Patai, *The Hebrew Goddess*, 38: "While it is not easy to reach a definite conclusion as to the physical shape in which Asherah was represented among the Hebrews, a careful perusal of the numerous Biblical references to the 'Asherahs' seems to indicate that they were carved wooden images which were set up by implanting their base into the ground. In early times they often stood next to altars dedicated to Baal; later, a 'statue of Asherah' was set up in the Jerusalem Temple itself. The word Asherah in Biblical usage can thus refer either to the goddess herself or to her image."

[35] Margaret Barker, "What Did King Josiah Reform?" 522.

[36] Benjamin L. McGuire, "Josiah's Reform: An Introduction," 161: "The discovery of the Book of the Law during King Josiah's reign (from 640 to 609 BC) jump-started a reform movement within Judaism. As part of this reform, Josiah carried out an aggressive shift within the popular religion—removing pagan religious institutions, eliminating sites of worship throughout Judah in order to centralize all worship at the Temple in Jerusalem, and attempting to reestablish the covenant between the Jewish people and God."

The one hard date is the year of Josiah's reform, 622. But the origins of Deuteronomy are older than the reform. Levitical reading and preaching of the law did not begin in 622; considering the allusions to Shechem the practice must have extended back at least a century into Northern Israel. The shock of the discovery of the law in 622 does not mean that such traditions were unknown in Israel previously; it means rather that the Judean monarchy had lost touch with them for as much as 50 or 75 years (assuming that Hezekiah knew of them and used them in his reforms)....

Was the law written specifically for the purpose of "planting" it in the temple? Perhaps—if we assume that only in this way could its claims be brought to the king convincingly and without danger of the law's advocates. Yet it is striking that even with the written law before him Josiah was unconvinced until specific supporters of the law had assured him of its validity (2 Kgs. 22:8–20).

It is more likely that the writing and rewriting of Deuteronomic laws and admonitions was going on underground throughout the reign of Manasseh (ca. 687–642). If we visualize the Yahwistic cultic calendar as lapsing or at least suffering from neglect, the old patterns of cultic renewal of covenant and law would be strained and even threatened with extinction. Oral materials remembered from year to year would no longer be recited, and authoritative texts of the laws inscribed at cult sites (cf. 27:2–3) would become defaced or even destroyed. Thus both oral and written records of D[euteronomic] traditions were driven underground and fostered there until they broke to the surface in 622.

This interpretation does away with the view that the planted Deuteronomy was a "pious fraud." No one needed to concoct a book purporting to be by Moses; all he had to do was collect materials long attributed to Moses, through the device of the cult functionary speaking on behalf of Moses, and to assert that these traditions should once again be binding in Israel.[37]

---

[37] Norman K. Gottwald, "Deuteronomy," 102–3. David Bokovoy, *Authoring the Old Testament: Genesis–Deuteronomy*, 65: "Most scholars believe that an early form of the Book of Deuteronomy also served as the inspiration for King Josiah's reforms."

While Deuteronomy might have redacted earlier documents, there is internal evidence suggesting that it has a strong dependency on Assyrian treaty forms. Simo Parpola, "Assyria's Expansion in the 8th and 7th Centuries and Its Long-Term Repercussions in the West," 104–5:

> There cannot be any doubt that, not only the king of Judah, but the ruling class of Judah as a whole was familiar with the central provisions of the treaties with Assyria, for vassal rulers were explicitly told to propagate them to their people. Indeed, it can be assumed that the treaties had, figuratively speaking, "entered the intestines of their sons and daughters like bread and wine," as prescribed in [the succession treaty of Esarhaddon]. Hence the fact that this very language was chosen to formulate the laws in Deuteronomy 13, one of the core texts of Deuteronomic monolatry, has far-reaching implications. To spell it out: *in the mind of the writer of Deuteronomy 13, the God of Israel has taken the place previously occupied in the collective mind of the nation by the feared, almighty king of Assyria.* The same is implied by the paradoxical image of the Deuteronomic God, who, according to a recent analysis by Geller, *"is above all else a person."* Strikingly, the Covenant God's characteristics listed by Geller are also central characteristics of the Assyrian kin—"the very likeness of God"—as presented in Assyrian imperial propaganda. The conclusion seems inescapable that the Deuteronomic concept of God, which according to current scholarly consensus evolved in the late 7th or early 6th century B.C.E. and is basic to all later Judaism, is heavily indebted to Assyrian religion and royal ideology.

The influence of this new book of the law colors a large portion of our understanding of biblical history because that book's worldview dominated and replaced competing views of history. It was certainly in tune with the religio-political needs of the times. In Halpern's assessment:

> Deuteronomy invents the individual in the cause of collectivization. It levels old social distinctions, revaluing the status of women, slaves, debtors, resident aliens, and war captives, enlisting the underclasses and elite sympathy for them to hammer out a common code of moral indignation and political correctness, to impose a cultural identity that presses claims prior to the obligations of kinship and personal loyalty. Like Josiah's cult centralization, which prohibited access to Yhwh except through the king the lawbook "cuts down the high corn," the old male blood ties, to impose uniformity—uniform submission to the state—on the people. Deuteronomy, to put a point on it, is an implement of totalitarian administration.[38]

Josiah's reforms had already begun to fade shortly after his death. Like Mannaseh (the king who followed Hezekiah) Jehoiakim who became king after Josiah (when Pharaoh Necho removed Jehoahaz and installed Jehoiakim) reversed the religious reforms.[39]

Nevertheless, the pressures for these reforms logically would have remained salient among the elite class who had probably pushed for them in the first place. It was these elites who were carried off to Babylon and who were again installed as the ruling elite upon their return to Israel. The strongest evidence for this hypothesis is that the religion of Deuteronomy becomes normative after the Exile, where it may be seen as having failed to establish a permanent reform prior to the Exile (598/7 B.C. to 538 B.C.). Although the Deuteronomic reforms would not dominate Israelite religion until after the return from the Exile, they form the important religious and political backdrop against which we may understand Lehi and his call.

Lehi of Jerusalem

The Assyrian invasion of 701 B.C. did more than establish remarkable parallels in Israelite history. In a very real way, the story of the Book of Mormon begins with that invasion, even though the specific events described come a century later. The Assyrian invasion resulted in the destruction of the Northern Kingdom of Israel. Ten of Israel's tribes had their ancestral lands in that kingdom. As with the Babylonian conquest, the Assyrians carried away a large number of people. As with the Babylonian conquest, the removal of a large number of people did not mean that everyone was taken away. One result was a small exodus of people who fled from the

---

[38] Halpern, "Sybil, or the Two Nations?" 329.
[39] Horn, "The Divided Monarchy," 143.

troubles and headed south. Many relocated to Jerusalem, in the Southern Kingdom of Judah. An influx of population around that time can be traced archaeologically.[40]

Lehi (which may have meant "cheek/jawbone," or perhaps in its unshortened form: "[incline thy] cheek, [O Jehovah]"[41]), traced his ancestry to the tribe of Joseph (1 Ne. 5:14), one of the tribes of the Northern Kingdom. It is plausible that Lehi's grandparents may have been among those who fled from Israel, seeking eventual safety in Jerusalem,[42] providing a logical reason that Lehi and his family would be in Jerusalem even though they belonged to a northern tribe. It also explains the references to Lehi's "land of inheritance" (1 Ne. 2:4).

Jeffrey R. Chadwick suggests that the migration patterns of the members of the tribe of Manasseh (inheritors of Joseph's blessing) suggest the probability that "Lehi's land of inheritance was most likely not located within the borders of the southern kingdom of Judah. The most likely location for Lehi's ancestral real estate in the ancient land of Israel was the region of Manasseh . . . . The ancient tribe of Manasseh possessed large tracts of land on both sides of the Jordan River."[43] These lands outside of Jerusalem account for the textual information that suggest both a difference between their home and the lands of their inheritance, as well as the journey to that land of inheritance to retrieve their gold and silver to attempt to exchange them for the brass plates.[44]

---

[40] Jeffrey R. Chadwick, "Lehi's House at Jerusalem and the Land of His Inheritance," 91. The increase in population came "at the last quarter of the eighth century B.C.—the exact period of the Assyrian attacks on the northern kingdom."

[41] Paul Y. Hoskisson, "Lehi and Sariah," 31. John A. Tvedtnes, "Lehi and Sariah Comments," 37 argues for Lehi as "cheek/jawbone" as the simplest etymology. While this is an unusual name, Jeffrey R. Chadwick, "The Names Lehi & Sariah—Language and Meaning," 33–34 suggests that the name may have either derived from something associated with Lehi's birth (similar to other names he references) or was perhaps a nickname rather than a given name.

Jeffrey R. Chadwick, "Lehi in the Samaria Papyri and on an Ostracon from the Shore of the Red Sea," 17, argues: "In contrast to Nibley's examples from South Semitic origins, I have suggested (and continue to suggest) that the personal name Lehi is a Hebrew term, equivalent to the place name Lehi in Judges 15, and that it carries the same meaning—'cheek' or 'jaw.'"

[42] Chadwick, "Lehi's House at Jerusalem, 87. Chadwick notes that the Bible lists another time when Manassites migrated to Judah (2 Chr. 15:9). He suggests that, while the biblically attested migration might be possible, it is highly improbable: "In leaving Baasha's northern kingdom to join Asa's Judah, the defectors essentially forfeited all rights and privileges they might have claimed in the north, including title to their lands. It is most unlikely that Lehi would have had any claim to land in Manasseh if he were descended from those who left the region to ally with Asa in the south. Moreover, since Lehi's family was living around 600 B.C., nearly three hundred years after Asa, it is unlikely that any record or even memory of land ownership would have remained with them if they had been descended from the early defectors."

[43] Ibid., 85.

[44] 1 Nephi 2:4 "And it came to pass that he departed into the wilderness. And he left his house, and the land of his inheritance, and his gold, and his silver, and his precious things. . . ." implies that the house and the land of inheritance were separate. 1 Ne. 3:16 has Nephi suggesting to his brothers, "let us go down to the land of our father's inheritance, for behold he

The refugees from the north settled on the western hill of the ancient city of Jerusalem, an area known in modern times as the Jewish Quarter of the Old City.[45] Therefore, it is very likely that Lehi was born in this Jewish Quarter. His birth has been estimated as somewhere between 650–640 B.C.[46]

Prior to his call as a prophet, Lehi appears to have been involved in the production of goods made from gold and silver.[47] Chadwick elaborates the nature of the argument: "Lehi left behind gold and silver, two precious metals likely to have been used in expert jewelry smithing. While the population at large often utilized silver as money, in the form of cut pieces and small jewelry (no coins were in use in Judah during Iron Age II), to possess gold was very rare—gold was not used as a medium of common monetary exchange. For Lehi to possess both gold and silver suggests that he worked with gold, which in turn suggests gold smithing."[48] The combination of income from metalsmithing and from the rentals in Samaria would have provided Lehi's family with a lifestyle approaching the upper class in Jerusalem.[49]

Lehi's family home would have followed the typical pattern of Israelite homes, which archeologists call a "pillared" or "four-room" house. Yet it was more than just a house in the modern sense. It was more of a compound, with living quarters in the rear and an open courtyard in the front. The courtyard was enclosed with walls that extended from the living quarters so that the whole was a contained unit. The living area often had two stories, and the open courtyard often had covered areas on both sides of an open area that were used to stable animals and perhaps contained a shop

---

left gold and silver, and all manner of riches." They did not proceed to their home, but to a specific "land of our father's inheritance."

[45] Chadwick, "Lehi's House at Jerusalem," 93.

[46] H. Donl Peterson, "Father Lehi," 56.

[47] His occupation has been the subject of some discussion. Hugh Nibley, *Lehi in the Desert/the World of the Jaredites*, 36–37, proposed that he gained his wealth as a caravaneer, trading in wine, oil, figs, and honey.

John A. Tvedtnes (former associate director of research at the Foundation for Ancient Research and Mormon Studies) was the first to call this assumption into question. Tvedtnes countered many of the specifics that Nibley used to propose Lehi as a traveling merchant and suggested that there is better evidence that he was involved in metalworking. Interestingly, most of Tvedtnes's evidence concerns Nephi's familiarity with metalworking, not his father's. However, sons typically learned their father's trade, so the evidence still points to Lehi's work with metal. John A. Tvedtnes, *The Most Correct Book: Insights from a Book of Mormon Scholar*, 88–98. The article "Was Lehi a Caravaneer?" an early version of this chapter, was presented as a FARMS preliminary report in 1984. See also Neal Rappleye, "Lehi the Smelter: New Light on Lehi's Profession."

[48] Chadwick, "Lehi's House at Jerusalem," 114. Chadwick proposes ten reasons to see Lehi as a metalsmith (114–17), all but the first of which deal with Nephi rather than Lehi. We simply have better information for Nephi and the best explanation for Nephi's expertise is that of his father.

[49] Ibid., 117.

area.⁵⁰ As a wealthy resident (1 Ne. 2:2, 3:22–25), Lehi's home might have encompassed 2,000 square feet between the two floors of living space.⁵¹

Lehi's wife's name, Sariah, probably meant "prince[ess] of Jehovah."⁵² As the wife of a wealthy man, she would have had the responsibilities of maintaining her household, including the servants that were likely attached to the family.⁵³ She would have been directly involved in clothing and feeding those in her household as well as managing the activities of the servants and children's chores.⁵⁴ In addition to caring for the physical comforts of her family, Sariah would also have played a large role in their religious education, as her children witnessed her keeping of daily religious rituals, participating in Sabbath activities, and in religious festivals.⁵⁵

Israel's Sin According to Lehi (and Nephi)

Nephi records that "in that same year [the first year of the reign of Zedekiah] there came many prophets, prophesying unto the people that they must repent, or the great city Jerusalem must be destroyed" (1 Ne. 1:4).⁵⁶ History clearly informs us that the threat to Jerusalem was real. Of what was Jerusalem unrepentant?

For Israel, sin (particularly in the pre-Exilic period) was a collective concept. As Bruce Halpern explains, "This corporate view of reward and punishment spawned the proverb, 'The fathers have eaten sour grapes, and the teeth of the children are set on edge.' (Jer. 31:29, Ezek. 18:14) This means that our economic, political and other woes result from our predecessors' errors, an eminently sane view. But in popular theology, it

---

⁵⁰ Ibid., 118–119.

⁵¹ Ibid., 119.

⁵² John Gee, Matthew Roper, and John A. Tvedtnes, "Book of Mormon Names Attested in ancient Hebrew Inscriptions," 43. While "Sariah" is attested only for males in the Bible, it appears as a female name in the Elephantine Papyri. See Jeffrey R. Chadwick, "Sariah in the Elephantine Papyri," 197.

⁵³ Camille Fronk, "Desert Epiphany: Sariah and the Women in 1 Nephi," 8.

⁵⁴ Ariel E. Bybee, "A Woman's World in Lehi's Jerusalem," 141:

> Six days a week, women sorted, cleaned, parched, and ground grain, kneaded and baked bread, drew water, collected fuel for cooking, butchered and cleaned small animals, milked, churned butter, made cheese and yogurt, tended vegetable gardens and fruit trees, and preserved meat and fruits for storage. The women prepared raw wool and flax fibers, which were then spun, woven, sewn, and tailored into clothing for their families. They often produced many of the common household tools, such as cooking and cleaning implements, lamps, and candles. The burden of daily cleaning and washing also fell on the shoulders of the women in the household (see Proverbs 31:10–31).

⁵⁵ Ibid., 142–43.

⁵⁶ David Rolph Seely and Jo Ann H. Seely, "Lehi & Jeremiah: Prophets, Priests, & Patriarchs," 33, compare Jeremiah and Lehi: "The prophecies of Jeremiah and Lehi have four common and central themes: repentance and the impending destruction and exile by the Babylonians; the coming of the Messiah; the future scattering and gathering of Israel; and the eventual restoration of the gospel in the latter days."

carried the implication in times of woe that Yhwh or some other god was avenging the ancestors' sins—construed perhaps as treason—upon the descendants."[57]

This collectivist understanding of sin tells us that we cannot look for the source in individual evils or deviations from expectations. Sin great enough to threaten the state (represented by its head city, Jerusalem) was likely a result of state sin. Where can we reasonably look for clues? The most likely source for understanding such sin is in the message of the prophets sent to decry it. Against what were the prophets preaching? Of course, there is no simple answer. However, the climate of the times combined with the evidence of prophetic messages can point us in a reasonable direction.

Jeremiah began his mission in the early years of Josiah's reforms and five years before the discovery of the book of the law.[58] It was a time when many recognized pagan influences throughout Israel, not the least of which was a continued reverence for the Canaanite Baal. For Jeremiah, Baal worship was the very definition of a national sin, one that he compared to an unfaithful wife: "They say, If a man put away his wife, and she go from him, and become another man's, shall he return unto her again? shall not that land be greatly polluted? but thou hast played the harlot with many lovers; yet return again to me, saith the Lord" (Jer. 3:1).

In spite of the clear fact that Jeremiah's agenda paralleled and likely supported some of the reforms,[59] it is not clear that he was always in complete support of all those reforms. John Bright suggests: "It may well be that for a short while after 622 [when the reform was legally instituted] Jeremiah, in sympathy with what the reform sought to do and impressed with its positive achievements, was able to rest his attack. But, if so, this can hardly have been for long."[60] Specifically, Bright notes:

> There are, in fact, a number of sayings in the book that fit, if not demonstrably, at least most plausibly in the period immediately following 622. These made Jeremiah's attitude abundantly clear, and show that he was neither blind to the state of affairs nor long silent about it. On the contrary, he declared (6:16–21) that the people had shown themselves both obdurate to the demands of the law and deaf to its warnings, and that the reform had resulted only in an ever more elaborate cultus without any real return to the ancient paths; the demands of Yahweh's covenant having been lost behind cultic externals (cf. 7:21 ff.), the crimes of society continued unabated (5:26–29) and the clergy, having come to terms with them, uttered no rebuke (5:30 f).[61]

Similarly, Karel van der Toorn, describes Jeremiah's reaction to the book of Deuteronomy: "the prophet Jeremiah did not accept the claim of antiquity and

---

[57] Halpern, "Sybil, or the Two Nations?" 295.
[58] Bright, *Jeremiah*, xc.
[59] Ibid., xci, "Whether Jeremiah so intended it or not, preaching of this sort undoubtedly helped to prepare the climate for the measures which Josiah was attempting to put into effect."
[60] Ibid., xciii.
[61] Ibid., xcv. However, see William J. Hamblin, "Jeremiah, Josiah, Barker, and Me." Hamblin argues that Jeremiah did not contradict some of the reforms, particularly as they called for a return from pagan influences. The argument is continued in two parts.

denounced the book [Deuteronomy, or the book of the Law] as a fraud manufactured by 'the deceitful pen of the scribes' (Jer. 8:8–9)."[62]

The biblically declared intent of the religious reform paralleled Jeremiah's prophetic message, but the concentration of religion in Jerusalem's temple and the changes in temple worship accompanying that change may not have been as comfortably part of Jeremiah's message. As examined above, these reforms followed both a religious and a political agenda. Unquestionably aspects of the rural religion manifested the influence retained from non-Yahwist religions in the area, and Jeremiah was alarmed when these religious observances continued, instead of returning to the ancient Yahwist paths. In fact, Barker has suggested that many of the reforms in temple worship actually removed the first temple's accepted cultic practice: "Almost everything that Josiah swept away can be matched in the religion of the patriarchs Abraham, Isaac, and Jacob."[63] However, this idea should be tempered, as William J. Hamblin suggests:

> I don't believe there was ever a single pre-exilic temple theology. . . . Sectarian tendencies in Israelite religion were undoubtedly just as strong in pre-exilic times (before 586 B.C.) as they were in early Judaism of the second temple period (c. 500 B.C. –70 A.D.), rabbinic Judaism (after 70 A.D.), and early Christianity. Thus, in my opinion, in pre-exilic times there were already many different interpretations of temple theology and mysticism in ancient Israel.[64]

Hamblin's intent is to caution against declaring that all of Josiah's reforms constituted "a type of apostasy, which placed the Deuteronomists in positions of power in the state and temple, allowing them to suppress the authentic pre-exilic temple theology, mysteries, and ritual, which were eventually restored by Christianity—which may imply that much of the Old Testament as we have it was written and edited by apostates."[65]

Many of Josiah's reforms were important, but some may have gone too far. The reality of the situation was much more complex than any completely un-nuanced understanding can replicate. Jeremiah agreed with the intent of the reforms (calling the people to return to the worship of Yahweh), but not with their effect in elevating a Jerusalem elite. When we examine the specifics of what Lehi preached, we may see in his message another subtle result of the climate of reform. To appreciate the nature of Lehi's message in the context of his times, it helps to review Lehi's visionary call, and then the message that resulted from that call.

---

[62] Karel van der Toorn, *Scribal Culture and the Making of the Hebrew Bible*, 35.

[63] Barker, "What Did King Josiah Reform?" 527 (italics removed). William J. Hamblin, "Vindicating Josiah," 169–70, notes: "Although I accept much of her broader thesis, I disagree with Barker on several key issues, which I don't think are fundamental to the validity of her broader perspective." For example, relevant to this issue, he notes: "Whereas Barker claims that Josiah's reforms represented an apostasy, I believe the situation is much more complex" (171).

[64] Hamblin, "Vindicating Josiah," 170.

[65] Ibid., 169.

> And being thus overcome with the Spirit, he was carried away in a vision, even that he saw the heavens open, and he thought he saw God sitting upon his throne, surrounded with numberless concourses of angels in the attitude of singing and praising their God.
>
> And it came to pass that he saw One descending out of the midst of heaven, and he beheld that his luster was above that of the sun at noon-day.
>
> And he also saw twelve others following him, and their brightness did exceed that of the stars in the firmament.
>
> And they came down and went forth upon the face of the earth; and the first came and stood before my father, and gave unto him a book, and bade him that he should read.
>
> And it came to pass that as he read, he was filled with the Spirit of the Lord.
>
> And he read, saying: Wo, wo, unto Jerusalem, for I have seen thine abominations! Yea, and many things did my father read concerning Jerusalem—that it should be destroyed, and the inhabitants thereof; many should perish by the sword, and many should be carried away captive into Babylon.
>
> And it came to pass that when my father had read and seen many great and marvelous things, he did exclaim many things unto the Lord; such as: Great and marvelous are thy works, O Lord God Almighty! Thy throne is high in the heavens, and thy power, and goodness, and mercy are over all the inhabitants of the earth; and, because thou art merciful, thou wilt not suffer those who come unto thee that they shall perish! (1 Ne. 1:8–14)

As Christians reading this account, we easily recognize the Savior and the twelve apostles appearing to Lehi. As an Israelite, Lehi would have understood the vision through a different vocabulary and perception. For Lehi, the bright first man was his Messiah whom he saw arriving "upon the face of the earth." Lehi's Messiah was Yahweh on earth, an understanding Nephi reinforced when his guide explained the dream of the tree:

> And the angel said unto me again: Look and behold the condescension of God!
>
> And I looked and beheld the Redeemer of the world, of whom my father had spoken; and I also beheld the prophet who should prepare the way before him. And the Lamb of God went forth and was baptized of him; and after he was baptized, I beheld the heavens open, and the Holy Ghost come down out of heaven and abide upon him in the form of a dove. (1 Nephi 11:26–27)

The condescension of God is witnessed by his descent to earth. More important to our understanding of the problem of Israel's corporate sin is the way Lehi discussed that vision. When it ended, Lehi exclaimed: "Thy throne is high in the heavens, and thy power, and goodness, and mercy are over all the inhabitants of the earth; and, because thou art merciful, thou wilt not suffer those who come unto thee that they shall perish!" (1 Ne. 1:14). It is in that context that we see Lehi's message:

> Therefore, I would that ye should know, that after the Lord had shown so many marvelous things unto my father, Lehi, yea, concerning the destruction of Jerusalem, behold he went forth among the people, and began to prophesy and to declare unto them concerning the things which he had both seen and heard.
>
> And it came to pass that the Jews did mock him because of the things which he testified of them; for he truly testified of their wickedness and their abominations; and he testified that the things which he saw and heard, and also the things which he read in the book,

manifested plainly of the coming of a Messiah, and also the redemption of the world. (1 Ne. 1:8–19)

Like Jeremiah, Lehi preaches against the people's "wickedness and . . . abominations." However, Nephi emphasizes another very specific message: "the coming of a Messiah, and also the redemption of the world." That was not Jeremiah's message. Jeremiah's call preceded Josiah's reforms. Lehi's came after those reforms and much closer to the destruction of Jerusalem. Perhaps we can understand Lehi's message a little better when we see Nephi's similar vision. When Nephi is seeing the meanings behind his father's Tree of Life vision, he records:

> And I saw the heavens open, and the Lamb of God descending out of heaven; and he came down and showed himself unto them.
> And I also saw and bear record that the Holy Ghost fell upon twelve others; and they were ordained of God, and chosen.
> And the angel spake unto me, saying: Behold the Twelve Disciples of the Lamb, who are chosen to minister unto thy seed. (1 Ne. 12:6–8)

Like his father, Nephi sees the Messiah descending with the twelve, but Nephi's vision is much clearer about the nature of these personages. Interestingly, one of the results of Nephi's vision is a discussion of important parts of the gospel that have been lost. Nephi specifically describes the scriptures:

> And he said: Behold it proceedeth out of the mouth of a Jew. And I, Nephi, beheld it; and he said unto me: The book that thou beholdest is a record of the Jews, which contains the covenants of the Lord, which he hath made unto the house of Israel; and it also containeth many of the prophecies of the holy prophets; and it is a record like unto the engravings which are upon the plates of brass, save there are not so many; nevertheless, they contain the covenants of the Lord, which he hath made unto the house of Israel; wherefore, they are of great worth unto the Gentiles. . . .
> And after they go forth by the hand of the twelve apostles of the Lamb, from the Jews unto the Gentiles, thou seest the formation of that great and abominable church, which is most abominable above all other churches; for behold, they have taken away from the gospel of the Lamb many parts which are plain and most precious; and also many covenants of the Lord have they taken away. (1 Ne. 13:23, 26)

This verse is often read against Joseph Smith's statement: "I believe the Bible as it read when it came from the pen of the original writers. Ignorant translators, careless transcribers, or designing and corrupt priests have committed many errors."[66] In that context, it is easy to assume that the parts now missing from the gospel are texts, or at least mistaken translations of texts.[67] (However, it is unlikely that Nephi intended

---

[66] Joseph Fielding Smith, comp. and ed., *Teachings of the Prophet Joseph Smith*, 327. See the quotation in the context of these verses in Joseph Fielding McConkie and Robert L. Millet, *Doctrinal Commentary on the Book of Mormon*, 1:94–95.

[67] Ironically, the sources of understanding changes in the New Testament is better than for the Old Testament. The Septuagint represents a different textual tradition, and the Dead Sea Scrolls show some differences, though not many. The best information on scribal alteration comes from

to highlight translation issues since he was reading the text in its original language.) Nevertheless, he was specifically concerned with the "record of the Jews, which contains the covenants of the Lord." His concern was for the covenants Yahweh had given to the house of Israel. Nephi was not concerned with textual integrity but theological integrity.

Although we have only this hint of what Nephi thought might have been removed, we do have the testimony of what he wrote. If we hypothesize that he would have wanted to restore that which was missing from the record as it proceeded from "the mouth of a Jew," we have a clear candidate: Nephi's very strong emphasis on the atoning mission of the Messiah.[68] This atoning function of the Messiah differs in both time and mission from the end-time triumphal Messiah who comes as King. The atoning Messiah comes to earth in the meridian of time as a humble man who nevertheless performs the ultimate act of atonement for humankind.

Lehi preached the mercy of God, and Nephi preaches the atoning Messiah. Both do so after a similar vision of the Savior and the twelve apostles. I argue that both Lehi and later Nephi saw the de-emphasis on the atoning mission of the Messiah as an unfortunate result of Josiah's reforms. Lehi preached against the removal, but Nephi restored it by emphasizing it in his own version of the Tree of Life vision.[69]

Barker reconstructs the pre-reform temple practices, she strongly argues that one of the changes removed a temple practice that emphasized the Messiah in his atoning role.[70] "The original temple tradition was that Yahweh, the Lord, was the Son of the God Most High, and [was] present on earth as the Messiah. This means that the older religion in Israel would have taught about the Messiah. Thus finding Christ in the Old Testament is exactly what we should expect, though obscured by incorrect reading of the scriptures. This is, I suggest, one aspect of the restoration of 'the plain and precious things, which have been taken away from them' (1 Ne. 13:40)."[71]

Given the nature of Josiah's reforms, Lehi's emphasis on the atoning Messiah becomes an appropriate protest against a reform that removed the emphasis on the atoning mission of the Messiah. It explains a major "abomination" of which the

---

New Testament texts. Although there is no indication that major sections were removed, there is some evidence that editing has attempted to bring certain texts into line with an assumed orthodoxy. See Bart D. Ehrman, *The Orthodox Corruption of Scripture: The Effect of Early Christological Controversies on the Text of the New Testament*, which is entirely devoted to developing this argument. Ehrman works through examples of specific instances of changes. A more popular version of the thesis Ehrman elaborates in *The Orthodox Corruption of Scripture* is found in Bart D. Ehrman, *Misquoting Jesus: The Story behind Who Changed the Bible and Why*, 151–75.

[68] Brant A. Gardner, *Second Witness*, 1:38–40.

[69] Kevin Christensen, "The Temple, the Monarchy, and Wisdom: Lehi's World and the Scholarship of Margaret Barker," 475–77, discusses the emphasis on atonement in both its temple and Book of Mormon contexts.

[70] Margaret Barker, *The Great High Priest: The Temple Roots of Christian Liturgy*, 51–52; and Margaret Barker, *Temple Theology: An Introduction*, 61–64.

[71] Margaret Barker, "Joseph Smith and Preexilic Israelite Religion," 79.

people (read here the official religion rather than popular religion, which would not have completely accepted the changes at this time) should repent.

Israel's Sin and Lehi's Family Dynamics

The reforms were altering the nature of political relationships. With the indivisibility of religion and politics, the political changes were the more likely candidates that underlay Lehi's intra-family discord. Richard S. Hess states that "the advent of kingship led to an abandonment of the egalitarian ideals of the highland culture and the embracing of a new form of government for Israel. The largely aniconic and simple nature of Israelite faith in the highland settlements changed under the influence of a more sophisticated monarchy that incorporated examples of polytheistic worship."[72] This abandonment of egalitarian ideals may have been another of the sins against which Lehi preached. Just as Nephi highlights the role of the Atoning Messiah in the Book of Mormon, he also uses egalitarian principles as the political and social underpinnings of his New World city. (See "The Nephite Egalitarian Ideal," in Chapter 6.)

Lehi's family becomes a microcosmic picture of what must have been divisiveness in the general population. The tensions that were present in Judahite society can be guessed at from hints in the Bible account but are explicit inside Lehi's family. The picture of Lehi (and Nephi) as opposed to certain elements of the Josianic reform is highlighted by the way in which Laman and Lemuel appear to support the Jerusalem establishment (and therefore the reforms). As Kevin Christiansen noted: "Laman and Lemuel demonstrate sympathy for the Jerusalem party, the same group of people who caused problems for Jeremiah and Ezekiel."[73]

With such preferences, they would have seen Lehi as stubbornly espousing parts of their religion that they sincerely believed needed reformation. They would naturally despise his visions, since those visions contained theological concepts that they felt needed to be "modernized." Those beliefs would have included Lehi's faith in the Atoning Messiah, a concept the reformers excised from the religion. Conflict over the identity and nature of the Messiah became the focus of religious debates in the New World. If Laman and Lemuel are actually *believers* rather than apostates, then it is their belief in contrast to the Atoning Messiah that explains how this particular conflict crosses the ocean to become the major theme of religious conflict during the entire Book of Mormon history.

This speculation about Laman and Lemuel's beliefs has some support in research about personality formation in the ancient world. Bruce J. Malina and Jerome H. Neyrey remind us the idea of individualism is a modern one; in the ancient world,

---

[72] Hess, *Israelite Religions*, 245.
[73] Christensen, "The Temple, the Monarchy, and Wisdom," 497. I have made the same argument, see Gardner, *Second Witness*, 1:xxx. See also Grant Hardy, *Understanding the Book of Mormon*, 39: "Whatever else they may have been, Laman and Lemuel appear to have been orthodox, observant Jews."

personalities were more group oriented, derived from shared traditions and particularly from geographic locations.[74] Laman and Lemuel identify with Jerusalem, a Jerusalem that had very recently been religiously transformed. Their personal association with that city and its ruling elite would plausibly make them believers—but believers in a different version of Israelite religion from Lehi's—rather than simple nonbelievers.

While being a nonbeliever would be very easy to understand in modern terms, religion defined reality in the ancient world. It would be an extremely unusual man who did not see his world religiously. As Dever explains: "Religion was so taken for granted that biblical Hebrew, for instance, has no specific word for 'religion.' Human life was filled with ideas and experiences that were, of course, 'religious,' and there are many terms in the Bible for these. But religion could not be abstracted and analyzed; nor could it have been an option, as we moderns suppose. Living in antiquity was being 'religious.'"[75]

Laman and Lemuel were Hebrews. They must have believed in *something* Hebrew. If they believed in the reform, in contrast to Lehi's belief in elements of the pre-reform religion, then this hypothesis explains their role in the Book of Mormon in a way that accounts for more tensions than any other explanation. Laman and Lemuel are definitely presented as villains in the Book of Mormon story;[76] but to their credit, they demonstrated filial obedience to their father, even though they may have had significant (and, given the religious climate in Jerusalem, legitimate) religious differences. Their behavior thus shows a strong sense of moral responsibility that, despite their disbelief, carries them to the New World and lasts until their father dies. With the dissolution of the family, Laman and Lemuel would see themselves as simply claiming their birthright as the eldest sons.[77] Of course, their willingness to turn to violence means that their evil reputation is not wholly undeserved.

Lehi as a Fleeing Prophet

Lehi's contemporaries Jeremiah and Ezekiel were persecuted.[78] Unsurprisingly, so was Lehi: "And when the Jews heard these things they were angry with him; yea, even

---

[74] Bruce J. Malina and Jerome H. Neyrey, *Portraits of Paul: An Archaeology of Ancient Personality*, 17.

[75] Dever, *Did God Have a Wife?* 3.

[76] Hardy, *Understanding the Book of Mormon*, 34: "Nephi has reduced thirty years of tumultuous family interactions among some two dozen people to a conflict between Laman and Lemuel on the one side and himself and Lehi on the other. From the beginning, he structures the narrative in such a way as to prevent readers from sympathizing with his older brothers."

[77] Ehab Abunuwara, "Into the Desert: An Arab View of the Book of Mormon," 62: "I read their story as a tragedy and overturning of the family structure. The status of eldest brother within a Middle Eastern family is culturally entrenched and derives its strength from the culture's patriarchal structure. The eldest brother is the father-in-waiting and demands equal respect with the father."

[78] Ezekiel received his call in the "fifth year of the exile of king Jehoiachin," (Ezek. 1:2). This was about five years after Lehi's call. The first year of King Zedekiah's reign would be the first year of Jehoiachin's exile.

as with the prophets of old, whom they had cast out, and stoned, and slain; and they also sought his life, that they might take it away." (1 Ne. 1:20) The biblical texts edited by the Deuteronomists make it appear that Josiah's reforms were easily implemented and gratefully accepted. The reality was surely more chaotic and ideologically combative. Leading some of the resistance to the reforms were the prophets, and Lehi was among those. Because the reforms were being pushed by the highest political authority, it was not a popular time for protesting prophets. Lehi was not the only one who left.

Aaron Schade notes:

> Urijah (ca. 609) had prophesied against Jerusalem (just as Jeremiah had done and Lehi would do), thus infuriating the king and his officials. Fearing for his life, Urijah fled to Egypt. He was pursued by a posse of the king headed by Elnatan and was captured and returned to Jerusalem, where he was executed and disrespectfully cast into a grave. [Jer. 26:21–23] A similar pursuit is related in Lachish ostracon 3.13-18. A commander named Konyahu, son of Elnatan, had gone down into Egypt; this letter seems to be describing the need for more men for an organized posse or a deputized search team.[79]

S. Kent Brown adds: "It was clearly unhealthy to preach against those who were in power in Jerusalem. As Urijah had done before him, Lehi fled Jerusalem. Unlike Urijah before him, Lehi escaped with his life and family. Perhaps Elnatan's pursuit of Urijah and his son's pursuit of an unnamed person into Egypt may account for Lehi's rather surprising selection of Arabia rather than Egypt as a place of refuge."[80]

Perhaps in addition to this disincentive to head toward the traditional shelter of Egypt, Lehi might have had a positive reason to flee down the Arabian peninsula. The copper-mining area of Timna was located in that direction. Chadwick suggests that Lehi's metal-working profession might have taken him to this region with some regularity.[81] Thus, both the vulnerability of other Egypt-bound prophets and

---

[79] Aaron P. Schade, "The Kingdom of Judah: Politics, Prophets, and Scribes in the Late Preexilic Period," 311.

[80] S. Kent Brown, "Jerusalem Connections to Arabia in 600 B.C.," 625. S. Kent Brown, "New Light from Arabia on Lehi's Trail," 60: "The mild surprise in the early part of the narrative is that anyone fleeing Jerusalem or its environs would head for Arabia, camping near the Red Sea. Almost all flights into exile that are recorded in the Bible show people going southwest to Egypt, not southeast into Arabia."

[81] Jeffrey R. Chadwick, "The Wrong Place for Lehi's Trail and the Valley of Lemuel," 201:
> Lehi and his sons had probably traveled to the Red Sea's gulf of Eilat (or Gulf of Aqaba) many times in the years prior to their final departure from Jerusalem. They seem to have known the trail well. It was a regularly traveled route that exited the city to the southeast, into the wilderness of Judah east of Bethlehem and Tekoa, and descended via the Arugot valley to Ein Gedi. From Ein Gedi, the path turned south along the western shore of the Dead Sea and continued straight south through the desert wilderness of the Arabah valley to the Gulf of Eilat. The copper-mining area of Timna was located half a day's journey north of the gulf shore, and other copper-mining sites were located in nearby northern Sinai.

My thanks to Neal Rappleye for suggesting this reference as the positive reason for their journey into Arabia.

familiarity with Arabia could have sent Lehi in a direction different from that taken by other fleeing prophets.

Lehi led his family out of Jerusalem prior to its destruction. He may have learned of its destruction only as the result of revelation after arriving in the New World (2 Ne. 1:4). However, with the length of time they spent traveling to Bountiful, it is highly likely that the gossip about the destruction of Jerusalem traveled the same paths that Lehi did. In that case, he would have learned of the destruction from multiple sources and had the confirmation through revelation.

Laman and Lemuel perhaps persisted in believing that it had not been destroyed. Perhaps they disbelieved their father's prophetic pronouncements. Perhaps they disbelieved or misinterpreted the gossip along the trail. In any case, they continued to nurture a desire for a symbolic if not physical return to Jerusalem.

Lehi the prophet was rejected in Israel. That is, tacit evidence that something he said was not in harmony with prevailing opinions. Nephi depicts himself not only as the faithful son but as the rightful inheritor of his father's mission. Nephi restored in the New World what he felt his father had, prophetically warned, that Yahweh's people had rejected in the Old World.

The First Camp

Lehi and his family arrived at a valley and camped next to a river (1 Ne. 2:6). The location of this camp is unknown, although all three scholars focusing on this stage have a favored candidate. Hilton and Hilton propose wadi al-Bad.[82] George Potter and Richard Wellington argue for wadi Tayyib al-Ism.[83] Chadwick prefers Bir Marsha, based on Lehi's plausible travel path and travel time.[84] Each has the important virtue of having accessible water, but only wadi Tayyib al-Ism appears to meet the most difficult requirement, a continually running river (1 Ne. 2:9). While that fact makes it an extremely tempting solution to the issue of the location of the first camp, there are problems.[85] Chadwick explains,

> The perennial stream Potter and Wellington found on their first trip into Tayyib al-Ism was the feature that initially convinced them they had found the valley of Lemuel. When addressing his son Laman, Lehi exclaimed: "O that thou mightest be like unto this river, continually running into the fountain of all righteousness" (1 Nephi 2:9). It is easy to see why some would think this statement is describing the river Laman as a continually flowing brook. (I admit that I used to think this myself.) And it is easy to understand why Potter and Wellington would think they had found the river Laman when they determined that the Tayyib al-Ism stream flows perennially.
>
> But a perennial stream is *not* required to fulfill Nephi's description or Lehi's exclamation. Lehi said "continually running," not "continually flowing." A Near Eastern

---

[82] Hilton and Hilton, *Discovering Lehi*, 50–53.
[83] Potter and Wellington, *Lehi in the Wilderness*, 33.
[84] Chadwick, "The Wrong Place for Lehi's Trail and the Valley of Lemuel," 214.
[85] Brown, *Voices from the Dust: Book of Mormon Insights*, 5–6.

wadi's streambed can run all the way to the sea whether water happens to be flowing in it or not. I have no doubt that water was flowing when Lehi made his statement (which may have been during the winter months). But whether or not water was flowing in that stream six months later does not make or break the issue in terms of identifying the site of the valley of Lemuel. The streambed itself would have been a continually running course to the ocean for the wadi's water, whether seasonal or perennial.[86]

This detail is particularly relevant to the stream Potter and Wellington propose because it fails to meet the textual description of running all the way to the sea (though it is conceivable that this was a literary rather than literal description). Potter and Wellington do specifically state that it does not currently run to the sea; however, they explain this discrepancy by hypothesizing a two-hundred foot change in the elevation of the canyon floor that occurred gradually over the centuries after Lehi's time.[87] Chadwick discusses some difficulties in their calculations and notes that archaeological evidence indicates only about a hundred-foot rise. Chadwick concludes: "No realistic assessment of the features of Tayyib al-Ism and its stream can match Nephi's description."[88] This conclusion, with which I agree, leaves the location for the first camp as a point of discussion and perhaps future discovery.[89]

Nevertheless, the presence of one such stream suggests that there may have been others in the past. John A. Tvedtnes notes:

> About 440 B.C., the Greek historian Herodotus wrote: "There is a large river in Arabia called the Corys, which issues into the Erythraean [Red] Sea. . . . The Arabian king had the hides of cows and other animals sewn together into a pipe, which was long enough to reach the desert from the river. Then he drew the water from the river through the pipe into big storage tanks, which had been excavated in the desert to receive and hold the water. It is twelve days' journey from the river to this desert, and he is supposed to have brought the water to three separate parts of the desert, through three pipes" (*Histories* 3.9). Although we cannot ascertain the location of this river (it may have been in the south, in Yemen), there are other ancient texts that mention rivers in the al-Maqnah region. . . .
>
> In the second century B.C., Agatharchides of Cnidus, a Greek historian and geographer, wrote his treatise *On the Erythraean Sea*. The original text has been lost over

---

[86] Chadwick, "The Wrong Place for Lehi's Trail and the Valley of Lemuel," 210–11. Internal references silently removed.

[87] Potter and Wellington, *Lehi in the Wilderness*, 39.

[88] Chadwick, "The Wrong Place for Lehi's Trail and the Valley of Lemuel," 212–14.

[89] S. Kent Brown, "The Hunt for the Valley of Lemuel," 65, suggests that there are currently three possibilities for a valley with a continuously running river. Nevertheless, they are not of the same quality. He concludes (p. 73):

> To date, the al-Bad' oasis and Wadi Tayyib al-Ism are the only candidates for the Valley of Lemuel that Latter-day Saints have explored. The others are unexamined. . . . The oasis at al-Bad' does not match the attractiveness of Wadi Tayyib al-Ism. . . According to my review, the only serious objection to Wadi Tayyib al-Ism is the apparent difficulty of reaching this site from the north end of the Gulf of Aqaba. Because we do not know how the family learned of the place their first camp, or how they may have reached Wadi Tayyib al-Ism, if indeed they camped there, we have to hold onto this point as a negative stroke against this site. But all other features that we can tease from the text point to this canyon.

time, but portions were quoted by subsequent writers who had access to it. In this way, portions of Book 1 of his work have been preserved, while Book 5 has survived almost intact and gives a description of the horn of Africa and the lands adjoining the Red Sea. Describing the northwest Arabian coast near the Sinai peninsula, Agatharchides wrote:

After these places there is a well-watered plain which, because of the streams that flow through it everywhere, grows dog's tooth grass, lucerne and also lotus the height of a man. Because of the abundance and excellence of the pasturage it not only supports flocks and herds of all sorts in unspeakably great numbers but also wild camels and, in addition, deer and gazelles. In response to the abundance of animals which breed there, crowds of lions, wolves and leopards gather from the desert.

Strabo, a Greek historian born in 63 B.C., cited an earlier work by Artemidorus. After describing the region of northwestern Arabia near the island of Tiran and opposite the southern end of the Sinai peninsula, he wrote: "One comes next to a plain [about modern al-Maqnah] which is well supplied with trees and water and is full of all kinds of domestic animals—mules among others; and it has a multitude of wild camels, deer, and gazelles, as also numerous lions, leopards, and wolves [jackals?]. Off this plain lies an island called Dia. Then one comes to a gulf about five hundred stadia in extent, which is enclosed all round by mountains and a mouth that is difficult to enter; and round it live men who hunt the land animals" (Geography 16.4.18). In the same section, Strabo mentioned a harbor named Charmothas (modern Umm Lajj) farther south along the same coast, saying that "a river flows into it."

These classical sources support the idea that there were rivers flowing in the western part of Arabia, both in Yemen to the south and in the land of Midian to the north, where Lehi encamped beside the river Laman.[90]

There is no current continually flowing river that compellingly meets all textual requirements.[91] Perhaps the argument for Wadi Tayyib al-Ism is stronger than I have portrayed it. The Book of Mormon text does not clearly tell us how Lehi would have known that it was an active watercourse throughout the entire year. He could have known that only if they camped at this location for a full year or learned that fact from unnamed people he might have consulted. In short, it remains an open question.

Certainly the very first thing the family did upon arriving at what become known as the Valley of Lemuel was to establish their camp. Of those mundane details, Nephi tells us nothing, assuming that any reader would understand the basics of what they had done. However, Nephi does make a point of one detail. Lehi "built an altar of stones, and made an offering unto the Lord, and gave thanks unto the Lord our God" (1 Ne. 2:7). By referencing the sacrifice, Nephi underscores that they continue to follow the law of Moses.

Nephi records three instances where Lehi offered sacrifices. These are occasions where the text assumes information that went without saying to an ancient Israelite, but which most modern readers would not even notice. S. Kent Brown points out that both the sacrifices noted in 1 Nephi 5:9 and 7:22 characterize the sacrifice as including burnt offerings—but not this first altar. For all three occasions (arriving at

---

[90] John A. Tvedtnes, "More on the River Laman," 2–3.
[91] Brown, "The Hunt for the Valley of Lemuel," 73, leans heavily toward the continuously flowing river in Wadi Tayyib al-Ism as the location described in the Book of Mormon.

the initial base camp, the return of the sons with the brass plates, and the return of the sons with Ishmael's family), thanks were the appropriate response to a safe return from a journey. For two sacrifices, an important difference explain the addition of the burnt offerings to the thank offering. The potential presence of sin accompanied two of the occasions, and burnt offerings were part of the process of removing the stain of such sin.

In the first of the two later occasions, Nephi and brothers return from Jerusalem with the plates, but also carrying the blood guilt of Nephi's murder of Laban. Even though he had acted under inspiration, the act of shedding human blood required the burnt offering noted in 1 Nephi 5:9. When Lehi's sons returned from the second trip to Jerusalem, bringing Ishmael's family, Laman and Lemuel's physical attack on Nephi constituted the sin requiring the burnt offering noted in 1 Nephi 7:22. In contrast, their mere arrival in safety was a thank-offering for their successful journey. No perceived communal sin pertained to that part of the journey.[92]

While the nature of the sacrifices subtly follow the logic of the law of Moses, the very fact that they made sacrifices at all raises a potential conflict. As part of the religio-political reforms, worship was not only centralized in Jerusalem but also made exclusive to Jerusalem. This policy seems to have been codified in Deuteronomy 12, which appears to prohibit building an altar outside Jerusalem.[93]

Had Lehi built the altar after the Exile rather than before, it would have been a more obvious violation of scripture. However, prior to either Hezekiah's or Josiah's reform movements, altars, and even temples outside of Jerusalem were normal Hebrew practice. Ephraim Stern notes: "The establishment of sanctuaries dedicated to Yahweh in settlements outside Jerusalem was a regular custom: for example, the famous cultic site at Kuntillet Ajrud, dating to the end of the 9th century B.C.E., dedicated to 'Yahweh of Samaria and his Asherah' or 'Yahweh of Teman and his Asherah.' Another sanctuary is mentioned in the even-earlier Mesha stela, in which the Moabite king claims to have taken the vessels of Yahweh from the city of Nebo and laid them before Chemosh. This implies that there was also a sanctuary dedicated to Yahweh in the Judean city of Nebo before it was plundered by the Moabites."[94]

Jared W. Ludlow discussed the temple found at Elephantine, Egypt:

> Although we don't know the exact date of the construction of the temple in Elephantine, it seems to have been built before the conquest of Egypt by Cambyses in 525 B.C., a number of years before the Jerusalem temple was rebuilt. Elephantine was noteworthy because it was a Jewish community outside of Israel that constructed its own

---

[92] S. Kent Brown, *From Jerusalem to Zarahemla: Literary and Historical Studies of the Book of Mormon*, 1–6.

[93] This prohibition would therefore also prohibit a temple outside of Jerusalem. Just as Lehi still performs sacrifices in the wilderness, Nephi would build a temple in the New World. Clearly, the prohibition was not part of their understanding of the nature of Israelite worship.

[94] Ephraim Stern, "The Phoenician Source of Palestinian Cults at the End of the Iron Age," 316.

temple, a development that runs counter to the belief "that foreign soil was ritually unclean precluding erection thereon of a temple."⁹⁵

The reforms initiated during Josiah's reign removed such religious sites throughout the land directly under Jerusalem's control. It was a move intended to centralize religious practice in Jerusalem. However, as the temple in Elephantine shows, even those centralizing regulations did not prevent the creation of a temple outside of Jerusalem after the Deuteronomic reforms and before the return from Babylonian exile. The Elephantine temple would have been roughly contemporaneous with the temple Nephi had built in the New World.

---

⁹⁵ Jared W. Ludlow, "A Tale of Three Communities: Jerusalem, Elephantine, and Lehi-Nephi," 31. The internal reference quotes Porten Bezalel, "The Jews in Egypt," in *The Cambridge History of Judaism* (Cambridge, England: Cambridge University Press, 1984), 1:386. Ludlow notes that the Elephantine temple was also destroyed. The Elephantine community petitioned Jerusalem for assistance in rebuilding it. On page 32 he suggests: "The fact that the Elephantine Jews sought a recommendation from Jerusalem shows 'that they did not regard themselves as schismatic, nor even opposed to the claims of the Temple at Jerusalem.'" Internal reference to Jena Jörg Frey, "Temple and Rival Temple—The Cases of Elephantine, Mt. Gerizim, and Leontopolis," in *Gemeinde ohne Tempel*, ed. Beate Ego and others (Tubingen, Germany: Mohr, 1999), 178–79.

4

The Lehite Exodus

Lehi's route into the Sinai peninsula may have been determined by inspired guidance or because he was already familiar with the region, but given the geographical vagueness that would characterize later periods of the Book of Mormon, this first step on their epic journey was remarkably clear. Hugh Nibley pioneered the examination of the textual details in attempting to reconstruct the path the family followed from Jerusalem to Bountiful. He concludes that the text "entirely excludes the Sinaitic Peninsula as the scene of their wanderings, and fits perfectly with a journey through the Arabian Peninsula. The slowest possible march 'in a south-southeasterly direction' in Sinai would reach the sea and have to turn north within ten days; yet Lehi's people traveled 'for many days,' nay, months, in a south-southeasterly direction keeping near the coast of the Red Sea all the while."[1] With that general geographical correlation, Nibley was content to fill in data on cultural convergences. Other authors, however, have worked to fill in missing geographic details.

In 1976, Lynn M. and Hope A. Hilton published the results of their initial attempts to trace Lehi's path. They have continued their efforts since that time, publishing an updated version in 1996.[2] The success of that initial project has led to subsequent attempts to fill in even more details of the journey. In 1994, Warren P. Aston and Michaela Knoth Aston published the account of their attempt to trace Lehi's trail,[3] a route followed by George Potter and Richard Wellington in 2003.[4] While each of these mapping efforts differ in specifics, they agree on the overall outline of a trek that followed the incense trail to Nahom and then, as indicated in the text, turned nearly eastward to arrive at a location that could be called Bountiful on the east coast of the Sinai Peninsula.

---

[1] Hugh W. Nibley, *Lehi in the Desert and The World of the Jaredites*, 55.
[2] Lynn M. Hilton and Hope A. Hilton, "In Search of Lehi's Trail—Part 1: The Preparation," 32–54. Lynn M. Hilton and Hope A. Hilton, "In Search of Lehi's Trail—Part 2: The Journey," 34–63. Lynn M. Hilton and Hope A. Hilton, *Discovering Lehi: New Evidence of Lehi and Nephi in Arabia*.
[3] Warren P. Aston and Michaela Knoth Aston, *In the Footsteps of Lehi: New Evidence for Lehi's Journey across Arabia to Bountiful*. Noel B. Reynolds, "Lehi's Arabian Journey Updated," 379–89, summarized some of the Aston's findings.
[4] George Potter and Richard Wellington, *Lehi in the Wilderness: 81 New, Documented Evidences That the Book of Mormon Is a True History*.

84 *Traditions of the Fathers*

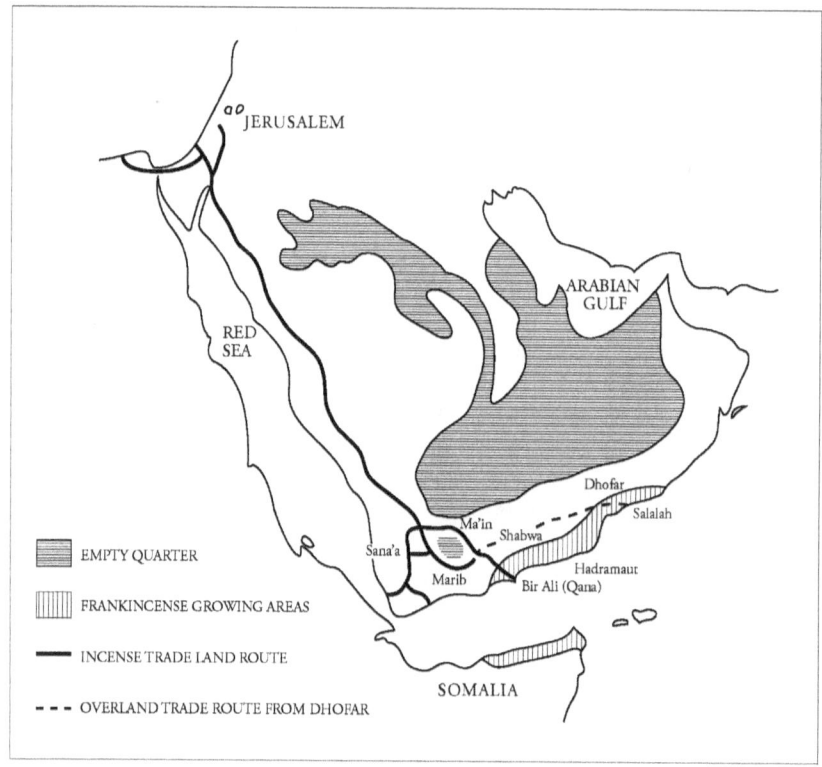

Figure 1: Lehi's trail

One complication in reconstructing the family's path is the multiple paths they could have taken as they left Jerusalem. S. Kent Brown describes the basic information available for the first leg of the Lehite exodus:

> The family's exact route to the tip of the northeastern arm of the Red Sea remains unknown. At least four options lay before them. They could depart eastward down through the Jordan valley, passing just south of Jericho and north of the Dead Sea, and climb the hills of Moab until they reached the well-trodden King's Highway where they would turn south. A second path would have taken them farther east, beyond the King's Highway, where a dusty desert road ran south toward the Red Sea. Another route ran south from Jerusalem, one spur descending steeply eastward into the Jordan valley from Tekoa, birthplace of the prophet Amos, leading travelers to the Ein Gedi oasis and then to a trail running south. A second spur of this southbound road would have taken them through Hebron toward Arad, eventually leading them into the Jordan valley some twenty-five miles south of Ein Gedi. By any route, the Red Sea lay almost 200 miles away. They continued on another "three days"—a ritually significant number. After arriving in the area south of

modern Aqaba, the family found itself about 250 miles from Jerusalem, virtually a two-week walk from the city, including Sabbaths. Here they set up camp.[5]

The option for each of these four routes out of Jerusalem is not quite equivalent to the others, each requiring a significant difference in the time and distance required. Jeffrey Chadwick compares Lehi's choice to modern example: "Traveling the practical and most likely route from Jerusalem straight south to the Red Sea via the Ein Gedi/Arabah valley route could be likened to a modern driving trip from Salt Lake City south to Phoenix. There is a direct and practical path for both journeys. By contrast, traveling from Jerusalem to the Red Sea via the King's Highway would be like driving from Salt Lake City to Phoenix via Denver—the eastward loop is a much longer and quite unnecessary addition to the route."[6] Some researchers have preferred the well-traveled King's Highway, while Potter and Wellington make a case for the most distant route.[7]

Although Urijah had been chased on his flight from Jerusalem to Egypt, there is no indication that Lehi was similarly pursued. Once outside of the city, Lehi's family would have been even safer, as they were another family traveling a well-known road.[8] In a time before photographs, there was no way to easily identify particular individuals. Melding with the general flow of traffic on those roads, Lehi and his family were able to travel to their first camp without incident. They had become essentially anonymous.

Returning for the Brass Plates

Perhaps not long after establishing a camp in the valley of Lemuel, Lehi received another vision:

> Behold I have dreamed a dream, in the which the Lord hath commanded me that thou and thy brethren shall return to Jerusalem.
> For behold, Laban hath the record of the Jews and also a genealogy of my forefathers, and they are engraven upon plates of brass.
> Wherefore, the Lord hath commanded me that thou and thy brothers should go unto the house of Laban, and seek the records, and bring them down hither into the wilderness. (1 Ne. 3:2–4)

Even without knowing how long they had been encamped before Lehi received this revelation, it is not hard to imagine how difficult the very concept of returning to Jerusalem would have been. When the purpose was added to the simple fact of

---

[5] S. Kent Brown, *Voices from the Dust: Book of Mormon Insights*, 3.

[6] Chadwick, "The Wrong Place for Lehi's Trail and the Valley of Lemuel," 203.

[7] Ibid., 198, notes that other investigators prefer the King's Highway. He may be referring only to Potter and Wellington, *Lehi in the Wilderness*, 22. Neither Hilton and Hilton, *Discovering Lehi: New Evidence of Lehi and Nephi in Arabia*, nor Aston and Aston, *In the Footsteps of Lehi*, speculate on the path from Jerusalem to the Red Sea.

[8] Chadwick, "The Wrong Place for Lehi's Trail and the Valley of Lemuel," 205: "Once outside the big city, on the wilderness paths to either Jericho or Ein Gedi, Lehi was probably as secure as anyone else traveling the byways of Judah."

retracing what much have been a rather long and boring journey, it had to have become even less appealing.

Lehi and Laban were both descendants of Joseph of Egypt (1 Ne. 5:16). Laban probably kept the records as a leader in the clan and as such was an important kinsman. Lehi and his sons would have known Laban. They knew that Laban could command fifty men (1 Ne. 3:31) even before they made their first foray to his home (although they mention those fifty after the first attempt had failed). Of this very specific number under Laban's command, Nibley noted:

> The number fifty suits perfectly with the Amarna picture, where the military forces are always so surprisingly small and a garrison of thirty to eighty men is thought adequate even for big cities. It is strikingly vindicated in a letter of Nebuchadnezzar, Lehi's contemporary, wherein the great king orders: "As to the fifties who were under your command, those gone to the rear, or fugitives return to their ranks." Commenting on this, Offord says, "In these days it is interesting to note the indication here, that in the Babylonian army a platoon contained fifty men"; also, we might add, that it was called a "fifty"—hence, "Laban with his fifty." Of course, companies of fifty are mentioned in the Bible, along with tens and hundreds, etc., but not as garrisons of great cities and not as *the* standard military unit of this time. Laban, like Hoshaiah of Lachish, had a single company of soldiers under him as the permanent garrison, and like Jaush (his possible successor) worked in close cooperation with "the authorities in Jerusalem."[9]

After fleeing Jerusalem on a trek that required several days without striking camp, the brothers not only had to travel to Jerusalem and then return to their family's camp, but when they were at Jerusalem they were to perform what must have seemed an impossible task. One cannot fault Laman and Lemuel's murmuring: "It is a hard thing which I [Lehi] have required of them" (1 Ne. 3:5). Knowing the extreme difficulty of both the journey and the mission, we can better understand that Nephi could rely only upon Yahweh to provide success (1 Ne. 3:7).

In spite of Laban's fifty, the final confrontation between Laban and Nephi did not end well for Laban.[10] Benjamin L. McGuire presented a fascinating analysis of the story of Nephi and Laban that strongly suggests that Nephi wrote the entire account to highlight its parallel to another scriptural text—the story of David and Goliath.[11] Given Nephi's probable scribal training and the evidence of careful construction of

---

[9] Hugh Nibley, *An Approach to the Book of Mormon*, 108.

[10] Val Larsen, "Killing Laban: The Birth of Sovereignty in the Nephite Constitutional Order," 26–41, reads the inclusion of this event in Nephi's narrative as a post hoc demonstration of Nephi's sovereign rights. "A close reading of the text makes it abundantly clear that the killing of Laban was not an individual act, but rather a sovereign act that had a clear political purpose" (pp. 28–29).

[11] Benjamin L. McGuire, "Nephi and Goliath: A Case Study of Literary Allusion in the Book of Mormon," Larsen, "Killing Laban," 35–36, agrees with McGuire's reading: "I will expand on Ben McGuire's analysis of parallels between David and Nephi in the Goliath and Laban stories. In most cases, not only are events similar but the similar events occur in the same sequence in the two narratives."

his first book (our 1 Nephi), McGuire's hypothesis is entirely plausible. McGuire summarizes the important literary allusions:

> Having recognized the literary allusion, we now reinterpret the Book of Mormon text through the lens of the David and Goliath narrative. Nephi can be seen as the heir apparent. He will be king. The others may not recognize his kingship, but, in "delivering into his hand" the antagonist, the enemy of true Israel, God has demonstrated his preference. (This, of course, simply reinforces 1 Nephi 3:30, prior to the beginning of the narrative, where Nephi, like David, has already been chosen.) Laman and Lemuel are representative of Saul and the rest of faithless Israel. They are afraid, in a way that prevents them from taking action, and their own wickedness has precluded them from being favored by God (and so precluded either of them from becoming king). Nephi's calculated language shows that he was not guilty of murder in the case of Laban (at least by his own estimation) and that he considered Laban to be guilty of theft, of attempted murder, and of the larger crime of wickedness before God. As a result, God's "delivering him" into Nephi's hands both alleviates the guilt that might have normally come upon Nephi and suggests the miraculous nature of its occurrence. Nephi overcomes not only Laban (Goliath) but also by extension his fifty or, like David, his tens of thousands (perhaps intended in Nephi's remarks in 1 Nephi 4:1). Regardless, Nephi takes the sword from fallen Laban and decapitates him. It is with this graphic image that the narrative unit closes. Nephi has proven his faith in God, and will return victorious to his people.[12]

Perhaps it was literary necessity as much as God's command that had Nephi cut off Laban's head. Surely there was another way to kill him, but not one that so completely fulfilled the allusion. When Nephi slew Laban, even he understood that it was a difficult situation (1 Ne. 4:10). Perhaps Yahweh's direction came in such a way that Nephi would be able to see the parallel scriptural story and have a context in which he could place the event in order to see past the obvious problem of being asked to take a life. Perhaps as part of Nephi's literary retelling of this story, it is important to note that, in his speech to his brothers prior to returning and meeting Laban, Nephi used scripture to bolster their faith in the ultimate success of what had been to that point an unsuccessful endeavor:

> And it came to pass that I spake unto my brethren, saying: Let us go up again unto Jerusalem, and let us be faithful in keeping the commandments of the Lord; for behold he is mightier than all the earth, then why not mightier than Laban and his fifty, yea, or even than his tens of thousands?
> Therefore let us go up; let us be strong like unto Moses; for he truly spake unto the waters of the Red Sea and they divided hither and thither, and our fathers came through, out of captivity, on dry ground, and the armies of Pharaoh did follow and were drowned in the waters of the Red Sea.
> Now behold ye know that this is true; and ye also know that an angel hath spoken unto you; wherefore can ye doubt? Let us go up; the Lord is able to deliver us, even as our fathers, and to destroy Laban, even as the Egyptians. (1 Ne. 4:1–3)

---

[12] McGuire, "Nephi and Goliath," 24.

88 *Traditions of the Fathers*

Of all the stories of Yahweh's power, Nephi selected one where the salvation of the Israelites depended upon the death of their antagonist.

The Importance of the Brass Plates

The brass plates were so important that success included Nephi taking Laban's life. The Spirit had convinced Nephi of the necessity of that action by declaring: "It is better that one man should perish than that a nation should dwindle and perish in unbelief" (1 Ne. 4:13). As Nephi processed that information, his understanding was that his people would be able to live Yahweh's law only if they had that law (1 Ne. 4:14–15).

When Nephites referred to scripture, they referred to the contents of the brass plates rather than any of the voluminous Nephite records kept in the New World.[13] While the brass plates parallel much of what we know in our Old Testament, they differed in that they also contained prophets such as Zenos and Zenock who do not appear in our Old Testament. It also contained the genealogy of Lehi's fathers, also not specifically present in our Old Testament (1 Ne. 5:11–14).[14]

It is likely that the differences between the contents of the brass plates and our Old Testament are due to the different provenance of the two records. Our received Old Testament has been compiled from records kept in the southern kingdom, or in Judah. The brass plates were transmitted through a tribe which had its inheritance in the northern kingdom of Israel.

As with the Old Testament at that time, we should not consider the brass plates as a fixed canon, but rather as a collected set of individual books that were considered scripture. There was no concept of a set list of accepted books during Lehi's day (supported, perhaps, by the willingness to accept the discovered book of the law as scripture, see 2 Kgs. 22:8).

There is no set of northern kingdom scriptures available. How the northern kingdom's collection of books considered to be scripture might have been different from those considered scripture in the southern kingdom can only be teased out of

---

[13] Nephi begins this practice noting that: "I did read unto them that which was written by the prophet Isaiah; for I did liken all scriptures unto us" (1 Ne. 19:23). Abinadi discusses passages that were certainly on the brass plates and notes: "Behold, the scriptures are before you" (Alma 13:20).

It is interesting to note that Nephi and Jacob, as authors, cite texts from the brass plates. While we have later examples of prophets such as Abinadi who quote from the brass plates, Mormon as an author does not appear to similarly quote from them. Mormon may quote people who quote from the plates, but when Mormon is quoting from a source, that source is the large plates of Nephi rather than the brass plates.

[14] Rex C. Reeve, Jr., "The Book of Mormon Plates," 103, identifies these citations: "The five books of Moses, which gave an account of the creation of the world, and also of Adam and Eve, who were our first parents (1 Ne. 5:11). And also a record of the Jews from the beginning, even down to the commencement of the reign of Zedekiah, king of Judah (1 Ne. 5:12). And . . . the words . . . of all the holy prophets, which have been delivered unto them by the Spirit and power of God (1 Ne. 3:20; see also 1 Ne. 5:13). And . . . a genealogy of [Lehi's] fathers (1 Ne. 5:14)."

the hints that are available through studying the redacted inclusion of those records in the southern tradition as we have received it.

The theory known as the documentary hypothesis examines various traits in Hebrew of the Bible and discerns by those traits that there were four main traditions that merged into what we currently have as a Bible.[15] A tradition called J (for Jahwist—for the typical name of God in this source) is considered representative of the older southern kingdom traditions. P is a priestly text. D is the Deuteronomic tradition, considered to be largely completed after the Babylonian exile, though likely begun before.[16] Finally, the E tradition (Elohist—the typical name for God in this tradition) is considered to represent texts from the northern kingdom.[17] All of these were eventually combined and edited into the text that we call the Pentateuch.

As a record kept by the house of Joseph, the brass plates would have been a northern kingdom record. It is reasonable that some of those fleeing the destruction of the kingdom of Israel would carry their scriptures south to Judah. David Bokovoy highlights the potential significance of the E source for the prophet Lehi:

> Unlike other traditions, the E source focuses upon the prophetic leadership of four of Israel's ancestors: Abraham, Jacob, Joseph, and Moses. Throughout the documentary strand, E either implicitly or explicitly refers to each of these men as prophets who receive revelation from God.
>
> Interestingly, in E, however, this prophetic revelation almost always comes in a unique and indirect way. E regularly presents God revealing his divine will by means of dreams or vision rather than direct appearances."[18]

Lehi, a descendant of Joseph was known (at least to his sons and in a derogatory epithet) as a "visionary man."[19]

---

[15] Bruce Corley, Steve Lemke, and Grand Lovejoy, *Biblical Hermeneutics: A Comprehensive Introduction to Interpreting Scripture*, 363. A more complete historical picture of the hypothesis (also known as the Graf-Welhausen hypothesis) and the reaction to it is Roland Kenneth Harrison, *Introduction to the Old Testament*, 1:19–61.

An overview of the LDS reaction to this hypothesis is Kevin Barney, "Reflections on the Documentary Hypothesis," 57–99. David Bokovoy, *Authoring the Old Testament: Genesis–Deuteronomy*, is an explanation of the documentary hypothesis specifically placed in the context of LDS traditions and understanding.

[16] Hess, *Israelite Religions*, 47, "The D document is so named because of its connection with Deuteronomy. Second Kings 22–23 recounts how, early in the reign of Josiah in Jerusalem, a copy of the law scroll was discovered while cleaning out and repairing the temple. The content of this scroll prompted Josiah to inaugurate his great reforms. It was de Wette who first suggested that this law book may have related to what we know as Deuteronomy. De Wette and others who followed him suggested that the text of Deuteronomy was written at the time of Josiah and, whether or not it was actually planted and subsequently discovered in the temple, it became a public justification for the reforms that were carried forward by Josiah's party, known as the Deuteronomists."

[17] Ibid., 47. Bokovoy, *Authoring the Old Testament*, 56.

[18] Bokovoy, *Authoring the Old Testament*, 56–57.

[19] See 1 Ne. 2:11; 5:2. Lehi self-applies the label in 1 Ne. 5:4.

Sorenson suggested that the brass plate texts as discernable in the Book of Mormon demonstrate features that correlate with known markers of the northern text, or the E source:

> Book of Mormon writers mention five prophets whose words appear in the brass plates: Zenos, Zenock, Ezias, Isaiah and Neum (the last might be Nahum). Of the first four only Isaiah is surely known from existing biblical texts. Internal evidence suggests a reason why: All four direct a great deal of attention to the Northern Kingdom. Since the Masoretic text, which lies behind our King James version, came out of the South, omission of three of the four (or four of the five, counting Neum) is explicable. Zenos is quoted as saying "And as for those who are at Jerusalem... [1 Ne. 19:13]" Nowhere else in the extensive quotes from Zenos does he mention Judah or Jerusalem. This in context strongly suggests that he was not located in the territory of Judah. (It is implied in 3 Nephi 10:16 that Zenos and Zenock were of a Joseph tribe, although nothing is said of location.)[20]

Reinforcing Sorenson's suggestion, Steve St. Clair further examined the plausible connection of the brass plates to the northern kingdom. He notes: "Much can be learned about a culture from the study of those whom it holds in high and low esteem. In the case of Northern Israel, a set of heroes and villains appears that is different from those of the Jews. Specifically, the northern tradition has great interest in and respect for Joseph, Moses, and Joshua, and a corresponding disdain for or lack of interest in Judah, Aaron, and David."[21] For the Book of Mormon, he finds:

> An examination of the attention paid to these Israelite forebears in the Book of Mormon is most instructive. Joseph, the ancestor of the nation, is considered as a hero whose blessings on his posterity had an ongoing effect on their success. In all, the Biblical Joseph is named twenty-five times in the Book of Mormon; and when Lehi gave his youngest son that name, he specifically borrowed from the Biblical Joseph.
>
> Moses is also looked upon in the Book of Mormon with supreme respect, and his leading of the exodus out of Egypt is seen as a pattern for much of the typology of the book, including the flight of Lehi's family through their own wilderness, across their own Red Sea, and to their own promised land. He is named sixty-three times, more often than any other Old Testament character. Incidentally, in all its accounts of Moses and his doings, the Book of Mormon never mentions the ark of the covenant—a trait it shares with the northern Israelite "E" pentateuchal source.[22]

St. Clair also finds similarities in the attitude of the northern kingdom toward the scriptures and the evidence found in the Book of Mormon:

> Bowman notes "the refusal of the Samaritans to accept any book other than the Torah." So strongly did they feel about the law of Moses that they "claim to believe literally that nothing can or must be taken away from the Law or be added to it. They claim that their text of the Law is perfect, while that of the Jews is defective...."

---

[20] John L. Sorenson, *Nephite Culture and Society*, 29–30.

[21] Steve St. Clair, "The Stick of Joseph: The Book of Mormon and the Literary Tradition of the Northern Kingdom." This paper was originally located online, but that location was closed. It is unavailable in the Internet Archive. Copy in my possession.

[22] Ibid.

Abinadi's use of the Decalogue as a core text for preaching to King Noah and his priests is reminiscent of the northern tradition's fixation on that section of the Law. . .

Probably most telling is the reaction of Book of Mormon people to "the manner of prophesying of the Jews." Nephi and Jacob, who respond favorably to the writings of Isaiah and other prophets from the brass plates, leave the impression that they are excited about the prophetic writings because they are hearing them for the first time. The words of Korihor are more reminiscent of the standard northern Israelite feelings about prophets: "Behold, these things which ye call prophecies, which ye say are handed down by holy prophets, behold, they are foolish traditions of your fathers." It also explains how Sherem could say he believes in the scriptures, and then be totally unaffected by appeals to the writings of the prophets.[23]

Sorenson's summary of what he sees connecting the Book of Mormon to the northern kingdom tradition differs from St. Clair, but comes to the same conclusion:

1. The Book of Mormon virtually ignores the Davidic covenant, which is a J element. David is mentioned but six times (twice only incidentally in quotations from Isaiah). Two instances involved strong condemnation of David.

2. Instead, considerable attention is paid to the Abrahamic covenant and to the patriarchs. All 29 references to Abraham are laudatory. Jacob is also so named, a positive E characteristic, whereas J uses "Israel" as his personal name.

3. The Jews, particularly the inhabitants of Jerusalem, are branded as evil in the strongest terms.

4. Emphasis is placed on Joseph being sold into Egypt, his saving Jacob's house, and the Lord's special covenant with Joseph which is not attested in the Old Testament. The coat of Joseph is a topic specific to E on which the Book of Mormon adds data not found in the Jewish version (J).

5. The name "Jehovah" (Yahweh), the preferred J title of deity, occurs only twice in the Book of Mormon (once in a quote from Isaiah 12—with one word changed—and again in the very last sentence in the volume). The name "Lord" is usually used for divinity in the Book of Mormon (almost 1400 times).

6. Unmistakable El (E source) names do occur in the Book of Mormon, notably "Most High God" (Hebrew "*El Elyon*") and "Almighty God" (the Septuagint's term for "*El Shaddai*"), the former six times and the latter eleven.[24]

The list of connections that point toward the northern kingdom tradition is important for two reasons. First, it provides a cultural and temporal explanation for the differences between the Book of Mormon and the Bible. They may be seen as flowing from the natures of the differing scriptural traditions that eventually merged into our Bible. Second, the fact that the brass plates specifically trace to Joseph in Egypt (1 Ne. 5:14) suggests the provenance that links this particular set to a clan and explains why Lehi was interested in this copy of the scriptures rather than any other written scripture that might have been available at the time. It also explains why Laban, who was also of Joseph's lineage (1 Ne. 5:16) was in possession of the plates. The Book of Mormon's

---

[23] Ibid.
[24] Sorenson, *Nephite Culture and Society*, 32–33. I should note that his numbers 5 and 6 depend upon a literalist translation model of the Book of Mormon, with which I disagree.

description of a different set of records of interest to a particular family with connections to the destroyed northern kingdom is appropriate to Jerusalem in 597 B.C.

Lehi's Prophecy: How Long is a Year?

A significant Book of Mormon prophecy followed Lehi's dream of the Tree of Life. Nephi reports:

> For behold, it came to pass after my father had made an end of speaking the words of his dream, and also of exhorting them to all diligence, he spake unto them concerning the Jews—
>
> That after they should be destroyed, even that great city Jerusalem, and many be carried away captive into Babylon, according to the own due time of the Lord, they should return again, yea, even be brought back out of captivity; and after they should be brought back out of captivity they should possess again the land of their inheritance.
>
> Yea, even six hundred years from the time that my father left Jerusalem, a prophet would the Lord God raise up among the Jews—even a Messiah, or, in other words, a Savior of the world. (1 Ne. 10:2–4)

No other prophecy of the coming of the Messiah was so explicitly timed. Lehi declared that the Messiah would appear six hundred years from the time they left Jerusalem. Even though the Nephites would change their calendar's starting point from the time they left Jerusalem to the beginning of the reign of the judges, they nevertheless mark off six hundred years between their departure and the birth of the Messiah. The prophecy was not generic. Its fulfillment was not approximate.[25]

That firm count leaves us with a conundrum for reconciling the Nephite calendar with our secular calendar. The Book of Mormon indicates that it begins "in the commencement of the first year of the reign of Zedekiah, king of Judah" (1 Ne. 1:4). History records that this event took place in 597 B.C. There are not 600 years between that date, or the even later date of Lehi's departure, and the probable year in which Jesus was born. Scholarly consensus places Jesus's birth a few years earlier than our calendar's year 1, making it even more difficult to find the 600 years that fulfill the prophecy. As Randall Spackman points out:

> The Gospel of Matthew records that "Jesus was born in Bethlehem of Judea in the days of Herod the king" (Matt. 2:1). Josephus reports that at the Passover feast following Herod's death, a riot broke out and many were killed. Varus, the Roman governor of Syria, marched his forces to Jerusalem and left one of his legions there to maintain order. Because coins bearing Varus' name indicate he was governor of Syria from 6 B.C. through 4 B.C., the death

---

[25] David Rolph Seely, "Chronology, Book of Mormon," 198–99, provides an overview of the various approaches LDS authors have taken to fitting the 600-year prophecy with historical evidence. These approaches range from suggesting that the Book of Mormon is a more accurate chronology to the reanalysis of the number of days considered as a "year," such as Spackman advocates. While Seely does not support a particular position, I find Spackman's argument most convincing.

of Herod very likely occurred before Passover in the year 4 B.C.—and hence the birth of Christ earlier than that.[26]

Thus, instead of a span between 600 B.C. and 1 B.C., the time between Lehi's departure and Christ's birth was perhaps from 587 B.C. to 4 B.C. (583 years). Nevertheless, the Nephite reckoning specifically counts six hundred years. How might the Nephite count be reconciled with external history?

The modern reader simply assumes that a "year" is roughly three hundred and sixty five days. This "year" is based on a solar calendar. While a solar calendar was known, Israel used a lunar calendar in Lehi's day.[27] A lunar calendar assigns an average of 354.367 days per year, which is eleven days fewer than a solar calendar (365.2422 days per year).[28] The later Qumran community (beginning some time before 134 B.C.[29]) advocated a 364-day solar calendar rather than the 354-day lunar calendar that was still in use by the Jerusalem religious leaders.[30]

There are 600 lunar years between the departure of Lehi's family and the probable birth of Jesus. That convergence between record and definition strongly suggests that the Nephite year was based, at least in part, on the Old World heritage of a lunar year.[31]

---

[26] Randall P. Spackman, "The Jewish/Nephite Lunar Calendar," 50.
Jeffrey R. Chadwick, "Dating the Birth of Jesus Christ," 9–13, summarizes LDS scholars who have reviewed the historical information whose views converge on a period from winter 5 B.C. to spring of 4 B.C. as the probable time of Jesus's birth.
[27] Michael D. Coogan, "Time, Units of," 744.
[28] Spackman, "The Jewish/Nephite Lunar Calendar," 51.
[29] Lawrence H. Schiffman, *Reclaiming the Dead Sea Scrolls*, 40.
[30] Michael Wise, Martin Abegg Jr., and Edward Cook, *The Dead Sea Scrolls: A New Translation*, 25.
[31] Chadwick, "Dating the Birth of Jesus Christ," 18, strongly disagrees: "It is also virtually certain that the years referred to in 3 Nephi were 365 days long, the same length as the ancient Jewish lunar-solar year, and the same length as the modern secular calendar year. The Nephites were still observing the law of Moses during the 3 Nephi period. The performances of the law of Moses, as found in biblical writings available to the Nephites (on the brass plates of Laban), were keyed to the seasons of the 365-day solar year, beginning with a 'first month,' which was the spring month that the biblical record called Aviv."
Chadwick notes that Hebrew months were lunar and that the ritual year was solar. This discrepancy was reconciled by the addition of an extra month every three years or so (18–19). The entire argument hinges on the fact that the continuation of observation of the law of Moses would necessarily have gone unchanged in the New World for 600 years. In the face of competing conceptions of a year in Mesoamerica, I do not see this requirement as conclusive as Chadwick does.
He does suggest, based on his assumptions: "So, notwithstanding differences that must have developed between the ways of the ancient Near Eastern Jewish calendar and the ancient American Nephite calendar separately evolved, it seems a reasonable conclusion that the Nephites were (1) observing a 365-day solar count, which (2) accommodated a first month that began in close proximity to the vernal equinox."
Chadwick does not examine the problem of the 600-year prophecy, focusing exclusively on Jesus's birth and death dates. He simply accepts that count without attempting to tie it to historical events. See his note 49, pp. 34–35.

Nevertheless, it is also possible that after their long sojourn in the New World, the Nephites were also influenced by Maya (and general Mesoamerican) calendars. The Maya used several types of calendars, but one closely approximated the length of the lunar year. The dating of the origin of this calendar is unknown, though it is contemporary with the carved texts. The earliest currently known date from a Maya inscription is 36 B.C. from Chiapa de Corzo.[32] The expectation is that the calendar existed for a long time prior to the time of the first remaining written texts from the Maya.

Maya mathematics was based on twenty rather than ten (counting fingers and toes instead of fingers only). The Maya *tun* was a 360-day year that consisted of 18 *uinals* ("months"), each of which had exactly 20 days. These 360-day years were accumulated into larger significant sets. The *k'atun* was 20 *tuns*. Even more important was the *bak'tun*, which was 20 *k'atuns*.[33] Clark, suggests that these units make an important appearance in the Book of Mormon:

> A correspondence that has always impressed me involves the prophecies in 400-year blocks. The Maya were obsessed with time, and they carved precise dates on their stone monuments that began with the count of 400 years, an interval called a *baktun*. Each *baktun* was made up of 20 *katuns*, an extremely important 20-year interval. If you permit me some liberties with the text, Samuel the Lamanite warned the Nephites that one *baktun* "shall not pass away before . . . they [would] be smitten" (Hel. 13:9). Nephi and Alma uttered the same *baktun* prophecy, and Moroni recorded its fulfillment. Moroni bids us farewell just after the first *katun* of this final *baktun*, or 420 years since the "sign was given of the coming of Christ" (Moro. 10:1).[34]

Sorenson has suggested that this Mesoamerican counting of *tun* years can explain how there are 600 years between Lehi's departure and Christ's birth.[35] Whether the Mesoamerican 360-day calendar or the Old World's 354-day lunar calendar formed the basis of the Nephite calculation of what a "year" meant, the 600-year prophecy works with a culturally appropriate definition of a year that is fewer than 365 days long.[36] The difference between the two possible types of shorter years can be

---

Lincoln H. Blumell and Thomas A. Wayment, "When Was Jesus Born? A Response to a Recent Proposal," 62, comment on Chadwick's insistence on a 365-day year: "Despite the best scholarly efforts, no one can claim with any degree of certainty which ancient American civilization the Nephite calendar should be tied to." Blumell and Wayment clearly indicate the six-hundred year problem (p. 63): "The Book of Mormon counts 600 years between Lehi's departure and the birth of Jesus, which according to our modern calendar occurred in less than 600 years."

John A. Tvedtnes, "When Was Christ Born?" 28–33 also disagrees with Chadwick on a number of points.

[32] John S. Henderson, *The World of the Ancient Maya*, 92. Henderson notes that the long count may not have been exclusively Maya but "was certainly of the greatest importance to the Maya of the Classic period" (277).

[33] Lynn V. Foster, *Handbook to the Life in the Ancient Maya World*, 257.

[34] John E. Clark, "Archaeology, Relics, and Book of Mormon Belief," 46–47.

[35] John L. Sorenson, *An Ancient American Setting for the Book of Mormon*, 270–76.

[36] My personal speculation is that the initial counts were lunar based, coming from their heritage. After some undeterminable time in the New World, the count would have shifted to the

accounted depending upon the portion of the year counted, or the fact that in ancient Near Eastern practice, both end years were counted when counting between years.[37] In either case, the different definition of a year accounts for why there are 600 Nephite years from the time of their departure to the birth of Christ.

A Tree in a Dream

Yahweh had commanded Lehi to leave Jerusalem with his family. Yahweh had commanded that Lehi's sons acquire the brass plates. Yahweh had commanded the sons to return to Jerusalem to bring Ismael's family. With such divine direction for so much of the family's journey, it is understandable that Nephi spends time discussing a vision that perhaps paralleled and presaged the family's physical and spiritual journey.

At some point during their stay in the first camp, Lehi received a vision we know as the vision of the Tree of Life. The Tree of Life had a well-known set of symbolic interpretations in ancient Israel.[38] However, this dream was sufficiently different from expectations that Nephi did not immediately understand it (1 Ne. 11:1). If it had precisely replicated the expected symbolism, Nephi would not have needed heavenly guidance for understanding.[39]

The vision of the Tree of Life placed Lehi in prophetic time, seeing both the reason for his journey and foretelling future family dynamics. Perhaps to assure that Lehi saw this dream as relevant to their current journey, aspects of the visual presentation invoked images that were, or would be, part of their physical journey.

In Lehi's vision he appears to travel at night: He "traveled for the space of many hours in darkness" (1 Ne. 8:8). S. Kent Brown notes: "It also appears that in his dream Lehi was doing what all people do when they travel through the desert in that part of the world: he went at night. A person travels at night in order to escape the terrible heat of the day. In this connection, all the major civilizations in South Arabia worshiped the moon as their chief god. Why? Because the moon provides light at night when one is traveling. Perhaps importantly, we recall that Nephi quotes Yahweh as saying, 'I will also be your light in the wilderness' [1 Ne. 17:13]. It was a matter of nighttime travel."[40]

Another feature of the dream's descriptions concerns the "great and spacious building" which Lehi termed "strange" (1 Ne. 8:33). Brown notes the cultural background that explains the features of this part of the dream:

---

widespread cultural model of the 360-day *tun* year. I believe the timing of the two is close enough that the inherited calendar was pretty easily displaced by the dominant model in the new land.

[37]"Contrary to modern practice, in totaling units both the first and the last were usually counted." Coogan, "Time, Units of," 744.

[38] Andrew C. Skinner, "The Tree of Life in the Hebrew Bible and Later Jewish Thought," 25–54.

[39] This would be true for any Israelite because the lore of the Tree of Life was well known. However, it is most particularly true if Nephi was, as I argue, trained as a scribe. See Gardner, "Nephi as Scribe," 45–55.

[40] S. Kent Brown, "Arabia and the Book of Mormon."

Recent studies have shown that the so-called sky-scraper architecture of modern Yemen, featured most vividly by the towering buildings in the town named Shibam in the Hadhramaut Valley, has been common since at least the eight century B.C. and is apparently unique in the ancient world. The French excavations of the buildings supported multistoried structures. In addition, "many ancient South Arabian building inscriptions indicate the number of floors within houses as three or four, with up to six in [the town of] Zafar.". . .

In this light, it seems evident that Lehi was seeing the architecture of ancient south Arabia in his dream. For contemporary buildings there "stood as it were in the air," referring to five or six stories in height. Such structures would naturally give the appearance of standing "high above the earth" (1 Ne. 8:26).[41]

Lehi's dream was more than a prediction of his family's acceptance of the gospel (1 Ne. 8:15–18). It also provided a picture of lands toward which the family would later travel.

Nephi's explication of the dream has a particularly rough transition when Nephi shifts from describing the Tree of Life and begins to speak of the mortal birth of the Messiah. These two seemingly different topics are presented with no linking explanation. Nephi finishes a discussion of the tree symbolism in 1 Ne. 8:38. The intervening chapter 9 is a transitional chapter, but when Nephi returns to the impact of his vision in chapter 10 he delves directly into a discussion of the Messiah. In both Lehi's dream and Nephi's vision of that dream, the discussion of the Messiah comes immediately after the vision of the tree. Nephi's recounting of both events provides the transition between the topics.[42] What feels like a jolting shift in the narrative is understandable when we understand how Nephi would have seen the tree's symbolism.

One of the items removed from the temple during Josiah's reform was the asherah. Margaret Barker explains: "In the northern kingdom of Israel as well as in Jerusalem, there had been struggles over the asherah, a tree-like symbol that had been constantly set up and then removed and destroyed (1 Kings 15:13; 2 Kings 13:6; 17:16; 18:4; 21:7; 23:6, 15). The asherah had been a tree or piece of wood set beside the altar (Deuteronomy 16:21)."[43] Of that particular symbol, Mark Smith remarks: "The inclusion of the asherah in the Jerusalem temple was perhaps no more than a conservative cultic preservation of Israel's ancient traditions; criticism of it was probably more the innovation."[44] In this case, whether or not the presence of an

---

[41] S. Kent Brown, "New Light from Arabia on Lehi's Trail," 68–69.

[42] Charles Swift, "'I Have Dreamed a Dream': Lehi's Archetypal Vision of the Tree of Life," 139: "When Nephi seeks to understand what the tree of life means, he is immediately shown Mary and the birth of the Son of God (see 1 Nephi 11:9–22). Nephi understands by what he sees that the tree represents the love of God, but it is also clear that the love of God is personified in the Savior. The fact that Nephi's vision continues with a preview of the Savior's mortal ministry and death supports the idea that the tree of life is a symbol for the Savior."

[43] Margaret Barker, "The Fragrant Tree," 58. Also Margaret Barker, "What Did King Josiah Reform?" 522.

[44] Smith, *The Early History of God*, 188.

asherah in the temple was part of normative Israelite belief, that temple presence assures us that the symbol and meaning were known.

Asherah was a goddess who was considered (by the time of Lehi) to be Yahweh's wife, a divine mother.[45] Kevin L. Barney summarizes the historical background of Asherah as the divine wife:

> The understanding of Asherah changed over time in response to these developments. At first She was the wife of El, the mother and procreator of the Gods. As El was merged into Yahweh (around the tenth century B.C.E.), Asherah came to be viewed as the consort, not of El, but of Yahweh. For instance, an inscription at Kuntillet 'Ajrud in the northern Sinai, fifty-five miles northwest of Eilat, dating to roughly the ninth to eighth centuries B.C.E., states: "I have blessed you by Yahweh of Samaria and his Asherah" [brkt 'tkm lyhwh shmrn wl'shrth]. Eventually, the functions of Asherah were also absorbed into Yahweh's; then, in an effort to put a stop to any independent worship of Her, reformers linked Her polemically to (the now thoroughly discredited) Baal, despite the fact that such a linkage does not seem to have had any historical basis. This reform movement against the worship of Asherah took place from the eighth to the sixth centuries B.C.E., and by the time of the conclusion of the Babylonian Exile, the worship of Asherah *as such* had been stamped out.[46]

The Asherah was the physical representation of Asherah, the divine consort and mother, who had a respected place in the Jerusalem temple for hundreds of years.[47] The most relevant part of Asherah's worship to Lehi's dream was that she was both represented by, and the embodiment of, the Tree of Life.[48]

As Nephi records his account of his father's dream and his revealed interpretation of it, he does not say, "Because I looked again, I learned that. . . . " Rather, when he tells the Spirit that he wants to know the interpretation of the tree, the answer is a vision of Mary in Nazareth. The explanation of the meaning of the tree begins with "the mother of God," as 1 Nephi 11:18 read in the 1830 edition of the Book of Mormon.[49]

The conceptual link that Nephi would have used to make this abrupt transition was his understanding of the symbolic link between the tree and Asherah, the divine mother. Daniel C. Peterson notes: "What was the 'asherah' that stood in the temple at Jerusalem and in Samaria? Asherah was associated with trees. A tenth-century

---

[45] Raphael Patai, *The Hebrew Goddess*, 31–32, 53. See also William G. Dever, *Did God Have a Wife? Archaeology and Folk Religion in Ancient Israel*, 166–67, for Asherah as Yahweh's consort and pp. 176–208 for a description of the cult of Asherah.

[46] Kevin L. Barney, "How to Worship Our Mother in Heaven (Without Getting Excommunicated)," 123–24 (emphasis his).

[47] Gardner, *Second Witness*, 1:34–35, 157–60, provides a longer discussion of the relationship of Asherah to the Tree of Life in the context of Lehi's vision and early Israelite culture. See also Margaret Barker, "The Fragrant Tree," 57–59, who discusses both Asherah and the extension into the title "Queen of Heaven."

[48] Margaret Barker, *The Great Angel: A Study of Israel's Second God*, 58.

[49] Daniel C. Peterson, "Nephi and His Asherah," 16–25.

cultic stand from Ta'anach, near Megiddo, features two representations of Asherah, first in human form and then as a sacred tree. She *is* the tree."[50]

The cultural linkage between the tree and Asherah explains how Lehi moved so easily from the Tree to the Messiah, and how Nephi so readily moved from the Tree to the "mother of God." In pre-reform Israelite religion, Asherah was the divine mother. Therefore, Asherah as the Tree of Life was a logical symbol for the Messiah's physical birth.[51] The issue of whether Asherah should be considered as a part of true Israelite belief is quite another discussion. The important information is that the complex of ideas surrounding Asherah would have informed Lehi and Nephi's cultural understanding. That cultural background allowed them to easily make a transition from the tree to the mother of Yahweh, a transition difficult for us but natural for them.

Other aspects of the tree also reflect an ancient understanding of the tree's symbols. Old Testament scholar Margaret Barker noted:

> The Tree of Life made one happy according to the Book of Proverbs (Prov. 3:18), but for other detailed descriptions of the tree we have to rely on the noncanonical texts. Enoch described it as perfumed, with fruits like grapes (1 Enoch 32:5), and a text discovered in Egypt in 1945 described the tree as beautiful, fiery, and with fruits like *white* grapes. I don't know of any other source which describes the fruit as white grapes, so you can imagine my surprise when I read the account of Lehi's vision of the tree whose *white fruit* made one happy, and the interpretation of the vision, that the Virgin in Nazareth was the mother of the Son of God after the manner of the flesh (1 Ne. 11:14–23). This is the Heavenly Mother, represented by the Tree of Life, and then Mary and her Son on the earth. This revelation to Joseph Smith was the exact ancient Wisdom symbolism, intact, and almost certainly as it was known in 600 B.C.E.[52]

A Tree in Stone

In modern LDS popular thought, Lehi's Tree of Life has merged with the discovery of a large standing stone from the archaeological site of Izapa in the state of Soconusco, Mexico. On one of those standing stones, called stelae, was found a beautiful and obvious depiction of a tree. M. Wells Jakeman introduced Izapa Stela 5 to an LDS audience in the 1950s with an interpretation stressing the correspondences between the tree and related objects on the sculpture and Lehi's dream.[53] His analysis

---

[50] Ibid., 21.

[51] See Gardner, *Second Witness*, 1:214–22, for a discussion of why the 1830 edition referred to the "mother of God" but later changed the text to "mother of the son of God."

[52] Margaret Barker, "Joseph Smith and Preexilic Israelite Religion," 76; emphasis hers. Barker expands somewhat on the association between Wisdom and the Tree of Life in her "The Fragrant Tree," 74–75. For the association between the Tree of Life and Wisdom in the New Testament, see John W. Welch, "The Tree of Life in the New Testament and Christian Tradition," 91–95.

[53] M. Wells Jakeman, *The Complex "Tree of Life" Carving on Izapa Stela 5: A Reanalysis and Partial Interpretation*. Jakeman presented another analysis that emphasized the Mesoamerican context without the Book of Mormon coloration in M. Wells Jakeman, *Stela 5, Izapa, Chiapas, Mexico: A Major Archaeological Discovery of the New World. Detailed Commentary on the Carving*.

Figure 2: Izapa Stela 5

has been so influential that Izapa Stela 5 came to be known among some Latter-day Saints as the "Lehi stone,"[54] prompting other authors to promote it as a representation of Lehi's dream.[55]

This connection between the depiction on the stone and dream from the book of Nephi was made in spite of the fact that Mesoamericans never called their depictions of trees a "tree of life."[56] The identification has been made more on the basis of wishful thinking than upon an actual reading of the symbology of the stela. Mark Alan Wright explains some of the reasons that LDS authors have promoted a mistaken reading of the meaning of the stela:

---

[54] John E. Clark, "A New Artistic Rendering of Izapa Stela 5: A Step toward Improved Interpretation," 23.

[55] Among defenses of Stela 5 as the tree of life, see Joseph L. Allen, *Exploring the Lands of the Book of Mormon*, 118–28; Joseph L. Allen, *Sacred Sites: Searching for Book of Mormon Lands*, 22–23; Alan K. Parrish, "Stela 5, Izapa: A Layman's Consideration of the Tree of Life Stone," 125–50, and Diane E. Wirth, *A Challenge to the Critics: Scholarly Evidences of the Book of Mormon*, 65–75.

For a history of the discovery of the stela and its place in LDS thought, see Stewart W. Brewer, "The History of an Idea: The Scene on Stela 5 from Izapa, Mexico, as a Representation of Lehi's Vision of the Tree of Life," 13–21.

V. Garth Norman, "Stela 5," 740–44, presents a moderately toned defense of Stela 5 as a representation of Lehi's dream, noting that Clark disagrees.

[56] Mark Alan Wright, "'Tree of Life' or 'Cosmic Tree:' Stela 5 in its Ancient Mesoamerican Context," 5.

There is a common misconception held by many members of the Church that Lehi's vision of the Tree of Life is recorded on a stone monument known as Stela 5 from Izapa, Mexico. This misconception is based on poorly drawn versions of the monument that left out important details and included fabricated details that were never actually there. Mesoamerican art and writing are extremely detailed, and getting the details right is extremely important when it comes to offering correct interpretations. A seemingly minor difference in a depiction can often alter the meaning significantly. Tiny details in our own alphabet provide a nice analogy. Consider the minor differences between the lower-case letters i and j, or between b and d, or even the virtually indistinguishable lower-case letter l and the numeral 1. There are subtle differences, but they matter, and context is critical.[57]

The problem with the line drawings of the stela are directly related to the weathered condition of the stone. Early drawings were honest to what the artist could see. However, the New World Archaeological Foundation at Brigham Young University undertook a project to "finesse more details from the old stones by using new lighting techniques" according to John E. Clark.[58] The improved drawing provides details that enhance the "Mesoamericanness" of the representation but decrease the chances that this stela has anything to do with the Book of Mormon.[59]

---

[57] Ibid., 1.

[58] Clark, "A New Artistic Rendering of Izapa Stela 5," 23.

[59] V. Garth Norman, *Book of Mormon-Mesoamerican Geography: History Study Map*, 27 (no printed page number) presents Norman's reading of Stela 5 which elaborates on Jakeman's correlation to Lehi's dream. Norman does not believe that the New World Archaeological Foundation's new drawing is an accurate representation. Personal communication, October 2012.
Allen, *Sacred Sites*, 23:

> The above interpretation [linking Stela 5 with Lehi's dream] has not, however, been without its critics. Hugh Nibley and John Sorenson, both prolific Book of Mormon researchers, chided Jakeman for his enthusiasm. More recently, John Clark, field director of the New World Archaeological Foundation, presented what he considered to be a more accurate drawing of the stone. He then challenged its relationship to the Book of Mormon, considering it as being more relative to the Popol Vuh, an ancient document of the Quiché Maya in Guatemala.
>
> Conversely, LDS archaeologists Bruce Warren and Richard Hauck rejected Clark's commentary and reported that there are too many consistencies with Lehi's dream for it to be coincidental. According to Dr. Alan Christensen, who has presented an updated translation of the Popul Vuh, the style of writing in both the Book of Mormon and the Popul Vuh manifest the same exquisite style of Hebrew writing called chiasmus. This in turn may suggest a relationship with those two documents and Izapa Stela 5.
>
> While we may not be able to prove or disprove a firm relationship with Stela 5 and Lehi's dream, there are several things which are intriguing and perhaps even definitive. (1) the major standard of measurement on the stone, as discovered by V. Garth Norman, is the Biblical cubit, and (2) the style of writing on the stone, as discovered by Todd B. Allen, manifests Hebrew chiasmus.

Clearly, Allen is interested in maintaining Izapa Stela 5 as a correlation to the Book of Mormon. However, the reasons presented do not deal with the specific arguments about the elements on the stone. Warren and Hauck's opinion that there are "too many coincidences"

In addition to reading the symbols on this particular stela, it is important to read those same details as they appear on other stela from Izapa. In the overall context of the artistic production of the people of Izapa, the images fit that Mesoamerican and non-Book of Mormon context better than the hopeful reading of the single stela against the Book of Mormon.[60] Even though Izapa began around the time Nephites arrived in the New World, that timing is coincidence, not causality. Indeed, Clark notes that the site, a coastal location, is in the wrong place, since the Nephites fled inland from the Lamanites.[61] Perhaps the site might be considered Lamanite, but why would Laman or Lemuel commemorate a dream that prophesied negatively about them? Izapa Stela 5 is marvelous art, important for understanding the development of Mesoamerican ideology. It is not relevant to the Book of Mormon.

Shazer and the Failed Bows

The purpose of the first camp was to provide a base from which the family could prepare for their much longer journey. In addition to the very important missions to Jerusalem, they "did gather together whatsoever things we should carry into the wilderness, and all the remainder of our provisions which the Lord had given unto us; and we did take seed of every kind that we might carry into the wilderness" (1 Ne. 16:11). Four days later they "did pitch our tents again; and we did call the name of the place Shazer" (1 Ne. 16:13).

Virtually all researchers into the path of their journey understand that the only viable option was along what is known as the Frankincense Trail, a well-traveled merchants' path connecting the frankincense production of the Omani coast with the Near Eastern markets.[62] The trail was more a way than a marked road, at times being quite narrow but at others several miles across.[63] Nevertheless, it was absolutely defined

---

simply rehashes the correlation without dealing with the significant divergences of the iconography from the tree of life.

Concerning Allen's invocation of Dr. Christensen, Christensen has found chiastic structures in the Popol Vuh, but has not said anything of which I am aware about any connection to Izapa Stela 5. Allen sees what he calls chiastic structures in the scene which is the basis of his statement. Since chiasm is a literary device and Stela 5 is an artistic representation, it is unclear how bilateral symmetry and literary chiasms might be correlated.

[60] I have provided a more extensive analysis of the iconography of Stela 5 in Gardner, *Second Witness*, 1:163–69.

[61] Clark, "A New Artistic Rendering of Izapa Stela 5," 29.

[62] S. Kent Brown, "Jerusalem Connections to Arabia in 600 B.C.," 632–33: "According to the Old Testament, by far the largest number of contacts between people in Arabia and those in and around Jerusalem were of a commercial character. Jerusalemites enjoyed prized Arabian imports as diverse as incense, sheep, goats, and gems (see 2 Chronicles 17:11; Isaiah 60:6; Ezekiel 27:21–22). And most of the Old Testament references to this trade date to the era of Lehi and Sariah." See also Aston and Aston, *In the Footsteps of Lehi*, 4. Hilton and Hilton, *Discovering Lehi*, 20–21. George Potter and Richard Wellington, *Lehi in the Wilderness*, 54.

[63] Brown, "New Light from Arabia on Lehi's Trail," 83.

by the essential quality of linking one watering location to the next.[64] It is that universal necessity of water that assures us that Lehi and his family followed the Frankincense Trail. It was the only way that led from one water source to another.

The descriptions of Shazer allow conjecture as to its location, but no certainty.[65] It is certainly interesting that the family decided that they should name it ("we did call the name of the place Shazer," 1 Ne. 16:13). Nothing actually happens here, save that they leave the area to go hunting and then return, presumably with what they had killed (1 Ne. 16:14).

It is only after they continue, with the journey marked by two different times that Nephi notes the passing of many days (1 Ne. 16: 15, 17) that the next major event occurs. The family lost its ability to kill game. Unlike the successful hunting at Shazer, this time: "it came to pass that we did return without food to our families, and being much fatigued, because of their journeying, they did suffer much for the want of food" (1 Ne. 16:19).

Nephi introduces the crisis with a statement that he writes as though it would be easily understood. It isn't. "And it came to pass that as I, Nephi, went forth to slay food, behold, I did break my bow, which was made of fine steel; and after I did break my bow, behold, my brethren were angry with me because of the loss of my bow, for we did obtain no food" (1 Ne. 16:18).

His brothers' anger stemmed from the previous loss of their own bows: "Now it came to pass that I, Nephi, having been afflicted with my brethren because of the loss of my bow, and their bows having lost their springs, it began to be exceedingly difficult, yea, insomuch that we could obtain no food" (1 Ne. 16:21). For Nephi, the problems with the bows were secondary to the immediate problem of obtaining food. For modern readers the problem with the bows remains a problem of bows. How do bows lose "their springs" and how does a steel bow break?

William J. Hamblin, provides the background to understanding how a bow might lose its spring and why that would be a problem:

> Bows are delicate weapons that need special care and constant attention. Both medieval and modern archers recognized this fact. To lose its "spring" probably means that the bow had lost some of its elasticity and thereby its strength and efficiency. Longman describes this problem: "All bows will lose both cast [range] and strength if shot with many days running, and they will not recover if overshot. . . . Even in one day a bow will sometimes go down one or two pounds, . . . hot weather especially affecting them." Most

---

[64] Hilton and Hilton, *Discovering Lehi,* 10; Potter and Wellington, *Lehi in the Wilderness,* 62.
[65] Brown, "New Light from Arabia on Lehi's Trail," 77.
Richard Wellington and George W. Potter. "Lehi's Trail from the Valley of Lemuel to Nephi's Harbor," 30–31, describe their possible hypothesis about the location of Shazer. Of their work, Jeffrey R. Chadwick, "An Archaeologist's View," 73, says: "Upon reading their description of the location and features of the wadi Agharr, I was impressed. Their suggestion that it was Lehi's 'Shazer' seems to me remarkably plausible. If Shazer was not at Agharr, it has to have been at a place just like Agharr. Kudos to Wellington and Potter on this identification—they may just have it."

likely, this is precisely what happened to the bows of Nephi's brothers. The change in climate, the hot weather, and continual hunting progressively weakened the elasticity and draw weight ("springs") of their bows to the point that the bows had insufficient range and penetrating power for effective hunting.[66]

When a bow loses its "spring" it does not break, as did Nephi's bow. Rather it becomes less effective. Why do Laman and Lemuel's bows only lose their spring, but Nephi's bow actually breaks? To begin to answer that we need to understand what the text plausibly means when it calls Nephi's bow a "bow of steel."

Solid steel bows are known from India and medieval Europe, but date no earlier than the fourteenth century A.D.[67] It is unlikely that Nephi's bow was made entirely of steel. Rather than a literal description, the phrase "bow of steel" is probably based upon similar phrases in the King James Version of the Bible:

> He shall flee from the iron weapon, and the bow of steel shall strike him through. (Job 20:24)
> He teacheth my hands to war; so that a bow of steel is broken by mine arms. (Psalm 18:34 and 2 Sam. 22:35)

The translators of the King James Version have used "steel" anachronistically. The underlying words, *nechushah/nechosheth* should be translated as "bronze."[68] I hypothesize that Joseph Smith was influenced by the description in 2 Samuel of a steel bow breaking, because it fits the pattern of Joseph's reliance on biblical passages throughout the Book of Mormon text.[69] The text's description of what happened to the bows is accurate for a composite bow from that time period, but not for the anachronous "steel bow."

What was the King James Version's "steel" bow like? Hamblin tells us:

> From archaeological remains, it is clear that the Hebrew "bronze bow" was not made entirely of bronze but was a term that, as Roland de Vaux notes, "refers to the metal coverings of certain bows." Nephi's "steel bow" could thus likely be Joseph Smith's Jacobean English translation of an original Hebrew "bronze bow," referring to an ordinary wooden weapon decorated or reinforced in certain parts (usually the upper limb, nock, and grip) with bronze. This explanation is supported by the fact that Nephi's "steel" bow is said to have broken, a good indication that Nephi was not referring to a pure steel bow of the fourteenth-century-A.D. type, which would be essentially impossible to break by human muscle power alone.[70]

Still, how does such a reinforced bow break? Remember that the brothers' presumably fully wooden bows simply lose their springs while Nephi's "steel" bow actually breaks. Hamblin continues:

---

[66] William J. Hamblin, "The Bow and Arrow in the Book of Mormon," 374–75.

[67] Ibid., 373.

[68] Robert Young, *Young's Analytical Concordance to the Bible*, 933. See also Hamblin, "The Bow and Arrow in the Book of Mormon," 373.

[69] For an explanation of how this aspect of the translation operated, see Brant A. Gardner, *The Gift and Power: Translating the Book of Mormon*, 187–92.

[70] Hamblin, "The Bow and Arrow in the Book of Mormon," 373–74.

Obviously both self bows [made from a single piece of wood] and composite bows can break under a number of circumstances. However, composite bows have a specific structural problem that leaves them susceptible to changes in temperature and climate, which may cause the bow to warp and break. Taybugha, a fourteenth-century Arab master-archer, advised that "an archer should never neglect his bow for a single moment, and in extremes of temperature he should inspect it day and night, hour by hour." Such care in protecting a composite bow from warping is necessary because "the neck has a natural tendency to lateral displacement.... Should side-warping of this kind not be detected and the bow be drawn the defective limb will be subjected to a most severe twisting strain and possibly break."[71]

Lehi and his family left the more temperate Palestine, where the bow was probably made, to the more arid climate of the Arabian Peninsula, which would dry out the wood of the bows. They had recently left the "more fertile parts" and entered an area that was even drier.[72] This changing humidity would produce the very conditions that Hamblin suggests would warp a bow, creating the structural weakness that would cause Nephi's bow to break.

This isn't the end of the mystery of the bows, however. The text also very matter-of-factly indicates that in addition to making a new bow, Nephi also made a new arrow (1 Ne. 16:23). The text makes no mention of a problem with arrows, only with Nephi's bow. If his bow broke, we understand why he made a new one, but why does he also make an arrow? David S. Fox suggests:

> Consider what happens to an arrow at the instant the string is released: the full force of the drawn string is applied to the end of the arrow, trying to accelerate it, but also tending to bend or buckle the arrow. If the bow's draw weight and the arrow's stiffness are not perfectly matched, the arrow will stray off the intended course or fall short of the mark. An arrow that is too flexible will leave the bow with a vibration that can cause the arrow to behave erratically. On the other hand, an arrow that is too stiff is probably too heavy for the bow.
> Nephi's steel bow likely used heavier, stiffer arrows than his simply fashioned wooden bow could handle.... The arrows to match the steel bow used by such a man would undoubtedly have been quite heavy in order for them to be of adequate stiffness. One experienced archer reports, "The arrows from the steel bow when shot from the wooden bow would be like shooting telephone poles." Hence, it is accurate that Nephi should mention, in one and the same breath, the fact that he made an arrow as well as a bow. Bow wood and arrow wood from the same tree or area could be matched as well.[73]

The incident with the bows provides an interesting glimpse into the conditions that would have generated the descriptions of these bows in the Book of Mormon.

---

[71] Ibid., 374.

[72] Available information suggests that the humidity levels in Medinah, Saudi Arabia would be perhaps only half of that in Jerusalem. See "Meoweather: Weather History of Medinah, Al Madinah, Saudi Arabia." The data were for the month of February. Of course, the actual humidity varies and the differences in the Book of Mormon depend upon factors we cannot control, such as the humidity levels at that time and in the particular place that the Book of Mormon calls Shazer. It is presumably inland from the sea and therefore lower in humidity than would be the case in locations closer to the shore.

[73] David S. Fox, "Nephi's Bows and Arrows," 41–42.

The change in humidity provides the underlying cause for both the loss of springs in the wooden bows, and the reason that the steel bow would break. The nature of Nephi's replacement bow also explains the need to make an arrow, a brief but important detail mentioned in passing in the text.

The Place Which Was Called Nahom

Nephi's narrative of their journey concentrates most actions and descriptions around encampments rather than events during travel itself. Perhaps the journey itself was sufficient to occupy the family since it was during the encampments that they had the time for other situations to develop or at least come to a head. After the camp at Shazer, the next important narrative unit also involves a specific place:

> And it came to pass that we did again take our journey, traveling nearly the same course as in the beginning; and after we had traveled for the space of many days we did pitch our tents again, that we might tarry for the space of a time.
> And it came to pass that Ishmael died, and was buried in the place which was called Nahom.
> And it came to pass that the daughters of Ishmael did mourn exceedingly, because of the loss of their father, and because of their afflictions in the wilderness....
> And it came to pass that we did again take our journey in the wilderness; and we did travel nearly eastward from that time forth. And we did travel and wade through much affliction in the wilderness. (1 Ne. 16:33-35, 17:1)

At the previous named encampment, Nephi noted that: "we did call the name of the place Shazer" (1 Ne. 16:13). This time they stop: "in the place which was called Nahom" (1 Ne. 16:34). The distinction is important. Nephi tells us that this name was already associated with this location.

Modern LDS correlations between this place described in the Book of Mormon and a known location in Arabia date to 1987 when Ross T. Christensen discovered a seventeenth-century map of Arabia listing a location featuring the name "Nehhm."[74] Hilton and Hilton note: "Supplying the missing vowels as is customary in ancient Semitic languages, he believes it would have been pronounced NAHOM. When we visited the place in 1987 we confirmed that 'Nahom' was the name still used by the Bedouins of the area for the town and large surrounding valley."[75]

This might be the only specific location other than Jerusalem which ties the Book of Mormon account to a known place in the real world. Nevertheless, the reading of Nahom as NHM is problematic because of the /H/. In Semitic languages there are three different sounds all represented by the single English character, potentially creating three different words. Stephen D. Ricks notes: "Nahom as the realization of the southwest Arabian proper name *nhm* is eminently plausible. In the ancient Sabaean and Qatabanian dialects of southern Arabia, *nhm* is again the only root of the three possibilities that appears, with

---

[74] Ross T. Christensen, "The Place Called Nahom," 21.
[75] Hilton and Hilton, *Discovering Lehi*, 21.

meanings of 'pecked masonry' or 'stone dressing.'"[76] That meaning fits the region and the word, but not necessarily the context.

Hugh Nibley first suggested that the name "Nahom" might be as much symbolic as literal. It was the place where Ishmael was buried and where the women "did mourn exceedingly" (1 Ne 16:35).[77] Ricks hypothesizes:

> It is possible that the name *Nahom* served as the basis of a play on words by Lehi's party that Nephi recorded. Likewise, the Hebrew root *nhm*, meaning "to mourn" (but "to roar" in Isaiah 5:29–30), attested in Ezekiel 24:23 and Proverbs 5:11, may reflect the actions of the daughters of Ishmael in 1 Nephi 16:35, who did "mourn exceedingly." Thus, Book of Mormon *Nahom* could have an etymological connection to "to mourn, to groan," but the place-name *Nehem* of the Arabian Peninsula might have had a different etymology. Nahom is thus a striking fit as a Book of Mormon proper name based on archaeological, geographical, historical, and, to a lesser extent, on linguistic or etymological considerations.[78]

Noel B. Reynolds elaborated on this particular etymology:

> The Semitic name *NHM* occurs in Arabic and Hebrew texts as *Nahum, Naham, Nihm, Nehem*, and *Nahm*. Its roots indicate mourning, consoling, and complaining from hunger. The name fits perfectly the events that Nephi associates with Nahom:
> The daughters of Ishmael did mourn exceedingly, because of the loss of their father, and because of their afflictions in the wilderness; and they did murmur against my father, . . . saying: Our father is dead; yea, and we have wandered much in the wilderness, and we have suffered much affliction, hunger, thirst, and fatigue; and after all these sufferings we must perish in the wilderness with hunger. (1 Ne. 16:35)[79]

Appropriate to the possible play on words, the possible location of the Book of Mormon Nahom was an appropriate location for a funeral. Reynolds continues:

> Warren Aston has shown that the name *NHM* can be associated with this same area as early as the first century A.D. Because this area features an ancient burial ground that was actively used between 3000 B.C. and A.D. 1000 and is removed from places of settlement, it is not now known whether it was named for the Nihm tribe that has occupied the general area for centuries or whether the tribe took its name from the locality. What is known, however, is that the place name is unique in all the Middle East. Consistent with

---

[76] Stephen D. Ricks, "On Lehi's Trail: Nahom, Ishmael's Burial Place," 67.

[77] Nibley, *Lehi in the Desert*, 90–91.

[78] Ricks, "On Lehi's Trail," 67. Neal Rappleye and Stephen O. Smoot, "Book of Mormon Minimalists and the NHM Inscriptions: A Response to Dan Vogel," 176–78, discuss the issue of pronunciation and elaborate on the importance of word play in Semitic and Near Eastern texts.

[79] Noel B. Reynolds, "Lehi's Arabian Journey Updated," 380. See also Aston and Aston, *In the Footsteps of Lehi*, 12–19. Brown, *Voices from the Dust*, 38, repeats the general etymology: "In one of its forms, the root n-h-m in Hebrew—vowels do not appear in writing—has the basic verbal sense to growl or to groan, as in mourning. The other possible form of the verb, n-h-m, with a rasped h sound in the middle, means to comfort or to regret. Each of these meanings, of course, generally matches the events that overtook the family at 'the place . . . called Nahom,' what with the need to comfort those who were groaning or mourning because of the loss of Ishmael and because of unrelenting hardships."

this understanding of Nehem as a traditional burial ground, Nephi states that Ishmael was buried in Nahom, not that he died there.[80]

More importantly, since the Astons' work discovered a connection to the first century A.D., a new find has made the dating of the name and place even more precise. S. Kent Brown tells us: "From Nephi's language, it seems clear that 'the place' already carried a local name. Its general locale is now known. It lies south of the Wadi Jawf, a place known variously as Nihm or Nehem. Three votive altars, dated to the seventh or sixth centuries B.C., all attest to the antiquity of this tribal and regional name. In effect, these altars offer the first archaeological correlation to specific events noted in the Book of Mormon."[81]

The coincidence of the Book of Mormon name and that of a particular location in Arabia is interesting, but on that basis alone might only be a coincidence. The factors which elevate this particular location into a convergence are the simultaneous coincidences of timing (there was such a location/people during Lehi's lifetime, as indicated by the votive altars) and that it is in the correct location in the text's scarce geographic clues. That location becomes important in the Book of Mormon because it is right after their time at Nahom that Lehi's family takes a marked turn to the east. Brown describes this choice:

> Nephi writes that from "the place which was called Nahom. . . we did travel nearly eastward" (1 Ne. 16:34; 17:1). In fact, from the region of Nahom-Nihm, all roads turned east. Even the shortcuts across the Ramlat Al-Sabas'tayn desert, which connected to the incense trail north of Nahom-Nihm, ran east-west, connecting to Shabwah, which lay more than 200 miles east of Nahom and was the main center for gathering incense harvested in south Arabia. The caravan traffic out of Shabwah traveled westward to the general area of Nahom and then turned north to Najran. The party of Lehi and Sariah were traveling the opposite direction of the loaded camels of the caravans, an observation that helps to explain why some members of the party thought that they could return to Jerusalem even though at Nahom they were about 1,400 miles away (see 1 Ne. 16:36).[82]

Warren and Michaela Aston suggest that this turn at Nahom provides the strongest locational evidence for this Nahom-Nihm as the Nahom of the Book of Mormon. At this place, and at no other, do the various incense routes all turn east.[83] This combination of

---

[80] Ibid., 381.

[81] Ibid., 37. For more on the votive altars, see Warren P. Aston, "Newly Found Altars from Nahom," 57–61. Brown, "New Light from Arabia on Lehi's Trail," 82. See also S. Kent Brown, "'The Place That Was Called Nahom': New Light from Ancient Yemen," 68.

[82] Brown, *Voices from the Dust*, 39, essentially repeated on 43. Hilton and Hilton, *Discovering Lehi*, 137. Warren P. Aston, "The Arabian Bountiful Discovered? Evidence for Nephi's Bountiful," 7.

[83] Aston and Aston, *In the Footsteps of Lehi*, 22. See also (No author), "Lehi's Trail and Nahom Revisited," 47–48.

Rappleye and Smoot, "Book of Mormon Minimalists and the NHM Inscriptions," 179, note:
1. Both Nahom in the Book of Mormon and Nihm in Southern Arabia match in the following interlocking details:

Eastward to Bountiful

There were at least two ways that the trail turned eastward from the location which was called Nahom. One of those was the better traveled and the better supplied. The second was more dangerous not only for the terrain but for the hostile tribes that inhabited the area. Lehi's family took the more difficult road.

Although Nephi had earlier described difficulties on the trail (such as the incident of the broken bow), it appears that the last leg of the journey from Nahom to Bountiful was the most difficult. Nephi writes that "we did travel and wade through much affliction in the wilderness" (1 Ne. 17:1) and noted that they lived on raw meat (1 Ne. 17:2). To a modern reader, living on "raw meat" communicates great hardship. However, Nephi's purpose is to explain that they became accustomed to this new life and thrived: "While we did live upon raw meat in the wilderness, our women did give plenty of suck for their children, and were strong" (1 Ne. 17:2).

We need not visualize them gnawing at a freshly cut bloody haunch. The Arabs today still eat a spicy, raw, partially dried meat called "bastern" (literally, "raw meat").[84] Lehi's band probably consumed something similar on their journey. The point of the raw meat was not a descent into barbarism, but the undesirability of fire. A fire would have called attention to Lehi's party. Brown explains:

> In almost identical language, both Ammoron and Alma write of God's preserving Lehi's party from "the hands of their enemies" (Omni 1:6; Alma 9:10). Who were these enemies? According to the fuller part of Nephi's narrative, it was not anyone whom party members met between the first camp and Nahom. The most attractive possibility is that the group met such people on the leg of the journey between Nahom and the seacoast, even though Nephi himself does not mention enemies. . . . Such a view strengthens the impression that the toughest and longest period of the trip came between Nahom and the sea. Another piece that fits into this part of the trip is Nephi's note that party members had not made "much fire, as [they] journeyed," an evident attempt to avoid drawing the attention of marauding raiders (1 Ne. 18:12). As a final addition to the portrait, Alma seems to tie a recollection of ancestors who were "strong in battle" to Lehi's party, whom God "delivered . . . out of the land of Jerusalem" (Alma 9:22). If so, then we are to think that the party struggled against more than the harsh realities of the desert as they forged on toward the seacoast. That is, one of their biggest challenges may have come in dealing

---

2. Both are places with a Semitic name based on the tri-consonantal root NHM.
3. Both pre-date 600 BCE (implied in 1 Nephi 16:34).
4. Both are places for the burial of the dead (1 Nephi 16:34).
5. Both are at the southern end of a travel route moving south-southeast (1 Nephi 16:13–14, 33), which subsequently turns toward the east from that point (1 Nephi 17:1).
6. Both have "bountiful lands, consistent in 12 particular details, approximately east of its location (1 Nephi 17:4).

[84] Joseph L. Allen, *Exploring the Lands of the Book of Mormon*, 266.

with tribesmen whom they met. This impression, too, matches what we know of tribal troubles in this part of Arabia.[85]

Although Nephi gives very little description of this part of the journey, he nevertheless claims that "we had suffered many afflictions and much difficulty, yea, even so much that we cannot write them all" (1 Ne. 17:6). Brown notes that later Book of Mormon writers provide even more detailed descriptions of these times than Nephi did:

> Evidently, it was during this stage of the journey that the family "did not prosper nor progress in their journey, but were driven back" (Mosiah 1:17). We must observe in this connection that the later Nephite authors enjoyed access to the fuller account of this trek. They offer a few glimpses that Nephi's spare narrative does not. For instance, in the words of King Benjamin (died about 121 B.C.), "the ball or director" ceased to work, at least part of the time, because party members did not give "heed and diligence" to the Lord's commands. As a result, "they were smitten with famine and sore afflictions," incurring "the displeasure of God upon them" (1:17). In the words of Alma, because they "forgot to exercise their faith and diligence. . . they did not progress in their journey. . . or did not travel a direct course, and were afflicted with hunger and thirst (Alma 37:41–42; also 18:37–38).[86]

The geography of the turn eastward provides the explanatory backdrop for these increased difficulties. The descriptions of their travel suggest that they ceased to follow the more well-worn parts of the Incense Trail and began to travel in the borders of the Empty Quarter, a land which has earned its name. They had to deal with summer daytime temperatures of perhaps 125 degrees Fahrenheit. In addition to the heat and scarcity of water, constant winds would have been blowing, creating moving sand dunes and valleys. The ridges of the dunes typically run in a north-northeast to south-southeast direction, requiring Lehi's party to continually climb up and carefully descend the loose, hot sand. The dunes' wind-blown ridges can reach between 600 and 800 feet high.[87]

Perhaps these human and physical conditions are behind a terse statement about the nature of the Lehi's eight years in the wilderness: "And if it so be that the children of men keep the commandments of God he doth nourish them, and strengthen them, and provide means whereby they can accomplish the thing which he has commanded them; wherefore, he did provide means for us while we did sojourn in the wilderness. And we did sojourn for the space of many years, yea, even eight years in the wilderness" (1 Ne. 17:3–4). Brown further suggests: "The terms *to sojourn, to dwell,* and *to stay* often describe servile relationships in the Bible, a feature mirrored in the Book of Mormon."[88]

---

[85] Brown, "New Light From Arabia on Lehi's Trail," 91–92. See also Brown, *Voices from the Dust,* 43.
[86] Brown, *Voices from the Dust,* 44.
[87] Ibid., 44–45.
[88] Brown, *From Jerusalem to Zarahemla,* 55. See also S. Kent Brown, "A Case for Lehi's Bondage in Arabia," 205–17.

Brown notes that "sojourning" occurs only twice in Nephi's narrative and that the term appears during the eight years when the family was experiencing privations in the wilderness. The time spent in this region was longer than needed to cross the distance from Nahom to Bountiful, yet it takes a very long period of time for which Nephi provides only the sketchiest of accounts (see 1 Ne. 17: 1–6). Brown suggests that, when Nephi used the phrase "we did sojourn in the wilderness" (1 Ne. 17:3–4), he meant it in a specialized sense: "The expression *to sojourn* often means 'to live as a resident alien' in territory where one owns no property and has no family roots." Further, "in not a few passages throughout the Old Testament the verb definitely has the connotation 'to live as a subject'—be it as a resident alien, hireling, slave or inferior wife."[89] The connotations of "to sojourn" provide a plausible answer about how the Lehites managed to secure provisions for their arduous trek along the borders of the Empty Quarter.[90]

Bountiful after Privation

After eight years of struggling through harsh conditions, Nephi's prose may have been restrained when he wrote: "We were exceedingly rejoiced when we came to the seashore" (1 Ne. 17:6). The conditions of the seashore encampment were such that the family named it "Bountiful, because of its much fruit and also wild honey" (1 Ne. 17:5).

The seemingly anomalous description of a land of plenty on the Arabian Peninsula has at times been the subject of derision and dismissal of the Book of Mormon account.[91] In spite of the low expectations of finding such a "bountiful" location anywhere in the Arabian peninsula, there are multiple candidates for Bountiful in the general location where the text suggests that they should be: on the eastern seacoast, nearly directly eastward from Nahom.

Lynn and Hope Hilton were the first couple who attempted to traverse Lehi's trail, and their suggestion for Bountiful is Wadi Sayq along the coast of Oman. They note: "Dhufar, Oman is unique. There is no place like it along the extended shores of the Arabian peninsula. When irrigated, it is a verdant region [a] 'Shangri-la,' containing

---

[89] Ibid., 57. Brown quotes David Daube, *The Exodus Pattern in the Bible*, 24.

[90] Brown, *Voices from the Dust*, 42. Potter and Wellington, *Lehi in the Wilderness*, 64, suggest that the most probable commodity of exchange the Lehites possessed was their ability to read and write and which may have been the services that were offered or sold as the medium of exchange for provisions.

However, since this correlation rests entirely upon a particular English word, it is not as strong as it might appear. Vocabulary exists in the translation layer and has an indeterminate connection to the underlying text. In this case, the intent of the "sojourning" might be plausible, but as it is based upon the translation vocabulary, it cannot be considered a strong indication.

[91] Aston and Aston, *In the Footsteps of Lehi*, 28, note: "As recently as 1985 one [critic] made this comment about the Book of Mormon Bountiful: 'Arabia is bountiful in sunshine, petroleum, sand, heat, and fresh air, but certainly not in 'much fruit and wild honey,' nor has it been since the creation of time." They cite Thomas Key, *A Biologist Looks at the Book of Mormon*, 1–2.

gardens, palm trees, fruits, flowers and animal life, graced by groves of stately jumaise sycamore fig trees, adjacent to hills where the small Arabian cattle feed in natural grass that reaches their shoulders. Inland some twenty miles from this coastal area, the former well-protected, almost secret, groves of bus-sized frankincense trees still grow."[92]

Warren and Michaela Aston later made a similar journey, similarly suggesting Wadi Sayq. The coastal mouth of that valley carries the name Khor Kharfot ("Fort Inlet") upon which they focused their attention.[93] Potter and Wellington's even later examination called for a different candidate. While agreeing on the region, they disagree that the camp was at Khor Kharfot because they deem it inappropriate for the task of building a large ocean-going ship. Based on that need, they suggest Khor Rori in southern Oman.[94]

The Astons noted that the sole requirement they were unable to confirm was the presence of metal in the region.[95] That deficit was resolved by a team of geologists William Revell Phillips assembled in 1998. They examined the region for deposits of ore and found that, no matter which of the major candidates for Bountiful was the actual site noted in the Book of Mormon, Lehi's family would be within "a few kilometers of a usable deposit of good iron ore."[96]

Phillips later proposed yet another location for Bountiful. He notes: "I have read Lynn Hilton's case for Salalah, Warren Aston's support for Wadi Sayq, and Richard Wellington and George Potter in defense of Khor Rori. Each has a sound argument and may indeed represent the true Bountiful, but I plan herein to muddy the water with yet another candidate for Land Bountiful—Mughsayl."[97] When Phillips compares the possible locations for Land Bountiful he finds that most fit the overall parameters fairly well, save Wadi Sayq which has a difficult access from the interior.[98] Where his proposal differs from others is that it was Mughsayl was on the known Frankincense Trail and supported a population.[99] Phillips sees this as an advantage in the requirements to construct a ship.[100]

We have multiple plausible locations for Bountiful.[101] At this point, it is perhaps only academic to select one over the other. Each provides sufficient convergence between

---

[92] Hilton and Hilton, *Discovering Lehi*, 149. Inadvertent punctuation and spelling errors silently removed.

[93] Aston and Aston, *In the Footsteps of Lehi*, 43.

[94] Potter and Wellington, *Lehi in the Wilderness*, 139, 152. Jeffrey Chadwick, while critical of some of Potter and Wellington's correlations, nevertheless was impressed with their argument concerning the harbor at Khor Rori. Chadwick, "The Wrong Place for Lehi's Trail and the Valley of Lemuel," 199–200.

[95] Aston and Aston, *In the Footsteps of Lehi*, 55.

[96] William Revell Phillips, "Metals of the Book of Mormon," 36.

[97] William Revell Phillips, "Mughsayl, Another Candidate for Land Bountiful," 49.

[98] Ibid., 55.

[99] Ibid., 58.

[100] Ibid., 56.

[101] In 2008, Warren P. Aston defended his position in response to Phillips and others. See Warren P. Aston, "Identifying Our Best Candidate for Nephi's Bountiful," 58–64.

location and text that we may be confident that the text is accurately describing a real location, even though we cannot determine which real location it was.

Sailing to the New World

Yahweh allowed the family some respite from their difficult journey, but not much. Nephi records that it was after the "space of many days" that Yahweh commanded him to go up to a mountain for further instructions (1 Ne. 17:7). Having come to a seashore, it was perhaps not a complete surprise that the next command would be to sail to their next destination. Of course, prior to sailing there was the small problem of constructing the vessel in which they would sail.[102] For Nephi, it was the building of the ship that occupied his narrative much more than the details of sailing. It was another occasion to define himself as the rightful sovereign in the New World based on the preparations leading to their arrival.

Reading with concerns that differ from those that influenced what Nephi wrote, we are much more interested than Nephi in the details of the ocean crossing. How did they manage to sail from the east coast of the Sinai peninsula when prevailing winds typically blew the wrong way. How could they have traversed and survived that much open ocean? The answers are in some small details and in some unstated details.

Sailing from the coast of Oman requires specific combinations of atmospheric conditions. As Sorenson reports, "Navigation on the Indian Ocean remained in many ways the same from very early times until the development of steamships. Sailing there has always depended upon the monsoons. The word *monsoon* is from the Arabic *mawsim*, which literally means 'the date for sailing from one port in order to reach another.'"[103] The typical prevailing winds would not allow the journey during most months of the year.[104] However, during the monsoon season, the winds shift direction, blowing from the west, thus allowing for eastward travel.[105]

The next leg of the journey would be more difficult, because the prevailing winds do not change seasonally. How did Lehi cross the Pacific Ocean against prevailing winds for the remainder of his trip? Similar to the seasonal wind changes that allowed

---

[102] Noel B. Reynolds, "By Objective Measures: Old Wine into Old Bottles," 128–29:

> Oman, the likely location of Bountiful, has in the twentieth century been finally recognized for its ancient shipbuilding, a fact that allowed the ancient Omani to earn recognition as the Phoenicians of the Indian Ocean. . .
> Ancient Oman played an important role in early trade routes and, along with the city of Dilmun (probably situated on Bahrain Island to the north of Oman), served as an international center for trade by sea. Long before 600 B.C., their trade linked India, Persia, Mesopotamia, Africa, Egypt, and eventually China. In ancient times it was the natural location to build and launch a ship for a journey eastward into the Indian Ocean.

[103] John L. Sorenson, "Winds and Currents: A Look at Nephi's Ocean Crossing," 53. See also Aston and Aston, *In the Footsteps of Lehi*, 20. They are referencing Nigel Groom, *Frankincense and Myrrh* (London: Longman, 1981), 56.

[104] Aston and Aston, *In the Footsteps of Lehi*, 56.

[105] David L. Clark, "Lehi and el Niño: A Method of Migration," 57–58.

the Lehites to travel eastward during the monsoon season are climate cycles that would have allowed Lehi's family to cross the Pacific. In this case, they are much larger cycles related to the El Niño effect. David L. Clark suggests:

> If Lehi had sailed from the Arabian Peninsula during the August monsoon of an ENSO year, by the time his ship had been driven into the Indonesian area, El Niño would have intensified the eastward current, thereby enhancing the possibility of the voyage across the Pacific to the Western Hemisphere. The great increase in the strength of the eastward drift of the Equatorial Counter Current commonly affects a broad area of the equatorial Pacific and may extend more than ten degrees north and south of the equator. This ENSO-orchestrated eastward flow of abnormally warm water from the western and central Pacific could have helped the Lehi vessel to cross the Pacific and then travel up the coast of central America.[106]

While God could alter regional or even global climates, typically He acts more conservatively, using existing conditions in the world to accomplish his purposes. In this case, simply directing the party to leave around August would have placed them not only in a time of harvest, but also at the beginning of the monsoon season. Perhaps there was a divine reason for the eight years in the wilderness of which the family was unaware. Perhaps Yahweh was waiting for the climatic conditions that would enable the journey.

The text gives few details of the actual ocean crossing. This gives the impression that the journey was made in a single journey across the open ocean. That is not the likely scenario. Kelly DeVries points out:

> One of the most important aspects of premodern navigation is the need to resupply. Ships did not move fast, because they did not need to. But they did need to resupply. One could not carry enough water or food on board a ship to last an entire voyage.
>
> Most people's perception of Nephi's voyage is that his party boarded the ship and sailed straight to the New World. Nothing in-between. That's simply not the case. In fact, it doesn't seem logical they could have made the journey without stopping. Nephi would have needed to stop and resupply along the route, obtaining fresh water and food. However, there are parts of the journey where he could not have done so.
>
> We also know that in some ships of this time, cisterns were constructed by using the sails and allowing the rainwater to gather in the sails and then to be drained into amphorae, buckets, or other vessels that kept the water safe and away from salt water. This is one of the ways that Nephi was able to replenish his water supply for the journey.[107]

John Sorenson teases out certain implications in the scanty record:

> The most economical explanation of the course followed depends on the idea that the Lord typically uses natural forces familiar to us to accomplish his ends. In this case, he would have directed the party over a course where winds and currents would carry any vessel toward the intended spot in America with a minimum of miraculous intervention.

---

[106] Ibid., 60–63. Sorenson, "Winds and Currents," 54, cites Ben R. Finney, "Anomalous Westerlies, El Niño, and the Colonization of Polynesia," *American Anthropologist* 87, no. 1 (March 1985): 9–26, who suggests that the El Niño effect would allow migration from the Polynesian islands to the West.

[107] Kelly DeVries, quoted in *Journey of Faith: From Jerusalem to the Promised Land*, 91.

No doubt other seafarers would already have passed over certain legs of the same route, though probably not the whole of it.

Across the Indian Ocean the traditional course taken by sailing ships in premodern times followed near 15 degrees north latitude, which carried them straight east to the Malabar coast of India. From there they would round Sri Lanka (Ceylon) and sail east near 10 degrees north latitude to the Straits of Malacca and past the site of modern Singapore. Or they may have gone around the south and east coasts of Sumatra. One feasible course thereafter would wend between major islands of today's Indonesia to the Admiralty group north of New Guinea, thence past Tonga and through Polynesia near the Marquesas.[108]

Nephi's silence about the journey across the ocean is even greater than his terse account of eight years in the wilderness.

Nephi Ends a Book: Nephi Starts a Book

Nephi is the only Book of Mormon writer to create two books. Just as he called both sets of plates he had created "the plates of Nephi" (1 Ne. 9:2), he named his two books "The book of Nephi," causing Joseph (or perhaps Oliver) to find a way to give them differentiating names.[109] The words *first* and *second* are inserted supralinearly on the Printer's Manuscript of the Book of Mormon, indicating that they were added after the copy was made from the dictated original.[110] Noel B. Reynolds notes that there appears to be "no clear reason for dividing 1 Nephi from the first several chapters of 2 Nephi, as the latter book continues the same story."[111] His suggestion for the division is that Nephi thereby created two books with parallel structures.[112] While I

---

[108] Sorenson, *Nephite Culture and Society*, 54–55.

[109] Noel B. Reynolds, "Nephi's Outline," 54, suggests that they became known as the "plates of Jacob" following Jacob's custodianship. This is based on:

> And a hundredth part of the proceedings of this people, which now began to be numerous, cannot be written upon these plates; but many of their proceedings are written upon the larger plates, and their wars, and their contentions, and the reigns of their kings.
> These plates are called the plates of Jacob, and they were made by the hand of Nephi. And I make an end of speaking these words. (Jacob 3:13–14; emphasis Reynolds's)

That designation does not appear after that time. Nephi himself had simply called them "the plates of Nephi" (1 Ne. 9:2). I think it more likely that when Jacob referred to the "plates of Jacob" his intent was to identify the book of Jacob. It appears to have been correct that Nephi made the plates on which Jacob and his descendants wrote. That is the best explanation for why the writers eventually ran out of room on those plates (Omni 1:30).

My suggestion that Oliver might have been the source of the designation of *first* and *second* to differentiate the books of Nephi is speculation based on the evidence that there was no differentiation on the plates, and that in a parallel situation where there were no chapter numbers, it was Oliver who generated the chapter numbers.

[110] Royal Skousen, ed., *The Printer's Manuscript of the Book of Mormon*, vol. 2, part 1: 52, 143.

[111] Reynolds, "Nephi's Outline," 55.

[112] Ibid., 57.

Frederick W. Axelgard, "1 and 2 Nephi: An Inspiring Whole," 54, sees a different structure, but he has structures that cross the boundaries between the two books of Nephi:

agree that there are structural parallels, I suggest that there is a more obvious and important reason to create two different books. To understand the division between the books, we need to look more closely at how 1 Nephi ends.

The final historical event in 1 Nephi is the arrival in the New World. However, it is the way that event is presented in the text that matters to our understanding of what Nephi was thinking when he created a new book rather than a new chapter in the same book. When the Book of Mormon was dictated, and in the 1830 edition, 1 Nephi had only seven chapters instead of the twenty-two in every LDS edition since 1879. Our chapter divisions make a distinction between two paragraphs that were not intended to be separate:

> And it came to pass that we did find upon the land of promise, as we journeyed in the wilderness, that there were beasts in the forests of every kind, both the cow and the ox, and the ass and the horse, and the goat and the wild goat, and all manner of wild animals, which were for the use of men. And we did find all manner of ore, both of gold, and of silver, and of copper.
>
> And it came to pass that the Lord commanded me, wherefore I did make plates of ore that I might engraven upon them the record of my people. And upon the plates which I made I did engraven the record of my father, and also our journeyings in the wilderness, and the prophecies of my father; and also many of mine own prophecies have I engraven upon them. (1 Nephi 18:25–19:1)

It is not a coincidence that mentioning that they "did find all manner of ore, both of gold, and of silver, and of copper" should be followed by "wherefore I did make plates of ore."[113] This becomes the last historical event in his first book. What follows the discussion of the plates is a discourse on the ultimate purpose of the plates.

It is possible that Nephi also used the making of the plates to mark a conceptual shift from working from his father's record to his own remembrances. There is a seemingly anomalous introduction to the plates in 1 Nephi 9:2-5. It makes more sense if we can reconstruct Nephi's conceptual organization for this part of his record.

The search for an overarching framework in Nephi's writing produces three fundamental findings. First, they contain two primary divisions, one heavily historical and the other exclusively spiritual in content. Secondly, Nephi's historical section (1 Ne. 1–2, 2 Ne. 5) appears to have two subsections. A major portion of Nephi's family history is contained in 1 Ne. 1–18. In 1 Ne. 19–2 [through] 2 Ne. 5, Nephi brings in other prophets' writings (Isaiah, Zenock, Zenos, Neum, and Joseph) and focuses on spiritual matters with an intensity that suggests a transitional lead-in to his final, completely spiritual-prophetic segment. Third, Nephi's final section (2 Ne. 6–33) functions as a genuine conclusion. It is devoid of temporal references, contains a major review of Nephi's earlier prophecies, and ends with an outpouring of personal concern and doctrinal climax.

[113] Robert F. Smith, "The Golden Plates," 276, discusses the possibility that the plates delivered to Joseph Smith were an alloy of gold and copper known as tumbaga. The presence of both gold and copper in this list might therefore be significant for the creation of the plates. Silver, however, is not part of the alloy and therefore the correlation is tenuous.

Nephi declares: "Behold, I make an abridgment of the record of my father, upon plates which I have made with mine own hands; wherefore, after I have abridged the record of my father then will I make an account of mine own life" (1 Ne. 1:17). First, we should understand that, when Joseph used the word "abridgment" in his translation, our understanding of that word does not fit how Nephi used it. Nephi never simply copies his father's record or shortens it by careful editing. He consults that record, but unlike Mormon's use of sources, seldom clearly quotes from it.

We can infer when he stopped consulting his father's record by the nature of the division between chapter 9 and the beginning of chapter 10, corresponding to a division in the 1830 edition between chapters 2 and 3.[114] Chapter 9 ends with a very final "And thus it is. Amen" (1 Ne. 9:6). Chapter 10 begins: "And now I, Nephi, proceed to give an account upon these plates of my proceedings, and my reign and ministry; wherefore, to proceed with mine account, I must speak somewhat of the things of my father, and also of my brethren" (1 Ne. 10:1).

Reinforcing the plausibility that Nephi is using this break to shift from the record of his father to "an account. . . of my proceedings, and my reign and ministry," chapter 9 discusses the plates. Although this material has been separated into a different chapter in our current edition, in the 1830 edition it was concluding information that was part of chapter 2.

Nephi concludes a narrative unit by indicating "And all these things did my father see, and hear, and speak, as he dwelt in a tent, in the valley of Lemuel, and also a great many more things, which cannot be written upon these plates" (1 Ne. 9:1). Nephi has previously used "dwelt in a tent" as unit-ending marker (1 Ne. 2:15).[115] He adds that there is more to be said that "cannot be written upon these plates." We then get our first description of the creation of the small plates:

> And now, as I have spoken concerning these plates, behold they are not the plates upon which I make a full account of the history of my people; for the plates upon which I make a full account of my people I have given the name of Nephi; wherefore, they are called the plates of Nephi, after mine own name; and these plates also are called the plates of Nephi.
>
> Nevertheless, I have received a commandment of the Lord that I should make these plates, for the special purpose that there should be an account engraven of the ministry of my people.
>
> Upon the other plates should be engraven an account of the reign of the kings, and the wars and contentions of my people; wherefore these plates are for the more part of the ministry; and the other plates are for the more part of the reign of the kings and the wars and contentions of my people.
>
> Wherefore, the Lord hath commanded me to make these plates for a wise purpose in him, which purpose I know not. (1 Ne. 9:2–5)

Nephi's reference "as I have spoken concerning these plates," must refer to 1 Ne. 6:1–6. He doesn't reference their creation, but their dedication to "the things which are pleasing unto God" (1 Ne. 6:5). Comparing the function of the discussion of the

---

[114] Reynolds, "Nephi's Outline," 56.
[115] Gardner, *Second Witness*, 1:96, discusses "dwelt in a tent" in its literary function.

creation of the plates in both 1 Ne. 9:2-6 and 1 Ne. 19:1-6 suggests that in both cases they mark the ending of a historical section.

In 1 Nephi 1–9, Nephi tells his father's story, using his father's record. It is not a simple copy because Nephi also adds material from his own experience that could not have been on his father's record, such as the details of the brothers' attempts to retrieve the brass plates. Nephi concludes that section with a description of the making of the plates.

The next description of the making of the plates (1 Ne. 19:1–6) also ends the historical record of Nephi's Old World record, concluding with a prophetic reflection on the purpose of the small plates and a prophecy grounded in Isaiah. First Nephi is a book of the Old World background to the New World branch of Israel.

Although written as though no time passes between the two accounts, Lehi's blessing of his sons certainly comes at some point after the necessities of establishing themselves in the New World have been accomplished. Lehi's blessing establishes the future-looking perspective that will flavor 2 Nephi. Where 1 Nephi is heavily historical, 2 Nephi is heavily prophetic. Lehi's blessings establish the future perspective, and Nephi ends the book with a long prophetic exploration of the future of his people crafted from both references to Isaiah and Nephi's experience with the vision of the Tree of Life.[116] The only history as history comes in the description of the separation of the Nephites and the Lamanites, found in a single chapter—our Chapter 5, which was also a whole chapter in the 1830 edition.

Second Nephi is not only a book for the New World, but it is also a book of prophecy more than history. The entire concept behind 2 Nephi is markedly different from the models and structures that informed 1 Nephi. Nephi divided the two books for both the Old World/New World division and by the differing concepts that drove their content.

---

[116] See the explanation in ibid., 2:324–35.

5

Book of Mormon Geography in the New World

In the evening of Thursday, October 11, 1492, a sailor named Rodrigo de Triana spotted land.[1] Admiral Christopher Columbus had his three ships anchor for the night. The next morning Columbus stepped ashore on an island east of the Gulf of Mexico. Although Columbus's original logs are lost, Bartolomé de Las Casas had access to them when he wrote his history.[2] Thus we have the following record of this portentous occasion:

> Presently many inhabitants of the island assembled. What follows is in the actual words of the Admiral in his book of the first navigation and discovery of the Indies. "I," he says, "that we might form great friendship, for I knew that they were a people who could be more easily freed and converted to our holy faith by love than by force, gave to some of them red caps, and glass beads to put round their necks, and many other things of little value, which gave them great pleasure, and made them so much our friends that it was a marvel to see. They afterwards came to the ship's boats where we were, swimming and bringing us parrots, cotton threads in skeins, darts, and many other things; and we exchanged them for other things that we gave them, such as glass beads and small bells. In fine, they took all, and gave what they had with good will. It appeared to me to be a race of people very poor in everything. They go naked as when their mothers bore them, and so do the women, although I did not see more than one young girl. All I saw were youths, none more than thirty years of age. They are very well made, with very handsome bodies, and very good countenances. Their hair is short and coarse, almost like the hairs of a horse's tail. They wear the hairs brought down to the eyebrows, except a few locks behind, which they wear long and never cut. They paint themselves black, and they are the colour of the Canarians, neither black nor white. Some paint themselves white, others red, and others of what colour they find. Some paint their faces, others the whole body, some only round the eyes, others only on the nose."[3]

---

[1] *The Journal of Christopher Columbus and Documents Relating to the Voyages of John Cabot and Gaspar Corte Real*, 36.
[2] Ibid., iv.
[3] Ibid., 36–38.

On an unknown day of a year that can only be approximated to about 587 B.C., no one knows who first sighted land from the ship in which Lehi had his extended family sailed from the Old World to the New. That landing has been completely lost to secular history and would have remained so forever save for the miraculous translation of the Book of Mormon. Even more striking than the differences in the global importance of these two New World landings is the difference between the accounts. Columbus's journal provides significant details, including the names of the participants and descriptions of the natives they met. Nephi simply says: "And it came to pass that after we had sailed for the space of many days we did arrive at the promised land; and we went forth upon the land, and did pitch our tents; and we did call it the promised land" (1 Ne. 18:23). Nephi's remarkable lack of detail makes it difficult to know even where his family landed.

Columbus met natives upon making landfall, and surely Lehi's family did as well. Differences in the availability of people to meet the landing cannot explain the differences between the record we have from Columbus and that from Nephi. Perhaps the timing of the reports provides some explanation. Nephi is writing thirty to forty years after leaving Jerusalem (2 Ne. 5:28, 34). Although Columbus's account was not delayed for so long, the account nevertheless demonstrates that some time had passed between event and text. The passage of time is likely not the sole answer to the differences.

Most importantly, there is a factor that does help understand the differences. Felipe Fernández-Armesto notes that Las Casas worked from a source that may have been defective or garbled. At times Las Casas appears to "reflect his priorities rather than those of Columbus."[4] The real similarity between the two accounts is subtly related to the fact that both texts are specifically focused on the author's goals. Columbus's account is shaped by Las Casas, who according to Fernández-Armesto, was: "passionately committed to the vindication of the natives' rights and the accumulation of ethnographic material. Thus the direct quotations he has handed down from Columbus's journal fall mainly into two categories: pious invocations of the Deity . . . and material on the Indians, with very little else. Thus Las Casas tends to distort by selection and there is too little extra material in the *Histories* to make up a fully rounded picture."[5]

Nephi's account is similarly distorted, but through his own selection process rather than a later editor's. Las Casas's purpose in recounting Columbus's meeting was to present the New World natives in a favorable light. When Nephi wrote, he had a very different message for a very different type of audience. Nephi was living among the only people to whom he might have made an announcement. They already knew the story.

The real beginning for Nephites in the New World would be the creation of Nephi's community. Nephi spends very little time on the events between the landing and his exodus to the place that would be called the land of Nephi. We must tease

---

[4] Felipe Fernández-Armesto, *Columbus on Himself*, 38.
[5] Ibid., 30.

out details of where they landed and how they had sufficient people to form a new community from other sources.

Where in the World?

Wherever Lehi's party may have landed, they certainly entered a populated land. By the time Lehi and his family arrived, there is ample archaeological evidence of populations throughout most habitable areas. Prior to the time of the Jaredites, there is also ample archaeological evidence that there were populations throughout the habitable regions of both the North and South American continent. Wherever Book of Mormon peoples landed, whenever they landed, there were people already there.[6]

Where was this not so empty land? Nephi could not tell us where they were—he didn't know. At least, he didn't know in any terms that would make sense to his much later readers. He had left behind any geography to which he might have referred. The new world was defined only by its own context. Unlike reconstructing the Old World geography through which Lehi and his family traveled, no New World Jerusalem survived into historical times to guide our search.

Joseph Smith's contemporary Frederick G. Williams left a note indicating that Lehi's party "landed on the continent of South America in Chile thirty degrees south Lattitude."[7] While that idea was made even more influential when Orson Pratt included it in the footnotes for his 1879 edition of the Book of Mormon, there was at least one other interpretation. An 1842 *Times and Seasons* editorial suggests that the party landed a little south of the Isthmus of Panama.[8] This location plausibly represents Joseph Smith's position at the time, although the editorial was unsigned.[9]

---

[6] Jared Diamond, *Guns, Germs, and Steel: The Fates of Human Societies*, 44–45. K. Kris Hirst, "How Were the Americas Populated? Kennewick Man, Part 4."

[7] Frederick G. Williams, "Did Lehi Land in Chilé?" 57. Author Williams is a descendant of Joseph's contemporary, for whom he was named. Although Williams's article attempts to disassociate this idea from Joseph Smith, it is nevertheless quite likely that it was a popular option. Matthew Roper, "Nephi's Neighbors," 36, cites a newspaper article from 1830: "Eight months after the publication of the Book of Mormon, an Ohio reporter described the teachings of Oliver Cowdery and his companions as they stopped in Ohio on their way to Missouri: 'This new Revelation, they say is especially designed for the benefit, or rather for the Christianizing of the Aborigines of America; who, as they affirm, are a part of the tribe of Manasseh, and whose ancestors landed on the coast of Chili 600 years before the coming of Christ, and from them descended all the Indians of America.'" Roper's source is A. S., "The Golden Bible, or, Campbellism Improved," *Observer and Telegraph* (Hudson, Ohio), November 18, 1830. The photocopy of this document is very difficult to read. I was able to find and read the quotation in the source. The transcription is available on the same web page.

[8] Williams, "Did Lehi Land in Chilé?" 57.

[9] Roper, "Nephi's Neighbors," 77. See pages 81–83 for stylometric analysis of some 1842 unsigned editorials. The results indicate that Joseph Smith is the likely author of some, but there is some evidence for collaborative efforts in others. Nevertheless, all indicate Joseph's participation.

Nevertheless, it is unlikely that either of these statements represent a prophetic declaration.[10] The subject appears to have been open to speculation.[11]

To discover where Nephite history unfolded we must attempt to reconstruct geography from textual clues that can be teased from events when the record keepers were telling us something else entirely. Unfortunately, those clues have proven so flexible a standard that although most readers expect that the promised land was somewhere in the western hemisphere, one proposal suggested it could have been Malaysia.[12] Some geographies have concentrated so much on the lay of the land that they have ignored the people who lived on that land.[13]

How might we begin? In his book *Mormon's Map*, John L. Sorenson suggests: "To start at the beginning seems like a good plan in solving any problem. The beginning in addressing Book of Mormon geography is the text of the Book of Mormon itself. . . . Whatever the Book of Mormon says about its own geography thus takes precedence over anything commentators have said."[14] Sadly, even that guide has been inconclusive.

---

[10] John L. Lund, *Mesoamerica and the Book of Mormon: Is This the Place?* 23, accepts the 1842 *Times and Seasons* editorial as Joseph's firm identification of the landing place.

[11] Matthew Roper, "Limited Geography and the Book of Mormon: Historical Antecedents and Early Interpretations," 225–76, discusses the evidence for multiple opinions about the relationship of the Book of Mormon to a known geography.

[12] Ralph A. Olsen, "A Malay Site for Book of Mormon Events," 30–33. For an analysis of this hypothesis, see Brant A. Gardner, "Testing a Methodology: A Malaysian Setting for the Book of Mormon." Olsen's more complete argument is Ralph A. Olsen, *The Malay Peninsula as the Setting for the Book of Mormon*.

[13] Perhaps the most difficult geographies to accept are those that require extensive changes to land masses during historical times. Venice Priddis, *The Book and the Map: New Insights into Book of Mormon Geography* resolves geography by appealing to massive changes of lands rising from the ocean during historical times (9–20). She suggests that the Amazon basin was a lake and that a sea covered the lands south, creating a complete separation of the Pacific coast of South America from the Atlantic coast. John L. Sorenson, *The Geography of Book of Mormon Events: A Source Book*, 161, describes the Priddis geography: "At the time of the crucifixion, within three hours Tiahuanaco rose 3400 feet above its previous level, southern Chile emerged from the ocean's bottom, and previously submerged Panama rose above the surface of the oceans; however, Zarahemla and the Sidon River remained unchanged." Quite apart from the geological impossibility of such changes occurring within three hours, archaeology clearly indicates living populations in places such as Panama during times when this model would have that location under water.

Cecil G. Le Poidevin, *Zion, Land of Promise: An Atlas Study of Book of Mormon Geography*, similarly has the Amazon basin flooded to create a much narrower land mass for Book of Mormon lands. This is seen in multiple maps, beginning with the map on page 16.

[14] John L. Sorenson, *Mormon's Map*, 9. John L. Sorenson, *Mormon's Codex: An Ancient American Book*, 17: "A typical investigator peruses a map of the Americas, finds what he or she intuits to be a correlation, then proceeds to select from the Book of Mormon statements thought to support his correlation of choice. But a valid geography must do more than this. In order to have a realistic hope of establishing a real-world location for the Book of Mormon events, one must reconcile *everything* the text says or implies about geography."

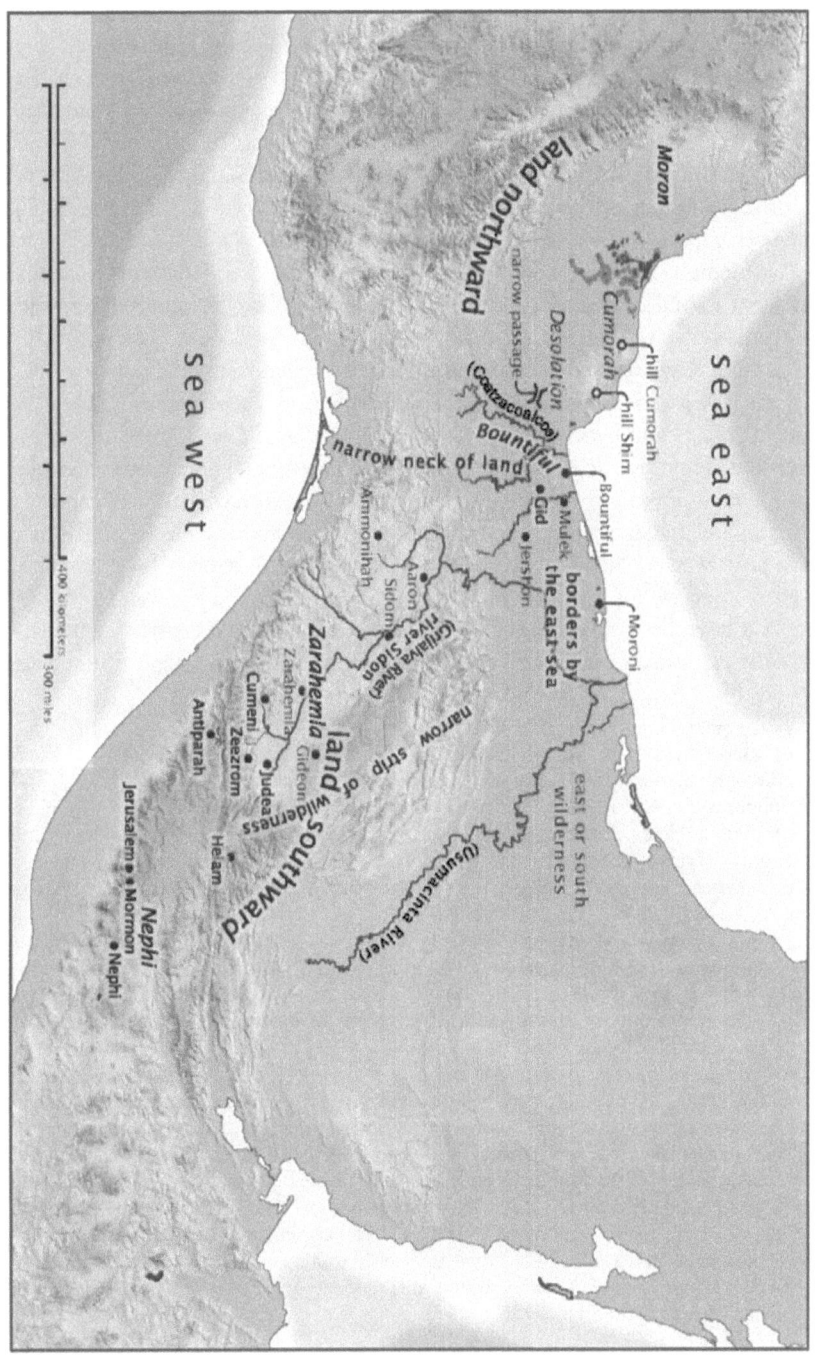

Figure 3: Mesoamerica and the Book of Mormon

Nevertheless, of the myriad possible geographies, there is a growing consensus among scholars with training in history, archaeology, and anthropology, that the Book of Mormon likely took place in a geographic and cultural region known as Mesoamerica (stretching from central Mexico to El Salvador and Honduras on the south).[15] Rather than repeat the arguments for looking at Mesoamerica, I will simply state my agreement with that consensus. My work supports the overall usefulness of the model John L. Sorenson proposes, particularly in his most recent version.[16]

In Sorenson's model, Lehi's party landed on the west coast of Guatemala. Sorenson arrived at that location by back-tracking from more solid geographic information about other reconstructible locations in the Book of Mormon.[17] With this landing place, we can provide some of the detail that Nephi did not.

Frederick Joseph Bové surveyed the archaeological sites along the Guatemalan coast for the period between 750 B.C. and 500 B.C. and found "a total of 12 sites consisting of 6 primary centers, 2 secondary, 3 tertiary, [and] one fourth order place. Development of primary centers near the coast occurs with one primary center, . . . 17 km inland and another, . . . only 3 km from the shoreline."[18] The populations of these centers might have ranged from 75 households to perhaps 1200 households based on comparisons with data from the Valley of Mexico.[19] However, the numbers may also have been much lower based on archaeology from coastal Guatemala.[20] Nevertheless, these estimates place enough people living in eyesight of the watery

---

[15] A good overview of the various theories is Stephen L. Carr, "A Summary of Several Theories of Book of Mormon Lands in Mesoamerica."

[16] Sorenson, *An Ancient American Setting of the Book of Mormon*, 1–48, lays out the basics of the correlation. Here he appears to support a Pacific crossing for the Jaredites. More recently, Sorenson, *Mormon's Codex*, 119–43, provides his most recent thinking on the geographic correspondences between the Book of Mormon text and Mesoamerica. He now sees an Atlantic cross, with which I agree (27).

[17] Sorenson, *An Ancient American Setting for the Book of Mormon*, 138–39. Note that while Sorenson creates a landing place based on other criteria, he nevertheless states it with a precision that echoes the Frederick G. Williams statement: "Nephi's ship likely threaded through the islands of the western Pacific, then across the open reaches north of the equator to landfall around 14 degrees north latitude" (138).

Lund, *Mesoamerica and the Book of Mormon*, 23, accepts Joseph Smith as the author of the 1842 designation of a landing site a little south of the Isthmus of Panama. Accepting that "Joseph Smith is an unimpeachable source" (11), the Nephites would then have journeyed to what is now Highland Guatemala. This is a distance of perhaps over 1,000 miles, or the driving distance between Arizona and Wisconsin. Lund understands that there isn't much logic in that conclusion: "I have often wondered why they didn't settle where they first landed near Panama, and why the Lord did not have them sail directly to the Land of First Inheritance?" (25). His overriding geographical imperative is to follow statements deemed to come directly from Joseph Smith.

[18] Frederick Joseph Bové, "The Evolution of Chiefdoms and States on the Pacific Slope of Guatemala: A Spatial Analysis," 302.

[19] Ibid., 80–81.

[20] Joyce Marcus, "The Size of the Early Mesoamerican Village," 85–86.

horizon that an approaching sail would have been noticed; if noticed, then carefully watched; if watched, then met. The Lehite interaction with other peoples in the land began when they made landfall.

Which Sidon River?

Sorenson's correlation between the Book of Mormon and a Mesoamerican geography uses the Grijalva River as the Book of Mormon's River Sidon. It is not the only possible choice for the Sidon that would provide a Mesoamerican setting for the Book of Mormon, and other LDS authors have suggested that the Usumacinta River should be used as the identifiable river that would have been called the Sidon.[21] Both have their headwaters in the Cuchumatanes mountains.[22] The Grijalva is west of the Usumacinta. The Grijalva and the Usumacinta rivers are sufficiently close together, running a sufficiently parallel path into the Gulf of Mexico, that if the Book of Mormon took place in that region we must ask why the text mentions only one river.

There are two answers to that question. First, the absence of a second major river in the text strongly suggests that the Book of Mormon lands are indeed limited—and limited in such a way that the second river did not figure in any significant event in Nephite history. The second answer is much more important. It is probable that the second river does make an unnamed appearance in the Book of Mormon.

---

[21] Sorenson, *Mormon's Codex*, 21–22: "The only two Mesoamerican rivers proposed so far that might qualify as the Sidon are the Usumacinta and the Grijalva, both located in southern Mexico and part of Guatemala. However, the proposal involving the Usumacinta River runs into problems—distances, lack of archaeological sites of the right age and type, and types of terrain—that rule it out."

For proponents of the Usumacinta, see the following:

V. Garth Norman, *Book of Mormon Geography—Mesoamerican Historic Geography*. A graphic of the map is available at his website: V. Garth Norman, "The Definitive Mesoamerican Book of Mormon Lands Map." A review of this geography is Lawrence L. Poulsen, "'The Light is Better Over Here,' Review of 'Book of Mormon Geography—Mesoamerican Historic Geography' by V. Garth Norman," 11–20.

F. Richard Hauck, *Deciphering the Geography of the Book of Mormon: Settlements and Routes in Ancient America*, 121. John E. Clark, "A Key for Evaluating Nephite Geographies: Review of F. Richard Hauck, Deciphering the Geography of the Book of Mormon," 20–70. See also William J. Hamblin, "A Stumble Forward? Review of F. Richard Hauck, Deciphering the Geography of the Book of Mormon: Settlements and Routes in Ancient America," 71–77. Jerry L. Ainsworth, *The Lives and Travels of Mormon and Moroni*, 81. See also Jerry L. Ainsworth, "Response to Allens' [sic] Article on River Sidon." Kirk Magleby, "Book of Mormon Model."

[22] Joseph E. Vincent, "Some Views on Book of Mormon Geography," notes an interesting division in the proponents of each river: "The archaeology department of BYU has thought that the Rio Usumacinta was the River Sidon, while members of the New World Archaeological Foundation have felt that it was the Rio Grijalva."

126 Traditions of the Fathers

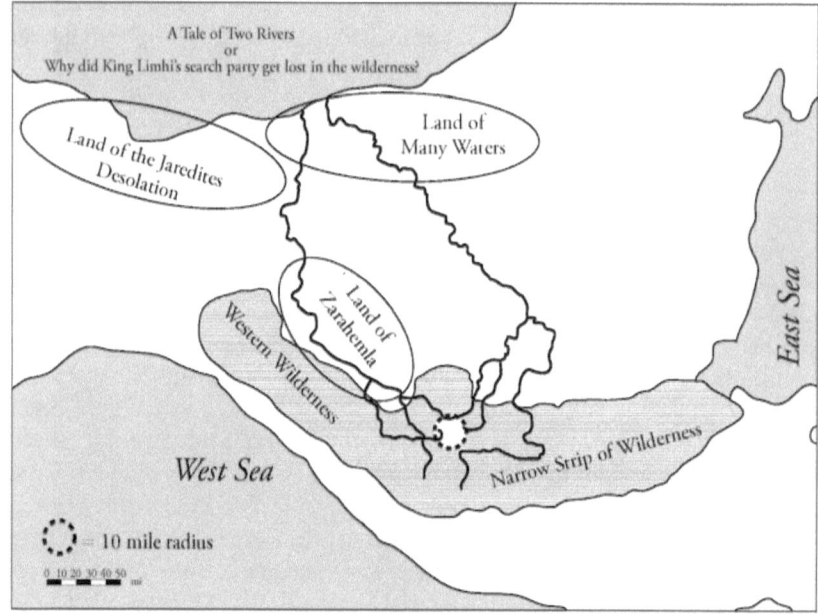

Figure 4: Limhi's expedition and two rivers

The presence of a second, nearly parallel, river explains an otherwise enigmatic Book of Mormon event. During the oppression of his people, king Limhi of Lehi-Nephi sent a party to petition the Nephites in Zarahemla for assistance:

> And the king [Limhi] said unto [Ammon]: Being grieved for the afflictions of my people, I caused that forty and three of my people should take a journey into the wilderness, that thereby they might find the land of Zarahemla, that we might appeal unto our brethren to deliver us out of bondage.
>
> And they were lost in the wilderness for the space of many days, yet they were diligent, and found not the land of Zarahemla but returned to this land, having traveled in a land among many waters, having discovered a land which was covered with bones of men, and of beasts, and was also covered with ruins of buildings of every kind, having discovered a land which had been peopled with a people who were as numerous as the hosts of Israel. (Mosiah 8:7–8)

Limhi's grandfather, Zeniff, left Zarahemla and returned to the land of Nephi to establish a city in what had been his homeland. (This story is recounted in Omni 1:27–29 and more fully in Mosiah 9:1–9.) Perhaps most or even all of the first generation had died, but there were surely plenty of the second generation who could pass on instructions from those who had come from Zarahemla to the former land of Nephi. The instructions certainly mentioned finding and following the Sidon, as Zarahemla was located along that river. How could Limhi's ambassadorial party get so lost that they not only missed Zarahemla but arrived in a land containing the Jaredite remains?

The easiest explanation is that the headwaters of the Grijalva and the Usumacinta are in the same mountain range (the Cuchumatanes) and the headwaters are within twenty miles of each other.[23] The ambassadorial party got lost because it followed the wrong river.[24] The Usumacinta (as well as the Grijalva) empties into lands that had been occupied by the Olmec, considered to be the plausible culture into which the Jaredites merged after their arrival. Thus, the best understanding of this event would be that the search party followed the wrong river to its end and arrived in lands that had been occupied by a Jaredite population. An otherwise problematic story becomes quite understandable when read against this geography.

Of course, this explanation still works if they had followed the Grijalva as the wrong river.[25] The story tells us that there are two rivers, but it doesn't, by itself, tell us which of the two rivers is the Sidon. Lawrence L. Poulsen has done extensive work with modern three-dimensional maps in his search to understand the geography of the Book of Mormon. After carefully examining the texts related to the Sidon in the Book of Mormon and comparing those requirements to the two possible rivers in the Mesoamerican region (the Grijalva and the Usumacinta), he concludes:

> From its source in the Sierra Los Cuchumatanes mountains to its mouth in the Gulf of Mexico, the Grijalva river matches the descriptions of the river Sidon found in the text of the Book of Mormon. Although the Grijalva River runs south to north over most of its course, it has segments that run East to West (Alma 22:27) and other segments which run

---

[23] Poulsen, "Tale of Two Rivers."

[24] Poulsen first pointed this out to me. It was immediately apparent when he simply asked how they got so lost. Of course, he only asked because he already knew the answer, but the answer was so obvious that I was surprised that no one had noticed it before. I have seen the idea discussed after Poulsen's work, but I do believe that he should have credit as the first to make the connection.

[25] John P. Pratt, "Mormon's Map Puzzle Solved?" uses this story to suggest that the Usumacinta was the Sidon and that the "wrong river" they followed was the Grijalva. His reason is: "The destroyed city they found was in, or beyond, the narrow neck of land, in the part of the Land Northward later called Desolation, which was separated from Bountiful in the Land Southward by the Narrow Neck (Alma 22:30–32)." Using a map that locates the Olmec north of the Isthmus of Tehuantepec would indicate that it is much easier to explain how they left the Grijalva and traveled even further through the Isthmus of Tehuantepec to end up in ancient Olmec lands. Following the Usumacinta would have made that even more difficult.

The logic of this explanation is entirely dependent upon two suppositions. The first is that there were never any Jaredite remains in the land southward. The second is that the Jaredites and the Olmec are assumed to be identical, so that any Olmec ruin that appears to be important must have been Jaredite. That assumption places much Jaredite action northwest of the Grijalva, making it easier to understand how the ambassadorial party could have found those particular Jaredites. Archaeology makes it clear that the ambassadorial party could have found Olmec or epi-Olmice remains along the plains surrounding the last stretch of the Usumacinta.

Another issue with this theory is that, if the Usumacinta were the Sidon, then as the Nephites moved toward the narrow neck of land (the Isthmus of Tehuantepec in the Mesoamerican hypothesis), it would be difficult to understand how there could be no mention of the second large river blocking their way. Of course, if the Grijalva were the Sidon, the second river would be outside of the typical action in the Book of Mormon, yet another reason for selecting the Grijalva.

southeast to northwest (not explicitly mentioned in the Book of Mormon). It is a twisty mountain river with many turns, some quite sharp, and would certainly have been able to carry the bodies cast into it out to the sea (Alma 3:3 and Alma 44:33). The Usumacinta, however, from its source that runs from west to east and south to north, does not appear to match. In addition the Usumacinta runs for most of its course through the lowlands emptying into an area of extended floodlands near the Gulf of Mexico making it too slow to be able to carry bodies out to sea.[26]

In addition, the Grijalva has a feature that appears to fit another specific story in the Book of Mormon. John L. Hilton and Janet F. Hilton examined the sequence of battles in Alma, noting an important correlation between a fordable river and a hill that the text names Amnihu. In their exploration of the Upper Grijalva, they found:

> Coming down the river into the open valley area, one can see an unusual hill sufficiently separated from the other hills. This spectacular landmark with its unusual double column of limestone rock rising perhaps 20 or 30 meters above the hill base is located just on the east side of the river. Immediately downstream from the hill is a valley, which could correspond to the valley of Gideon, suggesting that this landmark hill might fit as the ancient Nephite hill Amnihu, which lay across the river and likely a little upstream of the city Zarahemla (Alma 2).
>
> The hill Amnihu would have to have been sufficiently different from other nearby hills that during his secret negotiations with the Lamanite king, Amlici could have identified it by description as a rendezvous area for the incoming Lamanite forces sent to join Amlici's rebel army in what turned out to be a very bloody, abortive attempt at a military coup....
>
> [From the top of the hill] the view of the river and large valley was very impressive and subjectively seemed to compare to what we expected as a candidate area for the city Zarahemla. A native was net-fishing near the middle of the river with water below his waist; he apparently needed no dugout to cross this location during this low-water time of the year (i.e., May 1992).[27]

Of course, this description by itself is less than a certain identification. Nevertheless, it is important that such a potential location exist. Taken as a whole, the three-dimensional features of the Grijalva river nicely correlate with the requirements of the text in ways that the Usumacinta does not. That convergence of text and physical location strengthens the case for the Grijalva as the Book of Mormon river Sidon. The addition of plausible details such as a candidate for hill Amnihu close to a ford on the northern section of the river becomes part of the several aspects of the river that point to the Grijalva as the Book of Mormon Sidon.[28]

---

[26] Poulsen, "The River Sidon."

[27] John L. and Janet F. Hilton, "A Correlation of the Sidon River and the Lands of Manti and Zarahemla with the Southern End of Rio Grijalva (San Miguel)," 157–58. Mesoamerica has two seasons, a rainy and a dry season. The dry season lasts for months, and therefore the rivers would run lower during the dry season. That would also be the typical season for warfare as that would be when the pathways would be dry and more readily passable. That fits with a battle requiring a fordable river. Having one available in the dry season matches well with the textual requirement. It need not be fordable at all times.

[28] Ibid., 142–62, and Poulsen, "The River Sidon," have increased the detail of the suggested correlation between the Sidon and the Grijalva River.

These physical details will dovetail with the cultural information to provide an even stronger argument for locating Book of Mormon events in this river valley.

Locating the Sidon is important not only for understanding a major geographical feature of the Book of Mormon but because locating the Sidon also locates the land of Zarahemla. Knowing where Nephite history occurred in real-world terms points us to the proper archaeological data to begin to understand whether that particular information will converge with the descriptions of history in the Book of Mormon. In this case, deciding for the Grijalva also resolves language and cultural conflicts described in the text in ways that the Usumacinta-as-Sidon cannot. (See "Merging Peoples in Zarahemla," in Chapter 8).

Directions in the Book of Mormon[29]

Although Sorenson's geographic correlation has proven highly productive, one aspect of the correlation remains problematic. Deanne G. Matheny explains:

> The most fundamental geographical problem associated with Sorenson's model has to do with issues of directionality. . . . In order for his model to fit the geography of Mesoamerica, one must assume that the Nephites had a system of directions with cardinal directions skewed "45 degrees or more" off of the usually observed cardinals. . . . In other words, the whole directional card must be shifted more than 60 degrees to the west for this model to fit the geography of the chosen area. Otherwise, as Vogel has pointed out, the land north will be on the west, and the south on the east, and so forth. . . . Making this shift in directions creates its own set of problems, however, because in such a Nephite directional system the sun would come up in the south and set in the north.[30]

These are serious considerations. How could Nephites possibly think that the sun would come upon in the south and set in the north? They couldn't. Yet we have a geographic correlation that fits both real world geography and cultural history

---

[29] This paper was published as Brant A. Gardner, "From the East to the West: The Problem of Directions in the Book of Mormon." It appears here with slight modifications.

[30] Deanne G. Matheny, "Does the Shoe Fit? A Critique of the Limited Tehuantepec Geography," 277. Perhaps the most important criticism of Sorenson's model has been the variance from cardinal directions. Doug Christensen, posted to Book of Mormon Archaeological Forum Group, Facebook:

> Despite the differences, there is almost unanimous agreement among scholars that Sorensen's so called "Nephite North" which is required in order to make his model work, unnecessarily muddies the picture. . . .
>
> Joseph and Blake Allen recently responded to an inquiry about the Sorenson model. Their answer is typical of the current thinking of most LDS scholars: "We don't feel that there is any strength to the idea of a rotated map. Sorenson pursued the hourglass concept and then superimposed it on a Mesoamerican map, thereby proposing a shift in Nephite directions from the standard cardinal directions, rotating the map and calling the result by the name of "Nephite north."
>
> This theory has received an abundant amount of negative criticism, as there is no evidence from either the Book of Mormon or Maya culture that hints at a directional shift.

remarkably well—except when we come to the terms north, south, east, and west.[31] I propose that if Mesoamerica is a good fit for the Book of Mormon's real-world geography, then information about Mesoamerica may be used to reexamine and refine the nature of that fit.[32] In short, an understanding of the Mesoamerican directional system offers an explanation for the way that Book of Mormon directions correspond to that geography, without recourse to an artificial shift in the directions.

The Mesoamerican Directional System

Scholars have found a very similar directional system among the various Mesoamerican cultures. Much of the data come from the Maya cultures because the ability to translate the carved and painted texts provides a unique view of pre-contact culture currently unavailable for any other Mesoamerican people. Nevertheless, what may be more carefully worked out in the Maya data has sufficient corroboration in data from other cultures to depict an essentially pan-Mesoamerican orientation system.

The Mesoamerican system is not a replica of our Western understanding of directions, even though it is often described using Western directional terms. While both systems are used to describe the real world and share some base characteristics, there is an incomplete overlap in meaning between the two systems. That incomplete overlap in meaning is too often hidden when we use the terms from the Western system of cardinal directions to describe the Mesoamerican system. This is not to suggest that Mesoamericans did not locate a "pure" direction as we do. Both systems are ultimately based on real-world conditions, such as the rising sun. It is a difference in the range of meaning that is covered when a particular direction is used.

To begin with, unlike our four cardinal directions, the Mesoamerican system had five "directions." Four have similarities to our north, south, east and west, but the fifth "direction" was the center, which has no Western counterpart. To our Western understanding, the center doesn't seem like a direction, but it was nevertheless a very important part of the Mesoamerican method of orientation in the world. David Freidel, Linda Schele, and Joy Parker describe this concept for the Maya:

---

[31] The cultural data have been sufficiently impressive that other LDS authors have attempted to retain the basic culture area, but find a way to correlate the geography with the cardinal directions rather than Sorenson's necessary shift of the Nephite cultural north. See Dee Stoddard, "'From the East to the West Sea' An Analysis of John L. Sorenson's Book of Mormon Directional Statements."

[32] John L. Sorenson, "Viva Zapato! Hurray for the Shoe!" 305, notes: "This supposed 'standard scheme' [cardinal directions] is actually a mental artifact of Western European culture developed largely since the rise of the compass and of science not many centuries ago." Sorenson's defense of his understanding of directions is based on appropriate anthropology. The refinement suggested here is the result of a more specific application of the Mesoamerican data. However, an important point of difference is Sorenson's belief that "aside from whatever these translated words for directions denoted in relation to the natural world, their use in the language of the Nephites does not seem to show that they paid prime attention to the sun's rising or setting" (308). I will examine the evidence that the Nephite terms are based on a prime attention to the path of the sun.

Just as the gods marked the periphery by placing the four sides and corners around the center, the Maya shaman creates a five-part image to sanctify space and open a portal to the Otherworld. Mayanists have adopted the Latin word *quincunx* for this five-point-plan concept, although the Maya have many ways of expressing it in their own languages. The discerning of the four sides or the four corners and the establishing of their position relative to the center point is what we mean by "centering." The Yukatek farmers today "center" their fields ritually even before they begin to cut them out of the fallow brushland. They mark off their fields and the units within them with small piles of stones, just as villages mark off their lands from those of neighboring communities with large piles of stones.[33]

For Westerners, the very idea of a "direction" almost implies movement. Our system tells us where we are headed. The Mesoamerican system helped people define where they were. From small to large or large to small, Mesoamerican peoples centered themselves, their homes, and their cities at the crossroads of the world. Mary Miller and Karl Taube describe the way that the five-part concept influenced multiple levels of the Mesoamerican world:

> One of the underlying organizational principles of Mesoamerican religion is replication, in which essential patterns of everyday life and the surrounding world are copied and incorporated as models of religious thought and action. Basic features of the social world are often repeated on an increasingly larger scale to encompass the world and the workings of the universe. For example, in the Maya region, the house with its four walls and corner posts could stand for a maize field, the community, and the structure of the cosmos. Grand and abstract concepts are placed in human terms, and conversely, the ordered structure of the universe serves to sanctify and validate human social conventions.[34]

There was no universal center. Each city was its own world—its own center. Each family home replicated the world and placed that family at its center. For Mesoamerican cultures, direction was equally symbolic as descriptive.

Not only does the "center direction" differ from our Western understanding, even the Mesoamerican directions that roughly correspond to our north, south, east, and west were differently conceived. Susan Milbrath describes the Mesoamerican mode of orientation using a Maya community as her example: "Analysis of Chamula astronomical concepts indicates that the primary axis is an east-west direction based on the sun's daily path. . . . Even though they recognize that the zenith position is overhead, the east is visualized as the 'up' direction and the west as 'down.'"[35] A universal aspect of Mesoamerican directional systems is that they are based on the path of the sun. They encode that path throughout the year, tracing the shifting rising and setting of the sun from solstice to solstice.

---

[33] David Freidel, Linda Schele, and Joy Parker, *Maya Cosmos: Three Thousand Years on the Shaman's Path*, 128–29.
[34] Mary Miller and Karl Taube, *An Illustrated Dictionary of the Gods and Symbols of Ancient Mexico and the Maya*, 30.
[35] Susan Milbrath, *Star Gods of the Maya: Astronomy in Art, Folklore, and Calendars*, 17, 19.

Western cardinal directions are conceptually a +, with each direction directly and cleanly associated with the "pure" direction equidistant from all other directions. The Mesoamerican system, on the other hand, is better represented in the form of an 'x.' East is not a line toward the sun at the equinox, but the entire wedge created by tracing the passage of the sun along the horizon from solstice to solstice from the center. Prudence M. Rice puts it clearly: "Maya quadripartite organization of horizontal space is not strictly based on the four fixed cardinal directions recognized in the modern world. Instead, the divisions seem to invoke the solstice-equinox positions and movements of the sun as it rises on the eastern horizon and sets on the western."[36] Although the plausible origin of this conception is the travel of the sun along the horizon, Mesoamerican systems regularized their depictions (and therefore their perceptions) into a quadripartite system surrounding the center.

Figure 6: Compass

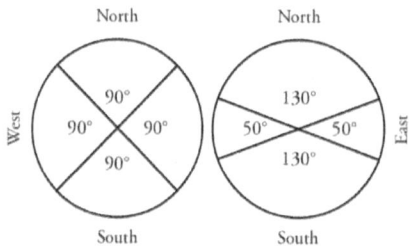

Figure 5: Mesoamerican directions

The world was depicted as a square with lines drawn from corner to corner. The Codex Mendoza shows the Aztec capital city at the center of the world. Tenochtitlan, indicated by the eagle on the cactus (the symbol for Tenochtitlan), sits at the center of the crossed lines that extend from each corner of the cosmos to the opposite corner.[37] This quadripartite visual orientation is seen in texts describing the world even though the orientation of the building sites themselves align to the center points of the wedges.

While the five-part concept defined the understanding of one's orientation in the cosmos, the actual directional system appears to have been built on only a single "direction," which was the path of the sun throughout the day and throughout the year. Other spatial relationships were made against that defining axis.

Steven Pinker provides some interesting background on this terminological problem. His emphasis was on understanding how the brain encodes meaning rather than anything to do with geography, but the example is informative:

---

[36] Prudence M. Rice, *Maya Political Science: Time, Astronomy, and the Cosmos*, 20.

[37] "Codex Mendoza," 4:189. This codex opens with a depiction of a deity at the center of the cosmos, depicting not only the center and the quadripartite directions, but also the world trees anchoring the corners of the cosmos.

Figure 7: Tenochtitlan from Codex Mendoza

A set of studies by the anthropologist Stephen Levinson and his colleagues aim[ed] to show that a language's spatial terms determine how its speakers use the three dimensions of space to remember the locations of objects. Levinson's group examined Tzeltal, a language spoken in the Chiapas region of Mexico. . . Tzeltal has no general words for "left" or "right." The closest it has are terms for the left or right arm or leg, but the terms are rarely used to refer to the left side of an object, table, or room. Instead the Tzeltal speakers describe spatial arrangements relative to the mountain slope that dominates their villages. The spatial vocabulary of Tzeltal includes words that mean "up-the-slope" (which is roughly southward), "down-the-slope" (roughly northward), and "across-the-slope." These coordinates are used not just when traipsing up and down the mountain but also when on flat terrain or indoors, and even when describing the arrangements of small objects. According to Levinson, Tzeltal speakers say "The spoon is downslope of the teacup," not "The spoon is on the right of the teacup."[38]

We should not assume that Tzeltal speakers don't understand right and left. They certainly do. They simply use different terminology to describe those spatial relationships. What Pinker didn't know was that the upslope/downslope spatial orientation was repeated in their concept of world directions. Upslope/downslope are not only the terms the Tzeltal use instead of "left/right," but are also used instead of "south/north."[39] The Tzeltal conceive of the east/west axis as the critical direction for orientation. Upslope (left and south) and downslope (right and north) are simply the same terms they would use for anything else that is spatially oriented against the main reference (the sun in the case of the directions, or the human body in the case of the location of the spoon in the cup). They are not precisely terms for "north" or "south," but for spatial orientation against a reference position.

David Stuart analyzed two Maya glyphs and argued for their meaning as "right" and "left" by noting their visual associations with other glyphs typically given as "south" and "north." He concludes: "As students of Maya cosmology have often noted, the sun's path defines the principal axis of the universe, with its 'right' and 'left' determining the perpendicular axis that corresponds to our 'north' and 'south.' In Chamula and other Maya communities, the celestial 'sides' are perceived from the sun's own perspective."[40]

This idea is corroborated by a larger study of direction terms in various Mesoamerican languages. Nicholas A. Hopkins and J. Kathryn Josserand, found a general agreement in vocabulary for east and west that was related to the path of the

---

[38] Steven Pinker, *The Stuff of Thought: Language as a Window into Human Nature*, 141–42.

[39] Nicholas A. Hopkins and J. Kathryn Josserand, "Directions and Partitions in Maya World View," 13. This paper expands an earlier presentation on March 24, 2001, in the symposium "Four Corners of the Maya World," 19th Maya Weekend, University Museum, University of Pennsylvania. The current publication is posthumous for Dr. Josserand. In it, they explain, "Some languages form the words for 'north' and 'south' on the basis of local geographical conditions" (13). They do not collect the Tzeltal terms for north and south. They do collect a "down-slope'" meaning for "north" and "right-handed" for Nahuatl(14).

[40] David Stuart, "Glyphs for 'Right' and 'Left'?" 4.

sun.⁴¹ They noted: "Terms for 'north' and 'south' are much more elusive. First, there are far fewer reports of these terms. Second, there are no consistent patterns in the nomenclature. Many languages have no recorded terms for 'north' and 'south,' even when 'east' and 'west' are noted."⁴² They concluded:

> The extreme chaos of terms for "north" and "south" reinforces the idea that these "directions" are almost irrelevant. Directional orientation is based on the movements of the sun, east to west, and the other two "directions" are of lesser importance. How then, do we derive the system of four directions that is recorded in village barrios regional states, and other matters? The solution seems to be, as Karen Bassie has argued, that "east" and "west" are not directions at all, but are broad quadrants of the sky centered on, but not limited to, the cardinal directions "east' and "west." "East" is the entire section of the horizon where the sun rises during the year, from solstice to solstice and back again. This quadrant is represented in site layout by the E-group complexes found at Uaxactun and elsewhere. "West" is the corresponding quadrant where the sun is observed to set. "North" and "south" are simply the quadrants that lie between these two, that lie "at the sides of the sky," "to the right hand" or "to the left." That is, two defined quadrants imply two others, giving a total of four. The "four corners of the Maya world" are simply the limits of the east-west quadrants, and do not imply four cardinal directions.⁴³

Hopkins and Josserand report an interesting example of what happened when an informant was asked to give the word for "north." The informant spoke Tojolabal, (a Mayan language). He did not provide a word, but rather a definition: "We are looking north when we stand with our left hand toward where the sun goes down."⁴⁴

There was no "north" in the Mesoamerican system—only a spatial relationship to that side of the sun's path. That is why the vocabulary varies so greatly. It wasn't that Mesoamericans didn't know where north was, they conceived it—and described it— entirely differently. It existed only as a quadrant on the right or left of the sun's path: some Mesoamerican cultures called it "right" and some "left."

It is both interesting and important to note that Mesoamericans were not the only peoples to use left/right rather than specific names for directions. William J. Hamblin notes:

> The Hebrews, like most Semitic peoples, oriented themselves by facing east, toward the rising sun. Thus *east* in Hebrew was simply *front* (*qedem*), with *south* as *right* (*yamîn*), *north* as *left* (*ś^emôl*), and *west* as *rear* (*achôr*) or "sea" (*yam*). . . .
> The Egyptians oriented themselves by facing south, toward the source of the Nile. "One of the terms for 'south' [in Egyptian] is also a term for 'face'; the usual word for 'north'

---

⁴¹ Hopkins and Josserand, "Directions and Partitions," 9–11.
⁴² Ibid., 13.
⁴³ Ibid., 15–16.
⁴⁴ Ibid., 14, periods as they appear in the original. This is prefaced with the explanation "The Tojolabal entries are clearly not lexical; the compiler of the dictionary, Carlos Lenkersdorf, is concerned with explaining to Tojolabal speakers the meaning of terms in Spanish (and vice versa) rather than simply listing lexical items." (p. 13–14).

is probably related to a word which means the 'back of the head.' The word for *east* is the same as for *left*, and *west* is the same word as *right*.[45]

One need not assume any linguistic connection between the Middle Eastern and Mesoamerican languages to account for the similarities. Using the body as the directional model from an accepted focal point is easily seen as independent invention. For both Middle Eastern and Mesoamerican terminology, directional terms were created based upon a particular orientation of the body.

So Where Is Mesoamerican North?

Perhaps the most important indication of the difference between our modern Western perception of directions and that of the Mesoamerican cultures is our persistent desire to find north. It likely reflects our reliance on the compass pointing to north but is buttressed by our familiarity with maps that conventionally place north at the top. Thus we understand where we are on a map when we can find north and place the map into its "proper" relationship with the land around us.

For the Mesoamericans, the question would be "where is east," and the answer was determined by the sun. What was in the east could range from solstice to solstice, but it could also be rectified to the central point. Even though what might lie in the east (or on the north) could fall into a quadrant emanating from the center point, it could also be standardized into the average between the two. Nevertheless, when glyphs are associated with building walls, or when Mesoamerican cities were built, the glyphs appear to be associated with the cardinal directions. For example, city builders often arranged an east-west road which was often intersected by a perpendicular north-south road. A road may be built only in one place, and the center point of the range of what was east or on the north was used.

This pattern is easily demonstrated in a complex called an E Group, one of the early features of many Mesoamerican cities. Francisco Estrada-Belli describes this type of construction: "E-Groups are generally formed by a western pyramid with radial stairways to the west and an elongated platform with one or three small substructures on the east side of the plaza. Their name is derived from Group E of Uaxactun, which was the first of this type to be recognized. Triadic Groups are normally situated on an elevated platform and are formed by a main pyramidal temple flanked by two smaller ones facing each other."[46] This platform was used as a marker for the passage of the sun along the horizon.[47] Importantly, there is a central pyramid in the group. Thus

---

[45] William J. Hamblin, "Directions in Hebrew, Egyptian, and Nephite Language," 183.

[46] Francisco Estrada-Belli, *The First Maya Civilization: Ritual and Power Before the Classic Period*, 67.

[47] Susan Toby Evans, *Ancient Mexico and Central America: Archaeology and Culture History*, 237. However, Estrada-Belli, *The First Maya Civilization*, 67, notes: "The most common orientation of the Triadic Groups is west-facing, although other cardinal orientations are not uncommon, especially at sites where several Triadic Groups are present." He also suggests: "While in the sample of Lowland E-Groups analyzed . . . the equinoctial and solsticial target

while Mesoamericans might comprehend a quadrant of the sky as east, they could—and did—use what we would see as cardinal directions to lay out sites according to those center points of the quadrant.

The conceptual directions included those that we consider the cardinal directions. They also include a wider span. Another way to understand this variation is the way the electronic compass acts when installed in some cars. As we travel, we can be traveling in a "pure" direction even though the road is not precisely aligned to that cardinal direction. For example, we continue to travel east as long as we stay within the arc that distinguishes east from northeast. (See the description in Alma 2:35–37, quoted and discussed below.)

If you remove the intermediary line from the linguistic equation, you have a better example of the Maya quadrants. You are traveling east until you trip over the conceptual division between east and north, at which time you are traveling north. Nevertheless, our compass shows east as a single, precise, location. The reality is that, in usage, it must be considered an arc of the horizon, just as I am suggesting for the Maya. The Maya similarly used the center point of the arc as the pure indication of the direction.

Modern drivers witness this phenomenon all the time but perceive it differently. If we have a vehicle that provides compass directions, it may display our direction of travel as north in spite of various small twists and turns in the road. We travel to the northeast only when the degree of variation from true north is sufficient to trip us into the arc of another designation. Since we use a designation between north and east, we can define that direction. However, for any direction of travel, there is an arc of tolerated variation from the cardinal direction that is included in the definition of north. Though we don't perceive it on maps, we experience it in our vehicles on a daily basis.

The important concept for understanding directions in the Book of Mormon is that, although Mesoamerican cultures could certainly find and use our cardinal points, their descriptions of personal orientation were given against the most obviously available spatial referent, the sun. Lacking the magnetic compass, their quickest assessments of location were made using the more obvious locational tool.[48] That

---

points were generally found not to be the norm, the targeted positions did mark specific twenty-day intervals (or multiples of) in relation to the sun's passage to the zenith, thus underscoring the paramount importance of this solar phenomenon in providing meaningful time-markers in the calendar" (78).

[48] Jaroslav lKokocník, Jan Kostelecký, and František Vítek, "On an Unresolved Orientation of Pyramids and Ceremonial Centers in Mesoamerica. Published as Jaroslav Klokocník, Jan Kostelecký, and František Vítek, "Pyramids and Ceremonial Centers in Mesoamerica: Were they Oriented Using a Magnetic Compass?" 515–33.

The authors note (p. 5 of downloaded paper) that a possible magnetic needle was found in the Olmec archaeological site of San Lorenzo. This makes a compass a possibility. They conclude (p. 16) that the hypothesis that the Maya used a magnetic compass to lay out their sites "cannot be simply rejected in the light of existing facts; it still provides an explanation for the strange alignments, where the other interpretation [sic] are not helpful. Our new measurements and computations from 2003–2005 support the hypothesis."

means that the orientation of actions in the Book of Mormon would use directions according to the location of the sun which traveled along the horizon, rather than the fixed conceptual center point of its travel. Just as when we use the compass in our vehicles, travel-direction "north" need not be map-direction "north."

Book of Mormon Directions in Translation

Ted Dee Stoddard adamantly declares that Joseph correctly replicated a system that closely mirrors the Western model:

1. The directional system of the Nephites has six Nephite cardinal directions: north, northward, south, southward, east, and west.
2. "Northward" reflects the general direction of northwest rather than northeast. "Northward" could be either a northwest or a northeast direction by its very nature, but northwest is the correct orientation from an Isthmus of Tehuantepec perspective. Or, as Noah Webster in his 1828 dictionary says about "northward" as an adjective, as in land northward: "Being towards the north, or nearer to the north than to the east and west points."
3. "Southward" reflects the general direction of southeast rather than southwest. "Southward" could be either a southeast or a southwest direction by its very nature, but southeast is the correct orientation from an Isthmus of Tehuantepec perspective. Interestingly, Noah Webster does not show an adjectival definition for "southward" in his 1828 dictionary.
4. North, south, east, and west are the directions that readers of the twenty-first century are accustomed to, based on compass bearings. When these cardinal directions are viewed from the perspective of a horizontally positioned hourglass that is placed over a map of Mesoamerica, they coincide with the same four cardinal directions employed by Book of Mormon readers of the twenty-first century.[49]

The certainty of these declarations rests on the assumption that the words in the English translation precisely replicate the plate text meaning.[50] I cannot find support

---

While this possibility underscores the ability of ancient Mesoamericans to align buildings, the use of the compass would not have been practical for daily orientation. It remains a case of the semantic field defined by the words used for the directions. The magnetic orientation was likely available, as was an understanding of "pure" directions, but it was not the sole definition of the range associated with those terms.

[49] Stoddard, "'From the East to the West Sea': An Analysis of John L. Sorenson's Book of Mormon Directional Statements."

[50] It is worth noting that the shift in directions is also likely related to Stoddard's preferred Mesoamerican geography, which follows the Allens' geography and not Sorenson's. See Joseph Lovell Allen and Blake Joseph Allen, *Exploring the Lands of the Book of Mormon*, 360–61. That model relies upon the assumption of Western cardinal directions as an important underpinning to the relationship between the Book of Mormon and Mesoamerican geography. However, that geography has some features that I am unable to reconcile between text and geography—hence, my preference for Sorenson's correlation.

for such an absolute declaration that English communicates the original meaning from the plates. Rather, I suggest that Joseph used his common vocabulary to express the Book of Mormon system of spatial orientation. When we read those modern terms, we impute our modern meaning to them without attempting to understand any possible nuances that might be available in the way the Book of Mormon uses those terms. In the case of Book of Mormon directions, I suggest that there are sufficient hints in the text to allow a reconstruction of a plate text system that encoded meaning differently than we might perceive when we see the directional terms in English translation.

Of course, the very suggestion that the English words might not exactly represent the plate meaning embodies another assumption: that the translation occurred in a way that allows such a slight disconnect. The nature of that translation has been the subject of discussion among faithful scholars, with opinions ranging from Brigham H. Roberts's declaration that Joseph "expressed [the translation] in such language as the Prophet could command"[51] to Royal Skousen's understanding that Joseph Smith precisely read a translation that had already been done and which appeared in some manner when using the interpreters.[52] My own analysis of the available data is more in line with Roberts.[53]

Although we certainly find the words "north," "south," "east" and "west" in the Book of Mormon, there is an important and very specific phrase that I believe more closely replicates the essential Mesoamerican directional system (and the implicit directional understanding of the Book of Mormon authors): "From the east to the west." Against the background of Mesoamerican directions, it is a reasonable initial hypothesis that this phrase represents plate text terms that indicated the path of the sun. This phrase implying solar movement occurs six times.[54]

There is a single occurrence of "from the west to the east" in 3 Nephi 1:17 and three related phrases mentioning a sea:

> Helaman 3:8 "from the sea west to the sea east"
> Helaman 4:7 "from the west sea, even unto the east"
> Helaman 11:20 "from the sea west to the sea east"

Importantly, all but one of these (Helaman 4:7) come in the context of an expression of the "whole earth":

---

[51] Brigham H. Roberts, *New Witnesses for God*, 2:116; brackets mine.

[52] Royal Skousen, "Translating the Book of Mormon: Evidence from the Original Manuscript," 64–65. A revised version is Royal Skousen, "How Joseph Smith Translated the Book of Mormon: Evidence from the Original Manuscript," 24. Skousen's understanding is best represented by his definition of "tight control" in these documents: "Joseph Smith saw specific words written out in English and read them off to the scribe—the accuracy of the resulting text depending on the carefulness of Joseph and his scribe."

[53] Brant A. Gardner, *The Gift and Power: Translating the Book of Mormon*, 227–47.

[54] Alma 22:27, 29, 32, 33; 50:8; 3 Nephi 20:13. Instances compiled using an electronic search for the terms "east" and "west" and compiling only those with this particular configuration.

And they began to know that the Son of God must shortly appear; yea, in fine, all the people upon the face of the whole earth from the west to the east, both in the land north and in the land south, were so exceedingly astonished that they fell to the earth. (3 Nephi 1:17)

And it came to pass that they did multiply and spread, and did go forth from the land southward to the land northward, and did spread insomuch that they began to cover the face of the whole earth, from the sea south to the sea north, from the sea west to the sea east. (Helaman 3:8)

And thus it did come to pass that the people of Nephi began to prosper again in the land, and began to build up their waste places, and began to multiply and spread, even until they did cover the whole face of the land, both on the northward and on the southward, from the sea west to the sea east. (Helaman 11:20)

Helaman 4:7 has a different context that appears to describe an intended direction rather than a generalization: "And there they did fortify against the Lamanites, from the west sea, even unto the east; it being a day's journey for a Nephite, on the line which they had fortified and stationed their armies to defend their north country." This may be a counter-indication, or it may be a requirement of the more specific starting point of the sea west rather than the indeterminate "unto the east" which does not specify the ending point.[55]

Although the "from-to" construction implies movement, most of the cases of "from the west to the east" do not come in connection with any movement but rather with descriptions of "the face of the whole earth." With only three examples it is a weak hypothesis, but I suggest that there was a literary reversal used in describing the "whole earth." I believe that by reversing the known path of the sun, it placed "the face of the whole earth" firmly in the metaphorical rather than the physical realm.[56]

In contrast to the movement implied when using the phrase "from the east to the west," the common usage for the other two "directions" is "on the north/on the south."[57] There are no instances of "from the north to the south" or "from the south to the north," except in Helaman 3:8, dealing with the whole earth rather than

---

[55] Another possible counter-indication is 3 Nephi 20:13: "And then shall the remnants, which shall be scattered abroad upon the face of the earth, be gathered in from the east and from the west, and from the south and from the north; and they shall be brought to the knowledge of the Lord their God, who hath redeemed them." This verse combines the correct order of east to west with "the face of the earth." However, this is not a *"from the east to the west."* There is a difference in the phrase, and I am suggesting that it is the presence of the "from-to" construction that is important.

[56] The phrase "on the east and on the west" occurs in Mosiah 27:6, but this is also in the context of the "face of the earth." When it occurs in 22:27, it is a description of "all the regions round about." Helaman 1:31 uses "on the east, nor on the west" as part of a description of Lamanites who were surrounded.

The only context that is not clearly related to "all" or being surrounded, is Alma 50:34: "And it came to pass that they did not head them until they had come to the borders of the land Desolation; and there they did head them, by the narrow pass which led by the sea into the land northward, yea, by the sea, on the west and on the east."

[57] Alma 22:29, 33; 46:17; 3 Nephi 6:2.

directions. For example, Alma 46:17: "And it came to pass that when he had poured out his soul to God, he named all the land which was south of the land Desolation, yea, and in fine, all the land, both *on the north* and *on the south*—A chosen land, and the land of liberty."[58] Hopkins and Josserand report that many of the languages they surveyed use terms such as "on the left," or "on the right" to designate south and north.[59] Where the Mesoamerican cultures used terms such as "on the right/on the left" or some other spatial indicator (such as the "upslope/downslope'" of the Tzeltal) the Book of Mormon translation supplies the words "north/south." Although the specific word comes from Joseph's Western understanding, the words are couched in phrases that replicate the functional relationships of the Mesoamerican system.

The Book of Mormon vocabulary of spatial orientation also replicates the four quarters assigned to east-west and the sides of the sky we know as north and south. In Mosiah 27:6 we find: "And there began to be much peace again in the land; and the people began to be very numerous, and began to scatter abroad upon the face of the earth, yea, on the north and on the south, on the east and on the west, building large cities and villages in all quarters of the land."[60] Of course, this is not definitively a translation from the plate text because we also find quarters of the land in the Bible and it is always possible that the term was borrowed from biblical usage.[61] Nevertheless, it fits with the entire system, even if it cannot be proof of the source of the concept.[62]

This conception of the Nephite usage of directional terms helps explain a passage that would otherwise be difficult. The flight of the Lamanite/Amlicite army is described in Alma 2:35–37:

---

[58] The Book of Mormon can also use "on the east" or "on the west" as terms of spatial orientation rather than direction:

Therefore when Zerahemnah saw the men of Lehi **on the east** of the river Sidon, and the armies of Moroni **on the west** of the river Sidon, that they were encircled about by the Nephites, they were struck with terror. (Alma 43:53)

And now, behold, the Lamanites could not retreat either way, neither **on the north**, nor **on the south**, nor **on the east**, nor **on the west**, for they were surrounded on every hand by the Nephites. (Helaman 1:31)

[59] Hopkins and Josserand, "Directions and Partitions," 13–14.
[60] This is the only verse indicating the four quarters. However, a phrase indicating that something is "in" a quarter occurs more frequently. See Alma 43:26; 52:10; 56:1; 58:30; 58:35; Ether 2:5; 14:15.
[61] Genesis 19:4; Numbers 34:3; Joshua 15:5; 18:14–15; Isaiah 47:15; 56:11; Mark 1:45.
[62] Hopkins and Josserand, "Directions and Partitions," 16: "This concept of quadrants survives even where the directional terms have been lost. In Tenejapa Tzeltal, directional orientation has shifted to *ta alan*, 'downhill' (north) versus *ta ajk'ol* 'uphill' (south). However, these are conceived of as quadrants, separated and opposed to the other quadrants (east and west), both called *ta jejch* 'transverse', 'to the side'."

142 Traditions of the Fathers

> And it came to pass that when they had all crossed the river Sidon that the Lamanites and the Amlicites began to flee before them, notwithstanding they were so numerous that they could not be numbered.
>
> And they fled before the Nephites towards the wilderness **which was west and north,** away beyond the borders of the land; and the Nephites did pursue them with their might, and did slay them.
>
> Yea, they were met on every hand, and slain and driven, until they were scattered **on the west, and on the north,** until they had reached the wilderness, which was called Hermounts; and it was that part of the wilderness which was infested by wild and ravenous beasts.

In this description, a fleeing army heads both west and north. Because we see "northward" with some frequency in the Book of Mormon, it could have been used to indicate travel to the northwest.[63] Instead, the text opts for travel both north and west. This is conceptually difficult in the plus style (+) cardinal directions, but quite understandable if the x-style quadrants are meant. In that case, they would simply wander back and forth over the conceptual line dividing the west from the northern quarter.[64]

Just as with the description given by the Tojolabal speaker, if one were to stand with his left hand to the sun's setting during the summer solstice, one would be looking "north," and that "north" corresponds quite nicely to the north that Sorenson suggested. No skewing of north 60 degrees to the west is required. However, it should be noted that it would be a misrepresentation of Nephite directions to use north to indicate only the direction based upon the summer solstice. For the Nephites, "north" would indicate anything to that side of the sun's path.

An inherent misperception of any ancient directional system occurs simply by our attempts to represent them on a map. Our maps take a birds-eye view, and often literally a satellite's view of the land we are interested in. Almost any map we use to describe the Book of Mormon geography assumes an understanding of an area of land much larger than the ancients would have comprehended. Their world was limited to what they could see, travel to, or have described to them. No remaining map created by any Mesoamerican people has any of the details of our modern maps. They are spatially inaccurate and locate landmarks without precise distance interrelationships. The maps place the reader at the center and describe the conceptual bounds of the world in distances that might be a day or two of travel.[65]

Combined with the differences in terminology and cultural perceptions, it is little wonder that the Book of Mormon directions appear difficult to fit onto a modern map. That inherent difficulty becomes even greater when we insist upon reading literal

---

[63] Northward, eastward, and southward are all used as directions of travel. There is no occurrence of travel westward, but there is no reason to assume that it wasn't a possible lexical item. As directions of travel: northward—Alma 52:23; 56:36; 63:6; southward—Alma 17:1; Ether 15:10; eastward—1 Nephi 17:1; Ether 9:3; 14:26.

[64] Poulsen, "The War with the Amlicites."

[65] Some of this information is presented in Lawrence L. Poulsen, "Lawrence Poulsen's Book of Mormon Geography," 9.

geographic statements where the text does not intend a literal reading. That is the issue that clouds our understanding of the Nephite seas.

Where are the Nephite Sea East and Sea West?[66]

Another possible contraindication for Sorenson's geographic correlation is the relationship of that geography to surrounding seas. Helaman 3:8 clearly mentions four seas: "And it came to pass that they did multiply and spread, and did go forth from the land southward to the land northward, and did spread insomuch that they began to cover the face of the whole earth, from the **sea south** to the **sea north,** from the **sea west** to the **sea east.**" Some Book of Mormon geographers therefore insist on identifying four surrounding bodies of water.[67] However, John E. Clark notes of these seas:

> I am convinced that the reference to a north sea and a south sea is devoid of any concrete geographical content. All specific references or allusions to Book of Mormon seas are only to the east and west seas. Any geography that tries to accommodate a north and south sea, I think, is doomed to fail. But we cannot dismiss the reference to these seas out of hand. If they are metaphorical, what was the metaphor?
>
> [The accompanying figure] shows a conceptualization of Nephite lands. The city of Zarahemla and the lands immediately surrounding it were the "center" (Helaman 1:24–27) or "heart" (Alma 60:19; Helaman 1:18) of the land. The surrounding lands, to the various wildernesses, were considered quarters of the land. A Bountiful quarter (Alma 52:10, 13; 53:8; 58:35) and a Manti quarter (43:26; 56:1–2, 9; 58:30) are mentioned. Moroni was another "part" of the land (Alma 59:6). We lack information on the eastern quarter; my designation of "Melek" is merely my best guess.
>
> We have seen that the Nephite lands were surrounded by wilderness on every side. And, conceptually, beyond each wilderness lay a sea to the south, north, west, and east. Thus the land was conceived as surrounded by seas or floating on one large sea. The land was divided into a center and four quarters. Each quarter duplicated the others. The quartering of the land was not the way most of us would do it, by making a cross following the cardinal directions, but was a cross. . . . Such a conception of the world would not be out of place in the Middle East at the time of Lehi; and it is remarkably close to the Mesoamerican view of their world. . . . The main point is that the reference to north and south seas fits nicely into the Mesoamerican scene as part of a metaphor for the whole earth and was probably used in a metaphorical sense in the Book of Mormon.[68]

---

[66] Many of the concepts presented in this section were worked out in conversation with Lawrence Poulsen, for whose counsel I am grateful.

[67] V. Garth Norman, *Book of Mormon Geography—Mesoamerican Historic Geography*. See also E. L. Peay, *The Lands of Zarahemla: Nephi's Land of Promise*, 2:24, has a sea west, east, and south, but no listing for a sea north.

[68] John E. Clark, "Revisiting 'A Key for evaluating Nephite Geographies,'" 41.

Clark's proposal that the north and south seas are metaphorical rather than physical finds an interesting parallel in the metaphorical use of the phrase "the other side of the sea" in various Maya documents. Frauke Sachse and Allen J. Christenson note that it is a metaphor that "remains hitherto largely unrecognized because a presumed literalness has obscured its metaphorical interpretation."[69] They conclude by noting that "the phrase 'the other side of the sea' in the Colonial sources is only a metaphor for a place of origin in the sense of creation and not departure, and thus does not necessarily refer to an actual location that could be found on any map."[70]

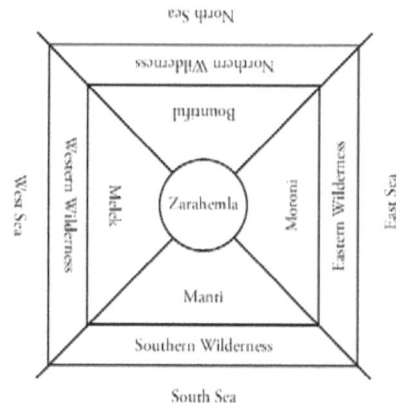

Figure 8: Nephite conceptual world

It is perhaps not coincidental that the metaphorical meaning that Clark suggests for the sea north and sea south is also associated with a conceptual organization of the world.

As Hopkins and Josserand worked through the vocabulary terms used for east and west, they presented their reconstruction of what the Classic Maya terms might have been. For east and west they reconstruct both the words and the plausible original meanings: "*'el-ab k'in "the front porch of the house of the Sun (where the Sun exists)', and *'och-ib k'in "the door of the house of the Sun (where the Sun enters).'"[71] They argue that these proto-forms may be traced to as early as 2000 B.C.[72]

In a world conceptually surrounded by seas, the house of the sun would lie across the sea, or on "the other side of the sea." Thus Sachse and Christenson explain: "We understand that in the Maya world view all creation involves the underlying concept of birth from a primordial sea in darkness. The world came into being because the earth and the mountains arose from the sea and the sky was lifted up from the water. Creation thus involves 'dawning.'"[73] The "other side of the sea" refers metaphorically to an origin in the conceptual east sea, the place of dawning and creation. Thus there was a very strong cultural preference for having a sea east and the parallel sea west. The question is how that conceptual world might have related to the physical seas that the Book of Mormon text requires.

---

[69] Frauke Sachse and Allen J. Christenson, "Tulan and the Other Side of the Sea: Unraveling a Metaphorical Concept from Colonial Guatemalan Highland Sources," 1–2.

[70] Ibid., 25–26.

[71] Hopkins and Josserand, "Directions and Partitions," 7–8. The * at the beginning of the word indicates that it is a reconstruction of an early form and is not actually found in that form in the later data.

[72] Ibid., 8.

[73] Sachse and Christenson, "Tulan and the Other Side," 2.

Book of Mormon Geography in the New World 145

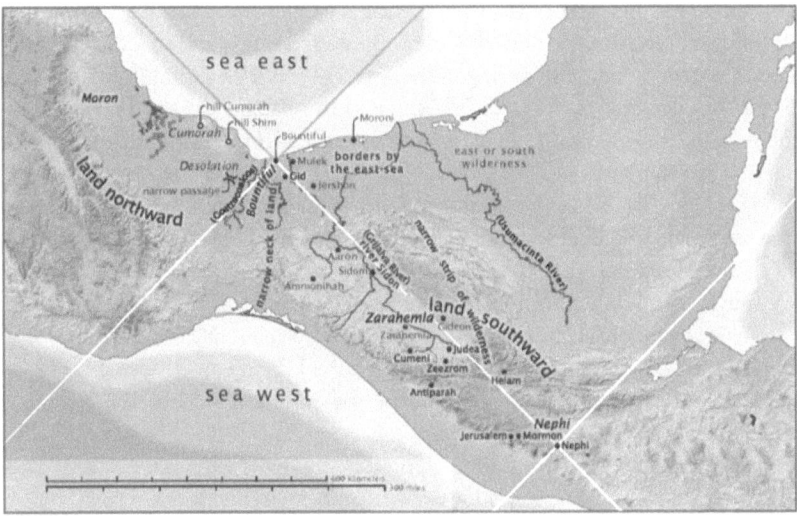

Figure 9: Directions from Bountiful or Nephi

In contrast with the metaphorical meanings for sea north and sea south, and the metaphorical meaning associated with the east sea, the Book of Mormon text clearly supports the physical presence of a sea east. Sorenson's correlation has the expected sea east but applies that designation to the Gulf of Mexico. Anyone examining a modern map perceives the Gulf of Mexico to be north of the lands surrounding the Isthmus of Tehuantepec. How can this body of water in the north be the sea east? In Sorenson's correlation, this is part of the skewing of directions. I suggest that no skewing is necessary, only the application of the principles of Mesoamerican directions.

The first important part of the explanation is the Mesoamerican concept of the center. Any directions given in the Book of Mormon necessarily related to some location that is conceptually the center of the world for those who live there. Directions related to a different center might result in different locations being placed in the direction quadrants. We can see this same principle even in our modern directional system. We may describe Denver as being in the east when we are located in Salt Lake City, but in the west when we are located in St. Louis. What is in the east (or west) depends upon the vantage point from which we view the direction. I propose that the term "sea east" is a description rather than a name, and that two different bodies of water might have been considered the sea east based upon the different center points from which they are described.

The original Nephite center point was not Zarahemla, but rather the City of Nephi. In Sorenson's correlation, we have the highland valley of Guatemala as a plausible land of Nephi. From that center, the east sea would be right where several

Book of Mormon geographers suggest—off the coast of modern Belize.[74] From that original center point, the Nephites would then have had the option of calling the Pacific either the sea west or sea south, since it creates the coastline that would be both south and west of the land of Nephi. Because the definition of Mesoamerican direction system had the sun setting in the sea west, it is logical that they would have selected that designation for what we know as the Pacific Ocean. The interesting combination of the sea west being both west and south helps explain Alma 53:22: "And now it came to pass that Helaman did march at the head of his two thousand stripling soldiers, to the support of the people in the borders of the land on the south by the west sea." The land south of Zarahemla bordered the west sea, not a south sea even though there was a coastline on the south.

While there is a reference to a sea east from the land of Nephi, most references to the sea east come from the time when directions were given in relation to the City of Bountiful, not the city of Nephi or even the city of Zarahemla.[75] Using Sorenson's correlation, Bountiful would be located at the northern side of the Isthmus of Tehuantepec. With that location as the center point, the Gulf of Mexico lies both on the north and on the east. Just as the cultural necessity of the sun rising across a sea east and setting in the sea west allowed the Nephites to define a sea west from the center point of the city of Nephi, that same cultural preference would naturally select sea east as the appropriate designation of that major body of water. No skewing of directions is necessary to see the Gulf of Mexico as the sea east based on the perspective of Bountiful as the center. Regardless of the body of water, the sea east existed as a description that was related to the cosmological understanding of the east as a place of creation and of the rising/birth of the sun. In the Book of Mormon, it is plausible that two different bodies of water served that function and were designated (not named) sea east to conform to the cosmological principle.

---

[74] The verse used to establish this correlation is Alma 22:27, which provides a description of the lands, but from the center point of a Lamanite king in the land of Nephi. Some of those making this correlation based on that passage are: Joseph L. Allen, *Exploring the Lands of the Book of Mormon*, 195; Allen and Allen, *Exploring the Lands of the Book of Mormon*, 393; Norman, *Book of Mormon Geography—Mesoamerican Historic Geography*; Poulsen, "Lawrence Poulsen's Book of Mormon Geography." While the verse is found in the book of Alma where the action focuses on Zarahemla as the center of Nephite culture, Alma 22:27 is given as part of the missionary journey to the land of Nephi and describes geography from that vantage point. See also Stephen L. Carr, "A Summary of Several Theories of Book of Mormon Lands in Mesoamerica."

[75] Nephi as the center: Alma 22:27.
Bountiful as the center: Alma 22:32-33; 27:22; 50:34; 52:13; Helaman 4:6–7.
There are two other references I am not listing because the east sea occurs in a context that reads better as a metaphor for "the whole world": Helaman 3:8; 11:20.

The Land Northward and Land Southward

Another feature of the Book of Mormon may be plausibly related to an underlying Mesoamerican directional system. The vast majority of the times we see the words *northward* and *southward* in the Book of Mormon, they are referring to locations and not to movement (i.e. the *land northward* and the *land southward*).[76] The term *northward* only appears three times as a description of motion and *southward* only twice.[77] *Eastward* occurs three times, always as an indication of direction of travel, and *westward* does not occur at all.[78]

The phrases "land northward/land southward" can parallel the functions of the "north/south" spatial orientation markers, but they are textually distinct from them. We find in 3 Nephi 6:2 "And it came to pass that they had not eaten up all their provisions; therefore they did take with them all that they had not devoured, of all their grain of every kind, and their gold, and their silver, and all their precious things, and they did return to their own lands and their possessions, both *on the north and on the south, both on the land northward and on the land southward.*" There is no reason to indicate the spatial orientation twice, and the reference here clearly separates the "land" from the spatial orientation.[79]

The two lands conceptually meet along a dividing line: "Thus the land on the northward was called Desolation, and the land on the southward was called Bountiful,

---

[76] Land northward: Omni 1:22, Alma 22:30–33, 46:22; 50:11, 29, 31, 33–34; 51:30; 52:2, 9; 63:4–5, 7, 9–10; Helaman 3:3, 9–11; 6:6; 7:1–2, 11:20; 3 Nephi 3:24; 4:23; 6:2; 8:12; Mormon 2:29.

Land southward: Alma 22:31, 32; Helaman 3:8; 4:8; 5:16; 3 Nephi 3:24; 6:2; 8:11; Mormon 1:6; 2:29; 3:5; 8:2; Ether 9:31–32; 10:19, 21.

Another verse may represent the metaphorical "whole world. "And thus it did come to pass that the people of Nephi began to prosper again in the land, and began to build up their waste places, and began to multiply and spread, even until they did cover the whole face of the land, both on the northward and on the southward, from the sea west to the sea east" (Helaman. 11:20). In this case, northward and southward are locations, even though not stated as lands. I hypothesize that this constitutes a generic reference rather than a directional one.

[77] Northward motion: Alma 63:6; Mormon 2:20; Ether 1:42 (in the Old World). Southward motion: Alma 17:1; Ether 15:10.

[78] Eastward motion: 1 Nephi 17:1; Ether 9:3, 14:26.

[79] Sorenson, *An Ancient American Setting*, 41–42, notes the occurrences of "northward/southward," but always considers them as indicators of directions rather than as labels as I am suggesting. Sorenson states:

> A semantic point from the Book of Mormon is important. The Book of Mormon usually refers to the "land north*ward*" and "land south*ward*," rarely to the "land north" or "land south." (The latter terms occur only seven times; -*ward* terms appear 47 times.) The suffix *ward*, of course, signifies "tending or leading toward." Gage correctly thought of Guatemala as "southward" from Mexico City, even though technically it was more nearly east. Similarly, if you board a plane in Los Angeles for Caracas, Venezuela, do you not mentally consider your direction southward? After all, your destination is South America; but actually you'll end up traveling more east than south. Still, south*ward* is correct.

Sorenson appears to want to use –ward as a specific direction rather than as an indicator of direction of travel, or as a name.

it being the wilderness which is filled with all manner of wild animals of every kind, a part of which had come from the land northward for food" (Alma 22:31). When the land northward has a name, it is Desolation. When the land southward has a name, it is Bountiful. They are adjacent lands. *Land northward* and *Desolation* are interchangeable labels, as are *land southward* and *Bountiful*.

The obvious conceptual inversion of Desolation/Bountiful suggests that another aspect of Mesoamerican direction systems is in play. Prudence M. Rice indicates that each of the four conceptual directions had other attributes:

> Among the lowland Maya, this solar basis for naming directions is evident by incorporating, *k'in* "sun," into the term. East (*lak'in*) was associated with sunrise, birth, and the color red (*chak*), while West (*chik'in, ochk'in*) was associated with sunset, death, and the color black (*ek'*). By contrast, *xaman* (North) was associated with "up" (as in the sun at zenith), the Sun God's "right" side on his journey, heavens, the number 13, the place of ancestors, and the color white (*sak*). *Nojol* (South) was associated with "down" or the sun's nadir, the sun's "left," the Underworld, the number 9, night ("death" of the sun and its Underworld journey back to the east), and the color Yellow (*k'an*).[80]

Although the association between "north" and "right" is common, it was not universal. David Stuart indicates:

> The "south" glyph is widely thought to read *nohol*, the word for "south" in the Yucatecan language, attested also in Chontal and Cholti. The –lo suffix on a "south" glyph written in Naj Tunich cave offers good support for this reading. . . . The root of the term is *noh*, which has the related meanings of "large," "great," "principal," or "right-side". . . .
>
> The NOH reading seems fitting in the context of the "hand" terms on Tikal's Marcador. The first glyph of the pair would simply read NOH-K'AB, a widespread and familiar term in Mayan languages for "right hand."[81]

In the case Stuart describes, the orientation that leads to the terms for "north" and "south" is based on facing the sun rather than from the perspective of the sun.

It appears that there were two possible methods of deriving a term for "north" or "south," both based on the same principle, but from either facing the sun or from the sun's perspective. In that light Hopkins and Josserand note the data from the later Mexica, who were Nahuatl speakers: "While Classical Nahuatl has a mythological reference to the "place of Death" as the base of "north," one variety of modern Nahuatl makes an association of "south" (for which no term is recorded) as "sinister, left-handed," and regards "north" as positive and right-handed [while calling it "down-slope"]."[82] As with the data for Mayan languages, the Nahuatl languages also demonstrate a reversal of the "handedness" of north and south.

There are strong indications of a bad/good perception about left/right (and therefore north/south which shared those terms) among the Classic Maya, paralleling

---

[80] Rice, *Maya Political Science*, 20.
[81] Stuart, "Glyphs for 'Right' and 'Left'?" 2.
[82] Hopkins and Josserand, "Directions and Partitions," 14.

these terms in Classical Nahuatl. Objects to the left of the viewer are consistently of lower status than those on the right.[83] Maya epigraphers Stephen Houston, David Stuart, and Karl Taube note: "Consistently the right hand is 'straight, correct large' (*no* or *to* in Ch'olti') or 'fine, pure' (*batz'i k'ob* in Colonial Tzotzil) and *wikiaq'ab*, 'decorated, adorned' in K'iche', while the left hand is not quite obedient and thus, as in Colonial Yukatek, 'ill behaved, graceless' (*tz'ik*) or 'clumsy like a cloven hoof' (*tz'itz'*), and in K'iche', *moxq'ab*, 'crazy hand.'"[84]

In a spatial relation system that uses the right/left hand designation for the terms we call south and north, it is not surprising at all that the Nephites used a word for "left hand/north" that would have a pejorative association. That was mirrored by the favorable association of "right hand/south." That the land northward was also associated with a "dead" Jaredite culture simply vindicated the pejorative association. This gives us a very simple explanation for why the land northward is Desolation and the land southward is Bountiful. The labels replicate the cultural perception of the spatial relationships based upon one facing the rising sun (and indicate that the Nephite preference was to associate left/north similar to the Mayan languages of Yukatek,[85] Chontal, and Cholti).

Sorenson's Directions Redux

The most serious contraindication for Sorenson's correlation between Mesoamerica and the Book of Mormon has been his apparent shifting of north some 60 degrees to the west. The quality of the correlations with the rest of the geography and cultural data suggest that we look to Mesoamerica to see if the cultural data from the region in which the Book of Mormon took place (according to this correlation) might provide an understanding of what has come to be called "Nephite North" (though it is not a term Sorenson used[86]). The combination of the Mesoamerican center and the perception of the quadrants as wedges emanating from that center explain how the Book of Mormon "north" might include a region that our cultural predisposition for cardinal directions would not recognize. Combined with the shifting center points from which directions or spatial relationships may be discussed, we have a culturally appropriate understanding of the underlying plate text directions that yielded the English translations of north, south, east, and west. In addition to explaining the spatial terms, it also provides a cultural underpinning for why the land northward was Desolation and the land southward was Bountiful. Sorenson's geographic correlation not only remains the best supported, but what has been a

---

[83] Stephen Houston, David Stuart, and Karl Taube, *The Memory of Bones. Body, Being, and Experience among the Classic Maya*, 29.

[84] Ibid., 30.

[85] "Yukatek" is the more modern spelling and "Yucatec" is the more traditional. Both terms appear depending upon the preference of the author. I have left the spelling as in the original citations.

[86] Sorenson, "Viva Zapato! Hurray for the Shoe!" 305: "The concept 'Nephite north' is not mine, consequently it is not appropriate on a map representing my views."

directional conundrum actually provides further indication that the plate text was written in a region steeped in the Mesoamerican understanding of spatial orientation.

Clarifying an Element of Sorenson's Geography

With a stronger assurance that we can work with Sorenson's basic geographic correlation, I propose a modification. In his map in *An Ancient American Setting for the Book of Mormon*, Sorenson placed the east wilderness on the east of the Usumacinta River. In *Mormon's Codex*, his map places the east wilderness on the west of the Usumacinta.[87] I hypothesize that the nature of the military situation would suggest that the Usumacinta was an important barrier on the east, and that the danger was having Lamanites in the region between the Grijalva and the Usumacinta. This hypothesis suggests that Sorenson's more recent map is the better of the two.

The Usumacinta would have created a natural boundary. It would have been difficult to easily ferry an entire army across the river. While crossing in boats is certainly possible, there is never an indication of any Lamanite attack beginning with or involving boats of any kind. Therefore, it is most likely that they would take a land route, and a land route that leads to an attack on the land Bountiful makes most sense if it comes from west of the Usumacinta. The compacted geography of Nephite lands to the west of the Usumacinta provides a better indication of how the land could be fortified given the few cities that were built there. It also explains why the Nephite perceptual world appears to know so little of the Maya lowlands. Separated by the Usumacinta, there was a natural barrier inhibiting easy traverse.

---

[87] Sorenson, *Mormon's Codex*, Map 4.

6

Nephites in a New World

When Lehi's family set sail from Bountiful they left a little-known land and sailed into an unknown ocean to an unknown destination. They arrived in an unimaginable land. Water and sky remained constant, but plants and animals were completely foreign. They planted seeds that they brought with them (1 Ne. 18:24), but they surely needed to eat long before those crops were harvested. Everything they had known about edible plants or animals was useless, and not knowing could be dangerous. Their very survival depended upon what they learned from the unnamed, unmentioned people they met soon after they arrived.

Perhaps Nephi told more of that meeting in his other, more historical record. Unfortunately, we have no record that allows us to know. While the lost 116 manuscript pages that were translated from the book of Lehi covered that time period, Mormon wrote them, not Nephi. Writing nearly one thousand years after Nephi, Mormon had his own selection bias.[1] Even if Nephi had left a detailed account of the first meeting in the New World, Mormon might have elected not to include it.

The New Neighbors

In 1947, Dewey Farnsworth published *The Americas before Columbus*. On the first page he asked the rhetorical question: "Who were the Mayas?" He answered: "The origin of the Mayas is still shrouded in mystery."[2] He attempted to resolve that mystery on that very same page: "Authorities generally agree to this extent: There were at least two separate and distinct migrations from Asia to the new world . . . one known as Archaic, about 4,000 to 5,000 years ago, and the other, the Mayan-Toltec migration, which occurred about 600 B.C."[3]

Doubtless there was some information available at that time which might have proposed those dates and divisions, but nothing in that statement can be accepted now. Current research shows three waves of migration into the Americas (not two),

---

[1] I discuss the nature of Mormon's selection bias in Brant A. Gardner, "Mormon's Editorial Method and Meta-Message," 87–94.
[2] Dewey Farnsworth, *The Americas before Columbus*, 3.
[3] Ibid.

and they were all over 15,000 years ago.⁴ The Maya and the Toltec were different peoples occupying different Mesoamerican regions, though Toltec influence may be seen among the Maya after A.D. 900.

Nevertheless, the suggestion that the Maya began around 600 B.C. excited Book of Mormon believers because the Book of Mormon traces one family's migration from the Old World to the New around 600 B.C.⁵ Perhaps because of these dates and the kind of amateur history and archaeology that Farnsworth's book represents, a folk nomenclature has developed in LDS writings about the Book of Mormon that uses New World names as representations of Book of Mormon peoples.⁶ Often writers suggest that the Mesoamerican people called Olmec *are* the Jaredites and the people called Maya *are* the Nephites.⁷ Such simplistic identifications are incorrect.

Richard A. Diehl describes the problems of even using the term *Olmec* as a representation of any ancient people:

> We do not know what these people called themselves, or if they even had a term that encompassed all of Olman. There is no evidence that they formed a single unified ethnic

---

⁴ No author, "Native American Populations Descend from Three Key Migrations, Scientists Say."

⁵ David A. Freidel, "Maya Warfare, Myth and Reality" provides a little perspective on the 600 B.C. date: "The origins of lowland Maya civilization are a matter of constant revision in the wake of new information from archaeological excavation in early sites. At the moment, the gap is narrowing between the time when pioneering Maya farmers first began entering the lowland forests around 1000 B.C. and the time that they started building temples and plazas in ritual centers, roughly 600 B.C."

⁶ Folklorist Jan Harold Brunvand. "Modern Legends of Mormondom, or, Supernaturalism Is alive and Well in Salt Lake City," 201, ties these ideas directly to Farnsworth:

> There seems to be a considerable variety of fantastic tales told concerning *Ancient American Archaeology* and how it supports the *Book of Mormon* account of pre-Columbian history, a subject too vast and baroque to be gone into here. Suffice it to say that much of this probably derives from certain widely read books by one Dewey Farnsworth, an amateur archaeologist. His works are large, lavishly illustrated compendia of quotations and homemade conjectures about archaeological finds on South and Central America. The folk mind, I believe, revises Farnsworth even more in the direction of fantasy, so that for every example in legend of something like an unsupported spiral stairway discovered in a quite explainable clearing which baffles modern science, there is an illustration in Farnsworth of a well-wrought, but quite explainable, Mayan or Aztec staircase. Such wonders as unknown metals and alloys, cryptic echoes of Hebraic or Egyptian culture, medical skills, and use of Christian symbols, all supposedly present before Columbus, crop up in the oral tales, as in Farnsworth's and others' books.

⁷ For example, Jerry Ainsworth, *The Lives and Travels of Mormon and Moroni*, 45, titles one chapter: "The Jaredite (Olmec) Civilization." Similarly, he says "It is certain something happened to the lowland 'Maya' (the Mulekites) after 200 B.C. that dramatically changed their society" (88).

A more subtle extension of this idea is the chapter "Two Traditions of Civilization" in John L. Sorenson, *Mormon's Codex: An Ancient American Book*, 144–49. Hidden among the valuable information presented is the oversimplification of Mesoamerican history into just the two traditions that he discusses. It was much more complex than that, and even more complex than his summary suggests within the traditions discussed.

group, and almost certainly no Olmec considered people living more than a few hours' walk away as members of his or her own group. Nevertheless, the numerous independent local cultures were so similar to one another that modern scientists consider them a single generic culture. When the Spaniards arrived in Mexico, the Nahuatl-speaking Aztecs called the inhabitants of Olman the *Olmeca-Huixtotin* (Olmeca: inhabitant of the Rubber country; Huixtotin: People of the Saltwater). Although the Olmeca-Huixtotin lacked any direct connection with their Formative-period predecessors, early archaeologists mistakenly applied the term Olmec to the remains of both cultures. Today it remains the accepted name of choice for the Formative-period cultures, despite occasional attempts to replace it with one that is less confusing.[8]

The term *Mayan* similarly provides an umbrella label that masks separate languages belonging to the same basic family (analogous to the Romance family of languages). Even though there was a general set of material culture traits, the various Maya cities were in no way a uniform culture.[9] Before anyone arrived in Central America who might be called Jaredite, there were people who could be culturally identified as Olmec. Before anyone arrived in Central America who might be called Nephite or Lamanite, there were people who could be culturally identified as Maya. Any suggestion that Book of Mormon peoples created Mesoamerican cultural horizons contradicts the available archaeological evidence.

Archaeological evidence tells us that Book of Mormon peoples did not infuse Old World culture into the New World or provide a spike in New World capabilities.[10] Diehl suggests that the Olmec are "one of only six pristine civilizations in human history. Pristine civilizations were the earliest civilizations in their respective regions, cultures that developed *sui generis* without any older models to guide their development."[11] When the Book of Mormon peoples entered the not-empty New World, they entered a land that was not only populated, but which already boasted highly developed civilizations. The Book of Mormon does not explain Mesoamerican peoples—but Mesoamerican peoples help explain the Book of Mormon.

---

[8] Richard A. Diehl, *The Olmecs: America's First Civilization*, 14. Diehl also notes: "It is unlikely that all of Olman's inhabitants spoke the same dialect or even the same language" (13).

[9] Mark Alan Wright, "The Cultural Tapestry of Mesoamerica," 7: "The thousands of separate ancient cities that we label as 'Maya' never conceptualized themselves as being part of a single culture (incidentally, even the origin of the word *Maya* is uncertain)."

[10] According to Diehl, *The Olmecs*, 14: "Not a single *bona fide* artifact of Old World origin has ever appeared in an Olmec archaeological site, or for that matter anywhere else in Mesoamerica."

Sorenson, *Mormon's Codex*, 499–503 appears to argue for some kind of external impetus to the rise of the Olmec. In the context of argument following those pages, he appears to suggest the Jaredites as that external impetus. He specifically suggests evidence for the "arrival of Semitic Foreigners" (532). It is a theme on which we disagree. I see Book of Mormon peoples as receiving culture rather than imparting it. For Sorenson, the immigration of Book of Mormon peoples appears as a causal factor in the rise of different Mesoamerican groups.

[11] Diehl, *The Olmecs*, 11–12. "They include Egyptian and Sumerian cultures in the Near East, Indus civilization in modern India and Pakistan, China's Shang culture, and Chavin culture in Peru" (12).

Although Jaredites were not the Olmec and Nephites were not the Maya, the Jaredite culture might yet be termed Olmec, and at least the Lamanite culture might be called Maya. As a definition of an assemblage of cultural and regional traits, both Olmec and Maya serve as blanket terms encompassing a number of distinct groups that give us a context against which we may read Jaredites and Nephites.

With such a small Lehite population entering an established region with a significantly larger population, the most logical direction of cultural borrowing would have been from the established indigenous populations to the small population that had originated in Jerusalem. With a different climate and different natural resources, the people who arrived on the shores of the New World had much more to learn than they did to give. Just as it is most likely that the indigenous material culture became the Lehite material culture, it is also most logical that the Lehites were under significantly more pressure to learn the local indigenous language than those populations were to learn Hebrew. Hebrew clearly continued, but it is unlikely that it would have been the common language even early in Book of Mormon history.

Becoming Nephites and Lamanites

Nephi's description of the family's early days is terse: "And it came to pass that we did begin to till the earth, and we began to plant seeds; yea, we did put all our seeds into the earth, which we had brought from the land of Jerusalem. And it came to pass that they did grow exceedingly; wherefore, we were blessed in abundance" (1 Ne. 18:24).

This simple statement isn't intended to describe their actions, but to support the conclusion that they were "blessed in abundance." In his thin description, Nephi establishes the essential beginnings of his people in the New World. They had shelter and food. That generally favorable statement concludes Nephi's story of the Old World. Although not an allusion, it is similar in intent to Genesis's conclusion to a day of creation: "it was good."

The first historical event in Nephi's second book is the occasion of Lehi's patriarchal blessings to his sons (2 Nephi 1–4). While this was certainly an event, Nephi uses that event to lay out the future story of Lehi's family rather than realized history. It is the next event, however—not only history, but also a historical event—that lays the foundation for all future Nephite history.

With the passing of the family's patriarch, conflict that had long existed between the brothers not only arose again, but arose without Lehi's steadying influence which had previously ameliorated it. At this point we see the schism that led to the demonyms (names for a people) "Lamanite" and "Nephite" that are used throughout the Book of Mormon.

Nephi records that these conflicts occurred "not many days after [Lehi's] death" (2 Ne. 4:13). He also reports that Yahweh warned him that the conflict had become fratricidal (2 Ne. 5:2–5). Consequently:

> And it came to pass that the Lord did warn me, that I, Nephi, should depart from them and flee into the wilderness, and all those who would go with me.

> Wherefore, it came to pass that I, Nephi, did take my family, and also Zoram and his family, and Sam, mine elder brother and his family, and Jacob and Joseph, my younger brethren, and also my sisters, and all those who would go with me. And all those who would go with me were those who believed in the warnings and the revelations of God; wherefore, they did hearken unto my words. (2 Ne. 5:5–6)

The physical separation of Nephite from Lamanite begins with this warning and subsequent flight into the wilderness. It is therefore important that we tease from it all of the information we can. Perhaps the most important detail is the composition of those who followed Nephi and those who remained behind.

Sorenson estimated that the plausible group constituting Lehi's family as they entered their ship would have been perhaps a maximum of around forty-three, allowing for each of the men to have fathered two children in the wilderness.[12] Of that number he suggests only fifteen as vigorous adults (excluding the elderly Lehi, Sariah, and Ishmael's wife).

When Nephi flees from his fratricidal brothers, he names the men who went with him. He mentions his sisters but does not name them. Since women are rarely named in the Book of Mormon, the explicit mention of sisters might indicate that they are unmarried. We expect that the wives of the named men accompanied them and are unnamed because their husbands' names implies their presence. Specifically named are Zoram, Sam, Jacob, and Joseph. Of course, Lehi has died and presumably Sariah as well. Surely Nephi would have mentioned his mother (the only woman he names in his account, save the prophetically revealed Mary) had she still been alive. Remaining behind, and unnamed, were Laman and Lemuel and the sons of Ishmael (Sorenson suggests that there were two).[13]

Although the list doesn't account for children, it does divide up the list of vigorous adults, those who would be available for the difficult task of creating a new community. For the nascent Nephites, there were five adult males; for the Lamanites, perhaps four. These small numbers make it difficult to understand how either Lamanites or Nephites could be called a people at this early date. It also makes it difficult to understand how, after traveling such a long distance away from his brothers, Nephi feared that the "people who were now called Lamanites should come upon us and destroy us" (2 Ne. 5:14).

There are very few clearly identifiable people. However, although not specifically named, Nephi also took "all those who would go with me . . . who believed in the warnings and the revelations of God." Who might these people have been? There are four possibilities for the identity of "all those who would go":

> (1) Ishmael's sons and their families. This is unlikely. Tribal Ishmaelites are associated with Lamanites and Lemuelites, as in Alma 47:35 and 4 Nephi 1:38.

---

[12] John L. Sorenson, *Nephite Culture and Society*, 22. See 3–20 for the analysis leading to the estimated total.
[13] Ibid., 14–15.

(2) Some of the Lamanite children. This possibility seems unlikely, since children born in the wilderness were probably no older than ten and would stay with their mothers who presumably stayed with their husbands.

(3) Unnamed and otherwise completely unidentified individuals who might have come over on the ship. This reading is possible, but would be the only time such people were mentioned or even hinted at as the family boarded the ship in the Old World.

(4) Local residents who allied themselves with the Lehites in the first months of settlement.[14]

As we examine the nature of the early Nephite community, only this fourth option is viable in explaining Nephi's community.

Assuming that this hypothesis is correct, we may further assert that many of the local people who originally joined with the Lehites remained with the Lamanites. Given only the people Nephi names as going with him, there should have been more Nephites than Lamanites. Nevertheless, in just two generations Jarom states that the Lamanites "were exceedingly more numerous than were they of the Nephites" (Jarom 1:6). It is difficult to arrive at that conclusion based on the named people who went with Nephi and those who would have stayed to become the Lamanites. It is therefore important to highlight that Nephi refers to the "people who were now called Lamanites" (2 Ne. 5:14). Even this early, Lamanite has become a demonym rather than a patronym, a point Jacob will later emphasize (Jacob 1:13–14).

When Nephi describes the arrival of the family in the New World, he uses food to suggest that they had been blessed. He, and subsequent writers, will refer to ease in obtaining food, not only to continue to describe a blessed condition, but also to make a cultural contrast. Nephi and subsequent writers contrast agriculture with the hunter-gatherer lifestyle. Agriculture attaches a people to a place and creates some permanence. Hunter-gatherers are nomadic and do not create permanent dwelling places. Agriculture supports a larger number of people, and hunter-gatherer bands tend to be smaller.

In Nephite usage, however, it isn't the mode—agricultural or hunter-gatherer—that is important. What is important is that the two can be used to create a conceptual division between civilized and uncivilized. Agriculture "civilizes" in that it encourages permanent communities.

---

[14] The presence of others in the land has often been an implicit rather than an explicit argument. One of the more detailed explanations of the textual evidence for others in the land is in Sorenson's chapter "When Lehi's Party Arrived in the Land, Did They Find Others There?" in his *Nephite Culture and Society*, 65–104.

I presented the core of my arguments based on "those who would go" and found additional corroboration of their presence in the likely setting for Jacob's sermon (2 Ne. 6–10) at the Foundation for Apologetic Information and Research (FAIR) conference in August 2001. See Brant A. Gardner, "A Social History of the Early Nephites." John Gee and Matthew Roper presented virtually the same argument at the 32nd Sidney B. Sperry Symposium, "'I Did Liken All Scriptures unto Us': Early Nephite Understandings of Isaiah and Implications for 'Others' in the Land," 53–54.

The enmity with the Lamanites is expressed in this contrast between an agricultural and a hunter-gatherer lifestyle.[15] Nephites, who plant, are civilized. Lamanites, who don't, are not. Nephi reports that the Lamanites: "did become an idle people, full of mischief and subtlety, and did seek in the wilderness for beasts of prey" (2 Ne. 5:24). Although this might have been a more or less accurate description of the early Lamanites,[16] it soon became a stereotype.[17] It persisted as a stereotype throughout the Book of Mormon.[18] Nephites continued to portray Lamanites as uncivilized hunters even when the textual evidence suggests that they lived in a larger

---

[15] See Enos 1:20; Alma 25:12, 47:36. Note especially Hel. 3:16 where apostates to the Lamanites "mixed with the Lamanites until they are no more called the Nephites, becoming wicked, and wild, and ferocious, yea, even becoming Lamanites."

[16] Sorenson, *An Ancient American Setting for the Book of Mormon*, 140, certainly sees this description of early Lamanites as literal:

> The coastal plain where the landing of Lehi would have occurred was uncomfortably hot and humid. That climate favored rapid crop growth, but the weather would be unpleasant for colonizers. The Nephites soon fled up to the land of Nephi, where the elevation permitted living in greater comfort. As Nephi tells the story, the Lamanites down in the hot lowlands were nomadic hunters, bloodthirsty, near naked, and lazy (2 Nephi 5:24; Enos 1:20). The circumstances of life in that environment could account for some of those characteristics. Many centuries later the Spaniards spoke in like terms of natives in the same area. The Tomas Medel manuscript, dating about A.D. 1550, just a generation after the first Spaniards arrived in the area, reported that the Indian men on the Pacific coast of Guatemala "spent their entire lives as naked as when they were born." That practice may have seemed a sensible response to the oppressive climate. In the late seventeenth century Catholic priest Fuentes y Guzman contrasted the "lassitude and laziness" of the same lowlanders with the energy of the highland inhabitants. As for getting a living, the tangle of forest and swamp along the coast itself may have been too hard for the Lamanite newcomers to farm effectively, since they wouldn't immediately get the knack of cultivation in that locale.

[17] Sorenson, *Mormon's Codex*, 235, makes the same observation: "These attributed characteristics sound more stereotypical than plainly descriptive and very much resemble a Near Eastern cultural formula according to which Mesopotamian city dwellers of the third millennium B.C. characterized Amorite desert dwellers of their day as dark savages who lived in tents, ate their food raw, and left their dead unburied."

Although the stereotype fits with a Middle Eastern model, such stereotyping is so typical of human behavior that no direct connection between the Middle East and the New World is required to explain it.

[18] While the entire catalog is not repeated, elements are used in various descriptions of the Lamanites: Jarom 1:6, Mosiah 9:2, 9:12, 10:12, Alma 17:14, 47:36 (apostates are more "Lamanite" than Lamanites), Hel. 3:16. As the Book of Mormon progresses, a new stereotype is added. Non-Nephite behavior becomes characterized by the paired set of "murder" and "plunder": Mosiah 2:3, 10:7, Alma 23:3, Hel. 6:23, 7:21, 11:25, 3 Ne. 4:5, Ether 8:16.

and more complex civilization than the Nephites.[19] For the Nephites, the stereotype defined Lamanites more than actual conditions described them.[20]

The Nephites were prejudiced. Extremely prejudiced.[21] Such prejudice is not surprising. It would be surprising if they were not. The process of community creation necessarily defines not-community. Historically, this process also engenders antagonism between *us* and *them*. Bruce J. Malina and Jerome H. Neyrey note: "A fundamental cultural correlate of geocentrism was the in-group/out-group perspective. In-group belonging and commitment are rooted in the perception of solidarity born of a common fate and rooted in similarity with others, specifically with one's family, extended family, neighborhood, town or city section, and ethnic group. In-group members are treated with loyalty, openness, allegiance, and support. Those falling outside the in-group boundaries belong to the out-group. With the out-group, dealings are indifferent, even hostile. For all practical purposes, ethnically out-group persons are, once more, a different species of being."[22]

The Lamanites might never have been described as a different species of being, but they were certainly cast as the mirror opposite of the Nephites—so much so that they are described in black and white terms—literally. There are "black Lamanites" and "white Nephites." When "black" Lamanites became Nephite, "their curse was taken from them, and their skin became white like unto the Nephites" (3 Ne. 2:15). Crossing the boundary from out-group to in-group changed their social description.

---

[19] The classic description of the differences between Nephite and Lamanite culture is found in Enos 1:20–21. See Brant A. Gardner, *Second Witness: Analytical and Contextual Commentary on the Book of Mormon*, 1:15–22, for a discussion of the features and anthropological intent of the comparative descriptions.

[20] Bruce J. Malina and Jerome H. Neyrey, *Portraits of Paul: An Archaeology of Ancient Personality*, 117–20, describe how Mediterranean cultures employed stereotypes as a short-cut to knowing what to expect of a person based on his place of origin. The stereotype was often "supported" by "evidence." They notethat, "when Polemo [a second-century Greek rhetorician] describes the peoples of the north, south, and east and west, he tends to give us a brief description of the physical traits caused by the distinctive climate of the region, and then a catalogue of the character traits 'natural' to that locale" (120).

[21] The concept of prejudice in the United States is entangled with the issues of slavery and its justification by denigrating an entire people on the basis of skin color. The assumption that prejudice and skin color are associated is perpetuated when the Book of Mormon indicates that "the Lord God did cause a skin of blackness to come upon [the Lamanites]" (2 Ne. 16:21). Our own powerful cultural associations between skin color and prejudice link this statement to a literal change in skin color. I argue that there was no such change. See "The Lamanite Skin of Blackness," in Chapter 6.

[22] Malina and Neyrey, *Portraits of Paul*, 122.

Also David Livingston Smith, *Less Than Human: Why We Demean, Enslave, and Exterminate Others*, 49: "the tendency to favor members of one's own community and discriminate against outsiders (otherwise known as the 'us and them' mentality). *We* are more industrious, conscientious, attractive, and so on, than *they* are. When things go badly for one of *us* it's an injustice, but when the same thing happens to one of *them* it's because they brought it on themselves. On the flip side, when one of *us* experiences good fortune, it's richly deserved, but when one of *them* benefits from a windfall, it's an undeserved stroke of luck."

The Lamanite Skin of Blackness

Good and bad in the Book of Mormon is as simple as black and white. Conveniently, the people are black and white. Inconveniently, bad black Lamanites chafe modern sensibilities. The problem, however, isn't in the binary opposition of black and white. It is in the assumption that those colors describe skin color.

It is an assumption based on an understandable but unfortunate reading of 2 Nephi 5:21: "And [Yahweh] had caused the cursing to come upon them, yea, even a sore cursing, because of their iniquity. For behold, they had hardened their hearts against him, that they had become like unto a flint; wherefore, as they were white, and exceedingly fair and delightsome, that they might not be enticing unto my people the Lord God did cause a skin of blackness to come upon them." Lamanites were white. Through iniquity they became black.[23] Our perception is focused on, and by, the phrase "skin of blackness."

---

[23] David Tayman, "Adjusting the Narrative: Part 2a-Nephi and the Skin of Blackness," adds some additional insight:

> Within the narrative, the announcement and implication of any "curse" happens contextually after the Nephites have already sent themselves into exile away from the newly-titled Lamanites. There's even an implication that not only had Nephi been made King, but also that time had passed sufficiently to build the temple, and to establish a society before the "curse" was made known to him and announced. In other words, the major implication here is *that there are no Nephite eyewitnesses to the initiation and application of the "curse" and any associated "marking," including King Nephi himself*. This is very important. Nobody in the text claims to have witnessed anyone's skin change color.
>
> While Nephi states that the announcement of the curse and marking comes from God, he stops short of giving a quotation of the Lord when giving the explanation of a skin of blackness—*the explanation of what the Lord did appears to be an extrapolation and an interpretation of Nephi's own*!

Tayman concludes: "I propose the interpretive possibility within the narrative that, down the road, an indigenous tribe with significantly darker skin tones encountered and battled the Nephite colony, and King Nephi interpreted them as being the 'loathsome' and 'cut off' 'scourge' who may have been connected with his brothers' people."

This conclusion appears to follow from his stated preferred solution to the issue of the skin of blackness in the Book of Mormon:

> This skin of blackness in the book of Mormon is defended by some as literal, and others as being purely metaphorical. While I am highly sympathetic to wanting to find a strictly and completely intended metaphorical reading, in my experience, both arguments tend to break down at some point when applied to the entire story, and all of the texts. I would like to propose a more nuanced reading, that also takes the text seriously, and at face value, and making full use of Moroni's declaration that *"if there are faults they are the mistakes of men"*—and I take this to include the original participants in the action as well as their chroniclers and translators.

The solution posits a literal color distinction that occurs when the term Lamanite becomes an exonym. Unfortunately, it also would posit a skin color difference among the Nephites and have any indigenous peoples who united with the Nephites having come from some unknown people with a significantly lighter skin. There is no evidence for that. There is no evidence that any of the people who joined with the Nephites would have had a different pigmentation from

The verse has been read as indicating a literal, visible, change in skin pigmentation.[24] Nevertheless, the second half of the same phrase has not been read literally. Skin is really skin, but blackness isn't really black.

The willingness to see part of the phrase as less than literal should alert the reader that perhaps the entire phrase should be seen in a different light. All human populations have variations in color, and pigmentation differences occur in all populations. One set of people can have very black skin, but they are not native to the western hemisphere. Amerindians are called "red," but they are not red. Caucasians are called "white," but they are not white. Asians are called "yellow," but they are not yellow. Skin color designations are cultural descriptions, not scientific ones. As Steven Pinker points out, "It's convention, not color vision, that tells us that a sick Caucasian is *green*, a cold one *blue*, and a scared one *yellow*."[25]

Humans frequently create categories that are binary opposites. The black/white opposition is common enough to be considered a universal human trait.[26] To each of the opposite colors, a binary opposite meaning is attached. In the case of black and white, it is good and bad.[27] One of the powerful aspects of such binary opposites is the

---

anyone else, therefore there was no reason to suppose any pigmentation change occurred because there were people with that same skin coloration already among the Nephites.

[24] For example, Milton R. Hunter, *Archaeology and the Book of Mormon*, 191. Rodney Turner, "The Lamanite Mark," 138. While Turner reads the statement of pigmentation change literally, he does not read the word "blackness" literally: "The expression 'skin of blackness' does not necessarily, or even probably, mean a black skin, only a darker skin. The pre-flood people of Canaan (Cain's posterity) had a 'blackness' come upon them after the Lord cursed their land 'with much heat' (Moses 7:8). After Enoch's city was translated from the earth Enoch beheld that 'the seed of Cain were black' and were separate from all other peoples (Moses 7:22). I believe that 'blackness' and 'black' are not synonyms and that the Lamanite mark was only a relatively darker pigmentation, not a literally black skin. By the same token, a 'white' skin is only relatively so (Jacob 3:8)." Turner, "The Lamanite Mark," 138 footnote 2.

Sorenson, *An Ancient American Setting for the Book of Mormon*, 90, sees a pigmentation change related to exposure to the elements.

Royal Skousen, *Analysis of Textual Variants of the Book of Mormon*, 4–2:897, appears to follow the suggestion that there was a physical change in skin color. Discussing the change of *white* to *pure* in 2 Nephi 6:30 for the 1840 edition, he notes: "Of course, the 1840 change of *white* to *pure* avoids... the need to interpret the remnant of the Nephites as being dark skinned. In other words, the editing change to *pure* may represent a conscious attempt at avoiding what was perceived as a difficult reading (the Nephites as being dark skinned), which therefore explains why the change from *white* to *pure* was made here—and only here—in 2 Nephi 30:6. There has never been any attempt to emend any of the passages that directly comment on the dark skin of the Lamanites."

Skousen's argument for the reason for the editorial change is persuasive. It persuades, however, that the *reader's* understanding of the text related to a change in pigmentation.

[25] Steven Pinker, *The Stuff of Thought: Language as a Window into Human Nature*, 115.

[26] Donald E. Brown, *Human Universals*, 134: "Prominent elements in [Universal People] taxonomy and other aspects of their speech and thought are binary discriminations, forming contrasting terms or semantic components (... black and white, nature and culture, male and female, good and bad, etc.)."

[27] It is the same process that uses right hand/left hand as a linguistic parallel to good and bad.

ability of one pole to suggest the other. Thus, it allows for imagery to be created without specific reference to the other pole and, for instance, we know that a "black heart" is a bad/good contrast rather than a description of color.

Armand L. Mauss discusses this very issue:

> In modern colloquial English (or American) we sometimes speak of people as having "thick" or "thin" skins, without intending any literal dermatological meaning. Attributions of "white" versus "black" or "dark" skins could be read in a similarly figurative manner, as they might have been by Joseph Smith himself (or by his Nephite authors). The reader therefore need not attribute racist intentions when the Book of Mormon uses such terms as *dark* or *filthy* versus *white* or *pure*, especially when "racial traits," such as skin color, are not even explicitly mentioned—which is the case most of the time.[28]

Language provides multiple ways in which the black/white dichotomy might be applied to humankind. Only one of them is associated with skin pigment and even that assumes a less-than-literal use of color terminology. The question for the Book of Mormon is: what did the author mean by the phrase that would be translated as "skin of blackness"?

The Black/White Dichotomy in the Text

If Lamanites and Nephites were as visually distinct as black and white skins would have made them, we should see descriptions in the text where that distinction is noted. It never happens. There is, however, an occasion where it should have made a difference—but didn't.

Chief Captain Moroni, working to free Nephite prisoners, sent wine to their Lamanite guards, hoping to intoxicate them (Alma 55). Because they would not accept such a gift from a Nephite, Moroni searched for and found a Lamanite among his own troops, a former guard of the Lamanite king. Accompanied by Nephites, this soldier took the wine to the guards. The deception worked.

The most important aspect of the story of understanding "skin of blackness" is that the sole Lamanite was accompanied by Nephites. If this Lamanite had become "white," then he would have been indistinguishable from his Nephite companions and the Nephites would not have needed to find a Lamanite. Had the Lamanite literally had a black skin as opposed to the white skin of his companions, the Lamanite guards would have seen that contrast immediately and the ruse would not have worked. A Lamanite's presence is central to the story, but the ruse would have failed if there had been a visible pigmentation difference between the sole Lamanite and his Nephite companions. The reason for having a Lamanite could plausibly be language or accent, but not skin color.

The Lamanite curse is expressed in two antithetically parallel phrases: "as they were white, and exceedingly fair and delightsome the Lord God did cause a skin of blackness to come upon them" (2 Ne. 5:21). The phrases describe a previous condition and its succeeding condition, pivoting upon causation. Yahweh changed the Lamanites from what they had been to what they had become.

---

[28] Mauss, *All Abraham's Children*, 128.

The before/after relationship is "fair and delightsome"/"skin of blackness." Both conditions are structural opposites. 3 Nephi 2:14–15 reads: "And it came to pass that those Lamanites who had united with the Nephites were numbered among the Nephites; And their curse was taken from them, and their skin became white like unto the Nephites." This reversal of the curse (not repeated here but "skin of blackness") implies its opposite (articulated here): "skin became white." The Lamanites have crossed the insider/outsider boundary, becoming those who were "united with the Nephites" and "numbered among" them. Because they have become Nephites, they therefore "became white like unto the Nephites."

This shift in "skin of blackness" to "skin became white" on the basis of a change from outsider to insider explains why the first appearance of the idea of the curse on the Lamanites has a different inception date than the curse mentioned in 2 Nephi 5:21. In 1 Nephi 12:23, Nephi prophesied: "And I beheld, after they had dwindled in unbelief they became a dark, and loathsome, and a filthy people." This is a reference to the Lamanites who survive the wars that destroy the Nephites (1 Ne. 12:19–20). In prophecy, Nephi places the darkness of the Lamanites over 1,000 years later than when we find it in 2 Nephi 5:21. Why the discrepancy in time?

The answer is that there is no discrepancy. The condition of darkness comes with dwindling in unbelief. When that occurs, darkness falls—on their hearts and metaphorically on their skins. It is not a physical change and therefore does not have a specific point of inception. It is as accurate when described in 2 Nephi as it is prophetically at the end of Nephite culture.

Another example is the dark/white pairing from the 1830 first edition of 2 Nephi 30:6: "Their scales of darkness shall begin to fall from their eyes; and many generations shall not pass away among them, save they shall be a white and a delightsome people."[29] This verse parallels "fair and delightsome," making "fair" and "white" structural equivalents. Although the "fair/delightsome" pair occurs twice (2 Ne. 5:21, 4 Ne. 1:10) and "white/delightsome" occurs only once, nevertheless these phrases are repeating the same concept.

"Fair/white" is paired with "dark/black" in the antithetical parallel. The textual opposite of "delightsome" is "loathsome." The term "loathsome" is paired with "dark" in 1 Nephi 12:23 and is the reason for the cursing in 2 Nephi 5:22.[30] The curse's purpose is to set a social barrier between the two peoples. When the curse is operating and the Lamanites are outsiders, they are "loathsome" (the opposite of "delightsome")—not desirable marriage partners. When they are insiders, they are "delightsome," available as marriage partners. Just as the white/black or fair/dark terms function along the

---

[29] The 1981 edition of the Book of Mormon changed "white" to "pure," following the 1840 edition. This change continues in the 2013 edition. The constructions examined here suggest that "white" would actually be a better translation but that the meaning is essentially equivalent to "pure."

[30] The parallel in the phrasing indicates the parallel in the intent, even though the 1 Nephi 12:23 passage refers to an event over 1,000 years in the future beyond the discussion in 2 Nephi 5:21.

insider/outsider boundary, so too does the delightsome/loathsome dichotomy describe social repercussions. Mauss concludes: "A comprehensive review of the Book of Mormon text as a whole shows that it uses *white* almost always as a figurative synonym for *pure, clean, luminous,* and similar concepts, not in reference to such "racial" traits as skin color"[31] (emphasis his).

If it is a metaphor, why did Nephi specifically use the word "skin"? We actually don't know the word Nephi used, only that Joseph translated it as "skin." What we do know is that there is an Old Testament model for the metaphorical use of "blackness" and a reference to at least some human skin. The KJV for Joel 2:6 reads: "Before their face the people shall be much pained: all faces shall gather blackness."[32] The blackness is associated only with the face rather than the skin, but certainly does not refer to a visual change to the color of one's face.

The metaphorical meaning is underlined in modern translations which render the meaning rather than just the words. The *Revised English Bible* translates the phrase from Joel 2:6: "face is drained of colour." The *New International Bible* translates: "every face turns pale." In this case, the Hebrew "blackness" is best understood with an opposite "color," or paleness. Job 30:30 notes that "My skin is black upon me." The description is of a sickness and not a change in pigmentation. Whatever Nephi wrote and Joseph Smith translated, there is every reason to believe that it was a metaphor. There is no evidence that it was literal.

Mesoamerican Depictions of "Skin Color"

Some LDS authors have used Mesoamerican artistic representations to support the idea of a pigmentation difference between Nephites and Lamanites. Multiple paintings show people with dramatically different skin tones, from white to black and browning/redding—a more natural color for Native Americans. Sorenson makes the case for literally white-skinned Nephites by referring to the artistic depiction of light and dark-skinned warriors in a combat scene from Chichén Itzá:

> A marked difference in skin pigmentation is shown in various participants represented in an 11th-century-AD mural at Chichén Itzá, Yucatan. Dark-skinned warriors are shown dominating or abusing people with white skin. Ann Axtell Morris, the artist who copied the mural for the Carnegie Institution, notes that in the original painting one class of painted figures had "natural, light-colored skins, [and] . . . extraordinary yellow hair, very long and thick. . . . It is difficult. . . to reconcile all of these physical qualities with a member of [the Maya] race. The painter, in depicting the hair and skin with such care in order to contrast them with their black, . . . armed captors, evidently had some notion of a distinct physical difference in his two sets of actors."[33]

---

[31] Mauss, *All Abraham's Children*, 118.
[32] Similarly, Nahum 2:10.
[33] Sorenson, *Mormon's Codex*, 239–40. John L. Sorenson, *Images of Ancient America: Visualizing Book of Mormon Life*, 16–17, shows two color pictures of what he suggests is different pigmentation (one of which comes from the Chichén Itzá mural).

Sorenson's favorable citation of Morris's 1931 description clearly accepts her assumption that the different colors were related to physical pigmentation. Unfortunately for this assumption, the accumulation of artistic evidence since that time strongly suggests that it is more likely that the Chichén Itzá mural uses the color as a convention to easily separate the opposing armies.

Important evidence is found on Maya pottery where there are similar light and dark contrasts, but which are demonstrably related to body painting. Mesoamerican scholars Stephen Houston, David Stuart, and Karl Taube note: "Body paint is widely attested in Classic Maya imagery, but, like the schematic and abstract patterns on textiles, it is nearly impossible to understand semantically; available contexts are too vague to pinpoint meaning."[34] They also note that "there [does not] seem to have been a clear relationship between the pigments emblazoned on pots and those that, when preserved, cover stone sculptures. On sculptures, red is the dominant color, possibly because it was the least difficult or expensive to produce. When contrasted with other pigments (the palette on such sculptures tends to be quite limited), human skin is red or yellow; the hair and lips are red; and blue is reserved for jewelry, feathers, or deity heads."[35]

The unrealistic colors on the stone monuments should warn us that something happens with colors applied to the body that transcends a desire for a naturalistic depiction. This is confirmed on Maya pottery where bodies are shown as dark and light, but the "dark" bodies also show unpainted areas on the body; the face is left the lighter color, or in one case, the arms are also in the "default" unpainted color of the natural clay.[36]

Although it is true that one can find artistic depictions of light and dark-skinned people, the examination of the wider corpus of artistic representations tells us that body paint (or some other artistic need such as distinguishing combatants) is a more probable explanation than pigmentation. Mesoamerican art should not be used to bolster the reading of a pigmentation change in the Book of Mormon.

Establishing the People and the City of Nephi

When Nephi, and those who would go with him, left their initial settlement(s) in the coastal region of Guatemala, they traveled for "many days" before finding the location where they established themselves (2 Ne. 5:7). Although they might have gone northwest or southwest along coast, later textual details strongly suggest that they traveled inland. In Sorenson's model:

---

[34] Stephen Houston, David Stuart, and Karl Taube, *The Memory of Bones: Body, Being, and Experience among the Classic Maya*, 22.

[35] Ibid., 24.

[36] The evidence may be seen in the online database of Maya vases. See Justin Kerr, "Maya Vase Data Base: A Precolumbian Portfolio." In this catalog, the images are indexed by what has become known as a Kerr number, a K followed by a number. For the clear examples where the dark "skin" is the result of body paint, see K558, K1563, K1599, and K2711.

Where the party of Nephi settled was quite surely the Valley of Guatemala, or, as they named it, the land of Nephi. The continental divide runs right through the valley, present-day Guatemala City. . .at an elevation of about 5,000 feet. Water on one side of the city flows eastward to the Caribbean, that on the other to the Pacific. This is the largest and most productive valley in highland Guatemala. The climate is famous: spring-like and temperate, with only infrequent cold rains and squalls—a marvelous spot in which to settle. The river that drains the valley southwestward provides a pass between the mountains that would all but invite Nephi's party to "come up" as they moved along the lowlands in their flight.[37]

Nephi literarily, and I believe intentionally, parallels this new settlement in a new land to his description of his family's settlement in the New World. After noting the journey across the ocean, Nephi indicated that his family began to till the earth and prosper: "And it came to pass that we did begin to till the earth, and we began to plant seeds; yea, we did put all our seeds into the earth, which we had brought from the land of Jerusalem. And it came to pass that they did grow exceedingly; wherefore, we were blessed in abundance" (1 Ne. 18:24). In this second new beginning, the two themes are repeated:

> And we did take our tents and whatsoever things were possible for us, and did journey in the wilderness for the space of many days. And after we had journeyed for the space of many days we did pitch our tents. . . .
> And the Lord was with us; and we did prosper exceedingly; for we did sow seed, and we did reap again in abundance. And we began to raise flocks, and herds, and animals of every kind. (2 Ne. 5:7, 11)

The essential elements are strikingly similar. Nephi's people travel through a wilderness—Lehi's traveled through a wilderness in the Old World (and then the vast oceanic wilderness). After many days, Nephi's people encamp and plant—Lehi's people similarly made shelters and planted. The tilling of the earth is a particularly important parallel because Nephi uses this element to create a cultural distinction between "civilized" Nephites and "uncivilized" Lamanites. (Lamanites "did become an idle people, full of mischief and subtlety, and did seek in the wilderness for beasts of prey" (2 Ne. 5:24).)

The Nephite dedication to the law of Moses is confirmed when Nephi records that they built a temple "after the manner of the temple of Solomon save it were not built of so many precious things" (2 Ne. 5:16).[38] While Nephi's intent in mentioning the temple was to reinforce the religious identity of the community, it also tells us that there were significantly more men available than the four named individuals who accompanied him.[39] With only four able-bodied men, their religious needs might have

---

[37] Sorenson, *An Ancient American Setting*, 141.
[38] Noel B. Reynolds, "By Objective Measures: Old Wine into Old Bottles," 130. Also see the discussion in Chapter 4, "The First Camp."
[39] In that literary context, it is probable that the inclusion of this explicit declaration of their foundation on the Old World Israelite religion is also an unstated contrast to the Lamanites, who would not be seen as following the law of Moses. Although Laman and Lemuel would

been met with a much smaller structure, perhaps even just an altar, such as had sufficed for Lehi when he offered sacrifices after leaving Jerusalem. The very fact that so soon after separation (though there is no way to know how soon) they were building a temple continues to suggest a reasonably sizable population, one that could afford to take time to construct a community building rather than concentrating on the immediate needs of their own food and shelter.[40] As John S. Henderson reminds us: "Public buildings imply political leaders with the authority and power to command the human and economic resources of large areas."[41]

The temple is the only structure Nephi mentions. Certainly there was housing for the people, but he doesn't describe those structures. He declares generally: "I did teach my people to build buildings" (2 Ne. 5:15). This statement should be seen in the context of a leader directing his people rather than any necessary education of his people. It is unlikely that Nephi knew any more about constructing buildings than the others in his Old World family, and also very likely that he knew less about how to appropriately build for the New World climate than the indigenous members of the community. At this point, we must call on what is known of that cultural area at that time to speculate on what Nephi's early village would have looked like.

The change from Old World to New and the inclusion of plausible peoples of the New World strongly suggests that the early Nephites (and Lamanites) participated in the existing material culture.[42] It would make the most sense to adopt local building materials and techniques that were appropriate to the region rather than attempt to import building methods and types that were designed for a different culture and different climate.

With varying degrees of elaboration, communities in the Maya cultural sphere consisted of various plaza groups. The residential plaza group consisted of the household

---

certainly retain their beliefs, the conceptual division into Nephite and Lamanite allowed for a stereotyping of Lamanites that would have included people having ties to Laman and Lemuel. For this definition of *Lamanite*, there was a certain contrast between their religion and that of the Nephite community.

[40] Garth L. Mangum, "The Economics of the Book of Mormon: Joseph Smith as Translator or Commentator," 82 and 83: "On an implicit level the Book of Mormon is replete with economic references, as any history of human life must be." "The very existence of a city is an economic phenomenon based on some combination of specialization and exchange; buying, selling, and profit-making; and political and military adventure and subjugation. . . . In the new land, there appears to be no period of isolated pioneering with subsistence living off the land but an almost immediate establishment of cities with construction of buildings and including temples, an assumption by Nephi of the role of overseer and a specialization of labor including working with wood, iron, copper, brass, steel, gold, silver and 'precious ores' (2 Nephi 5:15–18)."

[41] John S. Henderson, *The World of the Ancient Maya*, 89.

[42] Mangum, "The Economics of the Book of Mormon," 83–84. "A city-building society, such as that of the Nephites, requires specialization and exchange. The countryside provides the food which the city can and must obtain either by exchange or expropriation. A people governed in any way other than harsh dictatorship can develop a substantial urban sector only by providing in exchange for foodstuffs either handicrafts or manufactured products, desired services, or a marketing function with facilitates exchange with other areas, rural or urban."

structures and exterior spaces required to support family production activities. These groupings might support extended families or be expanded to include lineages living in a group or associated groups. (See Chapter 11 for more information on kin-based living arrangements in Mesoamerica.) Public architecture occurred in a space surrounded by and perhaps defined by the locations of the residential plaza groups so that all residential groups symbolically looked to a central place associated with public activities, including government and religion.[43] Individual houses were probably single room, thatch-roofed, wattle and daub constructions.[44]

Although the general Maya region has examples of more permanent public architecture at this time, it is unlikely that the earliest Nephite community was able to build on such a large scale. It is more probable that the earliest Nephite community structures were also thatch-covered wooden buildings, following the typical Mesoamerican spatial organization.[45] Francisco Estrada-Belli describes a late Preclassic [early Book of Mormon times] wooden temple from Cahal Pech in Belize: "This structure. . . was a lime-plastered pole and thatch building resting on a 20-centimeter-high stone-and-plaster platform. Inside, against the back wall, was a lime-plastered bench. Its exterior plastered walls were painted red."[46] As with other communities, the city of Nephi would plausibly build more elaborate communal structures of stone and plaster, but those would come later.[47]

Sorenson has suggested that the archaeological site known as Kaminaljuyú in highland Guatemala (near modern-day Guatemala City) may have been the city of Nephi.[48] Placing Nephites in this location again presumes interactions with existing

---

[43] Heather McKillop, *The Ancient Maya: New Perspectives*, 150.

[44] Kent V. Flannery, "The Early Mesoamerican House," 16. Flannery denotes this style as the standard between 1350 and 850 B.C. Its descendants are still built in many native communities.

[45] Francisco Estrada-Belli, *The First Maya Civilization: Ritual and Power before the Classic Period*, 68–69, describes the ritual plazas of three coordinated temples (known as E-groups) at the late Preclassic sites of Nakbé, Tikal, Cival, Cenote, and El Mirador.

[46] Ibid., 39.

[47] There is also a possibility that the Nephites merged into an existing population in highland Guatemala. Of course, that is also not mentioned in Nephi's account. However, it becomes more difficult to explain how Nephi becomes the ruler of the community if he and his followers merge into yet another large existing population.

[48] Sorenson, *Mormon's Codex*, 22. Sorenson, *An Ancient American Setting for the Book of Mormon*, 141:

> Two strong reasons stand out why the Valley of Guatemala should be considered the original land of Nephi. The first is that the site of Kaminaljuyu was for many centuries the dominant cultural center for all highland Guatemala, the most important spot for several hundred miles around. The great size (at least a mile square) and impressive constructions of Kaminaljuyu underline its key importance and that of the valley. The land of Nephi is portrayed in the Book of Mormon as dominant among its neighbors to the same degree. A second big reason for considering Nephi to have been here is that customs, details of terrain, and the dating of the archaeological remains correlate closely with what is reported in the Book of Mormon.

populations, but Kaminaljuyú had been settled for at least 400 years by the time Nephites could have arrived there.[49] Nevertheless, it still represented a community of wattle and daub structures rather than the later more monumental architecture.[50] The ability of Kaminaljuyú to rise in regional importance was related to its ability to control some of the important trade in obsidian, as witnessed by the presence of obsidian workshops.[51] The trade connections between Kaminaljuyú and other communities provides an important base on which the later Nephite economy could have been built. (See "Early Economic and Social Tension" in Chapter 7).

New World Peoples in Nephi's Community

The first hint of non-Lehites in the nascent Nephite community came with "all those who would go" with Nephi. Hints continue as that new community is built. The building required more than the named men. Nephi's appointment of his brothers, Jacob and Joseph, as priests and teachers "over the land of my people" (2 Ne. 5:26) indicates a larger population than would have been possible had there only been Old World immigrants in the new city.

The implicit presence of non-Lehite others not only explains the building projects and the religious organization with appointed priests and teachers, but that implicit presence supplies the logic behind an important early sermon. In 2 Nephi 6 we have the beginning of a sermon Jacob delivered. Although Jacob preached as a religious leader, it was Nephi who selected the Isaiah passage that formed the topic of the discourse (2 Ne. 6:4). The sermon was deemed sufficiently important that of all of the possible sermons Nephi or Jacob delivered, this is the one Nephi elected to record on the small plates. The handpicked text for the sermon initially appears enigmatic:

> Thus saith the Lord God: Behold, I will lift up mine hand to the Gentiles, and set up my standard to the people; and they shall bring thy sons in their arms, and thy daughters shall be carried upon their shoulders.
> And kings shall be thy nursing fathers, and their queens thy nursing mothers; they shall bow down to thee with their faces towards the earth, and lick up the dust of thy feet; and thou shalt know that I am the Lord; for they shall not be ashamed that wait for me. (2 Ne. 6:6–7; no change from Isaiah 49:22–23)

As Jacob elaborates these verses, he makes it clear that they apply to the reinstatement of scattered Israel. Certainly Nephi saw his people as part of the scattering, but why preach about what we would consider a still-future time when the

---

The second reason Sorenson lists is the more salient. The first is simply the assumption that anything connected to the Nephites must have been very important, and therefore anything important must have been Nephite. That is an understandable prejudice, but not one that can necessarily be demonstrated in the text. Such thinking has led to an assumption that Mesoamerican civilization received a cultural boost from Book of Mormon peoples. While that is, again, an understandable prejudice, it is not demonstrable from any of the archaeological data.

[49] Susan Toby Evans, *Ancient Mexico and Central America: Archaeology and Culture History*, 180.
[50] Ibid. Henderson, *The World of the Ancient Maya*, 95.
[51] Jane W. Pires-Ferreira, "Obsidian Exchange in Formative Mesoamerica," 303.

Gentiles would be the instrument of saving the scattered of Israel? In a fairly new community, there must have been more pressing needs than discussing something that might be a couple of thousand years in the future.

Nephi "did liken all scriptures unto us, that it might be for our profit and learning" (1 Ne. 19:23). It is highly unlikely that the king of a new community would specifically select a topic for a sermon and deem it important enough to copy onto the plate record, if it had no current relevance. What might that relevance have been?

The implicit non-Lehites provide the context in which this sermon becomes absolutely timely. Nephi instructed Jacob to give this sermon *because* the congregation consisted of Nephites joined with "Gentiles" (natives). Not only is it a conciliatory sermon that would help the Old World Nephites rethink the role of the Gentiles in their midst, but it also allows the Gentiles to see themselves as saviors of lineal Israelites and as recipients of Israel's blessings. Jacob told his audience a story—one that applied to their existence as a new people—but without making direct reference to his point. Later in the sermon he makes it clear that he intends this to be a message for the current people, not something for the far-distant future (2 Ne. 9:1–3).[52]

This potential background provides an interesting context for 2 Nephi 6:13: "Wherefore, they that fight against Zion and the covenant people of the Lord shall lick up the dust of their feet; and the people of the Lord shall not be ashamed." Nephi has already recorded contentions with the Lamanites. Now Jacob identifies the Gentiles as allies of Israel and their means of redemption. Giving the community this vision of itself as the salvation of Israel's blessings provides a compelling reason for Jacob's sermon, one in which these particular passages from Isaiah have striking relevance.[53]

John Gee and Matthew Roper see a similar application of these passages to Nephi's people: "In addition to explaining the latter-day application of Isaiah's prophecy, Jacob's sermon can be read as addressing the question of how Lehite Israel is to relate to non-Lehite peoples in the promised land. The answer, Jacob taught, is that the non-Lehites may, if they so choose, join with the people of God in seeking to build up Zion as joint inheritors of the land. Once they do so, they are numbered with Lehi's seed."[54]

---

[52] These are the verses:

And now, my beloved brethren, I have read these things that ye might know concerning the covenants of the Lord that he has covenanted with all the house of Israel—

That he has spoken unto the Jews, by the mouth of his holy prophets, even from the beginning down, from generation to generation, until the time comes that they shall be restored to the true church and fold of God; when they shall be gathered home to the lands of their inheritance, and shall be established in all their lands of promise.

Behold, my beloved brethren, I speak unto you these things that ye may rejoice, and lift up your heads forever, because of the blessings which the Lord God shall bestow upon your children. (2 Ne. 9:1–3)

[53] Brant A. Gardner, "A Social History of the Early Nephites."
[54] Gee and Roper, "'I Did Liken All Scriptures unto Us.'" 56. It is possible that Gee and Roper recognized this connection independently, although Roper attended the Conference for the

Gee and Roper also suggest that this perspective becomes foundational for the insider/outsider terminology seen throughout the Book of Mormon. The demonym *Lamanite* not only refers to non-Nephite, but also to non-covenant:

> Some have wondered why, if other people were present in the land during Book of Mormon times, they are not mentioned more frequently in the record. This teaching, delivered by the Nephites' first priest, would be foundational for later Nephite prophets and would likely have set a precedent for viewing all other peoples in the land, ideally in covenant terms. Previous cultural identity from the Lehite perspective would be swallowed up in this frame of reference. An example of this can be seen in the case of Nephi's righteous brother Sam. . . . Lehi, who blessed all of his children, uses the term "numbered" only in Sam's blessing. Interestingly, when Lehite tribal designations are mentioned, there is no tribe of Sam (Jacob 1:13, 4 Ne. 1:35–38). Why? Apparently because when one is "numbered" with a people, one takes upon himself the name and identity of that people. Gentiles, once numbered with Abraham (Abr. 2:10), Isaac, Jacob (3 Ne. 21:22), Moses and Aaron (D&C 84:34), or Lehi (1 Ne. 14:2, 2 Ne. 10:18–19), are thereafter identified with their covenant fathers, without respect to biological origin. From then on they are simply Israel.[55]

Therefore, the identification of the "Gentile" population of the New World as part of the Nephites occurs when they join with the Nephites who represent Israel. Similarly, those "Gentiles" who mix with the lineage of the Lamanites are also absorbed into that "lineage" of Israel. Nevertheless, because they have mixed with the Lamanites, they become cursed (2 Ne. 5:23) and do not have access to the blessings of Abraham even though they are classified under the Lamanite Israelite identity.

DNA and the Book of Mormon

Ugo A. Perego provides an overview of questions relevant to DNA and the Book of Mormon: "Over the past decade, critics of the Book of Mormon have promoted the idea that since the majority of Amerindian DNA lineages are closely related to Asian populations, and since no perfect genetic affinity to the Middle East has been found, it must be concluded that the Book of Mormon account is fictional. This argument is sometimes bolstered in part by a common sentiment among Latter-day Saints

---

Foundation for Apologetic Information and Research in August 2001 where I presented this basic concept. See Brant A. Gardner, "A Social History of the Early Nephites." Gee and Roper have added the important function of this sermon in establishing the Nephites as a collective name for a covenant people, inclusive of the non-Old World peoples who were now included in the covenant and promises to Israel through adoption into the community.

[55] Ibid., 58–59. Gee and Roper recognize the import of these verses for Jacob's direct audience (59–60): "Nephi's emphasis on the universal nature of God's love is even more meaningful if written and taught to a people grappling with issues of ethnic and social diversity. . . . Nephites would understand Jews to be those who came out from Jerusalem, yet the additional reference to Gentiles and heathens would make sense to a Nephite only if there were others in the land."

generally that all Native Americans are descendants of the Old World migrants described in the Book of Mormon text, particularly Lehi's colony."[56]

Thomas W. Murphy initiated this controversy when he noted that various methods of discerning genetic heritage all point to an Asian origin for Native American populations.[57] Murphy's initial statement was simply that "I have concluded that Latter-day Saints should not realistically expect to find validation for the ancient historicity of the Book of Mormon in genetics."[58] Had that been his only conclusion, both the article and the topic would have faded quickly. What Murphy argued was not simply that one could not find support for the Book of Mormon in genetics, but that the absence of such data indicated that the Book of Mormon was not historical.[59]

Murphy's argument is most effective if one were to assume that belief in the Book of Mormon requires Book of Mormon peoples to be the source of all New World inhabitants. Many Latter-day Saints have believed that there is ample evidence, even without DNA, that such a proposition cannot be correct.

In 2014, the Church placed an article on its website that is intended to be the official response to the question about DNA and the Book of Mormon, even though no author and no date of composition are identified:

> The Book of Mormon itself, however, does not claim that the peoples it describes were either the predominant or the exclusive inhabitants of the lands they occupied. In fact, cultural and demographic clues in its text hint at the presence of other groups. At the April 1929 general conference, President Anthony W. Ivins of the First Presidency cautioned: "We must be careful in the conclusions that we reach. The Book of Mormon . . . does not tell us that there was no one here before them [the peoples it describes]. It does not tell us that people did not come after."
>
> Joseph Smith appears to have been open to the idea of migrations other than those described in the Book of Mormon, and many Latter-day Saint leaders and scholars over the past century have found the Book of Mormon account to be fully consistent with the presence of other established populations. The 2006 update to the introduction of the Book

---

[56] Ugo A. Perego, "The Book of Mormon and the Origin of Native Americans from a Maternally Inherited DNA Standpoint," 193. I have provided a longer analysis of the reasons why Nephite genetics would not have survived over time in Gardner, *Second Witness*, 1:340–46. More resources are available through the "Science and Religion/DNA," *FairMormon Wiki*.

[57] Thomas W. Murphy, "Lamanite Genesis, Genealogy, and Genetics," 52–59.

[58] Ibid., 48.

[59] Ibid., 60. Murphy describes Y-chromosome testing that indicated a marker for Jewish heritage among the Lemba in Africa and the absence of that information in the Americas. He concludes: "At these markers, the Lemba showed more intermarriage with local populations than other members of the Jewish Diaspora but still clustered halfway between sub-Saharan Africans and others [sic] Jews. Both Bradman and Tudor Parfitt have also publicly noted the lack of a comparable link between Native Americans and ancient Israelites" (61). Although Murphy's direct arguments discuss the lack of evidence, he does mix in criticisms of Book of Mormon historicity, making it easy to see the intent of the article, an intent that was quickly recognized and adopted in the discussions following the article's publication. See pp. 52–53, 61–63, and his conclusion, 67–79.

of Mormon reflects this understanding by stating that Book of Mormon peoples were "among the ancestors of the American Indians."[60]

Even the original argument that the Book of Mormon could not be true because there was no European genetic material in the Americas has now fallen to the almost inevitable additional information that provides a richer picture of the genetic inheritance of Amerindians. An article published October 28, 2013, in the online *Science* magazine, reports:

> A complete nuclear genome of a Siberian boy who died 24,000 years ago—[is] the oldest complete genome of a modern human sequence to date. His DNA shows close ties to those of today's Native Americans. Yet he apparently descended not from East Asians, but from people who had lived in Europe or western Asia. The finding suggests that about a third of the ancestry of today's Native Americans can be traced to "western Eurasia," with the other two-thirds coming from eastern Asia, according to a talk . . . by ancient DNA expert Eske Willerslev of the University of Copenhagen. It also implies that traces of European ancestry previously detected in modern Native Americans do not come solely from mixing with European colonists, as most scientists had assumed, but have much deeper roots.[61]

Thus the absolute statements based on earlier research that there was no European DNA to be found among Native Americans is completely overturned by these more recent data. The old aphorism is substantiated again: The absence of evidence is not evidence of absence.

In this case, however, the only thing that significantly changes with respect to the Book of Mormon is that critics can no longer claim a total absence of European or western Asian DNA in Amerindian populations. It remains true that there is currently no data linking European or western Asian DNA to the time period of the Book of Mormon. However, it does call in to question the simple assumption that any European DNA evidence that had been found must have come in the wake of the Spanish invasion of the Americas.

An interesting opposite application of DNA data to the Book of Mormon asserts that DNA evidence actually proves that the Book of Mormon is a true record. Perego notes: "To contend with these arguments, some Mormons . . . are quick to embrace any news of possible Middle Eastern DNA in the Americas a conclusive proof that the migrations to America described in the Book of Mormon are real."[62]

One of the most visible proponents of this hypothesis is Rodney L. Meldrum. He declares in the introduction to his book, *Rediscovering the Book of Mormon Remnant through DNA*: "Over the past ten years much has been speculated about these questions [about the historicity of the Book of Mormon], especially in light of scientific findings involving human DNA testing. Recent research has been

---

[60] [No author identified], "Book of Mormon and DNA Studies," February 10, 2014.
[61] Michael Balter, "Ancient DNA Links Native Americans with Europe," *Science*, 409.
[62] Perego, "The Book of Mormon and the Origin of Native Americans," 193.

conducted on Native American DNA, studies potentially related to the Book of Mormon that may lend support to its claims. The research herein refutes the claim that DNA analysis proves the Book of Mormon false, and it explores genetic (DNA) evidence that may actually support the claims of the Book of Mormon."[63]

Meldrum describes this evidence that may actually support the Book of Mormon:

> Getting back to the controversy over medina [mitochondrial DNA] findings we begin from the initial research conducted on Native American populations throughout the Americas that found that they could be categorized into four primary haplogroups, identified as A, B, C, and D. All four of these "founding Haplogroups" were correspondingly found in native populations in Asia, lending support for the dominant theory of the peopling of the Americas over the Bering Strait land bridge during the last ice age. Confirming this concept is an article in the journal *Science* in 1998.
>
> Researchers had already identified four common genetic variants, called haplogroups A, B, C, and D, in the mitochondrial DNA (mtDNA) of living Native Americans. These haplogroups turned up in various Asian populations, lending genetic support for the leading theory that Native Americans descended primarily from these peoples. But researchers also found a handful of other less common variants, one of which was later identified as X.[64]

He demonstrates that this haplotype X has been found in European and Near Eastern populations,[65] as well as in Native American populations in the upper Mississippian area. This location of Near Eastern mtDNA therefore provides the scientific foundation for his placement of the Book of Mormon action in what has been termed the "heartland" of the United States.[66]

Perego provides a more recent perspective on DNA research as it pertains to the Book of Mormon: "In order for X2a to fit within Book of Mormon chronology, the currently accepted molecular clocks would need considerable recalibration, or other samples from the Old World carrying additional mutations shared with the Native American X2a would be needed. Neither of these two scenarios is currently likely, and neither may ever become a means for conclusively demonstrating a link between X2a and Lehi's party."[67]

Ironically, these data may yet help confirm a European DNA through Asia.[68] Unfortunately for Meldrum's hypothesis, the issue was and continues to be one of timing. In this case, "Before 24,000 years ago, the ancestors of Native Americans and the ancestors of today's East Asians split into distinct groups."[69] The newly discovered European or western Asian DNA antecedes the Book of Mormon Lehites by around 22,000 years.

---

[63] Rod L. Meldrum, *Rediscovering the Book of Mormon Remnant through DNA*, 3.
[64] Ibid., 72–73. I have removed his italics. He quotes Virginia Morell, "Genes May Link Ancient Eurasians, Native Americans," *Science*, 280.
[65] Ibid., 80–85.
[66] Ibid., 138.
[67] Perego, "The Book of Mormon and the Origin of Native Americans," 214.
[68] Balter, "Ancient DNA Links Native Americans with Europe," 409.
[69] Ibid.

Meldrum understands that "the primary remaining obstruction for haplogroup X to be evidence in support of the Book of Mormon is in dating."[70] If the X2a haplotype is to be associated with the Book of Mormon, then it must arrive when the Book of Mormon suggests a migration of peoples from the Ancient Near East and not millennia earlier. Meldrum's solution is to suggest that there is a prophetic declaration that the age of the earth is incompatible with current DNA timing; that therefore the molecular clocks must be wrong;[71] and to suggest that there are problems with the "evolutionary basis of the assumptions."[72] This approach creates an interesting conflict between accepting evolutionary science when it discovers mtDNA connections to Europe or Western Asia but then denying it entirely with respect to timing.

Perego notes that current science presents even greater issues for using X2a as an indicator of a Book of Mormon people: "The discussion of the X haplotype illustrates the challenges encountered when attempting to reconstruct genetic scenarios from modern populations that are compatible with the Book of Mormon time line and expected source population. Based on the molecular clocks currently used by the scientific community, it would be nearly impossible to distinguish a Eurasian lineage that arrived 2,600 years ago from those brought by the Europeans after the discovery of America's double continent, simply because there would not have been enough time for these lineages to differentiate enough to allow discernment between pre-Columbian and post-Columbian admixture."[73]

The ability of science to use DNA evidence to trace large population movements provides exciting windows on the past, but those windows necessarily provide only a limited view of what the actual landscape would have been. As Perego cautions:

> Using the mtDNA mutations as a guide, it is possible to trace all modern mtDNA lineages back to a single African female ancestor. Geneticists have named this ancestor the African "Eve," but despite this name, she was not necessarily the first woman on the planet. The mtDNA lineages corresponding to other women simply disappeared because their offspring failed to produce additional continuous female lineages (a phenomenon known in population genetics as genetic drift), because of natural or manmade calamities that wiped out a significant portion of the population (an event referred to as a population bottleneck), or because they were selected against due to the detrimental effect of specific mutations.[74]

The genetic data tell us about what survived, but not what once existed. Just as the African Eve was not the only female in Africa, the presence of European or western Asian DNA tells us about one division in the human population. It doesn't tell us about all of the population migrations that have occurred throughout history. Non-scientists have attempted to use the DNA evidence to come to conclusions that the underlying science does not allow. That frustration also occurs among those who

---

[70] Meldrum, *Rediscovering the Book of Mormon Remnant through DNA*, 93.
[71] Ibid., 93–98.
[72] Ibid., 102.
[73] Perego, "The Book of Mormon and the Origin of Native Americans," 214.
[74] Ibid., 201.

attempt to use the science to disprove the Book of Mormon as well as those who wish to prove it. The LDS Church's statement on "Book of Mormon and DNA Studies" declares: "DNA studies cannot be used decisively to either accept or reject the historical authenticity of the Book of Mormon."[75]

Nephi: Prophet and Author

Although it is all we have of Nephi's writings, our two books of Nephi were not all he wrote—were not the first he wrote—and explicitly were not history:

> And now, as I have spoken concerning these plates, behold *they are not the plates upon which I make a full account of the history of my people*; for the plates upon which I make a full account of my people I have given the name of Nephi; wherefore, they are called the plates of Nephi, after mine own name; and these plates also are called the plates of Nephi.
> Nevertheless, I have received a commandment of the Lord that I should make these plates, for the special purpose that there should be *an account engraven of the ministry of my people*.
> Upon the other plates should be engraven an account of the reign of the kings, and the wars and contentions of my people; wherefore these plates are for the more part of the ministry; and the other plates are for the more part of the reign of the kings and the wars and contentions of my people. (1 Nephi 9:2–4)

For Nephi, history told of the "reign of the kings, and the wars and contentions" of a people. In his not-history, separate, and somewhat duplicated narrative, Nephi shifts from history to "an account... of the ministry." Even that perspective, however, must have held some slightly different meaning than we expect. Joseph Fielding McConkie and Robert L. Millet lay out our expectation of what Nephi's two sets of plates contained: "Nephi was commanded to keep both the large plates (a record of the more secular matters, such as the reigns of the kings, the wars, the journeyings of the people, etc.) and the small plates (a record of the spiritual experiences of the people and of God's dealings with them)."[76]

In spite of our expectation based on what the text says, this isn't the kind of book Nephi gives us. Rather than what we might think of as a "record of the spiritual experiences" of Nephi's family, Nephi tells his family's story in 1 Nephi. There are certainly spiritual experiences in that story, but Nephi tells the story as much *for* the story as for the spiritual experiences. They are part of a larger theme, not the sole

---

[75] [No author identified], "Book of Mormon and DNA Studies."
[76] Joseph Fielding McConkie and Robert L. Millet, *Doctrinal Commentary on the Book of Mormon*, 1:62.
Other writers echo this same concept. Sidney B. Sperry, *Book of Mormon Compendium*, 95. "It will be observed from these passages that Nephi's main purpose in writing 1 Nephi was to bring men to God by telling them about the 'good news' of the ministry."
James E. Talmage, *Articles of Faith*, 239. "By command of the Lord, Nephi made other plates, upon which he recorded particularly what may be called in a broad sense the ecclesiastical history of his people, citing only such instances of other events as seemed necessary to the proper sequence of the narrative."

reason the events were recorded. There is something in 1 Nephi that was, for Nephi, more sacred than secular, more ministry than history; yet he encodes it inside the secular and the historical.

Nephi's "ministry" is a highly structured account designed to compare his New World people to Old World Israel. In this he is not reporting history, but creating history. Nephi intentionally recounts the story of his family's exodus from Jerusalem so that it evokes Israel's exodus from Egypt.[77] He parallels his rise from younger son to ruler to that of Joseph of Egypt.[78] He casts the entire story in such a way that it would be subconsciously understood as establishing a new people in a new place.[79]

As with the record Las Casas created of Columbus's voyage, what we have from Nephi is the result of a distortion by selection.[80] When we read Nephi's text for our modern concept of history, we should not be surprised that we find our kind of history only by reading between his lines. When Nephi doesn't tell us something we wish to know, it isn't because it didn't happen, but because it wasn't important to the reason he wrote. Dever's admonition about the Bible applies equally to the Book of Mormon: "The [biblical] writers were highly selective about what they included. They simply do not tell us many things that we 'moderns' wish to know."[81]

The overarching function of 1 Nephi is ethnogenesis, not history. Nephi creates a new people by following a pattern that was culturally engrained. Ann E. Killebrew summarizes research into the common aspects of this ancient Near Eastern genre (in brackets I have suggested the elements in the Book of Mormon that fit into the pattern):

> Following Hedwig Wolfram's definition, the process of ethnogenesis that forms the core ideology of a group often comprises three characteristic features: (1) a story or stories of a primordial deep, which can include the crossing of a sea or river, an impressive victory against all odds over an enemy, or combinations of similar "miraculous" stores (e.g., the exodus [Lehite exodus from Jerusalem]); (2) a group that undergoes a religious experience

---

[77] S. Kent Brown, "The Exodus Pattern in the Book of Mormon," 111–126; Terrence L. Szink, "Nephi and the Exodus," 1991, 39–42; Terrence L. Szink, "To a Land of Promise," 1987, 60–72; Bruce J. Boehm, "Wanderers in the Promised Land: A study of the Exodus Motif in the Book of Mormon and Holy Bible," 187–204.

[78] A longer treatment of this topic is Gardner, *Second Witness*, 1:42–48.

[79] Noel B. Reynolds, "Nephi's Political Testament," 221 sees 1 Nephi as a justification of Nephi's rule: "His small plates defend the Nephite tradition and refute the account advanced by the Lamanites and dissenters. Nephi carefully constructed what he wrote to convince his own and later generations that the Lord had selected him over his older brothers to be Lehi's successor."

This is very much a part of what Nephi is doing, but his need for ethnogenesis is even larger than the justification of his rule. He must not only establish his right to rule, but the cosmic place of the people he rules.

[80] Brant A. Gardner, "Crucible of Distortion: The Impact of the Spanish on Native American Oral Tradition," discusses distortion by selection as one of the factors altering our record of native lore. I examine multiple records of a specific account of the Aztec deity Quetzalcoatl to show how different authors selected different aspects of the lore to repeat and then mold the tale into a result quite different from the most native account available.

[81] William E. Dever, *Recent Archaeological Discoveries and Biblical Research*, 6.

or change in cult as a result of the primordial deed (e.g., reception of the Ten Commandments and worship of Yahweh [beheading of Laban to obtain the brass plates]); and (3) the existence of an ancestral enemy or enemies that cement group cohesion (e.g., most notably the Canaanites and Philistines [redefinition of Laman and Lemuel into Lamanites, categorized as enemies]). These basic elements form the key themes in the biblical narrative about the emergence of early Israel.[82]

Ideologically, Nephi establishes a new people by following a traditional literary pattern.[83] Although it is possible that this pattern was a subconscious inheritance of Old World culture, a case can be made that, prior to leaving the Old World, Nephi received scribal training.[84] That training would have helped him understand the literary ethnogenetic form, which he used as an underlying theme in his tale of the creation of his own people. Nephi provided his people with an accepted *mythos* for a new people, although in a different order from that listed above. The story of the departure from Jerusalem highlighted divine direction. In the conflict with Laban, Nephi overcame great odds to obtain the brass plates, and then the family crossed an ocean. In the New World, the new people were defined against a specific "ancestral" enemy in the persons of Laman and Lemuel who provided a foil against which the Nephites could unite themselves.

Nephi's probable scribal training also underlay the way he used scripture to secure his right to rulership. While there is no indication that there was any controversy in his selection as leader, nevertheless as Nephi wrote his account he made certain to justify his right to rule in spite of not being the eldest. He did so by interweaving references and allusions to the story of Joseph, son of Isaac.

Joseph had received a dream revelation that he was to rule over his older brethren (Gen. 37:5–11). Nephi received revelation that he would be "made a ruler and a teacher over thy brethren" (1 Ne. 2:22). Significantly, this revelation came just before he and his brothers returned to Jerusalem for the brass plates which provided proof that Lehi (and therefore Nephi) was a descendant of that very Joseph of Egypt. During that episode, an angel came to save Nephi from his brothers who were in the process of harming him (a rough parallel to Joseph's brothers). The angel reiterated the important message: "Know ye not that the Lord hath chosen him to be a ruler over you?" (1 Ne. 3:24).

---

[82] Ann E. Killebrew, *Biblical Peoples and Ethnicity: An Archaeological Study of Egyptians, Canaanites, Philistines, and Early Israel, 1300–1100* B.C.E., 149. My suggestions for how this description fits the Nephite situation are in brackets.

[83] This pattern may have been explicitly understood, or may simply have been an unconscious expectation of how one went about writing about a new people. Alan Dundes, "The Hero Pattern and the Life of Jesus," 190, discusses how common patterned expectations molded the biography of Abraham Lincoln to the "hero" pattern. See also Vladimir Propp, *Morphology of the Folktale* for the socially defined structure that underlies Russian folktales.

[84] Gardner, "Nephi as Scribe," 45–55.

Many of the events Nephi elected to recount show him as a younger brother ascending to leadership over his elder brothers.[85] I have already noted Benjamin L. McGuire's analysis of the kingship implications of the way Nephi tells of his encounter with Laban ("Returning for the Brass Plates" in Chapter 4). The incident of the bows shows Nephi leading the way in the physical survival of the family. In Bountiful, it is Nephi who received the inspiration and directions to build the ship that took them from the Old World to the New.

The only significant event Nephi related about his family's ocean voyage was the divine displeasure incurred when his brothers attempted to displace Nephi as the family leader, an incident that Nephi expressly tied to the issue of rulership: "And I, Nephi, began to fear exceedingly lest the Lord should be angry with us, and smite us because of our iniquity, that we should be swallowed up in the depths of the sea; wherefore, I, Nephi, began to speak to them with much soberness; but behold they were angry with me, saying: We will not that our younger brother shall be a ruler over us" (1 Ne. 18:10). Whether or not there was any controversy among the people who became the city of Nephi, Nephi felt it important to use his understanding of scripture to build the political foundation of his people upon the divine investiture of Nephi's right to rule.

It is interesting in light of the emphasis that Nephi placed on ruling over his brothers that it never happened. By the time Nephi was accepted as his people's ruler, he was far distant in time and space from his brothers. However, there is a hint that Nephi might have already been ascending to leadership prior to the division between the Lamanites and Nephites. In Zeniff's record, written after he had returned to the land of Nephi and the midst of the Lamanites, Zeniff declared that Nephi's brothers: "were wroth with him when they had arrived in the promised land, because they said that he had taken the ruling of the people out of their hands; and they sought to kill him" (Mosiah 10:15).

For Nephi, the underlying theme behind this "ministry" of his people was their sacred formation and charter. While he recounted history, it was a history crafted to demonstrate the ministry—the divine directives, guidance, and authority behind the foundation of this new branch of Israel.

The carefully crafted nature of 1 Nephi may also help us to understand more about Nephi's personality. Schooled as we are in modern literature, we might assume as we

---

[85] Noel B. Reynolds, "The Political Dimension in Nephi's Small Plates," 15, suggests:

> Every people needs to know that its laws and rulers are legitimate and authoritative. This is why stories of national origins and city foundings are so important to human societies throughout the world. Such stories provide explanations of the legitimate origins of their laws and their rulers. Not untypically, such traditions also deal with ambiguous elements of the founding, explaining away possibly competing accounts. When Nephi undertook late in his life to write a third account of the founding events of the Lehite colony, it appears that he wanted to provide his descendants with a document that would serve this function.

Reynolds expanded on his ideas in Noel B. Reynolds, "Nephite Kingship Reconsidered," 152–58.

read Nephi's narrative that he was accurately representing his personality in his writings. When we do so, we might arrive at the conclusion that he is not a particularly likeable character. For example, Tierza Askren voices what perhaps many have felt: "Can I just say how very much I loath [sic] Nephi?! Have for ages. Actually (and this really happened), I once shocked a Sunday School teacher and class when I made the suggestion that, if I had been Nephi's sister, I'd probably have wanted to kill him too. Who wouldn't? The man is pompous, self-absorbed and not at all hesitant to share his deep self-love with anyone who will listen."[86] It is a devastating assessment of Nephi as a man. Grant Hardy suggests: "It might be tempting to dismiss Nephi as a biased, self-aggrandizing character, but that would be a mistake. Instead, we ought to ask why he writes the way he does."[87]

Nephi's training as a scribe dictated the way in which the first book of Nephi was written. Karel van der Toorn explains: "We may say that scribes, even in their most instrumental of roles, impose their style, language, and ideas on the text. Acting as secretaries and transcribers, they are not phonographs in writing; they mold the material that reaches them orally. As prophecy turns into scripture, when tale becomes text, the scribe transforms his data to suit the conventions of the written genre and his interpretation of the oral tradition."[88] Nephi is taking his material from his father's record and from his life, but he is still imposing "style, language, and ideas on the text." In Van der Toorn's words, Nephi "transform[ed] his data to suit the conventions of the written genre and his interpretation."

The conventions which guided Nephi's text are unfamiliar to modern readers. E. Randolph Richards and Brandon J. O'Brien explain why lack of information this can generate a perhaps unfortunate assessment of Nephi's personality:

> *The most powerful cultural values are those that go without being said.* It is very hard to know what goes without being said in another culture. But often we are not even aware of what goes without being said in our own culture. This is why misunderstanding and misinterpretation happen. When a passage of Scripture appears to leave out a piece of the puzzle because something went without being said, we instinctively fill in the gap with a piece from our own culture—usually a piece that goes without being said. When we miss what went without being said for *them* and substitute what goes without being said for *us*, we are at risk of misreading Scripture.[89]

When we understand that Nephi's scribal training would have led him to cultural forms in the way he developed his arguments, we find an important division between Nephi the writer and Nephi the person.[90] Nephi wrote to define himself as the king.

---

[86] Tierza Askren, "Top 5 Things I Hate About Nephi."
[87] Grant Hardy, *Understanding the Book of Mormon: A Reader's Guide*, 44.
[88] Karel van der Toorn, *Scribal Culture and the Making of the Hebrew Bible*, 115.
[89] E. Randolph Richards and Brandon J. O'Brien, *Misreading Scripture with Western Eyes*, 12–13; emphasis theirs.
[90] John Gee, "Abraham and Idrimi," 35, notes that, while autobiographies existed in antiquity, they were rather rare. Only one is known to exist from the time of Abraham, that of

180 *Traditions of the Fathers*

The structure of ethnogenetic texts required that he not only demonstrate his ascension to the rightful ruler, but to establish an ancient enemy, the role to which his brothers Laman and Lemuel were assigned. These literary necessities color what were probably very different familial interactions.

Defending the Community

Even before describing the building of his community, Nephi discussed the need to defend it. He said: "I, Nephi, did take the sword of Laban, and after the manner of it did make many swords, lest by any means the people who were now called Lamanites should come upon us and destroy us; for I knew their hatred towards me and my children and those who were called my people" (2 Ne. 5:14). Both the creation of the swords and the reason for them require some explanation.

Why did Nephi feel the need to defend his people from the Lamanites?[91] The estranged family members had been left behind as Nephi and his group fled "in the wilderness for the space of many days" (2 Ne. 5:7). It is highly unlikely that those family members' hatred was so great that in the midst of their own very necessary establishment of homes and community that they would take the time to travel those many days for the sole purpose of harassing the Nephites. Nevertheless, we should take Nephi at his word that it was essential that his community be protected.

It is significant that Nephi calls his enemies "the people who were now called Lamanites" (2 Ne. 5:14). *Lamanite* served as a demonym in that it identified a people, but perhaps even more importantly as an exonym; a name for those who were "not us." Rather similar to the exonym *gentile*, it could cover a wide range of more specific demonyms. In Nephite usage, *Lamanite* and *enemy* were equivalent terms (see Jacob 1:14).

Regardless of who was classified as Lamanite, the archeological record from this early period suggests that warfare was part of the cultural legacy.[92] Archaeology

---

Idrimi, a ruler of Alalakh, a town that would have been in the patriarch Abraham's homeland. Idrimi ruled in the middle of the second millennium B.C. Gee notes that "Idrimi's autobiography compares well with Abraham's autobiography in both subject and form, even though Idrimi's autobiography dates about two hundred years later." The comparison in form is of particular importance to understanding Nephi's autobiography. Nephi also employed literary forms and traditions that differ from ours. In literature purporting to be first-person statements of rulers, there is no room for the assumed humility that we might expect of an author. The opposite is clearly the case, with the ruler often taking full credit for events in which he did not personally participate (or perhaps did so only from a position of safety). See any of the first-person accounts of the Babylonian or Assyrian kings found in D. Winton Thomas, ed., *Documents from Old Testament Times*.

[91] M Kathryn Brown and James F. Garber, "Evidence of Conflict during the Middle Formative in the Maya Lowlands: A View from Blackman Eddy, Belize," 91, discusses evidence for warfare from 650 B.C. The data are for the lowlands rather than the probable highland location of the Book of Mormon, but the data indicate that Nephi's fear was likely well founded.

[92] Estrada-Belli, *The First Maya Civilization*, 128. Christopher A. Pool, *Olmec Archaeology and Early Mesoamerica*, 138, discusses the case for warfare among the even earlier Olmec: "Warfare and raiding are common in transegalitarian societies (tribes and simple chiefdoms), and it is

therefore agrees that Nephi had to defend his community even if a too-literal reading of "Lamanites" should not have required it.

Much more problematic is Nephi's declaration that he made swords after the manner of the sword of Laban. The issue with this particular statement is that it appears to suggest that Nephi would have made metal swords, and there are no attested metal swords in Mesoamerica for any period, let alone this early.

There is so little information given that we must make guesses about the nature of these swords. Laban's sword had a "hilt . . . of pure gold, and the workmanship thereof was exceedingly fine, and . . . the blade thereof was of the most precious steel" (1 Ne. 4:9). How much of that model made it into Nephi's swords?

Important information comes in the very next verse, which notes that the people of Nephi had access to "iron, and . . . copper, and . . . brass, and . . . steel, and . . . gold, and . . . silver, and of precious ores, which were in great abundance" (2 Ne. 5:15). Nephi lists available metals, although "steel" is an alloy of iron with carbon rather than a separate metal (which might suggest a translation issue).

Among the available metals is gold, and Laban's sword had a hilt of pure gold. Might we expect that all of the swords Nephi created had hilts of pure gold? It is possible, but quite unlikely. Laban's sword was a status symbol, and Nephi was creating functional military weapons. It is unlikely that the essentially decorative status of the gold hilt had any function in a weapon that was created specifically for battle. It would be more reasonable to have the tang covered with wood and leather to create the grip rather than use gold. Nephi's use of the sword of Laban as a model must have been at least somewhat conceptual.

Of course, the most important part of the sword is the blade. It was possible to harden iron into steel by Lehi's day.[93] The Book of Mormon mentions steel, but only rarely in the New World.[94] In addition to 2 Nephi 5:15, Jarom 1:8 tells us: "And we multiplied exceedingly, and spread upon the face of the land, and became exceedingly rich in gold, and in silver, and in precious things, and in fine workmanship of wood, in buildings, and in machinery, and also in iron and copper, and brass and steel, making all manner of tools of every kind to till the ground, and weapons of war—yea, the sharp pointed arrow, and the quiver, and the dart, and the javelin, and all preparations for war." The list of metals is so parallel to what we see in 2 Nephi 5:15 that it is either a confirmation that this was the particular list of available metals, or

---

likely that Olmec groups fought with one another. Nevertheless, the archaeological evidence for warfare among the Olmecs is notable for its scarcity and ambiguity." Ross Hassig, *War and Society in Ancient Mesoamerica*, 13, notes that while there is no direct evidence for early warfare, tools that could double as weapons have been found as early as 4000 B.C., "suggesting that warfare was relatively unorganized, conducted by small groups armed with unspecialized tool-weapons, and aimed not at conquest but at raiding, for glory as much as for booty."

[93] Jeffrey R. Chadwick, "Lehi's House at Jerusalem and the Land of His Inheritance," 114.

[94] See Chapter 6 for more information on metal in the Book of Mormon.

that this is a literary list—a conventional statement.[95] Interestingly, the sword is not mentioned in the list of weapons for war. Since only projectile weapons are mentioned, the absence is curious, but not clearly indicative of the absence of the sword (metal or not) at that later date.

The only other reference to steel in the New World is among the Jaredites: "Wherefore, he came to the hill Ephraim, and he did molten out of the hill, and made swords out of steel" (Ether 7:9). The plausible dating for the statement in Ether places steel making in a time period when steel was quite rare in the whole world, suggesting that we might be seeing a translation anachronism.[96] Either we are seeing a record of metal swords which faded from use, or we should see in this text an artifact of the translation.

William J. Hamblin and A. Brent Merrill propose that at least the reference in Ether was related to translation: "Mosiah translated Ether's plates into social and linguistic concepts with which he was familiar. Mosiah, as king, possessed Laban's sword, a steel weapon that was passed down as one of the insignia of royalty. In translating Ether's record, Mosiah might thus have given the Jaredite kings steel swords, like the one he himself possessed, because in Mosiah's society a king was expected to have a steel sword as his royal weapon."[97]

Allowing for the possibility of metal swords, why didn't they survive in the known archaeological record? The answer is necessarily speculative, but it is a speculation built on plausible data. Two conditions are required for metal swords to persist. First, they would have to be superior to other weapon options, and second, they would have to be widely adopted.

Two possible factors might make a metal sword superior. The first is durability and the second is the quality of the cutting edge. It does not appear that either of these traits had significant advantages over the native weapon. Ross Hassig notes: "The Aztec swords [macuahuitl] were described by the conquistadores as cutting better than the Spanish swords and being so cleverly constructed that the blades could be neither pulled out nor broken."[98] The obsidian blades were much sharper than most steel swords of the era, and certainly for those that might have produced in volume. According to a report from The *Titulo C'oyoi*, created by the Quiché [a Maya people] during the Spanish conquest, a blow of a macuahuitl severed a horse's head during a battle sometime between 1523 and 1527.[99] It seems doubtful that the quality of steel Nephi could have produced would have provided any benefits over obsidian blades.

---

[95] A literary list has ties to literal meaning, but the meaning transcends the literal. For example, "lock, stock, and barrel" refers to gun making, but has become a literary list that is always given with only those items and always in that order. The meaning is "everything," rather than the specific items, or even anything related to gunsmithing.

[96] See "Horses, Chariots, and Other Anachronistic Nouns" in Chapter 12. Also see the discussion of translation anachronisms in Brant A. Gardner, *The Gift and Power: Translating the Book of Mormon*, 187–92, 234–39.

[97] William J. Hamblin and A. Brent Merrill, "Swords in the Book of Mormon," 347.

[98] Ross Hassig, *Aztec Warfare: Imperial Expansion and Political Control*, 84–85.

[99] Titulo C'oyoi, quoted in Robert M. Carmack, *Quichéan Civilization*, 303.

The second reason that a metal sword would not have created a military revolution is that there were important pressures against widespread adoption. The Old World sword and the New World macuahuitl required different battle techniques and therefore different strategies. The typical Middle Eastern sword is short, almost a dagger. However, there is at least one example of a longer-bladed weapon. In 1994, Avrahim Eitan reported that during excavations at Vered Jericho, a site three miles south of Jericho, workers discovered a metal sword. It measures "three feet long, about three inches wide, is made of iron, and has a bronze haft with a wooden grip. Even the tip of the sword remains intact. The strata from which the sword was excavated dates to the late seventh century or about 620 B.C. Most swords from the Middle East, as portrayed in pictures and reliefs, were short and seem to have been used like daggers. Thus, this three-foot sword from Vered Jericho seems to be unique in its large size."[100]

Even with this longer blade, the typical use would have been to thrust, as with the later Roman gladius, which had a blade almost as long.[101] The Mesoamerican macuahuitl was, by contrast, a hacking/slicing weapon. The difference in the way the weapon functioned would dictate different tactics, and combatants would need to be trained in the appropriate strategy to use the different attack required for the Old World sword.[102] There is no indication that any of Lehi's family had military training.

Such parallels argue that the Nephites used known Mesoamerican military weaponry for most of their history. Nephi may have attempted to introduce a weapon that his heritage would have considered superior, but it was likely not superior in actual Mesoamerican battle. Without any tactical advantage, there would have been no reason to continue to use it. As Jared Diamond reminds us: "Merely having a bigger, faster, or more powerful device for doing something is no guarantee of ready acceptance. Innumerable such technologies were either not adopted at all or adopted only after prolonged resistance."[103] In this case, a metal sword might not even have been "a bigger, faster, or more powerful device." Perhaps confirmation of this hypothesis might be found in the fact that the Maya had copper blades by the time of Spanish contact, but continued to use the obsidian blades as their primary weaponry.[104]

---

[100] William J. Adams Jr., "Nephi's Jerusalem and Laban's Sword," 11–12.

[101] Madeleine S. and J. Lane Miller, *Harper's Encyclopedia of Bible Life*, 350. "The sword was double-edged and about two feet long. Many that have been found were fitted with a corrugated grip. The sword was used like a bayonet for thrusting when at close grips with an enemy."

Ross Cowen, *Roman Legionary: 58 B.C.–A.D. 69*, 28: "Tactically, the sword was used in conjunction with a shield, often forming a shield wall from behind which a thrust provided the best protected aggressive action. The gladius Hispaniensis could have a length of about 27 inches."

[102] Hassig, *Aztec Warfare*, 97, notes that the macuahuitl required special training and, hence, were used by more elite forces.

[103] Jared Diamond, *Guns, Germs, and Steel: The Fates of Human Societies*, 247. John L. Sorenson and Paul Y. Hoskisson, "Lost Arts," 101–4, discuss examples of lost technologies in both the Old World and the New.

[104] Lynne V. Foster, *Handbook to Life in the Ancient Maya World*, 146.

Nevertheless, the Book of Mormon clearly requires metal-working as an undeniably physical presence because the royal records are kept on metal plates. The plates delivered to Joseph Smith attest to Nephite abilities with metal. To date, archaeological confirmation of these abilities at the time mentioned in the Book of Mormon does not exist.[105]

Linguistic data provide hope that archaeology might yet make a discovery that would alter our understanding of metallurgy dating in Mesoamerican. A word for metal has been reconstructed in the Mixe-Zoquean vocabulary (*ting-kuy).[106] This is the language group that would have been spoken during Jaredite times. It is therefore certain that there was metal, else there would be no reason to have the word. However, it could have referred to the iron ore and not to smelted metal. Confirmation of early metal-working is still absent.

King by Popular Demand

In addition to organizing the material and spiritual welfare of his people, Nephi briefly indicated how the community organized political affairs: "And it came to pass that they would that I should be their king. But I, Nephi, was desirous that they should have no king; nevertheless, I did for them according to that which was in my power" (2 Ne. 5:18). Nephi didn't explain his reluctance to accept the kingship, particularly in light of the prophecies that he should rule over his brethren.[107] However, he very clearly reported that it was the desire of the people that they should have a king. That popular pressure begs for analysis. Why did they want a king?

Small hamlets do not have kings. To qualify for that title one must be able to marshal the population into the construction of public structures denoting the power associated with, and expected of, a king. Richard N. Hansen comments:

---

[105] John L. Sorenson, "Metals and Metallurgy Relating to the Book of Mormon Text," collects information about metal working in the Old and the New Worlds. For the Old World, there is little controversy. In the New World, metals are known after Book of Mormon times and much of the data Sorenson collects come from the later periods. The data suggesting earlier dates are not firm enough to alter current archaeological assumptions of the later use of metals in the area.

[106] Søren Wichmann, *The Relationship among the Mixe-Zoquean Languages of Mexico*, 564. (Wichmann uses a symbol for the "ng" cluster).

[107] Noel B. Reynolds, "Nephite Kingship Reconsidered," 160–67, suggests that Nephi might not have accepted the role of king. Nevertheless, Reynolds notes: "While Nephi may not have been formally installed as a king, he clearly performed the important functions that his people associated with kingship" (167).

I disagree with Reynolds (p. 167) that "the widespread assumption that Nephi was a king cannot be supported conclusively from a reading of the text." Jacob notes that there were changes "under the reign of the second king" (Jacob 1:15), after Nephi's death. That wording indicates that there was a first king. Jacob also notes that after Nephi died, "whoso should reign in his stead were called by the people, second Nephi, third Nephi, and so forth" (Jacob 1:11). Combined with the clear statement of a second king, the evidence suggests that Nephi, Jacob's brother, was king in spite of his original protestation.

Others [quoting Mary W. Helms] have noted the connection between authority and architectural construction programs: "Historically, we can trace the origins of kings as actual or nominal builders to the lineage of headmen, master artisans, and religious specialists who direct the construction of community dwellings, men's houses, initiation quarters, or communal ceremonial-political centers in tribal and chiefdom societies."

Privileged individuals most likely attained rank or status originally on the basis of skills, talents, and accrued personal wealth. Their position encouraged them to reduce societal resistance to their accumulation of personal power and the expansion of wealth and prestige. As this process evolved, personal qualifiers became less significant than selected lineages, and leadership acquired by achievement became subordinate to ascribed or inherited status sanctioned and recognized by those ruled. The display of power was manifested in stone monuments and monumental architecture imbued with religious, cosmological, and ritual symbolism that displayed true regal and religious authority. The commission of other public works, however—such as water collection systems, agricultural terrace systems, and causeways—demonstrated that the governance was also concerned for the governed; this reciprocity both fueled and maintained kingly power and wealth.[108]

Assuming that the pressure for a king is evidence of a certain population level, we still have the issue of the explicit change from whatever type of rulership Nephi had previously provided to a king. His people did not ask for an Old Testament judge—they asked for a king.

I suggest that the desire for a king reflected a surge in the rise of kings all around the city of Nephi. Mesoamerican kings have been noted as early as the Preclassic (2000 B.C.–A.D. 250), and monarchies were typical of the Late Preclassic (400 B.C.–A.D. 250).[109] An interesting study is Cerros, a city located on the eastern coast of the Yucatan Peninsula, dating to the Preclassic. This village was transformed into a city center complete with monumental architecture. That transition from village to city, from simple architecture to monumental and symbolic architecture, suggests that there was also a shift in the government of the village. Villages typically have headmen as rulers. The symbolism of the architecture after the transformation suggests that they moved from that simpler form of government to a Mesoamerican-style king around 300 B.C. David Drew summarizes the "speculative reconstruction" of the archaeologists who investigated the site:

> They suggest that its inhabitants deliberately chose to adopt the institution of rulership. They did so because they were forced to confront the reality of developing social inequality within their society. Instead of allowing this to lead to conflict, to the break-up of social fabric, they sought not to deny such inequality but to embrace it, to institutionalize it by creating

---

[108] Richard D. Hansen, "Kingship in the Cradle of Maya Civilization: The Mirador Basin," 140–41.
[109] Ibid., 145: "By the Early Middle Preclassic Period (1000–600 BC) there are ample variations in residence size and structural sophistication at several sites in the Mirador Basin, including small, stone-lined residential platforms with packed clay floors, wattle-and-daub residences, as well as major platforms with vertical stone walls. The labor marshaled into public construction projects during this time was controlled by administrative elites, not only in the Mirador Basin but elsewhere in the Maya Lowlands as well."

one central force so powerful and given such extraordinary symbolic legitimacy that it overrode all others. What is suggested here is a kind of social contract of rights and obligations. Humbler members of the community had to pay tribute to maintain the ruler and his lineage or followers, to participate in the building of temples and other communal construction. But in return the ruler provided security, managerial authority to resolve disputes and organize public works and above all, as we have seen, he provided a religious focus—he took care of the spiritual matters of so fundamental an importance to such a society.[110]

David Webster describes the cultural development of this general time period:

> Prior to about 650 B.C. we can detect no signs of particular social or political complexity in the archaeological remains of these early settlers, although obsidian and other objects imported from Highland to Lowlands show that scattered populations were by no means isolated from one another. During the next two centuries a few communities in the central Maya Lowlands and Belize began to build masonry civic structures 10–14 m (33–46 ft.) high, some with stucco masks and other decorative elements that have a generic resemblance to those found at later Classic period sites. About the same time even bigger structures were erected in the valleys of El Salvador. Boulder sculptures there, and also along the Pacific coast of Guatemala and Mexico, show sophisticated symbolic motifs that possibly reflect influences from the Olmec culture of the Mexican Gulf Coast. At various highland centers elaborate burials, large buildings, stone stelae, and what might be early glyphs and numerals all appear by about 400 B.C. Some archaeologists believe that the basic ideological and iconographic conventions of kingship originated in highland centers such as Kaminaljuyú (where Guatemala City is now located).[111]

The Book of Mormon places Nephi's kingship in the right location for the nascent Mesoamerican forms of kingship, albeit early in its development.[112] Seeing Nephite

---

[110] David Drew, *The Lost Chronicles of the Maya Kings*, 139.
[111] David Webster, *The Fall of the Ancient Maya*, 44.
[112] The movement from chiefdoms to states is typically traced to around 300 B.C. Evans, *Ancient Mexico and Central America*, 205–6. That designation refers to social complexity rather than the institution of kingship itself. Norman Hammond, "Preclassic Maya Civilization," 139, finds evidence of kingship around 400 B.C.:

> By the beginning of the Late Preclassic in 400 B.C. we do, however, start to see a totally different society from that envisaged in the village farming model extant a decade and a half ago. In the next six or seven centuries through to the formal beginning of the Classic period, a true civilization emerges. . . .
> Rulers used these mats, and the mat had the equivalent meaning to "throne" in our iconography. Here at this small site we have the icon of royal power displayed; were there already rulers by 400 B.C. who had established both the reality of power and its symbolic expression?

For both Evans and Hammond, the relevant evidence comes from architecture. It is entirely plausible that the forces moving towards kingship preceded the kings who assembled the labor required to document their power in community architecture. The beginning dates are not entirely clear, with the earlier side comfortably supporting Nephi's kingship.
Hansen, "Kingship in the Cradle of Maya Civilization," 146–47: "By the Late Middle Preclassic Period, 600 to 400 BC, kingcraft had evolved to the point where pyramidal structures up to 18 m high were constructed at Nakbé, Xulnal, Wakna, El Pesquero, and, on a lesser scale, at La Florida. A ballcourt was built at Nakbé during this time, consistent with the Middle

kingship early should not be taken as evidence that it triggered Mesoamerican kingship (especially since the reverse is the more likely scenario). Nephi originally resisted the title of king rather than suggesting it. He also specifically tells us that he didn't teach much of the Old World culture to his people (2 Ne. 25:6).

In the city of Nephi we see evidence of the general trend to kingship that would continue in other Mesoamerican communities. Although it appears early, it is probably only because we have the textual information for its beginning rather than being required to wait for the monumental architecture that provide the archaeological evidence for kingship.[113]

The hypothesis that selecting Nephi as a king is evidence of a much larger number of non-Old World peoples who joined with Nephi answers one question and asks another. It can tell us why the community believed it needed a king, but it doesn't tell us why this larger population of non-Old World peoples would have selected a newcomer to their land as their king. Of course I continue to speculate, but I believe that there were two important factors behind Nephi's selection as king.

The first must have been related to some value that he brought the community. There had to be some reason that they were willing to follow him. I hypothesize that it was his ability to work metals, which would provide the community with an economic base that would give them a trade advantage over those who did not have those skills (and provided another economic advantage to the obsidian interchange already in place, metal goods likely following the same trade routes).[114] Of course, this reason is highly tenuous because there is no evidence for it at this time period.

The second reason is that Nephi had physical emblems of his right of rule. These were embodied in the artifacts that he mentions: "And I, Nephi, had also brought the records which were engraven upon the plates of brass; and also the ball, or compass,

---

Preclassic ballcourt discovered at Takalik Abaj. However, with the maturation of kingship, a major new focus became the economic and social organization of massive labor forces to construct ritually significant architecture."

[113] Charles W. Golden, "The Politics of Warfare in the Usumacinta Basin: La Pasadita and the Realm of Bird Jaguar," 32, makes a parallel observation: "Though an increasing number of titles apparent in the epigraphic record may reflect an increase in the number of titled personages within Maya polities during the Late Classic, there is no reason to believe that many such individuals were not present in Early Classic society." Miguel Angel Astor-Aguilera, *The Maya World of Communicating Objects: Quadripartite Crosses, Trees, and Stones*, 38, makes a similar argument based on the embedding of cosmology in iconography: "Cosmological concepts may be long present before imagery depicting these ideas become visible in the material record."

[114] The suggestion that working metals was Nephi's economic contribution makes logical sense but relies upon a metal industry for which there is currently no available evidence. See Chapter 6. I would hypothesize that one of the reasons that it might be difficult to find for the Nephites is that their metallurgical skills were intentionally kept secret due to their economic value. If there were a larger use of metals, the value of individual pieces would decrease. I would also hypothesize that the pieces were probably decorative and from softer metals such as gold or silver, remembering that these were the metals that Lehi worked in Jerusalem. (See "Lehi of Jerusalem" in Chapter 3).

which was prepared for my father by the hand of the Lord, according to that which is written" (2 Ne. 5:12). Nephi mentions these objects right after he comments on planting crops and husbanding animals and just before his declaration that "we began to prosper exceedingly, and to multiply in the land" (2 Ne. 5:13). Although the brass plates were certainly valuable for what they contained, they were also valuable for what they signified, which was a legitimate connection to a distant source of authority. Both the brass plates and the Liahona were made of a substance and in a manner that was not known in the New World at that time; hence, they would be objects of special attention. The arrival of Lehi's party on an ocean-going ship was also unusual, not simply for the people, but for the type of vessel. Nephi possessed artifacts tying him to some source of power that was manifest in these sacred objects.

Although the literary analogies come from almost two thousand years later, Mesoamerican peoples had a tradition of linking the authority of a new community and people to a distant respected source of that authority. The Popol Vuh, the story of the Quiché, describes travel to a distant sacred city where the great ruler Nacxit invested the symbols of rulership.[115] The Annals of the Cakchiquels similarly recounts receiving the emblems of sovereignty from distant Nacxit.[116] There is no direct connection between Nephi's declaration of his symbols of ancient authority and the accounts from the Quiché and the Cakchiquel. Nevertheless there is a common underlying respect for an ancient source justifying the authority of a new community's rulers.

The Nephite Egalitarian Ideal

Perhaps the most difficult part of the Book of Mormon to explain is the inclusion of twelve entire chapters of Isaiah. Jerald and Sandra Tanner thought it was due to a poverty of innovation: "That Joseph Smith would have to throw in so many chapters of Isaiah as filler shows that he was having a very difficult time trying to find something suitable to replace the material in the lost 116 pages."[117] Frankly, explaining the presence of Isaiah in 2 Nephi is no more difficult that explaining any of 2 Nephi. Where 1 Nephi is a well-written, well-crafted story, 2 Nephi is more disjointed.

There are five major sections in 2 Nephi: (1) Lehi's blessing of his sons, (2) a historical chapter about the division of the Nephites from the Lamanites, (3) Jacob's sermon on the salvation of Israel by Gentiles, (4) extensive quotations from Isaiah, and (5) Nephi's concluding prophetic vision. These seemingly diverse sections may be unified by Nephi's effort to provide a defining charter for the new community. The

---

[115] *Popol Vuh: The Sacred Book of the Maya*, 257, "Then they arrived before the face of the lord, whose name was Nacxit. He was the only judge over a great dominion. He then gave to them the signs and symbols of their lordship." Also *Popol Vuh: The Definitive Edition of the Mayan Book of the Dawn of Life and the Glories of Gods and Kings*, 203–4.

[116] *Annals of the Cakchiquels and Title of the Lords of Totonicapán*, 64–5. The *Title of the Lords of Totonicapán* retells Quiché history from a different city's viewpoint. That document also includes the journey to Nacxit to receive the signs, symbols, and insignia of rulership (177).

[117] Jerald and Sandra Tanner, "A Black Hole in the Book of Mormon." No pages in the online document.

subtext of 1 Nephi was the justification of Nephi's right to rule. The subtext of 2 Nephi is the principles upon which the community should be ruled. 1 Nephi is the ethnogenetic myth of a new community. 2 Nephi is *about* the community. Nephi intends these five units to become the foundation of Nephite society.

In particular, the Isaiah quotations that Nephi selected form the basis for his prophetic blessing (2 Ne. 25–33) and also reiterate the social and economic principles characterizing Yahweh's people. Isaiah emphasizes that those who seek wealth and ignore the poor are departing from Yahweh's ways (2 Ne. 15). Adopting Isaiah's commentary as a charter for a community puts egalitarianism as a foundational principle. Nephi establishes an ideal with which Nephite society struggles throughout the Book of Mormon.

In Jacob, the early Nephite community is becoming segregated by displays of wealth. Jacob's condemnation of "costly apparel" is a condemnation of social inequality: "Ye are lifted up in the pride of your hearts, and wear stiff necks and high heads because of the costliness of your apparel, and persecute your brethren because ye suppose that ye are better than they" (Jacob 2:13, see "Early Economic and Social Tension" in Chapter 7). Desires for social inequality show in Nehor's preaching, where he argues that there ought to be a class of people who "ought not to labor with their hands, but that they ought to be supported by the people" (Alma 1:3).

The push to reestablish a king soon after the creation of the reign of the judges is led by a man who espoused the same hierarchical society as Nehor. Amlici, "being after the order of the man that slew Gideon by the sword [Nehor]" (Alma 2:1), begins a civil war in his attempt to alter Nephite politics. From that point on in the Book of Mormon, an attempt to establish a king was simultaneously an attempt to overthrow the principles of social egalitarianism in favor of social hierarchies.

7

The Nephites in a Dark Tunnel: From Jacob to Omni

Although 1 Nephi expressly was not written as a history, it contains a rich mine of historical data compared to the other books recorded on the small plates of Nephi. Jacob provides some important historical information, but only if we can tease it out of what he considered religiously important. Beginning with Enos, we find decreasing history (and decreasing text) from the successive keepers of the plates, until we come to the book of Omni. This book includes multiple writers, most of whom write little more than a couple of sentences.

The books from Jacob to Omni cover the time period from around 550 B.C. to around 200 B.C.[1] During those 350 years, something important occurred that triggered a shift in what it meant to be Nephite. By the end of the book of Omni, the Nephites who had founded the city of Nephi had fled from it. They entered a previously unmentioned land and merged with a previously unmentioned people. The last writer in the book of Omni and the last half of Words of Mormon fill us in on what happened, but the seeds of why it happened were planted before our record of the Nephites entered that dark tunnel of historical time.

Pre-Christian Christianity

Nephi had declared: "And we talk of Christ, we rejoice in Christ, we preach of Christ, we prophesy of Christ..." (2 Ne. 25:26). The early Nephites were very Christian nearly 600 years before Christ established a way for his followers to be Christian. Not

---

[1] Both dates are approximations based on surrounding available listed years. The text is thin on chronological information. We can date Mosiah$_2$'s installation as king to 124 B.C. Prior to that we can date the destruction of "the more wicked part of the Nephites" to 276 B.C. Any dating of events in between are necessarily approximate. Dates are given according to the chronology as I understand it. See "Lehi's Prophecy: How Long is a Year," in Chapter 4, and Brant A. Gardner, *Second Witness: Analytical and Contextual Commentary on the Book of Mormon*, 1:189.

only are they Christian early, they are adamantly Christian throughout their existence.[2] That is a lot of Christian in the New World. Their prescient Christianity has been considered anachronous. In a video published by Living Hope Ministries, "The Bible vs. the Book of Mormon" Honduran archaeologist Eliseo Fajardo Madrid declared: "Here you do not find any evidence of Christianity."[3]

Although many of the early Spanish friars who preached in the New World saw remnants of Christian teaching among Mesoamerican peoples,[4] it is correct to state that there is no clear archaeological evidence of Old World Christianity in the New World. The problem is less in the absence of evidence than in the expectation of what evidence should be found. It is impossible to know how we might recognize pre-Christian Christianity if we found it. In the Old World, we might expect to find crosses or paintings of a plate of loaves and fishes in a religious building. Unfortunately all explicitly Christian iconography from the Old World was developed over six hundred years after the Lehites left the Old World.

The best way to understand the problem of identifying religion in an archaeological context is to examine the iconographic history of Israel and of early Christianity. Both Israel and early Christianity were very comfortable borrowing and incorporating iconography from their neighbors, even when that iconography originally depicted elements of their neighbor's religion.

Ramsay MacMullen notes:

> The tangible record gives the same impression of shared territory. For example, among the grave-goods of large Roman Egypt, very much the same things are found whether the burial be Christian or not. In a Pannonian grave was placed a box ornamented with a relief of the gods, Orpheus in the center, Sol and Luna in the corners, but the Chi-Rho as well; elsewhere, in Danube burials, similar random mixtures of symbolism appear, with gods and busts of Saint Peter and Saint Paul all in the same bas-relief. The Romans who bought cheap little baked clay oil-lamps from the shop of Annius Serapiodorus in the capital apparently didn't care whether he put the Good Shepherd or Bacchus or both together on his products; and the rich patrons of mosaicists in Gaul, North Africa, and Syria were similarly casual about the very confused symbolism they commissioned or their floors.[5]

---

[2] The Nephite understanding of deity is controversial for more than its adamant and apparently prescient Christianity. There are passages which make it difficult to understand how the Nephite perception of Yahweh meshes with the modern LDS concept of the Godhead. Gardner, "The Nephite Understanding of God," in *Second Witness*, 1: 214–22.

[3] Quotation in Brant A. Gardner, "Behind the Mask, Behind the Curtain: Uncovering the Illusion," 177–82. Although I have borrowed heavily from that analysis, it has been further edited and expanded here.

[4] Jacques Lafaye, *Quetzalcoatl and Guadalupe: The Formation of Mexican National Consciousness, 1531–1815*, 153: "The conquistadores, followed by the missionaries, found in the temples, sacred images, and codices of the ancient Mexicans signs which they believed must be of Christian or Judaic origin. The most impressive of these finds were the crosses."

[5] Ramsay MacMullen, *Christianizing the Roman Empire*, 78.

The iconography of the region intermixed in early Christianity. Graydon F. Snyder describes a similar mixture of symbols for Hellenistic Judaism:

> A nearly complete list of symbols used by Jews through the sixth century shows ninety-seven decorations and symbols of which only the *etrong, lulab,* menorah, and shofar became consistent signs of Jewish identity. For the most part, the remaining ninety-three symbols come from either the general Hellenistic culture (zodiac signs, garlands) or, occasionally, come from Jewish life (the Torah shrine).[6]

Both early Christian and at least the Hellenistic Jews accepted iconographic elements from surrounding cultures and incorporated them into their own art. This does not mean, however, that the use of these borrowed visual symbols was reflected in their textual descriptions of religion:

> In their synagogues Jews of the first centuries in the Christian era were quite willing to use a large number of Greco-Roman decorations and symbols. Some scholars, like Goodenough, see in such symbols signals of a more mystical Judaism. Others assume that Jewish leaders had no choice but to use ateliers who offered, as a matter of course, pagan decorations and symbols. Or in terms of interaction, Jews were willing to utilize the decorations and symbols of their non-Jewish neighbors. By so doing they indicated their active participation in the Greco-Roman culture. But *none* of these symbols became a part of the Jewish iconic conversation. In that sense, by the first two centuries of the Christian era Judaism had developed a firm symbolic identity. It could accept and utilize pagan symbolic material, but did not incorporate it.[7]

Among the Jews and early Christians, the use of pagan artistic forms did not alter their religion, that is, the use of a pagan symbol did not necessarily bring with it the pagan meaning of that symbol. As Snyder indicates, they could "accept and utilize pagan symbolic material, but . . . not incorporate it."[8]

Christianity had a similar approach to its iconography. The earliest artistic representations of Christ appear to have borrowed the representations of Apollo.[9] The early borrowing of symbols was so complete that John Dominic Crossan says of a sarcophagus from A.D. 150–275 that it can be "read as either pagan or Christian."[10]

---

[6] Graydon F. Snyder, *Inculturation of the Jesus Tradition: The Impact of Jesus on Jewish and Roman Cultures,* 13.

[7] Ibid., 92.

[8] Lee I. Levine, "Archaeology and the Religious Ethos of Pre-70 Palestine," 120: "All the regnant motifs in Second Temple Jewish art were borrowed from the surrounding Greco-Roman culture, yet they were chosen selectively and carefully. Similarly, the use of ossuaries for secondary burial may well have been a Jewish adaptation of a foreign practice, just as most motifs on these ossuaries were part of the artistic repertoire of the Hellenistic East."

[9] "From Apollo to Jesus." This site clearly has its own agenda, but the visual representations of the transformations of Jesus's appearance are still instructive.

[10] John Dominic Crossan, *The Essential Jesus: What Jesus Really Taught,* 30.

What of the fundamental icon of Christianity, the cross? The earliest Christians were still a sect within Judaism.[11] For that sect, the tragedy of Christ's death was intermingled with the ignominious method of his death. The cross was, early on, an embarrassment.[12] It was part of Paul's reformulation of the message for the gentiles that the cross was transformed from a symbol of ignomy to a symbol of resurrection.[13] Thus the pre-eminence of the cross in the Old World is dependent upon the necessity of recontextualizing a symbol of rebellion and shame into a proclamation of divinity.

That recontextualization was clearly successful. However, the conditions that elevated the cross to its preeminent status did not occur in the New World. Although Christ's death on the cross is prophesied in the Book of Mormon,[14] the people of the New World did not experience the crucifixion. They experienced their God arriving in glory. There was not only no need to recontextualize the cross, there was a much more spectacular experience to remember. Based on the Book of Mormon people's understanding of Christ, we shouldn't expect the cross as a representation of New World Christianity.[15]

If early Christianity borrowed its iconography from its surrounding Hellenistic culture and did so in ways that might make certain artifacts completely ambiguous (as in the sarcophagus Crossan discusses), what ought we to expect of the New World? When we look for New World Christians, for what do we look? Do we look for representations of Apollo? Do we look for any of the Greek-inspired icons of the Old World? Clearly we cannot. The conditions that inspired those borrowings occurred long after Book of Mormon peoples left the Old World. Based on the history of both Israel and early Christianity, we might expect the New World Israelites and Christians to do just as their Old World counterparts did—adapt the iconography of the surrounding cultures.[16] But how would we know what they borrowed and

---

[11] Lawrence H. Schiffman, *From Text to Tradition: A History of Second Temple and Rabbinic Judaism*, 152.

[12] James D. G. Dunn, *Jews and Christians, the Parting of the Ways A.D. 70 to 135*, 168: "The Son of God, appointed from the ignominy of death on the cross. . . ."

[13] David Wenham, *Paul: Follower of Jesus or Founder of Christianity?* 155: "For Paul the cross has happened and is now a massively important datum to be explained; the prominence of it in his thinking is not at all surprising."

[14] 1 Ne. 19:10, 13; 2 Ne. 6:9, 10:3, 5, 25:13; Mosiah 3:9, 15:7.

[15] Nevertheless, the presence of crosses in Mesoamerica has been used as evidence of an understanding of Christianity. Francisco Cervantes de Sálazar, *Crónica de Nueva España*, 293, and Fernando de Alva Ixtlilxochitl, *Obras Históricas*, 10, both see the red crosses on paintings of Quetzalcoatl's robes as evidence of his association with Christianity. LDS author Thomas Stuart Ferguson, *One Fold, One Shepherd*, 137–38, not only sees the Mesoamerican cross as representative of Christianity, but provides a depiction of a crucifixion. Unfortunately, the visual reference is for a Central Mexican ritual sacrifice by arrows, not a depiction of the crucifixion, although there are some visual similarities. See Gardner, *Second Witness*, 1:212–13 for more details.

[16] Chapter 10 discusses how syncretism with surrounding religious ideas provides the explanation for the features of Nephite apostasy. Those same pressures offer the explanation for how iconography might also be integrated. However, as noted for the Jewish borrowings,

reinterpreted if it was also an active icon for a different religious symbol? We would have the ambiguous sarcophagus without enough knowledge to even understand that it is ambiguous.

If the same forces developed the New World Israelite/Christian art, there would be a similar ambiguity. If the earliest Old World artistic depictions of Jesus Christ were based on Apollo, perhaps the New World artists would have borrowed the Maize God, who was clearly a god who died and was resurrected. There is enough correspondence between Christ and the Maize God to suggest that a Nephite artist might borrow that symbol.[17] If we therefore find a depiction of a Maize God, is it pagan or Christian? Is the sarcophagus pagan or Christian? It is, at this point, an unanswerable question. The absence of Old World Christian iconography is not evidence of the absence of Book of Mormon Christianity.

Perhaps the Nephites retained the early Israelite admonitions against graven images; "Thou shalt not make unto thee any graven image, or any likeness of any thing that is in heaven above, or that is in the earth beneath, or that is in the water under the earth" (Ex. 20:4). If so, they would not have produced many artistic representations of their religion at all. The examination of the plausible Nephite lands perhaps underscore this problem.

The Nephite land of Zarahemla was found in the Grijalva River Basin. Before a modern dam covered the region with a lake, the New World Archaeological Foundation excavated some sites along the Grijalva. The reports of those excavations can tell us a little of the iconographic picture of the peoples who lived there.

Two types of images are important in discovering the symbols that a Mesoamerican culture uses. The first is the set of large, public displays—e.g., masks of gods on the temples themselves[18] and images of deities on carved stelae.[19] My literature survey of the highland Chiapas region, which corresponds to the area

---

the iconographic integration could occur without necessarily creating a syncretism in the religious ideas. However, once borrowings began, others easily followed. If there had been a borrowing of iconography, that very iconography could accelerate the acceptance of outside religious ideas such as those that are seen among apostate Nephites.

[17] Diane E. Wirth, "Quetzalcoatl, the Maya Maize God, and Jesus Christ," 4–15, presents this very argument. Without endorsing the particulars of the argument, the use of the Maize God as a symbol for the Messiah would be logical, and perhaps even more compelling than the Old World association with Apollo.

[18] Ricardo Agurcia Fasquelle, "Rosalilia: Temple of the Sun King at Copan," 72–73.

[19] V. Garth Norman, *Izapa Sculpture. Part 1: Plates*, contains the photographs of the remarkable stelae of the early Preclassic site. Stelae are typical of the lowland Classic Maya sites, with numerous examples in virtually all major sites. Discussions of important stelae of these various sites is found in Simon Martin and Nikolai Grube, *Chronicle of the Maya Kings and Queens*.

proposed as Nephite lands between at least 200 B.C. and A.D. 400,[20] reported no deity masks on the temples; the only stelae reported come from the Late Classic.[21]

The ceramic legacy of the cultures of highland Chiapas is much richer, but still yields little that demonstrates a clear representation of the typical pantheon of the gods. Santa Rosa produces a number of ceramic figurine heads and animal representations.[22] A possible retention of an Olmec (1500–600 B.C.) religious motif is found in some "baby-face" figurines: "This class of figurine is found frequently in those sites that have an Olmec component, apparently as a relatively late trait of this influence toward the end of the Middle Preclassic and beginning of the Late Preclassic."[23] There is also a vessel that is shaped as a woman with the spout protruding from the shoulders. Donald Brockington says of this vessel: "As Delgado notes, the figure has '. . . general aspect of Teotihuacán III. . . .' It also bears considerable resemblance to Early Classic Monte Albán pieces, specifically Boos' 'Deity with the Headdress Composed of a Horizontal Band.'"[24] A carved shell pendant from Chiapa de Corzo has a representation of a zoomorph with an upturned nose that is visually related to some deity representations among the Olmec and Maya.[25] This appears to be the extent of the currently discovered artifacts that represent a possible iconographic meaning.[26] The region was not aniconic, but certainly icon-poor.

Our modern perspective clearly assumes that, if the Nephites were important in the Book of Mormon, they therefore should have influenced New World peoples in ways that we can find. That assumption is simply not born out in other cross-cultural studies. Gordon F. Ekholm cautions:

> There are still other reasons why through purely pragmatic archaeology we cannot hope to get a true picture of the extent of culture contacts in ancient times. One is that

---

[20] The Grijalva River Valley centers the geographic association with the Nephites. After the destruction prior to the Messiah's visitation, the Nephite capital moved north to Bountiful and probably out of this valley. The final days of the Book of Mormon occur closer to the Gulf Coast.

[21] The site of Colonia Lopez Matos, along the lower Grijalva, is a late Classic site with modest monumental statues and stelae. Roman Piña Chan and Carlos Navarrete, *Archaeological Research in the Lower Grijalva River Region, Tabasco, and Chiapas*, 44–51. Literature surveyed that did not yield reports of masks or stelae include:

Augustin Delgado, *Archaeological Research at Santa Rosa, Chiapas, and in the Region of Tehuantepec*.
Thomas A. Lee Jr., *Mound 4 Excavations at San Isidro, Chiapas, Mexico*.
Gareth W. Lowe, Pierre Agrinier, J. Alden Mason, Frederick Hicks, and Charles E. Rozaire, *Excavations at Chiapa de Corzo, Chiapas, Mexico*. I cite material in this volume hereafter by specific author and article.

[22] Delgado, *Archaeological Research at Santa Rosa*, 59–66.

[23] Ibid., 60.

[24] Donald L. Brockington, *The Ceramic History of Santa Rosa, Chiapas, Mexico*, 21.

[25] J. Alden Mason, "Mound 12, Chiapa de Corzo, Chiapas, Mexico," 23.

[26] There is a representation of a deity on a pottery fragment from the site of Yerba Buena, Chiapas. However, it dates after A.D. 500 and therefore is not relevant to a survey of the Book of Mormon time period. T. Patrick Culbert, *The Ceramic History of the Central Highlands of Chiapas, Mexico*, 10.

much of the culture of any society is nonmaterial. Many culture-contact situations might well be channeled in such a way that much nonmaterial culture is exchanged but that little or no material culture objects are traded. . . .

It is my view. . . that we can never fully document by concrete archaeological evidence the degree to which the cultures of neighboring peoples were dependent on each other.[27]

Perhaps even more relevant is the observation of David H. Kelley: "A further problem is caused by the fact that the individuals responsible for introducing an innovation to another culture are often dissidents in their own culture. If a group leaves an area because they dislike certain aspects of their own culture, they can hardly be expected to introduce these traits into another culture."[28] Perhaps it is in this context that we might see another coloring of Nephi's statement that he had "not taught them many things concerning the manner of the Jews; for their works were works of darkness, and their doings were doings of abominations" (2 Ne. 25:2).

Early Economic and Social Tension

The plates that Nephi designated as containing "an account of the reign of the kings, and the wars and contentions of my people (1 Ne. 9:4), were designed to be transmitted from ruler to ruler. This record tradition continued throughout Nephite history and from which Mormon created his book.

On the second set of plates Nephi wrote what we have in First and Second Nephi. That record was given a different transmission path. No known kings wrote on these plates. They passed from non-royal fathers to non-royal sons.[29] Nephi's Yahweh-directed intention for these plates was a "special purpose that there should be an account engraven of the ministry of my people" (1 Ne. 9:3). The plates had a different purpose and were guarded by a different family. Not only were they not royal, but they had decreasing importance in the community, and manifest a decreasing enthusiasm for keeping the record.

As Jacob began his record on the small plates, he noted: "The people of Nephi, under the reign of the second king, began to grow hard in their hearts, and indulge themselves somewhat in wicked practices, such as like unto David of old desiring many wives and concubines, and also Solomon, his son. Yea, and they also began to search much gold and silver, and began to be lifted up somewhat in pride" (Jacob 1:15–16). Jacob received the small plates fifty-five years after the departure from Jerusalem (Jacob 1:1), or approximately 532 B.C. How did this change begin so soon?

The hypothesis that the Book of Mormon took place in Mesoamerica gives us the opportunity to use the economic and social tensions in that area around the time of

---

[27] Gordon F. Ekholm, "Diffusion and Archaeological Evidence," 57.
[28] David H. Kelley, "Diffusion: Evidence and Process," 61.
[29] John S. Tanner, "Jacob and His Descendants as Authors," 55: "After passing into Jacob's hands, the small plates became increasingly focused on the history of Jacob's family rather than on the history of the whole Nephite group. Understanding this is critical. . . . From Jacob on, the plates were no longer kept by the rulers (see Jacob 1:9). Jacob and his descendants were not kings. From all we can tell, they did not play a leading role in political or military matters."

Jacob to provide an answer to this question. Those conditions provide the explanatory background for the particular features of Jacob's sermon at the temple—particularly the interesting combination of being lifted up in pride and accepting polygyny.

Jacob set the stage for his sermon by discussing a social problem that resulted from particular economic conditions:

> And now behold, my brethren, this is the word which I declare unto you, that many of you have begun to search for gold, and for silver, and for all manner of precious ores, in the which this land, which is a land of promise unto you and to your seed, doth abound most plentifully.
>
> And the hand of providence hath smiled upon you most pleasingly, that you have obtained many riches; and because some of you have obtained more abundantly than that of your brethren ye are lifted up in the pride of your hearts, and wear stiff necks and high heads because of the costliness of your apparel, and persecute your brethren because ye suppose that ye are better than they. (Jacob 2:12–13)

In this part of the sermon, Jacob describes the community's desire for economic prosperity. He does not decry the desire itself, but rather the result: "Some of you have obtained more abundantly than that of your brethren." Jacob would probably have been fine with the accumulation of wealth if all participated equally. The social problem was that those with more wealth "wear stiff necks and high heads because of the costliness of your apparel, and persecute your brethren because ye suppose that ye are better than they."

The early Nephite egalitarian ideal was quite at home among early Mesoamerican communities.[30] However, that same social stratification that Jacob decried was developing among other Mesoamerican communities during this same time period. The city of Nephi was apparently undergoing the same economic and social pressures as were other surrounding cities. Richard N. Hansen describes this development: "During this period [1000–600 B.C.] an embryonic leadership and status hierarchy in the Mirador Basin is suggested by the importation and distribution of exotic goods such as obsidian, jade, and basalt from the Maya Highlands, imported chert artifacts, and seashells from the eastern coast. The symbols representative of rank and the status of a patron elite also appear."[31]

To understand how the city of Nephi fit into the developing Mesoamerican culture, we must first understand their economic issues in ancient terms rather than modern assumptions. It is natural for modern readers to see that the Nephites were

---

[30] John S. Henderson, *The World of the Ancient Maya*, 81 describes the pre-900 B.C. communities: "These communities did not have centralized political leadership, and they did not undertake large public construction projects. They were essentially self-sufficient, relying on a combination of farming and foraging for subsistence on local raw materials for most tools." He then notes that, between 900 and 400 B.C., there were changes in the previous trade and economic networks: "The decline of these economic spheres might easily have contributed to intensified trade with the Maya area by removing such obstacles as competing markets for key commodities" (81).

[31] Richard D. Hansen, "Kingship in the Cradle of Maya Civilization: The Mirador Basin," 145.

searching for gold and silver and to assume that their wealth was therefore based on finding the intrinsically valuable metals. That could not have been the case.

Assuming, as I have, that those who arrived with Lehi merged with the much larger indigenous population, the values placed on certain materials would shift from the Old World ideas to those present among the larger society. In the case of gold and silver, Mesoamericans did not esteem those metals as highly as did the Old World. For Mesoamericans, the highest value appears to have been placed on jade. Historian David Drew notes: "As a precious material gold remained secondary to blue-green jade, the colour of fertility and the essence of life itself."[32] Mesoamerican languages often use a single word for both gold and silver.[33] That should warn us that there was no easily discerned differential value for the two metals as there is in modern society. It is possible that their value was in their easy malleability more than in intrinsic value. That is, they were valuable for what could be done with them more than just possessing them.

The second clear indication that we are dealing with a different economic principle comes from the availability of the two metals. Nephi specifically notes that "gold, and of silver . . . were in great abundance" (2 Ne. 5:15).[34] Jacob reiterates: "Many of you have begun to search for gold, and for silver . . . in the which this land . . . doth abound most plentifully" (Jacob 2:12).[35] Economic value is related to both desirability and availability. The more desirable and less available something is, the greater its value. Yet Nephi tells us that, although desirable, gold and silver were abundant. That fact would decrease their economic value.

The value of gold and silver in the Nephite economy could not have been based on intrinsic value.[36] It had to have been the potential value of what could be made with the raw material. Indeed, that is the very context Nephi provides: "And I did teach my people to build buildings, and to work in all manner of wood, and of iron, and of copper, and of brass, and of steel, and of gold, and of silver, and of precious

---

[32] David Drew, *The Lost Chronicles of the Maya Kings*, 15. See also George E. Stuart and Gene S. Stuart, *The Mysterious Maya*, 57, and Michael D. Coe, *The Maya*, 29.

[33] Maya languages usually use *tak'in* "sun excrement." In Nahuatl the word is *teocuitlatl* "divine excrement." To peoples who use night-soil as a fertilizer, excrement has a greater value it does than for many modern societies.

[34] Jeffrey R. Chadwick, "Lehi's House at Jerusalem and the Land of His Inheritance," 114, reminds us that gold and silver were not commonly used for exchange. Therefore, while Nephi would have seen the metals as valuable for what could be made from them, he would not see economic value in the simple possession of the metals.

[35] John Dombrowski, Elinor C. Betters, Howard I. Blutstein, Lynne E. Cox, and Elery M. Zehner, *Area Handbook for Guatemala*, 45, 294 notes that while modern Guatemala does not have a major mining industry for these metals, they are present and sporadically mined. Silver mines were exploited in the Spanish colonial period and are still productive in very small quantities.

[36] Gold and silver are an important unit of exchange according to the definitions in Alma 11:5–19. That was a system based on weights rather than intrinsic value, and the system appears to be based in barley rather than the metals. For more information, see the section "Controversial Coins" in Chapter 12.

ores" (2 Ne. 5:15). The Nephites created value by working the raw materials, not simply possessing them. The need for the raw materials to feed the economic engine provided the impetus for the new emphasis on searching for gold and silver.

Costly Apparel and the Nephite Economy

Jacob specifically notes that social stratification was being manifest in "costly apparel" (Jacob 2:13). This phrase holds the key to understanding the issues that Jacob sees in his community. The problem is that costly apparel is not possible inside an insulated community.

Each community had to make its own clothing. They had access to the same raw materials from which to create their fabrics and the same plants to create the dyes. Even styles that might be innovated can be rapidly diffused as each family copies innovations by other members of the community. In fact, it is not unusual that communities develop common dress styles.[37] "Costly apparel" cannot, by definition, be the same as what is commonly available. Economic value is created by relative scarcity. What everyone has cannot be considered "costly," no matter its quality.

The early descriptions of Nephite economics make most sense against a backdrop of trade with other communities. Rebecca Storey and Randolph J. Widmer describe the general economic situation in early Mesoamerica: "Reciprocal economic exchanges could also serve to create or sustain alliances among families or among groups. Sometimes similar commodities—for example, two ceramic vessels of identical function—were exchanged. At other times, jewelry or clothing was exchanged. In either case, the exchange was not purely an economic one but also served sociopolitical functions. This took on a more complex form when elite exchange occurred."[38]

The incipient elite exchanges are precisely the developing economic situation in the Maya world at this time.[39] John S. Henderson provides a general picture of the plausible economic background to Jacob's sermon:

> Although some parts of the Maya world—mostly in the highlands—were firmly tied into the economic networks and related patterns of interaction of the Olmec world, centered to the west on the Gulf Coast, most early Maya communities, especially in the lowlands, were small, simple, egalitarian villages. By the end of the Middle Preclassic period, after 500 B.C., communities like Mirador were beginning to reflect a new

---

[37] I spent a little time in Guatemala in the early 1970s and spoke with people who knew a lot about the woman's apparel item called a *huipil*, or blouse. Experts could see the patterns in the embroidery and know which community had created the huipil.

[38] Rebecca Storey and Randolph J. Widmer, "The Pre-Columbian Economy," 88.

[39] Susan Toby Evans, *Ancient Mexico and Central America: Archaeology and Culture History*, 233: "Part of long-distance exchange were ideas about how rulers should behave and be treated. This is not to argue that the idea of, say, a ruler claiming to be descended from mythological god-like beings was thought up in one place and then spread around—simple diffusionism—but rather that societal changes were making many regions fertile ground for the adoption and innovation of new means of justifying and realizing the stratification process."

developmental trajectory. Jewelry and other goods made from exotic raw materials indicate increasing prosperity, expanded economic ties to distant regions, and sharper differences in wealth and social status; large-scale, elaborately decorated public buildings reflect the emergence of powerful permanent leaders, chiefs or kings. These trends continued and intensified during the Late Preclassic period, setting the fundamental patterns of Classic-period Maya city-states.[40]

Henderson's description of the developing Maya kingdoms contains the same undercurrents that we see in the Book of Mormon. What he adds is the missing piece in Jacob's discourse: the acquisition of wealth through trade of the "jewelry and other goods made from exotic raw materials." The wealth occurs not because of the possession of unworked and undervalued raw material, but because the raw material could be worked into exotic goods that could be exchanged for exotic goods from other communities.

It is in the context of developing inter-community trade that we can understand what Jacob sees as "costly apparel." Linda Schele and Peter Mathews describe the way Mesoamerican elite proclaimed their wealth of exotic trade goods: "The Maya used commodities both in their raw state and as worked objects for money. . . . People throughout Mesoamerica wore these currencies as jewelry and clothing to display the wealth and enterprise of their families."[41]

Clothing served a similar function in the Mediterranean during the Bronze Age. Bettany Hughes describes the Mycenaean world: "The finds from the Mycenaean citadels and graves illustrate the centrality of visual signals in pre-history. Before writing was employed as a tool of propaganda, appearance and experience are *all-important*. Images have to speak louder than words."[42]

Costly apparel resulted from the visual display of trade goods. This visual difference established clear distinctions between those who had access to the outside wealth and those who did not. Against a Mesoamerican background, at the correct time, we have precisely the conditions needed for Jacob's costly apparel both to exist and also to be the trigger to the social inequality that Jacob excoriates.

Polygamy and the Nephite Economy

Social inequality represented by costly apparel was only one of the two major themes of Jacob's discourse. The second was his condemnation of the nascent practice of polygamy. For modern readers, those two issues are not particularly related. Read against a modern interpretive framework, there is no particular reason to combine those two issues into a single sermon. In fact, in a modern economy, increasing the number of wives (and children) might be seen as decreasing wealth rather than increasing it. However, in the early Mesoamerican community, they were directly related. Placing Jacob's sermon in a Mesoamerican context during the time period in

---

[40] Henderson, *The World of the Ancient Maya*, 87–88.
[41] Linda Schele and Peter Mathews, *The Code of Kings: The Language of Seven Sacred Maya Temples and Tombs*, 19.
[42] Bettany Hughes, *Helen of Troy: Goddess, Princess, Whore*, 43.

which Jacob gave this sermon supplies the reason that social inequality and polygamy should not only both appear in his sermon, but also be linked together.

Jacob's condemnation of polygamy is, as was his discussion of the problem of wealth, somewhat unusual. Not only is it apparently tied to economic development, but it is described in what should have been inappropriate terms. Jacob consistently equates having more than one wife with whoredoms and unchastity. This is just as impossible as would be valuable gold that is readily found.

Jacob speaks of wives, not harlots. All societies that accept multiple wives have legal regulations that legitimize the union. A plural wife is a wife, and relations with a wife do not fall under the rubric of whoredoms in any society. Thus, Jacob is somehow in the position of preaching about a type of marital union in which someone recognizes the woman as a wife, but which he—and Yahweh—do not. Jacob also describes the fate of the wives and children in ways that make no sense. He speaks of the daughters of Jerusalem being led away captive (Jacob 2:33) and their children being brought into destruction (Jacob 3:10). It is hard to see how the very fact of multiple wives can be equated to captivity, or cause the destruction of their children. Seeing Jacob's sermon in a Mesoamerican context provides a framework for his particular concerns. As with costly apparel, the context of the increasing inter-community trade provides the important background.

The development of social segregation in Mesoamerica has been the subject of multiple theories and studies, but one study uses the archaeological information to support the hypothesis that the development of institutionalized social inequality and political privilege was due to the internal social pressures of personal advancement. In terms of this theory, such seekers of advantage are termed "aggrandizers."[43]

John E. Clark and Michael Blake describe the conditions leading to the rise of social inequality. Significantly, they link trade and polygamy, just as did Jacob: "Aggrandizers simply strive to become more influential. It is the successful deployment of resources and labor that ultimately ensure the social and political longevity of an aggrandizer. . . . Building renown commences in the nuclear unit of production. An aggrandizer first accumulates deployable resources by the sweat of his brow, and through the efforts of his wife (wives) and children. The more wives and children the better."[44] I suggest that this situation explains why Jacob's discourse specifically pairs the problem of increasing social hierarchy through wealth with the issue of polygamy. At this point in time, the two were inextricably intertwined. Both are social issues stemming from the developing trade of the local aggrandizers.

Clark and Blake further note: "The conversion of external resources into social leverage locally requires (near) exclusive access to outside goods, material, or information. This also allows the aggrandizer to operate partially outside the

---

[43] John E. Clark and Michael Blake, "The Power of Prestige: Competitive Generosity and the Emergence of Rank Societies in Lowland Mesoamerica," 252.

[44] Ibid., 253 and 255.

sanctioning norms of his local group."[45] The Mesoamerican picture of developing social distinctions is precisely the type of threat that Jacob denounces in the early city of Nephi. Pressure for social hierarchies appears by distinctions displayed in costly apparel,[46] and those distinctions are related to the practice of having multiple wives. The increase in wealth is tied to outside trade, or the same access to external resources that Clark and Blake describe.

Assuming that Nephite wealth was built on the trade of manufactured goods with neighboring communities and assuming that these neighbors would have practiced polygamy, Nephite traders would have immediately seen the advantages of adopting their neighbors' successful means of enhancing production, then displaying the results in their "costly apparel." Because these men would be following the regional marriage customs, their unions would have been seen as legal in that context. They would be a "whoredom" in Jacob's view because they violated the commandment that men should have only one wife (Jacob 2:27).[47]

I also conjecture that Nephite polygyny involved elite men arranging diplomatic marriages to assure commercial or political alliances. Patriarchal societies tend to be patrilocal—that is, the woman leaves her father's home and moves to the husband's home. Furthermore, given degrees of kinship within which marriage is prohibited, such societies tend to seek women from other communities. While this practice would bring women into the city of Nephi, it would mean that Nephite daughters and sisters would become wives in other communities. Under these circumstances, an unwilling or frightened "daughter of my people" might easily lament her marriage as a form of captivity in a strange locale (and almost certainly a strange religion).

Such women who are given in marriage in foreign communities are those whose "chastity" Yahweh is protecting. The relationship being created cannot have legal sanction in Nephite society, or their chastity would not need protection. Polygamy would be accepted as marriage according to regional law but not according to Nephite law.

Furthermore, perhaps a component of *whoredom* is implied by sending women away to non-Nephite communities, thus contracting marriages with unbelievers. The

---

[45] Ibid., 255.

[46] Parrish Brady and Shon Hopkin, "The Zoramites and Costly Apparel: Symbolism and Irony," 40–53, examine the literary function of clothing in the story of the Zoramites, both the rich and the poor. This segment of the Book of Mormon could be read (as they do) as a specialized metaphor in the discussion of the Zoramites, but the concepts associated with costly apparel begin much earlier and extend much later. The Zoramite descriptions fit into the larger use of the concept rather than define a particular way in which Mormon uses clothing as a localized symbol.

[47] This hypothesis also explains the typically unasked question of how the Nephites decided to adopt polygamy in the first place. Certainly our modern aversion to the practice should suggest that communal definitions of marriage are difficult to change. In the case of an imported Israelite population with a foundational mandate against polygamy, there had to be some trigger that would encourage the practice of polygamy. That trigger is much more easily seen from a pervasive external pressure than from any internal change in perspective. Mesoamerican communities at this time accepted polygamy and therefore there was a general climate that not only encouraged the practice, but which also demonstrated its economic value.

women would lament their forced entry into political unions not sanctioned by Yahweh's command to Lehi. Their children, who would not be brought up under Mosaic law, would be subject to spiritual destruction. Positioning this Book of Mormon situation in the context of the developing social-economic situation of Middle Preclassic Mesoamerica explains why Jacob addressed both social differentiation and polygamy in the same discourse.

Jacob's discourse sits at the transition between Nephi's longer and more detailed texts and the decreasing details to come. As the Nephites enter this textual dark tunnel, we see a continual increase in the social and economic tensions within Nephite culture. They will plague Nephite ideals from this beginning through the thousand years until their final destruction.

Early Religious Tension

After Jacob's sermon denouncing costly apparel and polygamy, Jacob creates another entry in his book. This entry is less obviously a recorded sermon, since it lacks the context that he provides for his sermon at the temple. Nevertheless, Jacob is addressing an audience—hence, a sermon. In this second recorded sermon, he introduces the parable of the olive tree. Immediately following that discussion, Jacob says: "And now, behold, my brethren, as I said unto you that I would prophesy, behold, this is my prophecy—that the things which this prophet Zenos spake, concerning the house of Israel, in the which he likened them unto a tame olive tree, must surely come to pass" (Jacob 6:1). Chapter 6 reads like a sermon, and ends with a conclusion that is even more final than the conclusion to a sermon would be: "Finally, I bid you farewell, until I shall meet you before the pleasing bar of God, which bar striketh the wicked with awful dread and fear. Amen" (Jacob 6:13). This sentence is an absolute farewell, most appropriate for some form of permanent separation. Nevertheless, in the next chapter, Jacob is still alive in the same city.

Why was that ending declaration so final? Sidney Sperry suggests: "It is very probable that Jacob meant to end his book at this point; the quotation seems to imply that fact. However, later events caused him to add the historical matter now found in the last chapter of his record."[48] This analysis recognizes the finality of the statement but misses an important structural clue. The headnote for Jacob's book is original to the plate text and contains a synopsis of what Jacob will write. In it, Jacob clearly indicates that he will discuss Sherem, which is the next material after this apparently final closing: "The words of his preaching unto his brethren. He confoundeth a man who seeketh to overthrow the doctrine of Christ. A few words concerning the history of the people of Nephi." (Headnote for the book of Jacob). The finality of the sermon

---

[48] Sidney B. Sperry, *Book of Mormon Compendium*, 266.

cannot be related to a previously intended close of the book, because Jacob had already declared that he would continue.[49]

The final statement of Jacob's sermon can be best read, in my opinion, as Jacob's final discourse as chief priest. Although this conclusion is speculative and based on only a few fragments of evidence, I hypothesize that the termination of his religious position accounts for the finality of his benediction. The only indication that we have for Jacob's position in society is that Nephi established both of his younger brothers, Jacob and Joseph, as priests and teachers over the people (2 Ne. 5:26, Jacob 1:18). Although there is later evidence for the kingship passing to a brother (see "A Mesoamerican Model for Nephite Judges" in Chapter 9 for more details), there is no indication that Jacob received the throne. Rather, when Jacob discusses the succession, he simply notes that out of respect for his brother, Nephi, all kings took upon themselves the throne name of Nephi (Jacob 1:11). Jacob mentions a second Nephi (and explicitly a second king in Jacob 1:15), and then a third, raising the possibility that there actually had been a third by the time he wrote. (Of course, it might also have simply been an example of the naming convention.)

Both Jacob's possession of the small plates and his ability to speak to what appears to have been much of the population in Jacob 2–3, suggest that he continued to be the chief priest and teacher for the people, a position he had received from Nephi himself. As chief priest, Jacob was in the position of authority that allowed him to give this particular sermon, which was directed at some of the most important people in the community. Jacob described a growing social division between those who didn't have access to sumptuary goods and those who did, with those who did considering themselves to be better than the rest of the community (Jacob 2:13). Jacob addresses those very people and calls them to repentance.

It is not much of a leap, given human history, to see Jacob condemning the very people who are in a position of leadership, if not rulership, in the community. The elite marginalize prophets, who stand against them and neutralize them if possible. Jacob's father, Lehi, appears to have left Jerusalem under such a conflict, and the discernible social evidence surrounding Jacob's sermon suggests that he was in the same position. When Jacob ended his discourse with such a final farewell, it is not because he was dying or leaving the city, but because of another important separation. Logically, the ruling elite against whom Jacob preached removed him from his position as the official chief priest/teacher to the people. As rulers tend to do, Jacob would logically have been replaced with a teacher more favorable to the elite's policies.

Sherem appeared in the aftermath of that plausible removal from office, when he "came... among the people of Nephi" (Jacob 7:1). That statement alone suggests that he came from another city.[50] The rest of the details corroborate that idea. He must

---

[49] In contrast, the heading for 2 Nephi only predicts what Nephi wrote through our chapter 5. "An account of the death of Lehi. Nephi's brethren rebel against him. The Lord warns Nephi to depart into the wilderness. His journeyings in the wilderness, and so forth" (Headnote to 2 Nephi).

[50] John L. Sorenson, *Nephite Culture and Society: Collected Papers*, 68, suggests that Sherem must be an outsider.

ask where he can find Jacob, something that would be unusual had he been a resident in the city of Nephi. No matter how large the city of Nephi could have been at this point in history, it is unlikely that it had grown so large that major political and religious figures would be unknown.

Further, Jacob 7:4 tells us: "And he was learned, that he had a perfect knowledge of the language of the people; wherefore, he could use much flattery, and much power of speech, according to the power of the devil." Sherem was well educated, a fact he demonstrates by his eloquence and knowledge of the scriptures. Jacob's comment about Sherem's "perfect knowledge of the language" suggests verbal artistry, that he was eloquent and persuasive. But it also suggests at least the possibility that Sherem is fluent in a language not his own—*prima facie* evidence of an outsider.

Sherem's purpose in coming among the Nephites is interesting. He has undertaken his public ministry to counter a very specific Nephite teaching: that there should be a Messiah. That purpose is historically interesting. Obviously, Sherem was familiar with Nephite teachings or he could not preach against them. He must have learned of the Messiah prior to coming among the Nephites. Where would he have gained such knowledge? There are only two possible sources: from the Nephites or from the Lamanites.

Sherem might have learned about the Messiah from the Lamanites, because they would have known of the teaching, but is unlikely. Sherem began by confirming that he believes the scriptures (Jacob 7:10). The only writings called by that term in the New World are the brass plates. The Nephites possessed those plates, as evidenced by their presence in Mosiah$_2$'s coronation ritual (Mosiah 1:16). Since the Lamanites did not, it would have been difficult for Lamanites to be the source of Sherem's belief in the scriptures. The most logical source from which Sherem learned the scriptures (and hence about the Messiah) was from Nephites.

If Sherem was not from the city of Nephi, then he must have been part of the extensive trade relations between the city of Nephi and the surrounding communities.[51] If Sherem spoke a different natal language, then concourse with traders becomes even more likely, as Mesoamerican traders (at least when we have later records about them) were able to communicate in other languages; it facilitated trade.[52]

---

[51] It is tempting to say that Sherem was not a Nephite if he came from outside the city. However, in Jacob's definition that Nephites were all who were friendly to Nephi (Jacob 14), it would appear that Sherem should be included in that idea of who was a Nephite.
Kevin Christensen, "The Deuteronomist De-Christianizing of the Old Testament," 87, suggests that Sherem might have been a descendant of the people of Mulek. While that is an intriguing possibility, it runs contrary to the general information we have for the people of Zarahemla, who are the only textually known descendants of the people of Mulek. Those people had lost both religion and language, the two reasons Christensen saw as possible evidence of Sherem's Mulekite ancestry.

[52] Warwick Bray, *Everyday Life of the Aztecs*, 150. The evidence for the Aztec must be considered somewhat skewed as their political dominance assured that their own language, Nahuatl, was the *lingua franca* of trade. However, Bray notes that there were some who spoke

Religion, backed by scriptures, appears to have been one of the exports in the region. Copies of the brass-plates scriptures may have gone with trade goods to a community at some distance from the land of Nephi. In Sherem's community (if not in the city of Nephi itself), the orthodox Nephite religion had been reinterpreted. Although we have only the rejection of the Messiah at this early point, later evidence strongly suggests that there was a trend toward syncretism of the Nephite religion with the pagan religions of the region. (See Chapter 10 for more details.)[53]

Sherem came specifically to preach—not against the law of Moses—but against the Atoning Messiah about whom Jacob and Nephi taught. Why would he focus on this teaching? I have suggested that Jacob's sermon (Jacob 2–3) pitted Jacob directly against an influential trading class in the city of Nephi (and plausibly the ruling elite). Jacob condemned their practices. As traders, they would have been the source for the brass-plate texts that Sherem had studied. Thus, Sherem's understanding of the religion to which he converted was a skewed version, one that reflected beliefs of traders who were already in conflict with Jacob. Because Sherem specifically seeks out Jacob, the implication is that he wants to discredit Jacob's teaching, reduce his authority, and thereby decrease Nephite internal opposition to the practices of the prideful traders.

But why? The clue is the public nature of the debate and the specific discussion of Sherem's learning. Sherem was a highly educated and apparently vocally persuasive person looking for a very public debate with a specific religious figure. Had Sherem only cared to make converts, he might have preached to gathered Nephites. Instead, he targeted Jacob.

I hypothesize that the true purpose of Sherem's mission was to discredit Jacob by discrediting his teaching of the Atoning Messiah. It seems likely that Jacob continued to be a threat to the traders even without an official position. Discrediting him would have destroyed his informal influence as well, leaving the traders free to act without Jacob's continuing condemnation. This discrediting needed to take place in public, before his supporters.

The attempt failed.[54] It not only failed but had the opposite effect. For a period of time, Jacob was restored to influence and there was a renewal of the Nephite religion. Nevertheless, this initial religious tension does not disappear. Traces of it may be seen throughout this dark historical tunnel. Enos complains that:

> And there was nothing save it was exceeding harshness, preaching and prophesying of wars, and contentions, and destructions, and continually reminding them of death, and the duration of eternity, and the judgments and the power of God, and all these things—

---

other languages well enough to pass as natives of the land. It is highly unlikely that the Old World language inheritance of the Nephites would have served as such a *lingua franca*.

[53] For a more detailed discussion of the particular aspects of this apostate religion, see Gardner, *Second Witness*, 4:41–51.

[54] Later attempts to introduce apostate religious ideas would take greater hold. During the reign of Alma$_2$ as chief judge, the effects of apostasy were such that Alma$_2$ gave up the judgment seat to spend full time preaching the true gospel to bring the apostates back to the fold.

stirring them up continually to keep them in the fear of the Lord. I say there was nothing short of these things, and exceedingly great plainness of speech, would keep them from going down speedily to destruction. And after this manner do I write concerning them. (Enos 1:23).

The situation was no better when Jarom wrote (Jarom 1:3): "It is expedient that much should be done among this people, because of the hardness of their hearts, and the deafness of their ears, and the blindness of their minds, and the stiffness of their necks." The respite following Jacob's public victory was evidence of a battle won, but other battles lay in the future.

Nephites in Armed Conflict

As Jacob closed his record he left another important clue about the next three hundred years: "And it came to pass that many means were devised to reclaim and restore the Lamanites to the knowledge of the truth; but it all was vain, for they delighted in wars and bloodshed, and they had an eternal hatred against us, their brethren. And they sought by the power of their arms to destroy us continually" (Jacob 7:24).

Neither Nephi nor Jacob dwelt on the "wars and bloodshed" that Jacob indicated occurred "continually." We have only this quick statement. From it, however, we are given to understand that the Nephite community has been involved in armed conflict with Lamanites during Jacob's lifetime. It is important to emphasize that Jacob defined Lamanites as those who "seek to destroy the people of Nephi" (Jacob 1:14). We should not suppose that all of these conflicts—or even any of them—were with descendants of Laman or those who stayed with them. They might have been, but Jacob's use of the term does not allow us to be more precise than to document the existence of armed enemies, whatever their city/lineage affiliation might have been.

The Nephite response was to "fortify against them with . . . [our] arms, and with all . . . [our] might" (Jacob 7:25). This description suggests a continuation of Nephi's policy of arming his people. The need to do so had begun in Nephi's lifetime and had not abated by the end of Jacob's life. There was no abating of the danger of armed conflict during Enos' lifetime either: "And I saw wars between the Nephites and Lamanites in the course of my days" (Enos 1:23–24).

The theme of war continues in Jarom's record:

> And [the Nephites] were scattered upon much of the face of the land, and the Lamanites also. And they were exceedingly more numerous than were they of the Nephites; and they loved murder and would drink the blood of beasts.
>
> And it came to pass that they came many times against us, the Nephites, to battle. But our kings and our leaders were mighty men in the faith of the Lord; and they taught the people the ways of the Lord; wherefore, we withstood the Lamanites and swept them away out of our lands, and began to fortify our cities, or whatsoever place of our inheritance. (Jarom 1:6–7)

Jarom traced increasing populations and the expansion of some form of Nephite presence into a wider geography. However, along with the expansion of the Nephites he recorded an expansion of those called Lamanites. The description of the Lamanites in verse 6 is part of the outgroup bias that began during Nephi's time. (See "Becoming Nephites and Lamanites" in Chapter 6). I would caution against reading the descriptions too literally as they form stereotypes that reappear throughout the Book of Mormon.[55]

As our brief texts approach the end of the small plate record, the theme of warfare continues to be prominent. Omni records tersely that he had "fought much with the sword to preserve my people" (Omni 1:1). Chemish tells us very little, but his son Abinadom again mentioned that "I saw much war and contention between my people, the Nephites, and the Lamanites; and I, with my own sword, have taken the lives of many of the Lamanites in the defence of my brethren" (Omni 1:10).

The most consistent historical theme from Enos to Amaleki (the last writer in the book of Omni) is that of armed conflict. This is precisely what archaeology is beginning to uncover for this time period in the Maya lands, including Highland Guatemala where the city of Nephi is considered to have been located. David Webster notes: "A sizable Late Preclassic [500 B.C.–A.D. 250] community existed at Punta de Chimino, and some archaeologists believe that the impressive earthwork fortifications that defended the Punta de Chimino peninsula were first built at that time. If so, warfare had very deep roots in the region."[56] Data from the site called Blackman Eddy in Belize, suggest evidence of warfare perhaps as early as 650 B.C.[57] The existence of fortifications is dramatic evidence of violent conflict, but it is highly likely that conflict also existed in areas that had not yet resorted to defensive fortifications. Warfare had become a constant presence in Mesoamerican culture.

Some Mesoamerican cities had fortifications,[58] but they were not stone-walled cities like Jerusalem. The fortifications at Becán, for instance, consisted of a dirt wall likely surmounted by a wooden parapet. (Webster has suggested that this structure may date to the Late Preclassic, or 500 B.C.–A.D. 250.[59]) Late Formative (300 B.C.–A.D. 1) fortifications are also known for El Mirador.[60] David A. Freidel summarizes:

> The Late Preclassic kings and their warriors have left us a considerably more circumspect archaeological record of combat and defense against attack. At the site of in Mexico, the Late Preclassic rulers of the community commissioned a formidable ditch and rampart surrounding the ceremonial center. This is certainly a defensive fortification and

---

[55] Gardner, *Second Witness*, 2:104–6.
[56] David Webster, *The Fall of the Ancient Maya: Solving the Mystery of the Maya Collapse*, 275.
[57] M. Kathryn Brown and James F. Garber, "Evidence of Conflict during the Middle Formative in the Maya Lowlands: A View from Blackman Eddy, Belize," 91–92.
[58] Webster, *The Fall of the Ancient Maya*, 45.
[59] Jeremy A. Sabloff, *The New Archaeology and the Ancient Maya*, 116, "By Late Preclassic times, competition for land, people, and resources may have led to warfare between cities. For example, Webster has argued that the moat and parapet at Becán may well date to this period." Lynne V. Foster, *Handbook to Life in the Ancient Maya World*, 151, discusses other Preclassic fortifications.
[60] James N. Ambrosino, Traci Ardren, and Travis W. Stanton, "The History of Warfare at Yaxuná," 111.

its presence implies a real concern with violent attack aimed at the capture of the center and its inhabitants. At the Late Preclassic site of Cerros in Belize, the inhabitants constructed an impressive perimeter of water reservoirs that could well have served a defensive function as well against surprise attack from the landward side of this coastal community. At the enormous Late Preclassic community of El Mirador in Peten, Guatemala, walls enclosed strategic sectors of the ceremonial center. So there is some evidence to suggest that war aimed at the attack of ceremonial centers concerned some lords at some capitols. However, these defensive works are still a rarity in early Maya centers. Indeed, fortifications do not become a commonplace until the Terminal Classic period, nearly a thousand years later.[61]

Similar defensive walls are found in other Early Classic and Late Preclassic sites (Late Preclassic corresponds to the end of Book of Mormon times).[62] All these sites display a primary Late Preclassic occupation followed by permanent or temporary abandonment. Some of them—Cerros, Becán, and Cival—boasted large-scale defensive moats or stone walls.[63] Estrada-Belli describes the defensive wall around Cival, dating it during the Book of Mormon time-period even though it lies outside the lands commonly accepted as being in the Book of Mormon: "On the main hill, the plaza, the main temples and elite palace platforms were encircled by a 2-meter-high stone wall. On top of the stone base was probably a timber palisade reaching several meters in height."[64]

In sort, warfare, and even fortified cities, characterize both this region of Mesoamerica and the Book of Mormon. During one of these conflicts, Omni's son Ammoron records:

> Behold, it came to pass that three hundred and twenty years had passed away, and the more wicked part of the Nephites were destroyed.
>
> For the Lord would not suffer, after he had led them out of the land of Jerusalem and kept and preserved them from falling into the hands of their enemies, yea, he would not suffer that the words should not be verified, which he spake unto our fathers, saying that: Inasmuch as ye will not keep my commandments ye shall not prosper in the land.

---

[61] David A. Freidel, "Maya Warfare, Myth and Reality," [no page].

[62] Heather McKillop, *The Ancient Maya: New Perspectives*, 189:

> In addition to Webster's classic description of the defensive wall at Becán, defensive stone or earth walls have been reported from many sites in the southern and northern Maya lowlands. Although dating a defensive wall is often problematic, many evidently date to the Late Classic, although some date to the Early Classic or even the Late Preclassic. Southern lowland sites with defensive walls include Tikal, Calakmul, Becán, El Mirador, Dos Pilas, Auateca, and Punta de Chimino, among others. Dahlin describes a defensive wall around Chunchucmil in relation to walls around nine other sites in the northern Maya lowlands.

[63] Francisco Estrada-Belli, *The First Maya Civilization: Ritual and Power before the Classic Period*, 52.

[64] Ibid., 131.

Wherefore, the Lord did visit them in great judgment; nevertheless, he did spare the righteous that they should not perish, but did deliver them out of the hands of their enemies. (Omni 1:5–7)

Thus, two themes that began in the book of Jacob are highlighted over 200 years later.[65] Warfare continued to be a constant factor in Nephite life, and there were "wicked" Nephites who could be described as the ones who were destroyed. Without telling us what made them "wicked," Ammoron invoked the promise associated with the land to underscore the fact that their destruction was due to that wickedness. Had they been righteous, they would have been preserved, as demonstrated by the fact that some were preserved.

Ammoron does not explain how the wicked were destroyed in a way that only the righteous survived. I speculate that, based on the ability to create social distinctions, the "more wicked" would be those who were most socially separated. This term would translate to the ruling classes almost by definition in Mesoamerica. Those in such positions would naturally be the first target of a conquering enemy. The more egalitarian farmers, the non-elite, would not be destroyed because they would be needed to continue working the land to provide food for the new conquerors.

Emerging from the Dark Tunnel

Members of modern Western societies have lived through times of whirlwind changes. Such rapid shifts are historically unusual. For agricultural societies in particular, many aspects of group life remains the same for hundreds of years, if not longer. It is therefore hardly surprising that while we see some differences in the Nephites as they emerge from the four hundred years for which we have little historical information, the same cultural issues perplexing them as they entered that dim historical tunnel were present as they emerged.

Even though they were instructed not to initiate warfare (Alma 43:47–48), armed conflict dogged the Nephites throughout their history. Jacob's concern with costly apparel continues to appear throughout the Book of Mormon as a harbinger of social disruption.[66] The costly apparel is significant because it signals divisiveness and the pressures for hierarchical social structures that are seen to be antithetical to the Nephite ideal. These difficulties not only continue throughout most of the Book of Mormon, but they are intensified as the Nephites enter a new phase of their history, relocate into a new land and attempt integration with a new people, the people of Zarahemla.

---

[65] Jacob 1:1 has Jacob receiving the records fifty-five years after leaving Jerusalem. Ammoron writes of the destruction of the more wicked part of the Nephites at 325 years from the departure (Omni 1:5).

[66] Alma 1:6, 1:32, 4:6, 5:53; Hel. 13:28; 4 Ne. 1:24.

8

Nephites Arrive in Zarahemla

When Martin Harris lost the 116 manuscript pages of the Book of Mormon, he created a crisis in the translation of the text that was not fully solved with the replacement translation from the small plates of Nephi. Unfortunately, in addition to losing the entire book of Lehi (the original first book in Mormon's text), he also lost the beginning of the book of Mosiah.[1] The small plates did cover much of the time period of the book of Lehi but did not also adequately cover the beginning of the book of Mosiah (named for $Mosiah_1$, not his grandson $Mosiah_2$ with whom we are more familiar).

It was a particularly unfortunate location to lose text. The beginning of Mosiah contained information critical to understanding the rest of Mormon's book. Without the initial material, we are suddenly in a different city in a different country, seeing

---

[1] Royal Skousen, "Critical Methodology and the Text of the Book of Mormon," 138, discusses the chapter numbering against a statement Brent Metcalfe made suggesting that there was only a single missing chapter:

> Here Oliver Cowdery originally wrote "Chapter III," then changed this to "Chapter I" by deleting the last two numbers. This is characteristic of how Oliver corrected mistakes. . . . Oliver Cowdery definitely did not first write "Chapter II" and then cross out the whole number and insert a I before the crossed-out II. All three I's have the same ink flow and spacing. Based on Oliver's scribal practice, I would argue that if Oliver had written II and wanted to change it to I, he would have either crossed out the second I or crossed out both I's and followed it with a single I with an intervening space.

I suggest that it is important to understand that this information comes from the printer's manuscript and not the original. These are therefore changes that were only introduced after the printer's copy had been made. Therefore, the cross-out of the chapter number is easily understood on the original; but when the printer's manuscript was copied, the end of Words of Mormon and the beginning of Mosiah are on the same page. The editorial markings are clearly indicated in Royal Skousen, ed., *The Printer's Manuscript of the Book of Mormon*, vol. 2, part 1, 284. Clearly the small-plate material was copied first even though it was translated later. That transition would have been apparent on the original but is blurred by the copying process that gives us the printer's manuscript. In reexamining the textual evidence for this numbering change, I have concluded that it was due to Oliver's numbering the Printer's Manuscript after the fact and following his misidentification of Words of Mormon as Chapter 2 of Omni. See Brant A. Gardner, "When Hypotheses Collide: Responding to Lyon and Minson's 'When Pages Collide.'"

the results of a devastating civil war about which we would know nothing. Fortunately, the essential outline of the information that was plausibly contained in lost pages can be recovered from two different replacement sources.

The first is Amaleki's record found in Omni 1:12–30. Amaleki's account supplies the events that move the Nephites from the land of Nephi to the land of Zarahemla. It describes, though tersely, their meeting with a different people. The second account is Words of Mormon 1:12–18, which gives a very quick account of the conditions that led to the great discourse Benjamin gives at the beginning of the extant book of Mosiah.[2]

A New World Fleeing Prophet

Even with our supplemental information, we are missing the context that would explain why conditions became so dire in the land of Nephi that Yahweh would command Mosiah$_1$ to flee. We are also missing the introductory material about who Mosiah$_1$ was and why it was he who led the Nephites to a new land.[3] For both we are left to reasoned speculation.

Mosiah$_1$ was obviously a prophet. Equally importantly, Mosiah$_1$ does not appear to have been a direct descendant of Jacob. The small plate tradition was transmitted through Jacob's descendants, and Amaleki is the last keeper of that record. He discusses Mosiah$_1$'s story as an outside observer.

It is also unlikely that Mosiah$_1$ was Nephi's ruling descendant. Although his role in leading people away from Zarahemla might lead to the supposition that he was king in the city of Nephi, Jacob tells us that kings in the city of Nephi took upon themselves the regnal name of Nephi, becoming second Nephi, third Nephi, etc. (Jacob 1:11). Of course, it is possible that the tradition had changed in the intervening four hundred years, but it is at least clear that, beginning with Mosiah$_1$, the tradition of obvious regnal names disappears. The most reasonable explanation is that Mosiah$_1$ was a prophet, but not the king. It seem likely that he was a member of the ruling clan and that this connection allowed him to stake a claim to rulership in the new community with access to the symbols of Nephite rulership that he brought with him.

The command to flee came to him as prophet, as it had come to Lehi in Jerusalem and to Nephi in the land of their first inheritance. Those who followed Mosiah$_1$ are,

---

[2] Brant A. Gardner, *The Gift and Power: Translating the Book of Mormon*, 243–46, 282–83 discusses the end of Words of Mormon as a conceptual translation—that is, one given more by inspiration than direct translation of the plate text. This translation type would account for the section of Words of Mormon that is a replacement for the lost chapters of Mosiah.

A different opinion is expressed in Jack M. Lyon and Kent R. Minson, "When Pages Collide: Dissecting the Words of Mormon," 121–36. They suggest that the material I see as a prophetic expansion was actually text that had been translated and copied onto a page where the next chapter of Mosiah began. Hence it was translated material that wasn't lost with the 116 pages. See Gardner, "When Hypotheses Collide," 105–19, for a response to their analysis.

[3] Important to the Book of Mormon, but not to the history in the Book of Mormon, is that we have also lost what should have been an introduction to Mormon. As a strong editorial presence in the text, Mormon must have introduced himself near the beginning of his edited version of the book of Lehi.

like Nephi's followers, "as many as would hearken unto the voice of the Lord" (Omni 1:12; see also 2 Ne. 5:5). Highlighting the less obvious, some didn't follow: perhaps many—perhaps most. There was also an oblique similarity in that Nephi brought the plates to the New World and Mosiah₁ brought those same plates (and apparently the large plate records) with him to Zarahemla. It would have been literarily appropriate for the large plate historian to make such parallels to Nephi, but if this were the case, the literary parallel is lost.

It is plausible that Mosiah₁ and his people fled from a Lamanite invasion. Around 200 B.C., there was a massive incursion of people into highland Guatemala (Sorenson's Land of Nephi) from the northwest. They were likely Quichéan peoples. Julia Guernsey indicates that these Quichéans "appear to have moved south and eventually invaded such places as La Lagunita and Kaminaljuyú. They displaced much of the local population and replaced the elites, which, in the case of Kaminaljuyú, were likely Cholan speakers. The displaced inhabitants of Kaminaljuyú fled the area with the arrival of [these] people."[4] Both Quichéan and Cholan are different Mayan language groups, as Spanish and French are both Romance languages. Thus, at the right time and in the right place, we have an incursion of foreigners that created an exodus of residents.

In the Book of Mormon, when Mosiah₁ led his people away from the city of Nephi, he led them "*down* into the land which is called the land of Zarahemla" (Omni 1:13). The Book of Mormon has several references to the difference in elevation between the original land of Nephi and the land of Zarahemla, and one always went *down* to Zarahemla from Nephi and *up* to Nephi from Zarahemla.[5] The terms *up* and *down* in the Book of Mormon consistently relate to topography, not to modern map conventions that consider *up* as north.[6] In this case, *down* is northwest of highland Guatemala to the Grijalva River Valley.

Perhaps because of the traditional animosity with Lamanites who appear to cover the lands to the south of the Nephites, Nephite migrations from threat and danger always head north in the Book of Mormon, not south.[7] That pattern alone might be sufficient reason to understand why Mosiah₁ took this particular path. However, it is also possible that he was heading in a direction where he knew that there were potentially friendly people.

---

[4] Julia Guernsey, "Rulers, Gods, and Potbellies: A Consideration of Sculptural Forms and Themes from the Preclassic Pacific Coast and Piedmont of Mesoamerica," 257.
[5] John L. Sorenson, *Mormon's Map*, 32–33.
[6] John L. Sorenson, *An Ancient American Setting for the Book of Mormon*, 23.
[7] Mosiah₁ flees northward from the city of Nephi to Zarahemla. When the Lamanites push the Nephites out of Zarahemla, the Nephites retreat northward. They recapture Zarahemla, but again are forced northward. The final wars see the Nephites consistently moving northward. There is one exception to this. Mormon 8:2 indicates that some survivors of Cumorah "escaped into the country southward." It proved to be no refuge, as they were hunted down and destroyed. See Sorenson's conclusion that Nephites never mention traveling south out of Nephi. Ibid., 12.

The more northerly direction (through the wilderness area) was a known trade route. In the case of Kaminaljuyú (Sorenson's city of Nephi), a major export was obsidian, which had a nearby source and was even worked in Kaminaljuyú.[8] The volcanic processes that produce obsidian are so distinctive that pieces can be accurately traced to their source, often from hundreds of miles away. The Kaminaljuyú obsidian is known as El Chayal. El Chayal obsidian was traded down the coast during the early years of the Book of Mormon period; but at Mosiah$_1$'s time period, a distribution channel had been developed that traded El Chayal obsidian into Veracruz, northwest of Kaminaljuyú.[9] The existence of an established route and the assurance of friendly towns to the northwest help explain Mosiah$_1$'s flight in that direction. Combined with the dispersal of peoples from Kaminaljuyú, it is not surprising that about, this same time we see, archaeologically, Maya peoples moving into the upper Grijalva River Valley.[10]

Zarahemla before the Nephites

All of our information about the people of Zarahemla comes from Nephite records after their historic merger, perhaps around 162 B.C.[11] It is useful to set the stage for that merger by reconstructing what is known or can be deduced about the people of Zarahemla prior to the Nephite arrival. The only information Amaleki gives about Zarahemla is that both the land and city share their names with the current ruler.[12] Many Book of Mormon cities bear the name of their founder,[13] a pattern suggesting that Zarahemla was a relatively new city.

Zarahemla, the individual, may have founded the city which bore his name,[14] but he was a member of a lineage with a much longer history. Just as the Nephites continued

---

[8] Jane W. Pires-Ferreira, "Obsidian Exchange in Formative Mesoamerica," 302–3.

[9] Ibid.

[10] John E. Clark, quoted in Susan Toby Evans, *Ancient Mexico and Central America: Archaeology and Culture History,* 222.

[11] The Book of Mormon does not give a date for the arrival of the Nephites in Zarahemla. After examining the available data, I have concluded that the arrival was no earlier than 162 B.C. See Brant A. Gardner, *Second Witness: Analytical and Contextual Commentary on the Book of Mormon,* 3:197.

[12] Omni 1:14 talks of the ruler Zarahemla and the people of Zarahemla (referencing the ruler). Mosiah 7:13 references the land of Zarahemla and Alma 8:1 references Zarahemla as a place.

[13] The known complication in the pattern is that, while the city of Nephi was named for Nephi$_1$, subsequent kings took his name as a throne name. If that had been the case in Zarahemla (and there is no evidence either for or against that proposition), then the fact that a king and the city had the same name would not determine that the king was the city's founder.

[14] It is also possible that Zarahemla simply bore an ancestral name. We see two Mosiahs, two Almas, two Helamans, and two Nephis in this later period. Even that model makes the foundation of the city fairly recent. Without any specific information, I suggest this Zarahemla as the founder on very subjective readings of the nature of the city and its willingness to accept a large immigrant population, particularly one to which they were willing to cede the kingship of the city.

to trace their origins to the Old World after sojourns in both Nephi and Zarahemla, the people of Zarahemla traced their history to Jerusalem (Mosiah 25:2). The ancestors of the people of Zarahemla plausibly arrived on the east coast of the Mexican Gulf Coast and traveled south to eventually settle in Zarahemla (Hel. 6:10).[15]

The Ancestor, Mulek

The people of Zarahemla claimed descent from a distant royal ancestor, Mulek (Mosiah 25:2). We do not learn that Mulek was the son of Zedekiah (king in Jerusalem) until Helaman 6:10 (confirmed in Hel. 8:21).[16] Mulek left Jerusalem later than Lehi and under even harsher circumstances. Zedekiah had been a Babylonian puppet king, but revolted against his overlords. He reigned from 597 B.C. to 586 B.C., when Babylon crushed his rebellion. After his defeat, he was not only dethroned but disgraced. In vengeance for Zedekiah's treachery, Nebuchadnezzar killed his sons before his eyes, then blinded Zedekiah and carried him off to Babylon (2 Kgs. 25:7).

Although the Bible indicates that all of his sons were killed, the Book of Mormon identifies Mulek as a son who escaped and arrived in the New World.[17] The memory

---

[15] Sorenson, *An Ancient American Setting for the Book of Mormon*, 148.

The people of Zarahemla seem to have been named after their leader, who reported to Mosiah that his ancestors had arrived from the Mediterranean area by boat and that he was a descendant of "Mulek," a son of Zedekiah, the last of the Jewish kings before the Exile. The voyage arrived first in the land northward, then moved south. Probably they first settled at the east-coast site known later as "the city of Mulek" (note Alma 8:7). "And they came from there up into the south wilderness" (Alma 22:31), where Mosiah later encountered them. Factions had warred among themselves; Zarahemla was now chief over one group (Omni 1:17). If the city of Zarahemla was named after him (or his father), then his group would not have been in that spot for very long, although they might have lived in the general locale for some time.

[16] With such importance lying behind this lineage connection, one must wonder why Mormon waited so long to describe it, and why it appears only in comments where it appears almost as an aside rather than an explicit explanation. I hypothesize that the introduction of this connection between Zarahemla and Mulek was discussed more fully in the lost chapters of Mosiah.

[17] Orson Scott Card, *The Book of Mormon: Artifact or Artifice?* provides an interesting alternative reading of the Zarahemlaite background:

Let me offer an aside on the matter of Zarahemla and the Mulekites. Much has been made of the statement by King Zarahemla that his people were descended from the youngest son of King Zedekiah. Extraordinary and completely unconvincing efforts have been made to find such a son, overlooked by the Babylonian captors of Jerusalem; just as much effort has been devoted to explaining how a good Jaredite name like Mulek could show up in the family of an Israelite king. But is this really necessary?

In Meso-American culture, every ruling class had to assert an ancient ancestor who was a god or, at the very least, a king in an admired culture. Whoever ruled in the Valley of Mexico always had to claim to be descended from or heirs of the Toltecs. Rival Mayan cities would play at ancestral one-upmanship. Imagine, now, the vigorous and dangerous Nephites, coming down the valley of the Sidon River from the highlands of Guatemala. King Zarahemla is negotiating with King Mosiah. Mosiah tells him of his ancestry, of

of that event continued among his descendants for nearly six hundred years. Nephi$_2$ (son of Helaman$_2$) uses that information as proof that Jerusalem had indeed been destroyed: "And now will you dispute that Jerusalem was destroyed? Will ye say that the sons of Zedekiah were not slain, all except it were Mulek?" (Hel. 8:21).

Of the name "Mulek" and this enigmatic son of Zedekiah, Sorenson notes:

> "Mulek" appears as "Muloch" in the printer's manuscript of the Book of Mormon and as "Mulok" in printed editions from 1830 to 1852; the name then became "Mulek." However it was pronounced, the name comes to us of course as Nephite ears heard it from the people of Zarahemla, and their pronunciation could have changed it somewhat from the Old World Hebrew familiar to us. What is clear throughout these variations in the spelling of the name is that we have here a reflex of the Hebrew root *mlk*, as in Hebrew melek, "king" . . . .
>
> Robert F. Smith has mustered evidence that a son of Zedekiah with a name recalling Mulek may actually be referred to in the Bible. Jeremiah 38:6 in the King James translation speaks of Jeremiah's being cast into "the dungeon [literally, "pit"] of Malchiah the son of Hammelech." The last five words should be rendered more accurately, "Malkiyahti, the son of the king." This personal name could have been abbreviated to something like "Mulek." Thus Jeremiah might have been put into "the [very] dungeon of Mulek[?], the son of the king [Zedekiah]" referred to in the Hebrew text of Jeremiah 38:6.[18]

---

course, and the story of how God led Lehi and Nephi out of Jerusalem at the time when Zedekiah was king of Israel.

To Mosiah, what he is doing is bearing his testimony and asserting the divine guidance that he receives as the legitimate king of a chosen people. To Zarahemla, what he is doing is claiming that his lineage gives him the right to rule over the people of Zarahemla and displace him from the kingship. So what does Zarahemla do? Well, Mosiah admits that his ancestors were not kings in Israel. So Zarahemla picks his most noble ancestor, Mulek, and then declares him to be the son of that last king of Israel. Thus if anybody has the right to rule over anybody, it's Zarahemla who has the right to rule over Mosiah and his people. But Mosiah kindly points out that if Zarahemla and his people are descended from Israelites, they certainly seem to have forgotten the language and writing, and therefore have obviously degenerated from the high culture of Israel. The Nephites, on the other hand, have preserved a writing system that no one else uses, and which Zarahemla can't read. They have a history accounting for every year since they arrived in America, which Zarahemla of course cannot produce.

In the end, whatever negotiation there was ended up with Zarahemla bowing out of the kingship and his people becoming subject to rule by the Nephites. But the story of Mulek served a very useful purpose even so—it allowed the people to merge, not with the hostility of conquerors over the conquered, though in fact that is what the relationship fundamentally was, but rather with the idea of brotherhood. They were all Israelites.

Card's explanation is plausible, particularly since the Hebrew root *mlk* referred to a king. Mulek might as easily be a reference as a name. However, given the thin evidence available, I think it best to accept the Book of Mormon record at face value on this point.

[18] John L. Sorenson, *Nephite Culture and Society: Collected Papers*, 110–11.

Robert F. Smith's suggestion has been controversial, even among LDS scholars.[19] Nevertheless, as archaeologist Jeffrey R. Chadwick recounts Smith's argument:

> Smith also suggested that the Book of Mormon name Mulek might be a shortened form of the biblical Hebrew Malkiyahu. In support of this possibility, he noted that while Jeremiah's scribe is called Baruch . . . in Jeremiah 36:4, a longer form of his name— . . . (Berekhyahu)—appears on an ancient stamp seal impression published by Israeli archaeologist Nahman Avigad. Since the Hebrew long-form name Berekhyahu could apparently be expressed in a hypocoristic (short form) version like Barukh, Smith reasoned that perhaps the long form Malkiyahu could have a short form like Mulek. In that event, the "Malkiyahu son of the king" in Jeremiah 38:6 could well have been the Book of Mormon's Mulek, son of King Zedekiah (see Hel. 8:21).[20]

This suggestion has been strengthened by archaeological evidence:

> Recently, an ancient Judean stamp seal has been identified as bearing the Hebrew form of the name "Malchiah son of Hammelech." Does this mean that an actual archaeological relic that belonged to an ancient Book of Mormon personality has been located? Has the seal of Mulek been found?
>
> To answer this question requires us to explore a number of different but related issues. First, a word of explanation. The reading of Jeremiah 38:6 in the King James Version is somewhat misleading. The Hebrew Bible . . . [text is] pronounced Malkiyahu ben hamelek. The name Malkiyahu was reasonably rendered into English as "Malchiah" by the King James scholars, and the word ben was accurately translated as "son." But the King James term Hammelech . . . is not really a name; it is a transliteration. In Hebrew, hamelek means "the king" (*ha* is the definite article "the," and *melek* is the word for "king"). Thus, accurately translated, Jeremiah 38:6 refers to "Malkiyahu son of the king." Noted biblical scholar John Bright translates the phrase as "Prince Malkiah" (the term prince referring to a royal son) in his Anchor Bible commentary on Jeremiah.[21]

This is a promising connection between Mulek and Zedekiah. However, another alternative is possible. Although identified as Zedekiah's son, he was obviously not numbered among them when they were killed before their father's eyes. Possibly, "son" was used metaphorically rather than literally. Hershel Shanks, editor of the *Biblical Archaeology Review*, provides three possible ways that "son" was used in connection with royalty: "(1) the word means what it says; (2) 'son' refers to a royal official unrelated by blood to the king; [or] (3) 'son' refers to any male scion [descendant] of the royal family."[22] The non-kin connection is supported by a bulla, or clay seal, identified as the official seal of the "son" of King Jehoiakim. This "son" is named Yerame'el.[23]

---

[19] Jeffrey R. Chadwick, "Has the Seal of Mulek Been Found?" 73.
[20] Ibid., 74.
[21] Ibid.
[22] Hershel Shanks, *Jerusalem: An Archaeological Biography*, 107–8, quoted in John L. Sorenson, "Was Mulek a 'Blood Son' of King Zedekiah?" 2.
[23] Shanks, *Jerusalem: An Archaeological Biography*, 107–8, finds it doubtful that that Jehoiakim of the bulla was King Jehoiakim.

By this reading, Mulek would be an important functionary or perhaps more distant family member rather than an inheriting son. This reading allows a culturally acceptable reason why all of Zedekiah's sons (inheriting sons) were killed, but his "son" Mulek (non-inheriting family or unrelated functionary) survived. It even supports the bulla that might be connected to Mulek.

Zarahemla's ancestor and accompanying immigrants have become known in LDS literature as the Mulekites, but that is a modern name imposed upon the Book of Mormon text. No Mulekites are ever mentioned, and the modern ascription of the title is based on the assumption that the immigrants would take the name of the ancestor with whom Zarahemla identified.[24]

Merging Peoples in Zarahemla

The people of Nephi descended from an Israelite who had fled from his home in Jerusalem during the reign of Zedekiah. They sailed to a new world. The people of Zarahemla descended from an Israelite who had fled from his home in Jerusalem at the end of the reign of Zedekiah. They sailed to a new world. For four hundred years, they lived within five hundred miles of each other but never met.[25] The people of Zarahemla moved toward Nephite lands and the two peoples were separated by somewhat less than 200 miles when the people called Nephites arrived in Zarahemla seeking refuge.

When the two peoples met, Amaleki indicated that the Zarahemlaite[26] "language had become corrupted; and they had brought no records with them; and they denied the being of their Creator; and Mosiah, nor the people of Mosiah, could understand them" (Omni 1:15–17). They found a way to communicate and learned of their parallel history.[27] Gary R. Whiting provides a typical reading of the situation: "The

---

[24] My thanks to Heather Hardy for pointing this terminological problem out to me, after I had included the term "Mulekites" in a manuscript. She was very clear that the Book of Mormon never referred to a people named "Mulekites," which forced me to review the evidence and therefore agree with her.

[25] The distance is roughly from Guatemala City to Coatzacoalcos on the Gulf Coast. That might represent a landing area for the people accompanying Mulek, but it is also probable that they moved inland fairly soon, and were part of the general trend of Zoque speakers to move south/southeast. Thus, for most of their history, they may have been even closer.

[26] I am intentionally separating the people of Zarahemla from their ancestral Mulekites. The people of Zarahemla are about four hundred years separated from Mulek, speak a different language, and have a different religion. They are living in a different place. Those factors suggest that we are more accurate if we see them as related, but separate.

[27] Although the two peoples had not formally met, the archaeological record does indicate trade with Maya lands, the location of the city of Nephi. This evidence suggests that there had been general contact and was perhaps the reason that Mosiah₁ and his people chose that direction to travel as they escaped from the city of Nephi. The trade relations may also suggest that some among them could speak each other's language so that the language disparity was not absolute.

lack of records had been a stumbling block for the Mulekites, in that without them to stabilize their language it had become corrupt."[28]

Crediting the lack of records for the corrupted language might have been the reason that the Nephites accepted, but it is not a satisfactory explanation for the mutual unintelligibility of language between two peoples who had originated in the same place and time only four hundred years before. Although that is long enough for certain changes, it is simply insufficient for mutual unintelligibility between daughter languages of the same parent language.[29]

Conversely, possession of texts would not have hindered language change. After all, numerous Latin texts remained in active use for centuries after Latin had already split into various daughter languages (Italian, French, Spanish, Catalán). The possession of and ability to read those texts did not halt the language shifts which created those daughter languages. The language differences between the peoples of Mosiah and Mulek requires more than an appeal to lost or retained records.

The most likely condition that would create unintelligibility would be if either or both the Nephites and ancestral Zarahemlaites had merged with a larger population and adopted that population's language as their daily language. Biologist Luigi Luca Cavalli-Sforza musters linguistic data along with the genetic information he discusses on the origins of the Finnish peoples:

> The probable scenario is the following. The very small group that gave origin to modern Finns entered the plains of Finland 2,000 years ago, from the south or east. A Saami population already inhabited this area, and eventually retreated to the north. Contact of Finns and Saami was enough for the Finnish immigrants to learn their language, even though substantial genetic mixing did not occur. Especially if several small groups of settlers speaking different languages entered the area, they all had to learn the language, or the local dialect, of the only people who knew how to survive and get around in Finland's maze of lakes.[30]

In spite of not creating the substantial genetic mixing that is posited for Book of Mormon peoples, the linguistic situation is still parallel. The smaller populations moving into an established area adopted the residents' language rather than impose their own language upon the larger population. Because the Nephites had records,

---

[28] Gary R. Whiting, "The Testimony of Amaleki," 300.
[29] Theodora Bynon, *Historical Linguistics*, 269, comments:

> [In glottochronology,]... an average retention rate [of basic vocabulary items] of 81 per cent per millennium was calculated, using a list of just over two hundred items. Later, when the list was reduced to one hundred items, the rate was adjusted to 86 per cent. Using this standard retention rate as a yardstick, the date of split of any two languages could then be calculated on the assumption that over a period of a thousand years each of the languages would have retained 86 per cent of the basic vocabulary of the common protolanguage.

This methodology has been criticized, noting testable languages where the changes would occur more quickly. Nevertheless, when the assumed time measure is a thousand years, four hundred years should not represent an equally drastic change.

[30] Cavalli-Sforza, *Genes, Peoples, and Languages*, 117.

they retained their some ability to read and write Hebrew, and also to recognize that it had changed over time (Mormon 9:33).

Amaleki suggests that after crossing the ocean, the people of Mulek "were brought by the hand of the Lord across the great waters, into the land where Mosiah discovered them; and they had dwelt there from that time forth" (Omni 1:16). This cannot be precisely correct. The people of Mulek necessarily landed on a coast. The people of Zarahemla lived near a river, but not near a coastline. The people of Zarahemla could not have "dwelt . . . from that time forth" in the same location where their ancestors had disembarked. Amaleki must be using the word *land* expansively and generically rather than as a specific reference to the city of Zarahemla.

Mesoamerican linguistic history can fill in the blanks in the Book of Mormon record. I propose that the people we call the Mulekites landed along the Gulf Coast of Mexico,[31] which was inhabited at that time by a people archaeologists call the Olmec. That land is the homeland for two major languages, Mixe and Zoque. The linguistic reconstruction of the languages in that region indicates that during the florescence of the Olmec, those two daughter languages were a single language which has been called Mixe-Zoque.[32]

The later split in the languages also represents a separation of peoples, politics, and territories somewhere around 500 B.C.[33] Mixe speakers spread west and north, and Zoque speakers spread east and south. In particular, shortly after the split some Zoque speakers began to move up the Grijalva River Valley. The people of Zarahemla were part of a centuries-long process of resettlement, arriving fairly close to 200 B.C. Archaeologist Susan Toby Evans describes the population movements in that region:

> A few centers of interior Chiapas [in which the Grijalva River is located] survived what appears to have been major population restructuring in the period 400–200 B.C., when La Venta's important influence on this region was dead, and Maya centers in the Petén were growing powerful. In fact, Maya peoples began to push into the northern part of the interior of Chiapas, and Zoque-culture communities that survived, such as Santa Rosa [Sorenson's Zarahemla], Chiapa de Corzo [Sorenson's Sidom], and Mirador [Sorenson's Ammonihah], show a strong presence of Maya trade wares and architectural styles. Yet continued elite ties with other Mixe-Zoque peoples of the Isthmian region are indicated by the very early calendric monument, Chiapa de Corzo's [in the Grijalva River Valley] Stela 2, dated to 36 B.C.[34]

---

[31] The Book of Mormon gives no information about the departure from Jerusalem. Arguably Lehi crossed the Pacific because his family traveled through Sinai and debarked from the eastern coast. The landing of the people of Mulek on the east coast of the Gulf of Mexico is reasoned back from the evidence of where they encountered the Nephites, and the logical path up the Grijalva River Valley to Zarahemla. Although this designation fits with what we know of the text and cultural history of the region, it is not independently attested.

[32] Lyle Campbell and Terrence Kaufman, "A Linguistic Look at the Olmecs," 80–88.

[33] Lyle Campbell, "Mesoamerican Linguistics," mimeographed notes, n.d. Copy in my possession.

[34] Susan Toby Evans, *Ancient Mexico and Central America*, 222, 224. Part of this text quotes John E. Clark. Internal quotation marks silently removed. The text skips an inserted page on

The people of Zarahemla were perhaps less than a generation away from their homeland in what the Book of Mormon terms Jaredite lands. Maintaining elite ties with those homelands explains how the people of Zarahemla discovered the last king of the Jaredite people who lived with them for a time (Omni 1:21). It would have been those very connections that led Coriantumr toward Zarahemla after the loss of his people. Those ties also explain why the people of Zarahemla would not only accept him, but understand his language so that they could learn his story.

The second difference between Nephites and Zarahemlaites would prove much more intractable than a different language; they had a different religion. Amaleki reports that "they denied the being of their Creator" (Omni 1:17). That difference led to the civil war that is described in Words of Mormon 1:15–16. It was a difference that haunted the Nephites until it resulted in their dissolution into tribes just prior to Christ's triumphant arrival in the New World.

The denial of their Creator has the same roots as the change in their language. Along with language and material culture, the descendants of the Mulekites must have adopted the religion of the indigenous peoples as well. In this case, the absence of scriptures to anchor their understanding helps explain the speed and totality of the loss of their religion.

In describing the merger of the Nephites and the Zarahemlaites, LDS researcher J. N. Washburn suggests that "the lamb ate the lion,"[35] meaning that the smaller population dominated the larger. This was true politically, but unlikely linguistically. Even though Mosiah₁ attempted to have the population of Zarahemla learn the Nephite language (Omni 1:18), it would have been unusual if Nephite became the dominant language of the area. Correlating language to geography suggests that the Nephites brought perhaps a Hebrew and a Maya language (probably Cholan) to the merger, while the Zarahemlaites contributed Zoque. The persistence of Zoque in that geography throughout discernible history[36] suggests that Nephite did not become the dominant language of the Zarahemlaites and therefore of the future Nephites. Zoque probably became the Nephites' daily language soon after their arrival in Zarahemla.

Religiously, eating the lion gave the lamb heartburn. The differences in religion initially caused massive internal disruptions and apostasy to the Lamanites (Words of Mormon 1:15–16), and continued to influence the form of Nephite apostasy. (See Chapter 9.) Much of later Nephite history may be attributed to the easy fissionability along former Nephite/Zarahemlaite religious and political systems. The distinctions were never far from the illusory political and or religious unity.

---

calendrics. I have added the bracketed material to help associate Mesoamerican names with plausible Book of Mormon counterparts.

John S. Henderson, *The World of the Ancient Maya*, 85, comments: "Interaction of Maya and Zoquean peoples continued as a historical process along a linguistic frontier that extended from the Gulf Coast through the highlands and piedmont to the Pacific Coast."

[35] J. N. Washburn, *Book of Mormon Guidebook and Certain Problems in the Book of Mormon*, 26.
[36] Evans, *Ancient Mexico and Central America*, 222, 239.

Translating a Stone

There is no indication that the people of Zarahemla could not communicate with Coriantumr (the last Jaredite king), but they apparently could not read a stone that contained information about him. We are not told how the people of Zarahemla obtained the stone nor given any real description of it. At some point after the merger of the two peoples, Mosiah₁ translated this carved stone: "And it came to pass in the days of Mosiah, there was a large stone brought unto him with engravings on it; and he did interpret the engravings by the gift and power of God" (Omni 1:20).

Later, his grandson, Mosiah₂, would also translate a text delivered to him by a merging people. Both texts referred to Jaredites, but the second was recorded on twenty-four gold plates rather than on a stone (Mosiah 8:9). That later event provides important information that applies to the earlier translation.

When king Limhi asked Ammon if he knew of one who might translate the plates, Ammon replied: "I can assuredly tell thee, O king, of a man that can translate the records; for he has wherewith that he can look, and translate all records that are of ancient date; and it is a gift from God. And the things are called interpreters" (Mosiah 8:13). It is quite likely that the phrases "gift from God," and the "gift and power of God" are intentionally similar and that both refer to the mode of translation.[37]

The twenty-four plates themselves were associated with interpreters, which Ether sealed up with the plates specifically that they might be interpreted (Ether 4:5). However, during Ammon's conversation with Limhi, who first tells him about the twenty-four plates, Ammon confidently tells Limhi that Mosiah₂ already has interpreters. Therefore, there were at least two different sets of "interpreters," used by two very different peoples although at not very different times.[38] Mosiah₂'s interpreters were passed on to Alma₁ as part of the set of sacred objects that descended from ruler to ruler (Mosiah 28:20).[39] Plausibly, Moroni eventually delivered these same interpreters to Joseph Smith.

---

[37] Joseph similarly translated by the "gift and power of God," and his translation method was also with interpreters, or later the seer stone. For Joseph's translating by the "gift and power of God," see *Book of Mormon* [rpt. 1830], 1. This is the only statement that Joseph Smith ever made (though repeated multiple times) to explain how he translated the Book of Mormon. James E. Lancaster, "The Translation of the Book of Mormon," 98: "None of Smith's statements give detailed information about the translation of the Book of Mormon. He consistently emphasized that it was 'by the gift and power of God' that the record of the Nephites was made available to the world."

[38] The plates of Ether describe the end of the Jaredites and the epic battle between Coriantumr and Shiz. Ether was probably writing his record during Mosiah₁'s lifetime, a date I deduce from my assumption of the relatively recent founding of the city of Zarahemla and the information that the same Coriantumr lived among them for nine months. Hence, Coriantumr was alive during Zarahemla's lifetime, and Mosiah₁ meets Zarahemla.

[39] Verse 20 specifically names the interpreters, the plates of brass, and "all the records." It adds: "all the things which he had kept." While that generalization is non-descriptive, it plausibly included the Liahona and sword of Laban, which were part of the set of sacred objects: "And moreover, he also gave him charge concerning the records which were engraven on the

When the stone was brought to Mosiah₁, no interpreters were mentioned. However, it is a logical inference that he would have used interpreters to read it, since we see his grandson translating in that manner.[40] Although the connection with Joseph Smith is undeniable, there is also a connection with Mesoamerican practice that is less well known. Mark Alan Wright reports:

> In modern-day Yucatan, the most common title for shaman or ritual specialists is *aj-meen* (usually shortened to *j-men*), which literally means "practitioner" or "one who knows and does." The *h-men* [another spelling of *j-men*, the /j/ following the Spanish phonetics and pronounced as a heavily aspirated /h/] use crystals or clear rocks or even fragments of broken glass bottles as a medium through which they receive revelation. They hold them up to a light source and wait for three flashes of light to shine through it, which indicates the revelation is about to begin. As most modern Maya have been heavily influenced by Catholicism, they interpret these three flashes as representing the Father, Son, and Holy Spirit. They call these stones *zaztun* [sometimes spelled *sastun*], which literally means "clear stone" or "stone of light." They are considered extremely sacred objects, and the ritual specialist that owns them does not allow the stones to be casually handled by others. But not all clear stones are believed to be *zaztuns*. I know of one shaman who keeps a jar full of glass marbles on his table, but says they are just toys and used as "practice" *zaztuns* for his apprentices.[41]

Wright sees *zaztuns* as analogs to Mosiah₂'s interpreters. "Special stones capable of assisting divine communication" is an apt description linking *zaztuns*, interpreters, and Joseph's seer stones. While the particular *zaztuns* Wright describes were crystals or broken glass, a *zaztun* need not be transparent. Linda A. Brown reports:

> Maya priests collect cultural and natural things to use in divination. The cultural objects correspond to the prehispanic and colonial periods, and more recent objects may be included, though this is rare. The prehispanic objects collected anew include prismatic blades, obsidian points and polyhedral cores, fragments of clay figurines, spindle whorls, polished axes and polished stones in the shape of perforated circular artifacts—the so-called "doughnuts." More recent objects collected for divination uses include: glass bottle stoppers used for medicine,

---

plates of brass; and also the plates of Nephi; and also, the sword of Laban, and the ball or director, which led our fathers through the wilderness, which was prepared by the hand of the Lord that thereby they might be led, every one according to the heed and diligence which they gave unto him" (Mosiah 1:16).

It is likely that the specific interpreters that were passed along as royal relics were those that accompanied the plates of Ether. Even though Mosiah₂ already had interpreters prior to acquiring those with the Jaredite plates, the greater antiquity of the Jaredite interpreters and their connection to a foreign source of authority would have given them more social import.

[40] See Gardner, *The Gift and Power*, 259–77, for my speculation on how the interpreters, or a seer stone, was used to create a translation.

[41] Mark Alan Wright, "Nephite Daykeepers: Ritual Specialists in the Book of Mormon," 4. Copy in my possession, used by permission.

Miguel Angel Astor-Aguilera, *The Maya World of Communicating Objects*, 102, notes: "Also similar, further exhibiting a pan-American indigenous world view, is the Oodham use of a divining-like quartz, used for both curing and corn and rain rituals as also found throughout many indigenous societies in the greater Southwest and Southeast."

perfume, and marbles. Usually these objects are used as crystals; priests use them for divination and to observe the flame of a candle through the glass.[42]

Arad Stowell described one way that Joseph used his seer stone as part of his testimony in the 1826 hearing to determine if Joseph was a disorderly person: "Arad Stowel [sic] sworn, Says he went to see whether Prisoner could convince him that he possessed the skill that he professed to have, upon which prisoner laid a Book open upon a White Cloth, and proposed looking through another stone which was white and transparent; held the stone to the candle, turned his back to book and read."[43] Certainly more research would need to be done to support the conclusion that the scrying process was similar among the Maya and with Joseph, but the similarities in objects (many seer stones had holes in them) and the overall description strongly suggest that we are dealing with the same brain processes that use these instruments as modes of communication with deity.[44]

The modern use of zaztuns is a supplemental convergence with the Book of Mormon. It is a similar use in a similar location, but from a dramatically different time. The conservative nature of traditional societies suggests that the modern use may be a continuation of an ancient practice. While in no way rising to the level of a complex correspondence, the use of zaztuns provides an ethnographic analogy to understand the stones that are mentioned in the Book of Mormon. It doesn't show a direct connection but rather a similarity of practice.

The Maya priests use these objects to receive revelation from the divine, and Joseph Smith used his seer stones to receive the early revelations recorded in the Doctrine and Covenants. The Maya priests do not use their stones to translate, but Joseph did, and $Mosiah_2$ explicitly—and $Mosiah_1$ implicitly—did. Although there are obvious ties between the Book of Mormon text and Joseph's day, there are equal ties in objects and process to the ancient Maya (and very plausibly other cultures of that region).

Our text doesn't give much information about this carved stone. It simply says:

> And it came to pass in the days of Mosiah, there was a large stone brought unto him with engravings on it; and he did interpret the engravings by the gift and power of God.

---

[42] Linda A. Brown, "When Collecting Artifacts is a Conversation with the Gods," 3.

[43] "Bainbridge, NY, Court Record, 20 March 1826," 4:253. Daniel Sylvester Tuttle, "Mormons, p. 1557–6 [sic]," has a slightly different transcription which leaves open the possibility that Joseph offered to read, but the offer was not accepted: "Arad Stowel sworn. Says that he went to see whether prisoner could convince him that he possessed the skill that he professed to have, upon which prisoner laid a book open upon a white cloth, and proposed looking through another stone which was white and transparent; hold the stone to the candle, turn his back to book and read. The deception appeared so palpable, that went off disgusted." It seems that one who went with the specific purpose of testing Joseph would insist upon the proof, even if he chose not to accept it. The preferred reading is therefore that the test was offered and accepted, but not believed, even though apparently successful.

[44] See Gardner, *The Gift and Power*, 259–77, for my speculation on how seer stones "worked" to produce both a visionary experience and a translation.

And they gave an account of one Coriantumr, and the slain of his people. And Coriantumr was discovered by the people of Zarahemla; and he dwelt with them for the space of nine moons. (Omni 1:20–21)

There are three pieces of important information in these two verses. First, it was a large stone. Second, it told a story of Coriantumr. Third, the people of Zarahemla discovered Coriantumr. With our Mesoamerican context, we can piece together more of the story of Coriantumr and the people of Zarahemla. Most of the high cultures of ancient Mesoamerica erected carved stones containing different artistic scenes. Many of them show the stories of actions of the kings. Some later stones have texts based on Zoque, such as Stela 1 of La Mojarra, a village of that name on the Acula River in Veracruz, Mexico.[45] The Mesoamerican evidence therefore supplies the background that allows us to visualize what kind of large stone this was. It would have been a stela with at least bas-relief artistic depictions of the king. It may have contained a short glyphic text. Because the people of Zarahemla were plausibly Zoque speakers, they should have been able to read the glyphic text. It is unlikely that they were less literate than their surrounding cultures, which means that, while most could not read, the elite could. Therefore it is likely that this particular stone did not have a glyphic text, but that meaning had to be extracted from the iconography on the stone.

The people of Zarahemla discovered Coriantumr. Combined with the fact that it was a large stone, the best explanation is that they journeyed to where Coriantumr had been. Perhaps after speaking with him, they were interested in the location where there had been such a great destruction. At that locale, they found a commemorative stela, obviously carved during the final years of the Jaredite civilization. Coriantumr would not have been able to carry a stela of any size if we were to assume it came with him to Zarahemla. Coriantumr would have known the meaning of the stone; but if he died prior to its discovery, we have the explanation for why Mosiah$_1$ read the stone rather than Coriantumr.

---

[45] John Justeson and Terrence Kaufman, "Un desciframiento de la escritura jeroglífica epi-olmeca: métodos y resultados," 15, 20.

9

A New Covenant Made, then Unmade

Losing the first chapter(s) of Mosiah not only removed the description of the merger of Nephites with the people of Zarahemla, but it also erased the description of what nearly tore apart that merger. Mosiah₁ appears to have enjoyed a honeymoon period without wars or contentions. His son, Benjamin, had both. A war with the Lamanites (Omni 1:24 and W of M 1:12–14) was followed by contentions so severe that many of Zarahemla left to become Lamanites (Words of Mormon 1:16).

The mention of war is really no surprise. War has been and would continue to be a part of Nephite life. However, these Lamanites certainly were not the same as those with whom they had contended in the land of Nephi. These new Lamanites were probably those with which the people of Zarahemla had already had conflicts, though the people of Zarahemla would not have called them Lamanites. That is a designation that came with the Nephite record-keepers.

Immediately following the brief account of victory over the Lamanites, we are told:

> And it came to pass that after there had been false Christs, and their mouths had been shut, and they punished according to their crimes;
> And after there had been false prophets, and false preachers and teachers among the people, and all these having been punished according to their crimes; and after there having been much contention and many dissensions away unto the Lamanites. (W of M. 1:15–16)

The internal religious contention is described as the appearance of false Christs among the people. When Sherem challenged Jacob, modern scholars (though not the record itself) label him an anti-Christ, not a false Christ.[1] An anti-Christ isn't the same as a false-Christ. What might he have meant by, not one, but many, false Christs?

A possible explanation comes from the Nahua concept of a *teixiptla*. This hypothesis is speculative as both term and culture postdate the Book of Mormon era: "The Aztecs appear to have been a people compelled to insist on the visible presences of their gods," explains ethnohistorian Burr Cartwright Brundage. "In the conceptualization of these

---

[1] For example: Daniel H. Ludlow, *A Companion to Your Study of the Book of Mormon*, 161; Joseph Fielding McConkie and Robert L. Millet, *Doctrinal Commentary on the Book of Mormon*, 2:85; George Reynolds and Janne M. Sjodahl, *Commentary on the Book of Mormon*, 1:489–90.

presences they went to extremes of detail.... But the Aztecs had a special type of idol which differed radically in that it was animate and incarnate. This was the *teixiptla*, 'image' or 'representative,' a person who wore the regalia, acted out the part of the god, and then was sacrificed."[2] Some aspects of the Aztec *teixiptla* probably did not pertain to Benjamin's time, such as the final sacrifice of the incarnate deity.

The plausibility of connecting the later Aztec practice to both an earlier time and a different culture comes from similarities to older Maya practices. Maya religion incorporated many rituals that included wearing the guise of a god or sometimes a sacralized ancestor.[3] These deity impersonation rituals involved donning the regalia and, typically, a mask that identified the deity being impersonated.

The custom of representing a deity by donning its masks appears very early in Mesoamerican history. David C. Grove provides information on the site of Chalcatzingo, abandoned in 500 B.C. It contains impressive art in the Olmec style. Of interest to our discussion is Monument 2 which features "four persons.... At the right is a seated personage who faces two central figures walking towards him and a third who walks away on the left. The standing figures wear their 'bird-serpent' masks so their faces cannot be seen. The seated individual has turned his mask to the back of his head, revealing his face and pointed beard. All the masks seem to cover the entire face instead of simply the mouth area."[4]

The masks indicate the presence of the extra-human in the scene. The seated personage with his mask turned to the rear communicates that these are men in costume, or men imitating deity, just like the later Maya kings or the Aztec *teixiptla*. Ancient Maya ceramics depict artists carving the masks the kings would wear.[5] While there are specific elements that differ, the idea that there would be a human ritually posing as deity has a history that appears to extend into and earlier than Nephite times.

Perhaps "false Christ" was an appropriate term because those individuals were impersonating deities from the displaced competitor religion. If this speculative scenario is, in fact, what Mormon meant, it is obvious why this practice would have caused both ethnic and religious contention in Zarahemla. The situation was serious enough that there were "many dissensions away unto the Lamanites." In other words, the dissenters resolved their resistance to the newly imposed religious/political regime by defecting to the Lamanites. Presumably, they retreated toward the old Jaredite (Olmec) homeland, where their linguistic, cultural, and religious heritage was still viable.

A New Covenant of Unity

After the horrors of war and the internal stress of contention, Benjamin found himself leading a people composed of Nephites and Zarahemlaites who still considered themselves Nephites and Zarahemlaites. It is likely that many of the

---

[2] Burr Cartwright Brundage, *The Fifth Sun: Aztec Gods, Aztec World*, 57.
[3] Mark Alan Wright, "A Study of Classic Maya Rulership," 73.
[4] David C. Grove, *Chalcatzingo: Excavations on the Olmec Frontier*, 119.
[5] Dorie Reents-Budet, *Painting the Maya Universe: Royal Ceramics of the Classic Period*, 38, 316.

A New Covenant Made, then Unmade 231

contentions occurred between those two culture groups. Benjamin needed to heal the wounds and find a way to unite the two peoples in such a way that they would consider themselves one population rather than two.

His solution was to recreate the community under a new unifying concept: a name and a covenant. Benjamin explained the meaning of taking upon themselves the name of Christ (a unifying name above "Nephite" or "Zarahemlaite"). He asked the gathered people to embrace this name and therefore the covenant relationship that this name represented (Mosiah 5:1). They became Messiahists, children of the Messiah. In the context of more time-appropriate vocabulary, they were Yahwists, children of Yahweh. Similar to the exclusivist declarations in the Old Testament,[6] this new community was now in a unique and exclusive relationship with Yahweh, for "there shall be no other name given nor any other way nor means whereby salvation can come unto the children of men, only in and through the name of Christ [Yahweh], the Lord Omnipotent" (Mosiah 3:11). Although it was not a new designation for the Nephites, it was important that it also include the people of Zarahemla.

There are hints that Benjamin delivered this address at an event related to the Israelite festival calendar.[7] Terrence L. Szink and John W. Welch link Benjamin's speech to the complex of autumn festivals of ancient Israel:

> Of the three annual festival times in ancient Israel, the autumn festival complex was the most important and certainly the most popular in ancient Israel. In early times it apparently was called the Feast of Ingathering. According to many scholars, the various components of the autumn festival were celebrated as a single season of celebration in the earliest periods of Israelite history. Its many elements were not sharply differentiated until later times, when the first day of the seventh month became Rosh ha-Shanah (New Year), followed by eight days of penitence, then followed on the tenth day of the month by Yom Kippur (Day of Atonement) and on the fifteenth day by Sukkot (Festival of the Tabernacles), concluding with a full holy week.[8]

The parallels to Israelite practice are important as they underscore the Nephite retention of the brass plates and, hence, of the Old World religion. Nevertheless, by Benjamin's reign, Nephites had been in the New World for around four hundred years, and it is inconceivable that they had not made some accommodation to New World customs. In that context, it is equally important to examine parallels to Mesoamerican practice. Allen J. Christenson, who is conversant in Quiché Maya, has examined the correlation between the Maya November harvest festival and rituals of coronation and kingly renewal: "Throughout the history of the Maya, who dominated southern

---

[6] For example, Deut. 14: 2 "For thou art an holy people unto the Lord thy God, and the Lord hath chosen thee to be a peculiar people unto himself, above all the nations that are upon the earth."

[7] John W. Welch and Darryl R. Hague, "Benjamin's Sermon as a Traditional Ancient Farewell Address," 89–117; Terrence L. Szink and John W. Welch, "King Benjamin's Speech in the Context of Ancient Israelite Festivals," 147–223; Stephen D. Ricks, "Kingship, Coronation, and Covenant in Mosiah 1–6," 233–75.

[8] Szink and Welch, "King Benjamin's Speech in the Context of Ancient Israelite Festivals," 159.

Mesoamerica, the most important public festival of the year was timed to coincide with the main corn harvest in mid-November. For the most part, this also served as the New Year's day of the solar calendar, when kingship was renewed."[9]

The Hebrew autumn festivals also included the New Year celebration. That similarity may have allowed a conjunction of practices, where aspects of the New World festival and the religious festival merged in Nephite practice. This proposed merger of two different harvest festival traditions has the potential to explain aspects of the description of the events surrounding Benjamin's speech.

To understand the nature of this possible conjunction, we should note the Mesoamerican background for New Year's celebrations.[10] A new year was heralded with great ceremony. However, another very important type of New Year celebration may enter into Benjamin's New World accounting. In the Mesoamerican world, a fifty-two-year cycle was conceptually similar to a century in our calendar. It was a time when two different types of calendars coincided, not to be repeated again for another fifty-two years.

According to archaeologist Muriel Weaver Porter:

> One cannot overemphasize the significance of this 52-year cycle for Mesoamerican peoples. It is called the Calendar Round or Sacred Round. Aside from the Maya and Mexica we know it was in use by the Mixtecs, Otomis, Huastecs, Totonacs, Matlazinca, Tarascans, and many other groups. The cycles of time are believed to have been primarily divinatory in purpose. When these coincided, it was an event of great importance, marked by special ceremonies and perhaps by the enlargement of architectural structures.
>
> It was expected that the world would end at the completion of a 52-year cycle. At this time, among the Mexica in the Valley of Mexico, all fires were extinguished, pregnant women were locked up lest they be turned into wild animals, children were pinched to keep them awake so that they would not turn into mice, and all pottery was broken in preparation for the end of the world. . . . It was probably rare for a person to witness more than one of these celebrations in his lifetime, so undoubtedly it was an event approached with great anticipation and relived many times after its passing.[11]

I hypothesize that Benjamin had the unique opportunity of living at the important juncture of a New Year/New "Century." This auspicious combination of events provides the background for the specific ceremonies and for the details of the speech. It also helps explain why king Benjamin chose to crown Mosiah three years before his

---

[9] Allen J. Christenson, "Maya Harvest Festivals and the Book of Mormon," 1.

[10] The possible correspondence of this festival with a New Year's celebration is compelling, but the timing of the new year may have been different in the New World. Randall Spackman places the new year in the New World with the new moon on February 25 in the twenty-sixth year of the judges. Randall P. Spackman, "Introduction to Book of Mormon Chronology," 30. This calendar conflicts with the idea of an autumn harvest festival. However, with the passage of time in the New World, perhaps the new year correlation was stronger than the harvest festival connection.

[11] Muriel Porter Weaver, *The Aztecs, Maya, and Their Predecessors: Archaeology of Mesoamerica*, 103–4.

own death (Mosiah 6:4–5). Although Benjamin describes himself as old (Mosiah 2:30), he was obviously not on the verge of death. Rather, he saw this time as appropriate for naming a new king and renaming his people because the year itself as a moment of renewal, the beginning of a new "century." Benjamin is the only Book of Mormon ruler to abdicate rather than die in office.[12]

Another fascinating part of the story of Benjamin's speech is that, in order to be heard, he had to build a tower (Mosiah 2:7). Later, his son Mosiah$_2$ spoke to what had to have been an even larger gathering, but no mention is made of a tower (Mosiah 25).[13] The discrepancy has a plausible explanation in a Mesoamerican setting. In Mesoamerican cities, a speaker would ascend the steps of the pyramid to address a crowd. Many of the Maya ceremonial centers had excellent acoustic properties. A person speaking from the steps of the temple could be heard at other temples in the complex or within the ceremonial courtyard.[14] In that context, then, the temple should have already provided the benefits of a tower. Yet Benjamin built a tower.

At this point the fifty-two-year "century" provides the context. That time of renewal was marked by establishing or enlarging structures such as temples. If, as I have hypothesized, Benjamin's speech was occurring as part of a new year/jubilee/new century festival, and if part of Benjamin's effort to unite the people and build or rebuild temples as part of the renewal of the new century, then Benjamin is standing on the temple site but not in front of a finished temple. It had not yet been built. Benjamin thus constructs a tower because the permanent "tower," or temple, is not there. When his son later speaks, the temple had been built and therefore there was no need for the temporary tower.

While it is perhaps only a coincidence, one of the temple pyramids at Santa Rosa, Sorenson's candidate for Zarahemla, provides an intriguing possibility. When the New World Archaeological Foundation excavated one of the pyramid mounds, the archaeologists discovered a plaster floor, intentionally laid and smoothed over the foundation layer. Such a floor is itself unusual because Mesoamerican pyramids are built to demonstrate external volume, not usable interior space. The plaster floor was

---

[12] Abdication is rare in the Maya tradition as well. David Webster, *The Fall of the Ancient Maya: Solving the Mystery of the Maya Collapse,* 283: "For the first time the former tradition of father-son succession was violated, and Ruler 7 seems to have assumed power upon the abdication of his predecessor, a kind of event very rarely recorded in royal inscriptions suggestive of internal trouble."

The change of Nephite kings to judges appears to make a change in the way succession was perceived. Mosiah$_2$ initiates the change as part of attempting to find a way to transfer power. Alma$_2$ and Nephi$_2$ leave the judgment seat. While inheritance continued to play a part in succession, it was lessened.

[13] Not only was there another generation of people to increase the population, but the gathering was also to integrate the arrival of the people Limhi and the people of Alma.

[14] A number of anecdotal descriptions of the acoustics of various sites has been collected in "The Acoustics of Maya Temples."

intended to be covered—never to be seen again. The plaster itself, while interesting, was much more interesting for what it covered.

In the words of the excavating archaeologist, Augustín Delgado: "The plaster floor continued in both trench extensions. In contact with it, both above and below, was a thin layer of gravel. That below was of different natures to either side of the medial line of the temple. To the north it was composed of larger fragments of broken stone, while to the south it was natural gravel. The difference was probably due to the source of the material."[15]

Normal construction techniques indicate that labor may have been divided along kinship lines, with differing clans responsible for different parts of the construction. According to art historian Linda Schele and archaeologist Peter Mathews, "Archaeologists consistently find thin walls creating 'construction pens' inside pyramids, and often neighboring pens have different fill materials. These pens have been found under courts and plazas, so that they may have served as much to organize labor as to provide containing walls inside a construction. A likely system would have been to assign a certain number of pens to different lineages, who would then be responsible for finding the fill and bringing it to the pens. Each lineage would have fed its own people and perhaps contributed additional food and materials to the main construction project."[16]

What sets the Santa Rosa gravel apart from the construction pens in other temples is not the method of construction, but a methodically constructed feature—one that was intended to be concealed beneath a major temple. Another archaeologist working at Santa Rosa, Donald Brockington, discusses how this particular feature might develop the normal lineage connections at construction sites: "To the north the gravel was broken and to the south it was rounded. I supervised that excavation and, upon noting the difference, carefully searched the gravel, finding no mixture whatever. Not only does the difference suggest two sources of materials but it may be taken to imply two separate groups, each working on its section. Further, the medial line runs roughly east-west."[17] The east-west medial line suggests that it represents the path of the sun, symbolically tying this feature to the greater world. These are not multiple lineages represented by multiple construction pits, but two precise layers of gravel, carefully gathered, carefully separated, and carefully plastered over.

Brockington also noted that the general settlement pattern "might be interpreted to suggest a clustered village divided into moieties and oriented in relationship to a ceremonial construction."[18] The social picture that may be extracted from the data suggests two major divisions in Santa Rosa. The east-west median dividing the

---

[15] Augustin Delgado, *Archaeological Research at Santa Rosa, Chiapas[,] and in the Region of Tehuantepec*, 9.

[16] Linda Schele and Peter Mathews, *The Code of Kings: The Language of Seven Sacred Maya Temples and Tombs*, 28.

[17] Donald L. Brockington, *The Ceramic History of Santa Rosa, Chiapas, Mexico*, 60–61.

[18] Ibid., 60.

carefully separated gravel types mirrors the building clusters that also suggest the presence of two major groups in the city. The construction of this particular temple plausibly dates to around the time of Benjamin's speech.[19]

This archaeological evidence suggests a very tempting, albeit speculative, scenario. Benjamin's discourse was given at the temple site where Benjamin built a temporary tower. As part of Benjamin's coronation of his son, he gave his people a new identity, making of two a single people. As part of this ceremony, the people symbolized their new unity by physically laying a ceremonial floor consisting of two different gravels. This representation of division was then plastered over as a representation of unity. The separation was no longer visible. It was symbolically buried in the temple and conceptually buried in the new sacred space. The new temple became the physical embodiment of the covenant.

Clues to Culture in Benjamin's Speech

Benjamin's speech begins enigmatically but ends with such force and clarity that modern LDS scholars consider it a masterpiece. The enigmatic beginning is typically given less attention than the much more interesting and accessible body and ending of the speech. The beginning's enigma, however, reveals key aspects of the speech's place and time.

King Benjamin began his discourse with an unusual set of introductory statements:

> I have not commanded you to come up hither that ye should fear me, or that ye should think that I of myself am more than a mortal man.
>
> But I am like as yourselves, subject to all manner of infirmities in body and mind; yet I have been chosen by this people, and consecrated by my father, and was suffered by the hand of the Lord that I should be a ruler and a king over this people; and have been kept and preserved by his matchless power, to serve you with all the might, mind and strength which the Lord hath granted unto me.
>
> I say unto you that as I have been suffered to spend my days in your service, even up to this time, and have not sought gold nor silver nor any manner of riches of you;
>
> Neither have I suffered that ye should be confined in dungeons, nor that ye should make slaves one of another, nor that ye should murder, or plunder, or steal, or commit adultery; nor even have I suffered that ye should commit any manner of wickedness, and

---

[19] Archaeological dating is rarely precise, so the ability to date this temple falls within a plus or minus 100 years of the Benjamin's speech. The literature did not give specific dates, but the information allows for understanding the basic parameters. Delgado indicated that the structures above that floor date to the Classic, with the substructures being earlier. This timing at least leaves open the probability that the floor is also Preclassic (or the time period of the Book of Mormon). Caches of later pottery found under the floor were located in pits dug through the floor. Thus the flooring already existed when the later pottery was cached. Delgado, *Archaeological Research at Santa Rosa, Chiapas[,] and in the Region of Tehuantepec*, 29.

have taught you that ye should keep the commandments of the Lord, in all things which he hath commanded you— (Mosiah 2:10-13).

Why should Benjamin begin his sermon by describing what he is not and what he hasn't done? Benjamin is setting up an implicit contrast between what he was and what his people know from cultural experience he could have been. Benjamin wasn't, but could have been, like the kings in non-Nephite cities.

Think [not] that I am more than a mortal man (Mosiah 2:10)

Benjamin creates a contrast between himself and some other king who might be considered more than a mortal man.[20] That is precisely the nature of Maya kingship as we understand it.[21] Mark Alan Wright, whose dissertation discussed Maya kingship, notes: "Altar Q from Copán depicts the polity's first 16 kings, each seated upon throne-like renditions of their respective name glyphs. Its central theme shows a literal 'passing of the torch' from the founding king of Copán, K'inich Yax K'uk Mo', to the sixteenth ruler, Yax Pasaj. While Yax K'uk Mo' may or may not have been considered divine in his own lifetime, he was clearly apotheosized as the Sun God after his death. . . . Claiming descent from a deified ancestor reinforces the divinity of the living king."[22]

The best evidence for kingship among the Maya shows the distinct necessity of connecting not only to a royal but also to a divine lineage.[23]

Have not sought gold nor silver nor any manner of riches of you

Mesoamerican societies were hierarchically ranked, with kings at the apex of a system of increased wealth and power as one reached higher levels in the social hierarchy. Benjamin is expressly contrasting himself to this type of kingship. He still holds to the Nephite egalitarian idea, illustrated by his statement that "Even I, myself, have labored with mine own hands that I might serve you, and that ye should not be laden with taxes" (Mosiah 2:14).

[Not] suffered that you should be confined in dungeons . . . make slaves

John W. Welch points out that Benjamin is stressing that Nephite society is unique in opposing these common elements: "The use of dungeons or prisons was

---

[20] See the section on "Ammon and King Lamoni" in Chapter 12 for another occasion when the phrase "more than a man" is important to the story.

[21] While I understand that the Nephites in Zarahemla were in Zoque territory, our best data are for the Maya. While they may not be completely parallel to what would be found in the immediate vicinity of Zarahemla, the general cultural patterns, as far as can be discerned, are quite similar among differing cultural groups. Therefore, I use the Maya as an exemplar, not an equivalence.

[22] Mark Alan Wright, "A Study of Classic Maya Rulership," 50.

[23] Linda Schele and Mary Ellen Miller, *The Blood of Kings: Dynasty and Ritual in Maya Art*, 103. This implied comparison is strengthened by similar implied comparisons as the speech progresses.

apparently tolerated in Israel (Jer. 37:15, 1 Ne. 7:14), generally in the land of Nephi (Mosiah 17:5), in the land of Ammonihah (Alma 14:18, 23), and among the Lamanites (Hel. 5:21); but by special dispensation, the use of prisons was not allowed in Zarahemla under king Benjamin or in other lands by special royal decrees (Alma 23:2)."[24] That such a special decree was needed suggests that Lamanites used prisons or dungeons more commonly than the Nephites.

Likewise, enslavement had to be a real threat or Benjamin's prohibition of it would carry no weight. In point of fact, both the Maya and the later Aztecs practiced slavery. The Maya may have practiced slavery in both the Classic and Postclassic periods, depending on the interpretation of certain iconography. Archaeologist Sylvanus Morley writes:

> Slavery seems to have been practiced in both the Classic [A.D. 250–800] and Postclassic stages, despite Bishop Landa's [born 1524, died 1579] assertion that it was introduced in late Postclassic times by one of the Cocom rulers of Mayapan. This is difficult to believe in view of the frequent representations of the so-called "captive figures" on Classic Maya monuments. These "captive figures" are very likely representations of enslaved prisoners of war. . . .
>
> In Postclassic times, when we have documentary evidence for slavery, the condition would seem to have arisen in one of five different ways: (1) by having been born a slave; (2) by having been made a slave in punishment for stealing; (3) by having been made a prisoner of war; (4) by having become an orphan; and (5) by having been acquired by purchase or trade. Provision was made by law and custom for the redemption of children born into slavery. . . Prisoners of war were always enslaved. Those of high degree were sacrificed immediately, but those of lower rank became the property of the soldier who had captured them.[25]

However, Norman Hammond warns against reading more modern practices back into ancient Mesoamerican society: "[Slavery] is evocative, and it may well be that Maya slavery was less exploitative, and more like the villeinage of medieval England, or the patron-client relationship with mutual obligations that Tambiah notes for medieval Southeast Asia."[26] Whatever the exact details of the practice, it is clear from Benjamin's lumping it with prisons that slavery was negative and that its absence from Zarahemla was a politically enlightened act.

[Not] suffered that you should. . . murder/ plunder/ steal/ commit adultery

The prohibitions against murder and plunder come as a set, most probably because Benjamin intended them to refer to the same context of political achievement. Although most societies have prohibitions against murder (as distinct from execution, war, or religious ritual), Benjamin may here be using the term to include—and therefore to disapprove of—Mesoamerican human sacrifice.

---

[24] John W. Welch, "Benjamin, the Man: His Place in Nephite History," 40.
[25] Sylvanus G. Morley, *The Ancient Maya*, 159.
[26] Norman Hammond, "Inside the Black Box: Defining Maya Polity," 265.

Plunder, the acquisition of goods through acts of war, or raids, is both a motive and a reward for armed action, which was unquestionably very common in Mesoamerica. Both murder and plunder will recur again as a set in the Book of Mormon text.[27] It seems reasonable to see Benjamin setting himself apart from the other kings in disassociating himself also from the Mesoamerican cult of war, which was becoming dominant in this Maya culture region.[28] Benjamin's prohibition of adultery may contain an echo to Jacob's denunciations of marital infidelity and multiple wives, suggesting that Benjamin had continued the norm of "one man, one woman" to specifically contrast with neighboring cultures.

The introduction Benjamin gives to his sermon outlines concerns that are fully at home in a Mesoamerican context. They make sense as denials only against the common understanding that such practices were typical of other kings in other cities.

Unmaking Unity: Churches

The Hebrew religion the Nephites understood was rooted in communal concepts. Religion was practiced as a community. Sin was communal and was therefore communally atoned for by the sacrifices the priests made on behalf of the people. Benjamin's covenant was intended to follow that model.

The political and religious situation in Zarahemla would not permit the idea of a unified community religion to last long. Even after Benjamin's unification speech—to which all of his assented—the events described in the text underscore that differences resurfaced as that unifying moment moved further into the past. The divisions between Nephite and Zarahemlaite had originally caused contentions so great that some Nephites dissented, becoming Lamanites. They were not yet as destructively divisive, but they would become so within a generation.

Eventually, the concept of communal religion had to change and adapt to the reality of the divided religio-political loyalties. The reign of king Mosiah$_2$ saw important shifts in religion and politics designed to cope with the pressures that continued to build between the two factions of Zarahemla society. While Mosiah$_2$ was the man behind the changes, Alma$_1$ was the mind behind the changes.

Mosiah$_2$ cut the ties between religion and the entire community, allowing it to become associated with subsets of the community. In doing so, the concept of a church was introduced to Zarahemla. The English word "church" is ultimately derived from the Greek *kyriakon (doma)* "house of the Lord."[29] That wasn't the term used in the New Testament, however. Daniel N. Schowalter explains: "In the Greek word, the term *ekklesia* meant a group of citizens 'called out' to assemble for political

---

[27] Mosiah 10:17; Alma 23:3; Hel. 6:23, 7:21, 11:25; 3 Ne. 4:5; Ether 8:16.

[28] M. Kathryn Brown and James F. Garber, "Evidence of Conflict during the Middle Formative in the Maya Lowlands: A View from Blackman Eddy, Belize," 93: "Epigraphic and iconographic evidence suggests that captive sacrifice is a ritualized institution associated with warfare and is deeply rooted within Maya mythology."

[29] "Church," *Funk & Wagnalls Standard Dictionary of the English Language*, 1:238.

purposes. In the New Testament, *ekklesia* signifies a group of believers in Jesus who are called together, and is translated as 'church.'"[30] The line of translations reaches back to Hebrew, where Schowalter indicates: "In the Septuagint [Greek translation of the Hebrew Old Testament] *ekklesia* is used interchangeably with *synagogue* to render Hebrew terms that mean assembly."[31]

The New Testament usage shows some flexibility in its application. It usually refers to Christian assemblies in different cities (in Paul). However, Matthew 16:18 has Jesus saying: "And I say also unto thee, That thou art Peter, and upon this rock I will build my church; and the gates of hell shall not prevail against it." Schowalter notes: "Whether the 'rock' refers to Peter or to his confession is strongly debated, but either way, the verse conveys a sense of the church as a universal institution."[32]

Without knowing the particular word that was being translated, Joseph used "church" in its expansive, universal meaning when translating Nephi's books. Nephi records the words of his angel guide: "And he said unto me: Behold there are save two churches only; the one is the church of the Lamb of God, and the other is the church of the devil; wherefore, whoso belongeth not to the church of the Lamb of God belongeth to that great church, which is the mother of abominations; and she is the whore of all the earth" (1 Ne. 14:10). By contrasting two diametrically opposite "churches," the angel is proposing a paradigmatic division—not a particular congregation.[33]

After Nephi's use of "church," the word disappears from the Book of Mormon text until the aftermath of Abinadi's trial when Alma$_1$ forms a "church."[34] By the time we have shifted from the plates of Nephi to the book of Mosiah we have traversed not only over four hundred years in time but are also reading a different author and a different editor. Given the different meanings associated with *ekklesia* in the New Testament, it is important to determine whether Alma$_1$ uses "church" in the same way as Nephi or whether there is a different connotation behind the meaning of this later church.

John W. Welch underscored an important caveat (although in the context of a different topic): "Thinking like an ancient person, whether in Lehi's Jerusalem in the seventh century B.C. or in any other ancient setting, is not a simple undertaking."[35] In the case of the use of the term "church" in the Book of Mormon, the difficulty

---

[30] Daniel N. Schowalter, "Church," 121.
[31] Ibid.
[32] Ibid., 122. Schowalter continues: "This universal sense is developed further in the Deutero-Pauline letters. . . . Ignatius of Antioch (ca. 100 C.E.) is the earliest known author to use the phrase 'catholic church' when referring to the universality of the body of Christ."
[33] See Stephen E. Robinson, "Early Christianity and 1 Nephi 13–14," 179; see also Dennis A. Wright, "Great and Abominable Church," 2:568.
[34] Grant Hardy pointed out that 2 Ne. 26:20–21; 28:3, 12, appear to use "church" in the more modern sense. "Church" is not used as a designation for a Book of Mormon congregation until much later.
[35] John W. Welch, *The Legal Cases in the Book of Mormon*, 5.

comes in stripping away our own cultural assumptions in order to better examine the way the term is used in the Book of Mormon.

The first important difference between our understanding of "church" and the Nephite experience is that we accept the term as covering multiple Christian denominations. The implication of the modern use of "church" is either a place or an organization that is dedicated to a particular type of Christianity (or perhaps a different religion). Most of Nephite history prior to Zarahemla did not use "church" because there was nothing it might have described. The intertwining of religion and daily life was so complete that it does not make sense to speak of a "church" that might have been separate from any other institution or way of belief. "Living in antiquity was being 'religious,'" as William G. Dever admonishes.[36] Specifically for the Maya, Miguel Angel Astor-Aguilera notes: "Maya religion. . . was inseparable from day-to-day activities, whether related to socioeconomics, politics, or warfare."[37] For much of antiquity, it also meant being religious in the same way as everyone else in your community.

Against the background of a communal religion, Alma$_1$ created something new in the land. He led a group of people out of their community and taught them religious principles that differed from their community's. In Alma$_1$'s creation, a new community centered on a new religious perception. Rather than religion by tradition or genealogy, it was a religion and community of choice. People could elect to leave one community and its religion for the new community and religion, signaling one's entry into that new religious community with a formal rite:

> And after this manner he did baptize every one that went forth to the place of Mormon; and they were in number about two hundred and four souls; yea, and they were baptized in the waters of Mormon, and were filled with the grace of God.
>
> And they were called the church of God, or the church of Christ, from that time forward. And it came to pass that whosoever was baptized by the power and authority of God was added to his church. (Mosiah 18:16–17)

It appears that, at least in the beginning, this was a community of believers still inside the larger community. They were forced to physically flee to a new land when the king, "having discovered a movement among the people, sent his servants to watch them. Therefore on the day that they were assembling themselves together to hear the word of the Lord they were discovered unto the king" (Mosiah 18:32). Alma$_1$ created a new concept: a church as a community of specific believers among a population containing those who believed differently.

When the king threatened them, this new community physically broke its ties to the city of Nephi-Lehi and moved to the land they named Helam. There they clearly established a political structure contrasting with the one they had left. The people clamor for Alma$_1$ to be their king, but he refuses (Mosiah 23:8–13). Nevertheless,

---

[36] William G. Dever, *Did God Have a Wife? Archaeology and Folk Religion in Ancient Israel*, 3.
[37] Miguel Angel Astor-Aguilera, *The Maya World of Communicating Objects. Quadripartite Crosses, Trees, and Stones*, 56.

Alma₁ does function in a leadership position, taking the title of high priest and possessing authority to establish structure in the community (Mosiah 23:16–18). We might see Alma₁ reversing the trend of secularizing the community's government by sacralizing it.

When Alma₁ and his people were integrated into the people of Zarahemla, his ideas about church and government came with him, and appear to have influenced Mosiah₂:

> And it came to pass that king Mosiah granted unto Alma that he might establish churches throughout all the land of Zarahemla; and gave him power to ordain priests and teachers over every church.
>
> Now this was done because there were so many people that they could not all be governed by one teacher; neither could they all hear the word of God in one assembly;
>
> Therefore they did assemble themselves together in different bodies, being called churches; every church having their priests and their teachers, and every priest preaching the word according as it was delivered to him by the mouth of Alma.
>
> And thus, notwithstanding there being many churches they were all one church, yea, even the church of God; for there was nothing preached in all the churches except it were repentance and faith in God.
>
> And now there were seven churches in the land of Zarahemla. And it came to pass that whosoever were desirous to take upon them the name of Christ, or of God, they did join the churches of God. (Mosiah 25:19–23)

Zarahemla did not have churches prior to Alma₁'s arrival. Why not and why only at that time?[38] I hypothesize that the divisive pressures of the dual cultural inheritance were still operational—in fact, intensifying. Alma₁'s concept of a church as a body of believers that could exist as separate from a different understanding of religion in the community provided Mosiah₂ with a model that could be used to try to accommodate Zarahemla's religious reality. It was precisely what Mosiah₂ needed to better administer that fissionable community.

It was also the beginning of the end for Benjamin's covenant of unity. By admitting and accepting religious pluralism in Zarahemla, Mosiah₂ removed the veneer of social unity from his people. They would no longer be a single people united

---

[38] An interesting adjunct to the story of the establishment of churches in Zarahemla occurs between Limhi and Ammon. Limhi comes from the same location and culture as Alma₁ and clearly knows what Alma₁ has created. Ammon is a representative of Mosiah₂:

> And now since the coming of Ammon, king Limhi had also entered into a covenant with God, and also many of his people, to serve him and keep his commandments.
>
> And it came to pass that king Limhi and many of his people were desirous to be baptized; but there was none in the land that had authority from God. And Ammon declined doing this thing, considering himself an unworthy servant.
>
> Therefore they did not at that time form themselves into a church, waiting upon the Spirit of the Lord. Now they were desirous to become even as Alma and his brethren, who had fled into the wilderness. (Mosiah 21:32–34)

What Limhi requests is a baptism into a church. Ammon may or may not have had the authority to baptize, but he would have had no concept of baptism as a sign of entry into an organization with which he was not familiar. Therefore, Ammon wisely defers to Mosiah₂.

under a single name. They would be a divided people known for their city and not for their covenant.

Unmaking Unity: The Reign of Judges

Benjamin's new covenant of a new unified people with a unified name began to erode during the reign of his son, whom he installed as king as part of the new covenant. At the end of Mosiah$_2$'s reign, a crisis necessitated a major shift in how Zarahemla was governed. Mosiah$_2$'s sons declined to become king (Mosiah 29:3). Whereas Israelite political history saw associated tribes under the rule of judges more formally unite under a king, Mosiah$_2$ reversed the process. This king gave way to judges.

Nephi's people desired that he be their king, even though he was reluctant to accept that title (2 Ne. 5:18). There is no reason to believe that the social pressures for a king had diminished in the interim. In fact, an early challenge to Alma$_2$, the first chief judge, came in the form of an attempt to reinstate a monarchy:

> And it came to pass in the commencement of the fifth year of their reign there began to be a contention among the people; for a certain man, being called Amlici, he being a very cunning man, yea, a wise man as to the wisdom of the world, he being after the order of the man that slew Gideon by the sword, who was executed according to the law—
> Now this Amlici had, by his cunning, drawn away much people after him; even so much that they began to be very powerful; and they began to endeavor to establish Amlici to be a king over the people. (Alma 2:1–2)

The succession crisis arose because all acceptable heirs had declined. Not providing the expected and sanctioned method of determining the next king, the community was now open to other options. The experience with Amlici clearly highlights the willingness of a lineage competing with Mosiah in both political and religious ideas to challenge for the throne.

This implicit internal instability and plausible move away from Nephite ideals to the more syncretized version of both Nephite and Zarahemlaite religion and politics was, perhaps, the primary reason that Mosiah$_2$ initiated the change in the government. By abandoning the kingship, he was able to circumvent clan-based contention for the throne. By directly appointing someone who was outside of all of the established lineages and by creating a new position for him to fill, Mosiah$_2$ managed to provide a power transition that he approved rather than accept whatever might have arisen from the competing clan claims. Mosiah$_2$ selected Alma$_2$. Alma$_2$ was a descendant of those who had followed Zeniff to the land of Nephi and who had returned with Limhi. Their absence from Zarahemla for at least two generations made them all outsiders to Zarahemlaite political infighting. It was a bold move.

As Mosiah$_2$ explained his reasons for abolishing the monarchy, he declared:

> Now it is better that a man should be judged of God than of man, for the judgments of God are always just, but the judgments of man are not always just.
> Therefore, if it were possible that you could have just men to be your kings, who would establish the laws of God, and judge this people according to his commandments, yea, if ye

could have men for your kings who would do even as my father Benjamin did for this people—I say unto you, if this could always be the case then it would be expedient that ye should always have kings to rule over you. (Mosiah 29:12–13)

Mosiah$_2$ did not devalue a monarchy. He was, after all, a king. He had attempted to continue the monarchy. The move to judges should be seen as a response to the succession crisis, not to an ideological denouncing of the principle. What he explicates is the danger inherent in a monarchy if you have the wrong kind of king. Perhaps we see in this justification Mosiah$_2$'s implicit understanding of his people and the faction that would later push so hard for Amlici's kingship. Perhaps he knew that Amlici was "a wicked man, [who] would deprive them of their rights and privileges of the church; for it was his intent to destroy the church of God" (Alma 2:4).

Mosiah$_2$'s justification intentionally reflected Alma$_1$'s refusal of a proffered kingship:

> Behold, it is not expedient that we should have a king; for thus saith the Lord: Ye shall not esteem one flesh above another, or one man shall not think himself above another; therefore I say unto you it is not expedient that ye should have a king.
> Nevertheless, if it were possible that ye could always have just men to be your kings it would be well for you to have a king.
> But remember the iniquity of king Noah and his priests. (Mosiah 23:7–9)

Alma$_1$ reminded the people: "If it were possible that ye could always have just men to be your kings it would be well for you to have a king." He corroborated Mosiah$_2$'s declaration: "If ye could have men for your kings who would do even as my father Benjamin did for this people—I say unto you, if this could always be the case then it would be expedient that ye should always have kings to rule over you." There are enough differences in the recorded statements to indicate that Mosiah$_2$ is reflecting rather than quoting Alma$_1$, but the sentiments match precisely. Wicked king Noah was Alma$_1$'s explicit model. Mosiah$_2$ offered king Noah as the example of the wrong kind of king in Mosiah 29:18.

Mosiah$_2$ appointed Alma$_2$ as the first chief judge. In a single stroke, Mosiah$_2$ thus sidestepped the brewing succession conflict and declared the essential unity of Nephite religion and the right to rule. He introduced the new political organization with the following injunctions:

> Therefore, choose you by the voice of this people, judges, that ye may be judged according to the laws which have been given you by our fathers, which are correct, and which were given them by the hand of the Lord.
> Now it is not common that the voice of the people desireth anything contrary to that which is right; but it is common for the lesser part of the people to desire that which is not right; therefore this shall ye observe and make it your law—to do your business by the voice of the people.
> And if the time comes that the voice of the people doth choose iniquity, then is the time that the judgments of God will come upon you; yea, then is the time he will visit you with great destruction even as he has hitherto visited this land. (Mosiah 29:25–27).

Verse 25 tells us three important things about the new government. First, authority would be vested in several judges rather than a single king. Second, they would be judged according to law. Third, an important mechanism of government would be the "voice of the people."

The rule of law is relatively easy to understand as our modern society is also governed by the rule of law. Even the system of judges is not too foreign to us. They formed a governmental hierarchy, with local judges reporting to higher judges:

> And now if ye have judges, and they do not judge you according to the law which has been given, ye can cause that they may be judged of a higher judge.
>
> If your higher judges do not judge righteous judgments, ye shall cause that a small number of your lower judges should be gathered together, and they shall judge your higher judges, according to the voice of the people. (Mosiah 29:28–29)

However, the simple fact that the translated record includes the term "judges" makes it too simple to impose our modern understanding not only of a judge but of a legal system upon the Nephite record. John W. Welch summarized the problem: "A challenge inherent [in reconstructing Nephite legal cases] is to reconstruct the Nephite legal system, so far as possible, as the Nephites themselves might have understood and experienced law in the context of their own world."[39] Welch explains the complications:

> We know of no legal treatises, hornbooks (scholarly explanations of the law), or law manuals from the ancient world, and it is doubtful that the so-called law codes of the Bible and the ancient Near East functioned in that world in the same way as do statutes in the modern world. No specialized schools of law existed, although the scribal tradition prepared people to record legal agreements and to advise others involved in legal transactions in the use of traditional manners of documentation. A systematic sense of jurisprudence was still centuries away, and no attempts to rationalize decisions in individual cases appear to have been made.[40]

Nevertheless, Welch carefully examined a number of legal cases as represented in the Book of Mormon, comparing them to known biblical law[41] and concludes:

> This study has also shown that the Nephite administration of justice, like the Israelite system upon which it was based, featured various modes of adjudication and dispute resolution, ranging from private contentions to formal divisions of jurisdiction between priests and the king. Having adopted the legal and political reforms of King Mosiah, the Nephite legal system became more structured with the establishment of a system of lower and higher judges known as the reign of the judges. . . .
>
> Over the course of Nephite history, most of the basic judicial procedures, however, remained stable. Little change is seen concerning such procedural particularities as the populace's obligation to initiate judicial actions; taking, binding, and carrying an indicted party before a judge; smiting on the cheek as a form of humiliation and indictment; judging one's accountability based on degree of knowledge; requiring parties to appear personally without advocates or representatives; insisting on the two-witness rule; the swearing of oaths

---

[39] John W. Welch, *The Legal Cases in the Book of Mormon*, 5.
[40] Ibid., 9.
[41] Welch analyzes the following as legal cases (as indicated in his Table of Contents): "The Case of Sherem," "The Trial of Abinadi," "The Trial of Nehor," "The Trial of Alma and Amulek," and "The Trial of Seantum."

and the predominance of oral testimony; diligent inquisition or examination of parties; severe consequences for false accusation or perjury; construing silence as an admission of guilt; the acceptance of self-incrimination under certain conditions; resolving deadlocked cases by ordeal, signs, or oracular detection of culprits; accepting unequivocally the divine determination of innocence or guilt; the absence of courts of appeal on the merits; heralding judicial outcomes; using certain types of punishments; justifying the death penalty on certain rationales and in prescribed modes of execution; using post-judgment and pre-execution confessions; using the accusers as executioners; and ensuring that the operation of the legal system resulted in the establishment of justice and the restoration of peace in the society.[42]

The Nephite system of law and adjudication was, from the examination of the details involved in the specific cases, quite different from any legal system known to Joseph Smith. It did, however, fit comfortably into legal systems based upon Old Testament concepts and practices. Ronan James Head, in reviewing Welch's book in 2009 remarked:

> Skeptical students of the Book of Mormon could reasonably mine the text for evidences of nineteenth-century American law, an approach Welch anticipates and roundly rejects. He notes that certain terms in the Book of Mormon (e.g. *contends* and *robber*) correspond more accurately to their Hebrew uses than any American use. Welch insists that Book of Mormon law is demonstrably Hebrew (specifically pre-exilic owing to Lehi's departure from Jerusalem prior to the Babylonian captivity), arguing that a modern author of the Book of Mormon would have needed "a level of comprehension and familiarity with biblical law that exceeded the articulated knowledge of biblical scholars in the nineteenth century, let alone the comprehension of the young Joseph Smith" [page 55 in Welch, *The Legal Cases*].[43]

The change from monarchy to the rule of law did not acknowledge social differences as did the creation of churches. It exacerbated the existing divisions. Kingmen would later be given that name identifying them as an internal division, but it was division that began early. The first major event recorded for the reign of the judges was an attempt to return to a monarchy (with a different lineage ruling). The reliance upon law rather than the presumed divine dictates of a king permitted the growing dissent. That internal political strife would, within two centuries, dissolve any Nephite government greater than tribes.

Benjamin had created a new covenant for his people. His son sowed the structural seeds that would totally unmake it.

The Voice of the People

The third element of the new political process, "the voice of the people," merits closer examination. We may too easily assume that it is similar to familiar, modern

---

[42] Welch, *The Legal Cases*, 385.
[43] Ronan James Head, "In the Nephite Courtroom," 184–85. The internal quotation is from Welch, *The Legal Cases*, 55. Head also notes: "A critic of the Book of Mormon would probably question the extent to which Welch began with an assumption of historicity and worked backwards from there, but believing Mormon readers will no doubt share Welch's view."

political functions. Anthony W. Ivins did so in associating it with American democracy: "This book [the Book of Mormon], as has been testified before, is the very embodiment of the spirit of Americanism. We hear a lot about that in these days. In its simplicity it lays down those fundamental principles of democracy upon which every republican form of government must be based and [g]rounded [sic]. It teaches us that there should be no king to dictate upon this land. It teaches us that the will of the people, the voice of the people shall govern."[44]

In contrast to this supposed change from monarchy to democracy, there was a great deal of continuity between the monarchy and the rule of the judges. Judges were still considered rulers who sat on thrones. The chief judge led armies in battle. Although the judges were appointed by the voice of the people, they were succeeded by their sons.[45] This, and other evidence, led Richard L. Bushman to declare: "The 'reign of the judges,' as the Book of Mormon calls the period, was a far cry from the republican government Joseph Smith knew."[46]

---

[44] Anthony W. Ivins, *Conference Report*, October 7, 1923, 146. Also J. Keith Melville, "Joseph Smith, the Constitution, and Individual Liberties," 65.

[45] Sorenson, *Nephite Culture and Society*, 202–3; internal references silently removed. Sorenson provides the following notes on the continuities: "See Alma 12:20 on a judge as 'a chief ruler' in the city of Ammonihah; Alma 35:5, 8, on 'rulers' among the Zoramites; Helaman 7:4–5, judges 'do according to their wills' and enrich themselves; Alma 60:1, 7, 11, 21, rulers 'sit upon your thrones'; Alma 1:2, judges 'reign,' the same term used regarding kings; Alma 2:16, and compare Words of Mormon 1:14, the chief judge leads his forces into battle as had the king; Alma 60:19, 34–35, control of tax resources."

[46] Richard L. Bushman, "The Book of Mormon and the American Revolution," 15. The footnote to this statement reads:

> The confirmation of the chief judges by the voice of the people is the only element of the Nephite constitution which comes close to republicanism and in the context of life tenure and hereditary succession this "election" is closer to the traditional acclamation of the king than to a popular plebiscite. We forget that kings have usually been thought to rule by the consent of their people and that at the ascent of a new king to the throne this consent is normally exhibited anew. Sometimes the election is merely ritualistic; in other cases such as the selection of William III by the Convention Parliament in 1688, the consent of the people's representatives was as essential as the popular election of an American President. There was a popular element in Nephite monarchy, too. While still monarch, Mosiah had sent "among all the people desiring to know their will concerning who should be their king" (Mosiah 29:1). Zeniff was earlier "made a king by the voice of the people" (Mosiah 7:9; cf. Mosiah 19:26). The army of Israel "made their commander Omri king of Israel by common consent" (1 Kgs. 16:16 [NEB]).

Richard L. Bushman, "My Belief," 27, describing his discovery after attempting to apply "political principles embodied in the Book of Mormon and make some application to our Revolution and Constitution":

> Gradually it dawned on me that the very absence of republican statements might in itself be interesting. I long ago learned that it is better to flow with the evidence than to compel compliance with one's preformed ideas. So I asked, instead, what does the Book of Mormon say about politics? To my surprise, I discovered it was quite an unrepublican book. Not only

Ryan W. Davis provides a nuanced approach to Nephite democracy:

> A common mistake is to map the transition from monarchy to the reign of the judges too easily onto familiar political structures. Mosiah's new regime is not a democracy as the term is understood in contemporary society. Unlike American democracy, there is no legislative branch. By modern standards, other nondemocratic elements include that the chief judge is not apparently limited in his term of office and that judges not only govern but also "reign," to point out a few examples (see Alma 1:2; 60:21). And although political dynasties do occur in democratic states, the anticipation of familial succession seems especially strong in Nephite governance.[47]

He continues:

> A state's level of democracy is best thought of as a continuum between poles of a complete democracy and autocracy. The relevant question is whether the state is democratic in ways that will meaningfully influence the policy outcome under consideration.
> It is in this limited but important sense that the regime established by Mosiah should be considered a democracy.[48]

While the limitations Davis suggests might perhaps find a definition of democracy that could be fit to the Nephite model, little in the Nephite model allows it to be firmly separated from the monarchy that preceded it. The voice of the people was not a vote. Judges inherited their seats. Both the judges and monarchies follow the rule of law. If we are to limit the definition of democracy so severely, it might be wise to jettison the attempt to make that term fit the Nephite government that Mosiah set in motion.

Although it is tempting to assume that the voice of the people represented a vote, there is no evidence that it functioned in that way. According to Davis, "it is unclear whether the 'voice of the people' implies democratic choice in creating the set of possible political options or only in choosing among a set arranged by leaders."[49] I suggest that it was an entirely different mechanism.

While the voice of the people plays a more prominent role after the establishment of the reign of the judges,[50] it was nevertheless a functioning part of the monarchical system. The earliest mention of the "voice of the people" in conjunction with a king is from Zeniff's story. Zeniff was the leader of those who eventually colonized the city of Lehi-Nephi. Limhi, in giving his genealogy, explains: "I am Limhi, the son of Noah,

---

was Nephi a king, and monarchy presented as the ideal government in an ideal world, but the supposedly republican government instituted under Mosiah did not function that way at all.

[47] Ryan W. Davis, "For the Peace of the People: War & Democracy in the Book of Mormon," 44.

[48] Ibid. John W. Welch, "Democratizing Forces in King Benjamin's Speech," 111, uses some of these concepts of a limited democracy to suggest that "King Benjamin prepared the way for democratic developments."

[49] Davis, "For the Peace of the People," 44.

[50] Byron R. Merrill, "Government by the Voice of the People: A Witness and a Warning," 117, suggests a similarity to the Old Testament judges. Merrill also suggests that, while the Book of Mormon judges represented an ancient form of government that differs from modern United States democracy, it was built on similar "underling principles of freedom and morality which permeate the two systems" (126).

who was the son of Zeniff, who came up out of the land of Zarahemla . . . who was made a king by the *voice of the people*" (Mosiah 7:9).

It might be possible to read this statement as Zeniff's "election" to kingship, since he apparently did not rule by lineal right, although his son, Noah, and grandson, Limhi, would. However, both Benjamin and Mosiah, who *did* rule by lineal right, also invoke this principle. Benjamin commented in his great public discourse: "But I am like as yourselves, subject to all manner of infirmities in body and mind; yet *I have been chosen by this people*, and consecrated by my father, and was suffered by the . . . Lord that I should be a ruler and a king" (Mosiah 2:11). Although Benjamin identifies Yahweh as the ultimate source of his position, the proximate source is being chosen by the people.

The people's participation in transferring the kinship reappears in Mosiah's attempt to find a successor when his four sons opt for Lamanite missions instead of the throne: "Mosiah . . . sent out throughout all the land, among all the people, desiring to *know their will* concerning who should be their king. And . . . the *voice of the people came*, saying: We are desirous that Aaron thy son should be our king and our ruler" (Mosiah 29:1-2).

Just as Benjamin was "chosen" by the people, Mosiah solicited the people's preference concerning which son should be the king. In most monarchies, the heir would have been undisputed. While these examples show that the voice of the people functioned in the most important political decision—the change of king—it was not confined to transferring political power. When Ammon and Limhi plan how to escape Lamanite bondage, they "began to consult with the people . . . ; and even they did cause that all the people should gather themselves together; and this they did that they might have the *voice of the people* concerning the matter" (Mosiah 22:1). And of course, the voice of the people was presumably mobilized for other decisions that would affect the entire community. The very fact that the voice of the people was functioning under the monarchy should remind us that it was not the same as modern voting or elections.

In the same way that the voice of the people functioned in installing a king, it was part of installing the judges, and presumably in the same way. During the reign of the judges, an official may have been appointed or may have assumed his position by lineal right. Still, he was confirmed by the voice of the people. For instance, "Helaman, who was the son of Helaman, was appointed to fill the judgment-seat, by the voice of the people" (Hel. 2:2).

Note that Helaman$_2$ was "appointed," even though he "inherited" his father's judgment-seat. Lineage gave Helaman$_2$ a presumption of appointment. The people confirmed; they did not appoint. This was not an elected position. Even clearer was the case of Pacumeni: "Pacumeni was appointed, *according to the voice of the people*, to be a chief judge and a governor over the people, to reign in the stead of his brother Pahoran; and it was *according to his right*" (Hel. 1:13). Thus, Pacumeni became chief judge both by lineal right and by the voice of the people.

A third example of this same conjunction of the voice of the people and an appointment in which they did not make the selection occurred when Alma$_2$ transferred the chief judgeship to Nephihah:

> And he selected a wise man who was among the elders of the church, *and gave him power according to the voice of the people*, that he might have power to enact laws according to the laws which had been given, and to put them in force according to the wickedness and the crimes of the people.
> Now this man's name was Nephihah, and he was appointed chief judge; and he sat in the judgment-seat to judge and to govern the people. (Alma 4:16–17)

In this case, Alma$_2$ apparently had and exercised the prerogative of appointing his successor. His authority to do so was "according to the voice of the people," although this passage contains no specific details of how they communicated that authority. The voice of the people functioned with some power in the retention of their political leaders, but should not be described as an election.

Nevertheless, in the Book of Mormon record, the voice of the people was active even when there were disputes. Indeed, those disputes are valuable in giving us new insights into how the voice of the people functioned. For example, Pahoran's service as chief judge generated such a dispute:

> And those who were desirous that Pahoran should remain chief judge over the land took upon them the name of freemen; and thus was the division among them, for the freemen had sworn or covenanted to maintain their rights and the privileges of their religion by a free government.
> And it came to pass that this matter of their contention was settled by the voice of the people. And it came to pass that the voice of the people came in favor of the freemen, and Pahoran retained the judgment-seat, which caused much rejoicing among the brethren of Pahoran and also many of the people of liberty, who also put the king-men to silence, that they durst not oppose but were obliged to maintain the cause of freedom. (Alma 51:6–7)

Significantly, Pahoran was already sitting as the chief judge. The dispute was whether to retain (confirm) him. In this case, the voice of the people seems to have functioned something like a vote of confidence in a parliamentary system.[51] If Pahoran had lost, he would have stepped down. Furthermore, the voice of the people had the power to quell (at least in this case) the opposing voice of the king-men.

This incident also reveals that the voice of the people was not only a representation of a statistical community voice; it was invoked in a general assembly. Similarly, Ammon and Limhi "did cause that all the people should gather themselves together; and this that they might have the voice of the people concerning the matter" (Mosiah 22:1). When it was impractical to physically gather the people together, then the leaders took the question to the people. This approach reaffirms

---

[51] Donald Arthur Cazier, "A Study of Nephite, Lamanite, and Jaredite Governmental Institutions and Policies as Portrayed in the Book of Mormon," 87, 103, suggests that the voice of the people functioned as a vote of no confidence under the monarchy but was a more democratic institution under the judges.

the communal nature of the voice of the people. When possible, they would gather to take the entire community "voice"; and when that was not possible, they still sought the "voice" of the community, presumably through representatives of the kin groups. Mosiah 29:1 describes how Mosiah sent "throughout all the land" for the people's voice on the next king. In Alma 27:21, the chief judge sent a proclamation "throughout all the land" to obtain the voice of the people about arrangements for the people of Anti-Nephi-Lehi.

While coming from a different time and place, the Greek and Roman world provides a model for this combination of unelected ruler and the "voice of the people." Ramsay MacMullen finds this type of democracy in the centralized governments of the post-Greco-Roman world: "In this world so unmercifully vertical, how could democracy find place? Yet it was possible. In the very face of the ruler of all, and in the most public places, democracy found a place. Successes, well remembered for their drama, entered the record of the empire's earlier centuries again and again, the *demos* [people] massed outside the palace or in some place of entertainment, the race track or the like in some great city, behaving just like a political assembly and getting what they wanted. Lung power was people power, however informal it all appears."[52]

Lung power was massed in public settings where a leader would begin a phrase and the group would attempt to follow the phrase in unison to be louder and more clearly heard.[53] Although there were mechanisms of tallying votes, it appears that the power of the lungs became the more frequent means of settling disputes in the early Christian church:

> Greeks . . . had always raised and counted hands, the act of *cheirotonia*. No doubt, being Greeks, they weren't silent about it. *Cheirotonia*, or alternatively the rough measuring of shouts equivalent to "The Ayes have it," were both methods adopted by the church. They were adopted in preference to Roman balloting quite naturally; for the Christian community had its birth and early growth in the Greek east. In councils, then, a show of hands was occasionally asked for by the presiding person; but a show of preference by shouting seems to have been the rule, and certainly prevailed in Episcopal elections.[54]

Against the background Greeks and Romans used the voice of the people to affect decision-making, the sole description of how the Book of Mormon "voice of the people" operated takes on a clearer meaning, one that underscores the reason that it was called the *voice* of the people:

> And it came to pass that the people assembled themselves together throughout all the land, every man according to his mind, whether it were for or against Amlici, in separate bodies, having much dispute and wonderful contentions one with another.
>
> And thus they did assemble themselves together to cast in their voices concerning the matter; and they were laid before the judges.

---

[52] Ramsay MacMullen, *Voting about God in Early Church Councils*, 12–13.
[53] Ibid., 14.
[54] Ibid., 20.

And it came to pass that the voice of the people came against Amlici, that he was not made king over the people. (Alma 2:5–7).

This passage describes the people's assembling in groups, possibly several groups in several locations, and presumably at the village/town/hamlet level along kin-compound lines. The population was already too large to allow for a single assembly split into two. At each location, the two opposing bodies had "much dispute and wonderful contentions." While this division may possibly have been figurative and the debates individual rather than communal, I argue that we should read this verse literally as collective and organized (though not necessarily orderly) debates. The "voice of the people" appears to quite literally be a group function, not a synonym for ballot-casting.

A Mesoamerican Model for Nephite Judges

Abolishing the monarchy was drastic, but not as dramatic a change as it might seem. Just as the "voice of the people" was a pre-existing mechanism that shifted in importance in the reign of the judges, the reign of the judges was itself built upon existing political structures that were simply given new definitions and tasks.

Nephite social and political systems followed the same general developmental paths as did their surrounding cultures. From the time of Jacob there were pressures for social stratification, and those pressures continued in Zarahemla (and were manifest in the kingmen, see Alma 51). The result was a system with strong kinship organizations, but existing on different social strata.[55] Mesoamerican monarchies existed on top of a system of rule that divided power among kin-based lineages, each with their own organizational structure. Mesoamerican society had multiple elite lineages which were an organizational structure that functioned underneath the monarchy. That governmental layer could be elevated to the highest court of community rule. The clearest examples of this process come later than the Book of Mormon. During the Postclassic Period (A.D. 900 to the Conquest), evidence at the site of Chichén Itzá in the northern Petén describes a method of rule that appears to have shared power among representatives of important lineages rather than consolidated power in the person of a king:

---

[55] Evans, *Ancient Mexico and Central America*, 206:

> States are the most complex political organizations—all modern peoples are encompassed, to a greater or lesser degree, within the aegis of one state or another. The evolution of this form in the world's six cradles of civilization, including Mesoamerica, involved an important change in social relations. In chiefdoms, kinship ties still integrate all families into a society wherein each family is socially ranked by how closely it is related to the rule. In contrast, in states, social strata emerge (hence the term *stratified society*) in which the whole stratum (or class) is ranked, vis-a-vis other classes. Kinship is still essential, but it provides social cohesion *within* strata—kinship does not provide a basis for relations between members of lower and higher ranking strata.

The inscriptions amongst the buildings to the south of the city centre help to explain how the political system at Chichén Itzá worked. They do not talk of dynastic rulers and their great deeds, as in previous centuries. Instead they mention a number of individuals, with names such as "Kakupakal" or "Kokom," in connection with the dedication of buildings and other ceremonies, often concerned with the maintenance of sacred fires and the drilling of "new fire" on important occasions in the calendar. The glyph for sibling, *y-itah* is used to describe the relationship between these people, suggesting rule by "brothers." Some may indeed have been related in this way and Diego de Landa also talks of the tradition of "brothers" ruling at Chichén Itzá. But the phrase may best be interpreted to mean "companions" or individuals each of roughly equivalent status. They are accorded the title *ahaw*, but significantly none is termed *k'ul ahaw* or supreme, "divine lord." What this would seem to represent is rule by council, by the heads of different lineages. At the time of the Spanish Conquest some small city states still used the term *multepal*, best rendered as "'group rule," to describe what was probably a very similar system.[56]

The late method of rule at Chichén Itzá might be the most parallel to what we see among the Nephites, but the structures that allowed it had been in place for a long time. Many sites include a building known as a *popol nah*, or council house, which is recognized as a location where non-ruling elite lineages might meet.[57] The discovery of a Late Preclassic *popol nah* at Uaxactún places this type of government in precisely the time period of Mosiah$_2$'s shift to the rule of judges.[58]

The voice of the people worked itself out in lineages and representatives of lineages.[59] The council of elders was quite likely already present in Zarahemla, just as it was in other Mesoamerican locations. David Drew suggests that "all Maya kings in the Classic period appear to have ruled formally 'in council.'"[60]

What Mosiah$_2$ did was remove the top layer of political authority by abolishing the position of king. This act easily moved rule to the next functioning level, a process very likely followed by Chichén Itzá a millennium later. It did not require the creation of any new level of government or even concept of government. It exalted an existing structure to the next higher level.

Even in later political systems that retained a king, a substrate of auxiliary rulers continued. John M. D. Pohl notes: "It is clear that more than one bureaucratic organization, the paramountcy of kingship, is being portrayed in the codices. The four

---

[56] David Drew, *The Lost Chronicles of the Maya Kings*, 372.

[57] Lynne V. Foster, *Handbook to Life in the Ancient Maya World*, 123: "It is quite possible that the ruler was selected from any number of elite lineages rather than from a single royal dynasty. El Mirador may have been able to consolidate its authority by including members of the elite class from other cities. At Uaxactún, a *popol nah*, or what was known in the Terminal Classic Period as a council house, has been excavated, suggesting that the elites had an active role in governance at this time, not just the ruler."

[58] Ibid., 136–37.

[59] Drew, *The Lost Chronicles of the Maya Kings*, 324: "Local politics would differ from city to city, but one might presume that the *Popol Na*, the Council House, was a place of very real debate throughout the Classic period."

[60] Ibid., 243.

priests discussed here specifically conform to descriptions in the *Relación de Tilantongo* (discussing events from close to the time of the Conquest) and elsewhere of a body of judges who administered the realm for the king."[61]

Another interesting aspect of Lamanite and Nephite political organization was that succession was not always father to son. There were several occasions where the brother of the king became the next king. For example, when Amalickiah, a Lamanite king, was killed, his brother Ammon became the new king (Alma 52:2–3). Among the Nephites, we see a similar transfer of rights between brothers in the case of Amaron to Chemish (Omni 1:8) and Helaman$_2$ (son of Helaman$_1$) and his brother Shiblon (Alma 63:1), though they were record keepers rather than rulers. The transfer of power and/or authority from brother-to-brother while also retaining a father-to-son inheritance pattern in other cases is documented for Mesoamerica.[62] Thus this somewhat unexpected lateral transfer of power was an available model in Mesoamerica.

The Nephite Confederacy

The transformative events in Nephite religion and politics provide the undergirding for an understanding of the way multiple Nephite cities were beholden to Zarahemla. We find that: "There were seven churches in the land of Zarahemla" (Mosiah 25:23). These church organizations were attached to communities; therefore, at least seven cities or towns were somehow connected to the land of Zarahemla. One was Zarahemla itself and we may presume that two were faithful cities/lands ceded to the people of Alma$_1$ and the people of Limhi: Jershon and Gideon. When Alma$_2$ relinquishes the chief judge's seat, he travels to cities that were in potential rebellion: Ammonihah and Antionum.

The Old World model would suggest that Zarahemla was the capital city of a unified nation. The Book of Mormon evidence does not support that type of unified political organization. It is also beyond the textual evidence to posit Zarahemla as politically significant in its greater world.[63] There is no evidence that Zarahemla was one of the most important cities in its world. In fact, Mormon specifically notes that:

> Now there were not so many of the children of Nephi, or so many of those who were descendants of Nephi, as there were of the people of Zarahemla, who was a descendant of Mulek, and those who came with him into the wilderness.
>
> And there were not so many of the people of Nephi and of the people of Zarahemla as there were of the Lamanites; yea, they were not half so numerous. (Mosiah 25:2–3)

---

[61] John M. D. Pohl, "The Four Priests: Political Stability," 355–56.

[62] See Susan D. Gillespie, *The Aztec Kings: The Construction of Rulership in Mexica History*, 205; John L. Sorenson, *Mormon's Codex*, 366–67.

[63] Perhaps an analogy to the position of Jerusalem amidst the large powers of Assyrian, Babylon, and Egypt provides an idea of how a textually significant history might be historically of less importance. The analogy breaks down when the type of political structures of the Old World are compared to those of the New.

Not even among the more numerous Lamanites were there kingdoms comparable to the Old World models. Lynne V. Foster reminds us: "The ancient Maya were united by a shared ideology and worldview, but they never were unified into a single political state. There was no Maya empire comparable to ancient Rome; there was no single centralized authority equivalent to the Egyptian pharaoh. There were, instead, numerous substantial Maya cities, and many of these cities were independent polities. The challenge of the Mayanist has been to understand the sociopolitical nature of these cities and what, if any, relationship they had to one another."[64]

With such a diversity of political entities, it is not surprising that there should be a similar diversity of cultural traits, even among cities sharing the overall markers of a Mesoamerican culture. Mark Alan Wright explains: "Cultural diversity in Mesoamerica is evident even at the local level. It is not uncommon to find evidence for different ethnic groups residing in different barrios within a single city. . . . The diversity of material culture unearthed at Copan, Honduras, indicates that the kings ruled over a multiethnic population, a melting pot of cultures from the Maya heartland in the west to Central American cultures in the east."[65]

Among the Classic Maya (post–Book of Mormon), all political relationships appear to have been built upon fragile alliances that were inherently unstable.[66] With later political hegemonies built of such fragile alliances, we may look at earlier Book of Mormon politics for evidence that similar alliances informed Nephite government. The description of a loose and unstable alliance appears to be the best description of what we see in the Nephite political hegemony. In spite of king Benjamin's masterful speech that appeared to have created a new people under a new name, the old division between newer Nephite and older people of Zarahemla endured. When Mosiah$_2$ gathered his people together to hear the stories of the new immigrants (the people of Limhi and of Alma$_1$), "All the people of Nephi were assembled together, and also all the people of Zarahemla, and they were gathered together in two bodies" (Mosiah 25:4).

With so little unity inside the city of Zarahemla, we are not surprised to see some disunity among the cities that form the land of Zarahemla. The very fact that Mosiah$_2$ has Alma$_1$ establish churches tells us that there was no clear unity of religious/political belief in the region. Ancient religion and political understandings had such a close relationship as to be virtually inseparable. Nevertheless, we see them becoming separate in the land of Zarahemla. That very fact should alert us to the lack of unity in the region. That lack of unity becomes evident near the end of the first decade of the rule of judges:

> And it came to pass in the commencement of the ninth year, Alma saw the wickedness of the church, and he saw also that the example of the church began to lead those who were unbelievers on from one piece of iniquity to another, thus bringing on the destruction of the people.

---

[64] Foster, *Handbook to Life in the Ancient Maya World*, 121. Also Mark Alan Wright, "The Cultural Tapestry of Mesoamerica," 7.

[65] Wright, "The Cultural Tapestry of Mesoamerica," 11.

[66] Foster, *Handbook to Life in the Ancient Maya World*, 123.

A New Covenant Made, then Unmade 255

> Yea, he saw great inequality among the people, some lifting themselves up with their pride, despising others, turning their backs upon the needy and the naked and those who were hungry, and those who were athirst, and those who were sick and afflicted. (Alma 4:11–12)

The Nephite political and religious ideal was always egalitarian. Any indication that there were some who were lifting themselves above one another points to both apostasy and political dissent in the Book of Mormon.[67] With the close connection between religion and politics, political dissent in the Book of Mormon never lags far behind the religious differences. Most telling, then, is Alma$_2$'s reaction to this potentially politically disruptive schism. He does not call out the army but resigns as chief judge so he can go on a personal mission to call people to repentance (Alma 4:16–19).[68]

The complicated nature of the relationships among the dependent cities is most apparent when Alma$_2$ reaches Ammonihah, only to encounter sneers from the people:

> Behold, we know that thou art Alma; and we know that thou art high priest over the church which thou hast established in many parts of the land, according to your tradition; and we are not of thy church, and we do not believe in such foolish traditions.
>
> And now we know that because we are not of thy church we know that thou hast no power over us; and thou hast delivered up the judgment-seat unto Nephihah; therefore thou art not the chief judge over us. (Alma 8:11–12)

Ammonihah recognizes some relationship to Zarahemla because they note that Alma$_2$ is no longer the chief judge. However, they do not recognize any religious connection to Zarahemla. In a world where religion and politics were completely intertwined, this description should warn us, not only of a division in religion, but also of a divisibility in political systems. There was no complete dependency upon Zarahemla.[69]

---

[67] Gardner, *Second Witness*, 4:46–48.

[68] John E. Kammeyer, *The Nephite Art of War*, 57 of PDF version, sees the same type of political system as I am suggesting:

> There is enough evidence to show the Lamanites were a Mesoamerican "hegemonical" empire, a core population group ruling their tributaries by influence rather than direct force. The Lamanite kings ruled not by the voice of the people but rather by the respect their princes held for them, and the fear held by their subjects and tributaries.
>
> And thus we see that the patterns of pre-Columbian imperial expansion recorded by the Spanish can be identified as far back as Book of Mormon times. Neither Nephites nor Lamanites could rule by force. Instead, they ruled by influence, the one by the threat of force and the other by the influence of common culture and religion.

[69] My analysis of the nature of the Zarahemla confederacy differs dramatically from Sorenson's discussion. Sorenson discusses Zarahemla as the head of a state-level political organization. John L. Sorenson, *Mormon's Codex*, 363–65. The strongest evidence he provides is the appointment of Chief Captain Moroni as the military commander for the whole of the Zarahemla confederacy. "This sort of sociopolitical complexity likely would not happen in a government at the lesser, chiefdom level: Nephite rule was undoubtedly of the state type at that moment" (p. 364). In spite of that firm statement, the emerging data on known important

It is significant that Alma$_2$ never used an army to attempt to quell the religious (and potentially political) dissent in the dependent cities.[70] Simon Martin and Nikolai Grube note of the Classic Maya: "Political expansion, where it occurred, was not an acquisition of territory per se, but rather an extension of these elite networks. The most powerful dynasties brought rival 'divine lords' under their domination, with ties often reaching far outside their immediate region. The bonds between lords and their masters were highly personal and remained in effect even after the death of one party. But whether cemented by oaths of loyalty or marital unions they were, in practice, rather tenuous and more reliant on military threat and the benefits available to subject lords."[71] The lack of military force in such an important endeavor (designed to hold together the fragile alliances) underscores the difference between the Zarahemlaite political hegemony and the later Maya over-kings.

Archaeologically, the Grijalva River Valley never had the obviously centralized city-states as the lowland Maya region—the relatively flat region of the Petén which does not appear to have ever been directly mentioned in the Book of Mormon. Nevertheless, even in those larger regions, it appears that alliances were often quite fragile. Foster tells us: "The nature of Maya dynastic rulership did seem to encourage the autonomy of many cities rather than their integration into a single, more powerful and enduring polity. And the smaller Late Classic cities, with their strong separate identities, shifted alliances from one great power to the next, as proven by Quiriguá's temporary alliance with Calakmul against Copán. Fragmentation, economic competition, and warfare were very often the result of this instability."[72] The best model for understanding the political system in the land of Zarahemla is one of a loose confederacy of convenience and trade.

Maya hegemonies suggests that state is the wrong designation for this type of government, and Maya cities as center places were able to muster large armies without other indications of state-level political organization. It is certain that we are speaking of something more than simple chiefdoms, but the data from the Maya strongly suggest that there are other political types between the chiefdom and state options.

[70] When the Amlicites rebelled against the word of the people, civil war ensued. The use of the military was against a military threat rather than to quell dissent prior to the point when it devolved into war. See Alma 2:7–15.

[71] Simon Martin and Nikolai Grube, *Chronicle of the Maya Kings and Queens: Deciphering the Dynasties of the Ancient Maya*, 20.

[72] Foster, *Handbook of Life in the Ancient Maya World*, 136.

10

The Cultural Context of Nephite Apostasy

Mark Alan Wright and Brant A. Gardner[1]

Nephite religion was an Old World import into the New World. The presence of the brass plates provided a touchstone to maintain the boundaries of Hebrew religion in a world where it was both a new and unique system of belief. In spite of the general Nephite faithfulness to the religion as recorded on the brass plates, very early on challenges emerged to keeping Nephite practices and beliefs pure. Jarom noted:

> Behold, it is expedient that much should be done among this people, because of the hardness of their hearts, and the deafness of their ears, and the blindness of their minds, and the stiffness of their necks; nevertheless, God is exceedingly merciful unto them, and has not as yet swept them off from the face of the land.
>
> And there are many among us who have many revelations, for they are not all stiffnecked. And as many as are not stiffnecked and have faith, have communion with the Holy Spirit, which maketh manifest unto the children of men, according to their faith. (Jarom 1:3–4)

Of course, even Old World Israelite religion was characterized by frequent call to repentance. Prophets repeated summoned Israel to return from a specific type of apostasy—the acceptance of practices and/or gods of another religion. A common report of Israelite apostasy is found in Judges 2:13: "And they forsook the Lord, and served Baal and Ashtaroth."[2] Israelite apostasy typically occurred when Israel

---

[1] This section is a slight reworking of Mark Alan Wright and Brant A. Gardner, "The Cultural Context of Nephite Apostasy," 25–55, published in 2012. (See Bibliography.) I have modified the introduction and made other changes to better fit the context of this book. Mark Wright's ideas have not been altered. I appreciate his permission to present our collaborative work in this chapter.

[2] See also, among others, Judges 2:11; 3:7; 6:25, 30; 8:33; 10:6–10; 1 Samuel 7:3–4; 12:10; 1 Kings 16:31–32; 18:18–6; 22:53; 2 Kings 3:2; 10:18–28; 11:18; 17:16; 21:3–5; Jeremiah 2:23; 7:9; Hosea 2:8; and Zephaniah 1:4.

embraced certain religious and cultural elements from a nearby people with whom they shared similar traits, merging them with their own.[3]

The opportunity for similar mergers with surrounding culture were constantly available, but Nephites in Zarahemla need look no further than outside their city. The combination of Nephite brass plate religion with plausible Mesoamerican beliefs that the people of Nephi had adopted created a crucible in which predictable attempts occurred to reconcile the two religious heritages. Evidence of the clash came in the form of false Christs (W of M 1:15–16) which created the religious crisis that preceded Benjamin's sermon.

King Benjamin's masterful discourse created a temporary healing unification of the people of Zarahemla under one God, one name. However, that does not mean that all internal religious pressures faded forever. We hear of the rise of another significant Nephite apostasy just a generation later. Mormon calls it the religion of the Nehors, and it was so serious that Alma$_2$ resigned as the leader of the people to devote his time to preaching repentance (Alma 4:10–19).

The word *apostasy* never appears in the Book of Mormon, but the process is described throughout the text by expressions such as "dwindling in unbelief" (occurring in some form twenty-six times) or being in "open rebellion against God" (occurring in some form fifteen times). It is important to recognize that individual apostasy in the ancient world was more dangerous than our contemporary versions. In many parts of the modern world, one may turn away from the teachings of a particular church yet remain a solid member of society. Such compartmentalization was inconceivable in the ancient world: religion, politics, economics, and even culture were thoroughly intertwined. As Bruce J. Malina and Richard Rohrbaugh note: "Our new social arrangements, with the separation of religion and economics from kinship and politics, would have been inconceivable to [biblical authors and their primary audiences]. In fact, the separation of church and state, and of economics and state, are truly radical and unthinkable departures from what ha[d] heretofore been normal on the planet."[4]

This complicated interaction of socioreligious elements may help explain why Nephite apostasy often led to intense social and political divisions and even to armed rebellion or civil war. The seriousness of Nephite apostasy suggests a need to better understand how it occurred and why it so often resulted in violent upheavals.

Elements of Nephite Apostasy

Descriptions of Nephite apostasy remain remarkably consistent throughout that people's thousand-year history. Daniel C. Peterson has noted that "common factors

---

[3] See, for example, Mark S. Smith, *The Origins of Biblical Monotheism, Israel's Polytheistic Background and the Ugaritic Texts*, and William G. Dever, *Did God Have a Wife? Archaeology and Folk Religion in Ancient Israel*.

[4] Bruce J. Malina and Richard L. Rohrbaugh, *Social-Science Commentary on the Gospel of John*, 1. See also the brief description of the same idea in Marcus J. Borg, *Reading the Bible Again for the First Time: Taking the Bible Seriously but Not Literally*, 245.

The Cultural Context of Nephite Apostasy 259

repeatedly spoken of in the Book of Mormon that lure people into apostasy include (1) pride and the quest for status . . . ; (2) an exaggerated trust in human learning or wisdom . . . ; and (3) material wealth/prosperity and ease."[5] The most complete summary of apostasy is found in how Alma$_2$ describes the religion to which he attaches Nehor's name:

> And he [Nehor] had gone about among the people, preaching to them that which he termed to be the word of God, bearing down against the church; declaring unto the people that every priest and teacher ought to become popular; and they ought not to labor with their hands, but that they ought to be supported by the people.
>
> And he also testified unto the people that all mankind should be saved at the last day, and that they need not fear nor tremble, but that they might lift up their heads and rejoice; for the Lord had created all men, and had also redeemed all men; and, in the end, all men should have eternal life.
>
> And it came to pass that he did teach these things so much that many did believe on his words, even so many that they began to support him and give him money.
>
> And he began to be lifted up in the pride of his heart, and to wear very costly apparel, yea, and even began to establish a church after the manner of his preaching. (Alma 1:3–6)

These verses contain what Mormon believed were the essential elements of the order of the Nehors. These elements appear as the common descriptions of virtually all Nephite apostasies.[6] They usually appear in this order:

- Nehor claims he preaches "the word of God." Nehorism appears to maintain a connection to the "brass plates" Israelite religion, though clearly "looking beyond the mark" (Jacob 4:14).
- Nehor emphasizes a different role for priests. They "ought to be supported by the people" rather than laboring to support themselves. This endorsement of social hierarchies blatantly rejects of equality.
- All are saved and redeemed and will have eternal life (i.e., there is no need for an atoning Messiah).
- A manifestation of Nehor's social and religious position was the wearing of "very costly apparel."

Cultural Manifestations of Apostasy

Although Alma$_2$ describes the religion Nehor preached, many elements of this religion were manifested in social or cultural traits that the modern mind might separate from religion. For example, moderns might quite naturally ascribe the wearing of "very

---

[5] Daniel C. Peterson, "Apostasy," 69.
[6] Although Alma$_2$ discusses an "order of Nehor" / "order of the Nehors" (Alma 14:16, 21:4, 24:29, 24:28), the same traits can be identified among the priests of king Noah. For a more detailed discussion of the characteristics and spread of this apostate religious/political/economic system, see Brant A. Gardner, *Second Witness: Analytical and Contextual Commentary on the Book of Mormon*, 4:41–51.

costly apparel" to a cultural norm, whereas Alma$_2$ saw it as a sign of apostasy.[7] The earliest occurrences of Nephite apostasy as recorded by Jacob prompted similar concerns: "The hand of providence hath smiled upon you most pleasingly, that you have obtained many riches; and because some of you have obtained more abundantly than that of your brethren ye are lifted up in *the pride of your hearts*, and wear stiff necks and high heads because of the *costliness of your apparel*, and persecute your brethren because *ye suppose that ye are better than they*" (Jacob 2:13).

Jacob specifically condemns those who imagine they are better than those who do not wear costly apparel. This tendency toward social segregation was probably much more economic in nature than religious at that early point.[8] However, it becomes clear after the Nephites relocate to Zarahemla that such economic pressures gave rise not only to social stratification but also to changes in Zarahemla's religious climate. The political and religious unity that king Benjamin achieved (Mosiah 4:12–16, 5:5–10) had sufficiently disintegrated during Alma$_2$'s tenure as the chief judge that he had to relinquish the judgment seat to spend all of his time in missionary efforts among fellow Nephites (Alma 4:6–19).

Two interrelated additions to the catalog of apostate ideas appear late in the book of Mosiah: a desire for a particular kind of king and a denial of the existence and mission of the heavenly king, Jesus Christ. The desire for a king was not inherently apostate. Indeed, king Mosiah$_2$ affirmed, "If it were possible that ye could always have just men to be your kings it would be well for you to have a king" (Mosiah 23:8). In the Book of Mormon, righteous kings sought to bring their people closer to Yahweh. Jarom rejoiced that "our kings and our leaders were mighty men in the faith of the Lord; and they taught the people the ways of the Lord" (Jarom 1:7). In contrast, unrighteous kings led their people away from correct beliefs and practices. The story of king Noah is the earliest manifestation of this particular type of apostasy in the Book of Mormon. Noah attacked the egalitarian ideals king Benjamin had espoused and modeled (Mosiah 2:14). King Noah's priests espoused a version of what might be called "brass plates religion," but they also quite clearly denied the atoning Messiah.[9]

The connection between apostasy in Zarahemla and the Nehorites' desire for a king begins early in the book of Alma:

> And it came to pass in the commencement of the fifth year of their reign there began to be a contention among the people; for a certain man, being called Amlici, he being a

---

[7] Ibid., 6:257–58, discusses costly apparel as a general sign of apostasy signaling a shift in social and economic patterns.

[8] Brant A. Gardner, "A Social History of the Early Nephites."

[9] While it is not clear from Alma's brief synopsis, Nehorite religion appears to have maintained belief in some aspects of the Mosaic law. During Alma$_2$'s discourse to the Ammonihahites, he pointedly remarked, "The scriptures are before you" (Alma 13:20). Unless the people of Ammonihah believed in those scriptures, Alma$_2$'s admonition makes no sense. Further, the Ammonihahite demand to hear more than one person declare Alma$_2$'s message may be related to the Deuteronomic law of witnesses (Deut. 19:15). The most obvious instance of Nehorite believers accepting the law of Moses comes from Noah's priests, who declared, "We teach the law of Moses" (Mosiah 12:28).

very cunning man, yea, a wise man as to the wisdom of the world, he being after the order of the man that slew Gideon by the sword, who was executed according to the law—
Now this Amlici had, by his cunning, drawn away much people after him; even so much that they began to be very powerful; and they began to endeavor to establish Amlici to be a king over the people. (Alma 2:1–2)

Syncretization of Nephite Beliefs

Until recently, we lacked the ability to trace the cultural influences that created Nephite apostasy in the same way that we could see how the Canaanite religion influenced Israelite apostasy. New information about the plausible location of the Book of Mormon in the New World opens the possibility of tracing the ways in which Mesoamerican religion served as the model for Nephite apostasy.[10] Important to our understanding of Nephite apostasy is the realization that, when Lehi and his family landed in the New World, they found other peoples in the land. Abundant evidence from the archaeological record attests that the New World was inhabited long before Lehi's colony arrived, including the Mesoamerican region.[11] Though the authors of the Book of Mormon do not explicitly discuss the preexisting populations they encountered, they do provide clues about their presence.[12] This suggestion, while novel to some, is certainly not new. Matthew Roper notes: "Many Latter-day Saints over the years, including a number of church leaders, have acknowledged the likelihood that before, during, and following the events recounted in the Book of Mormon, the American hemisphere has been visited and inhabited by nations, kindreds, tongues, and peoples not mentioned in the text. They also concede that these groups may have significantly impacted the populations of the Americas genetically, culturally, linguistically, and in many other ways."[13]

As with the Israelite acculturation to the cults of Baal and Asherah, the New World Nephites also became acculturated to aspects of the prevailing Mesoamerican cults.[14] The process of combining elements from different religions into a new religion is known as syncretism. Syncretism occurs when different beliefs are seen to have

---

[10] John L. Sorenson, *An Ancient American Setting for the Book of Mormon*; Lawrence Poulsen, "Lawrence Poulsen's Book of Mormon Geography." While their geographies differ in some aspects, Sorenson and Poulsen agree on the essential culture areas where Nephite history would have taken place.

[11] Frederick Joseph Bové, *The Evolution of Chiefdoms and States on the Pacific Slope of Guatemala: A Spatial Analysis*, 302.

[12] John L. Sorenson, *Nephite Culture and Society*, 65–104. See also Matthew Roper, "Nephi's Neighbors: Book of Mormon Peoples and Pre-Columbian Populations," 91–128; and James E. Smith, "Nephi's Descendants? Historical Demography and the Book of Mormon," 255–96.

[13] Roper, "Nephi's Neighbors," 127.

[14] *Cult* is here defined in the anthropological sense as a system of religious veneration and devotion directed toward a particular figure or object.

sufficient similarities to bridge the differences.¹⁵ The process begins with the ability to accept and merge different ideas into one's worldview and becomes formalized when a sufficient number of people come to accept the same amalgam. In that case, a new cult is created that merges elements from the two different systems. How did Nephite apostates manage to form a new religion by combining two systems of belief that modern readers would find totally incompatible? They were able to see similarities where we see only irreconcilable differences, just as their distant descendants were able to syncretize their pagan religion with the Spaniards' Roman Catholicism.¹⁶ Mesoamerican scholar Michael E. Smith describes that process:

> The Nahuas [i.e., the indigenous peoples of Mexico, also referred to as Aztecs] did not have the concept of a "faith" or "religion" as a domain separable from the rest of culture, and their new religion is best seen as a syncretism or blend of Aztec beliefs and Christian beliefs. Conversion involved the adoption of essential Christian rites and practices while the basic mind set remained that of traditional Nahua culture. Rather than passively accepting a completely new and foreign religion, people created their own adaptation of Christianity, compatible with their colonial situation and with many of their traditional beliefs and values.¹⁷

We propose that certain Nephite beliefs and practices were syncretized with those of the surrounding native cultures, analogous to what would happen well over one thousand years later in the aftermath of the Spanish conquest of Mesoamerica. As we examine the potential perceptual similarities between Nephite and Mesoamerican religion, it is important to bear in mind that we are not describing normative Nephite religion but, rather, the ways in which those perceived similarities accommodated apostate Nephite religion.

We are not suggesting that syncretism manifests himself and His will to the faithful according to the cultural context in which they find themselves.¹⁸ Our concern here is with those cultural borrowings that allow some to distort truth and lead people away from correct beliefs and proper worship. *Apostasy* (from the Greek *apostasia*) literally means "defection" or "revolt" and typically refers to the renunciation of a religious or political belief system.

---

¹⁵ Michio Kitahara, "A Formal Model of Syncretism in Scales," 121–22. Kitahara provides a model of five elements underlying syncretism. While his model is given in the context of syncretism in music, the concepts hold for any two disparate systems that merge to create a third system.

¹⁶ *Pagan* is a blanket term referring to polytheistic, non-Abrahamic religions.

¹⁷ Michael E. Smith, *The Aztecs*, 284. See also Enrique Florescano, *Memory, Myth, and Time in Mexico: From the Aztecs to Independence*, 114. The conversion of European pagans to Christianity followed an analogous syncretic path. See Lewis R. Rambo, *Understanding Religious Conversion*, 77: "Conversion of European peoples [to Christianity] did not involve the complete rejection of pagan religious practices; more often than not it brought about a blending of those elements into the new religion."

¹⁸ Mark Alan Wright, "'According to Their Language, Unto Their Understanding': The Cultural Context of Hierophanies and Theophanies in Latter-day Saint Canon," 51–65.

Bridging the Nature of God

Syncretizing Nephite and Mesoamerican religions had to deal with concepts of deity. On this most fundamental point, modern monotheists would see tremendous differences with the Mesoamerican polytheists, but there were sufficient perceived similarities that the Nephite explanation of Deity could accommodate, or be accommodated to, Mesoamerican ideas about the nature of the divine.

Although the Nephites cannot be equated with the Maya, Maya culture was already widespread in Mesoamerica in the Preclassic period (400 B.C.–A.D. 250) and appears to have exerted great influence on surrounding cultures.[19] We have the best data for this culture, thanks to the preponderance of carved stone monuments and ceramic vessels painted with historical and mythological scenes and texts that have been preserved archaeologically. As plausibly influential neighbors of the Nephites, the Maya exemplify the kind of religious ideas to which some Nephites accommodated. Though certainly not homogenous, Maya beliefs and practices bear fundamental similarities to other Mesoamerican cultures and therefore exemplify the points of congruence along which our proposed syncretism occurred.[20]

Maya scholars use *god* and *deity* interchangeably in their scholarly literature. The problem with the terminology is that our modern ideas of "god" and "deity" may not replicate the Maya notion of "supernatural sentient beings that appear in sacred narrative."[21] Maya scholars Stephen Houston and David Stuart lament a scholarly ethnocentrism that has hindered understanding of Classic Period Maya deities. They argue that the Western conception of gods as perfect, immortal, and discrete beings is not applicable to the Mesoamerican pantheon.[22] Gabrielle Vail's assessment of the Postclassic Maya (A.D. 900–1521) representations of gods found in their bark-paper books can usefully be applied to the earlier Classic depictions of gods found on ceramics and monuments: "The picture that emerges is one of a series of deity complexes or clusters, composed of a small number of underlying divinities, each having various aspects, or manifestations."[23] Vail argues that in a "deity complex," a variety of distinctive gods could be lumped together into a single category, predicated on a core cluster of bodily features or costume elements. Conversely, a single god could be represented with a variety of differing characteristics or manifestations. Their names, attributes, and domains of influence were fluid, yet they retained their individual identity. Each of the elaborations that a modern reader might see as a different deity was actually considered to be merely an elaboration of the complex essence of one particular deity.

---

[19] Francisco Estrada Belli, *The First Maya Civilization*, 61–63.
[20] Lars Kirkhusmo Pharo, "The Concept of 'Religion' in Mesoamerican Languages," 28–70.
[21] Karl Taube, *The Major Gods of Ancient Yucatan*, 8. This definition, evoked several times in this chapter, is a key insight for drawing comparisons to the Book of Mormon.
[22] Stephen D. Houston and David Stuart, "Of Gods, Glyphs, and Kings: Divinity and Rulership among the Classic Maya," 290.
[23] Gabrielle Vail, "Pre-Hispanic Maya Religion," 123.

Although not precisely the same concept, Nephite religion understood a proliferation of "names" for the Messiah. For example, Isaiah declares that "his name shall be called Wonderful, Counsellor, The mighty God, The everlasting Father, The Prince of Peace" (Isa, 9:6; 2 Ne. 19:6). Each of these names proclaims a different quality, yet all apply to the same God. The Maya deity complexes similarly expanded the qualities of the underlying deity, albeit with a more complete elaboration than just a name.

An example from the modern Ch'orti', a designation for a Maya people and language, demonstrates how this Mesoamerican deity complex expands the names and manifestations of an underlying deity according to different conditions. One particular god manifests itself as a solar being during the dry season but transforms into a maize spirit during the rainy season.[24] Even as a solar deity, it has multiple manifestations throughout the course of a single day that also demonstrate syncretism with Christian ideals: "They say that the sun has not just one name. The one which is best known by people continues to be Jesus Christ. They say that when it is just getting light its name is Child Redeemer of the World. One name is San Gregorio the Illuminator. One name is San Antonio of Judgment. One name is Child Guardian. One is Child Refuge. One is Child San Pascual. One is Child Succor. One is Child Creator. They say that at each hour, one of these is its name."[25]

Although it is foreign to the way we understand our Christian tradition, a people who lived in the context of a world that saw manifestations of the divine in deity complexes might easily reenvision the Nephite God (with multiple names) as a deity complex, being composed of distinctive manifestations in different circumstances. For example, God the Father and Christ the Son are considered "one Eternal God" (Alma 11:44). From a syncretic perspective, the Book of Mormon can be read as teaching that each deity had his own identity and at times was described by different manifestations. When the text declares, "Behold, I am Jesus Christ. I am the Father and the Son" (Ether 3:14), the syncretist might easily interpret it as a deity complex. Abinadi's explanation in Mosiah 15 of how Christ is both the Father and the Son could also be read as an example of multiple manifestations of a single deity:

> And because he dwelleth in flesh he shall be called the Son of God, and having subjected the flesh to the will of the Father, being the Father and the Son—
>
> The Father, because he was conceived by the power of God; and the Son, because of the flesh; thus becoming the Father and Son—
>
> And they are one God, yea, the very Eternal Father of heaven and of earth.
>
> And thus the flesh becoming subject to the Spirit, or the Son to the Father, being one God, suffereth temptation, and yieldeth not to the temptation, but suffereth himself to be mocked, and scourged, and cast out, and disowned by his people. . . .
>
> Yea, even so he shall be led, crucified, and slain, the flesh becoming subject even unto death, the will of the Son being swallowed up in the will of the Father. (Mosiah 15:2–5, 7)

---

[24] Rafael Girard, *People of the Chan*, 350.
[25] John G. Fought, *Chorti (Mayan) Texts*, 485. Among the Ch'orti', San Antonio is the fire god, San Gregorio emits beams of light, and San Pascual is Venus as morning star.

Once a Nephite apostate accommodated the idea of a deity complex, that concept could easily be read into the scriptural tradition, and the Nephite God of many names could be reinterpreted in much more fluid Mesoamerican terms. Such a syncretic perspective would reread descriptions of God as differing manifestations, such as a creator deity (Jacob 2:5), a destroyer (3 Ne. 9), a rain god (Ether 9:35), a god of agricultural fertility (Alma 34:24), a solar deity (1 Ne. 1:9; Hel. 14:4, 20), a fire god (1 Ne. 1:6; Hel. 13:13), a king (Mosiah 2:19), a god of medicine (Alma 46:40), a shepherd (Alma 5:38), a lamb (1 Ne. 14), and even a rock (Hel. 5:12). Clearly, some of these manifestations are metaphorical in their appropriate context, but the ancient Maya similarly used rich metaphorical language, and they often used visual metaphors in their art. In an apostate/syncretic mind-set, the metaphor shifted to express a different underlying meaning.[26]

Bridging Heavenly Expectations

A similar recasting of Book of Mormon theology can link the future goal of both Nephite and Mesoamerican religion. Just as the concept of a deity complex could tie together Mesoamerican and Nephite ideas about God, so could perceived similarities in the nature of the afterlife create another syncretic thread. The early Nephite declaration of a king allowed for a direct point of parallelism with surrounding cultures that similarly proclaimed a king. Apostate Nephite religion accepted a king who was modeled after Mesoamerican ideals of what a king was and did.

Classic-period rulers considered themselves holy, but they never explicitly claimed they were gods during their lifetimes.[27] After death, however, kings were clearly venerated and eventually were apotheosized as deities, merging with one of the gods.[28] Although rulers were apotheosized as a variety of deities, the maize god and sun god seem to have been the most popular choices because they were both linked to cycles of birth, life, death, and resurrection—the sun in its daily journey and maize in its seasons of planting and harvest.

Perhaps the best-known example of apotheosis as the maize god among the ancient Maya comes from Pakal's sarcophagus at the site of Palenque. The scene depicts Pakal's simultaneous descent into the jaws of the underworld and his resurrection as the maize god. A beautiful example of deification occurs as the sun god comes from the Rosalila temple, which was built to honor K'inich Yax K'uk Mo', the founder of the Copan dynasty. The artist plays with multiple themes to this god's development toward deity status. In addition to this visual sign, the artist included visual puns to identify this particular emerging ancestor as K'inich Yax K'uk Mo'. The head of the sun god (*K'inich*) is shown emerging from the mouths of serpent-winged birds, which are marked with features of both quetzal birds (*k'uk'*) and macaws (*mo'*).

---

[26] Kerry M. Hull, *Verbal Art and Performance in Ch'orti' and Maya Hieroglyphic Writing*, 337.
[27] Houston and Stuart, "Of Gods, Glyphs, and Kings," 296.
[28] Mary Miller and Karl Taube, *An Illustrated Dictionary of the Gods and Symbols of Ancient Mexico and the Maya*, 76.

The imagery not only visually depicts the name K'inich Yax K'uk' Mo' but also conveys the message that he had merged with—and had therefore been apotheosized after his death as—the sun god.

Apostate Nephites would see a parallel in a similar expectation of apotheosis after death: "And for this cause ye shall have fulness of joy; and ye shall sit down in the kingdom of my Father; yea, your joy shall be full, even as the Father hath given me fulness of joy; and *ye shall be even as I am, and I am even as the Father; and the Father and I are one*" (3 Ne. 28:10). The ancient Maya kings expected to be merged with the sun and/or maize gods—gods of death and rebirth. The Nephite apostates would draw a parallel expectation of being merged with the resurrecting Christ and the Father.

The Nephite heaven was "a place where God dwells and all his holy angels. . . . He looketh down upon all the children of men; and he knows all the thoughts and intents of the heart; for by his hand were they all created from the beginning" (Alma 18:30, 32). The ancient Maya parallel associated the sky with the glorious celestial realm and frequently depicted deified ancestors looking down from the skyband, or heavens. For example, on Tikal Stela 31 the deceased Yax Nuun Ahiin takes on the form of the ancestral sun god as he overlooks his son, Sihyaj Chan K'awiil II.[29] This Mesoamerican practice of depicting ancestors or gods overseeing the affairs of the earth from the heavens has its origins in Olmec art.[30]

The celestial paradise that Mesoamerican rulers hoped for has been termed "Flower Mountain" by scholars because it is portrayed in the iconography as a place lush with plant and animal life.[31] Flower Mountain is depicted in Maya art as both the paradise of creation and origin as well as the desired destination after a ruler's death, where he would be deified as the sun god. Evidence for the belief in Flower Mountain dates to the Middle Formative Olmec (900–400 B.C.), and is attested among the Late Preclassic and Classic Maya as well (300 B.C.–AD 900).[32] Maya scholar Karl Taube argues that, "although the notion of a floral paradise recalls Christian ideals of the original Garden of Eden and the afterlife, the solar component is wholly Mesoamerican."[33] To Nephites, however, that solar component would have resonated with their beliefs about Christ. Alma alluded to the correlation between Christ's celestial glory and the radiance of the sun when he stated, "Behold the glory of the King of all the earth; and also the King of heaven shall very soon *shine forth* among all the children of men" (Alma 5:50). He later uses the same language to liken the state of the faithful unto Christ after their resurrection: "then shall the righteous *shine forth* in the kingdom of God" (Alma 40:25).

---

[29] Simon Martin and Nikolai Grube, *Chronicle of the Maya Kings and Queens: Deciphering the Dynasties of the Ancient Maya*, 34–35.

[30] Ibid., 26.

[31] Jane H. Hill, "The Flower World of Old Uto-Aztecan." Similar imagery is also found among ancient and modern southwestern Native American tribes, and scholars refer to it as "Flower World."

[32] Karl A. Taube, "Flower Mountain: Concepts of Life, Beauty, and Paradise among the Classic Maya," 69.

[33] Ibid., 70.

Only minimal recontextualization of Book of Mormon categories is required to make them resemble the Mesoamerican worldview (and vice versa). All these points of perceptual parallelism in Nephite and Mesoamerican theology could have provided an adequate basis for the emergence of a syncretic religion. If so, the foundational elements of the Nephite apostasy were in place and would have facilitated the acceptance of the principal element of Mesoamerican theology, one that had the greatest impact on Nephite history—the Mesoamerican divine king.

The Divine King Replaces the Heavenly King

As was true for the vast majority of ancient civilizations, ancient Maya kings were linked to the supernatural realm and were believed to have divinely sanctioned authority.[34] By the Classic period (A.D. 250–900), virtually all rulers of large polities held the title *k'uhul ajaw*, which has been variously translated as "holy," "sacred," or "divine" lord.[35] Among Mesoamericanists, the issue of how "divine" these rulers actually were is still a matter of debate, but it is clear that, during certain rituals, they stood as intermediaries who bridged the gap between the natural and supernatural realms. The rulers often depicted themselves in communion with deities and emphasized their special role as intermediaries between the human and the divine realms.[36]

For the ancient Maya, the right to rule came by descent from the gods, but typically these gods were historical ancestors who became gods only after their deaths. On Altar Q from Copan, we see a literal passing of the torch of rulership from K'inich Yax K'uk Mo, the dynasty's long-dead but apotheosized ancestor, to the sixteenth ruler, Yax Pasaj Chan Yoaat. By claiming descent from a deified ancestor, a king endowed himself with a portion of his ancestor's divinity through birthright, and his legitimacy as ruler thus became firmly established in the mind of the people.[37] Nephite rulers similarly traced their right to rule through their lineages, albeit to an honored rather than deified ancestor. Nevertheless, the similarity of the genealogical component is a parallel concept that allowed for syncretism.

King Benjamin did not rehearse his own genealogy back to a prominent apotheosized ruler, but he did declare that all of his people were descended from the "heavenly King" (Mosiah 2:19). In addition, they had become "children of Christ, his sons, and his daughters; for behold, this day he hath spiritually begotten you" (Mosiah 5:7). Benjamin, as representative of his people, might have been seen as claiming a connection with the heavenly king, as could his entire people (who were about to make a covenant with God).

Perhaps at least the Mesoamerican idea of tracing one's lineage to a dynastic founder is easily set parallel to Book of Mormon practice. Lamoni traced his genealogy back to Ishmael (Alma 17:21), king Ammoron (Alma 52:3) traced his genealogy back

---

[34] Houston and Stuart, "Of Gods, Glyphs, and Kings," 289.
[35] Ibid., 307–8.
[36] Julia L. J. Sanchez, "Ancient Maya Royal Strategies: Creating Power and Identity through Art," 264.
[37] Houston and Stuart, "Of Gods, Glyphs, and Kings," 290.

to Zoram (Alma 54:23), and among the Nephites "the kingdom had been conferred upon none but those who were descendants of Nephi" (Mosiah 25:13). Zarahemla, a descendant of Mulek, who had even tighter links to indigenous Mesoamerican ideas, claimed links back to Zedekiah of Judah (Omni 1:15–18). Even after the institution of kingship was eliminated, many of the chief judges who sat in rulership were Nephi's descendants ($Alma_2$, $Helaman_2$, $Nephi_3$). Even Nephi, the first king among his people, is careful to tell us he is a son of Lehi, who is a descendant of Joseph, ruler over Egypt (1 Ne. 5:14). Among the Jaredites, Ether traced his genealogy through nearly thirty predecessors back to Jared, their dynastic founder (Ether 1). Because Israel was also patriarchal, the idea of transmitting rights through lineage was firmly established as part of early Israel's cultural tradition, and this practice seems to have continued in the New World.

We are not suggesting that either the Israelite or Mesoamerican tradition of lineage-based authority influenced the other to develop the concept. The idea was sufficiently widespread in the ancient world that it was clearly the result of multiple instances of independent invention. However, where the Nephites and native Mesoamericans were two otherwise disparate cultures, sharing that concept of lineage-based authority provided a point of similarity conducive to syncretism. The Nephite genealogical principle could easily have acquired the more mythological Mesoamerican overtones.

The King, Ritual, and the Replacement of the Messianic Expectation

Two things combined to create the most dangerous instances of Nephite apostasy. The first was the notion of the divine king, and the second was the communal rituals by which that king's place in the community and universe was made real. We have examined some of the ideas and related ideological parallels that possibly underlay the apostate Nephites' creation of a new, syncretized religion. What we have yet to understand is how that syncretism took place and why the syncretic religion took the specific form of denying the Nephite God—Yahweh being understood as the heavenly manifestation who would become the atoning Messiah in an earthly manifestation (Mosiah 3–4).[38] We suggest that it was the didactic nature of ritual that created both the focal point and indoctrination method for the religious change.

The Nephite community's background in the law of Moses necessarily provided an expectation of certain types of communal ritual. The Book of Mormon clearly describes temples as focal points of Nephite communal life, being the location for speeches, sacrifices, and eventually the sacred appearance of their God in their midst. In these communal rituals, the Nephites shared common traits with most state-level societies. Anthropologist William Y. Adams notes:

> The principal rituals of which we have evidence, from texts and mural depictions, were the great state ceremonies, which often lasted over many days. They were carried on in and around the temples, which were the principal architectural monuments as well as the foci of

---

[38] Gardner, *Second Witness*, 1:216–17.

religion in all the early states. The most sacred parts of the ceremonies were rites of adoration, offering, and sacrifice, conducted by the professional priests within sacred precincts from which the laity were often excluded. But there were also public parades, pageantry, and feasting. Costumed religious pageantry, already well developed in tribal societies and chiefdoms, undoubtedly reached its peak of elaboration in the early states.[39]

In addition to any possible entertainment value, communal rituals served as public instruction that underscored and reinforced the shared communal understanding of how the world worked. Lewis Rambo reports:

> Scholars have come to recognize that ritual can play a vital part in religious life. Indeed, some argue that ritual precedes all other aspects of religion: people first *perform* religiously, and then *rationalize* the process by way of theology. Whichever comes first, it is clear that ritual may have an important effect on the conversion process. It is my view that religious action—regularized, sustained, and intentional—is fundamental to the conversion experience. Ritual fosters the necessary orientation, the readiness of mind and soul to have a conversion experience, and it consolidates conversion after the initial experience.[40]

The law of Moses required communal, visual ritual that centered on the performance of sacrifices. One was the sacrifice of a lamb (or whatever constituted the lamb surrogate in the New World) intended as a symbol and enactor of communal atonement. The Nephite perception of this particular sacrifice had to have been expanded by their understanding that the symbol foreshadowed the Messiah's atoning mission. Thus Nephite communal ritual provided a focus on the sacrifice of an animal that represented a future sacrifice of a deity (Mosiah 3). The doctrine made it clear that it was the person and not the animal that provided atonement, regardless of the enacted symbol.

As Nephites accommodated to the surrounding cultures, the idea of social hierarchies became more and more appealing.[41] At the summit of Mesoamerican hierarchical society was a king who represented a divine lineage and whose ritual presence enacted both the presence of deity and the power of blood sacrifice. The connection between king, blood, and communal ritual provided a powerful means of educating, or reeducating, the Nephites, who were already economically motivated to some kind of accommodation with surrounding cultures.[42]

The parallel of place combined ideas of Nephite and Mesoamerican ritual space. For the Nephites, their temple was the focus of their ritual. Similarly, the Maya temple

---

[39] William Y. Adams, *Religion and Adaptation*, 263.
[40] Lewis Rambo, *Understanding Religious Conversion*, 114.
[41] For example: "And it came to pass in the commencement of the ninth year, Alma saw the wickedness of the church, and he saw also that the example of the church began to lead those who were unbelievers on from one piece of iniquity to another, thus bringing on the destruction of the people. Yea, *he saw great inequality among the people, some lifting themselves up with their pride*, despising others, turning their backs upon the needy and the naked and those who were hungry, and those who were athirst, and those who were sick and afflicted" (Alma 4:11–12).
[42] Gardner, *Second Witness*, 2:487–90.

complexes were designed with public performances in mind.[43] Mesoamerican temples "served as a 'focusing lens' to concentrate attention on ideal models of existence and behavior."[44] Mesoamerican rulers used temples as places to "communicate with and influence the gods on behalf of the community."[45] Similarly, Nephite kings acted as intermediaries between the people and their god in association with temples. Benjamin, in his address at the temple, taught his people the words that "the angel of the Lord" had given him (Mosiah 4:1).[46] For both cultures, place and practice were sufficiently similar to allow the temple and the rites performed at the temple to be conduits of syncretism.

Most important to the syncretistic emergence of a religion that denied the atoning Messiah was the replacement of that person and function with a more present substitute. The Mesoamerican king fulfilled that conceptual place with a presence at once more comprehensible and "real" than the predicted Messiah, whose presence was far in the future and geographically distant from the Nephites (Hel. 16:20).

The living Mesoamerican king became, in ritual circumstances, the living and present deity. There were rituals where the king not only put on the mask of deity but, for ritual time and in ritual space, became that deity—commonly called god impersonation or "deity concurrence."[47] In deity concurrence, a ritual specialist, typically the ruler, puts on an engraved mask or elaborate headdress and transforms himself into the god whose mask or headdress is being worn. There is a glyphic formula that essentially says, "His holy image (*u-b'aah-il*), [that of] God X, [is upon] Ruler Y." The Maya used the head metaphorically as a mark of individuality, and it stood as a representation of the whole body.[48] In their minds, they were not playacting—they would actually become that god, acting as he would act and performing the godly duties pertaining to that particular deity. As Houston, Stuart, and Taube state, "There is no evident 'fiction,' but there is, apparently, a belief in godly immanence and transubstantiation, of specific people who become, in special moments, figures from sacred legend and the Maya pantheon."[49] There are many situations where deity concurrence takes place and a wide variety of deities are impersonated, such as wind gods, gods of incense burning, gods of ball playing, even major gods such as the sun god or the supreme creator deity, Itzamnaaj.[50] This practice goes back to the Formative period (1500 B.C.–A.D. 200), as cave paintings in Oxtotitlan dating to the eighth century B.C. attest.[51]

---

[43] William M. Ringle and George J. Bey III, "Post-Classic and Terminal Classic Courts of the Northern Maya Lowlands," 278.

[44] Jeff K. Kowalski, "Temple Complexes," 3:196.

[45] Ibid., 3:194.

[46] Jacob delivers the Lord's message in a temple setting. See Jacob 2:2–5.

[47] Stephen Houston, David Stuart, and Karl Taube, *The Memory of Bones: Body, Being, and Experience among the Classic Maya*, 64.

[48] Ibid., 64.

[49] Ibid., 270.

[50] Ibid., 274.

[51] David C. Grove, *The Olmec Paintings of Oxtotitlan Cave, Guerrero, Mexico*.

Against that context, Alma's question "Have you received *his image* in your countenances?" (Alma 5:14) and its rhetorical companion, "Can you look up, having the image of God [Jehovah] *engraven* upon your countenances?" (v. 19), become highly nuanced. Alma may have been referencing a concept that he expected his listeners to understand and attempted to shift that understanding into a more appropriate gospel context. The masks and headdresses that deity impersonators wore were literally *graven*; numerous ancient Maya ceramics depict artists in the act of carving them.[52]

Explaining Nephite Apostasy

Nephite prophets exhorted their people to walk steadfastly in Yahweh's way. There was another option. As social and economic pressures led apostate Nephites to desire a Mesoamerican-style king, the king's accepted and expected ritual roles made deity present rather than distant and merely predicted. The deity before them became a more real and important symbol than the one who was predicted to come in the distant future. This is similar to the argument that Korihor employs to diminish the belief in the future Messiah:

> O ye that are bound down under a foolish and a vain hope, why do ye yoke yourselves with such foolish things? Why do ye look for a Christ? For no man can know of anything which is to come.
>
> Behold, these things which ye call prophecies, which ye say are handed down by holy prophets, behold, they are foolish traditions of your fathers.
>
> How do ye know of their surety? Behold, ye cannot know of things which ye do not see; therefore ye cannot know that there shall be a Christ. (Alma 30:13–15)

When Alma$_2$ praised the people of Gideon, he did so by contrasting them with Nephite apostates: "*I trust that ye are not in a state of so much unbelief* as were your brethren; I trust that ye are not lifted up in the pride of your hearts; yea, *I trust that ye have not set your hearts upon riches* and the vain things of the world; yea, *I trust that you do not worship idols*, but that ye do worship the true and the living God, and that ye look forward for the remission of your sins, with an everlasting faith, *which is to come*" (Alma 7:6). The people of Gideon were not in apostasy (as were their "brethren" at Zarahemla). They had not set their hearts upon riches (one of the standard traits of Nephite apostasy). They did not worship idols (implying that their "brethren" did). The final result was that the people of Gideon "worship[ped] the true and the living God . . . [who] *is to come.*" The people of Gideon had not altered their religion by supplanting the future God for a present idol. Although Alma$_2$'s statement does not specifically mention the Mesoamerican king, it does highlight all the points of similarity upon which the adoption of such a king eventually replaced the "true and the living God . . . [who] is to come" with the person of the king enacting ritual before them.

The refocusing of apostate Nephite belief from atoning Messiah to Mesoamerican divine king plausibly hinged on the fulcrum of similarities in God's sacred blood.

---

[52] Dorie Reents-Budet, *Painting the Maya Universe: Royal Ceramics of the Classic Period*, 38, 316.

Faithful Nephites "believe[d] that salvation was, and is, and is to come, in and through the atoning blood of Christ, the Lord Omnipotent" (Mosiah 3:18). The Mesoamerican king's blood was similarly highly significant and culturally potent. Importantly, it was also a voluntary sacrifice. The Maya kings voluntarily shed their blood as an offering on behalf of their people. They used thorns, stingray spines, and obsidian blades to draw blood from their tongues and genitals. The blood was sometimes dripped onto bark paper and burned, and the smoke was considered both an offering to the gods and a medium for the gods to manifest themselves to the living. The voluntary self-sacrifice was turned from physical blood into divine substance through its ritual transformation as sacrifice.

The conceptual distance between the voluntary blood sacrifice of the king and the voluntary blood sacrifice of the future Messiah was short. In fact, it appears likely that many Nephites had already made that substitution. Perhaps we are seeing clues to the process of apostasy when Amulek is teaching Zoramite outcasts and specifically defines Christ's sacrifice by what it was *not*: "it shall not be a human sacrifice" (Alma 34:10). Amulek explains (as did Benjamin) in contrast to an accepted belief: "There is *not any man* that can *sacrifice his own blood* which will atone for the sins of another. . . . Therefore, it is expedient that there should be a great and last sacrifice, and then shall there be, or it is expedient there should be, a stop to the shedding of blood; then shall the law of Moses be fulfilled; yea, it shall be all fulfilled, every jot and tittle, and none shall have passed away" (Alma 34:11, 13).[53]

As a point of coincidence by which syncretic tendencies could form, the presence of a king on earth enacting the role of a heavenly king who shed blood for his people was not only an available theological conduit, but one that came with powerful cultural and social overtones. In addition to the ritual presence of the king, there was the daily presence of the culture he represented, with all of the economic benefits and desired social stratification that he embodied.

Nephite apostasy was much more than a change in the way God was perceived. Not a simple change of religion, it could foment a violent disruption:

> And it came to pass that the voice of the people came against Amlici, that he was not made king over the people.
>
> Now this did cause much joy in the hearts of those who were against him; but Amlici did stir up those who were in his favor to anger against those who were not in his favor.
>
> And it came to pass that they gathered themselves together, and did consecrate Amlici to be their king.

---

[53] Although all blood was considered sacred by the Maya, the blood of kings was believed to be the most potent. While some scholars have argued that there may be evidence that human sacrifice among the Aztec served an expiatory function (Michel Graulich, "Aztec Human Sacrifice as Expiation," 352–71), there is currently no archaeological evidence that bloodletting by ancient Mesoamerican rulers was done to atone for the sins of their people. Bloodletting was associated with agricultural fertility, which is linked to the cycle of death and rebirth, not with an expiatory sacrifice believed to atone for the sins of a ruler's people. The Nephites, living among the larger Mesoamerican culture, would surely have been aware of the sacred nature of royal blood and the power it had to bring new life.

Now when Amlici was made king over them he commanded them that they should take up arms against their brethren; and this he did that he might subject them to him.

Now the people of Amlici were distinguished by the name of Amlici, being called Amlicites; and the remainder were called Nephites, or the people of God. (Alma 2:7–11)

Even when the apostates did not specifically engage in armed conflict, they were important factors in a violent disruption. Alma 51:13 informs us: "And it came to pass that when the men who were called king-men had heard that the Lamanites were coming down to battle against them, they were glad in their hearts; and they refused to take up arms, for they were so wroth with the chief judge, and also with the people of liberty, that they would not take up arms to defend their country."

Why was a religious apostasy so socially disruptive? The splintering of the restored church after the Prophet Joseph Smith's martyrdom certainly resulted in different religious bodies, but not in civil war. The difference is explained by the ability of the modern world to separate religion from politics and culture. For the Nephites, religious apostasy included an alteration of the social order. When the pressures for the new type of king became strong enough, the matter was not only religious and political—it also included a desire to transform society. As the apostate religion syncretized religious ideas, its adherents longed for the social prestige, wealth, and privilege associated with those religious ideas in surrounding cities and cultures.

Michio Kitahara lists five points that allow for syncretism.[54] Each point is followed by my application of the point to the Book of Mormon:

1. "Two different cultures must be involved. Members of one culture are exposed to the [culture] of the other, and the two . . . traditions merge." The best reconstruction of Nephite culture places them in Mesoamerica as initially a smaller population inside the larger, more dominant culture. This circumstance inevitably led to the culture clash that created the possibility of (and the desire for) syncretism. That process certainly began with the adoption of Mesoamerican material culture and eventually moved to the adoption of ideology.
2. "The process itself is based on 'associationism'. . . . One may fairly safely assume that a concept rooted in one culture will be associated with a different concept in another culture, whenever syncretism takes place." We should not expect Nephite religion to demonstrate overt adoption of Mesoamerican deities nor, conversely, Mesoamerican religions to adopt Nephite religion. The general direction of cultural transfer should be from dominant to less dominant. Both the historical information of Mesoamerica and a close reading of the Book of Mormon indicate that the Nephites were not in the dominant position. Nevertheless, there were concepts that might have been associated and that thus could have provided the pathways for syncretic creation.
3. "Syncretism results from two sets of conceptual configurations, rather than two single concepts." Nephite and Mesoamerican religions were clearly different

---

[54] Kitahara, "Formal Model of Syncretism in Scales," 121–22.

and operated on different principles. The differences preclude wholesale adoption. The similarities allowed for syncretism.
4. "The two conceptual configurations must be sufficiently similar to, as well as significantly different from, each other." As noted in this article, commonality might be found in a number of areas. None of these suggest or depend upon an ideological loan from one culture to the other. They began in completely separate worlds, but the perceived parallels allowed for the conceptual paths along which a synthesis could have emerged.
5. "The end result of syncretism must contain recognizable features of both configurations." We certainly recognize the remnants of Israelite religion in Nephite apostasy. Understanding the specific nature of that apostasy requires a cultural background that has previously been unavailable to LDS researchers.

The fascinating similarities in multiple Nephite apostasies at different times and in different locations are best explained by the continued presence of a religious and cultural model to which they were adapted. Not only does the Mesoamerican context provide the cultural background that explains why Nephite apostasy took the particular form it did, but it also helps us understand some of the specific references Nephite prophets used when combating that apostasy.

11
Kinship: Tribes and Households

When Lehi's family left Jerusalem, they left their larger family—their tribe. Although politically a monarchy, the tribe and clan-based society persisted. Ziony Zevit explains:

> Israelite society, according to data in the Hebrew Bible, organized itself by groups of related individuals living in proximity to each other as bate 'ab, "father's houses," generally understood as extended families; mispahot, "clans," groupings of bat 'ab, and sebatim, "tribes," (in)formal confederations of mispahot". . . .
>
> At each level, relatedness was expressed in terms of genealogical descent. Although at each level, degrees of consanguinity most likely correlated with geographical proximity, father's houses or clans could cluster in small individual sites or occupy smaller or later villages or share towns and villages with others from different clans, even clans from different tribes. . . .
>
> At one and the same time, an individual belonged to different, nested, social groupings, each of which had cultic celebrations and obligations.[1]

When Lehi's family arrived in the New World, this underlying kin-based organization continued. Although it is rarely explicit, there are glimpses of it throughout the Book of Mormon. In conjunction with similar organizational principles in the New World, we may be certain that there were kin-based groupings throughout Book of Mormon history. We first see the development of tribal organizations as Lehi's family begins to separate themselves into tribes based upon Lehi's sons (paralleling the sons of Israel becoming the foundations of the twelve tribes that defined the people of Israel).

Jacob explains: "Now the people which were not Lamanites were Nephites; nevertheless, they were called Nephites, Jacobites, Josephites, Zoramites, Lamanites, Lemuelites, and Ishmaelites" (Jacob 1:13). In socio-political terms, there were only two divisions: Lamanites and Nephites. Therefore, "the people which were not Lamanites were Nephites." Jacob then adds the "nevertheless." The qualifier indicates that within each of these larger categories are tribal designations based upon the son who stood at the head of that lineage. Thus, there are Jacobites and Josephites who

---

[1] Ziony Zevit, "False Dichotomies in Descriptions of Israelite Religion: A Problem, Its Origin, and a Proposed Solution," 231.

are divisions within the Nephite polity just as there are Lemuelites and Ishmaelites inside the Lamanite socio-political designation.

The best evidence for the continuation of these kin-based organizations, even under both the Nephite monarchy and the subsequent reign of the judges is found when the overarching political organization is removed just before Christ appears in the Americas.

> Now behold, I will show unto you that they did not establish a king over the land; but in this same year, yea, the thirtieth year, they did destroy upon the judgment-seat, yea, did murder the chief judge of the land.
>
> And the people were divided one against another; and they did separate one from another into tribes, every man according to his family and his kindred and friends; and thus they did destroy the government of the land.
>
> And every tribe did appoint a chief or a leader over them; and thus they became tribes and leaders of tribes.
>
> Now behold, there was no man among them save he had much family and many kindreds and friends; therefore their tribes became exceedingly great. (3 Ne. 7:1–4)

There was no need to invent these tribal organizations because they had continued through all other political organizations. They were a ready-made structure upon which society could fall back when the higher political organization was removed. These tribes will also continue through at least the 4 Nephi record—which was, interestingly, also a period witnessing the disintegration of unity:

> And now it came to pass in this year, yea, in the two hundred and thirty and first year, there was a great division among the people.
>
> And it came to pass that in this year there arose a people who were called the Nephites, and they were true believers in Christ; and among them there were those who were called by the Lamanites—Jacobites, and Josephites, and Zoramites;
>
> Therefore the true believers in Christ, and the true worshipers of Christ, (among whom were the three disciples of Jesus who should tarry) were called Nephites, and Jacobites, and Josephites, and Zoramites.
>
> And it came to pass that they who rejected the gospel were called Lamanites, and Lemuelites, and Ishmaelites; and they did not dwindle in unbelief, but they did wilfully rebel against the gospel of Christ; and they did teach their children that they should not believe, even as their fathers, from the beginning, did dwindle. (4 Ne. 1:35–38)

While the continuation of the tribal units is clear, it is perhaps too apt to have the division follow precisely the traditional lineage divisions from prior to Christ's arrival and the unification of the people into a conceptual whole based upon their allegiance to the gospel. I suspect that, while the tribal distinction is accurate, the particulars are literary. Restating Ziony Zevit: "At each level, relatedness was expressed in terms of genealogical descent. Although at each level, degrees of consanguinity most likely correlated with geographical proximity, father's houses or clans could cluster in small individual sites or occupy smaller or later villages or share towns and villages with others from different clans, even clans from different tribes."[2]

---

[2] Ibid., 230.

The structure of the tribe continued, but the particular boundaries and internal associations would certainly have become complex in the thousand years of Nephite civilization.

Other subtle descriptions of society operating on the level of kin groups may be seen in the text. When king Benjamin gathered his people to the temple, they organized themselves in families; "And it came to pass that when they came up to the temple, they pitched their tents round about, every man according to his family, consisting of his wife, and his sons, and his daughters, and their sons, and their daughters, from the eldest down to the youngest, every family being separate one from another" (Mosiah 2:5). Other occasions also highlight kin relations. Sorenson notes:

> When Alma had approached him, Amulek identified himself as a "Nephite" (Alma 8:20). "I am Amulek . . . a descendant of Nephi," Alma 10:2–3 reports him saying. Mosiah 17:2 gives Alma's descent in identical language. We understand, then, that the two were establishing that they belonged to the same lineage. A Mayan practice at the time of the Spanish conquest shows the same principle governing how to get along in strange territory: "When anyone finds himself in a strange region and in need, he has recourse to those of his name [kin group]; and if there are any, they receive him and treat him with all kindness."[3]

The Household and Proximate Kin

Amulek's description of his household provides more information about family relations, at least at Ammonihah: "For behold, he hath blessed mine house, he hath blessed me, and my women, and my children, and my father and my kinsfolk; yea, even all my kindred hath he blessed, and the blessing of the Lord hath rested upon us according to the words which he spake" (Alma 10:11). When Amulek describes Alma$_2$'s blessing upon his relatives, he suggests an interesting pattern of kin connections. Structurally, the sentence progresses from named categories to a generalization ("all my kindred") that is the largest and most inclusive category. The interjection "yea" appears to extend the specifics of the first set of named categories. It is possible, therefore, that Alma$_2$'s blessing was direct and immediate for the first (present) set and indirect for the second (extended) set.

Possibly "all my kindred" may have been more tightly defined in Nephite society than in ours. Among the Aztecs, certain penalties could be applied to all of one's relatives.[4] Different sources give slightly different definitions, but all one's relatives could apply to either the fifth or the fourth generation.[5] Although the Aztecs had a different language and lived in a different time period, the same necessity of defining a maximum kin group may also have dictated Amulek's definition of "all my kindred."

---

[3] John L. Sorenson, *An Ancient American Setting for the Book of Mormon*, 212, citing William A. Haviland, "Principles of Descent in Sixteenth Century Yucatan," *Katunob* 8, no. 2 (December 1972): 64.

[4] Bartólome de Las Casas, *Apologética Historia Sumaria*, 2:401.

[5] See Diego Muñoz Camargo, *Historia de Tlaxcala*, 95 and Edward E. Calneck, "The Sahagún Texts as a Source of Sociological Information," 200.

Amulek's list of specific kindred contains even more specific suggestions about Nephite kin relationships. His first category is "my house." For kin-based societies, a literal house typically symbolizes the family. It may include people outside of the nuclear family. Groups of kin frequently live in compounds.

Anthropologists have reconstructed a picture of some Aztec households close to the time of the Spanish Conquest. The Aztec term for the "family" was *cencaltin*, "all the people of the house." One account from 1580 indicates that the "house" was not a single building, but rather a compound of different buildings, often containing six or seven married couples and their unmarried children.[6] Pedro Carrasco describes a typical compound: "The house often is an extended family of four married couples. The head of the family lives with two married nieces and one married nephew. The head of this house also has a renter who lives with his two married brothers-in-law."[7]

The archaeological excavation of living structures consisting of multiple buildings led archaeologists to conclude that such structures were family compounds, a very common feature of Maya archaeological sites dating to the time period of the Book of Mormon. For example, the site of Salinas La Blanca (which predates the Book of Mormon Nephites) has two household mounds with multiple thatched houses, one with three houses, and one with four.[8] It is likely that Amulek's "house" was a typical Mesoamerican household compound. When Amulek speaks of Alma blessing his "house" and then lists specific relatives, these are almost certainly people living in the same "house" or entire compound, not a single structure.

Associated with Amulek's "house" are "me, and my women, and my children, and my father and my kinsfolk." Clearly Amulek is the head of the household, as he describes all of his kin by their relation to him. "My children" and "my father" are almost certainly terms that we ourselves would use. However, a more problematic term is "my women." John A. Tvedtnes has suggested:

> The Hebrew word used for wife really means woman. In three Book of Mormon passages, the word women appears to mean wives:
> "Our women did bear children" (1 Ne. 17:1).
> "Our women have toiled, being big with child; and they have borne children" (1 Ne. 17:20).
> "For behold, he hath blessed mine house, he hath blessed me, and my women, and my children, and my father and my kinsfolk; yea, even all my kindred hath he blessed" (Alma 10:11).[9]

---

[6] Francisco de Casteñeda, "Official Reports on the Towns of Tequizistlán, Tepechpán, Acolman, and San Juan Teotihuacán, sent by Francisco de Casteñeda to His Majesty, Philip II, and the Council of the Indies, in 1580," 11:2:55.

[7] Pedro Carrasco, "Las clases sociales en el México Antiguo," 2:372.

[8] Kent V. Flannery, "The Early Formative Household Cluster on the Guatemalan Pacific Coast," 32.

[9] John A. Tvedtnes, "The Hebrew Background of the Book of Mormon," 91.

A similar linguistic convention exists in Spanish (*mi mujer*, "my woman/my wife") and Nahuatl (*nocihua*, "my woman/my wife") and certainly other languages. Was Amulek a polygamist? It seems likely that he was.[10] Amulek had been a much more worldly man before his conversion (Alma 10 4–6). The people of king Noah practiced polygamy (Mosiah 11:2). Given the resemblances between the order of the Nehors and the apostate religion of the people of Noah,[11] it seems likely that polygamy was also part of the set of objectionable religious/political "innovations" condemned by the Nephite prophets for both groups: the desire for kings, the desire for a hierarchical society, costly apparel, and apparently multiple wives.

Later in the Book of Mormon we get a picture of what the family compound of an elite Nephite might have looked like. We have a physical description of the compound where Nephi the son of Helaman lived. Nephi was seen praying "upon a tower, which was in the garden of Nephi, which was by the highway which led to the chief market, which was in the city of Zarahemla; therefore, Nephi had bowed himself upon the tower which was in his garden, which tower was also near unto the garden gate by which led the highway" (Hel. 7:10). During his service as chief judge, it would have been socially important for Nephi to be centrally located in the city.

Archaeological investigations have uncovered internal roads in Mesoamerican cities of this period, matching the mention of "the highway which led to the chief market." Wallace Hunt notes:

> Significantly, this is the only place in the Book of Mormon where the word "market" appears.
>
> One hardly notices the words "chief market" in this particular chapter, and upon deeper perusal of the verse, the use of the two words at first seems unnecessary. Why add this description? If Joseph Smith were authoring the book, there would be no need to include such a description. In fact, any unusual word or description could jeopardize the integrity of the work. After all, the native Americans with whom he was familiar had no marketplaces!
>
> We can, however, draw several conclusions from Mormon's inclusion of the phrase "chief market." First, the description was important to include, since he was limited for space and therefore would have included only words, phrases, and events that he felt were significant. Also, this description signifies that cities in this time period not only had more than one market, but that one of the markets was either larger or more significant than the others.[12]

Sorenson corroborates Hunt's conclusions with additional information on the Mesoamerican context for multiple market places:

> Cortez and his fellows were amazed by the market in Tlatelolco in the Valley of Mexico, by its diversity of goods, and by the complexity of its organization. Yet until

---

[10] Carol Pratt Bradley, a BYU student with a minor in ancient Near Eastern studies also considers the presence of "women" in this sentence as a possible indication of Amulek's multiple wives. Carol Pratt Bradley, "Women, the Book of Mormon, and the Law of Moses," 143.

[11] See Brant A. Gardner, *Second Witness: Analytical and Contextual Commentary on the Book of Mormon*, 4:41–51 for a discussion of the nature of the religion of the Nehors, including the evidence of such a religion in Noah's court.

[12] Wallace E. Hunt Jr., "Notes and Communications: The Marketplace," 140.

recently, only little attention has been given to the fact that a number of these cities had multiple markets.

The evidence, however, seems quite clear. Blanton and Kowalewski, for example, have noted that Monte Alban had both a chief market and subsidiary ones. For Teotihuacán, René Millon identifies one location as "the principal marketplace" and suggests that other markets existed for special products, such as kitchen wares. George Cowgill, the other leading expert on Teotihuacán, concurs. The Krotsers point out the same phenomenon at El Tajín. Meanwhile Edward Calnek's reexamination of documentary evidence on the organization of the Aztec capital, Tenochtitlán, has established that each major sector of the city had its own market, in addition to the giant central one. Apparently Zarahemla was no different.[13]

Nephi's residence was a compound surrounded by a wall in which there was a gate. This wall enclosed at least the "garden of Nephi" and the "tower." Presumably, the wall also enclosed, or was attached to, the residence itself. These features have also been established by Mesoamerican archaeology for elite residences. Sorenson comments:

> Garden areas were cultivated immediately adjacent to single habitation complexes. At the archaeological site of El Tajín near the coast of the Gulf of Mexico east of Mexico City are the remains of a city that occupied at least five square kilometers at its maximum period, probably between A.D. 600–900. At that time, the houses of its middle-class people were surrounded by gardens and fruit trees. Likewise, the famous city of Tula, north of the capital of Mexico, was even larger, up to fourteen square kilometers around A.D. 1000–1100, and gardened houselots were common there too.[14]

Nephi's tower was almost certainly one of the many low pyramidal structures that archaeologists have found in the majority of Mesoamerican sites from Book of Mormon times on. Those attached to private compounds were lower than the stepped pyramids in public squares used for public rituals, but they were nevertheless similarly constructed, if not nearly so high. Nephi's tower was low enough to allow easy conversation with the crowd (Hel. 7:12–13). In a family compound, such towers would have been suitable for prayer and communion with God.

All details in this short description of Nephi's residence conform to what is known of elite residences in the center of Mesoamerican cities. Of course, a farmer's home outside the town would not necessarily be by a road, would not have a tower, and would not have a wall. It would probably have been a compound and would certainly have some type of kitchen garden near the house that was different from the field crops.

---

[13] John L. Sorenson, "Nephi's Garden and Chief Market," 237. See also Hunt, "Notes and Communications: The Marketplace," 140.

[14] Sorenson, "Nephi's Garden and Chief Market," 237.

12
Glimpses of Lamanite Culture

The Book of Mormon is entirely focused on the Nephite story. For most of the text, the Lamanites are the book's boogey men, seen either threateningly in the shadows, or terrifyingly present in actual warfare. Nephite writers have no reason to write sympathetically about the Lamanites, and don't. As a result, for the majority of Book of Mormon history we know little about the Lamanites. That changes during a brief period between 200–100 B.C. During part of that century there was a turning of emphasis towards the Lamanites that first led the people of Zeniff to attempt to recolonize the land of Nephi, and later led the sons of Mosiah$_2$ to undertake a missionary journey to the Lamanites. During both of those times when the Nephites were engaged with Lamanites in Lamanite lands, we have a rare opportunity to picture Lamanite culture.

Zeniff Returns to the Land of Nephi

The origin story of the people of Zeniff is told twice in the Book of Mormon. We have a brief introduction to the story in Omni 1:27–30, although Zeniff is not named in that account. The second account comes from Zeniff's first-person record (Mosiah 9–10). What happens to those people after Zeniff's death is recounted in Mosiah chapters 11–21.

Zeniff begins his account: "I, Zeniff, having been taught in all the language of the Nephites, and having had a knowledge of the land of Nephi, or of the land of our fathers' first inheritance, and having been sent as a spy among the Lamanites that I might spy out their forces, that our army might come upon them and destroy them—but when I saw that which was good among them I was desirous that they should not be destroyed." (Mosiah 9:1). His explanation requires a review of the Nephite history that precipitates this action.

Zeniff is part of the generation of Nephites who had lived in the land of Nephi until no later than 162 B.C.[1] He and (probably) the leaders of this expedition were

---

[1] See Brant A. Gardner, *Second Witness: Analytical and Contextual Commentary on the Book of Mormon*, 3:197.

among those who had fled for their lives from the land of Nephi with Mosiah$_1$.[2] It is quite plausible that their decision to lead a military expedition to the land of Nephi was in retaliation for the perceived injustice of their expulsion. Perhaps now that the people of Zarahemla had swelled their population, the displaced Nephites considered that they had the military strength to "correct" their dispossession. This expedition appears to be a manifestation of both nostalgia for their former home and a grudge against those who had forced them out. This military action was apparently mounted with Mosiah$_1$'s blessing.

Zeniff, one of the army's spies, is supposed to learn about the people they want to attack, particularly the ways in which they would be most vulnerable. But what Zeniff learned changed the group's plans: "when I saw that which was good among them I was desirous that they should not be destroyed" (Mosiah 9:1). What could have changed his mind?

We have no details about how Zeniff conducted his spying mission. It seems probable that he adopted local clothing and went into the city of Nephi. As one who had previously lived in the land of Nephi he was able to pass as a native in both dress and language. Zeniff was among the people of the city of Nephi at least twice. Mosiah 9:5 mentions a second expedition, which leads to the establishment of a colony. Plausibly they left Zarahemla around 157 B.C. and remained separate from the main body of Nephites for at least twenty-seven years.[3]

Assuming that invading Lamanites were the reason that Mosiah$_1$ and his people left the land of Nephi does not suggest that all former Nephites left with him. (See "A New World Fleeing Prophet" in Chapter 8.) It is highly likely that many remained, and Zeniff's ability to blend in so well substantiates that assumption. The pressures for social differentiation that had always been part of the city of Nephi certainly remained, and Zeniff's suggestion that there was much good among them can be seen as evidence that those who remained had prospered under Lamanite rule.

I hypothesize that the wealth and power of the inhabitants helped Zeniff's expedition see "that which was good." The foundational promise of the Nephites was that: "Inasmuch as thy seed shall keep my commandments, they shall prosper in the land of promise" (1 Ne. 4:14). Zeniff may have assumed that the reverse was also true, that evidence of prosperity was evidence of some form of keeping the commandments and of "goodness."

If the tentative connections between Book of Mormon cities and archaeological sites are accurate, Nephi/Kaminaljuyú was much more spectacular than Zarahemla/Santa Rosa. Internal evidence in the Book of Mormon suggests that difference in size and

---

[2] The Book of Mormon always refers to these lands as the "land of Nephi," and to the "city of Nephi." However, it seems unlikely that the lands or city would have retained such a Nephite-oriented name once dominated by the Lamanites. We do not know what name would have been used, as we always see the story from the perspective of the Nephites.

[3] These dates are not given in the Book of Mormon, but are the result of an examination of the available evidence. See Gardner, *Second Witness*, 3:196–98.

wealth.⁴ Perhaps Zeniff thought that, with Mosiah₁'s people gone, the internal tensions had been relieved and the returning Nephites could settle peaceably in the general area, probably also accumulating some of the same wealth that characterized the city of Nephi. Indeed, the fact that the inhabitants granted lands to Zeniff's people is evidence that they felt no consuming hatred toward those who had fled with Mosiah₁. Although Zeniff doesn't dwell on it, Mormon's introduction to Zeniff's son, Noah, does suggest that Zeniff may have been at least partially correct in foreseeing Nephite prosperity:

> And it came to pass that king Noah built many elegant and spacious buildings; and he ornamented them with fine work of wood, and of all manner of precious things, of gold, and of silver, and of iron, and of brass, and of ziff, and of copper;
> And he also built him a spacious palace, and a throne in the midst thereof, all of which was of fine wood and was ornamented with gold and silver and with precious things. (Mosiah 11:8–9)

Although Mormon appears to add this information as a sign that Noah has become greedy and has violated expected Nephite egalitarian principles, the descriptions nevertheless show an ability to construct extravagant public buildings. Such displays are typical of larger and wealthier cities. The king must be able to muster the labor and acquire the resources required for such a display. It may have been the very thing that Zeniff and his followers hoped for when they returned to the land of Nephi.

Zeniff provides a description of the turning point in the relations between his people and the surrounding Lamanites:

> Therefore it came to pass, that after we had dwelt in the land for the space of twelve years that king Laman began to grow uneasy, lest by any means my people should wax strong in the land, and that they could not overpower them and bring them into bondage.
> Now they were a lazy and an idolatrous people; therefore they were desirous to bring us into bondage, that they might glut themselves with the labors of our hands; yea, that they might feast themselves upon the flocks of our fields. (Mosiah 9:11–12)

Zeniff describes the Lamanite intent, and then ascribes motive to that intent. He calls them a "lazy and an idolatrous people." Certainly worshipping idols could be an observed trait, but the idea that the Lamanites were "lazy" is simply a continuation of Nephite prejudice that began early and continues throughout the Book of Mormon. (See "Becoming Nephites and Lamanites" in Chapter 6).

The Book of Mormon talks of people who are in "bondage," and Zeniff suggests that the Lamanites fear that the Zeniffites will become strong enough to place them in bondage (Mosiah 9:11). What would that have meant? Zeniff defines bondage by describing what the Lamanites want to do to them: "They were desirous to bring us into bondage, that they might glut themselves with the labors of our hands; yea, that

---

⁴ The evidence must be deduced, but the nature of the loose political hegemony in the land of Zarahemla and the system of overkings among the Lamanites strongly suggests that there is a significant difference in political power, a power which would have the ability to generate public works that would demonstrate Lamanite wealth and power.

they might feast themselves upon the flocks of our fields" (Mosiah 9:12). The Book of Mormon term "bondage" is easily translated to the term Mesoamericanists use for a particular form of inter-city relationship—tribute.

As a dominant political power, the Lamanites could supplement their own production by requiring tribute of their subject peoples (as opposed to the Nephite ideal of working with one's own hands). The much later Aztecs of Tenochtitlan (the city of Motecuhzoma) collected extensive tribute from many city-states. They could hardly be called lazy. Alonso de Zorita, a Spanish judge (1511–c. 1585) described some of the Nahua lords and their relationships to their people:

> The benefits these lords received were these: Their people gave them personal service in their households and brought them fuel and water, the assignment of tasks being made by the lord. Their people also worked certain fields for the lords, the size of the fields depending upon the number of people. Because of this they were exempt from service to the ruler and from working his fields, and their only other obligation to the ruler was to serve in time of war, from which none was excused. In addition, the ruler furnished them with wages, meals, and lodgings, for they served as gentlemen in waiting in his palace.
>
> These lords were responsible for the working of the fields, both for themselves and for their people, and they had overseers who saw to this. The lords also had the duty of looking after the people in their charge, of defending and protecting them. Thus these lords were appointed and intended to serve the general as well as their private good.[5]

Because tribute allowed people to benefit from the labor of someone else's hands, it was a concept in direct conflict with a Nephite ideal.[6] Nevertheless, it is a well-known aspect of the inter-city relationships in Mesoamerica.

The idea of *bondage* is paralleled by the term *plunder* in the Book of Mormon.[7] When we examine the circumstances behind *plunder*, it is apparent that plunder as well as bondage describes the tributary relationship. Thus the bondage in which the people of Limhi find themselves (Limhi being Noah's son) is manifest in being required to deliver part of their produce to their Lamanite overlords: "And also Limhi, being the son of the king, having the kingdom conferred upon him by the people,

---

[5] Alonso de Zorita, *Life and Labor in Ancient Mexico: The Brief and Summary Relation of the Lords of New Spain*, 47.

[6] King Benjamin declares: "And even I, myself, have labored with mine own hands that I might serve you." (Mosiah 2:14). Alma$_1$ commands his newly formed people: "the priests . . . should labor with their own hands for their support" (Mosiah 18:16). This becomes codified in Zarahemla when Mosiah$_2$ establishes the rule of law for the reign of the judges:

> That they should let no pride nor haughtiness disturb their peace; that every man should esteem his neighbor as himself, laboring with their own hands for their support.
>
> Yea, and all their priests and teachers should labor with their own hands for their support, in all cases save it were in sickness, or in much want; and doing these things, they did abound in the grace of God. (Mosiah 27:4–5)

[7] For plunder, see: Mosiah 2:13, 10:17, 24:7, 29:14, 29:36; Alma 16:18, 17:14, 18:7, 23:3, 37:21, 50:21; Hel. 3:14, 3:16, 4:12, 6:17, 6:18, 6:21, 6:23, 7:21, 10:3, 11:25; 3 Ne. 4:4, 4:5, and Ether 8:16.

made oath unto the king of the Lamanites that his people should pay tribute unto him, even one half of all they possessed" (Mosiah 19:26).

After Alma₁ and his followers departed from the land of Nephi, they founded the city of Helam (Mosiah 23:19). They were able to remain hidden from Lamanites for a time, but eventually they, too, are required to enter a tributary relationship with the Lamanite king (Mosiah 23:37–39, 24:9–10). They also called their relationship *bondage* (Mosiah 24:13). The conqueror plunders and puts the conquered in bondage. The Book of Mormon vocabulary may be distinctive, but the experience is the same as the Mesoamerican tribute system.[8]

Culture as Explanation: Ammon and King Lamoni

One of the stranger stories in the Book of Mormon is Ammon's experience with king Lamoni. Although it is a popular story of faith, read without any historical context it appears highly implausible.[9] Ammon arrived as a lone Nephite among enemy Lamanites. Rather than treating him as an enemy warrior or spy, Lamoni proposes that Ammon marry his daughter, thus inviting him to become a member of the royal family. When Ammon refused, announcing that he preferred to be a servant, Lamoni gave him an assignment that had resulted in the execution of many (if not all) of the previous servants (Alma 17:28, 18:4, 19:20). Seemingly without hesitation Ammon is offered a place in the king's family, then with dizzying speed he falls from a potentially high social position to that of a servant sent on what amounted to a suicide mission. Ammon is sent to water the king's flocks at the waters of Sebus.

Mormon suggests that the incident at the waters of Sebus resulted from larcenous Lamanites (Alma 18:7), but he also tells us that the Lamanites scattered the flocks and then made no effort to gather any of them up. Instead of gathering up stolen bounty, they waited around to see what the guards would do. The text never mentions what kind of animals these flocks were.[10] What the text does tell us is that the story depends upon the fact that the flocks are scattered.

Mormon intends us to read this story of manifesting Yahweh's power—and we do. However, we should also read it for what it tells of us Lamanite society, because

---

[8] The desired result of all Lamanite (and Gadianton) military actions is to create this tribute system. The single exception is the lighting raid on Ammonihah that is part of the story of the Anti-Nephi-Lehies. See that discussion for an explanation of why this one military action is different.

[9] Hugh Nibley, *The Prophetic Book of Mormon*, 539: "The whole affair at the waters of Sebus must strike anyone as very strange; I always thought that it was rather silly until the other day when I gave it a moment's thought." After providing his own discussion of the strange aspects of the story, Nibley relates it to ritual games. He concludes, 541, "Granted that the Lamanites at Sebus were depraved barbarians and real Yahoos, what is the logical or ritual explanation, the aestetic appeal, or sporting spirit of the tag-team wrestling, demolition- or roller-derbies, or laser-tag of our own enlightened age? Nothing could be closer psychologically and historically to the ancient version of this insanity than the doings by the waters of Sebus."

[10] All we know of the flocks is that they can be driven to water and they can be scattered. Some Mesoamericans kept deer. Lynn V. Foster, *Handbook to Life in the Ancient Maya World*, 312. Perhaps the flocks were deer. Deer could certainly scatter when startled.

otherwise, parts of it make little sense. First, we must understand the basic scene. The waters of Sebus are clearly in Lamoni's territory, as whatever animal making up the flocks would need water twice a day, most logically in the morning and the evening. Obviously their pasturage lacks water, or they would not need to be brought to Sebus. Marauders appear regularly at this watering place and have done so for some time.

Mormon blames these incidents on Lamanites without making any distinction between the thieves and Lamoni's people. In fact, it is probable that the thieves were Lamoni's subjects. They may even have been related to Lamoni, as evidenced by their appearance in the king's bedchamber (Alma 19:21). Furthermore, in Alma 18:20, Lamoni called them "my brethren," a virtually inconceivable term to apply to common brigands or even to anyone from another city. It also seems extremely unusual that the kin of known thieves would be so close to the king that they are among the first to respond when Abish called the people together to witness Lamoni's unconsciousness. In short, the thieves' relatives lived in the royal compound. This situation is much more complicated than a simple livestock raid.

If the thieves lived physically near, perhaps in, the palace and appeared when a witness testified that something important has happened to the king, they are obviously among the city's nobility. Maya culture has several examples of frequently competing factions among the nobles, with different groups vying for power.[11] Historian David Drew describes the problem for Maya kings:

> Increasingly recognized today . . . is the likelihood of a constant, dynamic tension between the ruler, along with the family group, the royal lineage that surrounded him, and other powerful and long-established lineages within a city state. The centralizing success of royal dynasties almost certainly obscures the extent to which kings depended upon and negotiated with other political factions. For each dynasty of the Classic period had in earlier centuries been merely one among many such patrilineages or kin-groups. It is impossible to know with any precision how ruling lines established themselves at the end of the Preclassic period—as war-leaders, perhaps, or as mediators in local disputes. However they came by their authority, they could only have maintained it through consent and co-operation, despite the impression of absolute power that their monuments create. From the eighth century, at Copán in particular, there is now some evidence of the negotiation that must have gone on behind the scenes. There is little reason to believe that this kind of jostling was not seen in earlier centuries too.[12]

In this context, then, the incident at the waters of Sebus stops being a cowboys-and-rustlers story and instead becomes a sophisticated and subtle political contest. If nobles were scattering the king's flocks, Lamoni may have been restricted in his ability to respond with direct action against them. While the putative thieves did not get many animals, they still got what they wanted: they embarrassed the king and weakened his control over his territory. Since scattering the flocks was an affront to the king, some action was required to save his honor. Unable to act against the true

---

[11] Simon Martin and Nikolai Grube, *Chronicle of the Maya Kings and Queens: Deciphering the Dynasties of the Ancient Maya*, 18.

[12] David Drew, *The Lost Chronicles of the Maya Kings*, 324.

culprits (if, as I hypothesize, they were a powerful rival lineage), the king executed the hapless servants—pawns in this high-stakes game.

Even this action played into the hands of Lamoni's rivals. He could not ignore the action, since that would have been an advertisement of his weakness; but slaying his servants inevitably reduced the number of his servants, which also weakened his strength. As more and more servants were executed, the loyalty of those remaining would be increasingly strained. Either way, the rival is winning.

When Ammon appeared he presented a problem—and then a solution to a problem. He was a prince from an enemy polity. Were he to remain in Lamoni's kingdom, the king needed to be able to control him. The first tactic, perhaps looking to future alliances, was to offer him a daughter. As a member of the royal family, Ammon would have been bound by culture, tradition, and honor to serve this new family. When Ammon refused that marriage, the king came up with another use for Ammon.

If Ammon could not be controlled, then perhaps the king could use that fact to help him with a different problem. The king sent Ammon to the waters of Sebus expecting that Ammon would act where servants who understood the political issues could not. As an "uncontrollable" Nephite, Ammon could upset the status quo to the king's benefit but the king would not be held responsible.

In a Mesoamerican context, these events have a logical explanation. The offer of the king's daughter was an invitation to become family and beholden to the king. Without the ability to ensure Ammon's loyalty, the king inserted him into a politically charged charade. Those who knew the actors in the elaborate game could not change the results, but Ammon did not know the players or the nature of the game. Ammon went in armed with lethal weapons against clubs, which were certainly dangerous, but not the equivalent of a sling and sword that Ammon wielded. Without this cultural background, the story makes little sense.

More than a Man

Ammon's actions at the Waters of Sebus were reported to the king, who was certainly impressed. Lamoni was so impressed with the miracle of the encounter that he suspected that Ammon might be a being from a higher realm:

> And when they had all testified to the things which they had seen, and he had learned of the faithfulness of Ammon in preserving his flocks, and also of his great power in contending against those who sought to slay him, he was astonished exceedingly, and said: Surely, this is more than a man. Behold, is not this the Great Spirit who doth send such great punishments upon this people, because of their murders? (Alma 18:2)

Strikingly, he declared: "Surely, this is more than a man." His speculation is that Ammon might even be "the Great Spirit who doth send such great punishments upon this people, because of their murders?" Both of these statements reflect opinions very much at home in the Mesoamerican religious worldview.

The line between human and divine in ancient Mesoamerican was less firmly drawn than in the modern Western world. Many Mesoamerican religious stories deal with exploits of individuals who are "more than men." The hero twins of the Popol

Vuh are certainly depicted as men, but they just as certainly have supernatural powers.[13] The Mixtec deity male 9 Wind is shown in the Codex Vindobonensis as a being in the heavens who descends and acts upon the earth.[14] The myriad legends surrounding the Aztec god Quetzalcoatl suggest that he had both a heavenly aspect and one in which he operates on earth as "more than a man."[15] These "more than men" may be best understood as demi-gods, or deities that live and function on earth but who retain other-worldly powers.[16] It is in this light that we should see king Lamoni's speculation about Ammon—as one of the demi-gods familiar to him from Mesoamerican mythology.

Perplexingly for modern expectations, Lamoni characterized "the Great Spirit" as sending "great punishments upon this people, because of their murders." How did he come to that conclusion if Ammon were the Great Spirit?

Mesoamerican demi-gods did not act logically or consistently. They acted for their own other-worldly purposes and mysterious motives. Like Greek deities, Mesoamerican demi-gods' presence among human beings was ambiguous at best. They were not always beneficial—indeed, were often malevolent. In Mesoamerica, a demi-god's appearance would be, at the very least, risky even if it were not immediately dangerous. Ammon's prowess confirmed that he was dangerous. There was no guarantee that he would not be just as dangerous to Lamoni's people as he had been to Lamoni's enemies.

But what would prompt a demi-god to come among them? Lamoni made a connection between his political expedient of executing the servants and Ammon's appearance. If the first event caused the second, then Ammon was probably angry. He had saved the current set of servants from being executed by his swift and bloody action at the waters of Sebus. Lamoni would certainly have known that his executed servants had not truly been at fault and obviously had a guilty conscience as a result. In fact, Lamoni told the servants standing before him that Ammon had "come down at this time to preserve your lives, that I might not slay you as I did your brethren" (Alma 18:4).

Lamoni's response to the news about Ammon's prowess is authentically cautious and fearful. Were Ammon a demi-god, the extra-worldly power that destroyed the attackers as the Waters of Sebus might easily be turned against the king who sent innocent men to their deaths.

Mark Alan Wright suggests that the result of Ammon's preaching to Lamoni—the episode where Lamoni, his queen, and Ammon all fall to the ground as though they were dead (Alma 19:13–15)—may also echo Mesoamerican cultural expectations: "Bruce Love shared an account of a Yucatecan man who was working in his field one

---

[13] *Popol Vuh: The Definitive Edition of the Mayan Book of the Dawn of Life and the Glories of Gods and Kings*, 140–48, provides some examples. The entire mythological section is applicable.

[14] Jill Leslie Furst, *Codex Vindobonensis Mexicanus I: A Commentary*, 106–8, plate 123.

[15] Brant A. Gardner, "Quetzalcoatl's Fathers: A Critical Examination of Source Materials," and Alfredo López Austín, *Hombre Diós*, 75–101.

[16] Foster, *Handbook to Life in the Ancient Maya World*, 159.

day with his brother, only to be overtaken by a strong force that knocked him to the earth. That night they sought out a *j-meen*, a healer, and he consulted his sastun [also spelled zaztun, a physical divination aid] and other sacred objects to determine the cause of his ailment. After three days of prayers, offerings, and cleansing rituals, the man was restored to health and his 'spiritual balance returned.'"[17]

Wright further suggests that the cultural witness to the calling of a Mesoamerican holy man was often an event that was apparently life-threatening.[18] The holy man received his calling through a near-death experience. If that understanding informed the situation with Lamoni, then when the three come back to life it is not only a miracle but also a divine calling. It is the expected behavior of one who has been touched by the gods.

Horses, Chariots, and Other Anachronistic Nouns

Alma 18:9 introduces us to the two most obvious anachronisms in the Book of Mormon: "And they said unto him: Behold, he [Ammon] is feeding thy horses. Now the king had commanded his servants, previous to the time of the watering of their flocks, that they should prepare his horses and chariots, and conduct him forth to the land of Nephi; for there had been a great feast appointed at the land of Nephi, by the father of Lamoni, who was king over all the land."

To date, there is no uncontested evidence for horses in the Americas during Book of Mormon times, though there is indisputable evidence that there were many species of horse during the Pleistocene (with an assumed termination of between ten and twelve thousand years ago).[19] As for chariots, no archaeological evidence whatsoever has survived of a large, wheeled conveyance. Several small ceremonial objects with wheels have been recovered,[20] but they simply indicate that the wheel and axle were known, not that chariots (or other large, wheeled conveyances) were.[21]

---

[17] Mark Alan Wright, "Nephite Daykeepers: Ritual Specialists in the Book of Mormon," Quoting Bruce Love, *Maya Shamanism Today: Connecting with the Cosmos in Rural Yucatan* (Lancaster, Calif.: Labyrinthos Press, 2004), 1–3.

[18] Ibid., 10–11.

[19] Wade E. Miller, *Science and the Book of Mormon. Cureloms, Cumoms, Horses & More*, 75.

[20] Richard A. Diehl and Margaret D. Mandeville, "Tula, and Wheeled Animal Effigies in Mesoamerica," *Antiquity* 61, no. 232 (1987): 239–46; Paul R. Cheesman, *The World of the Book of Mormon*, 172–73; Paul R. Cheesman, "The Wheel in Ancient America," 185–97; John L. Sorenson, "Wheeled Figurines in the Ancient World." Diehl and Mandeville (p. 243) note that while these objects were once described as toys, it is more likely that they had a ritual function for adults.

[21] If Mesoamerican cultures knew of the wheel and axle, why didn't they use them for transport? Diehl and Margaret D. Mandeville, "Tula, and Wheeled Animal Effigies in Mesoamerica," 244, suggest:

> A final issue is why Mesoamerican Indians never adopted the wheel as a practical transportation device—a step which seems so natural from our technologically oriented worldview that we have difficulty comprehending why it did not occur. However, anthropologists have long known that most "unexplainable" facets of human culture are the result of factors

Nevertheless, some LDS authors have emphasized the evidence that does support the persistence of the horse into Book of Mormon times. John L. Sorenson notes:

> Within the last decade, further efforts have been made to clarify whether some possible American horse bones are really ancient. Under the auspices of the Foundation for Ancient Research and Mormon Studies (now the Neal A. Maxwell Institute for Religious Research), research has sought to reexamine specimens of purported pre-Columbian origin. Because the research is ongoing, little has been published from it. In the project, a physicist and a paleontologist have radiocarbon-dated as many horse remains in North or Middle America as paleontologists have suspected might predate the arrival of European explorers. Scores of specimens have been dated, although in the case of some of the most promising possibilities the purported bones have proved to be inaccessible (i.e., "cannot now be found"). In three instances the results yield apparently reliable pre-Columbian dates.[22]

Wade E. Miller gives more details on the study that Sorenson referenced:

> Small scattered populations of horse and ass, especially in remote areas, probably survived in North America until shortly before they were reintroduced by the Spaniards. Some recent datings, mostly unpublished, lead me to this conclusion. The Carbon-14 dating involved was first instigated by Dr. Steven E. Jones, former physics professor at Brigham Young University. I later worked with him on these.
> Some of the unpublished dates run on horse fossils that appear to be valid are: 5,890 B.C. (Pratt Cave in Texas); 830 B.C. (southern Saskatchewan, Canada); 815 A.D. (Ontario, Canada); 400 A.D. (Wolf Spider Cave, Colorado). A date of about 120 B.C. was determined using a thermoluminescence method on a horse bone from Horesethief Cave in Wyoming. While these dates are important, it will take a number of others in this age range to convince skeptics that the horse did continue in North America past the Pleistocene into historic times. In my opinion these dates eventually will come.[23]

Although this research suggests caution in declaring that there could not have been horses in Book of Mormon times,[24] it remains true that there is no evidence that

---

which are quite logical once they are known. We believe that a set of environmental and cultural factors so reduced the potential advantages of the wheel that it was not adopted...

[The absence of] draught animals and appropriate terrain, inhibited and probably prohibited the development of wheeled transportation.

The absence of draught animals was the major obstacle. Wheeled vehicles laden with cargo offer no substantial advantages over human porters if they must be propelled by people, particularly over long distances and on sloping or broken terrain. This is especially true of the very heavy vehicles with solid wooden wheels and axles, the earliest type known in the Old World and logically the first types in the technological evolution of vehicles. Animal traction is essential.

[22] John L. Sorenson, *Mormon's Codex: An Ancient American Book*, 317–18.

[23] Miller, *Science and the Book of Mormon*, 77. Wade E. Miller and Matthew Roper, "Animals in the Book of Mormon: Challenges and Perspectives."

[24] Others have also accepted that there would have been modern horses among the Nephites. See: Robert R. Bennett, "Horses in the Book of Mormon," accepts that the word "horse" accurately represented that animal: "In short, the Book of Mormon claims only that horses were known to some New World peoples before the time of Christ in certain limited regions of

a horse played any significant part in Mesoamerican culture. The Book of Mormon "horse" never fulfills the functions we expect of a horse, nor does it impact Nephite society as it did other societies from the nomadic Mongols (transport, valuable property) to sedentary farmers of Europe (plowing, riding, beasts of burden, etc.).

What's In a Name?

Two languages collide when new people invade an existing ecosphere. The flora and fauna have no existing names in the intruding language. In those situations, a common solution is to adapt known labels to apply to the new plants and animals. Sorenson therefore notes: "Was a Nephite 'horse' a specimen of our *Equus equus*? When they saw Spanish horses, the Aztecs called them 'the Spaniards' deer,' while to Europeans, small Mexican brocket deer were considered 'goats.' In the Isthmus of Tehuantepec, the tapir was called 'once an ass.' These examples show the difficulty of translating the names of unfamiliar beasts."[25]

The same process occurred with plants. In King James English, *corn* was a generic term for *grain*. When friendly Indians introduced maize to English speakers along the Atlantic seaboard, the British called it *corn*, recontextualizing it to differentiate it from wheat.[26] Now, four hundred years later, *corn* means *maize* to most English readers/speakers, and the generic meaning of *corn* as *grain* is fading into the realm of historical linguistics.

This process of linguistic adaptation is well understood and represents a plausible explanation for how a seemingly anachronistic term might end up in the Book of Mormon.[27] While Mesoamericans might not have known a horse, the Lehites certainly did and it is therefore plausible that they used their traditional word *horse* to describe the unfamiliar animal. It was this process that gives us our name hippopotamus, which means *river horse*. Although it hardly seems horse-like, it was nevertheless given that appellation.

This known process explains the word *horse* in the Book of Mormon (as well as other anachronistic nouns) by suggesting that Joseph Smith accurately translated the Lehite/Nephite misapplication of a term inherited from the Old World and applied to

---

the New World. Thus we need not conclude from the text that horses were universally known in the Americas throughout pre-Columbian history."

Daniel Johnson, "Hard Evidence of Horses in America."

Michael R. Ash, "Horses in the Book of Mormon."

John L. Lund, *Mesoamerica and the Book of Mormon: Is This the Place?* 243–58.

[25] Sorenson, *Mormon's Codex*, 313.

[26] Sorenson, *An Ancient American Setting for the Book of Mormon*, 288. Sorenson also suggested (p. 293): "The lowland Maya at first named all the big animals of the Spaniards—horse, mule, ass—with the name of the nearest native of equivalent size—the tapir. The Spaniards, however, thought the tapir looked like a pig, although it weighs up to 700 pounds. Others considered the tapir to resemble the ass; sixty years ago in southern Mexico the beast was called *anteburro* or 'once-an-ass.'"

[27] Ibid., 318: "A large literature discusses the terminological problem that explorers of new territories face when they come across un familiar animals; they usually dub these with names of similar and more familiar creatures. These names prove misleading if taken literally."

a plant or animal in the New World. The acceptability of this particular explanation is directly related to one's theory of the translation of the Book of Mormon. It requires a very literalist translation which preserved the Nephite cross-labeling.

Did the translation mislabeling occur with the Nephites or with Joseph? Certainly, the Middle Eastern Nephites (who knew what horses looked like and what they were used for) might have mislabeled as "horses" the closest local quadrupeds that they found in the New World. However, retaining this mistaken label assumes that Hebrew continued to be their common language and that they continued to name local animals using Hebrew words. Those local animals already had names in the native languages; and if the Nephites adopted one of those languages as their lingua franca (preserving Hebrew as a sacred language), then there would have been no reason why they insisted on the mislabel (which would, at a minimum, have confused the local people and their own locally born children) rather than adopting the animal's name in the native language. For example, even English-speakers identify the Mesoamerican ocelot by a word derived from Aztec *ocelotl*. The ocelot is not mislabeled; it is known by a borrowed identification. Similarly, our very common words "chocolate" and "tomato" are derived from Aztec loan words: *chocolatl* and *tomatl*. I find it much more likely that anachronistic vocabulary such as "horse" is the result of the modern translator's imposition of his language culture than that such words represent a literalist translation of a Nephite cross-label.

Translation Anachronisms

There are two times where languages collided in the description of the flora and fauna of the New World. One would be when the Lehites encountered the new animals and reapplied labels from Old World animals, such as Sorenson suggests. The other time was when Joseph translated the plate text into English. I suggest that the best explanation for the anachronistic nouns comes from the nature of Joseph's translation.

We need look no farther than the King James translation of the Bible for examples of anachronisms that occur only in the translation and not in the text being translated. The KJV frequently mentions candles[28] even though oil lamps provided light during both the Old and New Testaments. Thus, the word *candle* is an anachronism, but only in the translation. With the availability of the Hebrew and Greek source texts, it is clear that the original documents refer to the oil lamps rather than candles.

In the Book of Mormon case, we don't have the original text. We must peer through the translation to determine whether it is an anachronism on the original plate text or only in the English translation. The only way to do so is to examine the text to see if it tells us anything about a horse or chariot that would help us identify the animal and conveyance to which the words refer.

---

[28] Job 18:6, 21:17; Ps. 18:28; Prov. 20:27, 24:20, 31:18; Jer. 25:10; Matt. 5:15; Mark 4:21; Luke 8:16, 11:33, 15:8; Rev. 18:23, 22:5.

When a text uses such terms in contexts that justify our assumptions about the words, then we may reasonably conclude that the translated terms are functioning according to those assumptions. An excellent example from the Old Testament is Jeremiah 51:21: "And with thee will I break in pieces the horse and his rider; and with thee will I break in pieces the chariot and his rider." It is abundantly clear that men ride horses and ride in chariots. Similarly, Jeremiah 46:9 declares: "Come up, ye horses; and rage, ye chariots; and let the mighty men come forth; the Ethiopians and the Libyans, that handle the shield; and the Lydians, that handle and bend the bow." Here both the horse and the chariot function in a military setting in which, again, men ride on horses and in chariots.

These are the contexts that establish our assumptions about the relationship between horses and chariots. Deanne Matheny notes: "Twice King Lamoni's horses and chariots are prepared for traveling (Alma 18:9–10; 20:6). Horses and chariots also are among the items which the Nephites assembled before their battle with the Gadianton robbers (3 Ne. 3:22). These references indicate that horses functioned in several areas to pull conveyances of some sort." She footnotes this statement with: "Also found in 3 Nephi is Jesus' warning to the Gentiles that unless they repent, he will cut off their horses out of the midst of them and he will destroy their chariots (3 Ne. 21:14)."[29]

Unfortunately, the context to which Matheny assigns these verses are not their original context. For example, she says "horses and chariots are among the items with the Nephites assembled before their battle with the Gadianton robbers." The horses and chariots are clearly in a military context. However, 3 Nephi 3:22 reads:

> And it came to pass in the seventeenth year, in the latter end of the year, the proclamation of Lachoneus had gone forth throughout all the face of the land, and they had taken their horses, and their chariots, and their cattle, and all their flocks, and their herds, and their grain, and all their substance, and did march forth by thousands and by tens of thousands, until they had all gone forth to the place which had been appointed that they should gather themselves together, to defend themselves against their enemies.

Although the reason for gathering the material is a military situation, the actual context of horses and chariots is "and their cattle, and all their flocks, and their herds, and their grain, and all their substance." That is not a military context. Her footnote to 3 Nephi 21:14 neglects to note that the verse is an unlabeled quotation of Micah 5:9–14 (compare 3 Ne. 21:13–18).

The contextual data for Ammon's activities do not convey a military connection.[30] In Alma 18:9, the servants explain: "Behold, he is feeding thy horses. Now the king had commanded his servants . . . that they should prepare his horses and chariots, and conduct him forth to the land of Nephi." This context explains that

---

[29] Deanne G. Matheny, "Does the Shoe Fit? A Critique of the Limited Tehuantepec Geography," 305 and footnote 23.
[30] 2 Nephi 12:7 and 2 Nephi 15:28, which describe horses and chariots functioning in Old Testament contexts are, likewise, Old Testament quotations from Isaiah.

horses and chariots are near the palace and that horses must be fed. Lamoni is going to the land of Nephi on a formal state visit ("a great feast appointed . . . by the father of Lamoni") but the role played by the horses and chariots is not clear. We assume that the horse pulls the chariot because that's what horses do in the histories with which we are familiar. However, it isn't the relationship between the English words that is important. It is the discernible relationship in the text.

Rather than appear in the context of war, Book of Mormon horses and chariots appear in the context of a formal state visit. Horses and chariots reappear in that setting when Ammon and Lamoni hear that Ammon's brothers are in prison: "Lamoni . . . caused that his servants should make ready his horses and his chariots" (Alma 20:6) for another state visit to the king of the land where they were held.

Chariots never appear in the context of Book of Mormon warfare. Horses only move and eat. They never explicitly pull anything. They are never ridden. If we replaced the word *horse* with a made-up word (such as *glerk*) we would never suspect that a *glerk* was a horse. Thus, the text itself does not support *horse* as the only or even best translation for whatever word was on the plates.[31]

The use of chariot in the translation represents two different problems of meaning. The first is that the term Joseph used probably intended a meaning that has faded from use. William Henry Holmes (1846–1933) recorded: "[Désiré] Charnay [1828–1915] obtained from an ancient cemetery at Tenenpanco, Mexico, a number of toy chariots of terra cotta, presumably buried with the body of a child, some of which retained their wheels."[32] Holmes had no problem using the same word that Charnay had used: "These chariots are shaped like a flattened *cayote* [coyote] (a kind of long-bodied fox) with its straight ears and pointed face, and the wheels fit into four terra-cotta stumps; on my renewing the wood axle-tree, which had been destroyed long since, the chariots began to move."[33] Holmes and Charnay wrote that there were chariots in Mesoamerica. They did not mean Old World war chariots. The Book of Mormon translation need not either.

Holmes, Charnay, and Joseph were likely following standard vocabulary of the times. Webster's 1828 dictionary indicates that one meaning for chariot was "a half coach; a carriage with four wheels and one seat behind, used for convenience and pleasure."[34] It is this definition that lies behind the use of "chariot" in Doctrine and Covenants 62:7: "I, the Lord, am willing, if any among you desire to ride upon horses, or upon mules, or in chariots, he shall receive this blessing, if he receive it from the hand of the Lord, with a thankful heart in all things." The contemporary meaning of

---

[31] In contrast to the vocabulary issue with "horse," the use of metal plates in the Book of Mormon is not an anachronism because the context refers to creating them with ore (1 Ne. 19:1; Mosiah 21:27; Morm. 8:5) and they were metal when delivered to Joseph Smith. The process of identifying an anachronism to vocabulary choices cannot be used indiscriminately but must be based on the evidence from the text.

[32] William Henry Holmes, *Handbook of Aboriginal American Antiquities*, 20.

[33] Désiré Charnay, *The Ancient Cities of the New World, being Voyages and Explorations in Mexico and Central America from 1857–1882*, 171.

[34] Noah Webster, *American Dictionary of the English Language: 1828*.

chariot allowed for a four-wheeled conveyance. Although a "carriage with four wheels" is also unlikely to be an accurate translation for whatever was on the plates, it certainly demonstrates that the Book of Mormon chariot need not suggest Old World war chariots.

What Might Have Been Translated as "Horse" and "Chariot"?

Even assuming that *horse* and *chariot* represent translation anachronisms, the nouns still represent textual placeholders from some animal and conveyance in the original plate language. Fortunately, a Mesoamerican context provides a culturally plausible possibility.

The appropriate conveyance would be a royal litter, carried on men's shoulders rather than pulled by an animal. The royal litter is also often associated with an animal. Freidel, Schele, and Parker note:

> Lintel 2 of Temple 1 shows Hasaw-Ka'an-K'awil wearing the balloon headdress of Tlaloc-Venus warfare adopted at the time of the Waxaktun conquest, and holding the bunched javelins and shield, the original metaphors for war imported from Teotihuacán. He sits in majesty on the litter that carried him into battle, while above him hulks Waxaklahun-Ubah-Kan, the great War Serpent....
>
> Graffiti drawings scratched on the walls of Tikal palaces, depicting the conjuring of supernatural beings from the Otherworld, prove that these scenes were more than imaginary events seen only by the kings. Several of these elaborate doodles show the great litters of the king with his protector beings hovering over him while he is participating in ritual. These images are not the propaganda of rulers, created in an effort to persuade the people of the reality of the supernatural events they were witnessing. They are the poorly drawn images of witnesses, perhaps minor members of lordly families, who scratched the wonders that they saw during moments of ritual into the walls of the places where they lived their lives.[35]

---

[35] David Freidel, Linda Schele, and Joy Parker, *Maya Cosmos: Three Thousand Years on the Shaman's Path*, 311–13. David A. Freidel, "Maya Warfare, Myth and Reality," [no page]:

> Gods also accompanied lords and armies in Classic period struggles. One truly great king of Tikal, prosaically termed Ruler A by archaeologists, named himself Hasaw-Chan-K'awil, the spiritual embodiment of the battle standard. In so doing, he virtually claimed to be war itself incarnate. In two beautifully carved lintels spanning the doorways of his funeral temple, Temple 1 of Tikal, Hasaw-Chan-K'awil portrayed himself seated in majesty upon ornate litters. Behind him on one of the litters looms a huge image of the 18-Rabbit Serpent portrayed as a limbed and clawed monster covered with mosaic spangles. The monster leans over him to grasp the battle standard attached to the front of the litter. On the second litter, an enormous jaguar, Nu-Balam-Chak, ("deadly friend great jaguar?") menaces in the same pose, reaching over the king's head to hold the battle standard. These Tikal idols no doubt housed gods, but they were made of material. There are numerous informal graffiti scratched on palace walls at Tikal that show lords being carried around in litters with these huge idols. And we can be sure that Maya armies carried these litters into battle. King Flint-Sky-God K of the city of Dos Pilas south of Tikal exulted in one of his victory texts that he captured the predecessor of Hasaw-Chan-K'awil, King Shield-Skull of Tikal. His successor Shield-Sky-God K proudly declared himself guardian

296 *Traditions of the Fathers*

Figure 10: Battle litter graffiti from Tikal

Karl Taube discusses the practice among the later lowland Maya:

> Along with warriors and hunters, Maya kings had a distinct relation with the forest, as they were capable of passing beyond political and natural boundaries to visit or conquer distant realms. With this unique ability, they were identified with the jaguar (the "king" of the forest)—a concept vividly expressed by royal litters and palanquins topped by jaguar beings. First appearing on Stela 212 of Late Preclassic Izapa, such jaguar vehicles are common in Classic Maya art, including figurines.
>
> The most elaborate portrayals of jaguar palanquins appear on wooden lintels from Temples I and IV of Tikal. In the lintel scenes, the seated rulers are backed by massive supernatural jaguar figures. . . . The jaguar palanquins reveal that, during the Classic Maya period, Maya kings prowled the landscape as fierce beasts guarding and extending their domain.[36]

---

of the Kin Balam, the Sun Jaguar, of Tikal. This is the war god Shield-Skull evidently accompanied on his litter into that catastrophic conflict. No wonder, then, that Hasaw-Chan-K'awil celebrated the construction and activation of new war images for his city. Those gods served Tikal well, for Hasaw-Chan-K'awil's successor later depicted himself seated on the captured Sun Jaguar litter of an enemy king from the city of Naranjo.

[36] Karl Taube, "Ancient and Contemporary Maya Conceptions about Field and Forest," 480. See also Justin Kerr, "Maya Vase Data Base: A Pre-Columbian Portfolio." The litter accompanied by an animal may be seen on the vase designated as Kerr Number 767.

Another possibility is that the king in the litter is accompanied by a dog, as seen on Maya vases: Kerr Number 594; Kerr Number 5534; Kerr Number 6317. Justin Kerr pioneered a rollout technique for photographing Maya pots [Kerr developed a method that "unrolls" the pot to create a photography of the full painting as though it were on a flat surface]. That process allows for a better assessment of the entire scene based on a photograph. Photographs in his large collection are identified by Kerr numbers, which allow scholars to easily access the rollout of the indicated pot in the online collection.

Maya art represents the king riding on a litter associated with an animal as an accompanying spirit. The graffiti litters at least open the possibility that these were simply formal litters and not limited to battle context. These litters were accompanied by a "battle beast," or an animal alter ego, embodied in the regalia of the king and litter.[37] I suggest that the plausible underlying conveyance in the story of Ammon was a royal litter, accompanied in peacetime by the spiritual animal associated with the king. I suggest that the appearance of "horse" in this context comes from Joseph's assumptions in the translation rather than the meaning of the text on the plates.

This animal was a type of alter-ego for the king, and was called the *way* (pronounced "Y"):

> The *wayob* [plural of *way*] of the Classic Maya imagery appeared in many guises, including humanlike forms, animals of all sorts, and grotesque combinations of human and animal bodies. . . . It is interesting that pottery scenes from most of the major kingdoms depict creatures who are the *way* of their ruling lords; but with the exception of the rulers of Palenque, individual kings never recorded the names of their *way* in the texts on their monuments. From this we deduce that particular companion spirits were associated with particular lineages and kingdoms, and that their names were generally known to the artist who painted the pots. . . .
>
> The ancient Maya also transformed into their *wayob* when they fought their wars, and they very likely saw the planets and constellations as the *wayob* of the gods and their ancestors.[38]

There is no way to know precisely what was on the plates. However, there is ample evidence that Joseph's translation process allowed him to impose modern terms and concepts on ancient but unfamiliar terms.[39] Thus, plausible combinations of elements may explain the horse/chariot combination in the Book of Mormon in a way that fits the context and the descriptions rather than just the assumptions embodied in the English words *horse* and *chariot*. Strengthening this hypothesis is the mention of horses and chariots in Alma 18:9 where the context is a "great feast appointed at the land of Nephi, by the father of Lamoni, who was king over all the land." (See "The Overking and Subordinate Kings" below in this chapter.) The fact that the horses were fed suggests either a live accompanying animal or another instance of assumptive translation.

---

[37] Taube, "Ancient and Contemporary Maya Conceptions about Field and Forest," 310–13.
[38] Ibid., 191–92.
[39] Alma 14:29: "fled from the presence of Alma and Amulek even as a goat fleeth with her young from two lions." Neither goats or lions are native to Mesoamerica and are also candidates for a translation issue. The idiom could easily have involved hunter and prey, but they must be a different hunter and prey from the animals used in translation. In this case, it is unclear how the pairing of goats and lions occurred. Lions are certainly not a New York predator and there is no biblical pairing of the goats and lions that might explain the paired translation. There might be a hint in the requirement that there be two lions, but I am not aware of what that might be.

298 *Traditions of the Fathers*

Controversial "Coins"

A similar issue that hinges on both translation and reading assumptions is the notion of anachronous coins in the Book of Mormon. Alma 11:4 says: "Now these are the names of the different pieces of their gold, and of their silver, according to their value." Perhaps because a common currency in the world during Joseph Smith's time was the Spanish coin that was give the English name "piece of eight" (a single coin worth eight *reales*), Alma's "pieces of their gold" were assumed to be coins.

It is not hard to find faithful LDS authors who assume that this text indicated coinage. George Reynolds and Janne M. Sjodahl's *Commentary on the Book of Mormon* discusses this section in terms of coinage.[40] Sidney B. Sperry and Monte S. Nyman similarly refer to coins in the Book of Mormon.[41] Richard Pearson Smith even suggested that "in every case it turns out that the [Nephite coinage] system has an edge over the other systems from the standpoint of number of coins required for a purchase."[42] So pervasive was the assumptive reading of the text that the heading in the 1920 edition was "Nephite coins and measures," which was modified only slightly in the 1981 edition: "Nephite coinage set forth." The 1830 edition did not have a chapter break between our chapters 10 and 11, and the headnote of the chapter including our chapter 11 said nothing at all about this section.

The idea that there would be coins in the Book of Mormon has rightly been the focus of historical criticism of the text. Bill McKeever and Eric Johnson of the *Mormonism Research Ministry* note:

> Some have criticized the Mormon Church for its failure to provide evidence for any Nephite coins. But should we really expect the LDS Church to produce them? Coinage in the Western Hemisphere during the *Book of Mormon* time period was unknown. The use of coins did not become popular until the sixteenth century, more than a millennium after the last Nephite had allegedly died. However, the problem does not lie in a lack of Nephite coins. Rather, it lies in Joseph Smith's implication that such coins existed in the first place.[43]

McKeever and Johnson are correct that the presence of coins would be anomalous. They also correctly note that many LDS authors have assumed that the text refers to coins. They also correctly note that "over the years, many Mormons—including some scholars—have dismissed [the] description as coins."[44] They cite Daniel C. Peterson's discussion:

> It is, alas, quite true that there is no evidence whatsoever for the existence of Book of Mormon coins. Not even in the Book of Mormon itself. The text of the Book of Mormon never mentions the word "coin" or any variant of it. The reference to "Nephite coinage" in the chapter heading to Alma 11 is not part of the original text, and is mistaken. Alma

---

[40] George Reynolds and Janne M. Sjodahl, *Commentary on the Book of Mormon*, 3:175–78.

[41] Sidney B. Sperry, *Book of Mormon Compendium*, 335; Monte S. Nyman, *The Record of Alma: A Teaching Commentary on the Book of Mormon*, 135–37.

[42] Richard Pearson Smith, "The Nephite Monetary System," 316.

[43] Bill McKeever and Eric Johnson, "Are Ancient Coins Mentioned in the Book of Mormon?" (no page).

[44] Ibid.

11 is almost certainly talking about standardized weights of metal—a historical step toward coinage, but not yet the real thing. [Here ends McKeever and Johnson's citation of Peterson. Peterson continues:] Genuine coinage was not invented until some years after Lehi's departure from Jerusalem. And, even then, it scarcely circulated beyond Anatolia and reached Palestine only in the fifth century before Christ. Thus, while an ignorant nineteenth-century con artist might easily have blundered into putting coins in the pockets of his fictional Near Eastern immigrants, the Book of Mormon depicts precisely the monetary situation that it ought to for its claimed time and place of cultural origin. So Latter-day Saint scholars would be as surprised as anybody if we were someday to find a cache of "Book of Mormon coins."[45]

McKeever and Johnson suggest that Joseph Smith really intended coins, but this conclusion is based on their assumption that "pieces" necessarily refers to coins. Peterson's point is that the text not only does not say coins, but it does not describe coins.[46] The textual descriptions actually come much closer to descriptions of exchange systems from the ancient world where there is no assumption nor indication that the system included coins.[47] John W. Welch notes the initial provisions of Eshnunna's law code, instituted in Babylon in the early eighteenth century B.C.

> 1 kor of barley is (priced) at 1 shekel of silver;
> 3 *qa* of "best oil" are (priced) at 1 shekel of silver;
> 1 seah (and) 2 *qa* of sesame oil are (priced) at 1 shekel of silver. . .

---

[45] Daniel C. Peterson, "Chattanooga Cheapshot, or The Gall of Bitterness," 55. Peterson was responding to a similar discussion of coins in John Ankerberg and John Weldon, *Everything You Ever Wanted to Know about Mormonism*, 285–86.

[46] McKeever and Johnson, "Are Ancient Coins Mentioned in the Book of Mormon?" (no page): declare:

> We disagree with Dr. Peterson's claim that no variant of the word *coin* is used in the text. Taking his advice that Noah Webster's 1828 *American Dictionary of the English Language* is perhaps "our best source for the language of Joseph Smith and his contemporaries" (*Review of Books on the Book of Mormon*, 5:8), there are several definitions found under the word "piece" (the word Smith used in Alma 11:4). What's interesting is that none of them have any meaning that would fit Alma 11:4 until the eighth definition: "A coin; as a piece of eight." The meaning for "piece" in Joseph Smith's day was "coin." This shows that "coin" was interpreted not only by James Talmage but the "translator" of the Book of Mormon himself!

Their evidence for "piece" as "coin" is the eighth definition in Webster's 1828 dictionary, where it says "a coin; as in a *piece* of eight." This argument supposes that "piece" necessarily infers the entire phrase "piece of eight." It rather seems that the word was part of a nominative phrase that had meaning as a whole rather than as the separate words.

A second issue with their analysis is in the supposition that whatever term Joseph used necessarily replicated a meaning from the plate text. It is difficult to see what the plate might have had that necessarily invoked a specific Spanish coin.

[47] John W. Welch, "Weighing and Measuring in the Worlds of the Book of Mormon," 43: "The term *pieces* most likely refers to metallic weights of some sort. The first coins known to history—at least coins in the modern sense—appeared in Lydia in western Asia Minor by the seventh century B.C., spreading into the Mediterranean region only after Lehi had left Jerusalem. As in other ancient cultures, the Nephites seem to have used weighted pieces of metal as payment form measured amounts of grain."

> The hire for a wagon together with its oxen and its driver is 1 *massiktum* (and) 4 seah of barley. If it is (paid in) silver, the hire is one third of a shekel.[48]

Welch also notes a parallel between the Babylonian and Nephite systems which:

> has to do with the basic reason for establishing values for various goods. At Eshnunna, this valuation was designed to allow merchants to deal in a variety of commodities, each one being convertible into either silver or barley, sesame oil, wool, and other things. Thus precious metal and grain measures were interchangeable. Correspondingly, the Nephite system allowed traders to convert from silver or gold into many other goods: "also for a measure of every kind of grain" (Alma 11:7).[49]

Alma 11:7 specifies: "A senum of silver was equal to a senine of gold, and either for a measure of barley, and also for a measure of every kind of grain." The fact that these measures, in either gold or silver, are equivalent to a measure of grain tells us that we are dealing with weights. The primary Mesoamerican food crops were corn and beans, both of which could easily be measured by weight.

The Overking and Subordinate Kings

One of the most interesting facets of Lamanite political culture is the interrelationship among kings.[50] In Mosiah 24:2 we find: "For the Lamanites had taken possession of all these lands; therefore, the king of the Lamanites had appointed kings over all these lands." This Lamanite practice of a king over kings replicates what is known of many later Maya political interactions. Simon Martin and Nikolai Grube summarize the discernible pattern:

> The emergence of new information from the inscriptions, in which the Maya directly describe their political world, allows a reassessment of the topic. Our own research . . . points to a pervasive and enduring system of "overkingship" that shaped almost every facet of the Classic landscape [250 A.D. to 900 A.D.]. Such a scheme accords closely with wider Mesoamerican practice, while seeming to reconcile the most compelling features of the two existing views, namely the overwhelming evidence for multiple small kingdoms and the great disparities in the size of their capitals.[51]

---

[48] John W. Welch, "The Laws of Eshnunna and Nephi Economics," 147.

[49] Welch, "Weighing and Measuring in the Worlds of the Book of Mormon," 41. John W. Welch, "A Steady Stream of Significant Recognitions," 348–50. Michael R. Ash, *Of Faith and Reason: 80 Evidences Supporting the Prophet Joseph Smith*, 82–83, summarizes some of the evidence for the weights and measures as opposed to coinage.

[50] Noel B. Reynolds, "Nephite Kingship Reconsidered," 164: "The Lamanites seem to have installed a very different system—one of tributary kings appointed by the superior monarch, not by a prophet (see Mosiah 24:2–3), more like the system that appears to have prevailed in ancient Mesoamerica. At no time do we see the Nephites using a multilayered or federal system with subordinate kings."

[51] Martin and Grube, *Chronicle of the Maya Kings and Queens*, 18–19. See also, Linda Schele and Peter Mathews, "Royal Visits and other Intersite Relationships," 251: "Our present view of the Classic Maya lowlands is one of many small political units, each ruled over by a king, of ahau

More than a simple statement that the king of the Lamanites appointed other kings, we see specific types of relationships among kings in other parts of the Book of Mormon. For example, after Ammon has earned king Lamoni's trust, Lamoni suggests the way to free Ammon's brethren from imprisonment in the land of Middoni: "Now Lamoni said unto Ammon: . . . I will go with thee to the land of Middoni; for the king of the land of Middoni, whose name is Antiomno, is a friend unto me; therefore I go to the land of Middoni, that I may flatter the king of the land, and he will cast thy brethren out of prison" (Alma 20:4).

Lamoni proposes to use his personal influence with Antiomno to effect the release of Ammon's brethren. He does not propose a military solution. Specifically, he will "flatter" a king in a different land who "is a friend unto me." In the context of known Mesoamerican inter-city relationships, we can see Antiomno and the land of Middoni as part of the collection of cities who are beholden to the overking (who happens to be Lamoni's father).

The nature of these relationships is on display in a different way as Ammon and Lamoni, en route to the land of Middoni, meet Lamoni's father. This man remains unnamed in the text but is denominated as king over all Lamanite kings.

> And behold, the father of Lamoni said unto him: Why did ye not come to the feast on that great day when I made a feast unto my sons, and unto my people?
>
> And he also said: Whither art thou going with this Nephite, who is one of the children of a liar?
>
> And it came to pass that Lamoni rehearsed unto him whither he was going, for he feared to offend him.
>
> And he also told him all the cause of his tarrying in his own kingdom, that he did not go unto his father to the feast which he had prepared. (Alma 20:9–12)

The feast is first mentioned in Alma 18:9, when Ammon is feeding Lamoni's horses in preparation for the "great feast appointed at the land of Nephi, by the father of Lamoni, who was king over all the land." Clearly, when Lamoni ordered Ammon to prepare his horses and chariot for travel, he intended to attend the great feast. Presumably, the horses and chariots would have been the conveyance in which the king would make this trip or were otherwise associated with either the journey or Lamoni's reception at the feast.

The father's angry reaction makes it plain that Lamoni's absence was a serious breach of etiquette and, in fact, may be the reason the father is on the road in the first place—he is hunting Lamoni to demand an accounting. Later Classic Maya sites provide glyphic evidence of royal visits from subordinate rulers to their overlords.[52] According to Schele and Mathews, "The term 'royal visit' may be defined as the peaceful visit of one lord to the city of another. Although instances of royal visits

---

status, who had under him various other ahaus and cahals [ahau is the royal "lord" and cahal a provincial governor], some of whom were in charge of subsidiary centers within the polity."

[52] Martin and Grube, *Chronicle of the Maya Kings and Queens*, 249, also 228.

were only sporadically recorded, they were no doubt a common occurrence among the Classic Maya."[53]

In Maya culture, such visits could cement a relationship, or, in the breach, lead to war. Thus, a subordinate king who refused to come to the overlord's feast could have been considered in rebellion. Lamoni's father has not yet drawn this conclusion about his son but obviously feels that Lamoni owes him a convincing explanation about his absence. All facets of this story, the formal visit to another city and the expectation of a king's obeisance to the overking fit very comfortably into a Mesoamerican context.

The Treatment of Important Captives

Lamoni's royal visit to Antiomno provides another glimpse into Lamanite behavior that reflects Mesoamerican culture. The visit will request the release of Ammon's captive brethren. We learn that they had a very different reception than Ammon. No Lamanite princess was offered as a bride. Rather they were treated as enemies, captured, and tormented:

> And when Ammon did meet them he was exceedingly sorrowful, for behold they were naked, and their skins were worn exceedingly because of being bound with strong cords. And they also had suffered hunger, thirst, and all kinds of afflictions; nevertheless they were patient in all their sufferings. (Alma 20:29)

In the Maya world the mistreatment of captives was much more common than Ammon's remarkable reception. A polychrome Maya vase from Altar de Sacrificios (Early Classic period, A.D. 250–600) shows a captive dancing. The dancer's face is swollen, apparently as a result of torture.[54] A remarkable series of depictions on Maya stela shows the treatment of several named captives:

> Prestigious captives taken in battle were often kept alive for years on end. They were displayed in public rituals and often participated in these rituals in gruesome, humiliating, and painful ways. Smoking-Squirrel and Wac-Chanil-Ahau were enthusiastic practitioners of this sacred tradition. Kinichil-Cab of Ucanal survived his capture to reappear four years later, on May 23, 698, in an event that was in all probability a sacrificial ritual of some sort. Later in the same year, on September 23, Shield-Jaguar suffered through the same rite in "the land of Smoking-Squirrel of Naranjo." A year later, on April 19, 699, it was lady Wac-Chanil's turn. The hapless Kinichil-Cab appeared again in a public ritual she conducted. On Naranjo Stela 24 we see her standing on the bound, nearly naked body of this unfortunate warrior. Finally, on 9.13.10.0.0 (January 26, 702), the day Smoking-Squirrel dedicated both Stela 22 and Stela 24, the young king displayed his famous captive, Shield-Jaguar of Ucanal, in a public blood-letting ritual. As depicted, the ill-fated captive is nearly naked, stripped of all his marks of rank and prestige, holding

---

[53] Schele and Mathews, "Royal Visits and other Intersite Relationships," 228.

[54] David Freidel, Linda Schele, and Joy Parker, *Maya Cosmos: Three Thousand Years on the Shaman's Path*, 265. See also the Jaina captive figurine from the Late Classic (A.D. 700–900), Linda Schele and Mary Ellen Miller, *The Blood of Kings*, 228, photograph on 240.

his bound wrists up toward the magnificently dressed fourteen-year-old king who sits high above him on a jaguar-pillow.[55]

Although these events are separated from the story of Ammon and his brothers by more than seven hundred years, there still remain remarkable parallels, such as the stripping, binding, and blows to the face. Sadly, it would appear that Ammon's brethren might still have been getting better treatment than other royal captives could expect:[56]

> Victims were beaten, mutilated, their finger-nails torn out, and they were subjected to prolonged bouts of blood-letting before eventually being killed. The most prized prisoners, nobles or kings like K'an Hoy Chitam of Palenque, men who possessed particularly powerful and efficacious blood, could be held captive for years, their life-blood periodically tapped before an auspicious date was selected for their death. The final method of dispatch was normally decapitation, though it is evident that heart excision, the Aztec mode, was also practised. But as an alternative, or preliminary, men could be disemboweled, scalped, burnt, strapped to wooden scaffolds and shot with arrows, besides being trussed up as balls and bounced down stairways.[57]

Culture as Explanation: Anti-Nephi Lehies

The story of the Anti-Nephi Lehies is not simply one of great faith. Those faithful parents had children of great faith. Helaman's stripling warriors are their children. The Anti-Nephi Lehies' (later Ammonites) conversion to the gospel was sufficient that they were willing to give their lives for it. Dying for their new beliefs demonstrates great faith, but it also provides a confusing backdrop to their relationship with the stripling warriors.[58] The Ammonites had foresworn war, but were willing to take up

---

[55] Linda Schele and David Freidel, *A Forest of Kings: The Untold Story of the Ancient Maya*, 189–91.

[56] Ibid., 143: "The presence of this captive documents the crucial role played by war and captive taking in early Maya kingship. The Maya fought not to kill their enemies but to capture them. Kings did not take their captives easily, but in aggressive hand-to-hand combat. A defeated ruler or lord was stripped of his finery, bound, and carried back to the victorious city to be tortured and sacrificed in public rituals. The prestige value a royal captive held for a king was high, and often a king would link the names of his important captives to his own throughout his life. Captives were symbols of the prowess and potency of a ruler and his ability to subjugate his enemies."

[57] Drew, *The Lost Chronicles of the Maya Kings*, 313.

[58] Duane Boyce, "Were the Ammonites Pacifists?" 44 recognizes that the Ammonites do not fit the definition of a pacifist:

> Here's what we can say in summary, then, about the Ammonites and pacifism. It's true that the Ammonites deliberately made themselves noncombatants, and even suffered themselves to be slaughtered in consequence of that decision. And it's true that they supply what must certainly be among the most inspiring examples of repentance, contrition, humility, and sustained devotion to the Lord that can be found anywhere in scripture. In every way we feel on holy ground as we think of these devoted and sanctified people.

arms to defend the Nephites (Alma 53:13–14). "Helaman feared lest by so doing they should lose their souls" (Alma 53:15). The context that explains why the parents would lose their souls but the sons would not must have been so well known to Book of Mormon writers that they didn't feel a need for explicit description.

The Ammonite oath was evidently binding only upon those who had personally enunciated it. It did not cross generations. While we do not know the year they took the oath, they did so before Ammonihah was sacked, which occurred in the eleventh year of the reign of the judges (Alma 16:1–3, 25:2). The story of the stripling warriors occurs in the twenty-sixth year of the reign of the judges (Alma 56:9).

An unanswered question is how old these young men were. The record does not say whether children also took the oath. If they were too young to speak, it seems unlikely that they did. But taking the outside case, if the oldest of the young men were born after the oath, they would be fifteen. Men age twenty or more would not be considered "young," since it would not be unusual for even seventeen-year-olds to marry and have families, based on typical data from the ancient world. I hypothesize that some would be as old as seventeen (born prior to the covenant, but too young to repeat the words of the oath), but most would be younger. For the story to be as miraculous as it is in Mormon's telling, I speculate that these soldiers ranged from perhaps twelve to fifteen.[59]

It seems significant that these young men "called themselves Nephites." Their parents are the people of Ammon and perhaps maintained some connection to their identity as converted Lamanites. Their sons, however, have spent most (or all) of their lives in their new home and their self-definition is not Lamanite, but Nephite. Understanding why fighting endangered the parents' souls but not their sons' hinges on the sons' age and relationship to the oath.

The nature of the oath is best understood in a Mesoamerican context. The story begins with a remarkable conversion to the gospel. Aaron converted Lamoni's father, the king of the Lamanites.[60] When that king crowned one of his sons (original name

---

But it's also true that the Ammonites are not examples of pacifism. They were opposed to war only for themselves and for reasons particular to themselves. They were not opposed, in principle, to war itself.

[59] John W. Welch, "Law and War in the Book of Mormon," 66, sees them as perhaps twenty years old or older. Welch bases his analysis on a comparison to Hebrew terms that translate to "young man" and indicate one eligible for military service. Thus, he sees "young man" as a technical category, not descriptive. This suggestion is repeated in Stephen D. Ricks, "'Holy War': The Sacral Ideology of War in the Book of Mormon and in the Ancient Near East," 109. Since I am unable to support Hebrew as the language that informs the meaning of the text and have a difficult time arguing that a Hebrew legal definition could survive nearly six hundred years without modification in meaning, I prefer to see the term "young man" as descriptive rather than legalistic.

[60] The Book of Mormon never makes any clear distinctions among Lamanites, even when the logic of the description strongly suggests that they were not the unified group that the Nephite text seems to describe. In the case of the king of the Lamanites, it is not clear how large this particular king's lands might have been. However, it is unlikely that they approached the size of some of the later Classic city-states. The evidence of those city-states tell us that this

not known), that son adopted as his throne name—and, not incidentally, as the new name for those of his people who accepted the new identity, Anti-Nephi-Lehi (Alma 24:3).[61] The practice of taking a new name upon assuming the throne can be documented for the Classic Maya based on the evidence of the glyphic texts.[62]

The new name, Anti-Nephi-Lehi, betokened that they had become a new people with a new identity. These Anti-Nephi-Lehies were still living in their original cities, believers and nonbelievers mingled together as citizens of the same city. Not all Lamanites were converted, but the adoption of the new religion by the ruler would have made for internal dissent, just as it had earlier in Zarahemla. They had a premonition that this religious and political division would lead to rebellion (Alma 24:16). They were right.

Central to their story is their oath and the reason for taking it. The newly renamed brother of Lamoni who had adopted the name of Anti-Nephi-Lehi announced:

> And now behold, my brethren, since it has been all that we could do (as we were the most lost of all mankind) to repent of all our sins and the many murders which we have committed, and to get God to take them away from our hearts, for it was all we could do to repent sufficiently before God that he would take away our stain—
>
> Now, my best beloved brethren, since God hath taken away our stains, and our swords have become bright, then let us stain our swords no more with the blood of our brethren.
>
> Behold, I say unto you, Nay, let us retain our swords that they be not stained with the blood of our brethren; for perhaps, if we should stain our swords again they can no more be washed bright through the blood of the Son of our great God, which shall be shed for the atonement of our sins. (Alma 24:11–13)

To protect themselves against breaking this covenant, they buried their weapons (Alma 24:15–16).

Anti-Nephi-Lehies and the Cult of War

The first mystery to examine is why they would covenant based upon "the many murders which we have committed" (Alma 24:11) and why burying weapons of war was an appropriate response. Murder is, by definition, an unsanctioned and intended death inflicted on another person. An accidental death is not murder, nor are legal execution, or typically casualties inflicted on both sides in battle. All societies have ways of accepting and accommodating these deaths—certainly violent and even gruesomely hostile, but not murder.[63]

---

particular king would have had several dependent cities, but that there would be other kings with similar power and dependencies not all that far away, and others beyond that. There should be no assumption that the conversion of this particular king meant that everyone in the greater region was also converted.

[61] Lamoni is also a son, but apparently not directly in line for his father's throne.

[62] Martin and Grube, *Chronicle of the Maya Kings and Queens*, 91.

[63] Boyce, "Were the Ammonites Pacifists?" 39, is ambiguous on this point. Boyce recognizes that "the Ammonites were not repenting of acts of killing that had occurred in conventional

If we assume, as seems logical, that these former Lamanites had adopted the Preclassic Maya-like religion, then they also espoused the values of the Mesoamerican cult of war. Unlike European warfare, which was typically a struggle for territory, Mesoamerican warfare had different objectives. David Drew notes: "The aim of [Maya] warfare, in part, was to capture prominent individuals from an enemy state, put them to torture and finally to sacrifice them, normally by beheading."[64]

For the Maya, blood was the conduit for *ch'ulel*, or the "inner soul or spirit."[65] Sacrificial bloodletting became both nourishment/worship for the gods and the substitute sacrifice that renews creation.[66] According to anthropologist Dennis Tedlock, this principle of creation through sacrifice appears to have great antiquity in the Mesoamerican region: "*Puz*, all the way from its Mixe-Zoque (and possibly Olmec) sources down to modern Quiché, refers literally to the cutting of flesh with a knife, and it is the primary term for sacrifice. If it is read as a synecdoche in the present passage [of the *Popol Vuh*], it means that the creation was accomplished (in part) through sacrifice."[67] The sacrificial blood could and did come from the king and his queen but was augmented by the blood of captives taken in war. Classic Maya inscriptions glorify the personal conquests of the kings and the humiliation and sacrifice of their captives. The Bonampak mural commonly known as "the arraignment" is a graphic depiction of the ritual torture by which bloodletting was inflicted upon captives.[68]

I argue that the Anti-Nephi-Lehies had grown up with a religion that glorified warfare, saw bloodshed as a religious act, and exalted torture and human sacrifice. Men, women, and children all espoused this worldview, whether or not they participated in the actual warfare or death of captives.[69] In this context, Lamoni's brother, Anti-Nephi-Lehi, declare that they must make a supreme effort "to get God to take... away" their sins, especially "the many murders which we have committed... for it was all we could do to repent sufficiently before God that he would take away our stain" (Alma 24:11).

Imagine how far these people had traveled in their spiritual journey. They espoused a worldview in which the very existence of the world depended on shedding the blood of sacrificial victims. They must now forsake that concept and believe that the only

---

war as we normally think of it." Nevertheless, it was during wars that they committed "acts that had been motivated by hatred and by a desire for Nephite blood, and that they explicitly describe as 'murder.'" It is an interesting semantic division to separate some deaths in war from others. I do not find the argument convincing. It does not explain why the women would also be required to take the oath, or the older children, none of whom participated in the wars and who therefore had no opportunity to face the delicate division between killing and murdering.

[64] Drew, *The Lost Chronicles of the Maya Kings*, 171.
[65] Freidel, Schele, and Parker, *Maya Cosmos*, 201–2.
[66] Roberta H. Markman and Peter T. Markman, *The Flayed God: The Mesoamerican Mythological Tradition, Sacred Texts and Images from Pre-Colombian Mexico and Central America*, 179.
[67] Dennis Tedlock, "Creation in the Popol Vuh: A Hermeneutical Approach," 79.
[68] Schele and Miller, *The Blood of Kings*, 217.
[69] Ruben G. Mendozanotes: "The women of Yaxchilan and Bonampak were clearly implicated in blood sacrifice as were the men; and this pattern holds archaeologically, ethnohistorically, and ethnographically throughout the Americas." Email to the Aztlan mailing list, April 17, 2005, file copy in my possession.

sacrifice needed would be that of the future Atoning Messiah. Their old worldview had glorified warfare and human sacrifice. Their new worldview now condemned both practices. No wonder they considered themselves "the most lost of all mankind."

The Anti-Nephi-Lehies resolve never to touch arms again, not because self-defense is wrong or inherently evil, but because of the difficulty and depth of their chance of heart (Alma 24:11). They are choosing to stay as far as possible from the feelings aroused by and supporting the cult of war and sacrifice. Rather than risk a return to their former religious passion for sacrificial blood, they turn away from even the very first step along that path. It is a radical step to protect their newly gained cleanliness from the "stain" of that former life.

Burying Their "Weapons for the Shedding of Man's Blood"

Lamoni's brother urges the Anti-Nephi-Lehies:

> And now behold, since it has been as much as we could do to get our stains taken away from us, and our swords are made bright, let us hide them away that they may be kept bright, as a testimony to our God at the last day, or at the day that we shall be brought to stand before him to be judged, that we have not stained our swords in the blood of our brethren since he imparted his word unto us and has made us clean thereby.
>
> And now, my brethren, if our brethren seek to destroy us, behold, we will hide away our swords, yea, even we will bury them deep in the earth, that they may be kept bright, as a testimony that we have never used them, at the last day; and if our brethren destroy us, behold, we shall go to our God and shall be saved.
>
> And now it came to pass that when the king had made an end of these sayings, and all the people were assembled together, they took their swords, and all the weapons which were used for the shedding of man's blood, and they did bury them up deep in the earth. (Alma 24:15–17)

Daniel Ludlow has suggested that this ceremony "could have served as the source of the 'bury-the-hatchet' tradition of showing peace, which was a common practice among some of the tribes of American Indians when Columbus and other white men came to their lands."[70] In both time and space, the bury-the-hatchet symbol is a long way from the Anti-Nephi-Lehies.

Furthermore, "burying the hatchet" symbolized peace between two peoples. The Anti-Nephi-Lehies made their covenant and gesture with Yahweh.[71] There is only

---

[70] Daniel H. Ludlow, *A Companion to Your Study of the Book of Mormon*, 210.

[71] This may have become a model for converted Lamanites. Referencing a later group of converted Lamanites:

> And behold, ye do know of yourselves, for ye have witnessed it, that as many of them as are brought to the knowledge of the truth, and to know of the wicked and abominable traditions of their fathers, and are led to believe the holy scriptures, yea, the prophecies of the holy prophets, which are written, which leadeth them to faith on the Lord, and unto repentance, which faith and repentance bringeth a change of heart unto them—
>
> Therefore, as many as have come to this, ye know of yourselves are firm and steadfast in the faith, and in the thing wherewith they have been made free.

the slightest connection between the two events—certainly not enough to suggest a causal link.

It is much more likely that this action was related to a well-documented Mesoamerican devotional burying. There was a widespread Mesoamerican practice of caching, or burying, objects associated with specific ritual events originally possibly as early as 1500 B.C. and well established during the Preclassic and Late Preclassic periods which coincides with Book of Mormon times.[72] These rituals were typically associated with either dedications (beginnings) or terminations. Of the termination burials, Shirley Boteler Mock notes:

> Termination actions, although difficult to separate in all instances and often embedded in dedication events, generally include the defacement, mutilation, breaking, burning, or alteration of portable objects (such as pottery, jade, or stone tools), sculptures, stelae, or buildings. They may involve the alteration, destruction, or obliteration of specific parts; the moving of objects such as stelae or the scattering of their broken pieces; and even the razing and burial of a monumental structure before new construction....
>
> Based on the data ... these actions, as metaphors of sacrifice, often occurred at period endings, such as the termination of a calendric period or ritual cycle.[73]

Marshall J. Becker suggests that the Maya may have had a single category of "earth offerings" that included both the caches and human burials.[74] Although there is no indication that the Anti-Nephi-Lehies broke their weapons when burying them, those weapons were considered "dead" to them. Breaking them would not have been surprising, since the reason for burying them was to make them unusable, which breaking would ensure. Even though this action was not, as described, associated with a building, it was definitely associated with the termination of an old way of life and dedication to a new one. It is therefore plausible to see the Anti-Nephi-Lehies at the same kind of liminal point at which their Mesoamerican neighbors made dedicatory caches.

The Impromptu Attack on Ammonihah

The story describes the incredible bravery and faith of the Anti-Nephi-Lehies as they simply accept slaughter rather than break their covenant against raising arms. (See the covenant in Alma 24:18, and the description of the slaughter in vv. 22–23). One of the results was that the attackers broke off the attack, and some of them also converted to the gospel (Alma 24:24–26). It is the next act that is the most remarkable. In the aftermath of slaughtering defenseless people, the Lamanites decide

---

And ye know also that they have buried their weapons of war, and they fear to take them up lest by any means they should sin; yea, ye can see that they fear to sin—for behold they will suffer themselves that they be trodden down and slain by their enemies, and will not lift their swords against them, and this because of their faith in Christ. (Hel. 15:7–9)

[72] David M. Pendergast, "Intercessions with the Gods: Caches and Their Significance at Altun Ha and Lamanai, Belize," 55–57.

[73] Shirley Boteler Mock, "Prelude," 5.

[74] Marshall J. Becker, "Burials as Caches, Caches as Burials: A New Interpretation of the Meaning of Ritual Deposits among the Classic Period Lowland Maya," 186.

to leave their city and attack Nephites in the city of Ammonihah (Alma 25:1–2), about a three day's march distant. Why march for three days to attack Ammonihah as the acceptable postlude to interrupting the slaughter of unresisting men, women, and children—many of whom must have been considered kin—at this particular time?

We are told that: "And behold, now it came to pass that those Lamanites were more angry because they had slain their brethren; therefore they swore vengeance upon the Nephites; and they did no more attempt to slay the people of Anti-Nephi-Lehi at that time" (Alma 25:1). This reason seems improbable. The political reason for the attack was to overthrow the king. Since the Anti-Nephi-Lehies did not resist the army, the Lamanites took control of the government without any losses on their part.

But the key to understanding this strange situation is, in fact, the control of the government. That control provides the background information needed to explain why the Lamanites would risk their army after easily gaining their objective. To govern, the Lamanites had to seat a king, an act that had to meet a particular set of requirements.

The combination of iconographic depiction and translations of the glyphic texts provide a fairly complete picture of how the Maya would have conducted the basic ceremony.[75]

Simon Martin and Nikolai Grube give a more complete description of the pictographic exposition of the scaffolding that the king ascends to be seated upon his throne:

> The monuments that Yo'nal Ahk erected here proved especially influential and were emulated at the city for the next 150 years. His Stela 25 established an inaugural motif (the so-called "niche" scene) showing the newly installed king seated high on a decorated scaffold or litter, elevated symbolically to the heavenly realm. A jaguar cushion atop a reed effigy caiman [crocodile] forms his throne, roofed by a canopy representing the sky and crowned by the great celestial bird, the avian aspect of the god Itzamnaaj. The seat itself was reached by a ladder, draped with a cloth marked by the king's bloody footprints, the contribution of a sacrificial victim slain at its base.[76]

The earliest Classic period description of the ascension ritual is on the Leiden Plaque (a small Epi-Olmec engraved stone, named for its current location in Leiden, Netherlands), a smaller artistic depiction that was portable as opposed to the monumental art carved on stelae. Schele and Miller elaborate:

> The image on the Leiden Plaque refers to a second event that is vital to the process of accession. A captive, who is to be sacrificed as a blood offering sanctifying the transformation of the new king, lies bound and prostrate at his feet. The captive, marked as a noble by an ahau glyph on his head, was taken in battle specifically to serve in this ritual. Unhappy with his fate, he lifts his bound wrists and kicks his feet, twisting his body to look back across his shoulder, perhaps hoping for a reprieve. Other representations of accession ceremonies confirm that ritual sacrifice was a regular and necessary part of the process sanctifying the new ruler. At Piedras Negras, victims are shown stretched across an

---

[75] Schele and Miller, *The Blood of Kings*, 117.
[76] Martin and Grube, *Chronicle of the Maya Kings and Queens*, 142.

altar, their hearts excised. The heir designation rites recorded in the Bonampak murals were followed by sacrificial rituals that lasted for over a year. The battle to take the victims, their torture, and eventually their sacrifice are all depicted graphically.[77]

The attacking Lamanites have dethroned Lamoni's brother (king Anti-Nephi-Lehi) and must install a new king. For this particular ritual they need sacrificial victims who have been taken in battle. The pacifism of the Anti-Nephi-Lehies has denied them the right kind of captives; hence, the Lamanites have to find someone who will actually fight back and therefore set their sights on Ammonihah. But why Ammonihah?

Martin and Grube help us understand why the sneak attack on an unsuspecting Ammonihah would have been attractive to the Mesoamerican mind: "Like many a Maya ruler, Bird Jaguar's mystique was closely bound to his image as an indomitable warrior. His favorite military titles, 'He of 20 Captives' and 'Master of Aj Uk,' were seldom absent from his name phrase and much space was devoted to his various campaigns. Yet a modern understanding of these texts shows just how lowly most of these victims were. He made immense capital out of minor successes and Yaxchilan's reputation as a 'conquest state' only reflects how beguiling his efforts have proved."[78]

The Lamanites were in dire need of war captives to make their coronation ceremony valid. To get them with as little risk as possible, they did what Bird Jaguar would later do—they looked for easy victims. Ammonihah seemed like a quick and easy conquest—far enough away to be unsuspecting. As M. Kathryn Brown and James F. Garber note: "Evidence suggests that raiding for the purpose of capturing sacrificial victims was quite common and had strong ritual components."[79]

The story of this invasion (Alma 16:3–6) reports that the Lamanites took their captives and retreated to Lamanite territory when the Nephite army counterattacked. This is the only instance where a Lamanite invasion emphasizes that it transported its captives with the army back to its home base. It made no attempt to enforce a client or tribute relationship with Ammonihah. Indeed, such an effort would have been virtually impossible, given Ammonihah's location deep in Nephite territory. This war has only one real purpose: taking captives.

Stripped of cultural context, the story of the Anti-Nephi-Lehies still inspires, but it doesn't make historical sense. With that context restored from a Mesoamerican perspective, all of the aspects of the record become not only understandable, but many of them were inevitable. This is one of the stories where the context significantly improves the reading.

---

[77] Ibid., 110.
[78] Ibid., 130.
[79] M. Kathryn Brown and James F. Garber, "Evidence of Conflict during the Middle Formative in the Maya Lowlands: A View from Blackman Eddy, Belize," 106.

13

"The Tribulations of our Warfare"[1]

From the way Mormon wrote Nephite history, it seems that when Nephites weren't preaching, they were fighting Lamanites. Throughout the books of Alma and Helaman, they were fighting Lamanites with only a few short interludes of preaching. Even in the books where warfare is less dominant than it is in Alma and Helaman, it was always a present reality or a probability just lurking around the corner. The pervasiveness of warfare can be seen in Mormon's use of the descriptive phrase "continual peace," which was applied to a period as short as two years (Mosiah 19:29), and three times for a period of less than a year (Alma 4:5, 30:2, and 3 Nephi 6:9). Mormon's optimistic "continual peace" appears to apply only to the relatively short respite in continual war.

Although warfare is usually simply mentioned, the books of Alma and Helaman have sufficient details that we can learn a reasonable amount about how warfare was waged in Book of Mormon lands and times. Those details converge with and are illuminated by Mesoamerican history. Mesoamerica was similarly the scene of more continual war than peace.[2] Payson D. Sheets notes that "warfare was woven deeply into the social fabric of most Formative and all Classic and Postclassic Mesoamerican civilizations."[3]

---

[1] Alma 56:2

[2] During the fifties and sixties, many scholars studying the Maya held that they were a peaceful people, an opinion held in spite of the obvious evidence of warfare among the Lowland Maya. Travis W. Stanton and M. Kathryn Brown, "Studying Warfare in Ancient Mesoamerica," 12, comment: "The iconography of violent conflict is quite common in the Maya lowlands; however, it was often minimized or ignored for some time because of an adherence to the romantic belief that the Classic Maya were peaceful."

David A. Freidel, "Maya Warfare, Myth and Reality," [no page], corroborates: "The myth of the Maya was that of a peaceful people ruled by serene priest astronomers. The reality, as it comes into focus, is by no means disappointing. For now the ancient Maya are not merely projections of our wishful thinking, our own utopian dreams of a peaceful world. Now they are people with all of the ambitions, creative inspiration, and tragic flaws of the truly powerful. Like us, the Maya have lived with war and from the vantage of their experience we can contemplate together the seductive opportunities and catastrophic consequences of that art."

[3] Payson D. Sheets, "Warfare in Ancient Mesoamerica: A Summary View," 290.

One of the more important observations about Nephite and Mesoamerican warfare is that, despite the constant military activity or threat of it, neither Nephites or Mesoamerican cultures maintained a standing army. Even the feared Aztec war machine was composed primarily of commoners who were called up as needed.[4] The Book of Mormon rarely lays out the details of the cultural traits of the peoples it describes. In this case, the text doesn't tell much about the gathering of the army. In a possibly unique circumstance, Captain Moroni gathers men from throughout the country (Alma 62:3–6). This method of raising an army is perhaps more clearly seen when an army is disbanded. In an early conflict in Alma, after the Nephites bury their dead "they all returned to their lands, and to their houses, and their wives, and their children" (Alma 3:1). After successfully repelling the Lamanites at a later incursion: "the Lamanites were driven and scattered, and the people of Nephi returned again to their land" (Alma 28:3). Alma 44:23 states simply: "And the armies of the Nephites, or of Moroni, returned and came to their houses and their lands." They did not return to the fort, or their base. They went home.

Another similarity between Mesoamerican and Book of Mormon practice is seen in the method of arming the militia. David A. Freidel describes: "The Maya did not maintain standing armies. Rather, they assembled militia of able-bodied adult men and boys. From centralized arsenals kept in public buildings, they armed them with shock weapons like short stabbing spears and wooden axes edged with stone blades, and also with projectile weapons like throwing sticks and javelins, slings, and, in the latest period, bows and arrows. Maya soldiers typically carried long flexible shields of hide or smaller rigid round shields."[5] Compare the arming of this conscripted army with Alma 60:2 (which comes in the context of a failure to raise a conscript army): "For behold, I have somewhat to say unto them by the way of condemnation; for behold, ye yourselves know that ye have been appointed to gather together men, and arm them with swords, and with cimeters, and all manner of weapons of war of every kind, and send forth against the Lamanites, in whatsoever parts they should come into our land." A specific arsenal location is not mentioned, simply the responsibility to arm the militia. If nothing else, it tells us that the farmers did not bring their own weapons to the battlefield.

Why Did Lamanites War Against Nephites?

Lamanites never seemed to tire of fighting Nephites. Nephites never stopped to wonder why. From the Nephites we never learn whether they ever did anything that would provoke the Lamanites. From the Nephite perspective, they were always (until the very end, at least) in the right and the Lamanites were simply bloodthirsty.

---

[4] Ross Hassig, *Aztec Warfare: Imperial Expansion and Political Control*, 53–54. Nevertheless, there may have been some standing army for both Teotihuacan and the Aztecs. Sheets, "Warfare in Ancient Mesoamerica," 295–96: "Teotihuacan and the Aztecs, waged war with standing armies against external polities."

[5] Freidel, "Maya Warfare, Myth and Reality," [no page]. Grant Hardy notes that there is a possible similarity in the "place of arms" in Alma 47:5 and the centralized arsenal.

"The Tribulations of our Warfare" 313

That might be a literary explanation, but it isn't a reasonable one. War carries a heavy cost, particularly a war waged in another land with long supply lines and longer times when the conscripted army is kept from their fields. Such expensive wars cannot be accounted to be Lamanite rambunctiousness.

The differing political geographies of the land of Nephi and the land of Zarahemla dictate different reasons for battles recorded for those time periods. Although always called Lamanites, those warring against the Nephites were different cities in different lands and certainly different causes lay behind their aggression. However, for the wars recorded in the books of Alma and Helaman, there may be sufficient explanation in the need to control trade.

Warfare can cover a wide range of definitions of conflict.[6] For Mesoamerica, particularly during Zarahemla times and later, warfare can often be traced to the regulation and maintenance of trade through boundary control.[7] When Charles W. Golden examined the strategic location of the La Pasadita site in Guatemala, he noted:

> Approximately 20 kilometers to the north of La Pasadita [subordinate to Yaxchilán], on the western bank of the river, is El Cayo, Chiapas, whose governors were subordinate to the rulers of Piedras Negras. Somewhere in the space between these two secondary centers lay the ancient frontier between the Piedras Negras and Yaxchilán polities. La Pasadita was ideally placed to maintain control of the only overland access routes between those two polity centers and to serve as a staging point for attacks against, or defense from, the enemies of the lords of Yaxchilán. Epigraphic evidence suggests that the frontier between Yaxchilán and Piedras Negras was not always a peaceful one.[8]

Such evidence suggests that one way to examine the underlying cause of Book of Mormon wars with the Lamanites is to examine the problems of boundary maintenance. Although the Zarahemla Nephites were not expansionists (being specifically counseled against offensive warfare[9]), they were yet expanding in more peaceful ways. The Book of Mormon mentions only the city of Nephi while the

---

[6] Ibid., 2–3.
[7] Charles W. Golden, "The Politics of Warfare in the Usumacinta Basin: La Pasadita and the Realm of Bird Jaguar," 33: "This creation of these texts, particularly those dealing with the governors of subsidiary political centers, was ultimately aimed at tying the ruler and his subordinate nobility more securely together. This process was made material through the directed growth of secondary centers whose governors acted to regulate access and trade, thereby helping maintain the boundaries of regal authority through activities such as warfare."
[8] Ibid.
[9] Alma 43:46–47:
> And they were doing that which they felt was the duty which they owed to their God; for the Lord had said unto them, and also unto their fathers, that: Inasmuch as ye are not guilty of the first offense, neither the second, ye shall not suffer yourselves to be slain by the hands of your enemies.
> And again, the Lord has said that: Ye shall defend your families even unto bloodshed. Therefore for this cause were the Nephites contending with the Lamanites, to defend themselves, and their families, and their lands, their country, and their rights, and their religion.

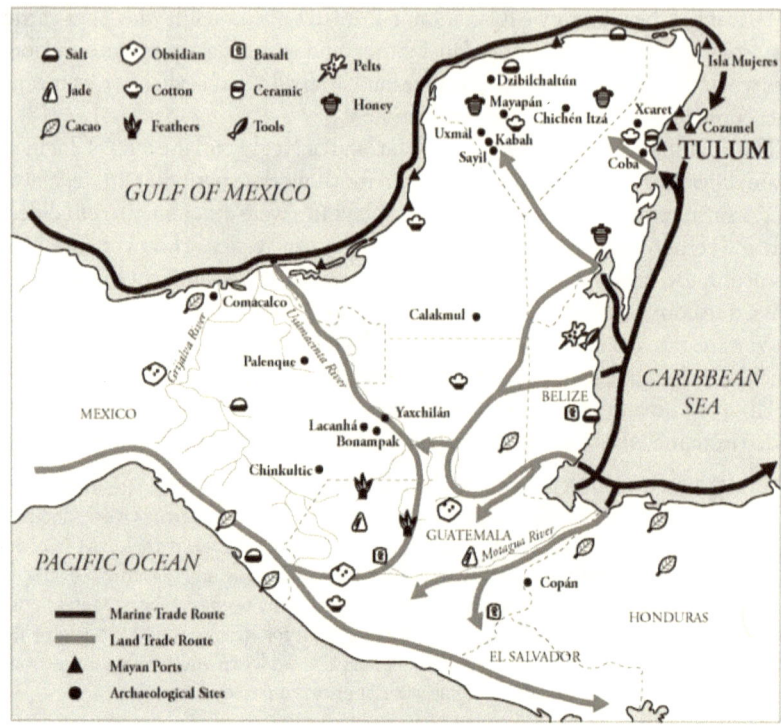

Figure 11: Trade Routes

Nephites occupied the land of Nephi. At that time, the Nephite "nation" consisted, at most, of smaller dependent villages beholden to the city of Nephi.

When we come to the book of Alma, we are no longer dealing with a center city and dependent towns. The independence and described wealth of Ammonihah and the land of Antionum (home of the Zoramites) tell us that Zarahemla headed a loose confederacy of cities which could easily alter their allegiance (which the Zoramites did). It is probably no coincidence that both of those locations were boundary cities adjoining Lamanite-controlled territories. While loyal to Zarahemla they served as buffer zones. When the Zoramites' loyalties shifted, it compromised the entire eastern defense line of the remaining Nephite lands.

Significantly, an important and ancient trade route linked the Maya lands to the southwest of the Grijalva Valley and Central Mexico. During the time period when the Nephite civilization was ending, Teotihuacan in Central Mexico was exerting extensive influence. Green obsidian from Teotihuacan has been found as far south as Honduras, and their pottery styles are found in many Maya locales. Even

Teotihuacan-influenced architecture may be seen in many Maya cities during this time period.[10]

That route ran along the Pacific coast through the Isthmus of Tehuantepec. Nephite holdings were in the isthmus, but for most of Nephite history in the Zarahemla region we see Nephi lands on the east of the coastal mountains rather than specifically along the coast used for the trade route.[11] Although unimportant to the recorded action in the Book of Mormon, this trade route was vitally important to the geopolitical forces that formed the Book of Mormon context. When Nephite influence increased in scope in the Grijalva Valley, it began to establish borders closer to, and therefore potentially influencing, this coastal trade route. That potential threat, whether realized or not, provides a regionally comprehensible reason that Lamanite polities would want to exert control over the Nephite hegemony: They wanted to protect their important trade route. These wars may have had internal feuds as part of their impetus (such as the Amlicite personal animosity) but the political and economic reasons likely had much more important goals. The scale of warfare seen in Alma and Helaman is much more plausible if the combatants were contesting Nephite incursion into a very important trade route. Prior to this time, the Nephite polity was small enough that it was not a perceived threat. However, it is also at this

---

[10] Janine Gasco and Michael E. Smith, "Origins and Development of Mesoamerican Civilization," 60.

[11] Robert J. Sharer, *The Ancient Maya*, 67: "The ancient Maya were a crucial part of a system of long-distance trade routes that ran the length and breadth of Mesoamerica and beyond. The primary long-distance trade routes in the Maya area were those that connected Central Mexico (to the northwest of the Maya) with Central America (to the southeast of the Maya). There were three primary route systems: the southern route, running along the Pacific coastal plain; the central route, running across the Petén; and the northern route, following the Yucatan coast."

"Maya Trade and Economy," *Authentic Maya*, no page, gives the following quotation from Frederick Bové, 1989, page 80, but does not provide the title of the work. I have not been able to find the source.

> Tak'alik Ab'aj in the Pacific Lowlands is a well studied trade center since the Early Preclassic, the original population apparently arrived during the Early Preclassic period, and around the Middle Preclassic, the inhabitants were already involved in a trade network that connected the *Olmec* groups. The trade network was concentrated in a lineal route that ran along the boca costa region in Guatemala and that connected Mexico with El Salvador. By the beginning of the Late Preclassic period, trade nexuses were switched to the Maya groups, with a strong orientation towards *Kaminaljuyú* in the *Highlands*. The commercial route was essentially the same, except for the fact that Kaminaljuyu and its trade connections with the Motagua basin were integrated into the network. This connection ceased to exist by the end of the Preclassic period. At the beginning of the Early Classic period, Tak'alik Ab'aj established new relationships with the Northwestern Guatemalan Highlands, more specifically with the Solano group that was in a process of expansion from the centers located in the northwest, and which eventually took control over Kaminaljuyu. At that time, the trade route no longer continued in line along the boca costa, but instead, it became vertical, connecting the South Coast not only with the Northwestern Altiplano but indirectly, with the Central Altiplano now under the control of the Solano group.

time that Chief Captain Moroni's defensive strategy created a line "from the east to the west sea" (Alma 22:32, see also Alma 50:10–11).[12]

The specific mention of the sea west tells us that they had defended, and blocked, this trade route, a point made subtly in Alma 22:33:

> And it came to pass that the Nephites had inhabited the land Bountiful, even from the east unto the west sea, and thus the Nephites in their wisdom, with their guards and their armies, had hemmed in the Lamanites on the south, that thereby they should have no more possession on the north, that they might not overrun the land northward.

If the Lamanites were hemmed in, the trade route was closed to them and provided a reason for the very extensive and expensive war described in Alma and Helaman. Even if it might have begun for a different reason, the scale would have increased with the desirability of opening the trade route. With a Nephite victory, it is also plausible (though completely unmentioned in the text) that the Nephites reopened the trade route and extracted some tribute from those using it.

Seasonality of Warfare

Ancient warfare was tied to seasonal weather patterns.[13] The universal reality was that agriculture was required to support populations that were large enough to field an army, but agriculture also required manpower to produce sufficient food. The data supporting the Book of Mormon's participation in this pattern depend upon a fairly narrow time period—the 110 years from the fifth year of the reign of the judges (in Alma 2) and continuing through the war accounts in Helaman. This period is the only time when Mormon provides sufficiently detailed information to ascertain the time of year during which the military engagements occur.[14] John L. Sorenson spells out the relationship:

> The first and probably prime determinant for scheduling wars was the need to provide food according to a natural cycle that allowed few exceptions. We learn quickly that the middle of the Nephite calendar year was the growing season and that the primary harvest became available toward the end of the year. Since no army could operate effectively without a reasonable secure supply of food, this meant that wars had to await the completion of the agricultural year. This fundamental principle is clearly expressed in Alma 53:7, which says regarding Moroni and his forces: "He did no more attempt a battle with the Lamanites in that year, but he did employ his men in preparing for war. . . . and

---

[12] My thanks to Neal Rappleye, email to Brant Gardner, September 23, 2013, who noticed the correlation between the defensive line extending to the west sea and its implications for the trade route.

[13] William J. Hamblin, "Warfare in the Book of Mormon," 243: "Ancient warfare was limited by agriculture. Men were needed to plant and harvest, yet the same men also had to serve as soldiers. So mass armies could be maintained only a few months a year when farming permitted it. Neither were armies equipped to operate in all weather conditions. Only certain months of the year permitted them to move, camp, and fight in the field."

[14] John L. Sorenson, "Seasonality of Warfare in the Book of Mormon and in Mesoamerica," 445.

"The Tribulations of our Warfare" 317

also delivering their women and their children from famine and affliction, and providing food for their armies."[15]

Sorenson notes the problem caused by a Lamanite attack that comes near the end of the Nephite year, when the crops were still in the field: "Alma 4:2: 'But the people were afflicted . . . for the loss of their fields of grain, which were trodden under foot and destroyed by the Lamanites.' (The Lamanites obviously had attacked near the end of the year, when ripe grain was standing in the fields. Suffering would continue until the next annual crop was ready.)"[16]

In addition to the growing cycle, Mesoamerica is a tropical region which has distinct rainy and dry seasons. The rainy season corresponds to the time after the crops have been harvested, but it complicates military maneuvers by swelling streams and muddying the trails. By contrast, the dry season, when the crops have been planted and growing toward maturity, makes travel much easier. Alma's fording of the Sidon (Alma 2:27) makes most sense during the dry season, corresponding to the general hypothesis that military actions would occur during the dry season.[17]

The Nephites followed a twelve-month calendar that the text identifies only with numbers: the first month, second month, etc. Sorenson's analysis of the timing of campaigns identifies about twice as many campaigns in the eleventh and second months as any other month. No campaigns at all are listed for the sixth, seventh, eighth, and ninth months.[18] This pattern corresponds well to a region in which there is a long rainy season during which the crops are growing. We can therefore make a tentative connection between our modern months and the Nephite calendar. The text itself gives us no way to know when the Nephite New Year was, but Sorenson suggests that the winter solstice (December 22) would have been an important day, as it was for most astronomically aware cultures, and he therefore identifies it as New Year's day. Thus, each of the Nephite months corresponds roughly to our own calendar, although Nephite months are about ten days earlier.[19]

Tactics and Order of Battle

Mormon described the military engagements in Alma and Helaman from his own perspective as a general.[20] His respect for Moroni as chief captain shows in how carefully he explains Moroni's preparations and engagements, as well as honoring Moroni by naming his own son for this earlier leader. Nevertheless, there are aspects of the engagements that we do not know, likely because Mormon simply thought

---

[15] Ibid., 446.
[16] Ibid., 447.
[17] Ibid., 447–48.
[18] Ibid., 455, Figure 1.
[19] Ibid., 457.
[20] John E. Kammeyer, *The Nephite Art of War*, provides an analysis of Nephite engagements from a military perspective. While much of the analysis is necessarily speculative, he informs that speculation with textual testimony and known military history and practice.

them obvious. For example, we don't know how the commanders communicated with their troops, though we may presume that it was with banners and drums.[21]

There are nevertheless a few descriptions of certain tactics that we also see in documents from the later Aztec battles. One of those occasions comes when Moroni wants to release captured Nephites being held in a Lamanite fortified city:

> And when the night came, Moroni went forth in the darkness of the night, and came upon the top of the wall to spy out in what part of the city the Lamanites did camp with their army.
>
> And it came to pass that they were on the east, by the entrance; and they were all asleep. And now Moroni returned to his army, and caused that they should prepare in haste strong cords and ladders, to be let down from the top of the wall into the inner part of the wall.
>
> And it came to pass that Moroni caused that his men should march forth and come upon the top of the wall, and let themselves down into that part of the city, yea, even on the west, where the Lamanites did not camp with their armies. (Alma 62:20–22)

Similarly, the Aztecs took the city of Quetzaltepec between 1454 and 1468 when Motecuhzoma Ilhuicamina, the Aztec king, died. Ross Hassig explains: "When the Aztecs tried to conquer the six-walled fortress of Quetzaltepec, scouts were sent at night to find a way to enter, as was standard practice, but they found none. As a result, the Aztecs constructed wooden ladders, used them to scale the walls, and conquered the fortress."[22]

The use of ladders to scale walls does not seem that inventive or unique. It is interesting to find the parallel, but not surprising. More interesting, however, is another case where an unusual Book of Mormon tactic occurs in an Aztec narrative. Mormon describes a particular type of deceit that allowed the Nephite army to attack the Lamanites from both the front and the rear:

> Now Gid and his men were on the right and the others on the left; and when they had thus secreted themselves, behold, I remained, with the remainder of my army, in that same place where we had first pitched our tents against the time that the Lamanites should come out to battle.

---

[21] John L. Sorenson, *Mormon's Codex: An Ancient American Book*, 109–10:

> We note the action of Moroni₁, a chief commander of the Nephite armies, who mustered forces by writing an inspiring motto on a piece torn from his coat. He "fastened it upon the end of a pole" and "went forth among the people" (Alma 46:12, 19), assembling loyalists to his cause. They responded by arming themselves and running together to follow his command (v. 21). Bernal Díaz reported that Tlaxcalan commanders led their men to battle with a "great standard" or flag on a pole strapped to their backs. This sounds like substantially the same custom.

While the information about Moroni₁ is correct and the information about the Tlaxcalans is also correct, it is not therefore correct that they were substantially the same custom. Moroni₁ used the standard to rally loyalists to the army. The Tlaxcalans used battle standards to help make sense of the battle itself. Moroni₁'s standard had a political function and the battle standards a military one. They are similar only in that they were cloth attached to a pole.

[22] Hassig, *Aztec Warfare*, 107–8.

> And it came to pass that the Lamanites did come out with their numerous army against us. And when they had come and were about to fall upon us with the sword, I caused that my men, those who were with me, should retreat into the wilderness.
>
> And it came to pass that the Lamanites did follow after us with great speed, for they were exceedingly desirous to overtake us that they might slay us; therefore they did follow us into the wilderness; and we did pass by in the midst of Gid and Teomner, insomuch that they were not discovered by the Lamanites.
>
> And it came to pass that when the Lamanites had passed by, or when the army had passed by, Gid and Teomner did rise up from their secret places, and did cut off the spies of the Lamanites that they should not return to the city. (Alma 58:17–20)

Helaman's forces behave predictably when the Lamanites engaged in a frontal assault—they broke and ran. Since the Lamanite assault forces thought they were facing a smaller Nephite army, they had no reason to hesitate in their pursuit. The ambushing Nephites first kill the spies—the eyes and ears of Lamanite army—and thus gain the element of surprise in attacking Manti.

The description of Gid and Teomner's units "ris[ing] up from their secret places" is tantalizingly close to another favorite tactic of the Aztec army. According to Hassig:

> One feint described many times in the historical accounts involved the use of foxholes and cover. During the war with Tecuantepec, King Axayacatl advanced at the front of his army. When the opponents attacked, he fell back to a place where his soldiers were hidden by straw, whereupon they attacked and won. In the war against the Huaxtecs, King Moteuczomah Ilhuicamina formed his units and attacked, before feigning a retreat. This drew the Huaxtecs forward until two thousand armed *cuahchicqueh* and *otontin* warriors, camouflaged with grass, arose and destroyed them. The same basic tactic was used in many other wars. In the war against Tolocan (Toluca), King Axayacatl and eight of his generals concealed themselves in straw-covered holds in the ground. When the Aztec army retreated past their location, they leaped out, killed the Toloca lords, and routed the army.[23]

Helaman does not mention either a grass/straw covering, or foxholes, though "rising up" strongly suggests that the Nephites may have used this tactic. Whatever form their concealment took, they had to be out of sight yet able to observe the passage of the Lamanite army. The correlation between the hidden unit of two thousand that Moteuczomah Ilhuicamina used and Helaman's unit of two thousand (and the reinforcement unit of two thousand) is also interesting as a possible standard size for a military unit.[24]

An important, though perhaps less striking, correlation is the Book of Mormon mention of night maneuvers. Alma 52:21–24 discusses a strategy Moroni used to capture the fortified city of Mulek which was under Lamanite control. Moroni has Teancum lead a small party past the city to decoy the Lamanites into pursuing them. To position his army where it wasn't expected, "Moroni and his army, by night,

---

[23] Ibid., 103.

[24] Ibid., 55, lists the largest unit as 8,000. He notes that the base-20 mathematical system used in Mesoamerica leads to a different set of round numbers than does our more familiar base-10 system. In this case, 2,000 would be a logical division inside the larger 8,000 unit.

marched in the wilderness" (Alma 52:22). Ross Hassig describes the timing of Aztec battles: "In general battles started in the morning, usually at dawn. But even though dawn attacks were anticipated by the enemy, surprise attacks could sometimes be effected. If the battle was not won during the day, the armies usually disengaged shortly before sunset. Night attacks were uncommon, because the dark severely limited large-scale movements and troop control."[25]

William J. Hamblin notes the general order of ancient battle as well as the way those features are seen in the Book of Mormon accounts of battle:

> Actual battles took only a small part of the time of a campaign, but the battle was of course the most important moment. . . . Information from spies was crucial to forming battle plans. Knowledge of the enemy sometimes depended solely upon reports from spies. The Book of Mormon too shows how crucial spying was in its battles.
>
> Battles often began with an exchange of missiles (stones, arrows, spears) to wound and demoralize the enemy. Only when the missiles were spent did the two sides close in for hand-to-hand combat. The battle described in Alma 49 describes such an archery duel preceding a hand-to-hand melee. If panic began to spread in the ranks, a complete and sudden collapse could result. The death of the king or commander could lead to such a collapse, as happened in Alma 49:25. Most casualties occurred during the flight and pursuit, after the main units had broken up. Battles in the Book of Mormon often end with just such rout, flight, and destruction of an army (see Alma 52:28; 62:31).[26]

Big Numbers and Missing Bodies

In the aftermath of the Nephite destruction at Cumorah, Mormon records:

> And when they had gone through and hewn down all my people save it were twenty and four of us, (among whom was my son Moroni) and we having survived the dead of our people, did behold on the morrow, when the Lamanites had returned unto their camps, from the top of the hill Cumorah, the *ten thousand* of my people who were hewn down, being led in the front by me.
>
> And we also beheld the *ten thousand* of my people who were led by my son Moroni.
>
> And behold, the *ten thousand* of Gidgiddonah had fallen, and he also in the midst.
>
> And Lamah had fallen with his *ten thousand*; and Gilgal had fallen with his *ten thousand*; and Limhah had fallen with his *ten thousand*; and Jeneum had fallen with his *ten thousand*; and Cumenihah, and Moronihah, and Antionum, and Shiblom, and Shem, and Josh, had fallen with their *ten thousand* each.
>
> And it came to pass that there were ten more who did fall by the sword, with their *ten thousand* each; yea, even all my people, save it were those twenty and four who were with me, and also a few who had escaped into the south countries, and a few who had deserted over unto the Lamanites, had fallen; and their flesh, and bones, and blood lay upon the

---

[25] Ibid., 95. Hassig also notes: "The militarily sophisticated Aztecs generally carried out night assaults only against nearby (and thus familiar) targets and not during distant campaigns." Moroni was retaking a Nephite city, and therefore may have been able to negotiate the terrain at night precisely because it was known territory.

[26] William J. Hamblin, "Warfare in the Book of Mormon," 246.

face of the earth, being left by the hands of those who slew them to molder upon the land, and to crumble and to return to their mother earth. (Mormon 6:11–15)

That is a lot of *"ten thousands"*—in fact, a total of twenty-three. Was it also that many people? It was certainly a large number, but the repetition of such a specific number in a military context strongly suggests that we are dealing with a military unit rather than a specific count of people. "Ten thousand" shows up in multiple military situations throughout the Book of Mormon:

Alma 3:25–26
Now all these things were done, yea, all these wars and contentions were commenced and ended in the fifth year of the reign of the judges.

And in one year were *thousands and tens of thousands* of souls sent to the eternal world, that they might reap their rewards according to their works, whether they were good or whether they were bad, to reap eternal happiness or eternal misery, according to the spirit which they listed to obey, whether it be a good spirit or a bad one.

Alma 28:2
And thus there was a tremendous battle; yea, even such an one as never had been known among all the people in the land from the time Lehi left Jerusalem; yea, and *tens of thousands* of the Lamanites were slain and scattered abroad.

Alma 56:28
And also there were sent two thousand men unto us from the land of Zarahemla. And thus we were prepared with *ten thousand* men, and provisions for them, and also for their wives and their children.

3 Nephi 4:21
And the Nephites were continually marching out by day and by night, and falling upon their armies, and cutting them off *by thousands and by tens of thousands*.[27]

The presence of such a very specific, although clearly conventional number in a military context suggests that military units were conceived as having *ten thousand* members. However, it may also be that this was a much more generalized way to indicate a large, uncounted number. In Helaman 3:26 we find *ten thousand* as an indication of a large number of baptisms: "And it came to pass that the work of the Lord did prosper unto the baptizing and uniting to the church of God, many souls, yea, even tens of thousands." The way *ten thousand* is used in the text, it should be seen as a generic number rather than a count.[28]

In the military context, A. Brent Merrill, a former major in the U.S. Air Force, cautions:

One must be careful when interpreting references to Nephite field armies normally composed of ten thousand men. To illustrate this point, the army of Antipus mentioned earlier almost certainly numbered about ten thousand when originally deployed. Through casualties and capture, this number was reduced to about six thousand. If, however, the Nephite reference to "ten thousand" was a form of unit designation—an organizational

---

[27] The use of *ten thousand* in a military context also occurs in Alma 60:22 and 3 Ne. 3:22

[28] For more information on the way numbers are used in the Book of Mormon, see the section "The Meaning of Numbers: Counts and Estimates," in Brant A. Gardner, *Second Witness: Analytical and Contextual Commentary on the Book of Mormon*, 5:30–37.

title—then one might properly say that, although his forces were seriously depleted, he still commanded an Army of Ten Thousand. An example of this can be seen in early Roman military organization. A unit called a "century," meaning one hundred, originally consisted of one hundred soldiers commanded by a "centurion." Later, because a unit of one hundred men was too large for a single officer to control readily, the size varied from sixty to eighty men, but the designation "century" was retained. In other words, it is not certain whether Nephite armies of "ten thousand" always maintained this number of troops. There could have been more, or less, depending on battlefield attrition or evolving Nephite usage of this description as an organizational title. The phrase "ten thousand" might not always be an accurate count of manpower.[29]

Anthropologist Ross Hassig corroborates that the Aztecs used military numbers generically, rather than specifically: "Too often figures cited for troops in battle conform closely to round numbers—10,000, 100,000, and so on—suggesting that general magnitudes were being indicated rather than precise numbers. And even where the figures do not appear to be round, they are often from the perspective of the Aztec vigesimal (base-20) numerical system (which had place values of 1, 20, 400, 8,000 and so on), resulting in typical troop numbers of 200, 400, 8,000, and so forth."[30]

Bernal Díaz del Castillo consistently referred to "ten thousand" warriors, even though the native "equivalent" was only 8,000, as Hassig notes.[31] Diaz certainly didn't count the individuals, but simply used his expected "large unit" number instead of the large unit number from the different mathematical base. The very fact of his using the benchmark number suggests estimates rather than counts. For example, in counting casualties, it is extremely unlikely that the dead always managed to occur in even thousands.

A related question for the dead is whether such huge battles could be attested archaeologically. While one might assume that they would leave distinctive remains, Diane Z. Chase and Arlen F. Chase remind us:

> Despite the flurry of interest in Classic period war by Mayanists, warfare is extremely difficult to see in the archaeological record. There are any number of reasons for this. Warfare activities often leave little tangible archaeological residues. Warfare may take place in vacant terrain. Other cultural activities may result in material manifestations that are very similar to those that would be expected to result from aggression, leading to problematic or nonconclusive interpretations of the archaeological record. Weapons and hunting items may not always be distinctive. Buildings may be burned, but the burning may be accidental or purposeful; Maya burning may as easily result from a purposeful reverential termination rights as from hostile aggression. Artifacts found smashed on building floors likewise may be the result either of termination rituals or of rapid abandonments. Archaeological data are more

---

[29] A. Brent Merrill, "Nephite Captains and Armies," 270–71.

[30] Hassig, *Aztec Warfare*, 55. It is also probable that these generic numbers correspond to the writer's mathematical system.

[31] Bernal Díaz del Castillo, *The True History of the Conquest of New Spain*, 119, 123, 162, 349.

often than not open to multiple interpretations with careful analysis of context providing the only potential resolution of meaning.[32]

For example, the Aztecs are well known for their warfare, yet evidence of battles is virtually absent—and they dominated Mesoamerican nearly a thousand years after the demise of the Nephites. Terry Stocker explains:

> Were it not for the written record, conquest as *the* major variable in the expansion of the Aztec state would never have been known. Aztec history spanned some 200 years, and they conquered 250 major centers. These centers had their own tributaries; therefore, they in essence conquered approximately 1000 to 2500 centers. The Aztecs placed governors and some of their own population at only eight of these conquered centers. . . . There is no evidence of an Aztec conquest at centers without governors; nor is there any evidence of Aztec presence at what I consider to be tributaries of the sites at which governors were placed.[33]

It is an issue that extends to all Mesoamerican burials, not simply those associated with battles. Miguel Angel Astor-Aguilera describes the problem: "Interpreting ancient burials [in Mesoamerica is] difficult since the relatively scarce human remains that have been found, from what must have been large city populations, do not add up. The scarcity of burials relative to population size, furthermore, applies to both elite and nonelites."[34]

For the Book of Mormon, it simply means that there are difficulties inherent in associating the large number of people who died in or participated in war with the archaeological data. The archaeological data are known to under-report burials of any type and those associated with battles are particularly difficult to find.

Further complicating the lack of physical remains is the cultural probability that the numbers simply mean "a large number" rather than a specific count. They might correspond to a military unit, but they also appear to be used in a much more generic sense, much as someone might say "I must have seen that movie a thousand times." The number is an exaggeration, a colloquialism that the listener understands as a generalization, not as a specific figure. The movie would certainly be viewed fewer than a thousand times. Such, I argue, are the numbers in the Book of Mormon.

---

[32] Diane Z. Chase and Arlen F. Chase, "Texts and Contexts in Maya Warfare: A Brief Consideration of Epigraphy and Archaeology at Caracol, Belize," 180–81. Internal references silently removed.

[33] Terry Stocker, "Conquest, Tribute and the Rise of the State," 367. Stocker continues: "Without written records we would have interpretations of the Aztec state similar to what we have for the Toltecs and Teotihuacan. What does this say about those interpretations of the Toltecs and Teotihuacan? I must state the obvious. Warfare as the major variable has not entered into an explanation of the development of these states, because it cannot be seen in the archaeological record."

Sorenson, *Mormon's Codex*, 382–86, discusses the problems of finding archaeological evidence for warfare. He cites Stocker, which I have independently verified.

[34] Miguel Angel Astor-Aguilera, *The Maya World of Communicating Objects: Quadripartite Crosses, Trees, and Stones*, 34.

14

The Gadianton Robbers in Typology and History

The Gadianton robbers are a specific instance of "secret combinations"—a larger set of events and concepts that chronologically showed up first in connection with the Jaredites. Though apparently not present during most of Nephite history, they reappeared scant years before the Savior's arrival in the New World, disappeared for more than two hundred years, then reappeared to play a major role in the Nephite denouement. While most conflicts in the Book of Mormon are between Nephites and Lamanites, Mormon emphasizes the Gadiantons as particularly dangerous. This combination of longevity, sporadic appearance, and ultimate danger makes the Gadianton robbers and secret combinations important in understanding the message of the Book of Mormon. The elucidation of this complex interaction of time, text, and meaning must necessarily center on both Mormon's text and the ancient cultural environment of that text.

Secret combinations are an enduring theme in nearly two thousand years of Book of Mormon history, but these pernicious groups have no consistent presence. They all seem to be related, but they are separated by hundreds or perhaps thousands of years. They have similar characteristics, but they are associated with different cultures. Nevertheless, Mormon's text ties them all together. We are looking for that binding thread.

The Narrative Role of Secret Combinations

As we approach the Gadianton robbers from the perspective of Mormon's construction of his text, we find that they and secret combinations are perhaps the most complex example of Mormon's authorial art. "Secret combinations" is a meta-theme that functions as both an organizational principle and a historical moral. The meta-theme of the secret combinations is not present because history happened in just such a way with Mormon dispassionately recording their role. Secret combinations are an interpretive layer that Mormon spreads over events to give them greater meaning. In creating this meta-theme, Mormon is following an Old World literary vision (paralleled in the New) that sees history in a larger context of types and patterns.[1] According to H. Wheeler Robinson, such a "unifying principle" acted "like a magnet in evoking a pattern amongst iron filings. It created a pattern of history out of all its complexities, a pattern which disclosed the previously hidden purpose of God."[2]

Mormon is dealing in patterns. This patterning of history becomes evident when disparate events at widely separated times are presented as obvious parallels. The repetition of the pattern is a marker of authorial formulation. For example, the same set of events and characteristics always accompanies a secret combination. The essential features are murders, a desire for wealth (frequently described as "robbings and plunderings," Alma 17:14, 50:21, and Hel. 6:17), and the destruction of political order (Alma 37:21). Mormon, and Moroni for the Jaredites, characterizes three different historical periods with these events and traits of secret combinations:

- The earliest manifestation of the pattern in Book of Mormon history is in Jaredite times (chronologically, not in narrative order). The destruction of the Jaredites is explicitly blamed on secret combinations (Ether 14:8–9). All three elements of the secret combinations are present.
- The second occurrence, actually the first in the text, is in Helaman's record, immediately preceding Christ's coming. The most complex and detailed of the three occurrences, this manifestation shows the Gadiantons making four separate appearances and disappearances within eighty years. These appearances and disappearances are a micro-example of the general patterning of the larger meta-theme. In spite of the four phases, however, Mormon treats this set as, for all practical purposes, a single appearance. The Gadiantons' rise leads to the collapse of the Nephite government just before the Savior's arrival in the New World.
- The third appearance of the Gadianton secret combination occurs during Mormon's day and results in the Nephites' final demise (Hel. 2:12–14).

Since three different episodes repeat this pattern, we may be certain that their similarities are no coincidence. In fact, those similarities are even more apparent in the specific details than in this overview. Of this intentional repetition, Richard Dilworth Rust notes: "Repetition appears purposefully within Book of Mormon narratives as a principle of reinforcement and confirmation. It seems that every important action, event, or character is repeated in the Book of Mormon. These repetitions emphasize the law of witnesses at work within the book. . . . They link narratives together with what Robert Alter calls 'type-scenes.' . . . Larger repeated

---

[1] Louis I. J. Stadelman, *The Hebrew Conception of the World*, 26.
Michael D. Coe, *The Maya*, 165: "The Post-Classic Maya thought in purely cyclic terms, so that if certain events had happened in a K'atun 13 Ahaw, they would recur in the next [K'atun] of the same name. The result is that prophecy and history are almost inextricably entwined in these documents."

[2] H. Wheeler Robinson, *Inspiration and Revelation in the Old Testament*, 129.

narratives treat escape and travel to a promised land; repentance; and the nature, rise, and effect of secret combinations."[3]

Mormon creates a meta-narrative by the tight repetition of secret societies' elements in relation to the collapse of political systems. The triple repetition creates a firm connection for the obvious reason that the pattern, the "type-scene," is not a coincidence. Mormon's narrative sophistication in using secret combinations suggests careful planning—planning intended to point to the greater pattern that reveals the purposes of God.

A Plausible Identification of the Gadiantons

The repetition of the patterns clearly shows the author's hand. But is Mormon inventing the patterns or simply revealing the pattern in the historical materials?

The textual linkage between type-scene and historical event is precisely where Mormon put it, in perhaps the most anomalous narrative sequence of his whole text. His introduction of the historical Gadiantons is actually a fairly simple story, but he tells it in an unusual and convoluted way.

Mormon's history of the Gadiantons begins at the forty-second year of the reign of the judges, or about 50 B.C. After their initial introduction (Hel. 2), Mormon concludes his chapter with these comments:

> And behold, in the end of this book ye shall see that this Gadianton did prove the overthrow, yea, almost the entire destruction of the people of Nephi.
> Behold I do not mean the end of the book of Helaman, but I mean the end of the book of Nephi, from which I have taken all the account which I have written. (Hel. 2:13–14)

Mormon has been speaking of a historical event but at this point shifts to his own present. In what is one of the more confusing narrative interruptions in the Book of Mormon, Mormon then abruptly terminates his chapter and begins a new one on what appears to be a completely unrelated topic. This new topic is a discussion of migrations to the lands northward. Even more surprisingly, Mormon brackets this migration narrative on both ends with a shift to his own present. Then he returns to his narrative with the explanation: "And now I return again to mine account . . . " (Hel. 3:17). The account to which he returns is that of the Gadiantons, the very subject he interrupted.

As if understanding the now-you-see-them-now-you-don't Gadiantons was not sufficiently difficult, Mormon introduces these enigmatic figures with an equally enigmatic narrative sequence. However, none of this is awkward or incompetent writing. He uses each of these apparent anomalies for his own narrative purposes. Awkward though it might appear, he carefully constructed this sequence to elaborate the meta-message of the secret combinations. In other words, this anomalous text intentionally identifies the historical Gadiantons as Mormon sees them.

---

[3] Richard Dilworth Rust, "Recurrence in Book of Mormon Narratives," 39.

Mormon's clue to historical events is this very text of the northward migration, bookended by his two references to his own time. These shifts in narrative time communicate that the narrative in-between is the hinge upon which the time-shift turns. Mormon is doing more than denoting place; he is connecting times.

The inserted, out-of-place narrative describes a northward migration of the Nephites. True, Mormon had earlier recorded Hagoth's northward migration, but his attention was on the departure, not the ultimate destination (Alma 63:5–8). In contrast, this inserted section emphasizes the emigrants' destination. This textually unusual focus on the land of destination is even more curious because there is no indication that any of these people came back to describe it. Where did Mormon find this detailed description of the land northward?

> And they did travel to an exceedingly great distance, insomuch that they came to large bodies of water and many rivers.
>
> Yea, and even they did spread forth into all parts of the land, into whatever parts it had not been rendered desolate and without timber, because of the many inhabitants who had before inherited the land.
>
> And now no part of the land was desolate, save it were for timber; but because of the greatness of the destruction of the people who had before inhabited the land it was called desolate.
>
> And there being but little timber upon the face of the land, nevertheless the people who went forth became exceedingly expert in the working of cement; therefore they did build houses of cement, in the which they did dwell. (Hel. 3:4–7)

The passage of time has made this description a little less obvious than it would have been to Mormon, but he still provides four crucial details about this land: (a) northward of the Nephite lands, (b) many waters, (c) nearly treeless, and (d) has cement buildings. From perhaps 100 B.C. to A.D. 600, only one area in Mesoamerica has all four of these characteristics: Teotihuacan in Central Mexico. It is north of the Nephite lands. It is near the lake that then occupied Mexico City's current site. It has buildings made of high-quality cement.[4] The environmental imbalance created by deforestation has been hypothesized as a major factor in Teotihuacan's downfall in A.D. 700.[5]

During Mormon's lifetime, Teotihuacan was exerting its influence from the Central Mexican Basin over nearly all of Mesoamerica. It rose from much humbler settlements beginning around 200 B.C. when the local populations began to harness the irrigation possibilities of the many springs in the Teotihuacan Valley. It may also have been about this time that rich outcroppings of obsidian were discovered in the

---

[4] Matthew G. Wells and John W. Welch, "Concrete Evidence for the Book of Mormon," 213. They are reporting research by David S. Hyman, *A Study of the Calcareous Cements in Prehispanic Mesoamerican Building Construction*, 7.

[5] George C. Vaillant, *Aztecs of Mexico*, 78–90.

area.[6] Obsidian is the material used for most Mesoamerican cutting blades and provided a highly prized trading commodity.

By the time of Christ, there were two important cities in the Central Basin, Cuicuilco in the southwest and Teotihuacan in the northeast. Cuicuilco supported a population of around 20,000 people and the general region supported several smaller population centers.[7] Not long after, however, the population of the valley shifted away from all other settlements and concentrated in the single location of Teotihuacan.[8] This dramatic restructuring of the population patterns followed the eruption of the volcano Xitle, near the city of Cuicuilco. Archaeologist Susan Toby Evans describes the site: "Many archaeological sites are buried, but few were so thoroughly entombed as Cuicuilco was by lava flows from Xitle, a nearby volcano. We don't know exactly when Xitle's [sic] erupted; possible dates range from 400 B.C. to A.D. 400. However, Popocatépetl was erupting from 250 B.C. to 50 A.D. severely disrupting southern basin communities. Cuicuilco was submerged by Xitle's eruptions: ash falls were followed by lava flows up to 10 m (33 ft.) deep, extending over about 80 sq. km (32 sq. miles), sealing the archaeological context so thoroughly that excavation proceeds with jackhammers."[9] Evans describes the evidence for the relocation of Cuicuilco's population to Teotihuacan:

> By the time Xitle erupted, with spectacular and frightening displays of fire and smoke, its effects and those of Popocatépetl's would have caused Cuicuilcans and others to flee for their lives; several lines of evidence suggest that many of the refugees went to Teotihuacan. First, changing settlement patterns from the Late to Terminal Formative indicate a massive demographic shift from the rest of the Basin to Teotihuacan. Also, Huehueteotl [Cuicuilco's patron god] braziers were found in Teotihuacan's household contexts but there was no great pyramid dedicated to this deity. This indicates the deity's importance as a family god, privately revered for his association with ancient ethnic roots, but in the volcanically inactive environment of the northern Basin of Mexico, this deity would not have been publicly venerated for his awful power to destroy.[10]

Teotihuacan's location provided an important combination of factors. Not only did it have the requisite water for farming (through irrigation), but the obsidian it controlled was both extremely high quality and had the added attraction of a coloration that ranged from green to green-gold. As all types of greenstones were valued more highly than gold in Mesoamerican cultures,[11] the combination of the

---

[6] René Millon, "The Place Where Time Began: An Archaeologist's Interpretation of What Happened in Teotihuacan History," 20.
[7] Susan Toby Evans, *Ancient Mexico and Central America: Archaeology and Culture History*, 209–10.
[8] Richard E. Blanton, Stephen A. Kowalewski, Gary Feinman, and Jill Appel, *Ancient Mesoamerica: A Comparison of Change in Three Regions*, 129.
[9] Evans, *Ancient Mexico and Central America*, 210.
[10] Ibid., 211.
[11] David Drew, *The Lost Chronicles of the Maya Kings*, 15. See also George E. Stuart and Gene S. Stuart, *The Mysterious Maya*, 57, and Michael D. Coe, *The Maya*, 29.

high-quality, useful material with the symbolically important visual aspect made Teotihuacan obsidian a trade good that was widely valued along trade routes reaching over 600 miles from the city itself.[12]

Perhaps equally important was the discovery of a cave system. Mesoamericans revered caves as connections to the sacred underworld. The inhabitants modified this natural cave to make it more ritually usable, and on top of this cave they built the Temple of the Sun, the largest pyramid ever constructed in the Valley of Mexico and one of the ancient world's largest and most impressive buildings (comprising 1,000,000 cubic meters). This impressive structure was principally built between A.D. 1 and 100.[13]

This spectacular confluence of location, timing, economics, religion, and opportunity created a city that would dominate Mesoamerica for nearly 700 years. Xitle's eruption and the resulting population shift meant that, between A.D. 1 and 100, Teotihuacan rose from a respectable city to a huge one. It extended to virtually the same geographic extent that it would have throughout its existence, showed evidence of deliberate planning, and accommodated a population of perhaps 80,000.[14]

Teotihuacan's influence increased steadily from this early time until it reached its farthest geographic influence and perhaps the height of its power and prestige from around A.D. 350 to 600. Beginning around A.D. 250–350, Teotihuacan's characteristic architectural features begin to appear in Maya cities, over six hundred miles to the south.[15] These early influences indicate trade with the Central Basin. Perhaps even stronger and more numerous connections began at the end of the fifth century A.D. when the highland Guatemalan city of Kaminaljuyú (Sorenson's candidate for the city of Nephi) came under such complete Teotihuacano influence as to suggest that it was either militarily conquered by the Teotihuacanos or voluntarily accepted Teotihuacan's political governance.[16] Even though Teotihuacan had a dramatic effect on the architecture and rulership of Kaminaljuyú, oxygen isotope studies of skeletal remains buried with Teotihuacan-style artifacts indicate that the majority of the elite spent their adult lives in Kaminaljuyú.[17] Therefore, even in Kaminaljuyú with a very clear Teotihuacano presence, the nature of the connection to the city in Central Mexico was one of influence rather than replacement of local peoples. Clearly, demonstrating ties to Teotihuacan provided Maya cities with such significant benefits that entire cities found it beneficial to be Teotihuacanicized in their public architecture and in their official or regal dress.

---

[12] Ibid., 258–59; Lynne V. Foster, ed., *Handbook to Life in the Ancient Maya World*, 42.
[13] Blanton et al., *Ancient Mesoamerica*, 129.
[14] Ibid.
[15] Prudence M. Rice, *Maya Political Science: Time, Astronomy, and the Cosmos*, 102–3.
[16] Simon Martin and Nikolai Grube, *Chronicle of the Maya Kings and Queens*, 8, and Heather McKillop, *The Ancient Maya: New Perspectives*, 183.
[17] McKillop, *The Ancient Maya*, 183–84. Two individuals spent their youth in Teotihuacan, but the majority were indigenous to Kaminaljuyu.

The Gadianton Robbers in Typology and History 331

Archaeologist Heather McKillop explains one way in which the Teotihuacano connection altered local politics: "From their research at the Lost World Complex [in Tikal], Laporte and Fialko (1995) see the local Tikal Maya royalty using their connections with Teotihuacan traders, perhaps including resident Teotihuacan merchants, to maneuver politically and perhaps to gain control and rulership. They think that the local Ma-Cuch lineage was able, through trading alliances with Teotihuacan, to outmaneuver two other lineages at Tikal and gain power."[18]

No other single city-state exercised as much control over as large a region of Mesoamerica until the rise of the Aztec triple alliance which Cortez found at perhaps the height of its power in 1521. By A.D. 600, Teotihuacan reached a population of perhaps 125,000, making it the sixth largest city in the world at that time.[19]

For Mormon, the identification of this city would have been sufficient from its well-known geography. I hypothesize that he did not specifically name it because he intended to associate it with the Gadiantons. Mormon the author is pointing to a specific location at a specific time because that location is the historical and geographical fulcrum on which he leverages his meta-narrative.

The major problem with Teotihuacan as the candidate location for Mormon's description is historical, not geographical. The description of a treeless area and cement buildings does not fit Teotihuacan of 49 B.C. when Mormon describes the northward migration but rather the Teotihuacan of A.D. 250 and later. That fact explains why Mormon broke his own narrative frame to establish the earlier the northward migration. Mormon does not have historical records describing the emigrants' location, but he still describes in detail a particular location for them based on that area in his own time. Mormon is describing the Teotihuacan that he knows personally and projecting it back into history.

However, it really is the Teotihuacan of his own time that concerns Mormon. He intentionally links this migration during Helaman's period to Teotihuacan, not because it is necessarily historically accurate but because he is making a connection between the Gadiantons of Helaman's time and those of his own. That authorial purpose is also his reason for shifting the narrative focus to his own time period both before and after describing the migration. Mormon is signaling that the land northward is relevant to his own day and that it is connected to Helaman's time period. For Mormon, this migration northward is the bridge over which Helaman's Gadiantons will walk through time and space to become Mormon's Gadiantons.[20] Those newer Gadiantons are causing the destruction of Mormon's people. Mormon

---

[18] Ibid., 184.

[19] Millon, "The Place Where Time Began," 33 note 2. He provides the following information on the six largest cities around A.D. 600: "Constantinople was the largest with an estimated population of 500,000. Second and third were the Chinese cities of Changan and Loyang. Ctesiphon, the Persian capital, twenty miles south of Baghdad, was fourth. . . . Alexandria was fifth with an estimated population of 200,000. Teotihuacan was sixth with an estimated population of 125,000."

[20] Not only does this bridge occur in the passage describing the northward migration, but it is reinforced by a migration of Gadiantons just before the destruction at Jesus's death (3 Ne. 7:12–13).

332 *Traditions of the Fathers*

links all three occurrences of the secret combinations (the Jaredite combinations, Helaman's Gadiantons, and Mormon's Gadiantons). They constitute a pattern of destructive combinations that culminate, in his own day, in the final demise of the Nephite nation. This connection between the three sets of Gadiantons is artificial. Mormon is describing the patterns rather than the iron filings. There is very little chance that the iron filings are the same, even though Mormon makes a pattern of them.

A brief note on the Gadiantons' history should suffice to show the artificiality of Mormon's patterning. After the first Gadianton secret combination destroys the Nephite government just before the Savior's arrival, it disappears for more than 260 years (4 Ne. 1:41–42). When the Gadiantons reappear, they grow in power and importance until they have spread "over all the face of the land" (4 Ne. 1:46). When Mormon reintroduces the secret combination in his own day, he calls them Gadianton robbers, applying a name to them that originated in a different land for a different group 260 years earlier. Seen with the dispassionate eye of modern historiography, it is highly unlikely that this latter group, which was apparently prominent throughout most of the land, would have remembered and honored an otherwise short-lived and obscure band of robbers inside the Nephite polity.

Is there any history behind this narrative device? If there is, we will find it by looking where Mormon tells us to look. We must look at a land northward that is well-watered but treeless and has many cement buildings—and which is on his mind in his own day. We must look at how Teotihuacan might explain the Gadianton robbers, because Mormon is telling us that they do. It is in Teotihuacan that we must look for the "iron-filing events" that underlay Mormon's patterned history.

Finding documentation on a secret society in ancient history when very few texts dating from before the Spanish Conquest are available is challenging enough. Most of our information must come from post-conquest sources, then we must move "upstream" (backward in time) to the earlier period. One of the most valuable sources of pre-contact cultural information on Mesoamerica is the *Florentine Codex*, a Nahuatl text written by the native informants of Fray Bernardino de Sahagún. From these Nahuatl texts, collected by 1540, Sahagún created his Spanish-language opus on the history and culture of the Aztecs between 1540 and 1585. The Nahuatl text has been translated into English, and one passage is important to our understanding of pre-contact secret societies. In the quotation below, I have intentionally left one word in Nahuatl: "The [*nonotzaleque*] went about carrying its hide [jaguar]—the hide of its forehead and of its chest, and its tail, its nose, and its claws, and its heart, and its fangs, and its snout. It is said that when they went about their tasks with them [these jaguar pelts]—that they did daring deeds, that because of them they were feared; that with them they were daring. Truly they went about restored. The names of these are [*nonotzaleque*], guardians of tradition, debasers of people."[21]

---

[21] Bernardino de Sahagún, *General History of the Things of New Spain: Florentine Codex*, 11:3.

The portrait of the *nonotzaleque* is negative, which is not surprising. Sahagún's informants were trained in Catholic schools and certainly understood the Spanish prejudices, hence their characterization of this group as "debasers of people." However, this pejorative description immediately follows "guardians of tradition," a trait that many would have considered admirable. The Spanish would not have been among the admirers, since they uniformly saw native religions as Satan-inspired.[22] These *nonotzaleque* apparently dealt with pre-conquest ideas and traditions.

Sahagún's translators, Arthur Anderson and Charles Dibble, translated *nonotzaleque* as "conjurers," no doubt because of the connection to the magically powerful jaguar pelt; but "conjurers" is not an adequate translation. The word's suffix, *-eque*, indicates a group of people who do something. It is analogous to the English *-ers* (e.g., "carpenters," "farmers," etc). The important information about these people is the verb stem—in this case, *nonotza*, which has meanings associated with speaking together, consulting, or agreeing.[23] Thus, the *nonotzaleque* are "those who agree or consult among themselves" or, in a more sinister and contextually appropriate context, "conspirators."

When Sahagún translated his Nahuatl document into Spanish, he rendered *nonotzaleque* as "assassins." This translation is appropriate in communicating two essential aspects of the conspiracy: the secret agreement and the intention to disrupt the government through murder. Significantly, Sahagún notes that this is a group "accustomed to and daring to kill."[24] Sahagún presents these conspirators as a preconquest group. Art historian Miguel Covarrubias links these *nonotzaleque* to the *nahaulista* (shamans) movement within the first hundred years after the conquest.[25] In fact, Covarrubias quotes Sahagún's passage and applies the term "assassins" to the *nahualistas*.[26] Perhaps even more important is the original group's connection to the jaguar. That connection allowed Anderson and Dibble to translate *nonotzaleque* as "conjurors," and it probably influenced Covarrubias in calling them *nahualista*.

A group that persisted in attempting to retain the old ways after the conquest is aptly named for practitioners of the old religion, and the association between the jaguar and the shaman provides another point of resemblance between the description of the *nonotzaleque*

---

[22] Diego de Durán, *Book of the Gods and Rites and the Ancient Calendar*, 51: "I am moved, O Christian reader, to begin the task of [writing this work] with the realization that we who have been chosen to instruct the Indians will never reveal the True God to them until the heathen ceremonies and false cults of their counterfeit deities are extinguished, erased. Here I shall set down a written account of the ancient idolatries and false religion with which the devil was worshipped until the Holy Gospel was brought to this land."

[23] Alonso de Molina, *Vocabulario en lengua Castellana y Mexicana y Mexicana y Castellana*, s.v. nonotza; and Rémi Simeon, *Dictionnaire de la langue Nahuatl ou Mexicaine*, s.v. nonotza.

[24] Bernardino de Sahagún, *Historia general de las cosas de Nueva España*, 3:222.

[25] This word is formed from the Nahuatl *nahaul* (shaman) plus the Spanish suffix, *-ista*, "adherents to." A more recent example would be *Peronista* to mean "supporter of Perón."

[26] Miguel Covarrubias, *Mexico South: The Isthmus of Tehuantepec*, 77–78. Covarrubias is quoted in both John L. Sorenson, *An Ancient American Setting for the Book of Mormon*, 303, and Bruce W. Warren, "Secret Combinations, Warfare, and Sacrifice," 229.

and the *nahualistas*. The *nahualistas* were a subversive organization after the conquest who therefore intended to keep their identities secret. Similarly, the *nonotzaleque* were apparently organized into a group whose goal was disrupting the government. Both characteristics generally are also true of the Book of Mormon secret combinations.

When we move upstream with this set of characteristics from the immediate post-conquest "conspirators" to the immediate pre-conquest period, the connection between a group of organized assassins who wore jaguar pelts suggests an examination of the various Aztec military organizations. One of these orders was the ocelomeh, or the "jaguar warriors," who wore jaguar pelts and other jaguar representations into battle.[27] Other military groups wore their own distinctive costumes.

Of course, wearing distinctive clothing hardly keeps one's affiliation a secret, but it can disguise an individual's identity, as the Ku Klux Klan learned. In this case, however, it is not secrecy but conspiracy (combination) that links these groups. They have an internal allegiance, code, and structure; they apparently operate as a group independent of other structural influences.

To this point, we have a tenuous description of a pre-conquest conspiracy that might be described as a secret combination. It is characterized by a readiness to kill, sorcery, and the jaguar pelt. How convincingly can this military order from Central Mexico be upstreamed 1200–1400 hundred years to Mormon's secret combinations in lands farther to the south?

In the larger context of Mesoamerican history, there is every reason to see Mormon as concerned with Teotihuacan's militaristic influences. Mormon's lifetime (and hence the flourishing of the third group of Gadianton robbers) parallels the period of Teotihuacan's expansion (A.D. 250–600) and its particular brand of militarism. The rise of the Gadianton influence beginning after A.D. 200 in the Book of Mormon coincides with the period of Teotihuacan's expanding influence, during which many of its cement buildings were constructed. These buildings include the Temple of the Feathered Serpent established approximately A.D. 250, now understood as dedicated to the cult of war.[28] This influence increased in geographic scope (Teotihuacano styles are seen in the Guatemalan site of Kaminaljuyú during this

---

[27] Ross Hassig, *Aztec Warfare: Imperial Expansion and Political Control*, 45.

[28] Saburo Sugiyama, "Rulership, Warfare, and Human Sacrifice at the Ciudadela: An Iconographic Study of Feathered Serpent Representations," 209–10, 220.

It may be one of the greatest ironies in LDS attempts to link the Book of Mormon to historical Mesoamerica that the famous feathered serpent symbol presented as a representation of Christ may actually have been a representation of the Gadianton robbers.

Some LDS authors linking Quetzalcoatl to Jesus Christ are: Joseph L. Allen, *Exploring the Lands of the Book of Mormon*, 159–67; Paul R. Cheesman, *The World of the Book of Mormon*, 30–39; Thomas Stuart Ferguson, *One Fold, One Shepherd*, 145–67; Milton R. Hunter, *Christ in Ancient America*, 9; Sorenson, *An Ancient American Setting for the Book of Mormon*, 326–30; Church President John Taylor, quoted in Bruce R. McConkie, *Mormon Doctrine*, 614; Diane E. Wirth, *A Challenge to the Critics*, 133–47; Diane E. Wirth, "Quetzalcoatl, the Maya Maize God, and Jesus Christ," 4–15; Blaine Yorgason, Bruce W. Warren, and Harold Brown, *New Evidences of Christ in Ancient America*.

time)[29] and physical presence from about this time until the time of Mormon, and continued after the close of the Book of Mormon.

The epigraphic record of Tikal records the installation of Siyaj K'ak', who founded a new dynasty in A.D. 378. By iconographic and epigraphic representation, it is absolutely certain that he came from Teotihuacan and that his descendants thereafter ruled in Tikal. (Tikal is located in Guatemala, south of Nephite lands.)[30] Many sites from this period provide evidence of either a change in ruling dynasties or an increase in militarism represented in new ways that clearly point to Teotihuacan influence.[31] When we place known Mesoamerican history beside Mormon's spiritual history, both accounts report militarism exacerbated by an organized foreign element from the lands northward.[32] The Book of Mormon timing for this description corresponds directly to the secular history of the expansion of Teotihuacan throughout all of Mesoamerica, but particularly the Maya region to its south.

Teotihuacan exported not only militarism and political leadership from Central Mexico but also its accompanying religious beliefs. The later *nonotzaleque* were willing to advance their political ideas through murder but also had a religious component in the powerful shamanic symbol of the jaguar. The modern world tends to forget that politics and religion were virtually inseparable in the ancient world. Where politics were involved, religion was involved. Teotihuacan's incursion into the Maya area farther south also carried in new religious symbols and perspectives, another correspondence with Mormon's description of the Gadiantons:

> And these Gadianton robbers, who were among the Lamanites, did infest the land, insomuch that the inhabitants thereof began to hide up their treasures in the earth; and they became slippery, because the Lord had cursed the land, that they could not hold them, nor retain them again.
> And it came to pass that there were *sorceries, and witchcrafts, and magics*; and the power of the evil one was wrought upon all the face of the land, even unto the fulfilling of all the words of Abinadi, and also Samuel the Lamanite. (Morm. 1:18–19)

While Mormon never describes the Gadiantons as a military caste, he notes their presence "among the Lamanites," implying that they were not the Lamanites. He also comments on an increase in "sorceries, and witchcrafts, and magics." With these pejorative terms, Mormon is describing new religious ideas that he sees becoming current in the land. While the Teotihuacanos would not have so negatively defined their beliefs (nor would those who adopted them), a Nephite perspective painted them menacingly. This description doesn't tell us what the Teotihuacanos believed, only that it was (to Nephite understanding) on the order of "sorceries, and witchcrafts, and magics."

---

[29] McKillop, *The Ancient Maya: New Perspectives*, 183.
[30] Martin and Grube, *Chronicle of the Maya Kings and Queens*, 29.
[31] Millon, "The Place Where Time Began," 26.
[32] The connection to the land northward is my assumption based on the explicit mention of Gadiantons, and then robbers among the Lamanites. See Mormon 1:18; 2:8.

Another characteristic of Mormon's secret combinations parallels the Teotihuacan incursions: "And it came to pass that the robbers of Gadianton did spread over all the face of the land; and there were none that were righteous save it were the disciples of Jesus. And gold and silver did they lay up in store in abundance, and did traffic in all manner of traffic" (4 Ne. 1:46). Mormon's personal experience with these Central Mexican invaders would have come near the height of their power when they were literally "spread over all the face of the land." These Gadiantons, who are not Lamanites but are "among" the Lamanites, are actively interested in commerce and gain. While little is known about what tribute Teotihuacan may have exacted from the Maya area, it is reasonable to assume that it existed. Thus, we have a foreign association—likely part of a military caste—that brings with it new religious ideas and "robs" the land of goods to send to their capital for their own gain, not to benefit either the Lamanite or Nephite polities. Assuming a Mesoamerican context, there is no better candidate for the Gadianton robbers who are contemporary with Mormon: a military association from Teotihuacan whose new militaristic philosophy was tied to a new emphasis on "sorceries, witchcrafts, and magics." What is known of Teotihuacan's history strongly supports Mormon's description of the Gadianton robbers with whom he was personally familiar.

However, as noted, this Teotihuacan influence has not been confirmed for the earlier two periods in which Mormon reports Gadiantons among the Nephites. How do we continue upstream if we know that the stream wasn't there? This is not necessarily the right question to ask, given Mormon's structure of his history. We are not looking for Teotihuacan's influence in the earlier appearance of the Gadianton robbers but for the connection that Mormon saw which enabled him to connect the earlier Gadiantons to those of his own time. One characteristic of the Teotihuacan Gadiantons was their focus on murder for gain and plunder. Mormon's description of the Gadiantons who gain control over the Nephite government in the book of Helaman casts them as a separatist organization characterized by greed and murder:

> For behold, the Lord had blessed them so long with the riches of the world that they had not been stirred up to anger, to wars, nor to bloodshed; therefore they began to set their hearts upon their riches; yea, they began to seek to get gain that they might be lifted up one above another; therefore they began to commit secret murders, and to rob and to plunder, that they might get gain.
>
> And now behold, those murderers and plunderers were a band who had been formed by Kishkumen and Gadianton. And now it had come to pass that there were many, even among the Nephites, of Gadianton's band. But behold, they were more numerous among the more wicked part of the Lamanites. And they were called Gadianton's robbers and murderers. (Hel. 6:17–18)

This organized group is among the Nephites, but its members are not Nephites. That same group is among the Lamanites, but its members are not Lamanites. Focused on gain, they murder, rob, and plunder. They are Gadiantons. These are the traits of the Central Mexicans of Mormon's time, and Mormon clearly links the Gadiantons of his own time to this earlier time period, both by name and attributes. Of course, these characteristics could easily fit the developing cultural pressures among the Maya at this period. There is no particular need to see them as foreign, except in the construction of Mormon's meta-theme. For Mormon, one characteristic of secret combinations ties together all the nearly two thousand years of history: a connection to the Jaredites.

Two Millennia of Disappearing and Reappearing Secret Combinations

I find it improbable that all of Mormon's Gadianton robbers came from Teotihuacan. Political disruptions have occurred throughout Mormon's story. While the "Gadiantons" who ultimately destroy Nephite civilization are the Teotihuacan invaders with whom Mormon has dealt first-hand, profit-focused disruption through intrigue and murder had long been a part of Mesoamerican politics.

We have already seen internal political machinations in the Book of Mormon. One example is the story of Ammon and the flocks of the Lamanite king (Alma 17–19). With the translation of the Maya monumental texts, similar political intrigues can be deduced. The Maya king-lists indicate periodic disruptions in dynasties that may have caused by internal power struggles. One example is a thirty-year period of dynastic instability in Tikal during which the eventual heir was kept from the throne, and two other males were associated with the rule through a woman of the dynasty.[33] This odd arrangement suggests that the two men attempted to assert power by using the woman from the "legitimate" line as their link to the traditional power base. It is not clear what altered the line of rule in the very next generation, but another man with an unclear connection to the dynastic line again used a woman to justify his claim to rule.[34] The competition between lineages for the right to rule may be seen in the aftermath of the collapse of Dos Pilas in 761 C.E. Once a unified kingdom, it fragmented into "local magnates, each of whom erected monuments and used the once restricted title 'divine lord of Mutal.'"[35] The site of Naranjo shows evidence of an attempt to create a new royal line or "bolster the pedigree of a lesser local lineage."[36]

Mormon saw "Gadianton" as the generic label for these forces that disrupted the legitimate political structure and traces this type of secret combination to the earliest possible source in his records: the Jaredites. Although Mormon takes pains to show that the secret combinations were not learned from the records of the Jaredites preserved by Nephite record-keepers, he takes equal pains to give them the same source: "that same being who did plot with Cain" (Hel. 6:25–29).

The connection between the Jaredites and the Gadianton robbers of Helaman's time would have been an easy correlation. Jaredite names frequently appear among

---

[33] Martin and Grube, *Chronicle of the Maya Kings and Queens*, 37.
[34] Ibid., 40.
[35] Ibid., 64.
[36] Ibid., 74.

the pro-king separatists.[37] Gadianton may be a name of Jaredite origin. Kishkumen almost certainly comes from the Jaredite heritage among the Zarahemlaites.[38]

Mormon's "problem" is making the connection between the Gadiantons of his own day and the Jaredites. If, as I argue, Mormon is seeing Teotihuacan in Central Mexico as Gadianton, then he must have some reason to connect this completely foreign culture to the Jaredites. He solves that narrative problem by inserting the northward migration into his text (Hel. 3:4–7). These Nephites who went north could, from Mormon's perspective, "carry" the secret combinations with them.

This mechanism connects Helaman's Gadiantons with Teotihuacan, but how can Mormon connect Teotihuacan and the Jaredites? This answer requires some historical context about Mesoamerica. "Olmec" is the name used for the people who occupied the territory that the Book of Mormon assigns to the Jaredites. Calling these people "Olmec" is actually a historical error. The Olmec name originally was associated with archaeological finds that are actually newer than the Olmec themselves, but the name stuck. The two groups are now called "the Olmec" and the "historic Olmec." What the older civilization called itself is unknown. Archaeologist Richard Diehl explains: "The Nahuatl-speaking Aztecs called the inhabitants of Olman the *Olmeca-Huixtotin* (Olmeca: inhabitant of the Rubber Country; Huixtotin: People of the Saltwater)."[39]

Furthermore, we should resist the temptation to equate the Olmec with the Jaredites because that would imply that the Olmec *were* Jaredites, which is not correct. The historic Olmec (Olmeca-Xicalanca) were a Postclassic culture (A.D. 900–1200). The culture we now call the Olmec dates from 1600 B.C. to 600 B.C., and the Jaredites from perhaps 1100 B.C. to 200 B.C. Just as the Lehites entered a world with other people in it, so did the Jaredites. They happened to enter the area dominated by the most highly evolved culture of their day. I argue that it would be accurate to say that they participated in Olmec culture, including the Olmec language.

One of the mysteries of the Olmec was the language they spoke. In 1976, linguists Lyle Campbell and Terrence Kaufman, published a ground-breaking paper. As they reconstructed the parent language of the modern languages Mixe and Zoque, they not

---

[37] Sorenson, *An Ancient American Setting for the Book of Mormon*, 265, has noted the Jaredite connection to the king-men.

[38] Hugh Nibley, *An Approach to the Book of Mormon*, 250:

> The Nephite Kumen, Kumen-onhi, Kishkumen certainly remind one of the Egyptian-Hittite name of an important city, Kumani; Nephite Seantum is cognate with Egyptian-Hittite Sandon, Sandas; the Jaredite Akish and Kish are both found in the Old World, where they are of very great antiquity, Akish being the Egyptian-Hittite name for Cyprus. Most interesting is the Nephite city of Gadiandi, whose name exactly parallels the Egyptian rendering of the name of a Hittite city, Cadyanda. It should be borne in mind that one of the great discoveries and upsets of the twentieth century has been the totally unsuspected importance and extent of the Hittite penetration of Hebrew civilization. Every year the Hittites receive new importance in the Hebrew story. The Book of Mormon has not overdone its *-andis* and *-antis*!

[39] Richard A. Diehl, *The Olmecs: America's First Civilization*, 14.

The Gadianton Robbers in Typology and History 339

only found a common ancestor but also that the common ancestor had provided an unusually large number of important loan words for other Mesoamerican languages (much as Latin is ancestral to Italian, Spanish, and French). They called this ancestral language Mixe-Zoque. The geographic spread of that language, the content and path of the loan words, and the time depth at which Mixe-Zoque would have been spoken all point to Mixe-Zoque being the language of the Olmec.[40] At the time when the Olmec culture was influencing much of Mesoamerica, their language also provided the vocabulary that described many of those important cultural aspects.

The plausible arrival point of the Jaredites in the New World was on the Gulf Coast of Mexico, in the area where the Olmec were established. Just as the Nephites merged with other native populations and adopted their culture, it would be logical that the Jaredites similarly entered Olmec culture and learned not only Olmec culture, but Olmec language.

The Mulekites would have also have settled in the Olmec cultural zone perhaps ten centuries later. They arrived as the Olmec culture was waning, and the Mixe-Zoque mother language was splitting into the Mixe and Zoque daughter languages. Linguistic history sees Zoquean speakers moving from the Gulf Coast area up the Grijalva Valley. The people of Zarahemla who descended from the Mulekites similarly made a move from Jaredite lands to found Zarahemla along the Sidon (plausibly the Grijalva). The most conservative reading of their history against known linguistic movements suggests that the people of Zarahemla inherited not only what the Book of Mormon knows as Jaredite traits, but what Mesoamerica knows as Olmec traits, including their language. The Book of Mormon indicates that "their language had become corrupted" (Omni 1:17), which plausibly resulted from their adoption of the Zoquean language with which they would have been surrounded and which was known to have been dominant in the plausible land of Zarahemla.[41]

Thus, the connection between the Jaredites and Mulekites (and later Zarahemlaites) is supported by linguistic as well as historical and cultural ties. The Book of Mormon specifically connects the Zarahemlaites to the Jaredites through Coriantumr (Omni 1:20–22). Mesoamerican linguistics and archaeology supply the rest of the connections.

---

[40] Lyle Campbell and Terrence Kaufman, "A Linguistic Look at the Olmecs," 80–88.

[41] I see the linguistic composition of Book of Mormon peoples as a complex interaction. Because Moroni specifically mentions a possibility of writing in Hebrew (Morm. 9:33), Hebrew had to have been retained among the Nephites. I posit that it was kept as a sacred language for the scholars, much as biblical Hebrew was retained in Israel even when the common language was Aramaic. I see the early Nephites speaking a Mayan language (perhaps Common Cholan, given that period of time and location). When they moved to Zarahemla, they met the people of Zarahemla, whose language had changed (been "corrupted," Omni 1:17). I suggest that the Mulekites and later Zarahemlaites spoke Zoquean. While the text specifically notes that the Nephites taught the Zarahemlaites their language (Omni 1:18), the differing population strongly suggests to me that the larger number of people spoke Zoque and that it therefore became the dominant language if "Nephite" had been retained as the court language. The use of French as the court language in England may be a model. The "Nephite" or Common Cholan would be retained for its trading usefulness.

The linguistic reconstruction of Mixe-Zoque opened up the ability to attach a language to the archaeological artifacts known as Olmec. Until the last decade, a similar ability to attach a language to the archaeological remains of Teotihuacan has been a matter of supposition and multiple guesses. The language spoken at Teotihuacan has been among the most formidable of Mesoamerican mysteries. This city might be called a Mesoamerican Rome because of its size and regional importance, but absolutely no trace remained of the language they spoke. They left no obvious written texts. They left no remnant peoples that could clearly define the ancestral language as an earlier form of the latter peoples (such as Spanish or French with their obvious connections to the earlier Latin). It would be a problem analogous to knowing about the Romans from their architectural and engineering feats, but never finding even a few chiseled words of Latin, or any Romance language. Unlike the argument that Campbell and Kaufman used to show that the reconstructed Mixe-Zoque was native to the region where the later Mixean and Zoquean language families existed, the central Mexican Basin had undergone sufficient repopulation and later influence of the Aztec language that reconstructing "Teotihuacano" from the later languages in the area was virtually impossible.

Terrence Kaufman examined the distribution of Mixe-Zoquean loan words in Nahuatl (the language of the Aztecs) that occurred between 400 B.C. and A.D. 500. He suggests that Mixe-Zoquean is a candidate for one of the main languages spoken at Teotihuacan. Another important language was Totonac. Teotihuacan was known to have multiple ethnic groups living in different regions of the city.[42] This linguistic connection between Teotihuacan and the Olmecs gives us Mormon's final connection between the secret combination of his day and the Jaredite combination of old. For Mormon, the secret combinations of the Jaredites (Olmec culture, north of Nephite lands, Mixe-Zoquean language) and those of the Gadiantons (Teotihuacan culture, north of Nephite lands, Mixe-Zoquean language) both bespoke the same source. With the two chronological bookends in place, the existence of Gadiantons in the middle (Helaman's day) would have been conclusive even if he had had less evidence of their parallel activities.

---

[42] Terrence Kaufman, "The History of the Nawa Language Group from the Earliest Times to the Sixteenth Century: Some Initial Results":

> Among groups known to have been in the neighborhood of the Valley of Mexico, Totonako [commonly spelled Totonac] is in fact the best candidate for the language of the most important group of Teotihuacanos, no matter how "important" is defined.
>
> But maybe Mije-Sokean [Mixe-Zoquean] is a better bet, since the degree of Mije-Sokean influence on Nawa [Nahua] is probably even greater than that from Totonako. There was no Mije-Sokean speaking population in central [Mexico] at the arrival of the Spanish. But the Mije-Sokean loans found in ALL types of Nawa indicate that there existed a Mije-Sokean population in or near the Valley of Mexico sometime in the period 400 B.C.E. to 500 C.E., and, of course, possibly later....
>
> *Meso-American languages do not borrow much from each other, and any amount of borrowing that permeates a whole language or dialect area is evidence of a serious amount of language contact.* (Emphasis his.)

Mormon certainly knew what the Zarahemlaite language was. Teotihuacan spoke a sister language. This language was different from the Maya languages spoken by most of the peoples Mormon would typically identify as Lamanite. Mormon would understand Teotihuacan as related to the ancient Olmec, or Jaredites, to call them by the name Mormon would have known. To Mormon, the Teotihuacanos were just descendants of the old Jaredites. Hence, the Gadianton secret combinations continued to rise from their ancient Jaredite roots.

From Threads to Tapestry

Mormon uses the literary concept of the type-scene to reinforce the spiritual pattern that emerges from historical events. As we have already seen, the historical episodes he uses consist of a secret combination with a strong internal organization, a focus on profit and power, and a modus operandi that typically disrupts and overthrows legitimate governments by political assassination. Mormon's point in depicting these type-scenes is that the secret combination destroys the people (defined by their religio-political structure). The quintessential type-scene to which all others refer is that of the Jaredites. Mormon links both of his parallel type-scenes (at Helaman's time and at his own) back to this Jaredite level.

The second type-scene he describes in his narrative is that of the Gadiantons of Helaman's time, just prior to the Messiah's arrival in the New World. He describes this second secret society in greater detail than his other two examples, with multiple internal parallels to stress the similarity of characteristics to the Jaredite secret combinations. Mormon explicitly connects these Gadiantons to the Jaredites through the Zarahemlaites' heritage. Both culturally and linguistically, Zarahemlaite society (at least prior to Nephite influence) had looked to Jaredite (or Olmec, to use the archaeological group) roots. The result of this secret combination, to which Mormon assigns the name "Gadianton robbers," is the destruction of the Nephite polity before the Messiah's arrival.

The third and final type-scene occurs in Mormon's day. He again applies the name, "Gadianton robbers," to this secret combination (though there is little historical chance of any connection to the Gadiantons of Helaman's day). Mormon links the secret combination of his day to that of Helaman's time by describing the northward migration by which, I argue, he saw the secret-combination concept traveling northward to take sinister root in the area we know as Central Mexico and to flower in Teotihuacan. This trajectory—almost like a disease vector—was carried back into Nephite lands during Mormon's lifetime by the appearance and influence of Teotihuacan that disrupted the cultures of the area. For Mormon, these northerners brought back the curse of the Gadianton combinations that resulted in the final demise of the Nephites that Mormon witnessed. Mormon's connection between the Gadianton secret combinations of his day that destroyed the Nephites and the earlier Gadianton combinations that had destroyed the Nephites just prior to the Messiah's resurrected (and culturally resurrecting) appearance at Bountiful would have been strengthened by Mormon's recognition of the linguistic ties between Teotihuacan and the Olmecs (in which culture the Jaredites participated).

Each of these three type-scenes is based on historical episodes, but Mormon presents them as a meta-narrative, a predictable pattern—one that explains the intensifying danger to his own nation and, finally, its collapse. As it had earlier destroyed the Jaredites, so it would destroy his own civilization. But that is not all. Not only is the presence of secret societies repetitive and predictive, so are its consequences. It is also probably the reason that only two of the three textually mentioned secret combination sets are named Gadiantons; Jaredite secret combinations do not receive the name.

Mormon describes how the Gadiantons of Helaman's day destroyed the Nephite polity, but after that terrible ending came a marvelous beginning. The Atoning Messiah arrived and transformed the Nephite world. Even though the Book of Mormon prophets clearly understood the difference between the mortal mission of the Atoning Messiah and the final mission of the Triumphal Messiah at the end of this world, they primarily preached the mortal Messiah and His atoning mission. Nevertheless, we give the Book of Mormon prophets little credit if we therefore presume that they did not also understand the second coming of Yahweh as the Triumphant Messiah.

Mormon certainly understood that these two "comings" involved the same person, but at two different times. The Triumphant Messiah will transform the world into a single political/religious entity, ushering in a complete and final peace. When the Atoning Messiah came, even though he was resurrected during his visit to the Nephites, he was simply completing his mortal mission; hence, the peace he brought then was temporary. For Mormon, the Messiah's return in glory will bring a permanent peace.

15

The Dreadful Groanings

And it came to pass that thus did the three days pass away. And it was in the morning, and the darkness dispersed from off the face of the land, and the earth did cease to tremble, and the rocks did cease to rend, and the dreadful groanings did cease, and all the tumultuous noises did pass away. (3 Ne. 10:9)

The Nephite people had known storms, but this was "one as never had been known in all the land" (3 Ne. 8:5). The Nephite people had heard thunder, but this was "terrible thunder, insomuch that it did shake the whole earth as if it was about to divide asunder" (3 Ne. 8:6). They had seen lightning, but this was "exceedingly sharp lightnings, such as never had been known in all the land" (3 Ne. 8:7). After the horrendous, cacophonous destruction came a thick, dark silence that no light could penetrate (3 Ne. 8:22). It seemed that there was no sound—until from the heavens Yahweh recounted the terrible list of the destructions He had visited upon the land (3 Ne. 9:1–12).

Only after that awful darkness came a ray of hope:

> O all ye that are spared because ye were more righteous than they, will ye not now return unto me, and repent of your sins, and be converted, that I may heal you?
>
> Yea, verily I say unto you, if ye will come unto me ye shall have eternal life. Behold, mine arm of mercy is extended towards you, and whosoever will come, him will I receive; and blessed are those who come unto me.
>
> Behold, I am Jesus Christ the Son of God. I created the heavens and the earth, and all things that in them are. I was with the Father from the beginning. I am in the Father, and the Father in me; and in me hath the Father glorified his name. (3 Ne. 9:13–15)

On the brass plates, Yahweh was known as a bringer of storms;[1] the land's dreadful groanings powerfully demonstrated that he was that same God. However, beginning with Nephi$_1$, if not his father Lehi, Nephites had emphasized that Yahweh was also a God of merciful atonement.[2] At the end of the storms, Yahweh the Atoning Messiah spoke of comfort and healing.

---

[1] Alberto R.W. Green, *The Storm-God in the Ancient Near East*, 258–80.
[2] Brant A. Gardner, *Second Witness: Analytical and Contextual Commentary on the Book of Mormon*, 1: 214–22.

Typologically, the coming of the Messiah at the end of times will be preceded by great destructions, including burnings. Malachi (whom the Messiah will quote to the Nephites) recorded: "For, behold, the day cometh, that shall burn as an oven; and all the proud, yea, and all that do wickedly, shall be stubble: and the day that cometh shall burn them up, saith the Lord of hosts, that it shall leave them neither root nor branch." (Mal. 4:1; 3 Ne. 25:1)

In accord with Mormon's cyclical view of history, the coming of the Messiah to Bountiful was a typological parallel to the coming of the Messiah at the end of time. But there was nothing metaphorical about the destruction inflicted upon the Nephite lands prior to the Messiah's majestic descent to Bountiful.

The Book of Mormon describes the destruction in detail. What Mormon could not do was explain the physical phenomena that generated those details. For Mormon, it was sufficient that they were harbingers of the Messiah's arrival. For Mormon, living some four hundred years after the physical devastation, it was the typology that mattered, not the science behind the devastation. Modern readers may appreciate the typology but also find the science interesting and important.

As real-world phenomena, the descriptions correspond to an explosive volcanic eruption in a subduction zone—or the zone where two tectonic plates are colliding.[3] Mesoamerica lies along a subduction boundary, precisely the type of location where these events might occur.[4] It is a region that Bart Kowallis ranks as "the most productive volcanic region on earth."[5] Volcanic eruptions are often difficult to date with precision, yielding timing only as plus or minus centuries.[6] Nevertheless, within the available dates, both the timing and nature of certain volcanos offer candidates for the events described in 3 Nephi.

The Book of Mormon appears to have a first-hand understanding of a particular more localized volcanic event, and evidence exists of similar volcanic activity in Book

---

[3] Bart J. Kowallis, "In the Thirty and Fourth Year: A Geologist's View of the Great Destruction in 3 Nephi," 145. On the general topic of the 3 Nephi phenomena, see also Isaac B. Ball, "Additional Internal Evidence for the Authenticity of the Book of Mormon."

[4] James L. Baer, "The Third Nephi Disaster: A Geological View," 130; Jerry D. Grover Jr., *Geology of the Book of Mormon*, 20.

[5] Kowallis, "In the Thirty and Fourth Year," 147.

[6] For example, the Xitle eruption has been studied extensively but yields a wide range of possible dates. Silvia Gonzalez, Alejandro Pastrana, Claus Siebe, and Geoff Duller, "Timing of the Prehistoric Eruption of Xitle Volcano and the Abandonment of Cuicuilco Pyramid, Southern Basin of Mexico," 217, note the difficulty in assessing the timing of eruptions. Specifically speaking of the Xitle eruption, they note twenty-eight radiocarbon dating studies that show a very wide range of time. However, they also note that most of them cluster to approximately 2000 years before present, or around A.D. 1 according to the time the article was written. All such figures add a plus/minus factor, typically of 65 years. The overall timing is confirmed in Hugo Delgado, Ricardo Molinero, Pablo Cerbantes, Jorge Nieto-Obregón, Rufino Lozano-Santa Cruz, Héctor L. Macias-González, Claudia Mendoza-Rosales, and Gilberto Silva-Rolmo, "Geology of Xitle Volcano in Southern Mexico City—A 2000-Year-Old Monogenetic Volcano in an Urban Area," 115. My thanks to Jerry Grover for pointing me to these articles.

of Mormon lands. One of the important candidates for the volcano at the heart of the 3 Nephi descriptions is San Martín, located just northwest of the Isthmus of Tehuantepec and in the borders near the Gulf of Mexico. That location would be near the plausible location of Bountiful from which the volcanic events were described. Understanding that there are difficulties in precisely dating historical volcanic events where there are no texts, we nevertheless find evidence that San Martín did erupt near 3 Nephi times.[7] Perhaps important to our understanding of the source of the volcanic activity is the information Jerry D. Grover Jr., a geologist, noted: "The description of [San Martín's 1793 eruption] has some interesting parallels with the account in 3rd Nephi including the onset of the eruption without warning, the initial description of the event as a storm, the zigzag-type lighting, the extremely loud continuous explosions, the ash fallout extending for hundreds of kilometers casing darkness, and the rendering of roads impassable."[8]

The Geology behind the Descriptions

Description: "And there were exceedingly sharp lightnings, such as never had been known in all the land" (3 Ne. 8:7).

Explanation: As a volcano explodes, lightning is triggered by the buildup of static electricity in the ash cloud.[9] Kowallis quotes Pliny the Younger, who recorded his observations of Mount Vesuvius's eruption in A.D. 79: "A fearful black cloud was rent by forked and quivering bursts of flame, and parted to reveal great tongues of fire, like flashes of lightning magnified in size."[10]

Lightning was not particularly remarkable in Mesoamerica, but Nephi describes this particular lightning as abnormal—"exceedingly sharp" and "such as never had been known in all the land." Perhaps neither Nephi nor anyone alive at that time had witnessed an erupting volcano. Perhaps their records, even over six hundred years, did not include such a description. Volcanoes may lie dormant for hundreds of years before erupting, as Mount St. Helens proved.

Description: "And the earth was carried up upon the city of Moronihah, that in the place of the city there became a great mountain" (3 Ne. 8:10).

Explanation: This verse describes earth "carried up" so that the result was a city buried under "a great mountain." There are two possible geological explanations. James L. Baer suggests:

> A subduction zone is characterized by periodic, severe earthquakes, by volcanic activity, usually by a deep trench, and, where conditions permit, by large-scale change of

---

[7] Grover, *Geology of the Book of Mormon*, 39, presents a chart of the potential eruptions, listing thirteen events. Some have a range long enough that they could easily have occurred before or after the 3 Nephi period. Nothing is conclusive for that time, but all have a possibility.
[8] Ibid., 38.
[9] Ball, "An Hypothesis concerning the Three Days of Darkness among the Nephites," 109.
[10] Kowallis, "In the Thirty and Fourth Year," 155.

ground elevation by means of faulting... Movement along some faults has been measured in thousands of feet....

On 31 May 1970 a severe earthquake, centered offshore from Chimbote, Peru, triggered massive land and mudslides. One massive mudslide moved at an estimated 250–300 miles per hour down from the mountains and along the valley. It completely buried the town of Yungay, killing more than 20,000 inhabitants. Was Moronihah "swallowed up" by a similar phenomenon? Subsequent subsurface drilling at and near the site of the Yungay disaster found ruins of two other cities buried by previous landslides.[11]

A second possibility suggests how the location of Moronihah might have "become a great mountain." Earthquakes can certainly cause relocations of land but can hardly create great mountains rapidly. Perhaps Moronihah was the site of a monogenetic volcano, meaning one created in a single eruptive event. A recent and well-documented example was the eruption of Paricutin in Mexico:

> Rarely do volcanologists get to watch the birth, growth, and death of a volcano. Paricutin provided such an opportunity. The eruption that created Paricutin began in 1943 and continued to 1952. Most of the explosive activity was during the first year of the eruption when the cone grew to 1,100 feet (336 m). The cone continued to grow for another 8 years but added only another 290 feet (88 m). Effusive activity began on the second day and continued to the end of the eruption. Lava flows covered about 10 square miles (25 square km) and had a volume of about 0.3 cubic miles (1.4 cubic km). The rate of eruption declined steadily until the last 6 months of the eruption when violent explosions were frequent and violent.[12]

While Paricutin was not an overnight phenomenon, it fits the description of a volcano that grew into a mountain. If Nephi$_3$ is describing results that were cumulative over time, not the events of a single period, it is easy to see how Moronihah's final fate would have been included as part of his set of original destructions. Nephi$_3$'s descriptions of the events were collected and collated into a cohesive account that stressed the symbolic nature of the events. I strongly suspect that indicating the timing of the events was due to literary pressures more than the historical duration of the various events described.

Description: "And there was a great and terrible destruction in the land southward.

But behold, there was a more great and terrible destruction in the land northward; for behold, the whole face of the land was changed, because of the tempest and the whirlwinds, and the thunderings and the lightnings, and the exceedingly great quaking of the whole earth" (3 Ne. 8:11–12).

Explanation: Although destruction occurred both in the south and north, the destruction in the north was so severe that "the whole face of the land was changed."[13]

---

[11] Baer, "The Third Nephi Disaster," 130.
[12] North Dakota and Oregon Space Grant Consortia, "Volcano World: Paricutin, Mexico."
[13] Kowallis, "In the Thirty and Fourth Year," 169–70:

This is an interesting geographical contrast to the description of the destruction in the south. It is particularly interesting if the eruption of Xitle (north of Nephite lands) is part of this description, since the lava flow from that volcano buried the city of Cuicuilco in the southern part of the Central Mexico Basin (which is north of Nephite lands).[14] The face of the land was dramatically altered for the area surrounding Xitle.

Does this alteration of the face of the land mean that it would be impossible to locate Book of Mormon sites in the real world? John L. Sorenson comments:

> Mormon and Moroni both lived and wrote after the catastrophic changes. They had no trouble identifying locations they personally knew in their lifetimes with places referred to by Alma or Helaman before the catastrophe. Nothing about the pre-crucifixion geography seems to have puzzled them. The volume itself says that the changes at the Savior's death were mainly to the surface. Bountiful was still in place, its temple still there, when the resurrected Savior appeared (3 Ne. 11:1). Zarahemla was rebuilt on the burned ruin of the former city (4 Ne. 1:8). The narrow pass was still in its key position during the final battles as it had been more than four centuries before. The River Sidon ran the same course, and Ramah/Cumorah, the landmark hill, presided unchanged over the annihilation of its second people. Thus, the record itself gives no justification for supposing that the form or nature of the land changed in any essentials, despite the impressive destruction that signaled the Savior's death. Nor is there reliable evidence from the earth sciences to lead us to suppose major changes took place.[15]

In addition to the thunderings and lightnings, Nephi records damage from the "tempest and the whirlwinds," which contributed to the great destruction. Kowallis observes:

> Large explosive volcanic eruptions are often accompanied by violent winds and whirlwinds. The winds are caused by the movement of clouds of volcanic ash, either hugging the ground as hot, fast-moving, enormously destructive clouds called *nuées ardentes*, or as blast clouds, moving at even higher velocities. For example, during the eruption of Mount St. Helens, the explosion was "almost beyond comprehension, five hundred times greater

---

One of the keys to understanding these passages of scripture is to understand the meaning of "whole face of the land" or "face of the whole earth." What did Nephi mean? Certainly, he did not mean literally the whole earth, for we know from historical records that no massive destruction occurred at this time in the Mediterranean region, nor in Asia, Europe, or the Middle East. So if we cannot interpret "the whole earth" as being literally the whole earth, what did the writer mean? I think it is obvious that he meant *his* whole earth, or the whole land that was known and inhabited by the Book of Mormon peoples. Here again one must not get carried away into thinking that all of North and South America were deformed, because, as has been shown by other authors, the area over which the Book of Mormon peoples roamed was most likely only a few hundred miles long and wide. It is only in this context that the great destruction makes sense and can be supported by scientific reasoning and, hopefully at some point in the future, some concrete evidence of the disaster. If we insist on holding to the claim that all of the topographic features of two great continents were formed at this time, we cannot count on any support from geology, and we will probably alienate anyone with even a rudimentary understanding of the subject.

[14] Evans, *Ancient Mexico and Central America*, 210.
[15] John L. Sorenson, *An Ancient American Setting for the Book of Mormon*, 45.

than the twenty-kiloton atomic bomb that fell on Hiroshima" and the blast cloud is estimated to have moved at velocities of over three hundred miles per hour.[16]

Mammoth and rapid movements of air certainly describe the tempests, particularly since they are not associated with rain. The idea that there might be whirlwinds associated with a volcanic eruption is less well attested than the powerfully accelerated ash clouds, but they are nevertheless a "fairly common feature of many explosive volcanic eruptions."[17]

Description: And it came to pass that there was thick darkness upon all the face of the land, insomuch that the inhabitants thereof who had not fallen could feel the vapor of darkness;

And there could be no light, because of the darkness, neither candles, neither torches; neither could there be fire kindled with their fine and exceedingly dry wood, so that there could not be any light at all;

And there was not any light seen, neither fire, nor glimmer, neither the sun, nor the moon, nor the stars, for so great were the mists of darkness which were upon the face of the land. (3 Nephi 8:20–22)

Explanation: In 1970 Russell Blong, began collecting legends of a gigantic eruption off the coast of northeastern Papua New Guinea, apparently about three hundred years ago. There is no historical account of that eruption, but the legends bear a remarkable similarity to those in the Book of Mormon.

> I am going to tell the story of darkness. I am going to tell the story of the great darkness which appeared on this ground/area. I did not see it. People told me and so I know it.
>
> It was while they were asleep, in the night, that it was so dark on this earth, and they slept/lay for about three nights. And when they took flares and went up the hills and made signs, going with flares in the pitch blackness, they said: Can you see my flare? But the flares did not light up the place! So they said: No!
>
> This went on many times. And when they were sleepy and it would have been night they slept. And when it should have been light they woke and got up, and kept looking and looking and lit flares and went up the hills saying; Do you see my flare? And others said: Do you see? And they looked all around. But they didn't see them.[18]

The three days of darkness is the most obvious connection between the legendary tale and the Book of Mormon record. Each record dramatizes the ash-filled air after the explosion.[19] The Book of Mormon describes wood that cannot be lit, while the New Guinea legend describes torches than cannot be seen (but were certainly lit).

---

[16] Kowallis, "In the Thirty and Fourth Year." 148. Internal quotation, Staffs of the *Longview (Wash.) Daily News* and the *Bellevue (Wash.) Journal-American*, *Volcano: The Eruption of Mount St. Helens* (Longview, Wash.: Longview Publishing, 1980), 26.

[17] Ibid., 152.

[18] Russell J. Blong, quoted in Kowallis, "In the Thirty and Fourth Year," 137.

[19] Grover, *Geology of the Book of Mormon*, 156–57: "The only realistic explanation for this phenomenon is a volcanic ash/tephra cloud disseminated as a result of a volcanic eruption." He

The inability to light the wood in the Book of Mormon indicates that there was a concentration of volcanic gases (carbon dioxide and sulfur dioxide) that prevented ignition. This may be confirmed by 3 Nephi 10:13, which suggests that some died from suffocation. Pliny the Younger likewise records that his uncle suffocated after Vesuvius erupted (A.D. 79).[20]

The comment about "exceeding dry wood" (v. 21) suggests that the tempest and thunder-and-lightning storm were related to the volcano, not to a tropical storm or hurricane. Either of the latter would have been accompanied by rain which would have drenched all wood that was not under cover.[21]

Description: And behold, that great city Moroni have I caused to be sunk in the depths of the sea, and the inhabitants thereof to be drowned...

And behold, the city of Gilgal have I caused to be sunk, and the inhabitants thereof to be buried up in the depths of the earth;

Yea, and the city of Onihah and the inhabitants thereof, and the city of Mocum and the inhabitants thereof, and the city of Jerusalem and the inhabitants thereof; and waters have I caused to come up in the stead thereof, to hide their wickedness and abominations from before my face, that the blood of the prophets and the saints shall not come up any more unto me against them. (3 Nephi 9:4, 6–7)

Explanation: Benjamin R. Jordan notes that the city of Port Royal in Jamaica also sank due to an earthquake. The process that caused the sinking of Port Royal might also explain at least some of the Book of Mormon cities that also sank.

> To understand the sinking of Port Royal, it is important to understand a phenomenon called "liquefaction." Liquefaction occurs in water-saturated soil or sand where grains are resting on each other with water filling the spaces between the grains. A large earthquake sets up vibrations that put those grains into motion so that they no longer rest on each other. The water becomes the support, and the sand becomes liquefied and behaves like a liquid. The grains can no longer bear weight, and effectively they become a form of quicksand. Anything resting on the sand or soil that is denser than the liquefied material will sink.[22]

More than simply plausible, the descriptions in 3 Nephi mirror known events, in this case, the combination of volcanic and seismic activity—seismic activity that accompanied the volcanic activity.

---

continues to explain that the three days of darkness required an ongoing eruption. He suggests the San Martin volcano as the best candidate to create this phenomenon.

[20] Ball, "An Hypothesis Concerning the Three Days of Darkness among the Nephites," 111.
[21] Kowallis, "In the Thirty and Fourth Year," 153.
[22] Benjamin R. Jordan, "'Many Great and Notable Cities Were Sunk': Liquefaction in the Book of Mormon," 120.

A Recent Reconstruction

Jerry D. Grover has made detailed reconstructions of certain possible scenarios that might have occurred in the proposed Book of Mormon geography. He notes at the beginning:

> In order to begin correlating 3rd Nephi events to locations on the ground, there are three potential primary hazards to consider that will drive all of the secondary hazards and damage: (1) volcanic activity, (2) earthquake activity, and (3) [a] large storm/hurricane.
>
> At the outset, in evaluating all of the events described in 3rd Nephi it is apparent that a volcano is an essential element, as there is really no other reasonable explanation for the mist and vapor of darkness that was widespread in the land northward and the land southward.[23]

In Grover's opinion, the conditions in 3 Nephi are best explained by the combination of a volcanic event, an earthquake accompanying that event, and the presence of a storm. Grover examines specific cities mentioned as part of the 3 Nephi events and explains how the descriptions fit with the geology of the region where they would be located in Sorenson's model. A sample of his analysis is the investigation of Bountiful:

> The Sorenson model identifies the city of Bountiful as being in the area of the current city of Tonalá, which is located on the west bank of the Tonalá River prior to its discharging into the Gulf of Mexico. . . . This location . . . is located on stable bedrock consisting of conglomerate, sandstone, and siltstone formations, which may have dampened surface oscillations somewhat limiting the earthquake damage.
>
> Importantly, directly across the Tonalá River is an entirely different seismic situation, as the soils and sediment are marsh deposits that are extremely susceptible to amplified ground shaking and potential liquefaction. . . .
>
> The identification of Bountiful located at Tonalá under the Sorenson model is directly supported by the underlying geology and the regional earthquake scenario. The indication that Bountiful exhibited a much lower level of damage than areas immediately adjacent is supported by the underlying stable rock where Bountiful is, and is also supported by the extensive damage caused by the earthquake amplification in the marsh alluvial deposits that would have occurred within sight easterly across the river for long distances east and south. This clearly squares with the people "marveling and wondering" and "were showing one with another the great and marvelous change which had taken place." No doubt some of the wonder would have been caused by seeing the relative difference in levels of destruction from one side of the river to the other.[24]

Grover's investigations not only support the 3 Nephi descriptions, but very specifically the Sorenson correlation. As with much of the cultural information, the geology provides specific explanations of the events that require the particular geological conditions in that region. Although timing must remain tentative due to the nature of dating of volcanic events, Grover suggests: "The variety of Book of Mormon events and descriptions ranging from 'tumultuous noises' to 'great mountain'

---

[23] Grover, *Book of Mormon Geography*, 77.
[24] Ibid., 183.

have all found a reasonable and plausible explanation in the geology and meteorology within the Isthmus of Tehuantepec."[25] Grover applies the same rigor to other models for a Mesoamerican setting for the Book of Mormon but does not find that their geology provides the combined plausibility of the Sorenson model. The geology strongly suggests that we are indeed looking in the right place to find Book of Mormon-related history.

---

[25] Ibid., 222.

16

A Bridge Too Far: Quetzalcoatl and Jesus Christ[1]

Jesus Christ's appearance to the remnant gathered around the temple at Bountiful is the pivotal event of the Book of Mormon. The temptation to link that event to the legends of the Mesoamerican "white god" has been overwhelming. No less a figure than Church president John Taylor wrote of Quetzalcoatl: "The story of the life of the Mexican divinity, Quetzalcoatl, closely resembles that of the Savior; so closely, indeed, that we can come to no other conclusion than that Quetzalcoatl and Christ are the same being. But the history of the former has been handed down to us through an impure Lamanitish source, which has sadly disfigured and perverted the original incidents and teachings of the Savior's life and ministry."[2]

In this statement, the two conceptual facets of the LDS literature on the subject of Quetzalcoatl as an evidence for Christ in America are clearly stated. The first is the faith-affirming declaration that there is, in the historical records, evidence that corroborates an important and transcendental event recorded in the Book of Mormon. The second is that this evidence has been somehow corrupted so that the correlation is not obvious, although it may still be discovered amid distorted remembrances.

Standing in the way of an absolute corroboration of that event is an incredibly complex set of texts which, in President Taylor's words, have "sadly disfigured and perverted the original incidents." Sorting through these potential distorted remembrances is notoriously difficult. Joseph L. Allen, whose doctoral dissertation examined (favorably) the evidence for the remembrance of Christ's visit in the textual sources, states: "On many occasions it is difficult, if not impossible, to determine whether the Spanish chroniclers were writing about human beings who were named Quetzalcoatl or whether the chroniclers were indeed referring to the myths and legends that date back to the god Quetzalcoatl."[3]

---

[1] This section is an abridgement of the discussion found in *Second Witness*, 5:353–95.
[2] John Taylor, *Mediation and Atonement*, 201.
[3] Joseph L. Allen, *Exploring the Lands of the Book of Mormon*, 165.

Is there a real remembrance of Christ's visit to the Americas as recorded in the Book of Mormon hiding behind the mutations and Christian glosses? Unraveling the mythology and history of Quetzalcoatl is unquestionably a complex and difficult riddle. Books have already attempted to unravel portions of the tales, but as John Sorenson notes, the whole remains "a complex, uncompleted task."[4] Fortunately, the task of determining whether a remembrance of Jesus Christ hides in the native lore is a much more limited and better-defined question than attempting to understand the whole history and development of the Quetzalcoatl mythology.

From Native to Spaniard: Through the Mirror, Darkly

Jan Vansina describes the difference between texts and traditions:

> The task of a historian working with written documents starts when he or she finds or takes up such a document and begins to read it. There is no relation at all between the historian on the one hand and the ready-made document that confronts him or her on the other. Hence the classical rules of evidence are straightforward. What is this document both physically and as a message? Is it an original, written by the person who composed it? Is it authentic, truly what it claims to be, or is it a forgery? Who wrote it, when, or where? Once the answers to these questions are known an internal analysis of the content can proceed. As long as they are not known one does not know to what any analysis of content they relate. So the analysis of the document itself comes first.
>
> But to historians dealing with oral tradition the situation is very different. Some of these are indeed faced with a piece of writing that claims to be the record of a tradition. The usual questions must be asked, but will refer only to the record not to the tradition itself. In most cases, however, the relationship of the historian to the document is totally different. He or she did not find the piece of writing, but rather created it. He or she recorded a living tradition.[5]

Although Vansina was discussing the topic in generalities, his description defines the very situation we find in Mesoamerican studies. Our best sources are texts, but they are texts that purport to encode oral tradition. The opening statement of the *Historia de los Mexicanos por sus Pinturas* (the "History of the Mexicans from Their Paintings"), written in Spanish by an anonymous author before 1535, portrays that very situation: "By the characters and writings that they use, by the accounts of the old ones and those who in the time of their paganism were priests and rulers, and from the sayings of the lords and principal men, who were taught the law and were raised in temples so that they dispense [the law], gathered together before me and bringing

---

[4] John L. Sorenson, *An Ancient American Setting for the Book of Mormon*, 327. In that book Sorenson accepted and promoted the correlation between Quetzalcoatl and Christ (326–30). He has reconfirmed that connection in John L. Sorenson, *Mormon's Codex: An Ancient American Book*, 660–65. Sorenson has not read my discussion of the topic. He notes in *Mormon's Codex*, xviii: "I have consciously avoided duplicating valuable points made by Brant A. Gardner in his multivolume *Second Witness* series on the Book of Mormon in a Mesoamerican setting. His work deserves separate consultation."

[5] Jan Vansina, *Oral Tradition as History*, 33.

their books and figures, which, as they demonstrated, were ancient and many of them have the greater part daubed with human blood, it appears . . ."[6]

After this introduction, the *Historia* author begins to discuss the native gods. For questions of methodology, the important information is that the written text is the result of what a Spaniard understood from a variety of sources and then wrote down. We are not reading a single account of the information. We are not hearing what a native would have said. We are hearing what a Spaniard extracted from multiple accounts and recorded. This author, just as Vansina suggests, has participated in the creation of the lore that we read. This combination of text and oral tradition requires that we create a basic methodology that will appropriately interpret the available material.

Therefore, the most critical aspect of an examination of the material describing Quetzalcoatl is discerning the relationship of the text's author to the native oral tradition. The Quetzalcoatl information was written after the conquest, for the most part in a language and a script that did not exist in the New World prior to the conquest. By definition, we are not in possession of a single text that does not show some influence from the Spanish who conquered either militarily or religiously. The least influence was the script taught to native converts. The most was a participation from the Spanish so heavy in recording native lore that they created a new lore out of it.

Robert Carmack discusses the problem of post-conquest native documents: "In varying degrees, all native documents show evidence of Christian influence. This points to acculturation, but also suggests another important purpose of the documents—they are pleas to the Spaniards to relax colonial demands, in exchange for the natives' acceptance of—and faithfulness to—Christianity. In many cases the missionaries taught the natives to merge their migration stories with the Biblical story of the dispersion of the Israelites from Babylon."[7] Inadvertently or by design, at the interface between native traditions and Spanish texts, mutations of the native material were easily inserted. From those beginnings, a third, hybrid form easily emerged. Failing to recognize that fact cripples any effort at recovering authentic native material.

One of the most fascinating and long-lived transformations of native lore was the Quetzalcoatl material. As early Spanish priests and religious writers attempted to understand the new cultures and religions around them, they began to develop their own myth: that Quetzalcoatl had actually been the wandering apostle St. Thomas, who was reputed to have taken Christianity to India. One of the earliest proponents of this myth about the New World was Fray Diego de Durán (1537–87), who barely contains his enthusiasm for the discovery of early Christianity among the natives:

---

[6] Ángel María Garibay K., ed., *Historia de los Mexicanos por sus Pinturas*, in *Teogonía e Historia de los Mexicanos*, 23; translation mine.
[7] Robert M. Carmack, *Quichéan Civilization: The Ethnohistoric, Ethnographic, and Archaeological Sources*, 21. See also Brant A. Gardner, "Crucible of Distortion: The Impact of the Spanish on the Record of Native Oral Tradition," for more information on the ways in which Spanish writers altered native oral traditions.

The great deeds and wondrous acts of Topiltzin[8] [Quetzalcoatl], his heroic acts, are famed among the Indians. These deeds are of such renown and remind one so much of miracles that I dare not make any statement or write of them. In all I subject myself to the correction of the Holy Catholic Church. But even though I wish to adhere to the Holy Gospel of Saint Mark, who states that God sent the Holy Apostles to all parts of the world to preach the gospel to His creatures, promising eternal life to all baptized believers, I would not dare affirm that Topiltzin was one of the blessed Apostles. Nevertheless, the story of his life has impressed me greatly and has led me and others to believe that, since the natives were also God's creatures, rational and capable of salvation, He cannot have left them without a preacher of the Gospel. And if this is true, that preacher was Topiltzin, who came to this land.[9]

Ironically, the methodology used to reshape Quetzalcoatl into St. Thomas was by parallels—the same method that modern LDS authors use in attempting to link Quetzalcoatl and Jesus. Jacques Lafaye describes part of the process of transformation from native god to Christian saint: "The use of a Christian vocabulary to depict Topiltzin's piety ('cell,' 'pray,' 'penance,' 'oratory'), and the mention of traits such as 'abstemious,' 'given to fasting,' 'genuflection,' had to impress Durán's contemporary readers. Add his statement that 'the exploits and prodigies of Topiltzin' had 'the appearance of miracles,' and the picture of a Christian Topiltzin takes very clear shape."[10]

Lafaye remarks: "Reading Durán, one gets the impression that years, even decades, separate him from the pioneer missionaries. Unlike them, he does not set himself the task of writing the history of the ancient Mexicans and their beliefs; he is intent in *interpreting* it as the history of his adopted country. By no accident it is precisely in Durán that we encounter the first great literary mutation of the figure of Quetzalcoatl."[11] He continues: "Later writers would complete his portrait of an apostolic Quetzalcoatl."[12]

Unfortunately, many LDS authors not only use the same methodology that led to this myth but often base their conclusions on Spanish authors whose writings already show the Christianization process. Of course, the Quetzalcoatl of their documents looks very Christian and therefore appears to be remembrances of Christ in the LDS version of the Spanish myth of St. Thomas.

Finally, after the work of reconstructing the native texts from their in-Spanish manifestations, we have the task of attempting to trace through the oral mutations a discernible thread leading back to the Book of Mormon event. An actual connection must be specific and distinctive. The more vague and nonspecific, the less value it has

---

[8] "Topiltzin" is a description used as a name. The literal meaning is "our son" but as used, it meant "my lord." It is frequently used as an alternate name for Quetzalcoatl. I suspect that Durán used "Topiltzin" rather than "Quetzalcoatl" because "our lord" reinforced his perspective of Topiltzin Quetzalcoatl as a Christian missionary.

[9] Diego de Durán, *Book of the Gods and Rites and the Ancient Calendar*, 59.

[10] Jacques Lafaye, *Quetzalcoatl and Guadalupe: The Formation of Mexican National Consciousness, 1531–1815*, 158.

[11] Ibid., 157.

[12] Ibid., 159.

A Bridge Too Far: Quetzalcoatl and Jesus Christ 357

in establishing that any tale collected after the conquest had its ultimate roots in Christ's literal appearance as recorded in the Book of Mormon.

Our search for Quetzalcoatl is complicated because even the best reconstructions of native legend cover multiple aspects or personages. Quetzalcoatl was both a god operating in the heavens and a deity on earth, associated in Aztec mythology with the legendary city of Tula (the Hispanicized name), also called Tollan (the Nahuatl name). This site is considered to be Tula Hidalgo, located fifty-two miles from Mexico City. The leading scholar on the Quetzalcoatl documentary sources, H. B. Nicholson, separated the material for the two versions of Quetzalcoatl, labeling the heavenly deity "Ehecatl Quetzalcoatl" or "Wind Quetzalcoatl" and the king in Tula as "Topiltzin Quetzalcoatl," or "Our Son/Lord, Quetzalcoatl." He attempts primarily to reconstruct a possible historical figure, the Tula-king, Topiltzin Quetzalcoatl, from the legends.[13]

I would add a third category to Nicholson's based on my own examination of the same texts: the heavenly god, the deity on earth, and the mortal king in Tula. Although there is always fuzziness in oral traditions, the particular father assigned to a given aspect of Quetzalcoatl is a useful clue about which of the three versions is being discussed.[14] Following Nicholson, I use Ehecatl Quetzalcoatl for the first, the deity in heaven. Because Nicholson was interested in the reconstruction of a plausible historical figure behind the Quetzalcoatl legends and myths, I use Nicholson's Topiltzin Quetzalcoatl to designate the mortal king in Tula. I adopt Ce Acatl Quetzalcoatl (One Reed Quetzalcoatl) to indicate the deity on earth. The father of Ehecatl Quetzalcoatl is Tonacatecuhtli, "Lord of our flesh," of Topiltzin Quetzalcoatl is Mixcoatl "cloud serpent" (and his analog, Camaxtli), and of Ce Acatl Quetzalcoatl is Totepeuh "Our Lord."

The ability to separate the three aspects of Quetzalcoatl helps clarify the complexity of the textual material. For the purpose of determining a possible connection between the Book of Mormon and the post-conquest texts, I examine each of the three bodies of folklore, according to the Quetzalcoatl persona.

Topiltzin Quetzalcoatl: King in Tula

The easiest aspect of Quetzalcoatl to discard as a possible remembrance of Jesus Christ is that of Topiltzin Quetzalcoatl, the mortal king in Tula. Richard A. Diehl dates the Toltec culture: "In modern archaeological parlance the term Toltec has acquired a chronological meaning, and we often speak of a 'Toltec period,' that time between A.D. 900 and 1200 when Toltec civilization reached its peak."[15] There is no way to fix the dates for Topiltzin Quetzalcoatl's reign in Tula, but Nicholson estimates it at ca. A.D. 1000.[16] Because the Book of Mormon had ended about six hundred years

---

[13] Nicholson, *Topiltzin Quetzalcoatl*, xxii, 3.
[14] Brant A. Gardner, "Quetzalcoatl's Fathers: A Critical Examination of Source Materials."
[15] Richard A. Diehl, *Tula: The Toltec Capital of Ancient Mexico*, 14.
[16] Nicholson, *Topiltzin Quetzalcoatl*, 273–74.

earlier, information specific to Topiltzin Quetzalcoatl cannot be a remembrance of Book of Mormon events.

LDS scholars have accepted that this version of Quetzalcoatl had no relevance to the Book of Mormon, even while holding out hope that a different version of the story might corroborate the Messiah's appearance. Joseph L. Allen writes: "From the time of Christ to the Conquest of Mexico, many priests and royalty were given the name of Quetzalcoatl. . . . One such culture hero, named Topiltzin Quetzalcoatl and born c935 A.D., left a trail from the Mexico City area to the Yucatán."[17] David A. Palmer concluded: "Unfortunately, the traditions and legends of the ancient life god have become closely intertwined with those legends surrounding the life of Ce Acatl Topiltzin Quetzalcoatl. [Palmer is using these names from the tradition, not in the sense that Nicholson and I use them.] He was the tenth-century king of Tula who abandoned the city with a retinue of followers and traveled to the Gulf Coast, promising to return. It is now believed that he continued on to the Yucatan where he took over such cities as Chichén Itzá."[18] If examining the texts discloses that events or stories are related to either this person or this timeframe, they must be excluded from consideration as remembrances of the appearance of the Messiah as recorded in the Book of Mormon.

Ehecatl Quetzalcoatl: The Deity in Heaven

A connection between Quetzalcoatl as a deity in heaven should be a more fruitful location for finding connections between Ehecatl Quetzalcoatl and Jesus Christ. Book of Mormon people understood that the Messiah was Yahweh come to earth. The distinction between Ehecatl Quetzalcoatl (deity in heaven) and Ce Acatl Quetzalcoatl (deity on earth) therefore has immediate salience as a conceptual parallel.

As a deity in heaven for the Aztecs, Ehecatl Quetzalcoatl was considered the god of wind, which is the meaning of the name *ehecatl*. Sahagún's native informants describe this aspect of the god: "Quetzalcoatl—he was the wind, the guide and roadsweeper of the rain gods, of the masters of the water, of those who brought rain. And when the wind rose, when the dust rumbled, and it crackled and there was a great din, and it became dark and the wind blew in many directions, and it thundered; then it was said: '[Quetzalcoatl] is wrathful.'"[19]

Do any of the legendary materials associated with Ehecatl Quetzalcoatl provide a link to the Book of Mormon event? Some LDS authors have thought so. Joseph L. Allen suggests: "Both Christ and Quetzalcoatl were recognized as creator of all things."[20] Diane Wirth more recently emphasized the god's creator role: "The Maya accounts corroborate the acts of creation in a somewhat different manner because they were recorded by another culture, but they still present a pan-Mesoamerican

---

[17] Allen, *Exploring the Lands of the Book of Mormon*, 160.

[18] David A. Palmer, *In Search of Cumorah: New Evidences for the Book of Mormon from Ancient Mexico*, 191. See also Paul R. Cheesman, *The World of the Book of Mormon*, 37.

[19] Bernardino de Sahagún, *General History of the Things of New Spain: Florentine Codex*, 1:3.

[20] Allen, *Exploring the Lands of the Book of Mormon*, 159.

mythological paradigm. Finally, we possess legends in 16th-century manuscripts declaring Quetzalcoatl as the Creator."[21]

Elements of the Ehecatl Quetzalcoatl material can be tested for a Book of Mormon connection. As far as can be determined, Mesoamerican cultures shared a common creation myth that might have been elaborated in slightly different ways but which kept the basic outline.[22] According to the creation myth, the current world was the result of repeated creations and destructions. Each previous creation was associated with both a deity and a "sun." The mythological story is traditionally called "The Legend of the Suns." Some versions of the myth have only four suns, with the current world being the fourth. The Aztecs apparently added a fifth sun for the current world, following the four previous suns.[23] In each of the previous suns, the world and its inhabitants were defective. Each made progress toward creating human beings, but the inhabitants during those suns were less than human. Only the current sun succeeded in making full humans.

In the Aztec version of the myth, each previous sun was created by either Quetzalcoatl or his nemesis Tezcatlipoca, who is considered to be Quetzalcoatl's brother.[24] One of the earliest sources for Aztec mythology is an anonymous Spanish document that has been given the name *Historia de los Mexicanos por sus Pinturas* (History of the Mexicans According to Their Paintings). This source appears to have been written prior to 1535.[25] Cortés conquered the Aztecs in 1521, so this document collects information during a time when numerous natives who recalled their mythology were still alive. It is the source mentioned above that was written from the natives who brought their books to assist in the retelling. The following gives some of the flavor of the creative tension between Quetzalcoatl and Tezcatlipoca:

> Returning to the giants who were created in the time when Tezcatlipoca was the sun, it is said that, as he stopped being the sun, they perished, and the tigers [jaguars] finished them off and ate them so that not a single one survived. These tigers were created in the following manner:
>
> After thirteen times fifty-two years, Quetzalcoatl became the sun and he removed Tezcatlipoca, because he hit him with a great staff and knocked him down into the water and there he made himself a tiger and came out to kill the giants....
>
> And Quetzalcoatl remained sun for another thirteen times fifty-two years, which are 676 years, at the end of which Tezcatlipoca (being a god) made of himself, as could his other brothers, whatever he cared to. Therefore he walked about as a tiger [jaguar] and he kicked

---

[21] Diane E. Wirth, "Quetzalcoatl, the Maya Maize God, and Jesus Christ," 8.

[22] Alfredo López Austin, Leonardo López Luján, and Saburo Sugiyama, "The Temple of Quetzalcoatl at Teotihuacan: Its Possible Ideological Significance," 93.

[23] Brant A. Gardner, "Reconstructing the Ethnohistory of Myth: A Structural Study of the Aztec 'Legend of the Suns,'" 20–21, 28–29.

[24] Garibay K., "Historia de los Mexicanos por sus pinturas," 23–24.

[25] Nicholson, *Topiltzin Quetzalcoatl*, 4.

Quetzalcoatl and knocked him down and he ceased to be the sun, and such a great wind came up and all of the people, save those who remained in the air, became monkeys and simians.[26]

This legend is certainly part of native lore and appears to have been transmitted correctly. Is there anything in the creation legends that might contain a reference to the Book of Mormon account or to the experience with the Messiah? As both Allen and Wirth point out, Ehecatl Quetzalcoatl is a creator-god. However, Ehecatl Quetzalcoatl is not a creator without Tezcatlipoca. Both are equally responsible for creation. In addition to requiring two creator-gods, the myth records multiple failed creations by those same deities, who are violently antagonistic to each other, repeatedly destroying the other's work. Ehecatl Quetzalcoatl and Tezcatlipoca are both destroyer-gods as much as they are creator-gods. The logic and specifics of these legends are so different from the Book of Mormon events that there is simply no connection at all. They become "parallel" only through the use of loaded vocabulary, just as Lafaye suggested for Durán.

Ce Acatl Quetzalcoatl: The Deity on Earth

While typically combined, I have made a distinction between Topiltzin Quetzalcoatl of Tula and Ce Acatl Quetzalcoatl, whom I see as a liminal category of god, one who retains divinity but whose actions occur on earth and in the time of legends. It is to these legends that most of the "Christianized" elements are attached. The popular "proofs" of the relationship between Quetzalcoatl and Jesus Christ (or another non-native person) are based on misunderstandings or misapplications of the textual data from the Ce Acatl Quetzalcoatl mythology.

Ce Acatl Quetzalcoatl as a "White" God. Although no aspect of Quetzalcoatl is more familiar than his description as a "white god," Nicholson does not reconstruct that element as part of his reconstruction of the Ce Acatl Quetzalcoatl basic myth. Nevertheless, it is precisely as a "white god" that President John Taylor made his correlation to Jesus Christ. Perhaps Nicholson didn't reconstruct it as an element of the Ce Acatl Quetzalcoatl myths because it is so difficult to find in the source texts. The idol that represented Quetzalcoatl was always painted black. The *Florentine Codex* reports that "his face was thickly smeared with soot."[27]

The best possibility for a "white" Quetzalcoatl is that he is associated with the cardinal direction associated with the color white. Anthropologists Mary Miller and Karl Taube explain the color associations of the Mesoamerican directions: "The identification of colors with directions is most fully documented among the ancient Maya, who had specific glyphs for the colors red, white, black, yellow, and green. In

---

[26] Garibay K., "Historia de los Mexicanos por sus Pinturas," 30; translation mine. I have regularized the spelling from Tezcatlipuca to Tezcatlipoca. The Nahuatl vowel commonly written /o/ had a value somewhere between /u/ and /o/ and therefore these letters vary with the transcriber and the way he or she heard the vowel.

[27] Sahagún, *Florentine Codex*, 1:3.

the Yucatec Maya codices, these colors are associated with east, north, west, south and center, respectively. . . . Like the Maya, Central Mexicans appear to have identified white with the north and yellow with the south."[28]

Historia de los Mexicanos por sus Pinturas records an unfortunately abbreviated version of the four sons of a heavenly god and goddess, the four Tezcatlipocas. Only two give their particular colors, and Quetzalcoatl is not one of them:

> This god and goddess gave birth to four sons:
> The oldest they named Tlatlauhqui Tezcatlipoca, and those of Huexotzinco and Tlaxcala, who held this one to be their principal god, called him Camaxtle: This one was born all red.
> They had the second son, whom they called Yayauhqui Tezcatlipoca, who was the best and the worst, and he was more powerful and able than the other three, because he was born in the middle of all: this one was born black.
> The third was called Quetzalcoatl, and as another name, Yohualli Ehecatl.
> The fourth and smallest was called Omitecutli and by another name, Maquizcoatl and the Mexicans [Aztecs] called him Huitzilopochtli, because he was left-handed. He was held by the Mexicans [Aztecs] to be their principal god.[29]

This tale appears to have undergone some changes or was perhaps garbled by the Spanish recorder. Huitzilopochtli was indeed the principal god of the Mexica but was not considered to have been one of the four brothers. He appears to be a later addition to the mythology as the Aztecs attempted to elevate their own tribal god to a more prominent place in the common Mesoamerican pantheon. The source shows the associations of the deities with the colors but does not correlate Quetzalcoatl with "white." Nevertheless, that is the most likely association.

A god who is "red" because of his association with a direction is not particularly interesting. A god who is "white" in a parallel relationship to a world direction is similarly not particularly interesting. While the association with directions can give us the probable reason that Quetzalcoatl was considered "white," the popularity of the "white god" comes because of the Western insistence that "white" must be a skin color. It would really be remarkable if the Mesoamerican deity on earth were Caucasian rather than Native American. That is the way the popular myth "reads," but it cannot be an accurate representation of pre-conquest mythology.

Quetzalcoatl as bearded. A distinguishing physical contrast between the natives and Spaniards was the natives' relative beardlessness. A bearded god might therefore be considered unusual (as were the "yellow-bearded" Spaniards noted above). In modern versions of the Quetzalcoatl tale, the beard is one of the most frequent

---

[28] Miller and Taube, *An Illustrated Dictionary of the Gods and Symbols of Ancient Mexico and the Maya*, 65.

[29] Garibay, "Historia de los Mexicanos por sus Pinturas," 23–24; translation mine.

indicators suggesting that Quetzalcoatl must have been foreign.[30] Unlike other elements of the Ce Acatl Quetzalcoatl mythology, this one appears to have firm roots in native lore. Sahagún's sixteenth-century informants say, "His beard was long, exceedingly long. He was heavily bearded."[31] So well-known was this element that, by 1615, Fray Juan de Torquemada could state: "This was held as very certain, that he was of good disposition . . . bearded."[32]

The sources ascribe a variety of beard colors to Quetzalcoatl: to Torquemada, blond; to Bartolomé de Las Casas (a Dominican priest, died 1566) black; and to Diego de Durán red and graying.[33] Such variations probably signal that the color was not part of pre-conquest lore. Nevertheless, beards really were part of the pre-conquest Mesoamerican religious tradition and are frequently depicted in pre-conquest Mesoamerican art. However, these same native depictions prove that, while there was a native emphasis on bearded figures, the beard was not unique to Quetzalcoatl and is not even diagnostic for Quetzalcoatl, meaning that Quetzalcoatl may be painted and recognized without a beard.

Prior to the arrival of the Spanish, the codices from Central Mexico had no script that consistently encoded language in the paintings. They consist of pictograms and rebus drawings that give clues to the meaning. In this system, the actors on the pages are identified by two types of characteristics. In many cases, their name (given as a date in the calendar and consisting of a number and a noun, such as "8 Deer") is attached by a line or by simple proximity to the person named. Even without the attached name, however, most of the deities can be identified by the visual "code" of distinctive body or facial paint, specific items of clothing, and certain accompanying cultural items. Much as different military uniforms can readily distinguish the branch of service, the visual clues of the individual gods declared their identity.

The first book of the *Florentine Codex* gives a brief description of the various Aztec gods, and each one is given the set of accoutrements that identify him or her. For example, they describe Quetzalcoatl: "And thus was he bedight: he had a conical ocelot-skin cap. His face was thickly smeared with soot. He was adorned with [spiral] wind and mesquite symbols. He had a curved, turquoise mosaic ear-pendant. He wore a gold neckband of small sea-shells. He had the quetzal-pheasant as a burden on his back. He had ocelot anklets with rattles. He wore a cotton bone[-ribbed] jacket. He carried the shield with the wind-shell design. He had the curved [inlaid] spear-thrower and also foam sandals."[34] Noticeably absent is a beard.

While numerous features might be associated with Quetzalcoatl, not every depiction uses them all. Each painter selected among the available clues used for a

---

[30] Milton R. Hunter, *Christ in Ancient America*, 17; Cheesman, *The World of the Book of Mormon*, 30; Clark V. Johnson, "Prophetic Decree and Ancient Histories Tell the Story of America," in *The Book of Mormon: Jacob Through Words of Mormon, To Learn with Joy*, 133.

[31] Sahagún, *Florentine Codex*, 3:13.

[32] Juan de Torquemada, *Monarquía Indiana*, 2:255.

[33] Ibid., 1:255; Bartólome de Las Casas, *Apologética Historia Sumaria*, 1:644; Diego de Durán, *Historia de las Indias de Nueva España*, 1:9.

[34] Sahagún, *Florentine Codex*, 13.

A Bridge Too Far: Quetzalcoatl and Jesus Christ 363

particular painting. This ability of the visual representation to indicate the painting's subject is relevant to our understanding of how beards functioned in pre-conquest art.

The Codex Nuttall, reportedly sent to Spain in 1519, had been composed in the Mixtec culture of Central Mexico at an unknown date prior to the conquest. It shows several bearded figures: male 13 Reed, male 1 Death, male 4 Jaguar, male 10 Rain, and male 10 Grass. Male 9 Wind, the name attached to the figure who is painted with the iconography identifying Quetzalcoatl, is not bearded. Therefore, in the Codex Nuttall, beards are certainly part of the iconographic representations of various figures, but not for male 9 Wind (who combines the aspects of Ehecatl Quetzalcoatl and Ce Acatl Quetzalcoatl).[35]

Quetzalcoatl's virgin birth. The most "Christian" suggestion in the Ce Acatl Quetzalcoatl legends is the Quetzalcoatl's "virgin birth." Joseph Allen lists this as one of the significant parallels between Quetzalcoatl and Jesus Christ: "Both Christ and Quetzalcoatl were born of virgins."[36]

The association between a virgin birth and Christianity was, unsurprisingly, important for the early Spanish writers. Father Gerónimo de Mendieta (1525–1604), a Franciscan missionary, reports a conversation between a Spanish priest and an old Indian about an indigenous sacred book:

> And when this priest asked the Indian what the book contained of his doctrine, he did not know how to reply in particular, but from what he responded, if that book had not been lost, [the priest] would have seen how the doctrine which he taught and preached to them and that which the book contained were the same. . . . Also he said that they knew of the destruction by the flood. . . . They knew also of the mission of the angel to Our Lady, by a metaphor, saying that a very small object like a feather fell from the heavens, and a virgin picked it up and placed it over her womb whereupon she became pregnant.[37]

Aztec mythology appears to have a category of miraculous births that post-contact authors have labeled "virgin births." In Aztec mythology, however, the virgin birth was not unique to Quetzalcoatl. The particular tale that Mendieta related describes the birth of the Aztec tribal deity Huitzilopochtli, not any version of Quetzalcoatl. That tale is reported by Sahagún's informants:

> To Uitzilopochtli the Mexicans paid great honor.
> Thus did they believe of his beginning, his origin. At Coatepec [serpent mountain place], near Tula, there dwelt one day, there lived a woman named Coatl icue ["serpent her-skirt"], mother of the Centzonhuitznaua [the four hundred Huitznahua]. And their elder sister was named Coyolxauhqui.
> And this Coatl icue used to perform penances there; she used to sweep; she used to take care of the sweeping. Thus she used to perform penances at Coatepec. And once,

---

[35] Zelia Nuttall, ed., *Codex Nuttall*. For male 13 Reed, see p. 7; male 1 Death, p. 10; male 4 Jaguar, p. 14; male 10 Rain, p. 14; male 10 Grass, p. 15; and male 9 Wind, p. 15.
[36] Allen, *Exploring the Lands of the Book of Mormon*, 159.
[37] Gerónimo de Mendieta, *Historia Eclesiástica Indiana*, 1:538; translation mine.

when Coatl icue was sweeping, feathers descended upon her—what was like a ball of feathers. Then Coatl icue snatched them up; she placed them at her waist. And when she had swept, then she would have taken the feathers which she had put at her waist. She found nothing. Thereupon by means of them Coatl icue conceived.[38]

Ce Acatl's birth is similarly miraculous, but is a very different story.[39] Does this element represent a remembrance of Jesus Christ? It is extremely doubtful. It isn't unique to a single deity, but represents a theme widely known from world mythology.[40] The Nephites experienced the Messiah as a resurrected being in his glory. If a remembrance was passed on, surely it would have been to that very memorable event, not to his birth, however, miraculous, on another continent.

Old Things Are New Again

The meeting of cultures resulting from the conquest of Mexico brought ardent Christians into contact with ardent pagans who very soon had reason to want to please their new Christian masters. Out of this crucible of intense religious feeling, a synthesis emerged that was espoused by sympathetic Spanish priests. The idea quickly developed that, although the Native Americans were clearly a fallen people, they had previously known Christianity. The Spanish religious imagination linked the stories of Quetzalcoatl to the figure of St. Thomas. In Lafaye's description:

> The identification of Saint Thomas as the apostolic missionary of the New World was based on an apocryphal text, the *Acta Thomae*. But the identity of the apostle was basically unimportant; men sought the traces of an "apostle type," so to speak. The European vision of an apostle was that of a Semite with long thick hair and beard, dressed in a long white tunic, and holding an apostolic staff in his hand. The apostle typically conducted himself like a Spanish missionary of the sixteenth century, but—this was a specific feature—he proved the truth of the religion he preached by prodigies and miracles. As might be expected, the principal Christian symbols, crosses in particular, were associated with his traces.[41]

Although faith hopes for a historical remembrance of Jesus Christ's visit to Bountiful, it will not be found in the Central Mexican mythology of Quetzalcoatl.[42]

---

[38] Sahagún, *Florentine Codex*, 1:1–2.

[39] Bierhorst, *History and Mythology of the Aztecs*, 153.

[40] Joseph Campbell, *The Hero with a Thousand Faces*, 1973, 297–314, esp. 311–14, which summarizes the story of Coatlicue.

[41] Lafaye, *Quetzalcoatl and Guadalupe*, 185.

[42] The most recent apologetic for connecting the Quetzalcoatl mythology with the Book of Mormon is Sorenson, *Mormon's Codex*, 468–78. Sorenson relies heavily on Laurette Sejourné's interpretation that is now over fifty years old and superseded by more recent work. Sorenson's list of traits indicating the correlation between Quetzalcoatl and the Book of Mormon covers many of the points I have listed in this chapter, notably that Quetzalcoatl was "described as a white, bearded man," and that "he departed with a promise to return" (477). Sorenson concludes: "Although a few similar characteristics are vaguely paralleled in religious complexes elsewhere in the world, this set as a whole is not duplicated in any other culture area or in any other sacred text. Some relationship between Quetzalcoatl and the biblical Christ

The LDS fascination with Quetzalcoatl is based in documents from history, but the connections are to the St. Thomas literature, not the Book of Mormon.

---

was apparent enough that when the Spaniards arrived, their priests in some cases supposed a connection" (478).

Sorenson's correspondence list suffers from the same problem as most such lists. The features are selected to highlight similarities even when more conspicuous differences also exist. He is also correct that some Spaniards saw a relationship between Quetzalcoatl and Christian preaching, but it was not between Quetzalcoatl and Jesus Christ, but to St. Thomas. What he misses in his use of secondary sources is that those secondary sources are based upon distortions initiated by the early Spaniards retelling the story in more Christian forms (as noted in this chapter).

17
Mormon and the Nephite Demise

Mormon had a story to tell—a story beyond history. Mormon testified of the Messiah through the patterns of Nephite history. It is through history that Mormon intended to "convinc[e]. . . Jew and Gentile that Jesus is the Christ, the Eternal God, manifesting himself unto all nations" (Title Page). Jesus the Christ had manifested himself to Nephites gathered in Bountiful. Scripture predicted that he would return, and through his history, Mormon elucidated the true pattern for his assured return.[1]

Nevertheless, Mormon's typological story is enmeshed in a physical reality. After the whirlwind chapter of almost non-information that is 4 Nephi,[2] Mormon returned to historical details augmented by personal details. At this point in his record, Mormon no longer compiled and edited. He wrote "the things which I have both seen and heard" (Mormon 1:1). As he focused on his current world, he noted that "The whole face of the land had become covered with buildings, and the people were as numerous almost, as it were the sand of the sea" (Mormon 1:7).

The archaeological record for Early Classic Mesoamerica agrees that there were increasing numbers of people in the Maya world along with an increasing number of new cities. Archaeologist John Henderson notes:

> Several regions experienced intensified population growth. Well-developed hierarchies of communities—from tiny hamlets and villages with no indications of special political functions to large cities with all the trappings of centralized power—appeared. Many cities enjoyed a boom in building, especially in civic architecture. Some cities sought and acquired power beyond their immediate hinterlands, and regional states emerged. Marriage, alliance, and warfare variously characterized relationships among autonomous states. Relationships with distant societies also intensified, as the great central Mexican city of Teotihuacan established a long-term presence in the Maya world, especially at Kaminaljuyú in the highlands.[3]

---

[1] Brant A. Gardner, "Mormon's Editorial Method and Meta-Message," 105.
[2] I argue that 4 Nephi is intended as a connector book to move from the account of the Messiah's appearance to Mormon's time without providing any actual information. See Brant A. Gardner, *Second Witness; Analytical and Contextual Commentary on the Book of Mormon*, for 4 Nephi as well as Gardner, "Mormon's Editorial Method and Meta-Message," 99–105.
[3] John S. Henderson, *The World of the Ancient Maya*, 111–14 (intervening photographs).

Future Mesoamerican populations would be still larger, but Mormon was seeing the densest population known in any record available to him. Mormon's tale begins in the way that we have learned to expect—war with Lamanites. Just as typically, it begins with the defeat of the Lamanites (Mormon 1:10–12). While there would be some victories after this time, this was the last true victory. Mormon describes the next war as one that they spent most of their time losing. They not only lost the war, they lost themselves as a people. He prepared his audience for this severe change in fortune by noting that the Nephites were no longer worthy of Yahweh's promise associated with the land: "Wherefore, this land is consecrated unto him whom he shall bring. And if it so be that they shall serve him according to the commandments which he hath given, it shall be a land of liberty unto them; wherefore, they shall never be brought down into captivity; if so, it shall be because of iniquity; for if iniquity shall abound cursed shall be the land for their sakes, but unto the righteous it shall be blessed forever" (2 Ne. 1:7).

For the most part, Nephites had been sufficiently righteous that Yahweh had ultimately protected them. Right after Mormon described that most recent victory over the Lamanites he declared:

> But wickedness did prevail upon the face of the whole land, insomuch that the Lord did take away his beloved disciples, and the work of miracles and of healing did cease because of the iniquity of the people.
>
> And there were no gifts from the Lord, and the Holy Ghost did not come upon any, because of their wickedness and unbelief. (Morm. 1:13–14)

The remainder of his record would show how Yahweh remained faithful to his word when his people were no longer faithful to Him. Mormon's explanation of the destruction of the Nephites looked to the disappointing fulfillment of the promise of the land. Forsaking their righteous relationship with Yahweh meant the loss of his promise of protection, and the consequence was the people's loss of liberty.[4]

While that is the message Mormon is declaring, it must have had more human origins. There must be something in this particular time period that fostered both the shift from Nephite to Lamanite military success and wars of boundary maintenance

---

[4] Mormon's reason for the eventual Nephite defeat is not human, but divine. Victory or defeat depended upon God's will. Of course, that pattern is recognizable from Old World Israelite scripture as well as from Mesoamerican warfare, though obviously couched in very different terms. F. Kent Reilly III and James F. Garber, "The Symbolic Representation of Warfare in Formative Period Mesoamerica," 132:

> Like all cultures, wars conducted by K'iche' and their ancestors against the Maya of the Classic period were fought for many of the same reasons that they have always been fought: control of labor and resources and the amassing of territory and power. However, the ideological explanation for victory or loss in warfare was a uniquely Mesoamerican supernatural expression.
>
> Thus, for the Maya as well as other Mesoamerican cultures, warfare occurred on two planes: the supernatural and the natural. Victory in the supernatural realm ensured victory in the natural world. Defeat in the supernatural realm could be the explanation for the reality of defeat in the natural order.

to a war of total destruction. I have suggested that the warfare seen in Alma and Helaman may have been the result of perceived Nephite incursions on a major Pacific coast trade route. (See Chapter 13.) Possibly the destruction of the Nephite nation at this particular time is also linked to this important trade route.

At this point in Mesoamerican history, the ties between Teotihuacan in Central Mexico and the Maya civilizations to the south of the Nephite holdings were stronger than ever before. This increased Teotihuacano presence in the Maya heartlands gave both the Maya and Teotihuacan a strong motive to secure the trade route that ran through Nephite territory. As Ross Hassig explains:

> Generally, foreign Teotihuacan sites were located in resource-rich areas at great distances from the Valley of Mexico. Teotihuacan did not expand out uniformly, nor did it dominate all adjacent regions. . . .
> Perhaps the most famous Teotihuacan-influenced center is Kaminaljuyu, located in highland Guatemala City. People from Teotihuacan apparently dominated Kaminaljuyu from a.d. 400 to 650–700, with at least part of their presence being tied to the greatly expanded exploitation of major obsidian sources during this period. Teotihuacan's interest was not simply in Kaminaljuyu, but in controlling the goods flowing through its existing trading network. . . . Empires control distant markets by maintaining exclusive rights to trade there, denying access to others, so that, limited to a single trading partner, colonial trade is inherently unequal, working to the advantage of the empire.[5]

The desire for control of the Maya markets may have finally reached the point that a war of destruction became cost-effective. Charles W. Golden suggests: "All-out destruction of the enemy may be expensive in the short term but reduces the need for warfare in the long term by eliminating threats to royal power."[6]

James N. Ambrosino, Traci Ardren, and Travis W. Stanton provide an example from later in time and a different location that nevertheless demonstrates a people who are subjected to multiple military campaigns followed by a final campaign of destruction:

> Yaxuná appears to have been located in a hotly contested strategic area in the center of the peninsula. All the previously described conflicts may have erupted over control of this location. Chichén Itzá, also existing within the center of the peninsula a mere 22 kilometers away, would have had no reason to control the nearby site of Yaxuná. From a simple standpoint of cost efficiency, annihilation rather than occupation may have been the preferable option. Additionally, we have suggested that previous wars at Yaxuná

---

[5] Ross Hassig, *War and Society in Ancient Mesoamerica*, 56.
[6] Charles W. Golden, "The Politics of Warfare in the Usumacinta Basin: La Pasadita and the Realm of Bird Jaguar," 45.
Hassig, *War and Society in Ancient Mesoamerica*, 166: "Economics may well be a major motive behind imperial expansion, but it is the military that makes empire possible, just as it underwrites a tribute system within the state. Moreover, the relationship between economics and military expansion is frequently reciprocal, with the potential for adequate gain determining whether or not the expansion is undertaken. But the potential profitability of a trade relationship does not determine whether political expansion will take place; military capacity does."

represented conflicts between local groups who were backed by foreign patrons or allies. We suggest that the victor of the fourth war was an entirely foreign group from Chichén Itzá who had no vested interest in the government of Yaxuná. Essentially, the Terminal Classic showdown at Yaxuná was not a dynastic struggle at all; it was a war for economic and political control of the entire Yucatán peninsula.[7]

In light of the Yaxuná case, it is significant that Mormon notes a change in the Lamanite army due to the reappearance of the Gadianton robbers. The Gadianton robbers are Mormon's shorthand for various groups outside of the typical Nephites and Lamanites. They are harbingers of the destruction of nations. The Gadiantons of Mormon's time (as I argued in Chapter 14) are associated with invaders from the north. He tells us that "these Gadianton robbers, who were among the Lamanites, did infest the land. . . . And it came to pass that there were sorceries, and witchcrafts, and magics" (Mormon 1:18–19). These are reasonable descriptions of the incursion of Teotihuacan (the principal city in Central Mexico) into the area. Teotihuacan had dominated Tikal by A.D. 378, when their "entrance" to the city is noted on a stela. Their influence in the region became pervasive after that time.

As Hassig explains, one of the ways Teotihuacan could maintain its interests was through the exercise of military might:

> A major key to the functioning of hegemonic versus territorial empires is their relative reliance on force versus power. Force is direct physical action—typically military might—that is depleted as it is used. Power is not necessarily force, operates indirectly, and is not consumed in use because it is psychological, the perception of the possessor's ability to achieve its end. The ability to wield force is a necessary element of power, although a single demonstration, rather than its continued application, may be sufficient to compel compliance.[8]

The Nephites had lived in the New World for nearly one thousand years, but now they were on the verge of destruction. The Nephites had been destroyed as a people just prior to the destructions of 3 Nephi and Christ's appearance at Bountiful, but rebuilt and became again Nephites rather than tribes. If earlier less-than-righteous destroyed Nephites survived, why is the Nephite nation completely and finally destroyed 400 years after Christ's appearance? Why not 500 years? Why not 200?

Although not the cause, an important omen is the Mesoamerican 400-year baktun cycle. It was perhaps similar to our millennium. Nevertheless, it was events that destroyed the Nephites, not the prophecy. What changed during Mormon's time was the increased presence of Teotihuacan in the Maya lands. Teotihuacan's influence was vast.

Teotihuacan is in the Central Basin of Mexico. Tikal is in the Maya lowlands, some 800 miles away along modern roads. Between those two major powers were the Nephites, by this time somewhere around the Isthmus of Tehuantepec, and therefore potentially controlling trade routes between north and south. Perhaps that was not to

---

[7] James N. Ambrosino, Traci Ardren, and Travis W. Stanton, "The History of Warfare at Yaxuná," 122–23.

[8] Hassig, *War and Society in Ancient Mesoamerica*, 57–58.

be tolerated. With increase in trade occasioned by the increased presence of Central Mexican goods and ideas among the Maya, it is reasonable to assume that the traditional trade route between Central Mexico and the large Maya centers—a route that necessarily passed through the Isthmus of Tehuantepec—had become even more important. At this point in time, and not earlier, there was sufficient reason to make the cost of eliminating the Nephites worth the expenditure.

The Teotihuacano presence among the Maya had strong militaristic overtones, even if the evidence for direct conquest is circumstantial.[9] The net effect, however, was a change in the nature of politics and artistic representations.[10] Whether solely based on improved weaponry or combined with other tactics, the evidence suggests that the Teotihuacanos were typically victorious over their Maya opponents (based on the widespread presence of Teotihuacano symbols among the Maya during this time period).

Teotihuacano influence would have been immediately visible on the battlefield. Even before the rain of darts from the powerful atlatls, the military "uniforms" of the

---

[9] William L. Fash and Barbara W. Fash, "Teotihuacan and the Maya: A Classic Heritage," 448:

The settlement pattern data, ceramics, and green obsidian lead us to speculate that a faction with ties to Teotihuacan established itself on the fortress-like hill of Cerro de las Mesas, and unified the diverse competing noble lines, moreover establishing a royal center in a thoroughly indefensible place, in the center of the Copán Valley Bottomlands. David Webster's hypothesis that warfare was critical in the formation of Maya kingdoms would seem to have much in its favor in the case of the Classic period Copán dynasty. What better way to resolve an internal conflict than to place themselves in the hands of a veteran warrior-merchant, who validated his right to rule by his mercantile and militaristic connections with the mighty Teotihuacan? The skeletal evidence that the man in the Hunal tomb had a parry fracture on his right forearm is interpreted by Jane Buikstra as evidence for a battle wound. As Sharer notes, it is also illuminating when we discuss archaeological confirmation of the pictorial record, since K'inich Yax K'uk' Mo' is portrayed with a small rectangular shield on his right arm. . . . Finally it is significant that the strontium analysis of the bones of this individual indicate that he was, in fact, not a native of the Copán Valley, adding important evidence in favor of his having been a "Lord of the West" [a Maya reference to one from Teotihuacan].

[10] David Stuart, "'The Arrival of Strangers': Teotihuacan and Tollan in Classic Maya History," 466:

The potential importance of the hieroglyphic texts is clear, but it is surprising how seldom they have been used to clarify the history underlying Teotihuacan-Maya interactions. With the exception of Proskouriakoff, most epigraphic work on central Petén history has assumed a more "internalist" perspective, often ignoring the Teotihuacan issue altogether. I offer a very different perspective in this essay, arguing that hieroglyphic texts at Tikal, Copán, and other Maya sites offer insights into Maya perceptions of a dynamic and often changing relationship with central Mexico. As we shall see, such sources strongly support a more "externalist" view that Teotihuacan played a very direct and even disruptive role in the political history of Maya kingdoms.

Teotihuacanos would have been visible.[11] Archaeologist Michael D. Coe describes the typical Teotihuacano military attire: "Teotihuacan fighting men were armed with atlatl-propelled darts and rectangular shields, and bore round, decorated, pyrite mosaic mirrors on their backs; with their eyes sometimes partially hidden by white shell 'goggles,' and their feather headdresses, they must have been terrifying figures to their opponents."[12]

Perhaps this visual indication of the presence of what must have been a known and foreboding enemy explains the Nephites' original reaction to this new war: "Therefore it came to pass that in my sixteenth year I did go forth at the head of an army of the Nephites, against the Lamanites; therefore three hundred and twenty and six years had passed away. And it came to pass that in the three hundred and twenty and seventh year the Lamanites did come upon us with exceedingly great power, insomuch that they did frighten my armies; therefore they would not fight, and they began to retreat towards the north countries" (Morm. 2:2–3). The Nephite flight described in verse 3 may not represent cowardice but rather a strategic retreat to understand and better prepare for this new type of enemy—an enemy with a more terrible reputation that any the Nephites had previously faced.

Mormon's account provides both details and his opinions about this final war. From his complaints we learn that the nature of warfare has changed. For Mormon, the accepted rules of engagement appear to have suddenly changed, and not for the better. For example, he wrote: "And they did also march forward against the city Teancum, and did drive the inhabitants forth out of her, and did take many prisoners both women and children, and did offer them up as sacrifices unto their idol gods" (Morm. 4:14). Human sacrifice was entrenched in Mesoamerican culture and was certainly practiced before this year.[13]

If human sacrifice had been a part of Mesoamerican culture for hundreds of years and if Nephite captives had been sacrificed during those centuries, why does Mormon mention it now? Mormon also notes, for the first time, that women and children (not just captured warriors) have been sacrificed. Mormon was probably not an eyewitness to the sacrifices, since the sacrifice of women and children would have occurred in cities with temples and altars, not on the battlefield. Thus, his statement that the women and children were being sacrificed reveals his unstated assumption that sacrifice was the reason for taking captives.[14] In this new and terrible war, women and children, not just men, are being sacrificed.

---

[11] Heather McKillop, *The Ancient Maya: New Perspectives*, 315, pictures Nun Yax Ayin of Tikal in "Teotihuacan style military regalia." Stuart, "The Arrival of Strangers," 468–69, discusses figures in Teotihuacan military attire. Fash and Fash, "Teotihuacan and the Maya," 443–45, discuss burials including Teotihuacan military regalia.

[12] Michael D. Coe, *The Maya*, 83.

[13] Susan Toby Evans, *Ancient Mexico and Central America: Archaeology and Culture History*, 292, for the Early Classic, A.D. 250–600. Ibid., 227, for the Late Formative, 300 B.C.–A.D. 1.

[14] There is no actual evidence that the Teotihuacanos brought child and female sacrifice with them into the Maya area. However, such sacrifices were performed in Teotihuacan itself. Carlos

Eventually, the Gadianton-infused Lamanites pushed the Nephites to the brink. The Nephites gathered for a last battle at Cumorah. Mormon requested that the Lamanite king set a time and place for the battle. This request, as well as the allowed time for preparation, fits within known practice for the later Aztecs, though there is insufficient textual information to assure that it was also a custom during Book of Mormon times.[15]

There is no light at the end of this story of destruction. Prior to Christ's death, the Nephites had been destroyed as a people, but they had returned after the Messiah's appearance. No such miracle closes Mormon's tale. The story ends without even waiting long enough for Mormon himself to close it. Mormon died. His people were destroyed. The only hope was Mormon's typological message that such destruction would surely presage a new coming of his Messiah, his God.

The Mesoamerican Cumorah

Cumorah was either an impressive defensive position or a metaphorical location for the destruction of a people—perhaps both. Moroni writes: "And it came to pass that the army of Coriantumr did pitch their tents by the hill Ramah; and it was that same hill where my father Mormon did hide up the records unto the Lord, which were sacred" (Ether 15:11). Moroni's equation of the two hills requires that the hill of Nephite destruction be in Jaredite lands, which places all of these events in a limited area that does not stretch from Mesoamerica to New York. (See the next section for the New York Hill Cumorah.)

John L. Sorenson simply accepts Moroni's equation of Ramah and Cumorah: "The hill Ramah, where the Jaredites destroyed themselves, was the same hill as Nephite Cumorah (Ether 15:11)."[16] Nevertheless, we have no source from which Moroni might have known that the two locations were indeed one and the same. Ether certainly knew Ramah but could not have known the name Cumorah. The identification couldn't have come from Ether's record.

Serrano Sánchez, "Funerary Practices and Human Sacrifice in Teotihuacán Burials," 113–14, comments:

> Skeletal evidence of human sacrifice at Teotihuacan dates back to the 1906 excavations of Batres, who found burials of children approximately six years of age at each of the corners of the four levels of the Pyramid of the Sun. Later, Ales Hrdlicka explored two simultaneously deposited burials of a man and a woman, placed side by side to the southeast of the same building.
>
> Burials of newborns associated with altars, recorded at two extensively excavated sites, La Ventilla B and Tlajinga, deserve special mention. Not only the context of the discovery—their close association with these structures—but also the high perinatal mortality confirmed at these sites makes us suspect deliberate death by infant sacrifice.

[15] Ross Hassig, *Aztec Warfare: Imperial Expansion and Political Control*, 48.
[16] Sorenson, *An Ancient American Setting for the Book of Mormon*, 14. He makes the same correlation in Sorenson, *Mormon's Codex*, 688, note 82.

Moroni knew the location as Cumorah, but there is no way to know how he understood it to be the very hill that Ether called Ramah. It is possible that there was some distinguishing feature of the hill that Ether noted and Moroni recognized (but did not record as he abridged Ether). Perhaps it was revelation, but Moroni doesn't mention that either. Perhaps it was only the similarity in the final destructions of the two peoples and that made them symbolically the same. It is currently unknowable.[17]

We may hope to learn more about Moroni's Cumorah. David A. Palmer comments that the site of El Mesón is near the proposed Hill Cumorah, which he identifies as Cerro Vigía in modern Veracruz.[18] El Mesón was occupied beginning as early as 400 B.C. and continued to be occupied through Nephite times until ca. A.D. 300.[19] The abandonment of this site around one hundred years earlier than the final events of the Nephite nations suggests that it was a location with the natural resources to support a city population, but that there were no significant competing peoples who had to be dislodged to allow the Nephites access to it.

Lawrence L. Poulsen has proposed a different hill along the eastern seashore of the Gulf of Mexico. Poulsen examined three-dimensional maps against the information in the text and found four possibilities. He then further refined the search, settling on one in Misantla, Veracruz, Mexico. One interesting correlation is to the requirement that there be "many waters, rivers, and fountains" (Mormon 6:4). Poulsen quotes from one of the early Spanish descriptions of the land commissioned by the king: "One of the aspects most prominent of the region, is the abundance of water, yes it is a district, humid by nature, where have existed the difficult problems of other places. In the entire jurisdiction there are abundant springs, lagoons, and streams. The great rivers form a true hydrographic net and it is notable that even in the hills, little fountains are found."[20] The actual hill that might have been Cumorah remains speculative.

---

[17] I do not think that questioning the correlation between Ramah and Cumorah alters the essential requirement that the final destruction of both people occurred in Mesoamerica. Other data are sufficient for that conclusion. However, arguments for a Mesoamerican location for the Book of Mormon that lean on this correlation (as Sorenson's does) are weaker than they appear if the two are not the same hill.

[18] David Palmer, *In Search of Cumorah: New Evidences for the Book of Mormon from Ancient Mexico*, 91.

[19] Michael L. Loughlin, "Recorrido Archaeológico El Mesón."

[20] Lawrence L. Poulsen, "Book of Mormon Geography and the Book of Ether." Poulsen translates the text written by Diego Pérez de Arteaga, "Relación de Misantla." He describes the source:

> The Viceroy of Mexico, shortly after the Spanish conquest, required that a report be submitted answering 50 questions about all locations still inhabited by Mesoamerican language groups. These were called Relaciones and are filed in the various archives throughout Mexico and in the Royal Archives in Spain. Information about location three is found in the "Relación de Misantla" prepared by Diego Perez de Arteaga and presumably was never submitted to the Royal Archives. It was eventually sold along with other "Relaciones" from Veracruz to the University of Texas at Austin for $10,000.

The New York Cumorah

Not long after the Book of Mormon was published, the community of believers began using the name "Cumorah" for the hill from which Joseph had retrieved the plates. The New York hill wasn't, and isn't, an imposing natural feature. There is nothing about the New York hill that suggests an important defensive position, particularly for the numbers of defenders mentioned. Although there is a strong tradition linking that hill with Cumorah, the tradition is stronger than any evidence for the correlation.

As later as almost a hundred years after the publication of the Book of Mormon, Orson F. Whitney indicated that it had different local names: "In the summer of 1914, it fell to my lot to visit some of the scenes made memorable by the early experiences of the Latter-day Saints. One object of surpassing interest was the Hill Cumorah, called 'Mormon Hill' by the inhabitants of the region in which it is situated—namely, western New York state about midway between the towns of Palmyra and Manchester."[21] Rex C. Reeve Jr. and Richard O. Cowan discuss the way it acquired the name Cumorah:

> At what point in modern times this New York hill was first called Cumorah is difficult to determine. In his account in the Pearl of Great Price, Joseph Smith refers to the hill where the plates were buried, but never calls it by any name. In the Doctrine and Covenants the name "Cumorah" only appears one time, in an 1842 epistle written by Joseph Smith: "And again, what do we hear? Glad tidings from Cumorah!" (D&C 128:20). No other uses of "Cumorah" have been found in any other of Joseph Smith's personal writings. When this name does appear it has been added by later editors or is being quoted from another individual.[22]

After acquiring copies of the "Relación de Misantla" David Ramirez Lavoignet prepared a revision of the relación and after adding extensive notes to bring it up to date, published it in 1962.

[21] Orson F. Whitney, "Some Historical and Prophetic Phases of the Book of Mormon," 216.

[22] Rex C. Reeve Jr. and Richard O. Cowan, "The Hill Called Cumorah," 73–74. The earliest possible connection between the New York hill and the Book of Mormon Cumorah comes from an 1878 interview with David Whitmer by Orson Pratt and Joseph F. Smith, "Report of Elders Orson Pratt and Joseph F. Smith," 772–73:

> When I was returning to Fayette, with Joseph and Oliver, all of us riding in the wagon, Oliver and I on an old-fashioned, wooden, spring seat and Joseph behind us; while traveling along in a clear open place, a very pleasant, nice-looking old man suddenly appeared by the side of our wagon and saluted us with, "Good morning, it is very warm," at the same time wiping his face or forehead with his hand. We returned the salutation, and, by a sign from Joseph, I invited him to ride if he was going our way. But he said very pleasantly, "No, I am going to Cumorah." This name was something new to me, I did not know what Cumorah meant. We all gazed at him and at each other, and as I looked around inquiringly of Joseph, the old man instantly disappeared, so that I did not see him again.

This report would be much more conclusive had it not been recorded nearly fifty years later. The passage of time and the accepted designation of "Cumorah" as the name of the New York

The sacralization of the New York hill by association with Cumorah tapped into the miraculous nature of the discovery and translation of the plates. It was an association that certainly occurred very early, but the source of the connection between the New York hill and the Cumorah of the Book of Mormon is unknown. One might suppose that had Moroni identified the New York hill as Cumorah, Joseph would have used the term earlier than he did.

Joseph's use of the term in 1842 is similar to his use of Urim and Thummim for the interpreters and the seer stones.[23] Although he was in a perfect position to know a different name and to correct the Saints, he didn't. However, that should not be seen as confirmation that the tradition was correct, but rather that the Saints' communal interpretation of history influenced Joseph's descriptions of that history. Joseph not only allowed the communal creation of the Church's history; he embraced it.

It is plausible that just as W. W. Phelps was the one to associate the interpreters with Urim and Thummim of the Bible, one of Joseph's companions made the association between the hill from which the plates were taken with the hill in which Mormon had hid plates. While that is a plausible connection, it is based on a misreading of the text. Mormon specifically says: "I made this record out of the plates of Nephi, and hid up in the hill Cumorah all the records which had been entrusted to me by the hand of the Lord, save it were *these few plates* which I gave unto my son Moroni" (Mormon 6:6, emphasis mine). Although the Book of Mormon specifically tells of plates being buried in the hill Cumorah, they were explicitly *not* the plates delivered to Joseph Smith.[24] On the basis of the only information we have in the text of the Book of Mormon, the hill from which Joseph retrieved the plates should never have been called Cumorah. Nevertheless, the association was made and became so entrenched in the Saints' understanding that it is difficult to separate the historical data from the communal story.

---

hill by the time of the recollection argue against this second-hand report from Whitmer as being a definitive statement.

Sidney B. Sperry, "Were There Two Cumorahs?" 268, suggests:

> Now, if it is agreed that the Book of Mormon evidence points inevitably to a Ramah-Cumorah in Middle America, the question then arises as to how the hill in New York from which the Prophet Joseph Smith received the sacred Nephite records came to be called Cumorah. No details are afforded us as to either how or when the hill was so named. But certainly no adherent of the Middle-American view of Ramah-Cumorah would object to the suggestion that Moroni himself may have called the hill Cumorah in honor of the one in Middle America. He may even have told the prophet Joseph Smith about it but of this we have no proof.

[23] Brant A. Gardner, *The Gift and Power: Translating the Book of Mormon*, 127–29.

[24] Of course, it is possible that Moroni returned to Cumorah and buried the plates there, but nothing in the text makes that assertion. The only information that the Book of Mormon itself offers is that Cumorah was not the resting place of the plates that Mormon gave to Moroni.

The strength of that communal story was sufficient that Sidney B. Sperry originally argued for a single hill that bore the name Cumorah. However, he changed his mind after reviewing the evidence. He records:

> The friendly controversy still goes on, the one camp holding that the only Cumorah in or out of the Book of Mormon is the traditional one in New York State, the other supporting the view that the Cumorah in New York has been named after the one in Middle America, but is not the one around which the last great battles of the Nephites and Lamanites took place.
>
> Now which of these two points of view is correct? It would be desirable if possible, to come to a unity in the matter. Truth should never be on the defensive, but sometimes it is hard to decide just where it is. Perhaps most people of the Church hold to the tradition a view of Cumorah, and, indeed, I have defended that view in some of my writings. But in recent years we have again gone over the Book of Mormon evidence very carefully and are prepared to present what we feel are the elements of the strongest case that can be made for a Cumorah in Middle America.[25]

Countering the force of traditional association is the archaeological data for the hill and the surrounding lands. John E. Clark discusses the reasons that the New York hill could not have been the location of the final Nephite battle: "Archaeologically speaking, it is a clean hill. No artifacts, no walls, no trenches, no arrow-heads. The area immediately surrounding the hill is similarly clean. Pre-Columbian people did not settle or build here. This is not the place of Mormon's last stand. We must look elsewhere for that hill."[26] Clark has also noted: "The cultural worlds of ancient Mesoamerica and early New York are far enough apart that it ought to be simple to discover from which one the book came. The cultures described in the Book of Mormon fit much better in Mesoamerica than in New York for any century."[27]

Nevertheless, we do understand that the plates from which Joseph translated the Book of Mormon came from the New York hill. How did they come to be there? Sorenson comments:

> A question many readers will have been asking themselves is a sound and necessary one: how did Joseph Smith obtain the gold plates in upstate New York if the final battleground of the Nephites was in Mesoamerica?
>
> Let's review where the final battle took place. The Book of Mormon makes clear that the demise of both Jaredites and Nephites took place near the narrow neck of land. Yet New York is thousands of miles away from any plausible configuration that could be described as this narrow neck. Thus the scripture itself rules out the idea that the Nephites perished near Palmyra.
>
> Then how did the plates get from the battleground to New York? We have no definitive answer, but we can construct a plausible picture. Mormon reports that he buried all the records in his custody at the Hill Cumorah of the final battle except for certain key golden plates (Morm. 6:6). Those from which Joseph Smith translated, he entrusted to his son Moroni. As late as 35 years afterward, Moroni was still adding to those records (Moro.

---

[25] Sperry, "Were There Two Cumorahs?" 261–62.
[26] John E. Clark, "Archaeology and Cumorah Questions," 144–51.
[27] John E. Clark, "Archaeological Trends and Book of Mormon Origins," 96.

10:1). He never does tell us where he intended to deposit them, nor where he was when he sealed them up (Moro. 10:34). The most obvious way to get the plates to New York State would have been for somebody to carry them there. Moroni could have done so himself during those final, lonely decades.

Would Moroni have been able to survive a trip of several thousand miles through strange peoples and lands, if he did transport the record? Such a journey would be no more surprising than the trip by Lehi's party over land and by sea halfway around the globe. As a matter of fact, we do have a striking case of a trip much like the one Moroni may have made. In the mid-sixteenth century, David Ingram, a shipwrecked English sailor, walked in 11 months through completely strange Indian territory from Tampico, Mexico, to the St. John River, at the present border between Maine and Canada. His remarkable journey would have been about the same distance as Moroni's and over essentially the same route. So Moroni's getting the plates to New York even under his own power seems feasible.[28]

How should we see Joseph Fielding Smith's firm declaration that the New York hill must be Cumorah? His opinion is unambiguous:

> The Prophet Joseph Smith himself is on record, definitely declaring the present hill called Cumorah to be the exact hill spoken of in the Book of Mormon.
>
> The fact that all of his associates from the beginning down have spoken of it as the identical hill where Mormon and Moroni hid the records must carry some weight. It is difficult for a reasonable person to believe that such men as Oliver Cowdery, Brigham Young, Parley P. Pratt, Orson Pratt, David Whitmer, and many others, could speak frequently of the spot where the Prophet Joseph Smith obtained the plates as the Hill Cumorah, and not be corrected by the Prophet, if that were not the fact. That they did speak of this hill in the days of the Prophet in this definite manner is an established record of history.[29]

Although Joseph Fielding Smith was adamant in his opinion, the data upon which the opinion was based are not nearly as strong as his statement suggests.[30] Joseph did make the association between Cumorah and the New York hill, but only late and well after it had become an accepted designation.

The weight of tradition certainly sees Cumorah in New York, but that tradition hangs on assumption rather than revelation or any firm evidence. There is an assumption that Joseph knew Book of Mormon geography, knew where the Book of Mormon Cumorah was, and declared the Book of Mormon Cumorah to be in New York. Those are three assumptions on which to base such a strong declaration, especially when the evidence does not support the thread on which the weight of tradition hangs.

---

[28] Sorenson, *An Ancient American Setting*, 44.

[29] Joseph Fielding Smith, *Doctrines of Salvation*, 3:234.

[30] Elder Smith's footnote to his declaration that Joseph Smith has definitely identified the New York hill as the very Cumorah cites the version of the Zelph story as found in Joseph Smith et al., *History of the Church of Jesus Christ of Latter-day Saints*, 2:79–80. That statement was a composite of multiple recollections of the incident. The reference to the Hill Cumorah is not an identification, but a reference of distance. See Kenneth W. Godfrey, "The Zelph Story," 31–56, for an analysis of the event and the construction of the account found in the *History of the Church*.

Archaeology and history declare a different story. The New York hill cannot be the Cumorah described in the text.

What history does support is that Joseph came late to using Cumorah to identify the New York hill. Rather than being able to use Joseph as the foundation of the naming tradition, it is easier, according to the evidence of history, to see Joseph as accepting the tradition. He would not have corrected it for the same reason he did not correct the use of "Urim and Thummim" when applied to the interpreters or seer stone.

18

Jaredites in the Text

The people known as the Jaredites appear in Mormon's text almost as an afterthought. Although Mormon indeed intended that the account be written (Mosiah 28:19), he left that task for Moroni. Nothing in the structure of Mormon's text nor in his eponymous book hints that he intended to add anything about Jaredite history himself, for the simple reason that Mormon's message for his future audience was complete without the book of Ether.[1] Even when Mormon discusses Mosiah$_2$ translating the plates of Ether, he barely discusses their contents.[2]

Mormon uses the book of Ether as the foundational evidence for exposing the nature of secret combinations, a topic which he expressed fully in his discussion of the Gadianton robbers. (See Chapter 16.) Perhaps he envisioned the addition of the book of Ether as a support document to give more information on the dangers of those secret combinations.

Even though the history contained in the book of Ether appears to have little impact on the story Mormon tells, it is nevertheless a crucial component of the search for the real-world setting of the Book of Mormon. No geographic correlation fits the text unless it accounts for the descriptions of the Jaredites along with the Nephites.

Some important criteria in the text constrain the possible candidates. For example, there is no known direct contact between Jaredites and Nephites. Coriantumr, the last Jaredite king, lived with the people of Zarahemla, but had died before the Nephites reached Zarahemla. Nevertheless, Nephites and Jaredites were contemporaries for about four hundred years.[3]

---

[1] I spell out my assumption about Mormon's intent in Brant A. Gardner, "Mormon's Editorial Method and Meta-Message."

[2] Other than the fact of their translation, here are the only content descriptions in Mormon's edited text: "Now after Mosiah had finished translating these records, behold, it gave an account of the people who were destroyed, from the time that they were destroyed back to the building of the great tower, at the time the Lord confounded the language of the people and they were scattered abroad upon the face of all the earth, yea, and even from that time back until the creation of Adam" (Mosiah 28:17).

[3] The four hundred year overlap is based on my reconstruction of the probable timing of Coriantumr's arrival among the people of Zarahemla, which I see as having occurred somewhere around 200 B.C. Gardner, *Second Witness*, 6:148.

The text also requires that the Jaredites arrive in the New World long before the Nephites. The Jaredite lands lie north of Nephite lands for much of Book of Mormon history, although the Nephites are pushed farther north in their final years. During those final years, Moroni believes that they are in former Jaredite country (called Desolation after the abandoned cities). As conclusive evidence of the eventual geographic overlap, Moroni suggests that the Jaredite Hill Ramah and the Nephite Hill Cumorah are the identical geologic feature (Ether 15:11). Beyond geography, the Jaredite history suggests complicated civilizations with ruling classes capable of marshalling the population for war as well as community construction.

There are certainly fewer textual constraints for identifying the historical peoples who were called Jaredites in the Book of Mormon than there are for identifying Nephite geographic and cultural affiliations. Compared to Mormon's large text, we have only the book of Ether to give a highly condensed Jaredite history. Nevertheless, there are sufficient data that they can be used to disqualify real-world candidates that might fit some of the criteria but not all—even if they are insufficient to absolutely identify how the Jaredites appear in archaeology.

The combination of the early date of the Jaredites and the more limited volume of written material we have about them in the Book of Mormon contribute to making the understanding of Jaredite history set against Mesoamerica geography the most difficult task in correlating the text to the real world. Their path to the New World is conjecture and there are different opinions on when they fit into history. Once in the New World they plausibly meld into a culture about which we are learning more and more, but about which many details remain cloudy. To these difficulties is added the complication that the story of Jaredites is farther removed from original sources than for any other Book of Mormon people.

The prophet Ether created a record of his people's history from some existing source or sources. Perhaps similar to Mormon, he may have created a new record based on original sources. Neither those originals nor Ether's complete work are known. $Mosiah_2$ translated Ether's record and then Moroni redacted $Mosiah_2$'s translation—interspersing Ether's account with his own reflections. Joseph Smith then translated Moroni's text. That is the longest string of intermediaries in the Book of Mormon between the original information and our current text.

The Translation of the Jaredite Record and the Tower[4]

Moroni records that "Jared came forth with his brother and their families, with some others and their families, from the great tower, at the time the Lord confounded the language of the people, and swore in his wrath that they should be scattered upon all the face of the earth; and according to the word of the Lord the people were scattered" (Ether 1:33). Referencing this verse, Hugh Nibley remarked: "Notice that

---

[4] This section abridges the larger treatment in Brant A. Gardner, *Second Witness: Analytical and Contextual Commentary on the Book of Mormon*, 6:146–54.

it doesn't say the Tower of Babel. That's very important."[5] It is important because our understanding of their time period and location can change dramatically if this is not a story that actually begins with the Tower of Babel. Was there another tower associated with the confusion of tongues? No.

What is important is that the reference to a tower may have been sufficient to trigger that connection in Mosiah$_2$'s translation. Moroni notes:

> And as I suppose that the first part of this record, which speaks concerning the creation of the world, and also of Adam, and an account from that time even to the great tower, and whatsoever things transpired among the children of men until that time, is had among the Jews—
> Therefore I do not write those things which transpired from the days of Adam until that time; but they are had upon the plates; and whoso findeth them, the same will have power that he may get the full account.
> But behold, I give not the full account, but a part of the account I give, from the tower down until they were destroyed. (Ether 1:3–5)

As Moroni describes it, then, the first part of Ether's record recounted the history from Adam to the time of the tower. At that point, the story begins in earnest. Moroni's statement corroborates the only other information we have about the plates' content in his description of Mosiah$_2$'s translation: "Now after Mosiah had finished translating these records, behold, it gave an account of the people who were destroyed, from the time that they were destroyed back to the building of the great tower, at the time the Lord confounded the language of the people and they were scattered abroad upon the face of all the earth, yea, and even from that time back until the creation of Adam" (Mosiah 28:17).

The tower also appears in the translation given for the Coriantumr stela: "It also spake a few words concerning his fathers. And his first parents came out from the tower, at the time the Lord confounded the language of the people; and the severity of the Lord fell upon them according to his judgments, which are just; and their bones lay scattered in the land northward" (Omni 1:22).

The Coriantumr stela does not, naturally, date from the time of Adam, but it does corroborate the description of the "first parents" coming from the tower, something that is important in both accounts. A citation to ancestors or founders is a common motif in Mesoamerican records, since citing a link between the current king and his illustrious progenitors established the legitimacy of his rule.[6] Thus, it is not surprising

---

[5] Hugh Nibley, *Teachings of the Book of Mormon—Semester 1: Transcripts of Lectures Presented to an Honors Book of Mormon Class at Brigham Young University, 1988–1990*, 433.

[6] Three major Maya documents contain information on their first ancestors. (1–2) *Annals of the Cakchiquels and Title of the Lords of Totonicapán*, 43, quotes, first the *Annals* and next the *Title*: "Here I shall write a few stories of our first fathers and ancestors, those who begot man of old, before these mountains and valleys were inhabited. . . . The Wise Men, the Nahuales, the chiefs and leaders of three great peoples and of others who joined them, called *U Mamae* [the old men], extending their sight over the four parts of the world and over all that is beneath the sky, and finding no obstacle, came from the other part of the ocean, from where the sun rises,

that two different records on different materials and written for different purposes would both invoke the ancestral past. Indeed, a Mesoamerican context would almost require such documents.

Nevertheless, what we have is Moroni's description of Mosiah$_2$'s translation. We do not have the very text from the book of Ether. Moroni is saying that Mosiah's translation shows similarities to the brass plates, which is perhaps an important distinction. Based on what we know of how Joseph Smith translated Nephi's plates, we might expect that Mosiah used a similar method. Thus, when Mosiah saw similar content, he used the familiar language from the brass plates, much as Joseph Smith used the familiar KJV language of Isaiah and Jesus's 3 Nephi sermon. It would be dangerous to assume that Mosiah used a better or more accurate or literal translation method than Joseph Smith did while translating a document from an unknown language by employing physical aids.

The process of having language from a later text emerge intact in a completely different account is a well-known phenomenon. An amazing example comes from an early Aztec chronicle—amazing because the chronicler actually recognized what was happening rather than accepting the story as a native account. Fray Diego de Durán received information from an informant when he was collecting material on Quetzalcoatl (Topiltzin, in Durán's work):

> Asking another old Indian what information he had of the departure of Topiltzin, he began saying that the Papa ["Pope", meaning Topiltzin] had arrived at the sea with many people and that he continued and had struck the sea with a staff and it had dried up and become a road through which he entered. Both he and his people. Also that his persecutors had entered after him and the waters had returned to their place and nothing more was ever known of them. And as I saw that he had read the same as I and I knew where he was going with the story, I didn't ask him more so that he would not relate Exodus to me, of which I felt he had received notice, yet he went as far as to mention the punishment which the children of Israel had with the serpents because of their murmurings against God and Moses.[7]

This passage is fascinating, both for its biblical content and for the fact that Fray Durán recognized and discounted it as a story from the Bible rather than as an authentic indigenous story. More interesting, however, is the fact that a native informant gave this material in response to a question about Quetzalcoatl. I propose the following speculative reconstruction of his thought processes.

The native informant obviously had learned the story, either directly or at second hand, and could relate it with enough details that Durán easily recognized it. Second,

---

a place called *Pa Tulán, Pa Civán* [an allusion to legendary Tula or Tollan] (3) *Popol Vuh: The Definitive Edition of the Mayan Book of the Dawn of Life and the Glories of Gods and Kings*, 165, reads: "These are the names of the first people who were made and modeled. This is the first person: Jaguar Quitze. And now the second; Jaguar Night. And now the third: Mahucutah. And the fourth: True Jaguar. And these are the names of our first mother-fathers."

[7] Diego de Durán, *Historia de las Indias de Nueva España*, 1:12. My translation.

For the Christian effect on native legends, see Brant A. Gardner, "Crucible of Distortion: The Impact of the Spanish on Native American Oral Tradition."

the native had to find enough correspondences with the Quetzalcoatl material that he could combine the two stories. In the reconstructible native legend, Quetzalcoatl reaches the seashore and departs from his people. In some versions, he is accompanied by a number of followers, and miracles occur both en route and on the beach. Quetzalcoatl also has a symbolic association with serpents. These points are conceptual nodes of meaning that parallel the story of Moses. Thus, the native had to know both tales, find the similarities, and use them to reconstruct his own version of the Quetzalcoatl material.

What we see in Durán's experience with his native informant is the same process I suggest for Mosiah$_2$'s translation. The material being translated and Mosiah$_2$'s understanding of the scripture had enough resemblances that Mosiah$_2$ shaped the Jaredites' original story to match the brass plates' story at the crucial point of finding a common origin in the great tower.

The Jaredite/Mesoamerican record itself seems fairly consistent and accurate, starting at the ending point (Ether and Coriantumr) and working backwards. But it is difficult to connect the Jaredite/Mesoamerican story with a chronology that would include the Tower of Babel.

I suggest that the native historian Ixtlilxochitl, writing in 1690, may provide some assistance—although for a different reason than that usually assigned to him. Milton R. Hunter and Thomas Stuart Ferguson's 1950 *Ancient America and the Book of Mormon* made Ixtlilxochitl a popular support for the Book of Mormon. For instance, they translate and quote Ixtlilxochitl's chronicle as stating:

> And [the Tulteca history tells] how afterwards men, multiplying made a very tall and strong Zacualli, which means the very high tower, in order to shelter themselves in it when the second world should be destroyed.
>
> When things were at their best, their languages were changed and, not understanding each other, they went to different parts of the world; and the Tultecas, who were as many as seven companions and their wives, who understood their language among themselves, came to these parts, having first crossed large lands and seas, living in caves and undergoing great hardships, until they came to this land, which they found good and fertile for their habitation.
>
> It is the common and general opinion of all the natives of all this Chichimeca land, which is now called New Spain, besides appearing in the demonstration of their pictures, that their ancestors came from Occidental parts, and all of them are now called Tultecas, Aculhuas, Mexicanos; and other nations that are in this land say that they are of the lineage of the Chichimecas, and are proud of it; and the reason is, according as it appears in their histories, that the first king they had was called Chichimecatl, who was the one who brought them to this New World where they settled, who, as can be inferred, came from the great Tartary, and they were of those of the division of Babylon, as it is declared more at length in the history that is written.
>
> And they say that they traveled for 104 years through different parts of the world until they arrived at Huehue Tlapallan their country, which happened in Ce Tecpatl [One Flint,

a year in the Mesoamerican calendar], for it had been 520 years since the Deluge had taken place, which are five ages.[8]

On its face, this passage obviously correlates to the Jaredite account. Both contain a tall tower, a flood ("the Deluge"), and a transoceanic migration, three details that encourage Hunter and Ferguson to accept it as a folk memory of the Jaredite migration story. However, they are mistaken. Ixtlilxochitl was a surviving descendant of the deposed Aztec kings and had access to an important archive of Aztec documents, but he had been born after the conquest and educated by the Spanish fathers. H. B. Nicholson characterizes Ixtlilxochitl as a "very controversial mestizo [mixed Spanish and Indian] author, perhaps the number-one problem child of Central Mexican ethnohistory. . . . The late date at which he wrote makes him necessarily largely a secondary source. The quality of his primary sources, few of which are known, seems to have been very uneven, apart from the question of how well he and his aged informants could understand them."[9]

Ixtlilxochitl's description of events has obvious parallels to authentic native creation traditions. The deluge is a reference to the Water Sun, which was destroyed by a flood. The travels of the Chichimecs recount the entrance of Aztec ancestors (considered to have been primitive desert dwellers) into Mesoamerica, perhaps from A.D. 1000–1200.[10] The very obvious biblical references have no counterpoints in any other native history or account of the Legend of the Suns, the creation mythology from which the Water Sun image was extracted. Those elements are uniquely found in Ixtlilxochitl and are clearly his addition to the material based on his familiarity with both the Bible and the Spanish interest in it.

Ixtlilxochitl begins with a word, *zacualli*, which he indicates means "high tower."[11] The *Codex Ríos*, in a much more authentic rendition of the myth, specifically describes a few inhabitants in a hollowed-out tree, called an *ahuéhuetl*.[12] The incident with the hollowed-out tree is corroborated in the account from the source commonly called the *Leyenda de los Soles*, "Legend of the Suns" (so-called because the untitled text begins with this myth).[13] No source other than Ixtlilxochitl has any mention of a tower, by any name. The hollowed-out tree can be reconstructed to the pre-contact mythology. The tower cannot.[14]

I see Ixtlilxochitl being used as a source as an immensely helpful model in solving the dilemma of connecting the Jaredite story to that of the Tower of Babel. He

---

[8] Milton R. Hunter and Thomas Stuart Ferguson, *Ancient America and the Book of Mormon*, 24–25.
[9] Henry B. Nicholson, *Topiltzin Quetzalcoatl: The Once and Future Lord of the Toltecs*, 113.
[10] Coe, *Mexico*, 132–34.
[11] "Zacualli" is rendered "tzacualli" in more standard orthography. It is a Nahuatl word used to describe the ceremonial temple, as well as hills upon which the temples where probably modeled. My thanks to Aedo Fernando for pointing out this spelling and meaning.
[12] "Codex Ríos," 3:18 [5r in the manuscript]. The meaning something like "old water tree."
[13] The "Legend of the Suns," is found in John Bierhorst, trans., *History and Mythology of the Aztecs: The Codex Chimalpopoca*, 143.
[14] Brant A. Gardner, "Reconstructing the Ethnohistory of Myth," 24.

constructed his history from two sources: native pre-conquest texts and the biblical stories learned from the Spanish Fathers. In telling the native history, he saw parallels between pieces of the native account and Bible stories. Either because of his own belief in the Bible (he was a Christian) or his awareness that a Christian-like narrative would be pleasing to the politically dominant Spanish, he gave the final form of his native history as much from the Bible as from the native histories to which he may have had access. Ixtlilxochitl was not alone in the process of reshaping texts, and most Mesoamerican native documents from the post-conquest period show similar influences.[15] It may be the process we are seeing at work in the tower story.

Mosiah$_2$, Moroni, and Joseph Smith all knew the biblical story. If any one of them made the same kind of translation/historical conflation as Ixtlilxochitl (or Durán's informant), then the tower story could have been read into the Jaredite story, rather than being original to it. I suggest that, if such a reading-in occurred, it was during Mosiah$_2$'s translation, as Mormon mentions the tower as part of Mosiah's translation (Mosiah 28:17). Thus, the tower appears in the narrative before Moroni's retelling of it.

Finding Large and Mighty Men

The brother of Jared is described as "a large and mighty man" (Ether 21:34). Hunter and Ferguson expand this detail about one person to suggest that the Jaredites were "large and mighty men," and thus connects them to Ixtlilxochitl's description of the "giants" who remained after the destruction of the world age known as the Water Sun.[16] They read Ixtlilxochitl's *quinametzin* "giants" as a Mayan word (it is clearly Nahuatl) and therefore provide it with a completely fanciful Mayan etymology.[17] Seeing the "large and mighty man" as a physical giant continued a tradition that began with the adoption of Josiah Priest's arguments by early Saints. Josiah Priest, in his 1833 *American Antiquities*, wrote: "There are those who imagine that the first inhabitants of the globe, or the antediluvians, were much larger than our race at the present time."[18] The *Evening and the Morning Star* reported: "As they were a very large race of men, whenever we hear that uncommon large bones have been dug up from the earth, we may conclude, That was the skeleton of a Jaredite."[19]

When Ixtlilxochitl spoke of giants, he was referring to part of the Mesoamerican creation mythology known as the "Legend of the Suns." In that story of multiple creations and destructions, some remnant from the earlier "Sun" survives into the next.[20] The connection between the Mesoamerican giant tradition and the Jaredites

---

[15] Brant A. Gardner, "Crucible of Distortion."
[16] Hunter and Ferguson, *Ancient America and the Book of Mormon*, 46.
[17] Ibid., 44. Both Alonso de Molina and Rémi Simeon give "giants" as a translation for "quinametzin." The *–tzin* ending is a honorific ending in Nahuatl. The translation given for the "Maya" elements would be correct, if these were only those elements and if the word were not Nahuatl.
[18] Josiah Priest, *American Antiquities and Discoveries in the West*, 284.
[19] "The Book of Ether," *The Evening and the Morning Star* 1 no. 3 (August 1832), 22. My thanks to Mark Alan Wright for pointing out this information.
[20] Gardner, "Reconstructing the Ethnohistory of Myth," 26.

is an imaginative reading of both the Mesoamerican mythology and the Book of Mormon. The "large and mighty" description in the Book of Mormon, however, does not appear to describe superhuman size. In addition to the brother of Jared, we see the phrase again in Ether 15:26: "And they were large and mighty men as to the strength of men." These phrases should be seen as a way of setting apart the ancients as more spectacular than the current generation. This process is seen in the later veneration of the Toltecs (A.D. 900–1100) by the Aztecs (A.D. 1300–Conquest). For the Aztecs, the Toltec culture was the epitome of perfection. The people themselves were described as more-than-human. A text from Sahagún reads: "They [the Toltecs] were tall, of more robust body than those who are today living, and because they were so tall they often ran or walked with long strides, for which they were called *tlanquacemilhuique*, which means, those who run an entire day without tiring."[21]

Geoffrey G. McCafferty further expounds on Ixtlilxochitl's giants:

> According to Ixtlilxochitl, the Cholula region was inhabited by "giants" (Nahuatl = *quinametitzúcuil*) following the Second Age, or Tlalchitonátiuc. These were the beings who built the pyramids of Teotihuacan and Cholula. In archaeological terminology, they correspond to the Classic period. When the Olmeca-Xicallanca arrived in the Cholula area, the giants who had survived the cataclysmic end of the Second Age enslaved them. Yet the Quinametinime giants were eventually defeated and "consumed," at which point the Olmeca-Xicallanca became the rulers of Cholula. The same historical tradition was shared by the Tlaxcaltecas, who kept a "femur the height of an ordinary man" (probably from a prehistoric mammoth) as evidence of giants, at least according to the testimony of Díaz del Castillo.[22]

Based on comparisons with other cultures, it is quite likely that the Mesoamerican mythologies were based on interpretations of fossils. Adrienne Mayor comments on a North American Paiute legend that includes giants similar to those recorded by Ixtlilxochitl: "The [fossilized] large limb bones of these mammals resemble giant counterparts of human."[23] The combination of fossil bones and the veneration of the ancestral past is the best explanation for the descriptions of the ancients as giants. There is no reason to expect that the Jaredites were physically larger than the average.

Approximating a Jaredite Chronology

Ether does not include any textual dating. Unlike the Nephite record that has a time anchor at the first year of the reign of Zedekiah and another (subject to debate) at the birth of Christ, the Jaredite record has no time anchor at either the beginning or the end. The only indication of time that we have is when specific numbers of years are mentioned for the reign of a specific king. Unfortunately, the record that we have is not consistent in providing the length of the reign, so we are left with a chronology that can only be built on conjecture.

---

[21] Bernardino de Sahagún, *Historia general de las cosas de Nueva España*, 3:188. My translation.
[22] Geoffrey G. McCafferty, "Ethnic Conflict in Postclassic Cholula, Mexico," 222.
[23] Adrienne Mayor, *Fossil Legends of the First Americans*, 342.

Including Ether himself, thirty names appear in the Jaredite genealogy (Ether 1:17–32), all presented as generational relationships. This genealogy offers the possibility of constructing a Jaredite timeline, but does not provide a beginning or ending point. Nevertheless, it gives us the possibility of establishing a chronology because we can establish a plausible time line for the thirty names. We can then locate that sequence when the Jaredite story intersects with the Nephite story. Unfortunately, even that intersection must be built on conjecture. It requires locating a time when the last Jaredite king, Coriantumr, stayed with the people of Zarahemla prior to the arrival of the Nephites in Zarahemla. There is no firm date for that encounter. Everything we might use to establish a Jaredite chronology is based on uncertain foundations.

Sorenson begins his Jaredite chronology with the probable dating for the Tower of Babel, which Sorenson accepts as around 2800–2500 B.C.[24] Assuming an average generous age from between sixty and seventy years per generation would stretch the timeline so that its beginnings come relatively close to that target date. However, that approach creates a timeline based on lifetimes rather than reigns. What we have is a king list, and there is some overlap between the life of a king and his inheriting son. Although the textual evidence suggests that the last-born son inherited[25] that still requires some overlap as it would be highly unlikely that every new king was born precisely in the year his father died.

The method I use for creating a timeline of Jaredite kings differs from Sorenson He indicated that "first it was necessary to settle upon beginning and ending dates for the Jaredite civilization in terms of chronological frameworks outside the Book of Mormon. Next an attempt was made to distribute the events in the Book of Ether over the whole time period marked out in a way which did no violence to the facts in the book."[26]

It appears from Sorenson's selection of beginning dates and ending dates that he is attempting to match his Ether chronology with Mesoamerican archaeology. He hypothesizes a date of 3100–2920 B.C. for the Tower of Babel and dates the Olmec "beginning date" at 3113 B.C. His later chronology places the Jaredites a little later at 3000 B.C.:

> Historical texts and archaeological research on Mesopotamia, [the Jaredite] homeland, tell us that big pyramid-shaped temple platforms called ziggurats were being erected well before 3000 B.C. Nothing but one of them qualifies as "the great tower" referred to in Ether 1:33. If the departure of the Jaredite party from their original home had been many centuries later than 3000 B.C. or earlier than about 3300 B.C., their account about "the

---

[24] Sorenson, *Mormon's Codex*, 27. The 2800 B.C. date is in Sorenson's text, and he comments on the possible change to 2500 B.C. on p. 27, note 2 of his *Codex*. This dating shortens the timeline that Sorenson had argued in, *An Ancient American Setting for the Book of Mormon*, 116, where he had suggested 3000 B.C.
[25] Grego, "Book of Mormon: Succession of Jaredite Kings in the Book of Ether."
[26] John L. Sorenson, "The Years of the Jaredites," 18.

great tower" would sound odd in terms of Near Eastern history. (Incidentally, the zero date from which the Mesoamerican calendars were calculated was 3113 B.C., which might or might not be a coincidence.) [27]

Sorenson also selected his ending date of 550–400 B.C. to coincide with the ending of the Olmec civilization (which he gives as 550 B.C.) rather than with the book of Ether.[28] I argue that these choices reflect an agenda of a too-direct connection between Jaredites and Olmec. It is one thing to say that the Jaredites participated in the Olmec world. I agree. But it is quite another to say that the Jaredites *were* the Olmec. There is no evidence for that assertion.

In contrast to selecting dates and working a chronology to fit it, I begin with the list of kings. While there is insufficient information to calculate a precise chronology from that list, I have used information on the later Maya kings to calculate an average thirty year reign as a generic model of the time from one king to the next.[29] There were Jaredite kings' reigns that exceeded thirty years.[30] On the other hand, Ahah "did reign over the people all his days. . . and few were his days" (Ether 11:2).

Beginning with the first generation after Jared and applying a thirty-year average reign produces a timeline of about 870 years. Although ultimogeniture might extend the average somewhat, the complications created by the political intrigues suggest caution. Therefore, I have continued to use the thirty-year average as the basis for a Jaredite chronology.

The next problem is deciding when to begin applying this average reign time to the Jaredite record. Jaredite chronology connects, though tenuously, to Nephite history. Ether and Coriantumr were contemporaries (Ether 14–15), and Coriantumr spent nine months in Zarahemla before the Nephites' arrival (Omni 1:21). I suggest that Mosiah$_1$ reached Zarahemla no later than 155 B.C.[31] The Mulekites arrived in the New World somewhere around the same time as the Lehites—say 580 B.C. Thus, the starting point for the chronology could range from 580 B.C. to 155 B.C.

Sorenson places Coriantumr's stay with the Mulekites early in their history to coincide with archaeological evidence for the collapse of the Olmec empire:

---

[27] Sorenson, *An Ancient American Setting*, 116.
[28] Ibid., 119.
[29] Simon Martin and Nikolai Grube, *Chronicle of the Maya Kings and Queens*, 26, 32, 38, 40, 44, 48, 52, 56, 60, 64, 70, 74, 78, 80, 86, 88, 94, 96, 102, 105, 108, 112, and others. They date the reigns of various Maya kings, and I have compared them to create the average I use here. It is hardly a scientific average but rather an attempt to find a usable number. I stress that it is used *generously*, rather than rigorously, to create a plausible timeline of Jaredite kings.
[30] Shule may have lived to be seventy or eighty, as Ether 7:22 records that Shule fought Nimrod, who was Shule's brother's great-grandson. Com reigns for forty-nine years (Ether 9:25), and Riplakish reigned for forty-two years (Ether 10:8).
[31] Gardner, *Second Witness*, 3:196–98 discusses the evidence for sorting out the Nephite/Zeniffite chronology. Mosiah$_2$ would have been born in 155 B.C. His father, Benjamin, likely accompanied Mosiah$_1$ to Zarahemla, but it is plausible that Mosiah$_2$ was born after their arrival.

The final destruction of the Jared ruling line could have been as early as 580 B.C. or as late as 400 B.C. The Book of Mormon does not tell us enough to allow a more precise determination, although I believe a date toward the earlier end of that span is preferable. The archaeological record is now quite settled on about 550 B.C. for the end of the First Tradition [the Olmec civilization].

Taking together the geographical setting, the cultural patterns, the agreement in dates, and many specific facts we cannot go into at this point, identifying the culture in which the Jaredites were involved with the First or Olmec Tradition is very reasonable.[32]

Sorenson's reasoning is sound—based on his apparent assumption that the Jaredites *were* the Olmec. However, I find that an assumption of complete identity cannot fit the available cultural data. There were Olmec prior to Jaredites, and the collapse of the general Olmec culture need not have required the collapse of Jaredite civilization. Indeed, there were descendants of the Olmec in the area, now distinguished as epi-Olmec. I place the end of the Jaredites in the Late Formative period, 300 B.C.–A.D. 1, specifically around 200 B.C., which is after the end of the Olmec domination. I see the devastating wars of annihilation in Ether as part the aftermath of the Olmec political collapse.

Support for dating the collapse of the Jaredite polity later than Sorenson's suggestion of around 550 B.C. is Coriantumr's stay in Zarahemla. Coriantumr was the last Jaredite king and stayed with the people of Zarahemla for "nine moons" (Omni 1:24). I hypothesize that the people of Zarahemla had cultural and linguistic ties with the Jaredite homeland and it was those ties, however far in the past, that were the reason that the refugee Coriantumr would set off toward their city and also why they would give him sanctuary.

The early history of the people of Mulek suggests that they had participated in Olmec culture to the point of adopting that language and religion and losing their own (Omni 1:17). When a group split off and moved up the Sidon River Valley to Zarahemla, they might reasonably retain some connection, if only sporadic trade connection, with that ancestral homeland. From the fact that both the city and the ruler at Mosiah$_1$'s arrival were named Zarahemla, I deduce that they had only recently relocated and that the city was named for the founding leader. Thus, Coriantumr may have lived with them perhaps less than fifty years before Mosiah$_1$'s arrival.

Therefore, I use 200 B.C. as an approximate death date for Coriantumr and his contemporary Ether and therefore as a plausible anchor for the generational chronology.[33] This anchor places the beginnings of the Jaredites about 1,100 B.C.—in short, after Abraham and the patriarchs, and after Joseph in Egypt—after Moses and

---

[32] Sorenson, *An Ancient American Setting*, 119.
[33] Palmer, *In Search of Cumorah*, 128, follows Sorenson's basic outline. He uses 600 B.C. as Ether's time, moving backwards in seventy-year "generations" to reach a departure date of 2700 B.C. from the Tower of Babel. Palmer apparently does not account for the overlap in lifetimes of those on the genealogical list.

the plausible timing of the Israelites' return from Egypt.[34] The timing and their separate history suggest that the Jaredites were not properly of Israel. They were obviously believers in Yahweh, although they may have known him by a different name.[35]

---

[34] Michael D. Coogan, "Exodus, The," 210, "Most scholars date [the Exodus] to the mid-thirteenth century B.C.E., during the reign of Rameses II, because of a convergence of probabilities, including the identification of the store cities of Pithom and Rameses (Ex. 1:11) with recently excavated sites in the Egyptian delta and the larger context of the history of Egypt and of the Levant."

[35] Mark S. Smith, *The Origins of Biblical Monotheism: Israel's Polytheistic Background and the Ugaritic Texts*, 144:

> El as a separate god disappeared, perhaps at different rates in different regions. This process may appear to involve Yahweh incorporating El's characteristics, for Yahweh is the eventual historical "winner." Yet in the pre-monarchic period, the process may be envisioned—at least initially—in the opposite terms: Israelite highland cult sites of El assimilated the outsider, southerner Yahweh. In comparison, Yahweh in ancient Israel and Baal at Ugarit were both outsider warrior gods who stood second in rank to El, but they eventually overshadowed him in power. Yet Yahweh's development went further. He was identified with El: here the son replaced and became the father whose name only serves as a title for the son.
>
> The word El became a generic word for "god," and is used as both the generic representation of "a god" or as a personal name. Perhaps the Jaredites, coming from an earlier time, preceded the Israelite understanding of their national god as Yahweh, and referred to God as El.

19

Jaredites in the New World

The only peoples named in the Book of Mormon originate in the Old World. Nephites trace their own history to the Old World and assume a similar history for the people they call Lamanites. The people of Mulek came from the Old World. The last people who appear in the Book of Mormon also came from the Old World but reached the New World before the other Book of Mormon peoples.

The Jaredite Old World homeland is not specified other than to associate it with a tower and the valley named Nimrod (Ether 1:33; 2:1). That association appears to place their native land somewhere among the Mesopotamian cultures of the Ancient Near East. Yahweh commanded Jared that: "thou shalt go at the head of them down into the valley which is northward. And there will I meet thee, and I will go before thee into a land which is choice above all the lands of the earth" (Ether 1:42). To begin in a valley famous for its towers would appear to place the Jaredites in Mesopotamia. That would have given them the option of following along the Tigris or the Euphrates to get to the sea. Traveling along the river would not only guide their journey but assure a dependable supply of water.

The Euphrates would provide the most direct route to place them in a position to use barges to cross waters. There are only two choices: the Black Sea or the Mediterranean.[1] Nibley hypothesized that they traveled east and departed from Asia.[2] This route is an argument for the Black Sea. I see a more western path of travel and therefore the Mediterranean. The text tells us:

---

[1] Joseph L. Allen, *Exploring the Lands of the Book of Mormon*, 259, notes the same possibilities, although he interprets the basic facts differently, arguing for a Pacific crossing rather than the Atlantic crossing I favor.

[2] Hugh Nibley, *Lehi in the Desert and the World of the Jaredites*, 176. Nibley suggests that the prevailing westerly winds argue strongly for a North Pacific crossing. They must therefore cross the steppes to leave from the east coast of Asia. Therefore, he entitles his third section "Jared on the Steppes" (179). Nibley's suggestion requires that the Jaredites spend a lot of time traveling on land, whereas the text (as I read it) describes travel by land only to the point where they build a barge and travel to the location where they remain for four years, after which they depart to the New World, again traveling by water.

And it came to pass that they did travel in the wilderness, and did build barges, in which they did cross many waters, being directed continually by the hand of the Lord.

And the Lord would not suffer that they should stop beyond the sea in the wilderness, but he would that they should come forth even unto the land of promise, which was choice above all other lands, which the Lord God had preserved for a righteous people. (Ether 2:6–7)

If we paused at this point, these verses might suggest that they immediately embarked for the New World. They did not. This embarkation was the first of two water journeys. After an unspecified time, they stopped when: "the Lord did bring Jared and his brethren forth even to that great sea which divideth the lands. And as they came to the sea they pitched their tents; and they called the name of the place Moriancumer; and they dwelt in tents, and dwelt in tents upon the seashore for the space of four years" (Ether 2:13). Thus they journeyed in the barges until they came to a place where "that great sea. . . divideth the lands," and there stopped for four years.

In arguing for an Asian departure point, Nibley declares that "we must not forget that a mountain of "exceeding height" stood near the point of Jaredite embarkation (Ether 3:1), and that there is no such mountain on the Atlantic seaboard of Europe, although there are many such mountains on the Asiatic shore."[3] Nevertheless, the exit point from the Mediterranean to the Atlantic is through the Straits of Gibraltar. While perhaps not much of a mountain in comparison to other mountains, in comparison to the surrounding landscape, Gibraltar is impressive. Gibraltar can accurately be called a mountain of "exceeding height"—not in inherent feet but in its unquestionable domination of the landscape.

After about four years without any movement toward their final destination, Yahweh chastised the brother of Jared. The brother Jared stood before Yahweh "for the space of three hours. . . [and Yahweh] chastened him because he remembered not to call upon the name of the Lord" (Ether 2:14). It seems unlikely that the brother of Jared had not prayed at all for four years. What is more likely is that, during those four years, they had failed to make any preparation for their final journey to the New World. They had not called upon Yahweh for instruction in how to proceed to the destination that had been promised them. Therefore, right after forgiving the brother of Jared, Yahweh instructed: "Go to work and build, after the manner of barges which ye have hitherto built" (Ether 2:16).

Crossing the Atlantic would suggest that the Jaredites landed on an eastern coast of the Western continents.[4] Based on the interactions in the Book of Mormon and the Mesoamerican geography, the Jaredites would have landed somewhere along the

---

[3] Ibid., 176.

[4] Sorenson, *An Ancient American Setting for the Book of Mormon*, Map 5, p. 37, shows the Jaredites landing on the Mexican west coast, northwest of the Isthmus of Tehuantepec. That correlation would support Nibley's suggestion of travel across the Pacific. In Sorenson, *Mormon's Codex: An Ancient American Book*, 27, he now suggests that they landed on the east coast, perhaps in Veracruz in the Gulf of Mexico. I would agree with this route, which means an Atlantic crossing. There is no indication that Sorenson was aware of my argument when he made this change. It represents his own rethinking of that part of the Jaredite story.

Gulf Coast of Mexico. When they arrived, they would have found the land already inhabited by the most dominant culture north of Panama; the Olmec.[5] Their homeland was in southern Veracruz and western Tabasco in Mexico.[6]

Olmec is a modern collective name given to a group of peoples who shared a set of cultural traits. The Olmec culture was the dominant politico-cultural influence around 1500 B.C. to 600 B.C., with a related late tradition called the epi-Olmec lasting through 200 B.C. The Olmec themselves built atop settlements and incorporated some cultural trends that preceded them.[7] Genetically, they can be associated with the Asian migrations that peopled the New World across the ancient land bridge between [Siberia and Alaska].[8] As with the later Nephites, Jaredites entered a land of strong cultures and powerful peoples.

The influence of Olmec culture on all Mesoamerican civilizations to follow is hard to overstate. David A. Freidel notes:

> The art of the Olmec civilization—now more broadly termed the "Middle Formative Ceremonial Complex of Mesoamerica"—continues to astound and inspire us after fifty years of intense study. We still can't quite believe that this convergence of brilliant conception and superb craft occurred at the very beginning of Mesoamerica's civilization. That fact is no longer in serious dispute, however, and we are left to wonder what there might be about this part of the Americas' geographical place and natural environment that encouraged the sudden flowering of this great artistic tradition. We also have to ponder the enduring beliefs of the people who wandered into and eventually settled Mesoamerica over millennia. We need to anticipate the spectacular consensus their descendants forged across languages and distances in a vision of their shared world as an ordered and comprehensible totality. Despite the eons of slowly accumulated skills and experience behind them, civilized worlds' mentalities are ultimately invented. They are conjured out of immediate political necessities, combined with special cultural opportunities, in the work of sages.
>
> Once invented, however, worldly visions are locally reinvented repeatedly over time, reflecting the particular histories of regional societies within the broader civilization. The result is a mosaic of cultures that, while different and distinct, shares elements of a common

---

[5] Sometimes Ether 2:5 is cited to suggest that the Jaredites were the first in their New World. The verse says: "And it came to pass that the Lord commanded them that they should go forth into the wilderness, yea, into that quarter where there never had man been." This does sound like they went to a land where there were no other populations. However, in context, it describes their journey in the wilderness prior to the first time they built barges. It occurred over four years before they ever departed for the New World.

[6] Christopher A. Pool, "Current Research on the Gulf Coast of Mexico," 192–93 (intervening chart): "Use of the term 'Olmec' can be particularly confusing, because this Aztec term for the Late Postclassic inhabitants of the south Gulf Coast has been adopted both for the archaeological culture that occupied the same region in the Early and Middle Formative periods and for a pan-Mesoamerican art style of the same time frame."

[7] Richard A. Diehl and Michael D. Coe, "Olmec Archaeology," 11.

[8] Ibid.

intellectual heritage. The Olmec crystallization of ideas influenced later Mesoamerican religions and cosmologies in ways we are still learning to appreciate.[9]

The Olmec, as a cultural collective, laid the foundations for many traits we see later in Maya and other Mesoamerican societies: temple building, bloodletting, warfare, and shamanic-based religion.[10] Moroni provides less cultural information for the Jaredites than Mormon's longer narrative provides for the Nephites. Nevertheless, just as Mesoamerican culture appears in Mormon's narrative, so Olmec influence can be glimpsed through Moroni's editing of the Jaredite narrative. Understanding some of what we know of the Olmec will make it easier to see the Olmec traits through the Jaredite descriptions.

The Olmec and Jaredite homelands cover a wide area north of the proposed Nephite land of Zarahemla. In both physical proximity and time period, these lands and peoples fit Mormon's descriptions of the "lands northward" and much of the influence that entered Nephite culture through the Jaredite-influenced Mulekites.

The earliest settlements with indications of a more complex culture have been found along the Río Barí (now completely silted in), near La Venta, Tabasco.[11] Archaeologist Richard A. Diehl describes what is known of their physical appearance:

> Virtually no Olmec skeletons survive in the acid tropical soils of Olman, the portion of southern Veracruz and Tabasco occupied by the Olmecs, thus their physical appearance remains a mystery. However, Olmec artists occasionally created realistic depictions of their fellow citizens in art. These renderings depict people similar in appearance to modern indigenous inhabitants of Olman, with short, squat muscular bodies, short wide noses, epicanthic folds that give the eyes an oriental cast, fleshy mouths with thick, at times down-turned, lips, short necks, and straight black hair. We cannot identify their language or languages with certainty.[12]

Archaeologists Richard Diehl and Michael D. Coe describe the Olmec rise from this beginning:

> Similar villages occurred along all the river valleys of the Olmec heartland in the following centuries. Although they appear to lack the monumental art and architecture, social hierarchies, and complex institutions that characterize Olmec culture, these villages clearly provided the local population base for later Olmec expansion. By the end of the Pre-Olmec period, San Lorenzo and La Venta were growing faster than other communities and

---

[9] David A. Freidel, "Preparing the Way," in *The Olmec World: Ritual and Rulership*, 3.

[10] While this view of the Olmec as a seedbed for later cultures has been a dominant position, there is an alternate reading of the Olmec influence in more recent years. Christopher A. Pool, "Current Research on the Gulf Coast of Mexico," 196–97, notes an alternate hypothesis that the Olmec were a "sister culture" rather than the "mother culture." That is, that they were part of a general regional development rather than the sole originators of it.

[11] Diehl and Coe, "Olmec Archaeology," 12.

[12] Richard A. Diehl, *The Olmecs: America's First Civilization*, 13.

fragments of basalt monuments in some of the deepest levels at San Lorenzo suggest that the Olmec sculptural tradition existed prior to 1200 B.C.[13]

By the close of the Olmec period in 600 B.C., their cultural system had become influential over a wide area of Mesoamerica, from modern Guatemala to Central Mexico and supplied cultural and religious ideas to all later Mesoamerican civilizations. Nevertheless, the culture we consider Olmec never thought of itself as a single ethnic population.[14]

Jaredites, Olmecs, and Warfare

The book of Ether documents Jaredite wars, but there have been no explicit depictions of such warfare among the Olmec.[15] Recently, an explanation has emerged. The Olmec used implicit symbol systems to display information related to warfare, similar to what has been discovered in much later Central Mexico's Teotihuacan. F. Kent Reilly III and James F. Garber note:

> Iconographic investigations suggest that, rather than the explicit warfare representations of the Classic Maya, Olmec-style images of conquest are expressed within an overarching iconographic complex. This complex is more closely akin to those seen at Teotihuacan. In other words, Olmec-style warfare depictions are implicit and contained within a larger motif set. Within this motif set, a close evaluation of elements, symbols, motifs and themes strongly suggests that the ideology of warfare, as expressed in Olmec-style art (1200–400 B.C.), was couched in a supernatural framework based on images depicting feline domination over humans as well as the ideological concept of jaguarian transformation itself.[16]

Ross Hassig notes that, while there are no fortifications or depictions of warfare in artistic representations: "rulers often bear weapons and are shown with naked, bound prisoners, testifying to the emergence of an unmistakable elite exercising military power by 1150 B.C."[17] He also notes that the most important evidence for Olmec militarism is the appearance of specialized military weapons.[18] Specialized

---

[13] Diehl and Coe, "Olmec Archaeology," 12.

[14] Ibid., 11.

[15] Morgan Deane, "Bleached Bones Covered the Field. An Analysis of the Jaredite Civil War using the 'War of the Eight Princes.'" January 1, 2010. Unpublished paper in my possession. Deane compares the descriptions of the Jaredite wars with the conditions and tactics noted for the "War of the Eight Princes" which took place in early Medieval China. Deane does not suggest any direct connection between the accounts, but only that they show similarities significant enough to suggest that the Jaredite wars may have developed from parallel causes, circumstances, and military tactics.

[16] F. Kent Reilly III and James F. Garber, "The Symbolic Representation of Warfare in Formative Period Mesoamerica," 128.

[17] Hassig, *War and Society in Ancient Mesoamerica*, 15.

[18] Ibid. He continues: "One major shift from earlier times was the Olmec emphasis on shock weapons, hand-to-hand arms such as spears that were meant for thrusting and slashing rather than throwing, as well as crushers such as clubs and maces. Shock weapons won the battles in

weapons also required specialized training in their use, testifying to some level of professionalism in their military.[19]

Jaredites, Olmecs, and Texts

Notable among the cultural achievements is the use of a writing system. Archaeologists Mary Pohl, Christopher von Nagy, Allison Perrett, and Kevin Pope report:

> One of the most significant findings at San Andrés was the confirmation that the Middle Formative Olmec were in the process of developing a system of writing. Early Franco phase feasting refuse yielded two classes of objects with early writing—small, engraved greenstone plaques about the size of a fingernail and a fist-sized roller stamp. . . . The artifacts are securely dated by both radiocarbon and the site ceramic chronology to ca. 650 B.C. The fact that the artifacts with glyphs were found in the context of feasting refuse suggest that writing among the Olmec was sacred and was closely tied to ritual activities.[20]

The presence of a writing system this early compares with, but does not independently corroborate the Jaredite records. Literate Jaredites are temporally and geographically plausible.

The transition from Olmec to Maya dominance in the general region was not abrupt in either time or space. It is on the linguistic frontier between these powerful cultures that this new information on hieroglyphs sheds potential insight on the Book of Mormon.

The best attested Mesoamerican script comes from the Classic (and later) Maya (A.D. 250–900). Four extant Maya codices contain texts using Maya hieroglyphs.[21] Glyphic texts are also found on stone monuments and on painted pots. While the Maya writing system is the best understood, it was not the only one in existence. Archaeologist Susan Toby Evans describes another important script:

> Evidence from the Terminal Formative Isthmus [A.D. 1–300, Isthmus of Tehuantepec] includes the oldest extensive texts of Mesoamerican glyph writing, a script referred to as "isthmian" (also "Epi-Olmec" or "Intermediate" or "Tuxtla" after the Tuxtla statuette, an important example of the script's use). The script is thought to be a written version of pre-proto-Zoquean, an ancestral form of the modern Isthmian languages, Mixe and Zoque.

---

pre-gunpowder wars, in large part because they were deadlier than projectiles that were relatively easy to dodge or deflect if thrown from a distance."

[19] Ibid., 17.

[20] Mary Pohl, Christopher von Nagy, Allison Perrett, and Kevin Pope, "Olmec Civilization at San Andrés, Tabasco, Mexico," 8.

[21] The Dresden Codex (located in the state library in Dresden, Germany), the Paris Codex (located in the Bibliothèque National, Paris), the Madrid Codex (also known as the Tro-Cortesianus Codex, located in Museo de América, Madrid), and the Grolier Codex (located in a museum in Mexico City).

Unlike Maya hieroglyphs, the Isthmian inscriptions have not yet been substantially deciphered, and in fact, the decipherments attempted to this point have used just 10 inscribed sources, the longest among them being that on the La Mojarra Stela.[22]

Linguists John Justeson and Terrence Kaufman have offered a translation of the La Mojarra Stela,[23] which has been challenged by Steven Houston and Michael D. Coe.[24] Although the translation is not confirmed, the probability that this script is a direct antecedent to the Maya system is suggested by the similarities in some of the glyphs and the phonetic value associated with them.

One particular sign is written similarly in both Epi-Olmec and Maya and reads phonetically as *wu* in both, meaning "great, large" in both systems. The correlation between that syllable and the graphic representation is not correct for Maya, but it is in Zoque. Apparently borrowing did occur and, at least in this example, was from Epi-Olmec to Maya.[25]

Jaredites, Olmecs, and Geography

The Book of Mormon location of interest here is Zarahemla. Prior to the Nephites' arrival, the Zarahemlaites had contact with at least one important Jaredite, Coriantumr (Omni 1:21), and some of the names recorded for Zarahemla residents suggest contact with Jaredite culture.[26] Thus, Zarahemla appears to have been influenced by the Jaredites, even though the city was located south of the Jaredite homeland.

The proposed location in Sorenson's geographic correlation places Zarahemla on the border between the Maya and Olmec. Zarahemla would lie along the old course of the Grijalva River (where there is now a lake resulting from damming the Grijalva) in Chiapas, Mexico. The Maya were in the Guatemalan highlands and in the central lowlands (the Petén region of Guatemala).

The final important correlation between the known history of the Gulf Coast peoples and the Book of Mormon peoples is the plausible linguistic connection between Jaredites, the people of Mulek (Zarahemlaites), and the Nephites. The earliest language of the Olmec people appears to have been one that later split into two daughter languages. The parent is simply known as a hyphenation of the two daughter languages, Mixe-Zoque.[27] As is typical in the division into different

---

[22] Susan Toby Evans, *Ancient Mexico and Central America: Archaeology and Culture*, 239–40.

[23] John Justeson Terrence Kaufman, "Un desciframiento de la escritura jeroglífica epi-olmeca: métodos y resultados," 15, 20.

[24] "Mesoamerican Relic Provides New Clues to Mysterious Ancient Writing System."

[25] John Justeson, "Lecture to the Northeastern Mesoamerican Epigraphy Group, Fall 1996."

[26] Sorenson, *An Ancient American Setting for the Book of Mormon*, 214: "The ancestors of chief Zarahemla surely had passed on their own traditional tales about the north, where their founders had landed before coming to Zarahemla (Alma 22:30–32). They had also encountered Coriantumr, the last surviving Jaredite ruler, north of the narrow neck (Omni 1:21)."

[27] The original argument for the connection is found in Lyle Campbell and Terrence Kaufman, "A Linguistic Look at the Olmecs," 80–88.

languages, the separation was physical before it became linguistic, with the Zoque portion being those people who remained, or moved in to, areas that would later be Nephite-controlled.

This suggests that the people of Mulek entered an area that the Book of Mormon peoples considered to have been Jaredite, and that they would have learned that language and culture. From their later actions, they would have spoken Zoquean. Zoque was spoken in the Grijalva Valley and particularly at Chiapa de Corzo.[28]

The Escalera phase, an identified development period at Chiapa de Corzo, begins approximately 500 B.C. and "apparently witnessed the introduction of large platform structures," according to archaeologist Gareth W. Lowe.[29] An earlier population had lived at this site; however, the introduction of large platforms suggests new influences. The confluence of language and visible innovation is the basis for my conclusion of a possible migration from Olmec lands about this time.

Linguist Lyle Campbell indicates that, by 500 B.C., common Zoquean was a separate language from the Mixe-Zoque language attributed to the Olmec.[30] While it is doubtful that the Mulekites landed and immediately moved up the Grijalva, Moroni's description of Lib (Ether 10:19–21) indicates a Jaredite interest in the south. Linguistically and culturally, the time period between 400 B.C. and 200 B.C. saw a population of Zoque speakers moving south from the Gulf Coast region into the Grijalva River Valley.[31] The descendants of Mulek moved into the Sidon River Valley somewhere around 200 B.C. (See also "Merging Peoples in Zarahemla" in Chapter 8.)

---

[28] Evans, *Ancient Mexico and Central America*, 222.

[29] Gareth W. Lowe, "Brief Archaeological History of the Southwest Quadrant," 9.

[30] Lyle Campbell, "Mesoamerican Linguistics," mimeographed notes, n.d. Copy in my possession.

[31] Evans, *Ancient Mexico and Central America*, 222–24. Internal quotation marks silently removed. Text skips an inserted page on Calendrics.

20

Historicity and Futurity

"Whatever else this work may have done, it lays a foundation. Though it does not contain all the answers, it improves the quality of our questions." John L. Sorenson[1]

A little over a decade before the 1985 publication of John L. Sorenson's groundbreaking *An Ancient American Setting for the Book of Mormon*, I stood in John Sorenson's office at Brigham Young University. During our conversation, I offered my opinion that we would never know where the Book of Mormon took place. He asked if I would feel the same if he could show me not only a geography that fit, but one in which there were cities in the appropriate locations to each other that dated to the appropriate Book of Mormon times. It was an exciting possibility, but the Doubting Thomas in me looked for more than just verbal assurance. Sorenson gave me a copy of the manuscript that eventually became *An Ancient American Setting*. He had shared the manuscript in various forms with many other interested students, and like them, I read it with absorbed interest. It turned my doubt to hope, then to agreement that he had a powerfully plausible argument.

What I have learned to see since reading that manuscript led to my dedication of this book to Sorenson. We have had very few conversations since then, but nothing in this book would have been possible without the foundation he laid or the questions that could only be built upon with that foundation. Just as Sorenson noted of his work, I clearly understand that this book does not contain all the answers. Perhaps this book may also allow us to ask yet more interesting questions—questions that could not be asked without a solid foundation for the Book of Mormon in time, geography, and culture.

In 1909, B. H. Roberts declared:

> The Book of Mormon of necessity must submit to every test, to literary criticism, as well as to every other class of criticism; for our age is above all things critical, and especially critical of sacred literature, and we may not hope that the Book of Mormon will escape closest scrutiny; neither, indeed, is it desirable that it should escape. It is given to the world as a revelation from God. It is a volume of American scripture. Men have a right to test it

---

[1] John L. Sorenson, *An Ancient American Setting for the Book of Mormon*, 355.

by the keenest criticism, and to pass severest judgment upon it, and we who accept it as a revelation from God have every reason to believe that it will endure every test; and the more thoroughly it is investigated, the greater shall be its ultimate triumph.[2]

Zechariah declared that Yahweh would bring his people "through the fire, and [would] refine them as silver is refined, and [would] try them as gold is tried" (Zech. 13:9). The Book of Mormon that B. H. Roberts envisioned has gone—and is going—through a similar refining furnace. Nevertheless, not only do we "have every reason to believe that it will endure" the fires of criticism, but we "have every reason to believe" that it will become as purer silver or purer gold.

The refining fire is an apt image for the removal of many of the traditional ideas and arguments that have built around the text. Removing the dross does not damage the historicity of the text. It is part of the refining process, and an important one. It has required that we must discard some old favorite "proofs," such as the Tree of Life stone (in Chapter 4), or Quetzalcoatl as Jesus Christ (in Chapter 15). The process of trying the text as gold is tried does not create a truer Book of Mormon, but it does help create a better understanding of the people whose lives are pictured in its pages.

We can kindle our own fire of discovery when we learn to ask interesting questions of the text. As John W. Welch pointed out: "Any piece of evidence is deeply intertwined with a question. No real evidence exists until an issue is raised which that evidence tends to prove or disprove."[3] Learning to see the Book of Mormon against the conditions and concerns that formed the information environment in which it was written allows us to formulate better questions, and with answers to those questions, deepen our understanding.[4]

I have told the story of the Book of Mormon as it moved through time and space, and through peoples and politics. I haven't often interrupted the narrative to declare the ways in which the story supports historicity. Nevertheless, my selection of the stories to tell has been informed by the desire to present the complex convergences between the text, times, places, and the social and political movements that are known to have been present in those times and places. At this point, it is useful to look back on the story to highlight the evidence for historicity that may be extracted from the story.

---

[2] Brigham H. Roberts, "The Translation of the Book of Mormon," 435–36.

[3] John W. Welch, "The Power of Evidence in the Nurturing of Faith," 32.

[4] James E. Faulconer, *Scripture Study: Tools and Suggestions*, 25–35, provides samples of the types of questions that might be asked of scripture to develop a better understanding of the message of the text. My approach to *Second Witness* was inspired by Faulconer's book. I have had the opportunity to thank him in person for that impetus. He has recently expanded those questions into books that provide questions for the reader to ask of the scriptures. For the Book of Mormon, see James E. Faulconer, *The Book of Mormon Made Harder: Scripture Study Questions*.

Historicity and Futurity 403

Geo-spatial Convergences

The essential foundation of Book of Mormon historicity is a plausible geography. Only with a geographical setting may other types of convergences come to bear. An illustrative historical case comes from the question of the historicity of Homer's *Iliad*. It was considered literature unrelated to history even though the ruins at Hisarlik had been traditionally associated with it.[5] That identification was not widely accepted until:

> In 1871, Heinrich Schliemann, a man who had started life as a sickly grocer's assistant but accumulated a fortune—in the indigo trade in St. Petersburg, during the gold rush in California, and finally dealing in saltpeter and brimstone at the inception of the Crimean War—went to the Eastern Mediterranean in pursuit of Helen of Troy and the old gold of the Age of Heroes. Schliemann was ravenous for knowledge and archaeological experience. He had taught himself eighteen languages, including Greek, Latin and Hebrew, and, as an adorer of the works of Homer, he determined to find physical proof of the *Iliad* and the *Odyssey*. At the age of forty-eight he travelled to Turkey in search of Troy and started to dig—in the right place.[6]

Schliemann's overenthusiastic and amateur declarations about which layers of the site related to Homer's Troy have since been corrected, but his excavations mark the modern acceptance that a real place lay behind the Homeric stories. The Book of Mormon analogue, albeit a tenuous one, was the creation of the New World Archaeological Foundation (NWAF) in 1952. An LDS lawyer, Thomas Stuart Ferguson,[7] became interested in the Pre-classic civilizations of Mexico and Central America. The NWAF grew from conversations among Ferguson and two respected non-LDS archaeologists; Alfred V. Kidder of the Carnegie Institution and Gordon Willey of Harvard University.[8] Although Ferguson certainly intended the archaeological work to supply evidence for the Book of Mormon, when the Church became involved with NWAF, the Church intentionally distanced itself from those overt purposes. Daniel C. Peterson explains:

> Several relevant facts stand out from this bare-bones recital of the earliest history of the New World Archaeological Foundation. First, non-Latter-day Saint archaeologists

---

[5] Bettany Hughes, *Helen of Troy: Goddess, Princess, Whore*, 177.
[6] Ibid., 34.
[7] Stan Larson, *Quest for the Gold Plates: Thomas Stuart Ferguson's Archaeological Search for the Book of Mormon*, 133–74, documents Ferguson as doubting both the Book of Mormon and the Book of Abraham later in life. Nevertheless, it is not certain that this picture accurately represents the entire picture. His son reported that a month before his death he said: "Larry, the Book of Mormon is *exactly* what Joseph Smith said it is." Daniel C. Peterson and Matthew Roper, "Ein Heldenleben? On Thomas Stuart Ferguson as an Elias for Cultural Mormons," 180–81. Ferguson's loss or retention of faith is irrelevant to his role in the establishment of the New World Archaeological Foundation which is the point I am interested in. However, the ways in which Ferguson's legacy has been used in Book of Mormon polemics requires that I at least note the possibility that his early enthusiastic belief in what archaeology would do for the Book of Mormon was tempered if not totally abandoned.
[8] Daniel C. Peterson, "On the New World Archaeological Foundation," 223–35.

were prominent—in fact, dominant—from the beginning, not only in choosing central Chiapas as the geographical focus of its excavations, but in making the pitch for support from the First Presidency of the Church of Jesus Christ of Latter-day Saints and in directing and carrying out NWAF's fieldwork. Second, far from betraying an eager zeal to back a hunt for Book of Mormon artifacts and "proofs," the leadership of the church was manifestly reluctant to fund NWAF. Third, the participation of the eminent non-Mormon archaeologists Alfred V. Kidder and Edwin Shook in proposals for financial support from the First Presidency ensured that those proposals did not focus at all on NWAF's potential usefulness in Book of Mormon apologetics.[9]

Unlike Schliemann's expedition to Hisarlik, this was not to be an enterprise based on faith and amateurism. If evidence were to be found, it would be found through solid archaeological work that was not only acceptable but respected in the Mesoamerican archaeological community. NWAF archaeologist Dee F. Green relates having been instructed by Church leaders that:

> interpretation should be an individual matter, that is, that any archaeology officially sponsored by the Church (i.e., the monies for which are provided by tithing) should concern itself only with the culture history interpretations normally within the scope of archaeology, and any attempt at correlation or interpretation involving the Book of Mormon should be eschewed. This enlightened policy, much to the gratification of the true professional archaeologist both in and outside the Church, has been scrupulously followed. It was made quite plain to me in 1963 when I was first employed by the BYU-NWAF that my opinions with regard to Book of Mormon archaeology were to be kept to myself, and my field report was to be kept entirely [free] from any such references.[10]

As with Schliemann, the NWAF began digging in the right place—to discover Preclassic cultures of Mesoamerica.[11] That work, and the abundance of information that have since come from Mesoamerica, yield a rich mine of data against which particulars in the Book of Mormon may be compared.

Of the various Book of Mormon geographies that focus on Mesoamerica, the most complete and productive is John L. Sorenson's *An Ancient American Setting for the*

---

[9] Ibid., 227.

[10] Dee F. Green, "Book of Mormon Archaeology: The Myths and the Alternatives," 76. He further notes (76–77): "Some of my colleagues and students, both in and out of the Church, have wondered if perhaps the real reason for the Church's involvement in archaeology (especially since it is centered in Mesoamerica with emphasis on the Preclassic period) is to help prove the Book of Mormon. While this may represent the individual thinking of some members of the Church Archaeological Committee, it has not intruded itself on the work of the foundation except to limit its activities to the Preclassic cultures of Mesoamerica."

[11] At the time it was a more interesting coincidence than it is today. When the NWAF began, the focus was so tightly on the Classic civilizations that the Preclassic was ignored and therefore not well known. Nevertheless, more recent archaeology tells us that there were Preclassic ruins in so many locations that finding them in the place predicted was hardly unique. The discovery of Preclassic civilization in the areas the NWAF excavated tell us about Mesoamerican Preclassic cultures, but do not directly demonstrate that the Book of Mormon took place in those areas.

Book of Mormon. He has made slight adjustments and updates in his more recent *Mormon's Codex: An Ancient American Book*.[12] I accept his basic geography except for a few points of disagreement (Chapter 5). The most serious drawback to his correlation has been the disjunction between textual directions and the cardinal directions for the proposed lands. I argue ("The Problem of Directions in the Book of Mormon" in Chapter 5) that the use of directions in the Book of Mormon plausibly fits a translated version of the Mesoamerican directional system that would have informed a text created in that region and time. I suggest that, rather than being a problem, the issue of the directions actually supports the geographic correlation by representing a culturally logical scheme that is not immediately apparent in the modern translation.

There are over seven hundred geographical statements in the text.[13] To be plausible, a geographical convergence should meet (or explain) all of them. As John E. Clark suggests: "It is important to stress that finding any sector of the Americas that fits Book of Mormon specifications requires dealing with hundreds of mutually dependent variables. Rather than counting a credible geography as one correspondence, it actually counts for several hundred."[14]

One example of a complex correlation is the examination of the destruction described in 3 Nephi.[15] The text does not tell us what caused the destruction, but it may be deduced from the descriptions that it was a massive volcanic event. To be a convergence, the descriptions must not only correspond to known features of such an eruption, but there must be volcanoes in the region. Grover's examination of the descriptions and the specific geological conditions of the lands included in Sorenson's map correlation provide a very close correlation between the descriptions and plausible events in that specific geography that would not apply in most other locations, including different models in Mesoamerica (Chapter 15).

---

[12] Sorenson, *An Ancient American Setting for the Book of Mormon*, 1–48; Sorenson, *Mormon's Codex: An Ancient American Book*, 119–43.

[13] John E. Clark, "Archaeological Trends and Book of Mormon Origins," 89: "The book provides over seven hundred references to its geography and is consistent from beginning to end, allowing construction of an internal geography." The correspondences are the correlation of the internal geography with a real-world physical geography. The correspondences are listed in John L. Sorenson, *Geography of Book of Mormon Events: A Source Book*, 230–328.

[14] John E. Clark, Wade Ardern, and Matthew Roper, "Debating the Foundations of Mormonism: The Book of Mormon and Archaeology."

[15] A second example is one that I find provides an important quick measuring stick for proposed Book of Mormon geographies. Helaman 3:3–7 provides a set of conditions that must all be present to find a particular Book of Mormon land. North of the Nephite lands must be a land of many waters, a very large number of people, very few trees (little timber), and houses of cement. Adobe might be claimed to be the meaning of cement, but it isn't a viable building material in places that have enough water to be a land of "large bodies of water and many rivers" (Hel. 3:4). There are those who favor the Great Lakes as a land of many waters and rivers, but there is no historical time when the region was nearly devoid of trees. These interconnected requirements can easily eliminate many geographies.

Geopolitical Convergences

Within the physical geography are human boundaries that represent important perceived divisions among the peoples who lived in those lands. The Book of Mormon describes perceived human boundaries with specific interrelationships at different points in time. Although mentioned late, the Jaredites are the earliest Book of Mormon people. The text requires that they lived in lands to the north of Nephite populations for most of Nephite history. They must have been there for up to a thousand years prior to the Nephite arrival, must overlap in time with the Nephites for about four hundred years, but have had no discernible direct contact between the two.

The text also requires that, as the Nephites move out of the land of Nephi, they must encounter a people who have already established a city, who speak a different language, and who have a different religion. Lamanites come from the south and Nephite expansion (or later retreat) moves north.

The Jaredites may be seen as participants in the Olmec civilization. As with other Mesoamerican cultures, the Olmec were never a single people and should be best understood as specific cities that followed a general cultural pattern. The Olmec homeland is north of proposed Nephite lands, and the Olmec were in those lands when the Jaredites arrived. Remnants of the Olmec cultures, usually termed the epi-Olmec, survived and overlapped for the appropriate centuries with the Nephite cultures.

There was certainly trade influence from the Olmec in the area that the Maya came to dominate, but there was no dominant presence such as Teotihuacan later represented. There was a Jaredite connection to the people of Zarahemla, but Coriantumr had died before $Mosiah_1$ led his fleeing Nephites to that city. The confluence of the people of Zarahemla—who spoke a different language than the Nephites and who, in Nephite opinion, had lost their religion—fit with the linguistic and archaeological movement of Zoque speakers from the north up through the Grijalva River Valley around 200 B.C.

Chronological Convergences

Even a perfect geographic convergence cannot be the correct location for the Book of Mormon if the region was not populated during Book of Mormon times. Just as the geographic convergences require a large number of small details to be correct, so does the intersection between geography and time. If the right things happen at the wrong time, there is no convergence.

It is important, therefore, that the Book of Mormon fit temporally into the Mesoamerican geography. Although the Book of Mormon has a precise record of dates, we have only archaeology with its general dates to compare against.[16] The Olmec and the Jaredites overlap in time depth and geography. The Nephites and the Maya similarly overlap in time depth and geography. I do not contend that the time depths are the same or that there is any equation of Olmec and Jaredite or Maya and

---

[16] There is only one monument with a date during Book of Mormon times. There are many dated texts, but the post-date the Book of Mormon.

Nephite. The Jaredites and Nephites lived during Olmec and Maya times and participated in cultures that are described as Olmec and Maya. Within that overall temporal correlation, there are more specific connections between historical movements seen in archaeology and Book of Mormon descriptions.

The Book of Mormon description of the events that precipitated the exodus of Lehi and his family from Jerusalem to the New World reflect in many small, but important, ways the religious and political climate during the very timeframe the text declares. (See Chapter 3.) The specific conditions in Jerusalem and the details of Lehi's family provide the explanatory backdrop for why Lehi was in conflict with Jerusalem's powerful leaders, why the family took the path they did when they left (rather than the traditional flight to Egypt), and plausibly provides the background to the greatest theological undercurrent in the Book of Mormon, that of the Atoning Messiah.

Once in the New World, the desire to elevate Nephi to king reflects cultural trends discerned for Mesoamerican peoples during that timeframe (Chapter 6). Jacob's sermon discussing the twin evils of costly apparel and polygamy fits into the economic pressures that were beginning during that time period in that region (Chapter 7). The movement of Quichéan speakers into Kaminaljuyú corresponds in time depth to the change in circumstances that lead to $Mosiah_1$ fleeing the city of Nephi for Zarahemla (Chapter 8). The merger of Nephites and the people of Zarahemla corresponds in time and place with the linguistic movement of Zoque speakers into the Grijalva River Valley (Chapter 8). At the end of the Book of Mormon, the historical influence of the powerful city-state of Teotihuacan provides the explanatory background for the changes that Mormon notes in the nature of warfare, as well as the plausible reason that the Nephites were subjected to destruction rather that dominance (Chapter 16).

Cultural Convergences

With a perfect geography and with appropriate temporal correlations, it is still possible that there would be no real convergence with the Book of Mormon. Were people present at the right places and times, but were hunter-gatherer tribes, there would be no convergence with a Book of Mormon that requires a complex agriculture-based culture.

It has long been noted that there are general correspondences between the Book of Mormon and Mesoamerica. The text requires cities. Mesoamerica has cities. The text requires frequent and prolonged warfare. The text describes warfare in terms appropriate to the weapons and tactics known for Mesoamerica (Chapter 13). The text requires a people who could read and write. Mesoamerica has the only known writing systems in all of the Americas. Significantly, many cultural convergences are even more specific.

A good deal is known about Mesoamerican kinship and social relationships. While less information is available for the Book of Mormon, there are nevertheless important convergences between those concepts as known for Mesoamerica and texts that reflect similarities in the Book of Mormon (Chapter 11). The political systems described in the Book of Mormon appear to both reflect and respond to Mesoamerican political ideas. Some of the Nephite political structures have parallels in the Mesoamerican cultures, and some aspects appear to be a distinct rejection of surrounding political systems. (See "King by Popular Demand" in Chapter 6 and Chapters 10 and 12.)

While the Nephite religion is based in the brass plates and remains reasonably faithful to those roots, its recurring pattern of apostasy is best explained by a subset of the Nephites establishing a syncretized religion with ideas from surrounding cultures (Chapter 10).

In numerous small but important ways, the convergences between the culture of Mesoamerica and that of the Book of Mormon continue to grow and become more impressive as the same location and cultural background provide an increasing set of convergences. In John E. Clark's words: "The cultural worlds of ancient Mesoamerica and early New York are far enough apart that it ought to be simple to discover from which one the book came. The cultures described in the Book of Mormon fit much better in Mesoamerica than in New York for any century."[17]

Productive Convergences

The most important convergences are those that not only create a connection between the text and a time and place, but which actually use that time and place to make the text more understandable. There are at least four stories which make more sense against the Mesoamerican place and time than they do against any other setting.

- The expedition Limhi sent to find Zarahemla that gets lost and finds the remains of a Jaredite battle (Chapter 5)
- Jacob's discourse condemning costly apparel and polygamy (Chapter 7)
- The story of Ammon and king Lamoni (Chapter 12)
- The story of the Anti-Nephi-Lehies (Chapter 12)

Each of these stories has features that are difficult to explain without a historical and geographic context. In each case Mesoamerica supplies the unstated cultural assumptions or geographic details behind enigmatic Book of Mormon episodes.

That one of these productive convergences would occur by coincidence is unlikely. With at least three of these instances, we significantly increase the likelihood that we have found the cultural background that implicitly informed the lives of Book of Mormon peoples.

From Traditions of the Fathers to Future Stories

In a presentation at the Bicentennial Conference celebrating Joseph Smith held at the Library of Congress, John E. Clark noted that "many items mentioned in the Book of Mormon have not been and may never be verified through archaeology, but

---

[17] Clark, "Archaeological Trends and Book of Mormon Origins," 96.

many have been. Verification is a one-way street in this instance. Positive and negative evidence do not count the same, as anyone tested for a serious medical condition knows. Given current means of verification, positive items are here to stay, but negative items may prove to be positive ones in hiding. 'Missing' evidence focuses further research, but it lacks compelling logical force in arguments because it represents the absence of information rather than secure evidence."[18]

There are still gaps in our understanding. There may always be gaps, just as biblical history still has gaps when compared with archaeology. What is recorded in a text does not always directly replicate what is recorded in material remains. Nevertheless, there are sufficient complex correspondences between the Book of Mormon and what is known of the greater historical and cultural trends in Mesoamerica to relegate the gaps to important areas for further research.

The hypothesis of historicity stands on firm evidentiary grounds. There are complex interconnected convergences between the Book of Mormon and a known place, time, and culture. In Clark's words: "The Book of Mormon is stronger today than it was in 1830, 1844, 1950, or even 2000, so I expect it will continue to become stronger in the future."[19] We have added significantly to our base of understanding in the last thirty years. There is more to learn.

There is an excellent cadre of LDS scholars with the training to examine the Book of Mormon in its Old World context. There are significantly fewer with the training to compare the Book of Mormon to its Mesoamerican background. It is a fertile ground for research and awaits new people, new ideas, and new perspectives. This is the place for beginnings even after all of the previous work is considered. As we have learned more about Mesoamerica, its cultures, and its history, we have been able to refine our understanding of the Book of Mormon's place in that history. It is this trend that pleads for more trained historians, ethnohistorians, archaeologists, linguists, and others to engage evidence that is perhaps only just now on the verge of discovery.

In the meantime, the keystone of our religion still supports the edifice.

---

[18] Ibid., 95.
[19] Ibid.

Bibliography

Abunuwara, Ehab. "Into the Desert: An Arab View of the Book of Mormon." *Journal of Book of Mormon Studies* 11 (2002): 60–65.
"The Acoustics of Maya Temples." http://www.luckymojo.com/esoteric/interdisciplinary/architecture/ecclesiastical/mayanacoustics.html (accessed March 2007).
Adams, William J., Jr. "Nephi's Jerusalem and Laban's Sword." In *Pressing Forward with the Book of Mormon*. Edited by John W. Welch and Melvin J. Thorne. Provo, Utah: Foundation for Ancient Research and Mormon Studies, 1999, 11–12.
Adams, William Y. *Religion and Adaptation*. Stanford, Calif.: CSLI Publications, 2005.
Ainsworth, Jerry L. *The Lives and Travels of Mormon and Moroni*. Mabank, Texas: Peacemakers Publishing, 2000.
Ainsworth, Jerry L. "Response to Allens' [sic] Article on River Sidon." January 20, 2012. *Book of Mormon Archaeological Forum*. http://www.bmaf.org/node/280 (accessed April 2011).
Akenson, Donald Harmon. *Surpassing Wonder: The Invention of the Bible and the Talmuds*. New York: Harcourt, Brace & Company, 1998.
Allen, James B., and Glen M. Leonard. *The Story of the Latter-day Saints*. 2d ed. rev., and enl. Salt Lake City: Deseret Book, 1992.
Allen, Joseph L. *Exploring the Lands of the Book of Mormon*. Orem, Utah: SA Publishers, 1989.
Allen, Joseph L. "Quetzalcoatl." In *Book of Mormon Reference Companion*. Edited by Dennis L. Largey. Salt Lake City: Deseret Book, 2003, 668–70.
Allen, Joseph L. *Sacred Sites: Searching for Book of Mormon Lands*. American Fork, Utah: Covenant Communications, 2003.
Allen, Joseph L., and Blake Joseph Allen. *Exploring the Lands of the Book of Mormon*. 2nd ed. Orem, Utah: Book of Mormon Tours and Research Institute, 2008.
Alexander, Thomas G. *Mormonism in Transition. A History of the Latter-day Saints, 1890–1930*. Urbana: University of Illinois Press, 1986.
Alexander, Thomas G. "The Reconstruction of Mormon Doctrine." In *Line Upon Line: Essays on Mormon Doctrine*. Edited by Gary James Bergera. Salt Lake City: Signature Books, 1989, 53–66.
Ambrosino, James N., Traci Ardren, and Travis W. Stanton. "The History of Warfare at Yaxuná." In *Ancient Mesoamerican Warfare*. Edited by Travis W. Stanton and M. Kathryn Brown. Walnut Creek, Calif.: Altamira Press, 2003, 109–23.
"Anales de Cuauhtitlan." In *Codice Chimalpopoca*. Edited by Primo Feliciano Velázquez. Mexico City: Universidad Nacional Autónoma de México, 1975.
Annals of the Cakchiquels. Translated by Adrian Recinos and Delia Goetz. Norman: University of Oklahoma Press, 1974.
Anderson, Richard Lloyd. *Investigating the Book of Mormon Witnesses*. Salt Lake City: Deseret Book, 1981.
Ankerberg, John, and John Weldon. *Everything You Ever Wanted to Know about Mormonism*. Eugene, Ore.: Harvest House, 1992.
Antley, Trevor. "The Talmage Journals: The Book of Mormon Geography Hearings, 1921." *Worlds without End: A Mormon Studies Roundtable*. Blog post July 21, 2012. http://www.withoutend.org/talmage-journals-book-mormon-geography-hearings-1921/ (accessed August 2012).
"Armed Forces Pest Management Board, Venomous Plants and Animals." http://www.afpmb.org/ pubs/living_hazards/snakes.html (accessed June 2007).

Arrington, Leonard J., and Davis Bitton. *The Mormon Experience: A History of the Latter-day Saints*. New York: Vintage Books, 1980.
Ash, Michael R. "Horses in the Book of Mormon." Paper presented at the Book of Mormon Archaeological Forum conference, October 2007. http://www.fairlds.org/authors/ash-michael/horses-in-the-book-of-mormon (accessed December 2012).
Ash, Michael R. *Of Faith and Reason: 80 Evidences Supporting the Prophet Joseph Smith*. Springville, Utah: CFI, 2008.
Askren, Tierza. "Top 5 Things I Hate about Nephi." *Mormon Expressions Blog*. Posted November 27, 2011. http://mormonexpression.com/blogs/2011/11/27/ top-5-things-i-hate-about-nephi/ (accessed September 2013).
Aston, Warren P. "The Arabian Bountiful Discovered? Evidence for Nephi's Bountiful." *Journal of Book of Mormon Studies* 7, no. 1 (1998): 4–11.
Aston, Warren P. "Identifying Our Best Candidate for Nephi's Bountiful." *Journal of Book of Mormon and Restoration Scripture* 17, nos. 1–2 (2008): 58–64.
Aston, Warren P. "Newly Found Altars from Nahom." *Journal of Book of Mormon Studies* 10, no. 2 (2001): 57–61.
Aston, Warren P., and Michaela Knoth Aston. *In the Footsteps of Lehi: New Evidence for Lehi's Journey across Arabia to Bountiful*. Salt Lake City: Deseret Book, 1994.
Astor-Aguilera, Miguel Angel. *The Maya World of Communicating Objects: Quadripartite Crosses, Trees, and Stones*. Albuquerque: University of New Mexico Press, 2010.
Axelgard, Frederick W. "1 and 2 Nephi: An Inspiring Whole." *BYU Studies* 26, no. 4 (Fall 1986): 53–65.
Baer, James L. "The Third Nephi Disaster: A Geological View." *Dialogue: A Journal of Mormon Thought* 19, no. 2 (Spring 1986): 129–32.
"Bainbridge, NY, Court Record, 20 March 1826." In Dan Vogel, comp. and ed., *Early Mormon Documents*, 5 vols. Salt Lake City: Signature Books, 1996–2003.
Baines, John. "Contextualizing Egyptian Representations of Society and Ethnicity." In *The Study of the Ancient Near East in the 21st Century: The William Foxwell Albright Centennial Conference*. Edited by Jerrold S. Cooper and Glenn M. Schwartz. Winona Lake, Wis.: Eisenbrauns, 1996, 339–84.
Ball, Isaac B. "Additional Internal Evidence for the Authenticity of the Book of Mormon." *Improvement Era*, May 1931. Retrieved from *GospeLink 2001* CD. Salt Lake City, Utah: Deseret Book, 2000.
Ball, Russell H. "An Hypothesis concerning the Three Days of Darkness among the Nephites." *Journal of Book of Mormon Studies* 2, no. 1 (Spring 1993): 107–23.
Balter, Michael. "Ancient DNA Links Native Americans with Europe." *Science* 342 (October 25, 2013): 409–10. http://www.sciencemag.org/content/342/6157/ 409.full.pdf (accessed October 2013). PDF copy in my possession.
Barber, Elizabeth Wayland, and Paul T. Barber. *When They Severed Earth from Sky: How the Human Mind Shapes Myth*. Princeton, N.J.: Princeton University Press, 2004.
Barker, Margaret. "The Fragrant Tree." In *The Tree of Life: From Eden to Eternity*. Edited by John W. Welch and Donald W. Parry. Provo, Utah: Neal A. Maxwell Institute for Religious Scholarship/Salt Lake City: Deseret Book, 2011, 55–79.
Barker, Margaret. *The Great Angel: A Study of Israel's Second God*. Louisville, Ky.: Westminster/John Knox, 1992.
Barker, Margaret *The Great High Priest: The Temple Roots of Christian Liturgy*. New York: T&T Clark, 2003.
Barker, Margaret. "Joseph Smith and Preexilic Israelite Religion." In *The Worlds of Joseph Smith:*

A Bicentennial Conference at the Library of Congress. Edited by John W. Welch. Provo, Utah: Brigham Young University Press, 2006, 69–82.

Barker, Margaret. Temple Theology: An Introduction. London: Society for Promoting Christian Knowledge, 2005.

Barker, Margaret. "What Did King Josiah Reform?" In Glimpses of Lehi's Jerusalem. Edited by John W. Welch, David Rolph Seely, and Jo Ann H. Seely. Provo, Utah: Foundation for Ancient Research and Mormon Studies, 2004, 522–42.

Barney, Kevin L. "How to Worship Our Mother in Heaven (Without Getting Excommunicated)." Dialogue: A Journal of Mormon Thought 41, no. 4 (Winter 2008): 121–46.

Barney, Kevin L. "Reflections on the Documentary Hypothesis." Dialogue: A Journal of Mormon Thought 33, no. 1 (Spring 2000): 57–99.

Barzun, Jacques, and Henry F. Graff. The Modern Researcher, 4th ed. San Diego: Harcourt Brace Jovanovich, 1985.

Beatty, Charles. A Journal of a Two Months Tour: With a View of Promoting Religion among the Frontier Inhabitants of Pensylvania, and of Introducing Christianity among the Indians to the Westward of the Alegh-geny Mountains. London: Printed for William Davenhill and George Pearch, 1768.

Becker, Marshall J. "Burials as Caches, Caches as Burials: A New Interpretation of the Meaning of Ritual Deposits among the Classic Period Lowland Maya." In New Theories of the Ancient Maya. Edited by Elin C. Danien and Robert J. Sharer. Philadelphia: University of Pennsylvania Museum, 1992, 185–96.

Bennett, Richard E. "'A Nation Now Extinct': American Indian Origin Theories as of 1820." Journal of the Book of Mormon and Other Restoration Scripture 20, no. 2 (2011): 30–51.

Bennett, Robert R. "Horses in the Book of Mormon." Research Report prepared by the FARMS Research Department, August 2000. http://maxwellinstitute.byu.edu/publications/transcripts/?id=129 (accessed November 2012).

Benson, Ezra Taft. The Teachings of Ezra Taft Benson. Salt Lake City: Bookcraft, 1988.

Bierhorst, John, trans. History and Mythology of the Aztecs: The Codex Chimalpopoca. Tucson: University of Arizona Press, 1992.

Bitton, Davis. "B. H. Roberts and Book of Mormon Scholarship: Early Twentieth Century: Age of Transition." Journal of Book of Mormon Studies 8, no. 2 (1999): 60–69.

Blanton, Richard E., Stephen A. Kowalewski, Gary Feinman, and Jill Appel. Ancient Mesoamerica: A Comparison of Change in Three Regions. New York: Cambridge University Press, 1981.

Blumell, Lincoln H., and Thomas A. Wayment. "When Was Jesus Born? A Response to a Recent Proposal." BYU Studies 51, no. 3 (2012): 53–81.

Boehm, Bruce J. "Wanderers in the Promised Land: A Study of the Exodus Motif in the Book of Mormon and Holy Bible." Journal of Book of Mormon Studies 3, no. 1 (Spring 1994): 187–204.

Bokovoy, David. Authoring the Old Testament: Genesis–Deuteronomy. Salt Lake City: Greg Kofford Books, 2014.

"The Book of Ether." Evening and the Morning Star 1, no. 3 (August 1832): 22–23. Retrieved from GospeLink Online, May 2013.

Book of Mormon. 1830. Rpt., Independence, Mo.: Herald House, 1970.

[No author indicated]. "Book of Mormon and DNA Studies." Gospel Topics. https://www.lds.org/topics/book-of-mormon-and-dna-studies (accessed February 2013).

Book of Mormon Critical Text: A Tool for Scholarly Reference. 3 vols. Edited by Robert F. Smith. Provo, Utah: Foundation for Ancient Research and Mormon Studies, 1987.

"Book of Mormon Students Meet. Interesting Convention Held in Provo Saturday and Sunday." Journal of the Book of Mormon and Other Restoration Scripture 22, no. 2 (2013): 108–110. Excerpts from "Book of Mormon Students Meet." Deseret Evening News, May 25, 1903.

"Book of Mormon Witnesses." FairMormon Wiki. http://en.fairmormon.org/Book_of_Mormon/Witnesses (accessed December 2013).

Borg, Marcus J. *Reading the Bible Again for the First Time: Taking the Bible Seriously But Not Literally*. San Francisco: HarperSanFrancisco, 2001.

Boudinot, Elias. *Star in the West; Or a Humble Attempt to Discover the Long Lost Ten Tribes of Israel Preparatory to Their Return to Their Beloved City, Jerusalem*. Trenton, N.J.: D. Fenton, S. Hutchinson, and J. Dunham. George Sherman, Printer, 1816.

Bové, Frederick Joseph. "The Evolution of Chiefdoms and States on the Pacific Slope of Guatemala: A Spatial Analysis." PhD diss., University of California, Los Angeles, 1981.

Box, G. H. *The Apocalypse of Abraham: Edited with a Translation from the Slavonic Text and Notes*. TRANSLATIONS OF EARLY DOCUMENTS, SERIES I, PALESTINIAN JEWISH TEXTS (PRE-RABBINIC). New York: Macmillan Company, 1919. http://www.marquette.edu/maqom/box.pdf (accessed September 2013).

Boyce, Duane. "Were the Ammonites Pacifists?" *Journal of Book of Mormon and Restoration Scripture* 18, no. 1 (2009): 33–47.

Brady, Parrish, and Shon Hopkin. "The Zoramites and Costly Apparel: Symbolism and Irony." *Journal of the Book of Mormon and Other Restoration Scripture* 22, no. 1 (2013): 40–53.

Bradley, Carol Pratt. "Women, the Book of Mormon, and the Law of Moses." *Studia Antiqua: The Journal of the Student Society for Ancient Studies*, Summer 2004, 125–71.

Bray, Warwick. *Everyday Life of the Aztecs*. New York: Peter Bedrick Books, 1991.

Brewer, Stewart W. "The History of an Idea: The Scene on Stela 5 from Izapa, Mexico, as a Representation of Lehi's Vision of the Tree of Life." *Journal of Book of Mormon Studies* 8, no. 1 (1999): 13–21.

Bright, John. *Jeremiah: A New Translation with Introduction and Commentary*. THE ANCHOR BIBLE. Garden City, N.Y.: Doubleday, 1971.

Brockington, Donald L. *The Ceramic History of Santa Rosa, Chiapas, Mexico*. PAPERS OF THE NEW WORLD ARCHAEOLOGICAL FOUNDATION, NO. 23. Provo, Utah: New World Archaeological Foundation, Brigham Young University, 1967.

Brown, Donald E. *Human Universals*. New York: McGraw-Hill, 1991.

Brown, Linda A. "When Collecting Artifacts Is a Conversation with the Gods." Reports of the Foundation for the Advancement of Mesoamerican Studies, 2009, No. 3. http://www.famsi.org/reports/03101/58brown/58brown.pdf (accessed April 2012).

Brown, M. Kathryn, and James F. Garber. "Evidence of Conflict during the Middle Formative in the Maya Lowlands: A View from Blackman Eddy, Belize." In *Warfare in Ancient Mesoamerica*. Edited by Travis W. Stanton and M. Kathryn Brown. Walnut Creek, Calif.: Altamira Press, 2003, 91–108.

Brown, S. Kent. "Arabia and the Book of Mormon." Paper presented at the annual conference of the Foundation for Apologetic Information and Research, August 2001. http://www.fairlds.org/FAIR_Conferences/2001_Arabia_and_the_Book_of_Mormon.html (accessed July 2008).

Brown, S. Kent. "A Case for Lehi's Bondage in Arabia." *Journal of Book of Mormon Studies* 6, no. 2 (1997): 205–17.

Brown, S. Kent. "The Exodus Pattern in the Book of Mormon." *BYU Studies* 30, no. 3 (Summer 1990): 111–26.

Brown, S. Kent. *From Jerusalem to Zarahemla: Literary and Historical Studies of the Book of Mormon*. Provo, Utah: BYU Religious Studies Center, 1998.

Brown, S. Kent. "The Hunt for the Valley of Lemuel." *Journal of Book of Mormon Studies* 16, no. 1 (2007): 65–73.

Brown, S. Kent. "Jerusalem Connections to Arabia in 600 B.C." In *Glimpses of Lehi's Jerusalem*. Edited by John W. Welch, David Rolph Seely, and Jo Ann H. Seely. Provo, Utah: Foundation for Ancient Research and Mormon Studies, 2004.
Brown, S. Kent. "New Light from Arabia on Lehi's Trail." In *Echoes and Evidences of the Book of Mormon*. Edited by Donald W. Parry, Daniel C. Peterson, and John W. Welch. Provo, Utah: Foundation for Ancient Research and Mormon Studies, 2002, 55–125.
Brown, S. Kent. "'The Place That Was Called Nahom': New Light from Ancient Yemen." *Journal of Book of Mormon Studies* 8, no. 1 (1999): 68.
Brown, S. Kent. *Voices from the Dust: Book of Mormon Insights*. American Fork, Utah: Covenant Communications, 2004.
Brown, S. Kent, and Peter Johnson, eds. *Journey of Faith: From Jerusalem to the Promised Land*. Provo, Utah: Neal A. Maxwell Institute for Religious Scholarship, 2006.
Brundage, Burr Cartwright. *The Fifth Sun: Aztec Gods, Aztec World*. Austin: University of Texas Press, 1979.
Brunvand, Jan Harold. "Modern Legends of Mormondom, or, Supernaturalism Is Alive and Well in Salt Lake City." *American Folk Legend: A Symposium*. Edited, with a preface, by Wayland D. Hand. UCLA Center for the Study of Comparative Folklore and Mythology, Publication II. Berkeley: University of California Press, 1971, 185–202.
Bushman, Richard L. *Believing History: Latter-day Saint Essays*. Edited by Reid L. Neilson and Jed Woodworth. New York: Columbia University Press, 2004.
Bushman, Richard L. "The Book of Mormon and the American Revolution." *BYU Studies* 17, no. 1 (Autumn 1976): 3–20.
Bushman, Richard L. *Joseph Smith and the Beginnings of Mormonism*. Urbana: University of Illinois Press, 1984.
Bushman, Richard L. "My Belief." *BYU Studies* 25, no. 2 (Spring 1985): 23–30.
Bybee, Ariel E. "A Woman's World in Lehi's Jerusalem." In *Glimpses of Lehi's Jerusalem*. Edited by John W. Welch, David Rolph Seely, and Jo Ann H. Seely. Provo, Utah: Foundation for Ancient Research and Mormon Studies, 2004, 131–48.
Bynon, Theodora. *Historical Linguistics*. CAMBRIDGE TEXTBOOKS IN LINGUISTICS. Series edited by W. Sidney Allen, C. J. Fillmore, Eugenie J. A. Henderson, Fred W. Householder, John Lyons, R. B. Le Page, F. R. Palmer, and J. L. M. Trim. New York: Cambridge University Press, 1977.
Calneck, Edward E. "The Sahagún Texts as a Source of Sociological Information." In *Sixteenth-Century Mexico*. Edited by Munro S. Edmonson. Albuquerque: University of New Mexico Press, 1974, 189–204.
Campbell, Alexander. "Delusions (February 10, 1831)." *Millennial Harbinger*, Vol. 2. Edited by Alexander Campbell, Bethany, Va.: Printed and published by the Editor, 1731 [sic]: 85–96.
Campbell, Joseph. *The Hero with a Thousand Faces*. BOLLINGEN SERIES, VOL. 17. Princeton, N.J.: Princeton University Press, 1973.
Campbell, Lyle. "Mesoamerican Linguistics." Mimeograph, April 1976.
Campbell, Lyle, and Terrence Kaufman. "A Linguistic Look at the Olmecs." *American Antiquity* 41, no. 1 (January 1976): 80–88.
Cannon, Donald Q. "In the Press: Early Newspaper Reports on the Initial Publication of the Book of Mormon." *Journal of Book of Mormon Studies* 16, no. 2 (2007): 4–15.
Cannon, George Q. "Editorial Thoughts—Book of Mormon Geography." *Juvenile Instructor* 25, no. 1 (January 1, 1890): 18–19.
Cantor, Norman F. *In the Wake of the Plague: The Black Death and the World It Made*. New York: Harper Perennial, 2002.
Card, Orson Scott. "The Book of Mormon, Artifact or Artifice?" Adapted from a speech given

at the BYU Symposium on Life, the Universe, and Everything, February 1993. http://www.nauvoo.com/library/card-bookofmormon.html (accessed June 2004).

Carmack, Robert M. *Quichéan Civilization: The Ethnohistoric, Ethnographic, and Archaeological Sources.* Berkeley: University of California Press, 1973.

Carr, Stephen L. "A Summary of Several Theories of Book of Mormon Lands in Mesoamerica." *Book of Mormon Archaeological Forum.* http://www.bmaf.org/node/108 (accessed April 2011).

Carrasco, Pedro. "Las clases sociales en el México Antiguo." In *Verhandlungen de 38th Internationalen Amerikanistenkongresses.* 2 vols. München: Kommissionverlag Klaus Renner, 1970, 2:315–20.

Casteñeda, Francisco de. "Official Reports on the Towns of Tequizistlán, Tepechpán, Acolman, and San Juan Teotihuacán, sent by Francisco de Casteñeda to His Majesty, Philip II, and the Council of the Indies, in 1580." Translated and edited by Zelia Nuttal. *Papers of the Peabody Museum of American Archaeology and Ethnology, Harvard University,* 11, no. 4. Cambridge, Mass.: The Museum, 1926, 45–84.

Cavalli-Sforza, Luigi Luca. *Genes, Peoples, and Languages.* Translated by Mark Seielstad. Berkeley: University of California Press, 2000.

Cazier, Donald Arthur. "A Study of Nephite, Lamanite, and Jaredite Governmental Institutions and Policies as Portrayed in the Book of Mormon." M.A. thesis, Brigham Young University, 1972.

Cervantes de Sálazar, Francisco. *Crónica de Nueva España.* 3 vols. Madrid: Hauser y Menet, 1914.

Chadwick, Jeffrey R. "An Archaeologist's View." *Journal of Book of Mormon Studies* 15, no. 2 (2006): 68–77.

Chadwick, Jeffrey R. "Dating the Birth of Christ." *BYU Studies* 49, no. 4 (2010): 5–38.

Chadwick, Jeffrey R. "Has the Seal of Mulek Been Found?" *Journal of Book of Mormon Studies* 12, no. 2 (2003): 72–83.

Chadwick, Jeffrey R. "Lehi in the Samaria Papyri and on an Ostracon from the Shore of the Red Sea." *Journal of Book of Mormon and Other Restoration Scriptures* 19, no. 1 (2010): 14–21.

Chadwick, Jeffrey R. "Lehi's House at Jerusalem and the Land of His Inheritance." In *Glimpses of Lehi's Jerusalem.* Edited by John W. Welch, David Rolph Seely, and Jo Ann H. Seely. Provo, Utah: Foundation for Ancient Research and Mormon Studies, 2004, 81–130.

Chadwick, Jeffrey R. "The Names Lehi & Sariah—Language and Meaning." *Journal of Book of Mormon Studies* 9, no. 1 (2000): 32–34.

Chadwick, Jeffrey R. "Sariah in the Elephantine Papyri." In *Pressing Forward with the Book of Mormon.* Edited by John W. Welch and Melvin J. Thorne. Provo, Utah: Foundation for Ancient Research and Mormon Studies, 1999, 6–10.

Chadwick, Jeffrey R. "The Wrong Place for Lehi's Trail and the Valley of Lemuel." In *The FARMS Review* 17, no. 2 (2005): 197–215.

Charlesworth, James H. *The Historical Jesus: An Essential Guide.* Nashville, Tenn.: Abingdon Press, 2008.

Charnay, Désiré. *The Ancient Cities of the New World, being Voyages and Explorations in Mexico and Central America from 1857–1882.* Translated by J. Gonino and Helen S. Conant. New York: Harper & Brothers, Franklin Square, 1887.

Chase, Diane Z., and Arlen F. Chase. "Texts and Contexts in Maya Warfare: A Brief Consideration of Epigraphy and Archaeology at Caracol, Belize." In *Ancient Mesoamerican Warfare.* Edited by Travis W. Stanton and M. Kathryn Brown. Walnut Creek, Calif.: Altamira Press, 2003, 171–88.

Cheesman, Paul R. "The Wheel in Ancient America." *BYU Studies* 9, no. 2 (Winter 1969): 185–97.

Cheesman, Paul R. *The World of the Book of Mormon.* Bountiful, Utah: Horizon Publishers, 1984.

Christenson, Allen J. "Maya Harvest Festivals and the Book of Mormon." In *Review of Books on the Book of Mormon* 3 (1991): 1–31.
Christensen, Doug. Post to "Book of Mormon Archaeological Forum Group." *Facebook.* http://www.facebook.com/groups/bmaf.org/permalink/ 10151035621679242/ (accessed July 2012).
Christensen, Kevin, "The Deuteronomist De-Christianizing of the Old Testament." *FARMS Review* 16, no. 2 (2004): 59–90.
Christensen, Kevin. "The Temple, the Monarchy, and Wisdom: Lehi's World and the Scholarship of Margaret Barker." In *Glimpses of Lehi's Jerusalem.* Edited by John W. Welch, David Rolph Seely, and Jo Ann H. Seely. Provo, Utah: Foundation for Ancient Research and Mormon Studies, 2004, 449–522.
Christensen, Ross T. "The Place Called Nahom." *Ensign,* August 1978, 73.
Clark, David L. "Lehi and el Niño: A Method of Migration." *BYU Studies* 30, no. 3 (Summer 1990): 57–65.
Clark, John E. "Archaeological Trends and Book of Mormon Origins." In *The Worlds of Joseph Smith: A Bicentennial Conference at the Library of Congress.* Edited by John W. Welch. Provo, Utah: Brigham Young University Press, 2006, 83–104.
Clark, John E. "Archaeology." In *Book of Mormon Reference Companion.* Edited by Dennis L. Largey. Salt Lake City: Deseret Book, 2003, 70–72.
Clark, John E. "Archaeology and Cumorah Questions." *Journal of Book of Mormon Studies* 13, no. 1 (2004): 144–51, 174 (endnotes).
Clark, John E. "Archaeology, Relics, and Book of Mormon Belief." *Journal of Book of Mormon Studies* 14, no. 2 (2005): 38–49.
Clark, John E. "Book of Mormon Geography." In *Encyclopedia of Mormonism.* Edited by Daniel H. Ludlow. 4 vols. New York: Macmillan Publishing, 1992, 1:176–79
Clark, John E. "A Key for Evaluating Nephite Geographies." *Review of Books on the Book of Mormon* 1 (1989): 20–70.
Clark, John E. "A New Artistic Rendering of Izapa Stela 5: A Step toward Improved Interpretation." *Journal of Book of Mormon Studies* 8, no. 1 (1999): 22–33.
Clark, John E. "Revisiting 'A Key for Evaluating Nephite Geographies.'" *Mormon Studies Review* 23, no. 1 (2011): 13–43.
Clark, John E., and Michael Blake. "The Power of Prestige: Competitive Generosity and the Emergence of Rank Societies in Lowland Mesoamerica." In *The Ancient Civilizations of Mesoamerica.* Edited by Michael E. Smith and Marilyn A. Masson. Malden, Mass.: Blackwell Publishers, 2000, 252–70.
Clark, John E., Wade Ardern, and Matthew Roper. "Debating the Foundations of Mormonism: The Book of Mormon and Archaeology." Paper presented at the annual conference of the Foundation for Apologetic Information and Research, August 2005. http://www.fairlds.org/fair-conferences/2005-fair-conference/2005-debating-the-foundations-of-mormonism-the-book-of-mormon-and-archaeology (accessed December 2012).
Clarke, Adam. *The Holy Bible Containing the Old and New Testaments: The Text Carefully Printed from the Most Correct Copies of the Present Authorized Translation, Including the Marginal Readings and Parallel Texts with A Commentary and Critical Notes Designed as a Help to a Better Understanding of the Sacred Writings.* 6 vols. n.d. Rpt., Nashville, Tenn.: Abingdon Press, 1977.
"Codex Mendoza." In *Antigüedades de México.* Mexico: Secretaria de Hacienda y Crédito Público, 1964.
"Codex Ríos." In *Antigüedades de México.* 4 vols. Mexico City: Secretaría de Hacienda y Crédito Público, 1964, 3:7–313.

Coe, Michael D. *Breaking the Maya Code*. 1992. Rev. ed., London: Thames & Hudson, 1999.
Coe, Michael D. *The Maya*. 6th ed. London: Thames and Hudson, 1999.
Coe, Michael D. *Mexico*. New York: Frederick A. Praeger, 1967.
Coe, Michael D. "Mormons & Archaeology: An Outside View." *Dialogue: A Journal of Mormon Thought* 8, no. 2 (Summer 1973): 40–48.
Coe, Michael D. "The Mormons: Interview with Michael Coe." PBS, "The Mormons." http://www.pbs.org/mormons/interviews/coe.html (accessed December 2010).
Coogan, Michael D. "Exodus, The." In *The Oxford Companion to the Bible*. Edited by Bruce M. Metzger and Michael D. Coogan. New York: Oxford University Press, 1993, 209–12.
Coogan, Michael D. "Time, Units of." In *The Oxford Companion to the Bible*. Edited by Bruce M. Metzger and Michael D. Coogan. New York: Oxford University Press, 1993, 743–44.
Corley, Bruce, Steve Lemke, and Grand Lovejoy. *Biblical Hermeneutics: A Comprehensive Introduction to Interpreting Scripture*. Nashville, Tenn.: Broadman & Holman Publishers, 1996.
Covarrubias, Miguel. *Mexico South: The Isthmus of Tehuantepec*. New York: Alfred A. Knopf, 1967.
Cowen, Ross. *Roman Legionary: 58 B.C.–A.D. 69*. Oxford, England: Osprey Publishing, 2003.
Cracroft, Richard H. "'Had for Good and Evil': 19th-Century Literary Treatments of the Book of Mormon." *Journal of Book of Mormon Studies* 12, no. 2 (2003): 4–19.
Cross, Frank Moore. *Canaanite Myth and Hebrew Epic: Essays in the History of the Religion of Israel*. Cambridge, Mass.: Harvard University Press, 1973.
Crossan, John Dominic. *The Essential Jesus: What Jesus Really Taught*. San Francisco: HarperSanFrancisco, 1995.
Crossan, John Dominic, and Jonathan L. Reed. *Excavating Jesus: Beneath the Stones, Behind the Texts*. San Francisco: HarperSanFrancisco, 2002.
Culbert, T. Patrick. *The Ceramic History of the Central Highlands of Chiapas, Mexico*. PAPERS OF THE NEW WORLD ARCHAEOLOGICAL FOUNDATION, NO. 14. Provo, Utah: New World Archaeological Foundation, Brigham Young University, 1965.
Daube, David. *The Exodus Pattern in the Bible*. London: Faber and Faber, 1963.
Davila, James R. "The Perils of Parallels (lecture)." *University of St. Andrews, School of Divinity*. April 2001. http://www.st-andrews.ac.uk/divinity/rt/dss/abstracts/ parallels/ (accessed December 2012).
Davis, Ryan W. "For the Peace of the People: War and Democracy in the Book of Mormon." *Journal of Book of Mormon Studies* 16, no. 1 (2007): 42–55.
Deane, Morgan. "Bleached Bones Covered the Field: An Analysis of the Jaredite Civil War using the 'War of the Eight Princes.'" Unpublished paper in my possession. January 1, 2010.
Delgado, Agustin. *Archaeological Research at Santa Rosa, Chiapas and in the Region of Tehuantepec*. PAPERS OF THE NEW WORLD ARCHAEOLOGICAL FOUNDATION, NOS. 17–18. Provo, Utah: New World Archaeological Foundation, Brigham Young University, 1965.
Delgado, Hugo, Ricardo Molinero, Pablo Cerbantes, Jorge Nieto-Obregón, Rufino Lozano-Santa Cruz, Héctor L. Macias-González, Claudia Mendoza-Rosales, and Gilberto Silva-Rolmo. "Geology of Xitle Volcano n Southern Mexico City—A 2000-year old monogenetic volcano in an urban area." *Revisa Mexicanoa de Ciencias Geológicas*. Vol. 15, No. 2 (1998):115–31.
Dever, William G. *Did God Have a Wife? Archaeology and Folk Religion in Ancient Israel*. Grand Rapids, Mich.: William B. Eerdmans Publishing, 2005.
Dever, William G. *Recent Archaeological Discoveries and Biblical Research*. THE SAMUEL AND ALTHEA STROUM LECTURES IN JEWISH STUDIES. Seattle: University of Washington Press, 1990.
Dever, William G. *What Did the Biblical Writers Know and When Did They Know It? What Archaeology Can Tell Us about the Reality of Ancient Israel*. Grand Rapids, Mich.: William

B. Eerdmans Publishing Company, 2001.
Diamond, Jared. *Guns, Germs, and Steel: The Fates of Human Societies*. New York: W. W. Norton and Company, 1999.
Díaz del Castillo, Bernal. *The True History of the Conquest of New Spain*. Translated by Janet Burke and Ted Humphrey. Indianapolis, Ind.: Hackett Publishing, 2012.
Diehl, Richard A. *The Olmecs: America's First Civilization*. London: Thames and Hudson, 2004.
Diehl, Richard A. *Tula: The Toltec Capital of Ancient Mexico*. London: Thames and Hudson, 1983.
Diehl, Richard A., and Michael D. Coe. "Olmec Archaeology." In *The Olmec World: Ritual and Rulership*. Princeton, N.J.: The Art Museum, Princeton University, 1996, 11–25.
Diehl, Richard A., and Margaret D. Mandeville. "Tula, and Wheeled Animal Effigies in Mesoamerica." *Antiquity* 61, no. 232 (1987): 239–46.
"Discovery of Ancient Ruins in Central America." *Evening and the Morning Star* 1, no. 9 (February 1833): 71. "Mormon Publications: 19th and 20th Centuries." Harold B. Lee Library, Brigham Young University, digital collection. Photographs. http://contentdm.lib.byu.edu/cdm4/document.php?CISOROOT=/NCMP1820-1846&CISOPTR=5919 (accessed December 2012).
Dombrowski, John, Elinor C. Betters, Howard I. Blutsein, Lynne E. Cox, and Elery M. Zehner. *Area Handbook for Guatemala*. Washington, D.C.: U.S. Government Printing Office, 1970.
Drew, David. *The Lost Chronicles of the Maya Kings*. Berkeley: University of California Press, 1999.
Dundes, Alan. "The Hero Pattern and the Life of Jesus." In *In Quest of the Hero*. Introduction by Robert A. Segal. Princeton, N.J.: Princeton University Press, 1990, 179–223.
Dunn, James D. G. *Jews and Christians, the Parting of the Ways, A.D. 70–135*. Grand Rapids, Mich.: William B. Eerdmans Publishing, 1992.
Durán, Diego de. *Book of the Gods and Rites and the Ancient Calendar*. Translated and edited by Fernando Horcasitas and Doris Heyden. Norman: University of Oklahoma Press, 1971.
Durán, Diego de. *Historia de las Indias de Nueva España*. Edited by Angel Maria Garibay K. 2 vols. Mexico City: Editorial Porrúa, 1967.
Echoes and Evidences of the Book of Mormon. Edited by Donald W. Parry, Daniel C. Peterson, and John W. Welch. Provo, Utah: Foundation for Ancient Research and Mormon Studies, 2002.
Ehrlich, Carl S. "Noah." In *The Oxford Companion to the Bible*. Edited by Bruce M. Metzger and Michael D. Coogan. New York: Oxford University Press, 1993, 558.
Ehrman, Bart D. *Misquoting Jesus: The Story behind Who Changed the Bible and Why*. New York: HarperCollins, 2005.
Ehrman, Bart D. *The Orthodox Corruption of Scripture: The Effect of Early Christological Controversies on the Text of the New Testament*. New York: Oxford University Press, 1993.
Ekholm, Gordon F. "Diffusion and Archaeological Evidence." In *Man across the Sea: Problems of Pre-Columbian Contacts*. Edited by Carrol L. Riley, J. Charles Kelley, Campbell W. Pennington, and Robert L. Rands. Austin: University of Texas Press, 1971, 54–59.
Estrada-Belli, Francisco. *The First Maya Civilization: Ritual and Power before the Classic Period*. New York: Routledge, 2011.
Evans, Susan Toby. *Ancient Mexico and Central America: Archaeology and Culture History*. London: Thames and Hudson, 2004.
Farnsworth, Dewey. *The Americas before Columbus*. Salt Lake City: Deseret Book, 1956.
Fash, William L., and Barbara W. Fash. "Teotihuacan and the Maya: A Classic Heritage." In *Mesoamerica's Classic Heritage: From Teotihuacan to the Aztecs*. Edited by David Carrasco, Lindsay Jones, and Scott Sessions. Boulder: University Press of Colorado, 2000, 433–63.
Fasquelle, Ricardo Agurcia. "Rosalila: Temple of the Sun King at Copan." In *Lords of Creation*:

The Origins of Sacred Maya Kingship. Edited by Virginia M. Fields and Dorie Reents-Budet. Los Angeles: Los Angeles County Museum of Art/London: Scala Publishers, 2005, 72–73.

Faulconer, James E. *The Book of Mormon Made Harder: Scripture Study Questions*. Provo, Utah: Neal A. Maxwell Institute for Religious Scholarship, Brigham Young University, 2014.

Faulconer, James E. *Scripture Study: Tools and Suggestions*. Provo, Utah: Foundation for Ancient Research and Mormon Studies, 1999.

Ferguson, Thomas Stuart. *One Fold, One Shepherd*. Salt Lake City: Olympus Publishing, 1962.

Fernández-Armesto, Felipe. *Columbus on Himself*. New York: Hackett Publishing, 2010.

Finkelstein, Israel, and Neil Asher Silberman. *The Bible Unearthed: Archaeology's New Vision of Ancient Israel and the Origin of Its Sacred Texts*. New York: Free Press, 2001.

Flannery, Kent V. "The Early Formative Household Cluster on the Guatemalan Pacific Coast." In *The Early Mesoamerican Village*. Edited by Kent V. Flannery. New York: Academic Press, 1976, 31–34.

Flannery, Kent V. "The Early Mesoamerican House." In *The Early Mesoamerican Village*. Edited by Kent V. Flannery. New York: Academic Press, 1976, 16–24.

Florescano, Enrique. *Memory, Myth, and Time in Mexico: From the Aztecs to Independence*. Translated by Albert G. Bork with the Assistance of Kathryn R. Bork. Austin: University of Texas Press, 1994.

Foster, Lynne V. *Handbook to Life in the Ancient Maya World*. 2002; rpt. in paperback, New York: Oxford University Press, 2005.

Fought, John G. *Chorti (Mayan) Texts*. Edited by Sarah S. Fought. Philadelphia: University of Pennsylvania Press, 1972.

Fox, David S. "Nephi's Bows and Arrows." In *Reexploring the Book of Mormon*. Edited by John W. Welch. Provo, Utah: Foundation for Ancient Research and Mormon Studies, 1992, 41–42.

Freidel, David A. "Maya Warfare, Myth and Reality." 1996. http://maya.csueastbay.edu/yaxuna/warfare.html (accessed January 2014).

Freidel, David A. "Preparing the Way." In *The Olmec World: Ritual and Rulership*. Princeton, N.J.: The Art Museum, Princeton University, 1996, 3–9.

Freidel, David A., Linda Schele, and Joy Parker. *Maya Cosmos: Three Thousand Years on the Shaman's Path*. New York: William Morrow, 1993.

"From Apollo to Jesus." http://www.jesusneverexisted.com/melange.html (accessed December 2005).

Fronk, Camille. "Desert Epiphany: Sariah and the Women in 1 Nephi." *Journal of Book of Mormon Studies* 9, no. 2 (2000): 4–15.

Funk and Wagnalls Standard Dictionary of the English Language, International Edition, Combined with Britannica World Language Dictionary. 2 vols. New York: Encyclopaedia Britannica/Funk and Wagnalls Company, 1960.

Furst, Jill Leslie. *Codex Vindobonensis Mexicanus I: A Commentary*. Albany: State University of New York at Albany, Institute for Mesoamerican Studies, 1978.

Gardner, Brant A. "Behind the Mask, Behind the Curtain: Uncovering the Illusion." Review of the Joel P. Kramer and Scott R. Johnson film, *The Bible vs. the Book of Mormon*. *FARMS Review* 17, no. 2 (2005): 145–95.

Gardner, Brant A. "Crucible of Distortion: The Impact of the Spanish on Native American Oral Tradition." http://independent.academia.edu/BrantGardner/Papers/962968/Crucible_of_Distortion_The_Impact_of_the_Spanish_on_ Native_American_Oral_ Tradition (accessed September 2011).

Gardner, Brant A. "From the East to the West: The Problem of Directions in the Book of Mormon." *Interpreter: A Journal of Mormon Scripture* 3 (2013): 119–53.

Gardner, Brant A. *The Gift and Power. Translating the Book of Mormon*. Salt Lake City: Greg Kofford Books, 2011.
Gardner, Brant A. "Monotheism, Messiah, and Mormon's Book." Paper presented at the annual conference of the Foundation for Apologetic Information and Research, August 2003. http://www.fairmormon.org/perspectives/fair-conferences/2003-fair-conference/2003-monotheism-messiah-and-mormons-book (accessed May 2014).
Gardner, Brant A. "Mormon's Editorial Method and Meta-Message." *FARMS Review* 21, no. 1 (2009): 83–105.
Gardner, Brant A. "Nephi as Scribe." *FARMS Review* 23, no. 1 (2011): 45–55.
Gardner, Brant A. "Quetzalcoatl's Fathers: A Critical Examination of Source Materials." http://www.ku.edu/~hoopes/aztlan/tripart.htm (accessed September 2003).
Gardner, Brant A. "Reconstructing the Ethnohistory of Myth: A Structural Study of the Aztec 'Legend of the Suns.'" In *Symbol and Meaning beyond the Closed Community: Essays in Mesoamerican Ideas*. Edited by Gary Gossen. Albany: Institute for Mesoamerican Studies, State University of New York. Albany, 1986, 19–34.
Gardner, Brant A. *Second Witness: Analytical and Contextual Commentary on the Book of Mormon*. 6 vols. Salt Lake City: Greg Kofford Books, 2007.
Gardner, Brant A. "A Social History of the Early Nephites." http://www.fairlds.org/pubs/conf/2001GarB.html (accessed January 2005).
Gardner, Brant A. "Testing a Methodology: A Malaysian Setting for the Book of Mormon." *Interpreter Foundation Blog*. http://www.mormoninterpreter.com/ testing-a-methodology-a-malaysian-setting-for-the-book-of-mormon/ (accessed January 2014).
Gardner, Brant A. "When Hypotheses Collide: Responding to Lyon and Minson's 'When Pages Collide.'" *Interpreter: A Journal of Mormon Scripture* 5 (2013): 105–19.
Garibay K., Ángel María. *Historia de la Literatura Nahuatl*. 2 vols. Mexico City: Editorial Porrúa, S. A., 1971.
Garibay K., Ángel María, ed., *Historia de los Mexicanos por sus pinturas*. In *Teogonía e Historia de los Mexicanos*. Mexico City: Editorial Porrúa, 1973, 23–66.
Gasco, Janine, and Michael E. Smith. "Origins and Development of Mesoamerican Civilization." In *The Legacy of Mesoamerica: History and Culture of a Native American Civilization*. Edited by Robert M. Carmack, Janine Gasco, and Gary H. Gossen. Upper Saddle River, N.J.: Prentice Hall, 1996, 40–79.
Gee, John. "Abraham and Idrimi." *Journal of the Book of Mormon and Other Restoration Scripture* 22, no. 1 (2013): 35–39.
Gee, John. "Egyptian Society during the Twenty-sixth Dynasty." In *Glimpses of Lehi's Jerusalem*. Edited by John W. Welch, David Rolph Seely, and Jo Ann H. Seely. Provo, Utah: Foundation for Ancient Research and Mormon Studies, 2004, 277–98.
Gee, John. "A Tragedy of Errors." *FARMS Review* 4, no. 1 (1992): 93–119.
Gee, John. "La Trahison des Clercs: On the Language and Translation of the Book of Mormon." *FARMS Review of Books* 6, no. 1 (1994): 51–120.
Gee, John. "The Wrong Kind of Book." In *Echoes and Evidences of the Book of Mormon*. Edited by Donald W. Parry, Daniel C. Peterson, and John W. Welch. Provo, Utah: Foundation for Ancient Research and Mormon Studies, 2002, 307–29.
Gee, John, and Matthew Roper. "'I Did Liken All Scriptures unto Us': Early Nephite Understandings of Isaiah and Implications for 'Others' in the Land." In *The Fulness of the Gospel: Foundational Teachings from the Book of Mormon*. Salt Lake City: Deseret Book, 2003, 51–65.
Gee, John, Matthew Roper, and John A. Tvedtnes. "Book of Mormon Names Attested in Ancient Hebrew Inscriptions." *Journal of Book of Mormon Studies* 9, no. 1 (2000): 42–51.

[No author indicated] "Geography." In *Book of Mormon Reference Companion*. Edited by Dennis L. Largey. Salt Lake City: Deseret Book, 2003, 288–91.
Gillespie, Susan D. *The Aztec Kings: The Construction of Rulership in Mexica History*. Tucson: University of Arizona Press, 1989.
Girard, Rafael. *People of the Chan*. Translated by B. Preble. Chino Valley, Ariz.: Continuum Foundation, 1995.
Givens, Terryl L. *By the Hand of Mormon: The American Scripture that Launched a New World Religion*. New York: Oxford University Press, 2002.
Givens, Terry L. "Foreword." In John L. Sorenson, *Mormon's Codex: An Ancient American Book*. Salt Lake City: Deseret Book/Provo, Utah: Neal A. Maxwell Institute for Religious Scholarship, 2013, xiii–xvi.
Givens, Terryl L. "Joseph Smith: Prophecy, Process, and Plenitude." In *The Worlds of Joseph Smith: A Bicentennial Conference at the Library of Congress*. Edited by John W. Welch. Provo, Utah: Brigham Young University Press, 2006, 55–68.
Goble, Edwin G. *Resurrecting Cumorah*. N.p.: CreateSpace, 2011.
Goble, Edwin G., and Wayne N. May. *This Land: Zarahemla and the Nephite Nation*. Colfax, Wisc.: Ancient American Archaeology Foundation, 2002.
Godfrey, Kenneth W. "The Zelph Story." *BYU Studies* 29, no. 2 (1989): 31–56.
Golden, Charles W. "The Politics of Warfare in the Usumacinta Basin: La Pasadita and the Realm of Bird Jaguar." In *Ancient Mesoamerican Warfare*. Edited by Travis W. Stanton and M. Kathryn Brown. Walnut Creek, Calif.: Altamira Press, 2003, 31–48.
Gonzalez, Silvia, Alejandro Pastrana, Claus Siebe, and Geoff Duller. "Timing of the prehistoric eruption of Xitle Volcano and the abandonment of Cuicuilco Pyramed, Southern Basin of Mexico." *Geological Society, London, Special Publications*, Vol. 171 No. 1 (2000): 205–224.
Goodwillie, Christian. "Shaker Richard McNemar: The Earliest Book of Mormon Reviewer." *Journal of Mormon History* 37, no. 2 (Spring 2011): 138–45.
Gottwald, Norman K. "Deuteronomy." In *The Interpreter's One-Volume Commentary on the Bible*. Edited by Charles M. Laymon. Nashville, Tenn.: Abingdon Press, 1971, 100–121.
Gottwald, Norman K. *The Hebrew Bible: A Socio-Literary Introduction*. Philadelphia, Penn.: Fortress Press, 1985.
Graulich, Michel. "Aztec Human Sacrifice as Expiation." *History of Religions* 39, no. 4 (2000): 352–71.
Green, Albert R. W. *The Storm-God in the Ancient Near East*. BIBLICAL AND JUDAIC STUDIES, NO. 8. Winona Lake, Ind.: Eisenbrauns, 2008.
Green, Dee F. "Book of Mormon Archaeology: The Myths and the Alternatives." *Dialogue: a Journal of Mormon Thought* 4, no. 2 (1969): 71–80.
Grego. "Book of Mormon: Succession of Jaredite Kings in the Book of Ether." http://bookofmormonnotes.wordpress.com/tag/book-of-mormon-succession-of-jaredite-kings-in-the-book-of-ether-by-grego/ (accessed October 2012).
Griggs, C. Wilfred. "The Book of Mormon as an Ancient Book." *BYU Studies* 22, no. 3 (1982): 259–78.
Grove, David C. *Chalcatzingo: Excavations on the Olmec Frontier*. London: Thames and Hudson, 1984.
Grove, David C. *The Olmec Paintings of Oxtotitlan Cave, Guerrero, Mexico*. STUDIES IN PRE-COLUMBIAN ART AND ARCHAEOLOGY, NO. 6. Washington, DC: Dumbarton Oaks, 1970.
Grover, Jerry D. Jr. *Geology of the Book of Mormon*. No Place. Self-Published. 2014.
Guernsey, Julia. "Rulers, Gods, and Potbellies: A Consideration of Sculptural Forms and themes from the Preclassic Pacific Coast and Piedmont of Mesoamerica." In *The Place of Stone Monuments: Context, Use, and Meaning in Mesoamerica's Preclassic Transition*. Edited by Julia Guernsey, John E. Clark, and Barbara Arroyo. Washington, D.C.: Dumbarton Oaks, 2010, 207–30.

Gutjahr, Paul C. *The Book of Mormon: A Biography*. LIVES OF GREAT RELIGIOUS BOOKS. Princeton, N.J.: Princeton University Press, 2012.

Gutjahr, Paul C. "The Golden Bible in the Bible's Golden Age: The Book of Mormon and Antebellum Print Culture." *FARMS Occasional Papers*, no. 5 (2007): 33–47.

Halpern, Baruch. *The First Historians: The Hebrew Bible and History*. San Francisco: Harper and Row, 1988.

Halpern, Baruch. "Sybil, or the Two Nations? Archaism, Kinship, Alienation, and the Elite Redefinition of Traditional Culture in Judah in the 8th–7th Centuries BCE." In *The Study of the Ancient Near East in the 21st Century: The William Foxwell Albright Centennial Conference*. Edited by Jerrold S. Cooper and Glenn M. Schwartz. Winona Lake, Wisc.: Eisenbrauns, 1996, 291–338.

Hamblin, William J. "The Bow and Arrow in the Book of Mormon." In *Warfare in the Book of Mormon*. Edited by Stephen D. Ricks and William J. Hamblin. Salt Lake City: Deseret Book/Provo, Utah: Foundation for Ancient Research and Mormon Studies, 1990, 365–99.

Hamblin, William J. "Directions in Hebrew, Egyptian, and Nephite Language." In *Reexploring the Book of Mormon*. Edited by John W. Welch. Provo, Utah: Foundation for Ancient Research and Mormon Studies, 1992, 183.

Hamblin, William J. "Jaredite Civilization." In *Book of Mormon Reference Companion*. Edited by Dennis L. Largey. Salt Lake City: Deseret Book, 2003, 433–37.

Hamblin, William J. "Jeremiah, Josiah, Barker, and Me." *Mormon Scripture Explorations: Exploring the Bible, Book of Mormon, Doctrine and Covenants and the Pearl of Great Price*. Blog post November 16, 2012, http://mormonscriptureexplorations.wordpress.com/2012/11/16/jeremiah-josiah-barker-and-me/ (accessed November 2012).

Hamblin, William J. "A Stumble Forward?" Review of F. Richard Hauck, *Deciphering the Geography of the Book of Mormon: Settlements and Routes in Ancient America*. In *Review of Books on the Book of Mormon* 1 (1989): 71–77.

Hamblin, William J. "Vindicating Josiah." *Interpreter: A Journal of Mormon Scripture* 4 (2013): 165–76.

Hamblin, William J. "Warfare in the Book of Mormon." In *Rediscovering the Book of Mormon*. Edited by John L. Sorenson and Melvin J. Thorne. Provo, Utah: Foundation for Ancient Research and Mormon Studies, 1991, 241–48.

Hamblin, William J., and A. Brent Merrill. "Swords in the Book of Mormon." In *Warfare in the Book of Mormon*. Edited by Stephen D. Ricks and William J. Hamblin. Salt Lake City: Deseret Book/Provo, Utah: Foundation for Ancient Research and Mormon Studies, 1990, 329–51.

Hammond, Norman. "Inside the Black Box: Defining Maya Polity." In *Classic Maya Political History: Hieroglyphic and Archaeological Evidence: Hieroglyphic and Archaeological Evidence*. Edited by T. Patrick Culbert. Cambridge, England: Cambridge University Press, 1991, 253–84.

Hammond, Norman. "Preclassic Maya Civilization." In *New Theories of the Ancient Maya*. Edited by Elin C. Danien and Robert J. Sharer. Philadelphia: The University Museum, University of Pennsylvania, 1992, 137–44.

Hansen, Richard D. "Kingship in the Cradle of Maya Civilization: The Mirador Basin." In *Fanning the Sacred Flame: Mesoamerican Studies in Honor of H. B. Nicholson*. Edited by Matthew A. Boxt and Brian D. Dillon. MESOAMERICAN WORLDS: FROM THE OLMECS TO THE DANZANTES SERIES. General editors David Carrasco and Eduardo Matos Moctezuma. Boulder: University Press of Colorado, 2012, 139–71.

Hardy, Grant. "Introduction." *The Book of Mormon: The Earliest Text*. Edited by Royal Skousen. New Haven, Conn.: Yale University Press, 2009, vii–xxvii.

Hardy, Grant. *Understanding the Book of Mormon: A Reader's Guide*. New York: Oxford University Press, 2010.
Harrison, Roland Kenneth. *Introduction to the Old Testament*. 2 vols. Grand Rapids, Mich.: William B. Eerdmans Publishing, 1969.
Hassig, Ross. *Aztec Warfare: Imperial Expansion and Political Control*. Norman: University of Oklahoma Press, 1988.
Hassig, Ross. *War and Society in Ancient Mesoamerica*. Berkeley, Calif.: University of Californian Press, 1992.
Hauck, F. Richard. *Deciphering the Geography of the Book of Mormon: Settlements and Routes in Ancient America*. Salt Lake City: Deseret Book, 1988.
Head, Ronan James. "In the Nephite Courtroom." Review of John W. Welch, *The Legal Cases of the Book of Mormon*. In *Dialogue: A Journal of Mormon Thought*, 42, no. 3 (Fall 2009): 183–88.
Heimerdinger, Chris. "A Lost Generation of Scholarship." *Book of Mormon Archaeological Forum*. http://www.bmaf.org/node/230 (accessed December 2010).
Henderson, John S. *The World of the Ancient Maya*. 2d ed. Ithaca, N.Y.: Cornell University Press, 1997.
Henline, Timothy W. *Absolute Proof that the Book of Mormon Is Fake*. Rock Cave, W.Va.: Fern Mountain Publishing, 2006.
Hess, Richard S. *Israelite Religions: An Archaeological and Biblical Survey*. Grand Rapids, Mich.: Baker Academic, 2007.
Hickman, Josiah E. *The Romance of the Book of Mormon*. Salt Lake City: Deseret News Press, 1937.
Hill, Jane H., "The Flower World of Old Uto-Aztecan." *Journal of Anthropological Research* 48, no. 2 (1992): 117–44.
Hilton, John L., and Janet F. Hilton. "A Correlation of the Sidon River and the Lands of Manti and Zarahemla with the Southern End of Rio Grijalva (San Miguel)." *Journal of Book of Mormon Studies* 1, no. 1 (1992): 142–62.
Hilton, Lynn M., and Hope A. Hilton, *Discovering Lehi: New Evidence of Lehi and Nephi in Arabia*. Springville, Utah: Cedar Fort, 1996.
Hilton, Lynn M., and Hope A. Hilton. "In Search of Lehi's Trail—Part 1: The Preparation." *Ensign*, September 1976, 32–54.
Hilton, Lynn M., and Hope A. Hilton. "In Search of Lehi's Trail—Part 2: The Journey." *Ensign*, October 1976, 34–63.
Hirst, K. Kris. "How Were the Americas Populated? Kennewick Man, Part 4." *About.com: Archaeology*, http://archaeology.about.com/od/ kennewickman/a /kennewick4.htm (accessed January 2008).
"Histoyre du Méchique." Titled in translation: *Historia de México*, in *Teogonía e Historia de los Mexicanos*. Edited and translated by Ángel María Garibay K. Mexico City: Editorial Porrúa, 1973, 91–152.
Hobbins, John F. "A Contrastive Approach to the Study of Ancient Texts." *Ancient Hebrew Poetry*, http://ancienthebrewpoetry.typepad.com/ancient_hebrew_ poetry/parallelomania/ (accessed December 2012).
Holmes, William Henry. *Handbook of Aboriginal American Antiquities*. SMITHSONIAN INSTITUTION BUREAU OF AMERICAN ETHNOLOGY BULLETIN, NO. 60. Part I: Introductory. Lithic Industries. Washington, D.C.: Government Printing Office, 1919.
Hopkins, Nicholas A., and J. Kathryn Josserand, "Directions and Partitions in Maya World View." *Foundation for the Advancement of Mesoamerican Studies, Inc.* 2011. http://www.famsi.org/research/hopkins/DirectionalPartitions.pdf (accessed April 2011). This paper is an expansion of a paper presented March 24, 2001 at the symposium "Four Corners

of the Maya World," 19th Maya Weekend, University Museum, University of Pennsylvania.
Horn, Siegfried H. "The Divided Monarchy: The Kingdoms of Judah and Israel." In *Ancient Israel*. Edited by Hershel Shanks. Washington, D.C.: Biblical Archaeology Society, 1998, 109–49.
Hoskisson, Paul Y. "Introduction." In *Historicity and the Latter-Day Saint Scriptures*. Edited by Paul Y. Hoskisson. Salt Lake City, Utah: BYU Religious Studies Center, 2001, vii–ix.
Hoskisson, Paul Y. "Lehi and Sariah." *Journal of Book of Mormon Studies* 9, no. 1 (2000): 30–34.
Houston, Stephen D., and David Stuart. "Of Gods, Glyphs, and Kings: Divinity and Rulership among the Classic Maya." *Antiquity* 70 (1996): 289–312.
Houston, Stephen D., David Stuart, and Karl Taube. *The Memory of Bones: Body, Being, and Experience among the Classic Maya*. Austin: University of Texas Press, 2006.
Hughes, Bettany. *Helen of Troy: Goddess, Princess, Whore*. New York: Alfred A. Knopf, 2005.
Hull, Kerry M. *Verbal Art and Performance in Ch'orti' and Maya Hieroglyphic Writing*. Ph.D. diss., of Texas at Austin, 2003.
Hunt, Wallace E., Jr. "Notes and Communications: The Marketplace." *Journal of Book of Mormon Studies* 4, no. 2 (Fall 1995): 138–41.
Hunter, Milton R. *Archaeology and the Book of Mormon*. Salt Lake City: Deseret Book, 1956.
Hunter, Milton R. *Christ in Ancient America. Archaeology and the Book of Mormon, Vol. 2*. Salt Lake City: Deseret Book, 1959.
Hunter, Milton R., and Thomas Stuart Ferguson. *Ancient America and the Book of Mormon*. Oakland, Calif.: Kolob Book Company, 1950.
Hutchinson, Anthony A. "The Word of God Is Enough: The Book of Mormon as Nineteenth-Century Scripture." In *New Approaches to the Book of Mormon: Explorations in Critical Methodology*. Edited by Brent Lee Metcalfe. Salt Lake City: Signature Books, 1993, 1–19.
Hyman, David S. *A Study of the Calcareous Cements in Prehispanic Mesoamerican Building Construction*. Baltimore, Md.: Johns Hopkins University Press, 1970.
Ivins, Antony W. *Conference Report*, April 4, 1909, 57–62. GospeLink Online (accessed January 2011).
Ivins, Anthony W. *Conference Report*. October 7, 1923, 139–47. GospeLink Online (accessed January 2011).
Ivins, Anthony W. *Conference Report*. April 5, 1929, 15–16. *GospeLink 2001*, CD-ROM. Salt Lake City: Deseret Book, 2000.
Ixtlilxochitl, Fernando de Alva. *Obras Históricas*. 2 vols. Edited by Alfredo Chavero. Mexico City: Editora Nacional, 1952.
Jakeman, M. Wells. *The Complex "Tree of Life" Carving on Izapa Stela 5: A Reanalysis and Partial Interpretation*. Provo, Utah: Brigham Young University, 1958.
Jakeman, M. Wells. *Stela 5, Izapa, Chiapas, Mexico: A Major Archaeological Discovery of the New World. Detailed Commentary on the Carving*. UNIVERSITY ARCHAEOLOGICAL SOCIETY SPECIAL PUBLICATIONS, NO. 2. Provo, Utah: Brigham Young University, 1958.
The Journal of Christopher Columbus and Documents Relating to the Voyages of John Cabot and Gaspar Corte Real. Translated by Clements R. Markham. London: Printed for the Hakluyt Society, 1893.
Johnson, Chris, and Duane Johnson. "How the Book of Mormon Destroyed Mormonism." http://buggingmos.wordpress.com/2013/10/25/chris-johnson-how-the-book-of-mormon-destroyed-mormonism (accessed November 2013).
Johnson, Clark V. "Prophetic Decree and Ancient Histories Tell the Story of America." In *The Book of Mormon: Jacob Through Words of Mormon, To Learn with Joy*. Edited by Monte S. Nyman and Charles D. Tate Jr. Provo, Utah: BYU Religious Studies Center, 1990, 125–39.
Johnson, Daniel. "Hard Evidence of Horses in America." Paper presented at the Book of

Mormon Archaeological Forum conference, October 2012. Video accessed December 2012, http://www.youtube.com/watch?v=6cHUxwDCq3g.
Johnson, David J. "Archaeology." In *Encyclopedia of Mormonism*. Edited by Daniel H. Ludlow. 4 vols. New York: Macmillan Publishing, 1992, 1:62–63.
Jordan, Benjamin R. "'Many Great and Notable Cities Were Sunk': Liquefaction in the Book of Mormon." *Dialogue: A Journal of Mormon Thought* 38, no. 3 (Fall 1999): 119–22.
Justeson, John, and Terrence Kaufman. "Un desciframiento de la escritura jeroglífica epi-olmeca: métodos y resultados." *Archaeología*, July–December 1992, 15–25.
Kammeyer, John E. *The Nephite Art of War.* PDF. Smashword e-book electronic edition, 2012. PDF in my possession.
Kaufman, Terrence. "The History of the Nawa Language Group from the Earliest Times to the Sixteenth Century: Some Initial Results." Revised March 2001. http://www.albany.edu/anthro/maldp/Nawa.pdf (accessed April 2007).
Key, Thomas. *A Biologist Looks at the Book of Mormon.* Issaquah, Wash.: Saints Alive in Jesus, 1985, 1–2.
Killebrew, Ann E. *Biblical Peoples and Ethnicity: An Archaeological Study of Egyptians, Canaanites, Philistines, and Early Israel, 1300–1100 b.c.e.* SOCIETY OF BIBLICAL LITERATURE ARCHAEOLOGY AND BIBLICAL STUDIES, NO. 9. Edited by Andrew G. Vaughn. Atlanta: Society of Biblical Literature, 2005.
Kelley, David H. "Diffusion: Evidence and Process." In *Man across the Sea: Problems of Pre-Columbian Contacts.* Edited by Carrol L. Riley, J. Charles Kelley, Campbell W. Pennington, and Robert L. Rands. Austin: University of Texas Press, 1971, 60–65.
Kerr, Justin. "Maya Vase Data Base: A Precolumbian Portfolio." http://www.mayavase.com/ (accessed December 2012).
Kimball, Stanley B. "The Anthon Transcript: People, Primary Sources, and Problems." *BYU Studies* 10, no. 3 (Spring 1970): 325–52.
Kirkham, Francis W. *A New Witness for Christ in America: The Book of Mormon.* Independence, Mo.: Zion's Printing and Publishing Co., 1942; enl. 2d ed., 1947.
Kitahara, Michio. "A Formal Model of Syncretism in Scales." *1970 Yearbook of the International Folk Music Council.* N.p.: International Council for Traditional Music, 1970, 121–26.
Kitchen, Kenneth A. *On the Reliability of the Old Testament.* Grand Rapids, Mich.: William B. Eerdmans Publishing, Company, 2003.
Klokoèník, Jaroslav, Jan Kostelecký, and František Vítek. *On an Unresolved Orientation of Pyramids and Ceremonial Centers in Mesoamerica.* N.p., n.d. Downloaded April 2013 from www.asu.cas.cz/~jklokocn/studia06a1.doc. Print version published as Klokoèník, Jaroslav, Jan Kostelecký, and František Vítek. "Pyramids and Ceremonial Centers in Mesoamerica: Were They Oriented Using a Magnetic Compass?" *Studia Geophysica et Geodaetica* 41, no. 4 (October 2007): 515–33.
Kowallis, Bart J. "In the Thirty and Fourth Year: A Geologist's View of the Great Destruction in 3 Nephi." *BYU Studies* 37, no. 3 (1997–98): 137–90.
Kowalski, Jeff K. "Temple Complexes." In *Oxford Encyclopedia of Mesoamerican Cultures.* Edited by David Carrasco. New York: Oxford University Press, 2001, 76–109.
Kuhn, Thomas S. *The Structure of Scientific Revolutions*, 3rd ed. Chicago: University of Chicago Press, 1996.
Lafaye, Jacques. *Quetzalcoatl and Guadalupe: The Formation of Mexican National Consciousness, 1531–1815.* Translated by Benjamin Keen. Chicago: Chicago University Press, 1974.
Lamb, Martin Thomas. *The Golden Bible; or The Book of Mormon. Is It from God?* New York: Ward and Drummond, 1887.

Lancaster, James E. "The Translation of the Book of Mormon." In *The Word of God: Essays on Mormon Scripture*. Edited by Dan Vogel. Salt Lake City: Signature Books, 1990, 97–112.

Larsen, Val. "Killing Laban: The Birth of Sovereignty in the Nephite Constitutional Order." *Journal of Book of Mormon Studies* 16, no. 1 (2007): 26–41.

Larson, Stan. *Quest for the Gold Plates: Thomas Stuart Ferguson's Archaeological Search for the Book of Mormon*. Salt Lake City: Freethinker Press in association with Smith Research Associates, 1996.

Las Casas, Bartólome de. *Apologética Historia Sumaria*. Edited by Edmundo O'Gorman. 2 vols. Mexico City: Universidad Nacional Autónoma de México, 1967.

Le Poidevin, Cecil G. *Zion, Land of Promise. An Atlas Study of Book of Mormon Geography*. N.p., n.pub., 1977.

Lee, Thomas A., Jr. *Mound 4 Excavations at San Isidro, Chiapas, Mexico*. PAPERS OF THE NEW WORLD ARCHAEOLOGICAL FOUNDATION, NO. 34. Provo, Utah: New World Archaeological Foundation, 1974.

"Legend of the Suns." *History and Mythology of the Aztecs: The Codex Chimalpopoca*. Translated by John Bierhorst. Tucson: University of Arizona Press, 1992, 139–62.

Levine, Baruch A. "The Clan-Based Economy of Biblical Israel." In *Symbiosis, Symbolism, and the Power of the Past: Canaan, Ancient Israel and Their Neighbors from the Late Bronze Age through Roman Palaestina*. Proceedings of the Centennial Symposium W. F. Albright Institute of Archaeological Research and American Schools of Oriental Research, Jerusalem, May 29–31, 2000. Edited by William G. Dever and Seymour Gitin. Winona Lake, Ind.: Eisenbrauns, 2003, 445–53.

Levine, Lee I. "Archaeology and the Religious Ethos of Pre-70 Palestine." In *Hillel and Jesus: Comparisons of Two Major Religious Leaders*. Edited by James H. Charlesworth and Loren L. Johns. Minneapolis: Fortress Press, 1997, 110–19.

Lindsay, Jeff. "Was the Book of Mormon Plagiarized from Walt Whitman's *Leaves of Grass*?" http://www.jefflindsay.com/bomsource.shtml (accessed December 2012).

Livingston, Tyler. "Book of Mormon Geography in Joseph's Day." *FAIR Blog* April 2, 2010. http://www.fairblog.org/2010/04/02/book-of-mormon-geography-in-joseph-smiths-day/ (accessed April 2011).

López Austín, Alfredo. *Hombre Diós. Religión y Política en el Mundo Nahuatl*. Mexico City: Universidad Nacional Autónima de México, 1972.

López Austín, Alfredo, Leonardo López Luján, and Saburo Sugiyama. "The Temple of Quetzalcoatl at Teotihuacan: Its Possible Ideological Significance." *Ancient Mesoamerica* 2, no. 1 (1991): 93–105.

Loughlin, Michael L. "Recorrido Archaeológico El Mesón." Foundation for the Advancement of Mesoamerican Studies, http://www.famsi.org/reports/ 02058/index.html (accessed May 2007).

Lowe, Gareth W. "Brief Archaeological History of the Southwest Quadrant." In *Excavations at Chiapa de Corzo, Chiapas, Mexico*. PAPERS OF THE NEW WORLD ARCHAEOLOGICAL FOUNDATION, NO. 8 (in a compilation of numbers 8–11). Provo, Utah: New World Archaeological Foundation, Brigham Young University, 1960, 7–12.

Lowe, Gareth W., Pierre Agrinier, J. Alden Mason, Frederick Hicks, Charles E. Rozaire. *Excavations at Chiapa de Corzo, Chiapas, Mexico*. PAPERS OF THE NEW WORLD ARCHAEOLOGICAL FOUNDATION, NOS. 8–11. Provo, Utah: New World Archaeological Foundation, 1967.

Ludlow, Daniel H. *A Companion to Your Study of the Book of Mormon*. Salt Lake City: Deseret Book, 1976.

Ludlow, Jared W. "A Tale of Three Communities: Jerusalem, Elephantine, and Lehi-Nephi." *Journal of Book of Mormon Studies* 16, no. 2 (2007): 29–41.
Lund, John L. *Joseph Smith and the Geography of the Book of Mormon*. Salt Lake City: Communications Company, 2012.
Lund, John L. *Mesoamerican and the Book of Mormon: Is This the Place?* Orem, Utah: Granite, 2007.
Lyon, Jack M., and Kent R. Minson. "When Pages Collide: Dissecting the Words of Mormon." *BYU Studies* 51, no. 4 (2012): 121–36.
MacKay, Michael Hubbard, and Gerrit J. Dirkmaat. *From Darkness unto Light: Joseph Smith's Translation and Publication of the Book of Mormon*. Provo, Utah: BYU Religious Studies Center/Salt Lake City: Deseret Book, 2015.
MacMullen, Ramsay. *Christianizing the Roman Empire, A.D. 100–400*. New Haven, Conn.: Yale University Press, 1984.
MacMullen, Ramsay. *Voting about God in Early Church Councils*. New Haven, Conn.: Yale University Press, 2006.
Madsen, Brigham D. "Reflections on LDS Disbelief in the Book of Mormon as History." *Dialogue: A Journal of Mormon Thought* 30, no. 3 (Fall 1997): 87–97.
Magleby, Kirk. "Book of Mormon Model." *Book of Mormon Resources*. July 28, 2012, Updated October 2, 2013. http://bookofmormonresources.blogspot.com/2012/07/book-of-mormon-model.html (accessed December 2014).
Malina, Bruce J. *The New Testament World: Insights from Cultural Anthropology*. Atlanta: John Knox Press, 1981.
Malina, Bruce J., and Jerome H. Neyrey. *Portraits of Paul: An Archaeology of Ancient Personality*. Louisville, Ky.: Westminster/John Knox Press, 1996.
Malina, Bruce J., and Richard L. Rohrbaugh. *Social-Science Commentary on the Gospel of John*. Minneapolis: Fortune Press, 1998.
Malina, Bruce J., and Richard L. Rohrbaugh. *Social-Science Commentary on the Synoptic Gospels*. Minneapolis, Minn.: Fortress Press, 1998.
Mangum, Garth L. "The Economics of the Book of Mormon: Joseph Smith as Translator or Commentator." *Journal of Book of Mormon Studies* 2, no. 2 (Fall 1993):78–89.
Marcus, Joyce. "The Size of the Early Mesoamerican Village." In *The Early Mesoamerican Village*. Edited by Kent V. Flannery. New York: Academic Press, 1976, 79–89.
Markman, Roberta H., and Peter T. Markman, *The Flayed God: The Mesoamerican Mythological Tradition, Sacred Texts and Images from Pre-Colombian Mexico and Central America*. San Francisco: HarperSanFrancisco, 1992.
Martin, Simon, and Nikolai Grube. *Chronicle of the Maya Kings and Queens*. London: Thames and Hudson, 2000.
Mason, J. Alden. "Mound 12, Chiapa de Corzo, Chiapas, Mexico." In *Excavations at Chiapa de Corzo, Chiapas, Mexico*, PAPERS OF THE NEW WORLD ARCHAEOLOGICAL FOUNDATION, NO. 9, IN NOS. 8–11. Provo, Utah: New World Archaeological Foundation, 1967.
Matheny, Deanne G. "Does the Shoe Fit? A Critique of the Limited Tehuantepec Geography." In *New Approaches to the Book of Mormon: Explorations in Critical Methodology*. Edited by Brent Lee Metcalfe. Salt Lake City: Signature Books, 1993, 269–328.
Mauss, Armand L. *All Abraham's Children: Changing Mormon Conceptions of Race and Lineage*. Urbana: University of Illinois Press, 2003.
Maxwell, Neal A. "All Hell is Moved." Speech given at BYU Devotional, November 8, 1977. http://speeches.byu.edu/?act=viewitem&id=1050 (accessed September 2013).
Maxwell, Neal A. *Deposition of a Disciple*. Salt Lake City: Deseret Book, 1976.
"Maya Trade and Economy." *Authentic Maya*. http://www.authenticmaya.com/maya_trade

_and_economy.htm (accessed December 2012).

Mayor, Adrienne. *Fossil Legends of the First Americans*. Princeton, N.J.: Princeton University Press, 2005.

Mazar, Amihai. "Remarks on Biblical Traditions and Archaeological Evidence Concerning Early Israel." In *Symbiosis, Symbolism, and the Power of the Past: Canaan, Ancient Israel, and Their Neighbors from the Late Bronze Age through Roman Palaestina*. Edited by William G. Dever and Seymour Gitin. Winona Lake, Ind.: Eisenbrauns, 2003, 85–98.

McCafferty, Geoffrey G. "Ethnic Conflict in Postclassic Cholula, Mexico." In *Ancient Mesoamerican Warfare*. Edited by Travis W. Stanton and M. Kathryn Brown. Walnut Creek, Calif.: Altamira Press, 2003, 219–44.

McConkie, Bruce R. *Mormon Doctrine*, 2d ed. Salt Lake City: Bookcraft, 1966.

McConkie, Joseph Fielding, and Robert L. Millet. *Doctrinal Commentary on the Book of Mormon*. 4 vols. Salt Lake City: Bookcraft, 1987–92.

McGuire, Benjamin L. "Finding Parallels: Some Cautions and Criticisms, Part 1." *Interpreter: A Journal of Mormon Scripture* 5 (2013): 2–59.

McGuire, Benjamin L. "Finding Parallels: Some Cautions and Criticisms, Part 2." *Interpreter: A Journal of Mormon Scripture* 5 (2013): 62–104.

McGuire, Benjamin L. "Josiah's Reform: An Introduction." *Interpreter: A Journal of Mormon Scripture* 4 (2013): 161–63.

McGuire, Benjamin L. "The Late War against the Book of Mormon." *Interpreter: A Journal of Mormon Scripture* 7 (2013): 323–55.

McGuire, Benjamin L. "Nephi and Goliath: A Case Study of Literary Allusion in the Book of Mormon." *Journal of the Book of Mormon and Other Restoration Scripture* 18, no. 1 (2009): 16–31.

McKeever, Bill, and Eric Johnson. "Are Ancient Coins Mentioned in the Book of Mormon?" *Mormonism Research Ministry*. http://www.mrm.org/coins (accessed October 2013).

McKillop, Heather. *The Ancient Maya: New Perspectives*. New York: W. W. Norton and Company, 2004.

McLellin, William E. *The Journals of William E. McLellin: 1831–1836*. Edited by Jan Shipps and John W. Welch. Urbana: University of Illinois Press/Provo, Utah: BYU Studies, 1994.

McMurrin, Sterling. "Brigham H. Roberts: A Biographical Essay." In Brigham H. Roberts, ed. *Studies of the Book of Mormon*. Urbana: University of Chicago Press, 1985, xiii–xxxi.

Meldrum, Rodney L. *Rediscovering the Book of Mormon Remnant through DNA*. Mendon, N.Y.: Digital Legend, 2009.

Melville, J. Keith. "Joseph Smith, the Constitution, and Individual Liberties." *BYU Studies* 28, no. 2 (Spring 1988): 65–74.

Mendieta, Gerónimo de. *Historia Eclesiástica Indiana*. 4 vols. Mexico City: Editorial Sálvador Chávez Hayhoe, 1945.

Mendoza, Ruben G. Email to the Aztlan mailing list, April 17, 2005, file copy in my possession.

"Meoweather: Weather History of Medinah, Al Madinah, Saudi Arabia." http://www.meoweather.com/history/Saudi%20Arabia/na/24.4686111/39.6141667/Medina.html (accessed February 2012).

Merrill, A. Brent. "Nephite Captains and Armies." In *Warfare in the Book of Mormon*. Edited by Stephen D. Ricks and William J. Hamblin. Salt Lake City: Deseret Book/Provo, Utah: Foundation for Ancient Research and Mormon Studies, 1990, 266–95.

Merrill, Byron R. "Government by the Voice of the People: A Witness and a Warning." In *The Book of Mormon: Mosiah: Salvation Only through Christ*. Edited by Monte S. Nyman and Charles D. Tate Jr. Provo, Utah: BYU Religious Studies Center, 1991, 113–37.

"Mesoamerican Relic Provides New Clues to Mysterious Ancient Writing System." Press release,

Brigham Young University. http://byunews.byu.edu/release.aspx?story=archive04/Jan/Isthmian (accessed November 2006).

Metcalfe, Brent Lee. "Reinventing Lamanite Identity." *Sunstone*, 131 (March 2004): 20–25.

Milbrath, Susan. *Star Gods of the Maya: Astronomy in Art, Folklore, and Calendars*. Austin: University of Texas Press, 1999.

Miller, Adam S. "An Experiment on the Word. Introduction." In *An Experiment on the Word: Reading Alma 32*. Edited by Adam S. Miller. Salem, Ore.: Salt Press, 2011, 1–8.

Miller, Madeleine S., and J. Lane Miller. *Harper's Encyclopedia of Bible Life*. Revised and updated by Boyce M. Bennett Jr. and David H. Scott. Edison, N.J.: Castle Books, 1996.

Miller, Mary, and Karl Taube. *An Illustrated Dictionary of the Gods and Symbols of Ancient Mexico and the Maya*. London: Thames and Hudson, 1993.

Miller, Wade E. *Science and the Book of Mormon: Cureloms, Cumoms, Horses and More*. Laguna Niguel, Calif.: KCT and Associates, 2009.

Miller, Wade E., and Matthew Roper. "Animals in the Book of Mormon: Challenges and Perspectives." *Interpreter: A Journal of Mormon Scripture*. Blog post. April 21, 2014. http://www.mormoninterpreter.com/animals-in-the-book-of-mormon-challenges-and-perspectives/ (accessed April 2014).

Millon, René. "The Place Where Time Began: An Archaeologist's Interpretation of What Happened in Teotihuacán History." In *Teotihuacán: City of the Gods*. Edited By Kathleen Berrin and Esther Pasztory. London: Thames and Hudson, 1993, 17–43.

Mock, Shirley Boteler. "Prelude." In *The Sowing and the Dawning: Termination, Dedication, and Transformation in the Archaeological and Ethnographic Record of Mesoamerica*. Edited by Shirley Boteler Mock. Albuquerque: University of New Mexico Press, 1998, 3–18.

Molina, Fray Alonso de. *Vocabulario en lengua Castellana y Mexicana y Mexicana y Castellana*. Mexico City: Editorial Porrúa, S.A., 1970.

Morell, Virginia. "Genes May Link Ancient Eurasians, Native Americans." *Science* 280, no. 5363 (April 1988): 520.

Morgan, Dale. *Dale Morgan on Early Mormonism: Correspondence and a New History*. Edited by John Phillip Walker. Salt Lake City, Utah: Signature Books, 1986. Online text. http://signaturebookslibrary.org/the-book-of-mormon-07/ (accessed July 2008).

Morley, Sylvanus G. *The Ancient Maya*. Stanford, Calif.: Stanford University Press, 1956.

Muñoz Camargo, Diego. *Historia de Tlaxcala*. Mexico City: Atenéo Nacional de Ciencias y Artes, 1947.

Murphy, Thomas W. "Lamanite Genesis, Genealogy, and Genetics." In *American Apocrypha: Essays on the Book of Mormon*. Edited by Dan Vogel and Brent Lee Metcalfe. Salt Lake City: Signature Books, 2002, 47–77.

"Native American Populations Descend from Three Key Migrations, Scientists Say." *ScienceDaily*, July 11, 2011. http://www.sciencedaily.com/releases/2012/07/120711134710.htm (accessed July 2012).

Nibley, Hugh. *An Approach to the Book of Mormon*. Salt Lake City: Church of Jesus Christ of Latter-day Saints, 1957.

Nibley, Hugh. *Lehi in the Desert and The World of the Jaredites*. Salt Lake City: Bookcraft, 1952.

Nibley, Hugh. *The Prophetic Book of Mormon*. THE COLLECTED WORKS OF HUGH NIBLEY, VOL. 8. Salt Lake City/Deseret Book and Provo, Utah: Foundation for Ancient Research and Mormon Studies, 1989.

Nibley, Hugh. *Teachings of the Book of Mormon—Semester 1: Transcripts of Lectures Presented to an Honors Book of Mormon Class at Brigham Young University, 1988–1990*. Provo, Utah: Foundation for Ancient Research and Mormon Studies, 1993.

Nicholson, Henry B. *Topiltzin Quetzalcoatl: The Once and Future Lord of the Toltecs*. Boulder: University Press of Colorado, 2001.
"Nineteenth Century: Statements during Joseph Smith's lifetime: Part I-1829–1840." http://en.fairmormon.org/Book_of_Mormon/Geography/Statements/Nineteenth_century/Joseph_Smith%27s_lifetime (accessed April 2011).
Norman, V. Garth. *Book of Mormon Geography—Mesoamerican Historic Geography*. American Fork, Utah: ARCON/Ancient America Foundation, 2006.
Norman, V. Garth. "The Definitive Mesoamerican Book of Mormon Lands Map." http://www.ancientamerica.org/library/media/HTML/7hvlmli5/book%20of%20mormon%20map.htm (accessed April 2011).
Norman, V. Garth. *Izapa Sculpture. Part 1: Plates*. PAPERS OF THE NEW WORLD ARCHAEOLOGICAL FOUNDATION, NO. 30. Provo, Utah: New World Archaeological Foundation, Brigham Young University, 1976.
Norman, V. Garth. "Stela 5." In *Book of Mormon Reference Companion*. General editor Dennis L. Largey. Salt Lake City: Deseret Book, 2003, 740–44.
North Dakota and Oregon Space Grant Consortia. "VolcanoWorld: Paricutin, Mexico." http://volcano.und.nodak.edu/vwdocs/volc_images/img_paricutin. html (accessed November 2005).
Norwood, L. Ara. "Ignoratio Elenchi: The Dialogue that Never Was: Review of James R. White, *Letters to a Mormon Elder*." *FARMS Review of Books on the Book of Mormon* 5, no. 1 (1993): 317–54.
Nuttall, Zelia, ed. *Codex Nuttall*. New York: Dover Publications, 1975.
Nyman, Monte S. *The Record of Alma: A Teaching Commentary on the Book of Alma—Book of Mormon Commentary*. Orem, Utah: Granite Publishing, 2004.
Olive, Phyllis. "The Book of Mormon Lands of Western New York." http://www.bookofmormonlands.com/ link%20sixteen.htm (accessed December 2010).
Olive, Phyllis Carol. *The Lost Tribes of the Book of Mormon*. Springville, Utah: Bonneville Books, 2001.
Olsen, Ralph A. "A Malay Site for Book of Mormon Events." *Sunstone*, Issue 131 (March 2004): 30–34.
Olsen, Ralph A. *The Malay Peninsula as the Setting for the Book of Mormon*. N.p.: n.pub., 1997.
Ostler, Blake T. "An Interview with Sterling M. McMurrin." *Dialogue: A Journal of Mormon Thought* 17, no. 1 (Spring 1984): 18–43.
Palmer, David A. *In Search of Cumorah: New Evidences for the Book of Mormon from Ancient Mexico*. Bountiful, Utah: Horizon Publishers, 1981.
Parrish, Alan K. "Stela 5, Izapa: A Layman's Consideration of the Tree of Life Stone." In *First Nephi: The Doctrinal Foundation*. Edited by Monte S. Nyman and Charles D. Tate Jr. Provo, Utah: BYU Religious Studies Center, 1988, 125–50.
Parry, Donald W., Daniel C. Peterson, and John W. Welch, eds. *Echoes and Evidences of the Book of Mormon*. Provo, Utah: Foundation for Ancient Research and Mormon Studies, 2002.
Pasztory, Esther. *Teotihuacan: An Experiment in Living*. Norman: University of Oklahoma Press, 1997.
Parpola, Simo. "Assyria's Expansion in the 8th and 7th Centuries and Its Long-Term Repercussions in the West." In *Symbiosis, Symbolism, and the Power of the Past: Canaan, Ancient Israel and Their Neighbors from the Late Bronze Age Through Roman Palaestina, Proceedings of the Centennial Symposium W. F. Albright Institute of Archaeological Research and American Schools of Oriental Research, Jerusalem, May 29–31, 2000*. Edited by William G. Dever and Seymour Gitin. Winona Lake, Ind.: Eisenbrauns, 2003, 99–111
Patai, Raphael. *The Hebrew Goddess*. Detroit: Wayne State University Press, 1990.

Pearson, Bruce L. *Introduction to Linguistic Concepts*. New York: Alfred A. Knopf, 1977.
Pendergast, David M. "Intercessions with the Gods: Caches and Their Significance at Altun Ha and Lamanai, Belize." In *The Sowing and the Dawning: Termination, Dedication, and Transformation in the Archaeological and Ethnographic Record of Mesoamerica*. Edited by Shirley Boteler Mock. Albuquerque: University of New Mexico Press, 1998, 55–63.
Perego, Ugo A. "The Book of Mormon and the Origin of Native Americans from a Maternally Inherited DNA Standpoint." In *No Weapon Shall Prosper: New Light on Sensitive Issues*. Edited by Robert L. Millet. Provo, Utah: BYU Religious Studies Center, 2011, 190–239.
Peterson, Boyd Jay. *Hugh Nibley: A Consecrated Life*. Salt Lake City: Greg Kofford Books, 2002.
Peterson, Daniel C. "Advancing Book of Mormon Scholarship." *MormonTimes*. May 19, 2011. http://www.mormontimes.com/article/20895/Advancing-Book-of-Mormon-research (accessed June 2011).
Peterson, Daniel C. "Apostasy." In *The Book of Mormon Reference Companion*. Edited by Dennis L. Largey. Salt Lake City: Deseret Book, 2003, 69–70.
Peterson, Daniel C. "Book of Mormon Economy and Technology." In *Encyclopedia of Mormonism*. Edited by Daniel H. Ludlow. 4 vols. New York: Macmillan Publishing, 1992, 172–75.
Peterson, Daniel C. "Chattanooga Cheapshot, or The Gall of Bitterness." *FARMS Review* 5, no. 1 (1993): 1–86.
Peterson, Daniel C. "'In the Hope That Something Will Stick': Changing Explanations for the Book of Mormon." *FARMS Review* 16, no. 2.
Peterson, Daniel C. "Introduction." *Review of Books on the Book of Mormon*. 1, no. 1 (1989): v–x.
Peterson, Daniel C. "Nephi and His Asherah." *Mormons, Scripture, and the Ancient World: Studies in Honor of John L. Sorenson*. Edited by Davis Bitton. Provo, Utah: Foundation for Ancient Research and Mormon Studies, 1998, 191–243.
Peterson, Daniel C. "On the New World Archaeological Foundation." *FARMS Review* 16, no. 1 (2004): 221–34.
Peterson, Daniel C. "The Protean Joseph Smith." Paper presented at the annual conference of the Foundation for Apologetic Information and Research, August 2002. http://www.fairmormon.org/perspectives/fair-conferences/2002-fair-conference/2002-the-protean-joseph-smith (accessed April 2014).
Peterson, Daniel C., and Matthew Roper. "Ein Heldenleben? On Thomas Stuart Ferguson as an Elias for Cultural Mormons." *FARMS Review* 16, no. 1 (2004): 175–219.
Peterson, H. Donl. "Father Lehi." In *The Book of Mormon: First Nephi, the Doctrinal Foundation*. Edited by Monte S. Nyman and Charles D. Tate Jr. Provo, Utah: BYU Religious Studies Center, 1988, 55–66.
Peterson, H. Donl. *Moroni: Ancient Prophet, Modern Messenger*. Salt Lake City, Deseret Book, 2000.
Pharo, Lars Kirkhusmo. "The Concept of 'Religion' in Mesoamerican Languages." *Numen* 54, no. 1 (2007): 28–70.
Phillips, William Revell. "Mughsayl. Another Candidate for Land Bountiful." *Journal of Book of Mormon Studies* 16, no. 2 (2007): 48–59.
Phillips, William Revell. "Metals of the Book of Mormon." *Journal of Book of Mormon Studies* 9, no. 2 (2000): 36–43.
Pike, Dana M. "Israelite Inscriptions from the Time of Jeremiah and Lehi." In *Glimpses of Lehi's Jerusalem*. Edited by John W. Welch, David Rolph Seely, and Jo Ann H. Seely. Provo, Utah: Foundation for Ancient Research and Mormon Studies, 2004, 193–244.
Piña Chan, Roman, and Carlos Navarrete. *Archaeological Research in the Lower Grijalva River Region, Tabasco and Chiapas*. PAPERS OF THE NEW WORLD ARCHAEOLOGICAL FOUNDATION, NO. 22. Provo, Utah: New World Archaeological Foundation, 1967, 44–51.

Pinker, Steven. *Learnability and Cognition: The Acquisition of Argument Structure*. Cambridge, Mass.: MIT Press, 1989.

Pinker, Steven. *The Stuff of Thought: Language as a Window into Human Nature*. New York: Viking, 2007.

Pires-Ferreira, Jane W. "Obsidian Exchange in Formative Mesoamerica." In *The Early American Village*. Edited by Kent V. Flannery. New York: Academic Press, 1976, 292–306.

Pohl, John M. D. "The Four Priests: Political Stability." In *The Ancient Civilizations of Mesoamerica: A Reader*. Edited by Michael E. Smith and Marilyn A. Masson. Malden, Mass.: Blackwell Publishers, 2000, 355–56.

Pohl, Mary, Christopher von Nagy, Allison Perrett, and Kevin Pope. "Olmec Civilization at San Andrés, Tabasco, Mexico." Report to the Foundation for the Advancement of Mesoamerican Studies. August 2004. http://www.famsi.org/reports/01047/pdf (accessed June 2013).

Pool, Christopher A. "Current Research on the Gulf Coast of Mexico." *Journal of Archaeological Research* 14 (2006): 189–241.

Pool, Christopher A. *Olmec Archaeology and Early Mesoamerica*. CAMBRIDGE WORLD ARCHAEOLOGY SERIES. Cambridge, England: Cambridge University Press, 2007.

Popol Vuh: The Definitive Edition of the Mayan Book of the Dawn of Life and the Glories of Gods and Kings. Translated by Dennis Tedlock. New York: Simon and Schuster, 1985.

Popol Vuh: The Sacred Book of the Maya. Translated by Allen J. Christenson. Norman: University of Oklahoma Press, 2007.

Popol Vuh, Volume II: Literal Poetic Version, Translation and Transcription. Translated by Allen J. Christenson. New York: O-Books, 2005.

Porter, Bruce H., and Rodney L. Meldrum. *Prophecies and Promises: The Book of Mormon and the United States of America*. New York: Digital Legend, 2009.

Potter, George, and Richard Wellington. *Lehi in the Wilderness: 81 New, Documented Evidences That the Book of Mormon Is a True History*. Springville, Utah: Cedar Fort, 2003.

Poulsen, Lawrence. L. "Book of Mormon Geography and the Book of Ether." http://poulsenll.org/files/Geography_Ether2.pdf (accessed April 2014).

Poulsen, Lawrence L. "Lawrence Poulsen's Book of Mormon Geography." http://www.poulsenll.org/bom/index.html (accessed December 2005).

Poulsen, Lawrence L. "'The Light Is Better Over Here.' Review of *Book of Mormon Geography—Mesoamerican Historic Geography* by V. Garth Norman." *FARMS Review* 19, no. 2 (2007): 11–20.

Poulsen, Lawrence. L. "The River Sidon." http://www.poulsenll.org/bom/ grijalvasidon.html (accessed April 2011).

Poulsen, Lawrence L. "Tale of Two Rivers." http://www.webring.org/l/rd?ring=mormonsites; id=2;url=http%3A%2F%2Fwww%2Epoulsenll%2Eorg%2Fbom%2Findex%2Ehtml (accessed November 2014).

Poulsen, Lawrence L. "The War with the Amlicites." *Book of Mormon Geography*. http://www.poulsenll.org/bom/amlicites.html (accessed April 2011).

Pratt, John P. "Mormon's Map Puzzle Solved?" http://www.ancientamerica.org/ librarymedia/ HTML/m59cha1b/Mormons%20Map%20Puzzle.htm (accessed July 2011).

Pratt, Orson, and Joseph F. Smith. "Report of Elders Orson Pratt and Joseph F. Smith, 7–8 September 1878, Richmond, Missouri." *Millennial Star* 40 (December 16, 1878): 785–89. Rpt. in Lyndon W. Cook, *The David Whitmer Interviews: A Restoration Witness*. Orem, Utah: Grandin Books, 1991.

Pratt, Parley P. *Autobiography of Parley P. Pratt*. Edited by Parley P. Pratt Jr. 3rd ed. 1884; Salt Lake City: Deseret Book, 1938.

Parley P. Pratt, *A Voice of Warning, and Instruction to All People, or, An Introduction to the Faith* and *Doctrine of the Church of Jesus Christ of Latter-Day Saints*, 8th ed. Liverpool: F. D. Richards, 1854.

Priddis, Venice. *The Book and the Map: New Insights into Book of Mormon Geography*. Salt Lake City: Bookcraft, 1975.

Priest, Josiah. *American Antiquities and Discoveries in the West*. 1834; rpt., 4th ed. Colfax, Wisc.: Ancient American Archaeology Foundation, n.d.

Propp, Vladimir. *Morphology of the Folktale*. Austin: University of Texas Press, 1977.

Raish, Martin H. "All that Glitters: Uncovering Fool's Gold in Book of Mormon Archaeology." *Sunstone* 6, no. 1 (January–February 1981): 10–15.

Raish, Martin H. "Review of Paul R. Cheesman and Millie F. Cheesman. *Ancient American Indians: Their Origins, Civilizations and Old World Connections*." *FARMS Review of Books* 4, no. 1 (1992): 21–23.

Raish, Martin H. "Tree of Life." In *Encyclopedia of Mormonism*. Edited by Daniel H. Ludlow. 4 vols. New York: Macmillan Publishing, 1992, 4:1486–88.

Ramachandran, V. S., and Sandra Blakeslee. *Phantoms in the Brain: Probing the Mysteries of the Human Mind*. New York: Quill, 1998.

Rambo, Lewis R. *Understanding Religious Conversion*. New Haven, Conn.: Yale University Press, 1993.

Rappleye, Neal. "Lehi the Smelter: New Light on Lehi's Profession." *Interpreter: A Journal of Mormon Scripture* 14 (2015): 223–25.

Rappleye, Neal, and Stephen O. Smoot. "Book of Mormon Minimalists and the NHM Inscriptions: A Response to Dan Vogel." *Interpreter: A Journal of Mormon Scripture* 8 (2014): 157–85.

Redford, Donald B. *Egypt, Canaan, and Israel in Ancient Times*. Princeton, N.J.: Princeton University Press, 1992.

Reents-Budet, Dorie. *Painting the Maya Universe: Royal Ceramics of the Classic Period*. Durham, N.C.: Duke University Press, 1994.

Reeve, Rex C., Jr. "The Book of Mormon Plates." In *First Nephi: The Doctrinal Foundation*. Edited by Monte S. Nyman and Charles D. Tate Jr. Provo, Utah: BYU Religious Studies Center, 1988, 99–111.

Reeve, Rex C., Jr., and Richard O. Cowan. "The Hill Called Cumorah." In *Regional Studies in LDS History: New York and Pennsylvania*. Edited by Larry C. Porter, Milton V. Backman Jr., and Susan Easton Black. Provo, Utah: BYU Department of Church History and Doctrine, 1992, 71–89.

Reilly, F. Kent, III, and James F. Garber. "The Symbolic Representation of Warfare in Formative Period Mesoamerica." In *Ancient Mesoamerican Warfare*. Edited by Travis W. Stanton and M. Kathryn Brown. Walnut Creek, Calif.: Altamira Press, 2003, 127–48.

Reynolds, George, and Janne M. Sjodahl. *Commentary on the Book of Mormon*. Edited and arranged by Philip C. Reynolds. 7 vols. Salt Lake City: Deseret Book, 1955–61.

Reynolds, Noel B. "By Objective Measures: Old Wine into Old Bottles." In *Echoes and Evidences of the Book of Mormon*. Edited by Donald W. Parry, Daniel C. Peterson, and John W. Welch. Provo, Utah: Foundation for Ancient Research and Mormon Studies, 2002, 127–53.

Reynolds, Noel B. "Introduction." In *Book of Mormon Authorship*. Edited by Noel B. Reynolds. Provo, Utah: BYU Religious Studies Center, 1982, 1–5.

Reynolds, Noel B. "Lehi's Arabian Journey Updated." In *Book of Mormon Authorship Revisited: The Evidence for Ancient Origins*. Edited by Noel B. Reynolds. Provo, Utah: Foundation for Ancient Research and Mormon Studies, 1997, 379–89.

Reynolds, Noel B. "Nephi's Outline." In *Book of Mormon Authorship*. Edited by Noel B.

Reynolds. Provo, Utah: BYU Religious Studies Center, 1982, 53–74.
Reynolds, Noel B. "Nephi's Political Testament." In *Rediscovering the Book of Mormon*. Edited by John L. Sorenson and Melvin J. Thorne. Provo, Utah: Foundation for Ancient Research and Mormon Studies, 1991, 220–29.
Reynolds, Noel B. "Nephite Kingship Reconsidered." In *Mormons, Scripture, and the Ancient World: Studies in Honor of John L. Sorenson*. Edited by Davis Bitton. Provo, Utah: Foundation for Ancient Research and Mormon Studies, 1998, 151–89.
Reynolds, Noel B. "The Political Dimension in Nephi's Small Plates." *BYU Studies* 27, no. 4 (Winter 1987): 15–37.
Rice, Prudence, M. *Maya Political Science: Time, Astronomy, and the Cosmos*. Austin, Texas: University of Austin Press, 2004.
Richards, LeGrand. *Conference Report, April 1955*. Retrieved from *GospeLink 2001*, CD-ROM. Salt Lake City: Deseret Book, 2000, 119–124.
Richards, E. Randolph, and Brandon J. O'Brien. *Misreading Scripture with Western Eyes: Removing Cultural Blinders to Better Understand the Bible*. Downers Grove, Ill.: IVP Books, 2012.
Ricks, Stephen D. "'Holy War': The Sacral Ideology of War in the Book of Mormon and in the Ancient Near East." In *Warfare in the Book of Mormon*. Edited by Stephen D. Ricks and William J. Hamblin. Salt Lake City: Deseret Book/Provo, Utah: Foundation for Ancient Research and Mormon Studies, 1990, 103–23.
Ricks, Stephen D. "Kingship, Coronation, and Covenant in Mosiah 1–6 in *King Benjamin's Speech*. Edited by John W. Welch and Stephen D. Ricks. Provo, Utah: FARMS, 1998, 233–75.
Ricks, Stephen D. "On Lehi's Trail: Nahom, Ishmael's Burial Place." *Journal of the Book of Mormon and Other Restoration Scripture* 20, no. 1 (2011): 66–67.
Ringle, William M., and George J. Bey III. "Post-Classic and Terminal Classic Courts of the Northern Maya Lowlands." In *Royal Courts of the Ancient Maya. Volume 2: Data and Case Studies*. Edited by Takeshi Inomata and Stephen D. Houston. Boulder, Colo.: Westview Press, 2001, 266–307.
Roberts, Brigham H. *New Witnesses for God*. 3 vols. Salt Lake City: Deseret News, 1909–11.
Roberts, Brigham H. *Studies of the Book of Mormon*. Edited by Brigham D. Madsen. Urbana: University of Chicago Press, 1985.
Roberts, Brigham H. "The Translation of the Book of Mormon." *Improvement Era* 9 (April 1909): 425–36.
Robinson, H. Wheeler. *Inspiration and Revelation in the Old Testament*. New York: Clarendon Press, 1946.
Robinson, Stephen E. "Early Christianity and 1 Nephi 13–14." In *First Nephi: The Doctrinal Foundation*. Edited by Monte S. Nyman and Charles D. Tate Jr. Provo, Utah: BYU Religious Studies Center, 1988, 177–91.
Rollston, Christopher A. *Writing and Literacy in the World of Ancient Israel: Epigraphic Evidence from the Iron Age*. Atlanta, Ga.: Society of Biblical Literature, 2010.
Roper, Matthew. "Early Publications on the Book of Mormon." *Journal of the Book of Mormon and Other Restoration Scripture* 18, no. 2 (2009): 38–49.
Roper, Matthew. "Limited Geography and the Book of Mormon." *FARMS Review* 16, no. 2 (2004): 225–76.
Roper, Matthew. "Nephi's Neighbors: Book of Mormon Peoples and Pre-Columbian Populations." *FARMS Review* 15, no. 2 (2003): 91–128.
Roper, Matthew, Paul J. Fields, and Atul Nepal. "Joseph Smith, the *Times and Seasons*, and Central American Ruins." *Journal of the Book of Mormon and Other Restoration Scripture* 22, no. 2 (2013): 85–97.

Roper, Matthew, Paul J. Fields, and Atul Nepal. "Wordprint Analysis and Joseph Smith's Role as Editor of the *Times and Season*." *Insights* 30, no. 6 (2010): 1–2.

Rust, Richard Dilworth. "Recurrence in Book of Mormon Narratives." *Journal of Book of Mormon Studies* 3, no. 1 (Spring 1994): 39–52.

S., A. "The Golden Bible, or, Campbellism Improved." *Observer and Telegraph* (Hudson, Ohio). November 18, 1830. Photocopy. http://contentdm.lib.byu.edu/cdm/compoundobject/collection/BOMP/id/244/rec/1 (accessed May 2014). The transcription is available on the same web page.

Sabloff, Jeremy A. *The New Archaeology and the Ancient Maya*. New York: Scientific American Library, 1990.

Sachse, Frauke, and Allen J. Christenson. "Tulan and the Other Side of the Sea: Unraveling a Metaphorical Concept from Colonial Guatemalan Highland Sources." *Mesoweb Publications*. http://www.mesoweb.com/articles/tulan/Tulan.pdf (accessed February 2012).

Sahagún, Bernardino de. *General History of the Things of New Spain: Florentine Codex*. Translated by Arthur J. O. Anderson and Charles E. Dibble. 12 vols. Salt Lake City: School of American Research and the University of Utah, 1975.

Sahagún, Bernardino de. *Historia General de las Cosas de Nueva España*. 4 vols. Mexico City: Editorial Porrúa, 1969.

Salmon, Douglas F. "Parallelomania and the Study of Latter-day Scripture: Confirmation, Coincidence, or the Collective Unconscious?" *Dialogue: A Journal of Mormon Thought* 33, no. 2 (2000): 129–56.

Sánchez, Carlos Serrano. "Funerary Practices and Human Sacrifice in Teotihuacán Burials." In *Teotihuacán: Art from the City of the Gods*. Edited by Kathleen Berrin and Esther Pasztory. New York: Thames and Hudson, 1993, 109–15.

Sanchez, Julia L. J. "Ancient Maya Royal Strategies: Creating Power and Identity through Art." *Ancient Mesoamerica* 16, no. 2 (2006): 261–75.

Sandmel, Samuel. "Parallelomania." *Journal of Biblical Literature* 81 (1962): 1–13.

Schade, Aaron P. "The Kingdom of Judah: Politics, Prophets, and Scribes in the Late Preexilic Period." In *Glimpses of Lehi's Jerusalem*. Edited by John W. Welch, David Rolph Seely, and Jo Ann H. Seely. Provo, Utah: Foundation for Ancient Research and Mormon Studies, 2004, 299–336.

Schaalje, G. Bruce. "A Bayesian Cease-Fire in the Late War on the Book of Mormon." Blog entry. *Interpreter: A Journal of Mormon Scripture*. Posted November 6, 2013. http://www.mormoninterpreter.com/a-bayesian-cease-fire-in-the-late-war-on-the-book-of-mormon/ (accessed November 2013).

Schele, Linda, and David Freidel. *A Forest of Kings: The Untold Story of the Ancient Maya*. New York: William Morrow and Company, 1990.

Schele, Linda, and Peter Mathews. *The Code of Kings: The Language of Seven Sacred Maya Temples and Tombs*. New York: Scribner, 1998.

Schele, Linda, and Peter Mathews. "Royal Visits and Other Intersite Relationships." In *Classic Maya Political History: Hieroglyphic and Archaeological Evidence*. Edited by T. Patrick Culbert. Cambridge, England: Cambridge University Press, 1991, 226–52.

Schele, Linda, and Mary Ellen Miller. *The Blood of Kings: Dynasty and Ritual in Maya Art*. New York: George Braziller, 1986.

Schiffman, Lawrence H. *From Text to Tradition: A History of Second Temple and Rabbinic Judaism*. Hoboken, N.J.: KTAV Publishing House, 1991.

Schiffman, Lawrence H. *Reclaiming the Dead Sea Scrolls*. New York: Doubleday, 1995.

Schowalter, Daniel N. "Church." In *The Oxford Companion to the Bible*. Edited by Bruce M.

Metzger and Michael D. Coogan. New York: Oxford University Press, 1993, 121–22.
"Science and Religion/DNA." *FairMormon Wiki*. http://en.fairmormon.org/DNA (accessed April 2014).
Seely, David Rolph. "Chronology, Book of Mormon." In *Book of Mormon Reference Companion*. General editor Dennis L. Largey. Salt Lake City: Deseret Book, 2003, 196–204.
Seely, David Rolph, and JoAnn H. Seely. "Lehi and Jeremiah: Prophets, Priests, and Patriarchs." *Journal of Book of Mormon Studies* 8, no. 2 (1999): 24–35.
Seely, David Rolph, and Fred E. Woods. "How Could Jerusalem, 'That Great City,' Be Destroyed?" In *Glimpses of Lehi's Jerusalem*. Edited by John W. Welch, David Rolph Seely, and Jo Ann H. Seely. Provo, Utah: Foundation for Ancient Research and Mormon Studies, 2004, 595–610.
Shanks, Hershel. *Jerusalem: An Archaeological Biography*. New York: Random House, 1995.
Sharer, Robert J. *The Ancient Maya*. 5th ed. Stanford, Calif.: Stanford University Press, 1994.
Sheets, Payson D. "Warfare in Ancient Mesoamerica: A Summary View." In *Ancient Mesoamerican Warfare*. Edited by Travis W. Stanton and M. Kathryn Brown. Walnut Creek, Calif.: Altamira Press, 2003, 287–302.
Simeon, Rémi. *Dictionnaire de la Langue Nahuatl ou Mexicaine*. 1885. Rpt., Graz, Austria: Akademische Druck-U. Verlagsanstalt, 1965.
Sjodahl, Janne M. *An Introduction to the Study of the Book of Mormon: A Suggested Key to Book of Mormon Geography*. Salt Lake City: Deseret News Press, 1927.
Skinner, Andrew C. "The Tree of Life in the Hebrew Bible and Later Jewish Thought." In *The Tree of Life: From Eden to Eternity*. Edited by John W. Welch and Donald W. Parry. Provo, Utah: Neal A. Maxwell Institute for Religious Scholarship/Salt Lake City: Deseret Book, 2011, 25–54.
Skousen, Royal. *Analysis of Textual Variants of the Book of Mormon*. THE CRITICAL TEXT OF THE BOOK OF MORMON, 4, 6 parts. Provo, Utah: Foundation for Ancient Research and Mormon Studies, 2004-9.
Skousen, Royal. "Critical Methodology and the Text of the Book of Mormon." *Review of Books on the Book of Mormon* 6, no. 1 (1994): 121–44.
Skousen, Royal. "How Joseph Smith Translated the Book of Mormon; Evidence from the Original Manuscript." *Journal of Book of Mormon Studies* 7, no. 1 (1998): 22–31.
Skousen, Royal, ed. *The Printer's Manuscript of the Book of Mormon*. THE CRITICAL TEXT OF THE BOOK OF MORMON, 2, 2 parts. Provo, Utah: Foundation for Ancient Research and Mormon Studies, 2001.
Skousen, Royal. "Translating the Book of Mormon: Evidence from the Original Manuscript." In *Book of Mormon Authorship Revisited: The Evidence for Ancient Origins*. Edited by Noel B. Reynolds. Provo, Utah: Foundation for Ancient Research and Mormon Studies, 1997, 61–93.
Smith, David Livingston. *Less Than Human: Why We Demean, Enslave, and Exterminate Others*. New York: St. Martin's Press, 2011.
Smith, Emma. "As Interviewed by Joseph Smith III, 1879." In *Opening the Heavens: Accounts of Divine Manifestations, 1820–1844*. Edited by John W. Welch. Provo, Utah: Brigham Young University Press/Salt Lake City: Deseret Book, 2005, 130-31.
Smith, Ethan, *View of the Hebrews*. 1923; 2d ed. 1825. Rpt., edited by Charles D. Tate Jr. RELIGIOUS STUDIES CENTER SPECIALIZED MONOGRAPH SERIES, VOL. 8. Provo, Utah: BYU Religious Studies Center, 1996.
Smith, George D. "Indians Not 'Lamanites'?" Letter to the editor. *Dialogue: A Journal of Mormon Thought* 18, no. 2 (Summer 1985): 5–6.
Smith, James E. "Nephi's Descendants? Historical Demography and the Book of Mormon." *Review of Books on the Book of Mormon* 6, no. 1 (1994): 255–96.

Smith, Joseph, et al. *History of the Church of Jesus Christ of Latter-day Saints*. Edited by B. H. Roberts, 2nd ed. rev. Vols. 1–6, 1902–12; 7, 1932. Salt Lake City: Deseret Book, 1973 printing.

Smith, Joseph Fielding, comp. and ed. *Teachings of the Prophet Joseph Smith*. 1924. Rpt., Salt Lake City: Deseret Book, 1972.

Smith, Joseph Fielding. *Doctrines of Salvation*. Compiled by Bruce R. McConkie. 1956. Rpt., Salt Lake City: Bookcraft, 1976.

Smith, Lucy Mack. *Lucy's Book: A Critical Edition of Lucy Mack Smith's Family Memoir*. Edited by Lavina Fielding Anderson. Salt Lake City: Signature Books, 2001.

Smith, Mark S. *The Early History of God: Yahweh and the Other Deities in Ancient Israel*, 2nd ed. Grand Rapids, Mich.: William B. Eerdmans, 1990, 2002.

Smith, Mark S. *The Origins of Biblical Monotheism: Israel's Polytheistic Background and the Ugaritic Texts*. New York: Oxford University Press, 2001.

Smith, Michael E. *The Aztecs*. Cambridge, Mass.: Blackwell, 1996.

Smith, Richard Pearson. "The Nephite Monetary System." *Improvement Era*, May 1954, 316–17.

Smith, Robert F. "The Golden Plates." In *Reexploring the Book of Mormon*. Edited by John W. Welch. Provo, Utah: Foundation for Ancient Research and Mormon Studies, 1992, 272–77.

Snyder, Graydon F. *Inculturation of the Jesus Tradition: The Impact of Jesus on Jewish and Roman Cultures*. Harrisburg, Pa.: Trinity Press International, 1999.

Sorenson, John L. "Ancient America and the Book of Mormon Revisited." *Dialogue: A Journal of Mormon Thought* 4, no. 2 (Summer 1969): 80–94.

Sorenson, John L. *An Ancient American Setting for the Book of Mormon*. Salt Lake City: Deseret Book/Provo, Utah: Foundation for Ancient Research and Mormon Studies, 1985.

Sorenson, John L. "Digging into the Book of Mormon: Our Changing Understanding of Ancient America and Its Scripture, Part 1." *Ensign*, September 1984, https://www.lds.org/ensign/1984/09/digging-into-the-book-of-mormon-our-changing-understanding-of-ancient-america-and-its-scripture (accessed July 2008).

Sorenson, John L. "Digging into the Book of Mormon: Our Changing Understanding of Ancient America and Its Scripture, Part 2." *Ensign*, October 1984, https://www.lds.org/ensign/1984/10/digging-into-the-book-of-mormon-our-changing-understanding-of-ancient-america-and-its-scripture-part-2 (accessed July 2008).

Sorenson, John L. *The Geography of Book of Mormon Events: A Source Book*. Provo, Utah: Foundation for Ancient Research and Mormon Studies, 1990.

Sorenson, John L. *Images of Ancient America: Visualizing Book of Mormon Life*. Provo, Utah: Research Press, Foundation for Ancient Research and Mormon Studies, 1998.

Sorenson, John L. "Instant Expertise on Book of Mormon Archaeology." *BYU Studies* 16, no. 3 (Spring 1976): 429–32.

Sorenson, John L. "Metals and Metallurgy Relating to the Book of Mormon Text." Unpublished paper distributed through Foundation for Ancient Research and Mormon Studies, 1992.

Sorenson, John L. *Mormon's Codex: An Ancient American Book*. Salt Lake City: Deseret Book Company and the Neal A. Maxwell Institute for Religious Scholarship, 2013.

Sorenson, John L. *Mormon's Map*. Provo, Utah: Foundation for Ancient Research and Mormon Studies, 2000.

Sorenson, John L. "Mormon's Sources." *Journal of the Book of Mormon and Other Restoration Scripture* 20, no. 2 (2011): 2–15.

Sorenson, John L. "Nephi's Garden and Chief Market." In *Reexploring the Book of Mormon*. Edited by John W. Welch. Provo, Utah: Foundation for Ancient Research and Mormon Studies, 1992, 236–38.

Sorenson, John L. *Nephite Culture and Society*. Edited by Matthew R. Sorenson. Salt Lake City:

New Sage Books, 1997.

Sorenson, John L. "Reading Mormon's Codex." Paper presented at the annual conference of the Foundation for Apologetic Information and Research, August 2012. http://www.fairlds.org/fair-conferences/2012-fair-conference/ 2012-reading-mormons-codex (accessed May 2013).

Sorenson, John L. "Religious Groups and Movements among the Nephites, 200–1 B.C." In *The Disciple as Scholar: Essays on Scripture and the Ancient World in Honor of Richard Lloyd Anderson*. Edited by Stephen D. Ricks, Donald W. Parry, and Andrew H. Hedges. Provo, Utah: Foundation for Ancient Research and Mormon Studies, 2000, 163–208.

Sorenson, John L. "Seasonality of Warfare in the Book of Mormon and in Mesoamerica." In *Warfare in the Book of Mormon*. Edited by Stephen D. Ricks and William J. Hamblin. Salt Lake City: Deseret Book/Provo, Utah: Foundation for Ancient Research and Mormon Studies, 1990, 445–77.

Sorenson, John L. "Was Mulek a "Blood Son" of King Zedekiah?" *Insights: A Window on the Ancient World* 19, no. 2 (1999): 2.

Sorenson, John L. "Wheeled Figurines in the Ancient World." FARMS Preliminary Report. Provo: Foundation for Ancient Research and Mormon Studies, 1981.

Sorenson, John L. "Viva Zapato! Hurray for the Shoe!" *Review of Books on the Book of Mormon* 6, no. 1 (1994): 297–361.

Sorenson, John L. "Winds and Currents: A Look at Nephi's Ocean Crossing." In *Reexploring the Book of Mormon*. Edited by John W. Welch. Provo, Utah: Foundation for Ancient Research and Mormon Studies, 1992, 53–56.

Sorenson, John L. "The Years of the Jaredites." *BYU Today* (September 1968): 18–24.

Sorenson, John L., and Paul Y. Hoskisson. "Lost Arts." In *Reexploring the Book of Mormon*. Edited by John W. Welch. Provo, Utah: Foundation for Ancient Research and Mormon Studies, 1992, 101–04.

Southerton, Simon G. *Losing a Lost Tribe: Native Americans, DNA, and the Mormon Church*. Salt Lake City: Signature Books, 2004.

Spackman, Randall P. "Introduction to Book of Mormon Chronology." FARMS Reprint Series. Provo, Utah: Foundation for Ancient Research and Mormon Studies, 1993.

Spackman, Randall P. "The Jewish/Nephite Lunar Calendar." *Journal of Book of Mormon Studies* 7, no. 1 (1998): 48–59.

Spencer, Joseph M. *An Other Testament: On Typology*. Salem, Ore.: Salt Press, 2012.

Sperry, Sidney B. *Book of Mormon Compendium*. Salt Lake City: Bookcraft, 1968.

Sperry, Sidney B. "Were There Two Cumorahs?" *Journal of Book of Mormon Studies* 4, no. 1 (Spring 1995): 260–68.

St. Clair, Steve. "The Stick of Joseph: The Book of Mormon and the Literary Tradition of the Northern Kingdom." http://members.tripod.com/~osher_2/ StickJoseph.html (accessed January 2009).

Stadelman, Louis I. J. *The Hebrew Conception of the World*. Rome: Biblical Institute Press, 1970.

Stanton, Travis W., and M. Kathryn Brown. "Studying Warfare in Ancient Mesoamerica." In *Ancient Mesoamerican Warfare*. Edited by Travis W. Stanton and M. Kathryn Brown. Walnut Creek, Calif.: Altamira Press, 2003, 1–16.

Stern, Ephraim. *Archaeology of the Land of the Bible. Volume 2: The Assyrian, Babylonian, and Persian Periods (732–332 BCE)*. ANCHOR BIBLE REFERENCE LIBRARY. New York: Doubleday, 2001.

Stern, Ephraim. "The Phoenician Source of Palestinian Cults at the End of the Iron Age." In *Symbiosis, Symbolism, and the Power of the Past: Canaan, Ancient Israel, and Their*

Neighbors from the Late Bronze Age through Roman Palaestina.. Edited by William G. Dever and Seymour Gitin. Winona Lake, Ind.: Eisenbrauns, 2003, 309–21.
Stiebing, William H., Jr. *Out of the Desert: Archaeology and the Exodus/Conquest Narratives.* Buffalo, N.Y.: Prometheus Books, 1989.
Stocker, Terry. "Conquest, Tribute and the Rise of the State." In *Studies in the Neolithic and Urban Revolutions: The V. Gordon Childe Colloquium, Mexico, 1986.* Edited by Linda Manzanilla. BAR INTERNATIONAL SERIES 349. Oxford: Biblical Archaeological Review, 1987, 365–76.
Stoddard, Dee. "'From the East to the West Sea': An Analysis of John L. Sorenson's Book of Mormon Directional Statements," 2009. http://www.bmaf.org/ node/251 (accessed August 2012).
Storey, Rebecca, and Randolph J. Widmer. "The Pre-Columbian Economy." In *The Cambridge Economic History of Latin America: The Colonial Era and the Short Nineteenth Century.* Edited by Victor Bulmer-Thomas, John H. Coatsworth, and Roberto Cortés Conde. New York: Cambridge University Press, 2006, 73–106.
Stuart, David. "'The Arrival of Strangers': Teotihuacan and Tollan in Classic Maya History." In *Mesoamerica's Classic Heritage: From Teotihuacan to the Aztecs.* Edited by David Carrasco, Lindsay Jones, and Scott Sessions. Boulder: University Press of Colorado, 2000, 465–514.
Stuart, David. "Glyphs for 'Right' and 'Left'?" January 2002. http://www.mesoweb.com/stuart/notes/rightleft.html (accessed February 2012; PDF in my possession).
Stuart, George E., and Gene S. Stuart. *The Mysterious Maya.* Washington, D.C.: National Geographic Society, 1977.
Sugiyama, Saburo. "Rulership, Warfare, and Human Sacrifice at the Ciudadela: An Iconographic Study of Feathered Serpent Representations." In *Art, Ideology, and the City of Teotihuacán.* Edited by Janet Catherine Berlo. Washington, D.C.: Dumbarton Oaks Research Library and Collection, 1992, 205–30.
Sweat, Anthony. "By the Gift and Power of Art." In Michael Hubbard MacKay and Gerrit J. Dirkmaat. *From Darkness unto Light: Joseph Smith's Translation and Publication of the Book of Mormon.* Provo, Utah: BYU Religious Studies Center/Salt Lake City: Deseret Book, 2015, 229–43.
Swift, Charles. "'I Have Dreamed a Dream': Lehi's Archetypal Vision of the Tree of Life." In *The Tree of Life: From Eden to Eternity.* Edited by John W. Welch and Donald W. Parry. Provo, Utah: Neal A. Maxwell Institute for Religious Scholarship/Salt Lake City: Deseret Book, 2011, 129–49.
Szink, Terrence L. "Nephi and the Exodus." In *Rediscovering the Book of Mormon.* Edited by John L. Sorenson and Melvin J. Thorne. Provo, Utah: FARMS, 1991, 39–42.
Szink, Terrence L. "To a Land of Promise." In *Studies in Scripture. Volume 7, 1 Nephi to Alma 29.* Edited by Kent P. Jackson. Salt Lake City: Deseret Book, 1987, 60–72.
Szink, Terrence L., and John W. Welch. "King Benjamin's Speech in the Context of Ancient Israelite Festivals." In *King Benjamin's Speech.* Edited by John W. Welch and Stephen D. Ricks. Provo, Utah: FARMS, 1998, 147–223.
Talmage, James E. *Articles of Faith.* Salt Lake City: Deseret Book, 1981.
Tanner, Jerald, and Sandra Tanner. "A Black Hole in the Book of Mormon." *Salt Lake City Messenger,* no. 73 (July 1989). http://www.utlm.org/newsletters/ no72.htm (accessed March 2015).
Tanner, John S. "Jacob and His Descendants as Authors." In *Rediscovering the Book of Mormon.* Edited by John L. Sorenson and Melvin J. Thorne. Provo, Utah: Foundation for Ancient Research and Mormon Studies, 1991, 52–66.
Taube, Karl. "Ancient and Contemporary Maya Conceptions about Field and Forest." In *The*

Lowland Maya Area: Three Millennia at the Human-Wildland Interface. Edited by A. Gómex-Pompa, M. F. Allen, S. L. Fedick, and J. J. Jiménez-Osornio. Binghamton, N.Y.: Food Products Press, 2003, 461–92.

Taube, Karl A. "Flower Mountain: Concepts of Life, Beauty, and Paradise among the Classic Maya." RES: Anthropology and Aesthetics, no. 45 (Spring 2004): 69–98.

Taube, Karl. The Major Gods of Ancient Yucatan. Washington, D.C.: Dumbarton Oaks Research Library and Collection, 1992.

Taylor, John. Mediation and Atonement. Salt Lake City: Deseret News, 1882. Retrieved from GospeLink 2001, CD-ROM. Salt Lake City: Deseret Book, 2000.

Tayman, David. "Adjusting the Narrative: Part 2a-Nephi and the Skin of Blackness." Worlds without End: A Mormon Studies Roundtable. Blog post April 9, 2013, http://www.withoutend.org/adjusting-narrative-part-2anephi-skin-blackness/ (accessed April 2013).

Tedlock, Dennis. "Creation in the Popol Vuh: A Hermeneutical Approach." In Symbol and Meaning beyond the Closed Community. Essays in Mesoamerican Ideas. Edited by Gary Gossen. Albany: Institute for Mesoamerican Studies, University at Albany, State University of New York, 1986, 77–82.

Thomas, D. Winton, ed. Documents from Old Testament Times. New York: Harper Torchbooks, 1958.

Thomasson, Gordon C. "Daddy, What's a 'Frontier'?" Privately circulated paper, 1970, revised 2000. Copy in my possession, courtesy of Thomasson.

Thompson, John S. "Lehi and Egypt." In Glimpses of Lehi's Jerusalem. Edited by John W. Welch, David Rolph Seely, and Jo Ann H. Seely. Provo, Utah: Foundation for Ancient Research and Mormon Studies, 2004, 259–76.

Thompson, Thomas L. Mythic Past: Biblical Archaeology and the Myth of Israel. New York: MJF Books, 1999.

"Title of the Lords of Totonicapan." In Annals of the Cakchiquels. Translated by Adrian Recinos and Delia Goetz. Norman: University of Oklahoma Press, 1974, 161–96.

"Titulo C'oyoi." In Robert M. Carmack. Quichéan Civilization. Translated by Robert M. Carmack. Berkeley: University of California Press, 1973, 287–306.

Torquemada, Juan de. Monarquía Indiana, 3 vols. Mexico City: Editorial Sálvador Chávez Hayhoe, 1943.

Turner, Rodney. "The Lamanite Mark." In Second Nephi: The Doctrinal Structure. Edited by Monte S. Nyman and Charles D. Tate Jr. Provo, Utah: BYU Religious Studies Center, 1989, 133–57.

Tuttle, Daniel Sylvester. "Mormons, p. 1557-6 [sic]." Schaff-Herzogg Encyclopaedia: A Religious Encyclopaedia or Dictionary of Biblical, Historical, Doctrinal, and Practical Theology. Funk and Wagnalls, 1883. http://www.lightplanet.com/response/1826Trial/Tuttle_1883.html (accessed January 2006).

Tvedtnes, John A. "The Hebrew Background of the Book of Mormon." In Rediscovering the Book of Mormon. Edited by John L. Sorenson and Melvin J. Thorne. Provo, Utah: Foundation for Ancient Research and Mormon Studies, 1991, 77–91.

Tvedtnes, John A. "Lehi and Sariah Comments." Journal of Book of Mormon Studies 9, no. 1 (2000): 37.

Tvedtnes, John A. "More on the River Laman." Insights 25, no. 3 (2005): 2–3.

Tvedtnes, John A. The Most Correct Book: Insights from a Book of Mormon Scholar. Salt Lake City: Cornerstone Publishing, 1999.

Tvedtnes, John A. "Reinventing the Book of Mormon: Review of Brent Lee Metcalfe, 'Reinventing Lamanite Identity.'" FARMS Review 16, no. 2 (2004): 91–106.

Tvedtnes, John A. "When Was Christ Born?" Interpreter: A Journal of Mormon Scripture 10 (2014): 1–33.

Underwood, Grant. "Book of Mormon Usage in Early LDS Theology." *Dialogue: A Journal of Mormon Thought* 17, no. 3 (Autumn 1984): 35–74.

Vail, Gabrielle. "Pre-Hispanic Maya Religion." *Ancient Mesoamerica* 11 (2000): 123–47.

Vail, Gabrielle, and Christine Hernandez. *Re-Creating Primordial Time: Foundation Rituals and Mythology in the Postclassic Maya Codices*. Boulder: University Press of Colorado, 2013.

Vaillant, George C. *Aztecs of Mexico City: Origin, Rise, and Fall of the Aztec Nation*. New York: Penguin Books, 1966.

Van der Toorn, Karel. *Scribal Culture and the Making of the Hebrew Bible*. Cambridge, Mass.: Harvard University Press, 2007.

Vansina, Jan. *Oral Tradition as History*. Madison: University of Wisconsin Press, 1985.

Vincent, Joseph E. "Some Views on Book of Mormon Geography." In *Fourteenth Annual Symposium on the Archaeology of the Scriptures*. Papers presented April 13, 1963. Edited by Forrest R. Hauck. Provo, Utah: Department of Extension Publications, Adult Education and Extension Services, Brigham Young University, 1963, 61–69.

Vogel, Dan. *Indian Origins and the Book of Mormon*. Salt Lake City: Signature Books, 1986.

Vogel, Dan. *Joseph Smith: The Making of a Prophet*. Salt Lake City: Signature Books, 2004.

Vogel, Dan, and Brent Lee Metcalfe. "Editor's Introduction." *American Apocrypha: Essays on the Book of Mormon*. Salt Lake City: Signature Books, 2002, vii–xvii.

Walker, John Phillip, ed. *Dale Morgan on Early Mormonism: Correspondence and a New History*. Salt Lake City: Signature Books, 1986. Online text. http://signaturebookslibrary.org/dale-morgan-on-early-mormonism/ (accessed July 2008).

Warren, Bruce W. "Secret Combinations, Warfare, and Sacrifice." In *Warfare in the Book of Mormon*. Edited by Stephen D. Ricks and William J. Hamblin. Salt Lake City: Deseret Book/Provo, Utah: Foundation for Ancient Research and Mormon Studies, 1990, 225–36.

Washburn, J. N. *Book of Mormon Guidebook and Certain Problems in the Book of Mormon*. Bound in one volume. Self-published, 1968.

Weaver, Muriel Porter. *The Aztecs, Maya, and Their Predecessors: Archaeology of Mesoamerica*. New York: Seminar Press, 1972.

Webster, David. *The Fall of the Ancient Maya: Solving the Mystery of the Maya Collapse*. London: Thames and Hudson, 2002.

Webster, Noah. *American Dictionary of the English Language: 1828 Noah Webster Dictionary*. Kindle Edition.

Weintraub, Karl J. *Reference Answers*. "Heuristic." http://www.answers.com/topic/ heuristic (accessed January 2009).

Welch, John W. "Benjamin, the Man: His Place in Nephite History." In *King Benjamin's Speech*. Edited by John W. Welch and Stephen D. Ricks. Provo, Utah: FARMS, 1998, 23–54.

Welch, John W. "Democratizing Forces in King Benjamin's Speech." In *Pressing Forward with the Book of Mormon*. Edited by John W. Welch and Melvin J. Thorne. Provo, Utah: Foundation for Ancient Research and Mormon Studies, 1999, 110–26.

Welch, John W. "Law and War in the Book of Mormon." In *Warfare in the Book of Mormon*. Edited by Stephen D. Ricks and William J. Hamblin. Salt Lake City: Deseret Book/Provo, Utah: Foundation for Ancient Research and Mormon Studies, 1990, 46–102.

Welch, John W. "The Laws of Eshnunna and Nephi Economics." In *Pressing Forward with the Book of Mormon*. Edited by John W. Welch and Melvin J. Thorne. Provo, Utah: Foundation for Ancient Research and Mormon Studies, 1999, 147–49.

Welch, John W. *The Legal Cases in the Book of Mormon*. Provo, Utah: Neal A. Maxwell Institute for Religious Scholarship, 2008.

Welch, John W. "The Miraculous Translation of the Book of Mormon." In *Opening the Heavens:*

Accounts of Divine Manifestations, 1820–1844. Edited by John W. Welch. Provo, Utah: Brigham Young University Press/Salt Lake City: Deseret Book, 2005, 77–213.
Welch, John W. "The Power of Evidence in the Nurturing of Faith." In *Echoes and Evidences of the Book of Mormon*. Edited by Donald W. Parry, Daniel C. Peterson, and John W. Welch. Provo, Utah: Foundation for Ancient Research and Mormon Studies, 2002, 17–53.
Welch, John W. "A Steady Stream of Significant Recognitions." In *Echoes and Evidences of the Book of Mormon*. Edited by Donald W. Parry, Daniel C. Peterson, and John W. Welch. Provo, Utah: Foundation for Ancient Research and Mormon Studies, 2002, 331–87.
Welch, John W. "The Tree of Life in the New Testament and Christian Tradition." In *The Tree of Life: From Eden to Eternity*. Edited by John W. Welch and Donald W. Parry. Provo, Utah: Neal A. Maxwell Institute for Religious Scholarship, 2011, 81–107.
Welch, John W. "Weighing and Measuring in the Worlds of the Book of Mormon." *Journal of Book of Mormon Studies* 8, no. 2 (1999): 36–46.
Welch, John W., and Darryl R. Hague. "Benjamin's Sermon as a Traditional Ancient Farewell Address." In *King Benjamin's Speech: "That Ye May Learn Wisdom."* Edited by John W. Welch and Stephen D. Ricks. Provo, Utah: Foundation for Ancient Research and Mormon Studies, 1998, 89–117.
Wellington, Richard, and George W. Potter. "Lehi's Trail from the Valley of Lemuel to Nephi's Harbor." *Journal of Book of Mormon Studies* 16, no. 2 (2006): 26–43.
Wells, Matthew G., and John W. Welch. "Concrete Evidence for the Book of Mormon." In *Reexploring the Book of Mormon*. Edited by John W. Welch. Provo, Utah: Foundation for Ancient Research and Mormon Studies, 1992, 212–14.
Wenham, David. *Paul: Follower of Jesus or Founder of Christianity?* Grand Rapids, Mich.: William B. Eerdmans Publishing, 1995.
Whiting, Gary R. "The Testimony of Amaleki." In *The Book of Mormon: Jacob through Words of Mormon, to Learn with Joy*. Edited by Monte S. Nyman and Charles D. Tate Jr. Provo, Utah: BYU Religious Studies Center, 1990, 295–306.
Whitmer, David. "As Interviewed by the *Chicago Tribune* (1885)." In *Opening the Heavens: Accounts of Divine Manifestations, 1820–1844*. Edited by John W. Welch. Provo, Utah: Brigham Young University Press/Salt Lake City: Deseret Book, 2005, 153–54.
Whitmer, David. "James H. Hart Interview, Richmond, Missouri, 21 August 1883." In *The David Whitmer Interviews: A Restoration Witness*. Edited by Lyndon W. Cook. Orem, Utah: Grandin Book, 1991, 95–96.
Whitney, Orson F. "Some Historical and Prophetic Phases of the Book of Mormon." In *A Book of Mormon Treasury: Selections from the Pages of the* Improvement Era. Salt Lake City: Bookcraft, 1959, 216–21.
Wichmann, Søren. *The Relationship among the Mixe-Zoquean Languages of Mexico*. Salt Lake City: University of Utah Press, 1995.
Widtsoe, John A. *Seven Claims of the Book of Mormon*. Salt Lake City: Deseret Book, 1936.
Williams, Frederick G. "Did Lehi Land in Chile?" In *Reexploring the Book of Mormon*. Edited by John W. Welch. Provo, Utah: Foundation for Ancient Research and Mormon Studies, 1992, 57–61.
Williams, R. John. "A Marvelous Work and a Possession: Book of Mormon Historicity as Postcolónialism." *Dialogue: A Journal of Mormon Thought* 38, no. 4 (Winter 2005): 37–55.
Winsor, Justin. *Narrative and Critical History of America*. Edited by Justin Winsor. 8 vols. Boston: Houghton, Mifflin, 1889.
Woodruff, Wilford. *Wilford Woodruff's Journal*. Edited by Scott G. Kenney. 9 vols. Salt Lake City: Signature Books, 1985.
Wirth, Diane E. *A Challenge to the Critics: Scholarly Evidences of the Book of Mormon*. Bountiful,

Utah: Horizon Publishers, 1986.
Wirth, Diane E. *Parallels: Mesoamerican and Ancient Middle Eastern Traditions*. St. George, Utah: Stonecliff Publishing, 2003.
Wirth, Diane E. "Quetzalcoatl, the Maya Maize God, and Jesus Christ." *Journal of Book of Mormon Studies* 11 (2002): 4–15.
Wise, Michael, Martin Abegg Jr., and Edward Cook. *The Dead Sea Scrolls: A New Translation*. San Francisco: HarperSanFrancisco, 1996.
Wright, Dennis A. "Great and Abominable Church." *Encyclopedia of Mormonism*, 4 vols. New York: Macmillan Publishing, 1992, 2:568–69.
Wright, Mark Alan. "'According to Their Language, Unto Their Understanding': The Cultural Context of Hierophanies and Theophanies in Latter-day Saint Canon." *Studies in the Bible and Antiquity* 3 (2011): 51–65.
Wright, Mark Alan. "The Cultural Tapestry of Mesoamerica." *Journal of the Book of Mormon and Other Restoration Scripture* 22, no. 2 (2013): 4–21.
Wright, Mark Alan. "Deification: Divine Inheritance and the Glorious Afterlife in the Book of Mormon and Ancient Mesoamerica." Paper presented at the annual conference of the Foundation for Apologetic Information and Research, August 2008, http://www.fairlds.org/FAIR_Conferences/2008-Mark-Wright.pdf (accessed May 2011).
Wright, Mark Alan. "Joseph Smith and Native American Artifacts." Paper presented at the BYU Church History Symposium. *Approaching Antiquity: Joseph Smith's Study of the Ancient World*, March 7–8, 2013. Provo, Utah.
Wright, Mark Alan. "Nephite Daykeepers: Ritual Specialists in the Book of Mormon." Draft of a presentation given at the Expound Symposium, Provo, Utah, 2011. PDF copy in my possession, courtesy of Wright.
Wright, Mark Alan. "A Study of Classic Maya Rulership." PhD diss., University of California Riverside, 2011.
Wright, Mark Alan. "'Tree of Life' or 'Cosmic Tree:' Stela 5 in its Ancient Mesoamerican Context." Paper presented at Brigham Young University Sperry Symposium, October 11, 2011. Unpublished and preliminary draft notes in my possession. Used with Wright's permission.
Wright, Mark Alan, and Brant A. Gardner. "The Cultural Context of Nephite Apostasy." *Interpreter: A Journal of Mormon Scripture* 1 (2012): 25–55.
Wunderli, Earl M. "Critique of a Limited Geography for Book of Mormon Events." *Dialogue: A Journal of Mormon Thought* 35, no. 3 (Fall 2002): 161–97.
Wunderli, Earl M. *An Imperfect Book: What the Book of Mormon Tells Us about Itself*. Salt Lake City: Signature Books, 2013.
Yorgason, Blaine M., Bruce W. Warren, and Harold Brown. *New Evidences of Christ in Ancient America*. Provo, Utah: Book of Mormon Research Foundation, Stratford Books, 1999.
Young, Robert. *Analytical Concordance to the Bible*. 22nd ed. Grand Rapids, Mich.: Wm. B. Eerdmans Publishing, 1970.
"Zarahemla." *Times and Seasons* 3, no. 23 (October 1, 1842): 927.
Zevit, Ziony. "False Dichotomies in Descriptions of Israelite Religion: A Problem, Its Origin, and a Proposed Solution." In *Symbiosis, Symbolism, and the Power of the Past: Canaan, Ancient Israel and Their Neighbors from the Late Bronze Age through Roman Palaestina, Proceedings of the Centennial Symposium W. F. Albright Institute of Archaeological Research and American Schools of Oriental Research, Jerusalem, May 29–31, 2000*. Edited by William G. Dever and Seymour Gitin. Winona Lake, Ind.: Eisenbrauns, 2003, 223–35.
Zorita, Alonso de. *Life and Labor in Ancient Mexico City: The Brief and Summary Relation of the Lords of New Spain*. Translated by Benjamin Keen. Norman: University of Oklahoma Press, 1963.

Index

Abinadom, 209
Adams, William Y., 268
aggrandizers, 202
ahuéhuetl, 386
Akenson, Donald Harmon, 52
Allen, Joseph L. and Quetzalcoatl, 353, 358, 360, 363
Alma$_1$
    and churches, 239, 240–41, 254
    and city of Helam, 285
    and kingship, 243
Alma$_2$
    and Ammonihah, 255
    order of Nehors, 259
    people of Gideon, 271
    political disunity, 260
    resigns as chief judge, 258
Ambrosino, James N., 369
Amlici, 242, 243
Ammonihah
    Alma$_2$ travels to, 253
    and dungeons, 237
    Anti-Nephi-Lehies and, 304
    attack on, 309–10
    kin definitions from, 277
    relationship to Zarahemla, 255, 314
Ammonites, 303–4
Ammoron, 211, 267
Amon, 56, 58
Amulek, 272, 277, 278
Anderson, Arthur, 333
Annals of the Cakchiquels, 188
Anti-Nephi Lehies, people, 303, 305
    attack on Ammonihah, 308, 310
    cult of war, 307
    origin of, 305
Anti-Nephi-Lehi, person, 305
Antiomno, 301–2

Antionum, 253, 314, 320
Apocrypha, 6
Apollo, 193, 195
Arden, Traci, 369
asherah/Asherah, 97–98
Ashurbanipal, 57
Askren, Tierza, 179
Assyrian invasion, 65
Aston, Warren P./Michaela Knoth Aston, 83, 111
Astor-Aguilera, Miguel Angel, 240, 323
Baal, 62–63, 69, 257, 261
Babylonian invasion, 55, 58
Baer, James L., 345
bak'tun, 94, 370
Barker, Margaret
    on Josiah's reforms, 63, 70, 73
    on Lehi's vision, 98
    on the asherah, 96
Barney, Kevin L., 97
Barzun, Jacques, 49
bastern, 108
Beauchamp, Ezery, xii
Becán, 209, 210
Becker, Marshall J., 308
Benjamin
    abdication, 233
    and blood sacrifice, 272
    and community healing, 258
    and egalitarianism, 236
    and festival calendars, 231–32
    and heavenly king, 267
    and kin groups, 277
    and sins 236–37
    and temple site/tower, 233, 235
    new covenant, 231
    religious unity undone, 241
    renames his people, 254

446 Traditions of the Fathers

Bir Marsha, 77
Bird Jaguar, 310
Black Sea, 393
black skin, 160, 161
Blake, Michael, 202
Blong, Russell, 348
body paint, 164
Book of Mormon
    archaeology compared to Bible, 37
    translation of, 29, 32, 34
Boudinot, Elias, 4, 5, 8
Bountiful (Arabian)
    and metals, 111
    building a ship, 178
    location/distance, 83
    candidates for, 110–11
Bountiful (New World)
    after destructions, 347
    and land southward, 147–49
    and San Martin volcano, 345
    and Tonala, 350
    Christ's appearance at, 342, 344, 367
    Pratt on location, 15
    Sorenson's location, 146
Bové, Frederick Joseph, 124
bows, 102–3
brass plates
    and Joseph of Egypt, 89
    and king Noah, 260
    and Mosiah's translation, 384, 385
    as scripture, 88, 206, 257
    as tokens, 231
    attempt to buy, 66
    from northern kingdom, 88, 90
Bright, John, 69, 219
Brockington, Donald, 234
Brown, Linda A., 225
Brown, M. Kathryn, 39, 310
Brown, S. Kent
    on journey, 84, 108–10
    on Lehi's dream, sacrifices, 79, 95
    on Nahom, 107
    on night travel, 95
    on persecution of prophets, 76
bury-the-hatchet, 307
Bushman, Richard L.
    on non-republican politics, 246
    on perceptions and misreading, 36
    on reign of judges/people, 246

Canaanite religion, 61
caching, 308
Cahal Pech, 167
Calakmul, 256
calendars, 92–94
Campbell, Lyle, 339, 340, 400
Cannon, George Q., 17
Captain Moroni, 312, 316, 317
captives, treatment, 302–3
Card, Orson Scott, 29, 217
Carmack, Robert, 355
Cavalli-Sforza, Luigi Luca, 221
Ce Acatl Quetzalcoatl, 357, 358, 360, 362, 363
Central American ruins, 14, 254
Cerro Vigía, 374
Cerros, 185, 210
Chadwick, Jeffrey, 77
Chalcatzingo, 230
Chamula, 131, 134
chariots
    and wheeled toys, 294
    contexts for meaning, 293–94, 297, 301
    in translation, 294
Charlesworth, James H., 59
Chase, Diane Z. and Arlen F., 322
Chemish, 209
Chiapa de Corzo, 400
Chichén Itzá
    and shared power, 251, 252
    and Topiltzin Quetzalcoatl, 358
    and white warriors, 164
Chile, as landing site, 121
Cholan, 215, 223
Christenson, Allen J.

on creation, 144
on harvest festival, 231
Christianity
and iconography, 192–5
and Quetzalcoatl, 364
and St. Thomas, 355
and syncretism, 262
Cival, 210
clan system (Israel), 61
Clark, David L., 113
Clark, John E.
on aggrandizers, 202
on archaeology, 37, 408–9
on Book of Mormon cities, 37
on 400-year prophecy, 94
on geographic correspondence, 405
on Izapa/Stela 5, 100–1
on Mesoamerica as better fit, 408
on new Izapa drawing, 100
on NY Cumorah, 377
on seas as symbol, 143
Clarke's Bible Commentary, 3
Clinton, De Witt, 11
Cluff, Benjamin Jr, 18
Codex Mendoza, 132
Codex Nuttall, 363
Coe, Michael D., 19, 40, 372
coins, 298
Columbus, Christopher, 119, 120, 307
conceptual translation, 34
convergences
as Sorenson uses, 47
complexity, 50, 407
Dever's definition, 49
geo-spatial, 402
Grijalva as the Sidon, 128
Nahom, 107
not proof, 51
600-year propohecy, 93
zaztuns, 226
Copan
alliance against, 256
and K'inich Yax K'uk Mo', 265, 267
ethnic groups in, 254

lineages and rule, 286
Coriantumr
and battle at Ramah, 373
and the stone, 227, 383
as last Jaredite king, 381, 389
in Zarahemla, 223–24, 390
costly apparel, 200–1, 203, 211, 260
Covarrubias, Miguel, 333
Cowan, Richard O., 375
Crossan, John Dominic
on sarcophagus, 193
on history in Luke, 39
on Nazareth, 38
on parallel layering, 31
Cuicuilco, 329, 347
Cumorah
and New York, 375, 377
as Ramah, 373
military significance, 373
burial of plates, 376
Davila, James R., 44
Davis, Ryan W., 247
de Triana, Rodrigo, 119
Dead Sea Scrolls, xviii
deity complex, 263, 264, 265
deity impersonation, 230, *See* teixiptla.
Delgado, Augustín, 234
Desolation, 148, 149, 382
Dever, William G.
Bible, limitations of, 60, 177
Hebrew has no word for religion, 75
on "plain meaning", 27
on choice of historical method, 43
on convergence, 47, 49
on religion in antiquity, 240
devotional burying. *See* caching.
DeVrieds, Kelly, 113
Diamond, Jared, 184
Dibble, Charles, 333
Diehl, Richard A.
on Olmec, 152–53, 338, 396
on Toltec, 357

Diehl, Richard, 396
DNA, 171
Dos Pilas, 337
downslope, 134
Drew, David
  on jade/gold, 199
  on kings/councils, 186, 252, 286
  on warfare/capture, 306
dry season, 317
dungeons, 235–37
Durán, Diego de, 355–56, 360, 362, 384–85
egalitarian ideal, 74, 198, 255, 260
Ehecatl Quetzalcoatl, 357–360, 363
Eitan, Avrahim, 183
Ekholm, Gordon F., 196
El Chayal, 216
El Mesón, 374
El Mirador, 209–10
Empty Quarter, 109–10
enthronement, 309
Eshnunna's law code, 299
Estrada-Belli, Francisco, 136, 167, 210
ethnogenesis, 177, 180, 189
ethnographic analogy, 47, 52, 226
Euphrates, 393
Eusebius, 3
Evans, Susan Toby, 222, 329, 398
fair and delightsome, 159, 162
FairMormon, 414
false Christs, 229
Farnsworth, Dewey, 151–52
Ferguson, Thomas Stuart, 20, 403-3
Fernández-Armesto, Felipe, 120
Flannery, Kent V., 39
Flower Mountain, 266
Foster, Lynne V., 254, 256
Fox, David S., 104
Frankincense Trail, 101–11

Freidel, David A., 130, 209, 295, 312, 395
functional translation, 34
Gadianton robbers. *See* secret combinations
Garber, James F., 310, 397
Gee, John, 170
Gibraltar, 394
Gid, 319
Gilgal, 349
Givens, Terryl L., xix, 12, 25
glottochronology, 221
Golden plates, physicality of, xvi
Golden, Charles W., 313
Gottwald, Norman, 63
Graff, Henry F., 49
Green, Dee F., 404
Grijalva River, 125, 127–28
Grijalva River Basin, 195, 216, 222, 400
Grolier Codex, 26
Grove, David C., 230
Grover, Jerry D., Jr, 345, 350
Grube, Nikolai, 256, 300, 309–10
Gutjahr, Paul, 10
Hagoth, 328
Halpern, Baruch, 30, 61–62, 65, 68
Ham, 3
Hamblin, William J.
  on bows, 102–103
  on Hebrew directions, 135
  on Laban's sword, 182
  on order of battle, 320
  on pre-exilic temple theology, 70
Hammond, Norman, 237
Hansen, Richard N., 185, 198
haplotype X2a, 173–74
Hardy, Grant, xii, xviii, 179, 239
Hardy, Heather, xii, 220
Harris, Franklin S., Jr., 20
Harris, Martin, xv, xvii, 213
Harris, Martin, 11

Harrison, Roland Kenneth, 57
Hassig, Ross
    on Aztec warfare, 183, 318–20, 322
    on fortifications in art, 397
    on Teotihuacan and Kaminaljuyú, 369
    on Teotihuacan military influence, 370
Head, Ronan James, 245
Hebrew, as literary language, 154
Helam, 240, 285
Helaman$_2$, 218, 248, 253, 268
Henderson, John S, 200, 367
Hernandez, Christine, 51
Heuristic fictions, 52
Hezekiah, 55, 58
    reforms of, 56, 62
    Manasseh reverses reforms, 63
    temples outside Jerusalem, 80
Hills, Louis E., 19
Hilton, Lynn and Hope, 77, 110–11
Hisarlik, 403
historical linguistics, 5, 48–50
historicity
    and Bible, xviii, 29
    and metallurgy, 40
    development of arguments, xix, 8, 22, 25, 47, 50
    explanatory pardigms, 2
    Mesoamerican focus, 20
    relation to proof, 171, 173
Hobbins, John F., 44
Holmes, Robert, 18
Holmes, William Henry, 294
Hopkins, Nicholas A., 134–35, 141, 144, 148
horses
    and chariots, 292–95
    as food animals, 293
    in the New World, 289–91
    Pre-Columbian, 290
    translation, 291
Houston, Stephen
    on body paint, 164
    on La Mojarra stela, 399
    on Mesoamerican gods, 270, 263

Hughes, Bettany, 201
Huitzilopochtli, 361, 363
human sacrifice, 40, 237, 272, 306, 372
Hunt, Wallace, 279
Hunter, Milton R., 385
hunter-gatherer lifestyle, 156
interpreters
    and Ether, 224
    and reading a stone, 225
    and W. W. Phelps, 376
    and zaztuns, 225
    called Urim and Thummim, 376
Ishmael, 80, 106, 155, 267
Isthmus of Tehuantepec, 138, 145–46, 345, 351, 370–71
iterative process, 50
Ivins, Anthony W., 23, 172, 246
Ixtlilxochitl, 385–87
Izapa Stela 5, 98–101
Jacob, 168–170
    and Isaiah, 169
    and Sherem, 204
    and warfare, 208
    on costly apparel, 189, 198, 200
    on polygamy, 202
jaguar warriors, 334
Jakeman, M. Wells, 20, 98
Japheth, 3
Jaredites
    and tower, 382
    genealogy, 389
    in Olmec lands, 382, 395
    two embarkations, 394
Jarom, 156, 208, 257, 260
Jehoahaz, 58, 65
Jehoiachin, 58, 75
Jehoiakim, 56, 58, 65, 219
Jeremiah
    and Malkiyahti, 218–19
    before Lehi, 69–70
    persecuted, 75
Johnson, Eric, 298–99

Jollserand, J. Kathryn, 134–35, 141, 144, 148
Jordan, Benjamin R., 349
Josiah, 58
    as reformer, 56, 63, 70, 73, 81, 96
    and Deuteronomy, 64
    family and rule, 55–57
Justeson, John, 399
K'inich Yax K'uk Mo', 236, 265–67
k'uhul ajaw-holy lord, 267
Kaminaljuyú
    and Teotihuacan, 330, 334, 369
    as city of Nephi, 167
    Cholan speakers, 215
    early settlement, 168
    El Chayal obsidian, 216
    Quichéan invasion, 215
Kaufman, Terrence, 340, 399
Kelley, David H., 197
keystone, Book of Mormon, xi, xvii, 409
Kidder, Alfred V., 403
Killebrew, Ann E., 177
kin compounds, 278–79
king Noah. *See* Noah (king).
kingmen, 245, 251
Kitahara, Michio, 273
Kitchen, Kenneth A., 58, 60
Korihor, 91, 271
Kowallis, Bart
    on Pliny's description, 345
    on volcanos/winds, 344, 347
Kuhn, Thomas S., 1–2
Kuntillet Ajrud, 80
Laban's sword, 181
Lafaye, Jacques, 356, 360, 364
Laman and Lemuel
    as believers, 75
    as enemies, 177
    as Jerusalem sympathizers, 74
    bows, 103
    cause for a burnt offering, 80
    separation from Nephi, 155

Lamb, Martin Thomas, 33
Lamoni
    and Ammon, 285–88
    and Ammon's brethren, 301
    as Anti-Nephi-Lehi's brother, 305–6
    father is over-king, 289, 297
    horses and chariots, 293
    state visit, 294, 301
    traces genealogy to Ishmael, 267
Las Casas, Bartolomé de, 119–20, 362
Layton, Lynn C., 20
Leaves of Grass, 45
Legend of the Suns, 359, 386–87
Lehi
    and brass plates, 85
    and dreams, 95–97
    and lunar calendar, 93
    and wilderness travel, 95, 102, 109, 125
    on Joseph of Egypt, 86, 89
    born in the Jewish Quarter, 67
    builds altar, 79
    land of inheritance, 66
    metalworker, 67
    name, 66
    prophetic call, 70–71, 73
    600-year prophecy, 92
Leiden Plaque, 309
Levine, Baruch A., 60
Liahona, 188
Limhi
    and bondage, 284
    and the voice of the people, 248
    delegation of, 126
Lindsay, Jeff, 44
literal translation, 34
lost tribes, xvii, 3–4, 7–8
Love, Bruce, 288
Lowe, Gareth W., 400
Ludlow, Daniel, 307
Ludlow, Jared W., 80
MacMullen, Ramsay, 192, 250
macuahuitl, 183
Madsen, Brigham D., 18

Maize God, 195, 265–66
Malaysia, 122
Malina, Bruce J., 35–36, 74, 158, 258
Manasseh, 58, 63–64, 66
Martin, Simon, 256, 300, 309–10
masks, 195, 230, 270, 271
Matheny, Deanne G., 129
Mauss, Armand L., 161, 163
Maxwell, Neal A., 53
Mayor, Adrienne, 388
McCafferty, Geoffrey G., 388
McConkie, Joseph Fielding, 175
McGuire, Benjamin L., 178
McKay, David O., 21
McKeever, Bill, 298–99
McKillop, Heather, 331
McNemar, Richard, 8, 9
Mediterranean Sea, 393
Meldrum, Rodney L., 173–74
Mendieta, Gerónimo de, 363
Merrill, A. Brent, 321
Mesoamerica
    aggrandizers and polygamy, 203
    and Nephite apostasy, 271
    art, beards, skin color, 163, 362
    Book of Mormon in, 19, 20, 48
    Bountiful/Desolation, 148
    buildings, 209, 278
    burials, 308, 323
    calenders, 94, 390
    caves and underworld, 330
    chief market, 279
    council of elders, 252
    creation/origin, 306, 359
    cultural region, 52, 124
    demi-gods and Ammon, 287
    directions, 130–31, 134, 360
    food crops, 300
    human sacrifice, 238, 372
    inter-city visits, 301
    jewelry, 199, 201, 329
    kings, 185, 188, 265
    languages and writing, 51, 398
    new year celebration, 232
    Quetzalcoatl, 353, 361
    ruins, 13
    slavery, 237, 284
    social stratification, 198, 236, 251
    Teotihuacan, 328, 331
    warfare, 181, 238, 302, 306, 311–12
metallurgy, 40, 184
Metcalfe, Brent Lee, 27, 37
Middoni, 301
Miller, Adam S., 27
Miller, Mary, 32, 131, 360
Miller, Wade E., 290
Millet, Robert L., 175
Misantla, 374
Mishnah, 38
Mitchill, Samuel, 11
Mixe-Zoquean, 184, 340
Mock, Shirley Boteler, 308
Moriancumer, 394
Morley, Sylvanus, 237
Moronihah, 345, 346
Mosiah, lost first chapter, 213
Mosiah$_1$
    and Nephite migration, 215, 282
    and seer stones, 225–27
    and Zarahemla, 223, 229, 390
    prophet, not king, 214
Mosiah$_2$
    and interpreters, 224, 226, 381–87
    and popol nah, 252
    religion and politics, 238, 242
    sons of, 281
    speaks to large gathering, 233
Moteuczomah Ilhuicamina, 319
Mulek
    lineage/descendents, 217, 219
    Muloch in the manuscript, 218
    seal of, 219
Mulekites. *See* people of Mulek.
Murphy, Thomas W., 171

Nabopolassar, 57
Nacxit, 188
Nahom, 105–7
nahualistas, 333
Nahum, 56
Native Americans
    and a book, 5
    and lost tribes, xvii, 3–4, 7, 12
Nazareth, 30, 38–9, 97–98
Necho II, 57
Nehor, 189, 259
Nephi
    and David and Goliath, 86
    and Joseph of Egypt, 178
    and Laban, 86
    and others, 151
    and temple, 165, 81
    bow, 102–4
    brass plates, 88
    egalitarian ideal of, 189
    king, 178, 180, 184, 188
    makes plates, xv
    makes swords, 181
    on lost ten tribes, 7, 169
    on Messiah, 72–73
    on mother of God, 97
    on the Tree of Life, 71, 95, 96
    personality of, 179
    scribal training/writer, 114, 116, 120, 176–77
    skin, as metaphor, 163
    Valley of Guatemala, 165
Nephihah, 249
Nephite apostasy, 258
Nephite twelve month calendar, 317
New World Archaeological Foundation. *See* NWAF.
Nibley, Hugh W., 21, 83, 106, 382
Nicholson, H. B., 357–58, 360, 386
Nimrod, 393
Noah (king), 243, 260, 279, 283
nonotzaleque, 332–33, 335
Northern Kingdom (Israel)
    and asherah, 96
    and brass plates, 88
    and the E tradition, 89–91
    Assyrian invasion, 7, 55, 65
Nyman, Monte S., 298
O'Brien, Brandon J., 35
obsidian, 168, 183–87, 198, 216, 225, 272, 314, 329, 369
Olive, Phyllis, 26
Olmec
    and Coriantumr, 391
    and Jaredites, 152, 338, 390
    and Mixe-Zoque, 222, 339–400
    art, 266
    dating, 153, 389, 395
    language/writing, 340, 342, 398–99
    cultural influence, 186, 196, 395–96
    Grijalva, 127
    name, 37, 153, 338
    warfare, 397
Onihah, 349
order of Nehors, 258–59, 260, 279
over-king, 300–2
pacifism, 310
Pacumeni, 248
Pahoran, 248, 249
Pakal, 265
Palenque, 265, 297, 303
Palmer, David A., 358, 374
Papua New Guinea, 348
parallelomania, 43
parallels, 44, 47–48
Paricutin, 346
Parker, Joy, 130, 295
Pearson, Bruce L., 48
people of Gideon, 271
people of Mulek
    adopted indigenous religion, 223
    and Jaredites, 396
    and Olmecs, 222, 339, 391, 400
    and Zarahemlaites, 399
    arrived after Nephites, 390
people of Zarahemla

and Benjamin's speech, 254
arrival of, 222
and Jaredites, 223, 227, 339, 391
become Nephites, 229, 231
Perego, Ugo A., 171, 173–74
Perrett, Allison, 398
Peterson, Daniel C., 97, 258, 298, 403
Phillips, William Revell, 111
Pinker, Steven, 26, 132, 160
plunder, 238, 284–85, 326, 336
Pohl, John M. D., 252
Pohl, Mary, 398
politics/religion (Israel), 59
polygamy, 198, 203
Pope, Kevin, 398
popol nah, 252
Popol Vuh
   and hero twins, 288
   Nacxit and rulership, 188
   sacred book of the Quiché, 28
   themes, 51
Port Royal, Jamaica, 349
Potter, George, 77–78, 85, 111
Poulsen, Lawrence L., xii, 127, 143, 374
Pratt, Orson, 15, 121
Pratt, Parley P., xi, 8, 378
prejudice, 158
Priest, Josiah, 387
prisons, 236, 237
production culture, 29, 31
productive convergences, 408
Psammetichus, 57
Punta de Chimino, 209
Quetzalcoatl
   and Jesus Christ, 353
   and St. Thomas, 355
   and Tula, 357
   aspects of, 288, 357
   beard and skin, 360–61
   Ce Acatl Quetzalcoatl, 360
   Ehecatl Quetzlcoatl, 358
   painted black, 360
   Topiltzin Quetzalcoatl, 357
   virgin birth, 363
Quiché, 215, 306, 407
quinametzin, 387
Quiriguá, 13–14, 256
rainy season, 317
Raish, Martin, 41
Rambo, Lewis, 269
Rappleye, Neal, xii, 67, 76, 106, 316
Redford, Donald B., 57
Reed, Jonathan L., 31, 38–39
Reeve, Rex C., Jr., 375
Reilly, F. Kent, III, 397
Relación de Tilantongo, 253
Reynolds, George, 298
Richards, E. Randolph, 35
Richards, LeGrand, 10
Roberts, B. H., 18, 139, 401
Robinson, H. Wheeler, 326
Rohrbaugh, Richard L., 35, 36, 258
Roman gladius, 183
Roper, Matthew, xvi, 170, 261
royal litter, 295–97
royal visits, 301
Rust, Richard Dilworth, 326
Sachse, Frauke, 144
Sahagún, Bernardino de, 332–33, 358, 362–63, 388
sailing, 112–14
Sais, 57
Saite kings, 57
Salinas La Blanca, 278
Salmon, Douglas F., 43
San Bartolo, 51
San Martín, as 3 Nephi volcano, 345
Sandmel, Samuel, 43
sarcophagus, 193–95, 265

454 *Traditions of the Fathers*

Sariah, 68
sastun. *See* zaztun
Schele, Linda, 130, 201, 234, 295, 301, 309
Schliemann, Heinrich, 403–4
Schowalter, Daniel N., 238
seas, 143
secret combinations, 325, 370, 381
    and Jaredites, 326, 338
    and Lamanites, 335
    and land northward, 327
    Gadianton robbers, 326
Shalmaneser V, 7
Shazer, 101, 102, 105
Sheets, Payson D., 311
Shem, 3
Sherem, 205–7, 229
Sierra Los Cuchumatanes, 127
Sihyaj Chan K'awiil II, 266
Siyaj K'ak', 335
Sjodahl, Janne M., 16, 298
skin. *See* black skin *and* white skin.
slavery, 237
Smith, Emma, xv
Smith, Ethan, 6
Smith, Joseph
    and Cumorah, 376, 378
    and interpreters, 224–26
    transcribers, 72
    translation, 291, 384
    Times and Seasons editorial, 121
Smith, Joseph Fielding, 378
Smith, Katherine, xv
Smith, Lucy Mack, xvi
Smith, Mark, 96
Smith, Michael E., 262
Smith, Richard Pearson, 298
Smoot, Stephen, xii
Snyder, Graydon F., 193
sojourn, 110
Sorenson, John L.
    Book of Mormon map, 122, 149, 404
    Ensign articles, 21
    on Dever's convergences, 47
    on gardens, 280
    on kin rituals, 277
    on marketplaces, 279
    on pre-Columbian horse, 290
    on Quetzalcoatl, 354
    on Ramah and Cumorah, 373
    on sailing to New World, 114
    on scholsrship, 22
    on skin color, 163
    on warfare, 316
Southerton, Simon G., 40
Spackman, Randall, 92
Spencer, Joseph M., xviii
Sperry, Sidney B., 204, 298, 377
St. Thomas, 4, 355–56, 364–65
Stanton, Travis W., 39, 369
steel, 181–83, 199
steel bow, 102–4
stereotype, 157–58, 209
Stern, Ephraim, 38, 80
Stiebing, William H., 38
Stocker, Terry, 323
Stoddard, Ted Dee, 138
Storey, Rebecca, 200
stories in Scriptures, xi, 52–53
Stowell, Arad, 226
stripling warriors, age of, 304
Stuart, David
    on body paint, 164
    on directions, 148
    on left/right, 134, 149
    on glyph for south, 148
    on Mesoamerican gods, 263, 270
subduction zone, 344–45
swords, 181–83
synagogue, 33, 39, 193, 239
syncretism
    and solar deity, 264
    definition, 261

conduits, 267–70
in Maya religion, 263
Nephite, 207, 268
Szink, Terrence L., 231
Talmage, James E., 18
Talmud, 38
Tanner, Jerald and Sandra, 189
Taube, Karl
on body paint, 164
on directions, 131, 149, 360
on Flower Mountain, 266
on gods, 32, 270
on jaguar palanquins, 296
Taylor, John, 353, 360
Tedlock, Dennis, 306
teixiptla, 229
Temple of the Sun, 330
temples outside of Jerusalem, 80
Tenochtitlan, 132, 284
Teomner, 319
Teotihuacan
and Jaredites, 338
and Maya region, 330, 335, 369
and secret combinations, 332, 337
and Tikal, 335, 370
cement, 328
Cuicuilco relocates to, 329
land northward, 332
language, 340–41
military, 334, 336, 370–71
Mormon's description of, 328, 331, 341
trade, 331
trees, lack of, 328
Tezcatlipoca, 359–61
The Evening and Morning Star, 12
The Itzan Society, 20
Thompson, Thomas L., 49
Tigris, 393
Tollan. *See* Tula
Topiltzin, 384
Topiltzin Quetzalcoatl, 357–58
Torquemada, Juan de, 362

Totepeuh, 357
Tower of Babel, 383, 389
trade routes
and Maya lands, 314–16
and Teotihuacan, 330, 369, 371
and Zarahemla, 315
translation anachronisms
chariots, 289
horse, 289, 291
in KJV, 291–92
Travels of Marco Polo, 43
tribes after Lehi, 275–77, 370
tribute
and hierarchy, 186
and trade, 316
and subordinate cities, 284–85, 310, 336
as plunder, 285
Tula
Huitzilopochtli myth, 363
Quetzalcoatl in, 357–58, 360
Tvedtnes, John A., 27, 67, 78, 278
type-scene, 327, 341–42
Tzeltal, 134
Uaxactun, 135, 136
Uitzilopochtli. *See* Huitzilopochtli
upslope, 134
Usumacinta River, 125–27
Vail, Gabrielle, 51, 263
van der Toorn, Karel, 69, 179
Vansina, Jan, 355
Veil, Gabrielle, 51
View of the Hebrews, 6
Vogel, Dan, 15, 37
voice of the people
and lineages, 246, 252
before Mosiah, 247–48
government mechanism, 244, 246, 249
operation of, 247, 250–51
volcano, 344, 346, 348, 350
von Nagy, Christopher, 398
votive altars, 107

wadi al-Bad, 77
wadi Tayyib al-Ism, 77
warfare
    and Maya religion, 240
    and Olmec, 396–97
    and trade, 313, 315, 369
    archaeological evidence, 209, 322
    chariots, lack of, 294
    differences in Mormon's time, 372
    in Alma, 311
    in Jacob, 208
    in Omni, 209
    in Helaman, 311
    Mesoamerican culture, 181, 306
    night attacks, 320
    standing army, lack of, 312
    seasonal, 316
Washburn, J. Alvin, 20
Washburn, J. N., 20, 223
Webster, David, 186, 209
Welch, John W., 50, 231, 236, 239, 244, 299, 402
Wellington, Richard, 77–78, 85, 111
white skin, 161
Whitman, Walt, 44
Whitmer, David, xvi, 10, 378
Whitmer, John, xvi
Whitney, Orson F., 375
Widmer, Randolph J., 200
Willey, Gordon, 403
Williams, Frederick G., 121
Williams, R. John, 42
Wirth, Diane, 358, 360
Words of Mormon, nature of, 214
Wright, Mark Alan, xii
    on divinitory stones, 225
    on early Mormons and artifacts, 16
    on Maya kingship, 236
    on Mesoamerican diversity, 254
    on shamanic near-death, 288
    on the Tree of Life stone, 99
Wright, Traci, xii
Wunderli, Earl M., 26, 33
Xitle, 329–30, 347
Yahweh, xiii, 71, 73, 231, 342
Yax Nuun Ahiin, 266
Yax Pasaj, 236, 267
Yaxchilan, 310
Yaxuná, 370
zacualli, 386
Zarahemla, king, 216, 220
zaztuns, 225–26
Zedekiah, 58, 388
    and Lehi, 220
    and Mulekites, 217, 268
    installed by Babylon, 56, 58
Zeniff
    and Lamanites, 283
    and voice of the people, 247
    as Nephite spy, 282
    leaves Zarahemla, 126
    origin of his people, 281
Zephaniah, 56
Zevit, Ziony, 275, 276
Zoque
    and Epi-Olmec, 399
    and Mixe-Zoque, 222, 339
    and Zarahemla, 223, 227, 400
    La Mojarra stela, 227
Zorita, Alonso de, 284

About the Author

Brant A. Gardner earned his M.S. in anthropology (specializing in Mesoamerican ethnohistory) from the State University of New York at Albany. He is the author of the six-volume *Second Witness: Analytical and Contextual Commentary on the Book of Mormon* and *The Gift and Power: Translating the Book of Mormon*. He has presented papers at the Foundation for Apologetic Information and Research (FAIR), the Book of Mormon Archaeological Symposium, and Sunstone. His other published works include chapters in *Estudios de Cultura Nahuatl* and *Symbol and Meaning beyond the Closed Community: Essays in Mesoamerican Ideas*, and articles in the *FARMS Review*, *Sunstone*, and *Meridian Magazine*. Brant and his wife, Valerie, have four children and eleven grandchildren.

Also available from
GREG KOFFORD BOOKS

Second Witness: Analytical and Contextual Commentary on the Book of Mormon

Brant A. Gardner

Second Witness, a new six-volume series from Greg Kofford Books, takes a detailed, verse-by-verse look at the Book of Mormon. It marshals the best of modern scholarship and new insights into a consistent picture of the Book of Mormon as a historical document. Taking a faithful but scholarly approach to the text and reading it through the insights of linguistics, anthropology, and ethnohistory, the commentary approaches the text from a variety of perspectives: how it was created, how it relates to history and culture, and what religious insights it provides.

The commentary accepts the best modern scholarship, which focuses on a particular region of Mesoamerica as the most plausible location for the Book of Mormon's setting. For the first time, that location—its peoples, cultures, and historical trends—are used as the backdrop for reading the text. The historical background is not presented as proof, but rather as an explanatory context.

The commentary does not forget Mormon's purpose in writing. It discusses the doctrinal and theological aspects of the text and highlights the way in which Mormon created it to meet his goal of "convincing . . . the Jew and Gentile that Jesus is the Christ, the Eternal God."

Praise for the *Second Witness* series:

"Gardner not only provides a unique tool for understanding the Book of Mormon as an ancient document written by real, living prophets, but he sets a standard for Latter-day Saint thinking and writing about scripture, providing a model for all who follow. . . . No other reference source will prove as thorough and valuable for serious readers of the Book of Mormon."
   -Neal A. Maxwell Institute, Brigham Young University

1. 1st Nephi: 978-1-58958-041-1
2. 2nd Nephi–Jacob: 978-1-58958-042-8
3. Enos–Mosiah: 978-1-58958-043-5
4. Alma: 978-1-58958-044-2
5. Helaman–3rd Nephi: 978-1-58958-045-9
6. 4th Nephi–Moroni: 978-1-58958-046-6

The Gift and Power: Translating the Book of Mormon

Brant A. Gardner

Hardcover, ISBN: 978-1-58958-131-9

From Brant A. Gardner, the author of the highly praised *Second Witness* commentaries on the Book of Mormon, comes *The Gift and Power: Translating the Book of Mormon*. In this first book-length treatment of the translation process, Gardner closely examines the accounts surrounding Joseph Smith's translation of the Book of Mormon to answer a wide spectrum of questions about the process, including: Did the Prophet use seerstones common to folk magicians of his time? How did he use them? And, what is the relationship to the golden plates and the printed text?

Approaching the topic in three sections, part 1 examines the stories told about Joseph, folk magic, and the translation. Part 2 examines the available evidence to determine how closely the English text replicates the original plate text. And part 3 seeks to explain how seer stones worked, why they no longer work, and how Joseph Smith could have produced a translation with them.

The Brigham Young University Book of Mormon Symposium Series

Various Authors

Nine-volume box set, ISBN: 978-1-58958-087-9

A series of lectures delivered at BYU by a wide and exciting array of the finest gospel scholars in the Church. Get valuable insights from foremost authorities including General authorities, BYU Professors and Church Educational System instructors. No gospel library will be complete without this valuable resource. Anyone interested in knowing what the top gospel scholars in the Church are saying about such important subjects as historiography, geography, and faith in Christ will be sure to enjoy this handsome box set. This is the perfect gift for any student of the Book of Mormon.

Contributors include: Neal A. Maxwell, Boyd K. Packer, Jeffrey R. Holland, Russell M. Nelson, Dallin H. Oaks, Gerald N. Lund, Dean L. Larsen, Joseph Fielding McConkie, Richard Neitzel Holzapfel, Truman G. Madsen, John W. Welch, Robert J. Matthews, Daniel H. Ludlow, Stephen D. Ricks, Grant Underwood, Robert L. Millet, Susan Easton Black, H. Donl Peterson, John L. Sorenson, Monte S. Nyman, Daniel C. Peterson, Stephen E. Robinson, Carolyn J. Rasmus, Dennis L. Largey, C. Max Caldwell, Andrew C. Skinner, S. Michael Wilcox, Paul R. Cheesman, K. Douglas Bassett, Douglas E. Brinley, Richard O. Cowan, Donald W. Parry, Bruce A. Van Orden, Kenneth W. Anderson, Leland Gentry, S. Kent Brown, H. Dean Garrett, Lee L. Donaldson, Robert E. Parsons, S. Brent Farley, Rodney Turner, Larry E. Dahl, Mae Blanch, Rex C. Reeve Jr., E. Dale LeBaron, Clyde J. Williams, Chauncey C. Riddle, Kent P. Jackson, Daniel K. Judd, Neal E. Lambert, Michael W. Middleton, R. Wayne Shute, John M. Butler, and many more!

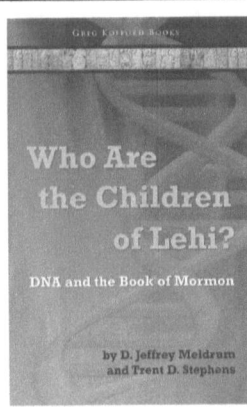

Who Are the Children of Lehi? DNA and the Book of Mormon

D. Jeffrey Meldrum and Trent D. Stephens

Hardcover, ISBN: 978-1-58958-048-0
Paperback, ISBN: 978-1-58958-129-6

How does the Book of Mormon, keystone of the LDS faith, stand up to data about DNA sequencing that puts the ancestors of modern Native Americans in northeast Asia instead of Palestine?

In *Who Are the Children of Lehi?* Meldrum and Stephens examine the merits and the fallacies of DNA-based interpretations that challenge the Book of Mormon's historicity. They provide clear guides to the science, summarize the studies, illuminate technical points with easy-to-grasp examples, and spell out the data's implications.

The results? There is no straight-line conclusion between DNA evidence and "Lamanites." The Book of Mormon's validity lies beyond the purview of scientific empiricism—as it always has. And finally, inspiringly, they affirm Lehi's kinship as one of covenant, not genes.

Re-reading Job: Understanding the Ancient World's Greatest Poem

Michael Austin

Paperback, ISBN: 978-1-58958-667-3

Job is perhaps the most difficult to understand of all books in the Bible. While a cursory reading of the text seems to relay a simple story of a righteous man whose love for God was tested through life's most difficult of challenges and rewarded for his faith through those trials, a closer reading of Job presents something far more complex and challenging. The majority of the text is a work of poetry that authors and artists through the centuries have recognized as being one of--if not the--greatest poem of the ancient world.

In *Re-reading Job: Understanding the Ancient World's Greatest Poem*, author Michael Austin shows how most readers have largely misunderstood this important work of scripture and provides insights that enable us to re-read Job in a drastically new way. In doing so, he shows that the story of Job is far more than that simple story of faith, trials, and blessings that we have all come to know, but is instead a subversive and complex work of scripture meant to inspire readers to rethink all that they thought they knew about God.

Praise for *Re-reading Job*:

"In this remarkable book, Michael Austin employs his considerable skills as a commentator to shed light on the most challenging text in the entire Hebrew Bible. Without question, readers will gain a deeper appreciation for this extraordinary ancient work through Austin's learned analysis. Rereading Job signifies that Latter-day Saints are entering a new age of mature biblical scholarship. It is an exciting time, and a thrilling work." — David Bokovoy, author, *Authoring the Old Testament*

Authoring the Old Testament: Genesis–Deuteronomy

David Bokovoy

Paperback, ISBN: 978-1-58958-588-1

For the last two centuries, biblical scholars have made discoveries and insights about the Old Testament that have greatly changed the way in which the authorship of these ancient scriptures has been understood. In the first of three volumes spanning the entire Hebrew Bible, David Bokovoy dives into the Pentateuch, showing how and why textual criticism has led biblical scholars today to understand the first five books of the Bible as an amalgamation of multiple texts into a single, though often complicated narrative; and he discusses what implications those have for Latter-day Saint understandings of the Bible and modern scripture.

Praise for *Authoring the Old Testament*:

"*Authoring the Old Testament* is a welcome introduction, from a faithful Latter-day Saint perspective, to the academic world of Higher Criticism of the Hebrew Bible.... [R]eaders will be positively served and firmly impressed by the many strengths of this book, coupled with Bokovoy's genuine dedication to learning by study and also by faith." — John W. Welch, editor, *BYU Studies Quarterly*

"Bokovoy provides a lucid, insightful lens through which disciple-students can study intelligently LDS scripture. This is first rate scholarship made accessible to a broad audience—nourishing to the heart and mind alike." — Fiona Givens, co-author, *The God Who Weeps: How Mormonism Makes Sense of Life*

"I repeat: this is one of the most important books on Mormon scripture to be published recently.... [*Authoring the Old Testament*] has the potential to radically expand understanding and appreciation for not only the Old Testament, but scripture in general. It's really that good. Read it. Share it with your friends. Discuss it." — David Tayman, The Improvement Era: A Mormon Blog

Saints of Valor: Mormon Medal of Honor Recipients

Sherman L. Fleek

Hardcover, ISBN: 978-1-58958-171-5

Since 1861 when the US Congress approved the concept of a Medal of Honor for combat valor, 3,457 individuals have received this highest military decoration that the nation can bestow. Nine of those have been Latter-day Saints. The military and personal stories of these LDS recipients are compelling, inspiring, and tragic. The men who appear in this book are tied by two common threads: the Medal of Honor and their Mormon heritage.

The purpose of this book is to highlight the valor of a special class of LDS servicemen who served and sacrificed "above and beyond the call of duty." Four of these nine Mormons gave their "last full measure" for their country, never seeing the high award they richly deserved. All four branches of the service are represented: five were Army (one was a pilot with the Army Air Forces during WWII), two Navy, and one each of the Marine Corps and Air Force. Four were military professionals who made the service their careers; five were not career-minded; three died at an early age and never married. This book captures these harrowing historical narratives from personal accounts.

Joseph Smith's Polygamy, 3 Vols.

Brian Hales

Hardcover
Volume 1: History 978-1-58958-189-0
Volume 2: History 978-1-58958-548-5
Volume 3: Theology 978-1-58958-190-6

Perhaps the least understood part of Joseph Smith's life and teachings is his introduction of polygamy to the Saints in Nauvoo. Because of the persecution he knew it would bring, Joseph said little about it publicly and only taught it to his closest and most trusted friends and associates before his martyrdom.

In this three-volume work, Brian C. Hales provides the most comprehensive faithful examination of this much misunderstood period in LDS Church history. Drawing for the first time on every known account, Hales helps us understand the history and teachings surrounding this secretive practice and also addresses and corrects many of the numerous allegations and misrepresentations concerning it. Hales further discusses how polygamy was practiced during this time and why so many of the early Saints were willing to participate in it.

Joseph Smith's Polygamy is an essential resource in understanding this challenging and misunderstood practice of early Mormonism.

Praise for *Joseph Smith's Polygamy*:

"Brian Hales wants to face up to every question, every problem, every fear about plural marriage. His answers may not satisfy everyone, but he gives readers the relevant sources where answers, if they exist, are to be found. There has never been a more thorough examination of the polygamy idea."
—Richard L. Bushman, author of *Joseph Smith: Rough Stone Rolling*

"Hales's massive and well documented three volume examination of the history and theology of Mormon plural marriage, as introduced and practiced during the life of Joseph Smith, will now be the standard against which all other treatments of this important subject will be measured." —Danel W. Bachman, author of "A Study of the Mormon Practice of Plural Marriage before the Death of Joseph Smith"

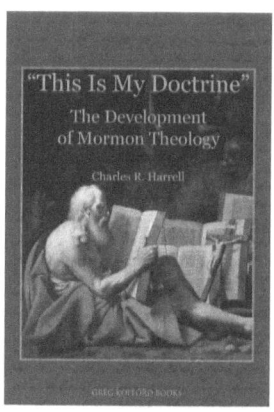

"This is My Doctrine": The Development of Mormon Theology

Charles R. Harrell

Hardcover, ISBN: 978-1-58958-103-6

The principal doctrines defining Mormonism today often bear little resemblance to those it started out with in the early 1830s. This book shows that these doctrines did not originate in a vacuum but were rather prompted and informed by the religious culture from which Mormonism arose. Early Mormons, like their early Christian and even earlier Israelite predecessors, brought with them their own varied culturally conditioned theological presuppositions (a process of convergence) and only later acquired a more distinctive theological outlook (a process of differentiation).

In this first-of-its-kind comprehensive treatment of the development of Mormon theology, Charles Harrell traces the history of Latter-day Saint doctrines from the times of the Old Testament to the present. He describes how Mormonism has carried on the tradition of the biblical authors, early Christians, and later Protestants in reinterpreting scripture to accommodate new theological ideas while attempting to uphold the integrity and authority of the scriptures. In the process, he probes three questions: How did Mormon doctrines develop? What are the scriptural underpinnings of these doctrines? And what do critical scholars make of these same scriptures? In this enlightening study, Harrell systematically peels back the doctrinal accretions of time to provide a fresh new look at Mormon theology.

"*This Is My Doctrine*" will provide those already versed in Mormonism's theological tradition with a new and richer perspective of Mormon theology. Those unacquainted with Mormonism will gain an appreciation for how Mormon theology fits into the larger Jewish and Christian theological traditions.

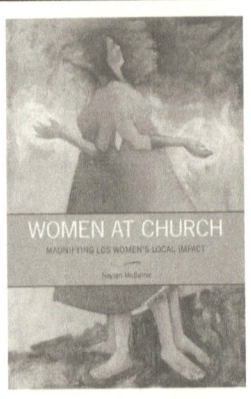

Women at Church: Magnifying LDS Women's Local Impact

Neylan McBaine

Paperback, ISBN: 978-1-58958-688-8

Women at Church is a practical and faithful guide to improving the way men and women work together at church. Looking at current administrative and cultural practices, the author explains why some women struggle with the gendered divisions of labor. She then examines ample real-life examples that are currently happening in local settings around the country that expand and reimagine gendered practices. Readers will understand how to evaluate possible pain points in current practices and propose solutions that continue to uphold all mandated church policies. Readers will be equipped with the tools they need to have respectful, empathetic and productive conversations about gendered practices in Church administration and culture.

Praise for *Women at Church*:

"Such a timely, faithful, and practical book! I suggest ordering this book in bulk to give to your bishopric, stake presidency, and all your local leadership to start a conversation on changing Church culture for women by letting our doctrine suggest creative local adaptations—Neylan McBaine shows the way!" — Valerie Hudson Cassler, author of *Women in Eternity, Women of Zion*

"A pivotal work replete with wisdom and insight. Neylan McBaine deftly outlines a workable programme for facilitating movement in the direction of the 'privileges and powers' promised the nascent Female Relief Society of Nauvoo." — Fiona Givens, co-author of *The God Who Weeps: How Mormonism Makes Sense of Life*

"In her timely and brilliant findings, Neylan McBaine issues a gracious invitation to rethink our assumptions about women's public Church service. Well researched, authentic, and respectful of the current Church administrative structure, McBaine shares exciting and practical ideas that address diverse needs and involve all members in the meaningful work of the Church." — Camille Fronk Olson, author of *Women of the Old Testament* and *Women of the New Testament*

For Zion:
A Mormon Theology of Hope

Joseph M. Spencer

Paperback, ISBN: 978-1-58958-568-3

What is hope? What is Zion? And what does it mean to hope for Zion? In this insightful book, Joseph Spencer explores these questions through the scriptures of two continents separated by nearly two millennia. In the first half, Spencer engages in a rich study of Paul's letter to the Roman to better understand how the apostle understood hope and what it means to have it. In the second half of the book, Spencer jumps to the early years of the Restoration and the various revelations on consecration to understand how Latter-day Saints are expected to strive for Zion. Between these halves is an interlude examining the hoped-for Zion that both thrived in the Book of Mormon and was hoped to be established again.

Praise for *For Zion*:

"Joseph Spencer is one of the most astute readers of sacred texts working in Mormon Studies. Blending theological savvy, historical grounding, and sensitive readings of scripture, he has produced an original and compelling case for consecration and the life of discipleship." — Terryl Givens, author, *Wrestling the Angel: The Foundations of Mormon Thought*

"*For Zion: A Mormon Theology of Hope* is more than a theological reflection. It also consists of able textual exegesis, historical contextualization, and philosophic exploration. Spencer's careful readings of Paul's focus on hope in Romans and on Joseph Smith's development of consecration in his early revelations, linking them as he does with the Book of Mormon, have provided an intriguing, intertextual avenue for understanding what true stewardship should be for us—now and in the future. As such he has set a new benchmark for solid, innovative Latter-day Saint scholarship that is at once provocative and challenging." — Eric D. Huntsman, author, *The Miracles of Jesus*

Hugh Nibley: A Consecrated Life

Boyd Jay Petersen

Hardcover, ISBN: 978-1-58958-019-0

Winner of the Mormon History Association's Best Biography Award

As one of the LDS Church's most widely recognized scholars, Hugh Nibley is both an icon and an enigma. Through complete access to Nibley's correspondence, journals, notes, and papers, Petersen has painted a portrait that reveals the man behind the legend.

Starting with a foreword written by Zina Nibley Petersen and finishing with appendices that include some of the best of Nibley's personal correspondence, the biography reveals aspects of the tapestry of the life of one who has truly consecrated his life to the service of the Lord.

Praise for *A Consecrated Life*:

"Hugh Nibley is generally touted as one of Mormonism's greatest minds and perhaps its most prolific scholarly apologist. Just as hefty as some of Nibley's largest tomes, this authorized biography is delightfully accessible and full of the scholar's delicious wordplay and wit, not to mention some astonishing war stories and insights into Nibley's phenomenal acquisition of languages. Introduced by a personable foreword from the author's wife (who is Nibley's daughter), the book is written with enthusiasm, respect and insight.... On the whole, Petersen is a careful scholar who provides helpful historical context.... This project is far from hagiography. It fills an important gap in LDS history and will appeal to a wide Mormon audience."
—Publishers Weekly

"Well written and thoroughly researched, Petersen's biography is a must-have for anyone struggling to reconcile faith and reason."
—Greg Taggart, Association for Mormon Letters

www.ingramcontent.com/pod-product-compliance
Lightning Source LLC
Chambersburg PA
CBHW030514230426
43665CB00010B/613